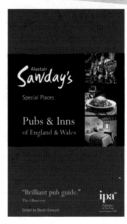

Fourteenth edition
Copyright © 2009 Alastair Sawday
Publishing Co. Ltd
Published in September 2009
ISBN-13: 978-1-906136-22-2

Alastair Sawday Publishing Co. Ltd,
The Old Farmyard, Yanley Lane,
Long Ashton, Bristol BS41 9LR, UK
Tel: +44 (0)1275 395430
Email: info@sawdays.co.uk
Web: www.sawdays.co.uk

The Globe Pequot Press,
P. O. Box 480, Guilford,
Connecticut 06437, USA
Tel: +1 203 458 4500
Email: info@globepequot.com
Web: www.globepequot.com

**Series Editor** Alastair Sawday
**Editor** Nicola Crosse
**Assistant to Editor** Wendy Ogden
**Editorial Director** Annie Shillito
**Writing** Nicola Crosse, Monica Guy.
**Inspections** Jan Adam, David Ashby,
Neil Brown, Gillian Bolam,
Angie Collings, Trish Dugmore,
Jane Elliott, Becca Harris, Vickie
MacIver, Robert & Glyn Newey,
Scott Reeve, Aideen Reid,
Linda Ridsdill Smith, Kate Shepherd,
Nicky Tennent, Mandy Wragg.
*And thanks to those people who did an*
*inspection or two.*
**Accounts** Bridget Bishop,
Sally Ranahan
**Production** Jules Richardson,
Rachel Coe, Tom Germain
**Sales & Marketing & PR** Rob Richardson,
Sarah Bolton, Bethan Riach, Lisa Walklin
**Web & IT** Chris Banks, Phil Clarke,
Mike Peake, Russell Wilkinson

*We have made every effort to ensure the accuracy*
*of the information in this book at the time of*
*going to press. However, we cannot accept any*
*responsibility for any loss, injury or*
*inconvenience resulting from the use of*
*information contained therein.*

Maps: Maidenhead Cartographic Services
Printing: Butler, Tanner & Dennis, Frome
UK distribution: Penguin UK, London

# Alastair Sawday's

Special Places
to Stay

# British
## Bed & Breakfast

# 4  Contents

| Front | Page |
|---|---|

| Guide entries | Entry | Map |
|---|---|---|

### The buildings

Beautiful as they were, our old offices leaked heat, used electricity to heat water and rooms, flooded spaces with light to illuminate one person, and were not ours to alter.

So in 2005 we created our own eco-offices by converting some old barns to create a low-emissions building. We made the building energy-efficient through a variety of innovative and energy-saving building techniques, described below.

Insulation   We went to great lengths to ensure that very little heat can escape, by laying thick insulating board under the roof and floor and adding further insulation underneath the roof and between the rafters. We then lined the whole of the inside of the building with plastic sheeting to ensure air-tightness.

Heating   We installed a wood-pellet boiler from Austria, in order to be largely fossil-fuel free. The pellets are made from compressed sawdust, a waste product from timber mills that work only with sustainably managed forests. The heat is conveyed by water, throughout the building, via an under-floor system.

Water   We installed a 6000-litre tank to collect rainwater from the roofs. This is pumped back, via an ultra-violet filter, to the lavatories, showers and basins. There are two solar thermal panels on the roof providing heat to the one (massively insulated) hot-water cylinder.

Photo: Tom Germain

Lighting   We have a carefully planned mix of low-energy lighting: task lighting and up-lighting. We also installed sun-pipes to reflect the outside light into the building.

Electricity   All our electricity has long come from the Good Energy company and is 100% renewable.

Materials   Virtually all materials are non-toxic or natural. Our carpets are made from (80%) Herdwick sheep-wool from National Trust farms in the Lake District.

Doors and windows   Outside doors and new windows are wooden, double-glazed and beautifully constructed in Norway. Old windows have been double-glazed.

We have a building we are proud of, and architects and designers are fascinated by. But best of all, we are now in a better position to encourage our owners and readers to take sustainability more seriously.

### What we do

Besides having moved the business to a low-carbon building, the company works in a number of ways to reduce its overall environmental footprint.

Our footprint   We measure our footprint annually and use it to find ways of reducing our environmental impact. To help address unavoidable carbon emissions we try to put something back: since 2006 we have supported SCAD, an organisation that works with villagers in India to create sustainable development.

Travel Staff are encouraged to car-share or cycle to work and we provide showers (rainwater-fed) and bike sheds. Our company cars run on LPG (liquid petroleum gas) or recycled cooking oil. We avoid flying and take the train for business trips wherever possible. All office travel is logged as part of our footprint and we count our freelance editors' and inspectors' miles too.

Our office Nearly all of our office waste is recycled; kitchen waste is composted and used in the office vegetable garden. Organic and fairtrade basic provisions are used in the staff kitchen and at in-house events, and green cleaning products are used throughout the office.

Working with owners We are proud that many of our Special Places help support their local economy and, through our Ethical Collection, we recognise owners who go the extra mile to serve locally sourced and organic food or those who have a positive impact on their environment or community.

Engaging readers We hope to raise awareness of the need for individuals to play their part; our Go Slow series places an emphasis on ethical travel and the Fragile Earth imprint consists of hard-hitting environmental titles. Our Ethical Collection informs readers about owners' ethical endeavours.

Ethical printing We print our books locally to support the British printing industry and to reduce our carbon footprint. We print our books on either FSC-certified or recycled paper, using vegetable or soy-based inks.

Our supply chain Our electricity is 100% renewable (supplied by Good Energy), and we put our savings with Triodos, a bank whose motives we trust. Most supplies are bought in bulk from a local ethical-trading co-operative.

For many years Alastair Sawday Publishing has been 'greening' the business in different ways. Our aim is to reduce our environmental footprint as far as possible, and almost every decision we make takes into account the environmental implications. In recognition of our efforts we won a Business Commitment to the Environment Award in 2005, and in 2006 a Queen's Award for Enterprise in the Sustainable Development category. In that year Alastair was voted ITN's 'Eco Hero'. In 2009 we were given the South West C+ Carbon Positive Consumer Choices Award for our Ethical Collection.

In 2008 and again in 2009 we won the Independent Publishers Guild Environmental Award. In 2009 we were also the IPG overall Independent Publisher and Trade Publisher of the Year. The judging panel were effusive in their praise, stating: "With green issues currently at the forefront of publishers' minds, Alastair Sawday Publishing was singled out in this category as a model for all independents to follow. Its efforts to reduce waste in its

Photo: Tom Germain

office and supply chain have reduced the company's environmental impact, and it works closely with staff to identify more areas of improvement. Here is a publisher who lives and breathes green. Alastair Sawday has all the right principles and is clearly committed to improving its practice further."

Becoming 'green' is a journey and, although we began long before most companies, we still have a long way to go. We don't plan to pursue growth for growth's sake. The Sawday's name – and thus our future – depends on maintaining our integrity. We promote special places – those that add beauty, authenticity and a touch of humanity to our lives. This is a niche, albeit a growing one, so we will spend time pursuing truly special places rather than chasing the mass market.

That said, we do plan to produce more titles as well as to diversify. We are expanding our Go Slow series to other European countries, and have launched *Green Europe*, both bold new publishing projects designed to raise the profile of low-impact tourism. Our Fragile Earth series is a growing collection of campaigning books about the environment: highlighting the perilous state of the world yet offering imaginative and radical solutions and some intriguing facts, these books will keep you up to date and well-armed for the battle with apathy.

THE QUEEN'S AWARDS
FOR ENTERPRISE:
SUSTAINABLE DEVELOPMENT
2006

There was a time when I wrote about grim-faced landladies, rules, linoleum and greasy breakfasts. Well, the Beast has been well and truly vanquished; she is almost nowhere to be seen, though may still lurk behind the curtains somewhere. We claim an honourable part in the victory. It is strange, however, that I am beginning to miss her in a funny way; I can't poke fun any more.

A new generation of B&B owners has brought new ideas and styles. There are younger people opening their houses to visitors, often with panache and a strong design sense, though perhaps with less willingness to break rules. It may be that mavericks are mostly older, in which case we welcome back to the fold quite a number of 'old' B&B owners who left us and have returned. I hope they have brought with them their old determination to do their own thing.

Given how most prices have gone through roofs in the last decade, it is good to know that some owners have dropped their prices. Some are pretty cheap anyway, and nearly all these houses offer amazing value. Even in London we can astonish you with low prices.

For some reason Norfolk and Kent figure more largely in this edition. I have no idea why, but it is good to know that we are not stuck in a time warp. Things do change; both counties are beautiful, and in very different ways.

A trend that I welcome is that more vegetables, even animals, are brought directly from garden to plate, via the sink or the butcher. Eggs from the owners' own chickens often spill over the local bacon. This is a delightful change in our food culture; it is satisfying to know that you, the travelling reader, will be supporting this change just by eating breakfast

*Alastair Sawday*

Photo: Tom Germain

It's been quite a year, so far, for worrying about rules. The random imposition of new fire regulations, which came into force in 2006, is beginning to creep up on small B&Bs. I say random as it appears that fire and rescue services across the country have very different ideas about interpreting these standards and enforcing them. In some counties, local fire authorities are telling B&B owners that they must install the sort of technology that is utterly disproportionate to any risk posed by their building. This is the same technology required for large commercial hotels with hundreds of bedrooms: electric sensors, video monitoring, expensive fire doors. And it is not just the cost of installing these gizmos that is daunting – if you have a listed building it is sometimes difficult to get planning permission for the changes, and then there are aesthetics to consider. Who ever admired a green notice with a running

stick man and an arrow? Or a beautiful Georgian door covered in fire-retardant hardboard? The irony of these new regulations is that they were specifically set up 'to make the law easier to understand and comply with'! Perhaps when the fire service itself is less confused about it they could let us know. However, there is good news. Some fire officers are being encouraged to use that common sense! Do look at www.firesafetysense.com

Then along came the news that pets are to be banned from 'food preparation areas' – kitchens to you and me. The traditional farmhouse kitchen – and there are many in this book – has now been branded a 'high risk' food preparation area, particularly dangerous if there is a snoozing pooch in the corner or a cat likely to leap through the window. Oliver Letwin, Conservative MP for Dorset West, has no sympathy for this piece of Brussels barminess. He said "The health and safety inspectors have determined that dogs and farmhouse kitchens are not compatible with one another. Faced with the prospect of such a beast in such a place, the inspectors have reached for the regulatory gun. My conclusion is that this particular aspect of the world has gone barking mad." Most owners in this book would agree that he has a point, and in any case we all know that food poisoning is usually caused by raw food coming into contact with cooked food. Allergies are on the increase because of, not in spite of, over-sterile environments. And the happiest breakfast I ever had in a B&B was

Photo left: Astalleigh House, entry 203
Photo right: 38 St Giles, entry 356

one where a hen sat on my feet and a donkey peered through the window.

Not surprisingly, many B&Bs (there are about 20,000 in Britain) have decided, reluctantly, to close down, some because they cannot afford to make the changes the law requires, some because they want to keep their way of life intact (like keep the family dog in the kitchen as they have always done). In a year when the domestic holiday market is booming, this doesn't make any sense.

So just how do regulations like these creep into our lives, and who is benefiting from their application here? It starts in Brussels apparently, with a short document, which turns into a bigger one to become British law and then a huge lump of guidelines in order for local government to implement the new law. But where is the common sense? Where the delicate balance

Photo: Kingsdown Place, entry 271

between the obvious need to protect people and the need for businesses, particularly small ones, to be creative and innovative?

If we are not careful, we will lose a vital part of our tourist industry – the small B&B. And as the majority of these are in rural areas this could undermine all the efforts made recently to revive interest in the countryside and to support local food growers, local shops and farmers' markets. We must hope then, that the Minister for Tourism and her Department are equally concerned.

In this book you will find a whole array of different places to stay, some very simple, others rather swish. It will not be like staying in a hotel: you probably will not have a lock on your bedroom door, you may share a table with other guests at breakfast, and there certainly won't be anyone to carry your bag, or room service. These are people's homes, so you will encounter family life in all its glory and divergence. There's something about the personal touch, the human contact and the lack of corporateness that is priceless, and your breakfast will usually be far better than any posh hotel. You may even run into a child, or a health and safety-threatening animal or two!

Enjoy the experience of B&B-ing, treasure it: it is part of our cultural heritage and we ignore the threats facing B&Bs at our peril.

*Nicola Crosse*

It's simple. There are no rules, no boxes to tick. We choose places that we like and are fiercely subjective in our choices. We also recognise that one person's idea of special is not necessarily someone else's so there is a huge variety of places, and prices, in the book. Those who are familiar with our Special Places series know that we look for comfort, originality, authenticity, and reject the insincere, the anonymous and the banal. The way guests are treated comes as high on our list as the setting, the architecture, the atmosphere and the food.

## Inspections

We visit every place in the guide to get a feel for how both house and owner tick. We don't take a clipboard and we don't have a list of what is acceptable and what is not. Instead, we chat for an hour or so with the owner and look round. It's all very informal, but it gives us an excellent idea of who would enjoy staying there. If the visit happens to be the last of the day, we sometimes stay the night.

Once in the book properties are re-inspected every four years or so, to keep things fresh and accurate.

## Feedback

In between inspections we rely on feedback from our army of readers, as well as from staff members who are encouraged to visit properties across the series. This feedback is invaluable to us and we always follow up on comments.

So do tell us whether your stay has been a joy or not, if the atmosphere was great or stuffy, the owners cheery or bored. The accuracy of the book depends on what you, and our inspectors, tell us. A lot of the new entries in each edition are recommended by our readers, so keep telling us about new places you've discovered too. Please use the forms on our website at www.sawdays.co.uk, or later in this book (page 437).

However, please do not tell us if the bedside light was broken, or the shower head was scummy. Tell the owner, immediately, and get them to do something about it. Most owners are

Photo: Arlington Avenue, entry 331

more than happy to correct problems and will bend over backwards to help. Far better than bottling it up and then writing to us a week later!

## Subscriptions

Owners pay to appear in this guide. Their fee goes towards the high costs of inspecting, of producing an all-colour book and of maintaining our website. We only include places that we like and find special for one reason or another, so it is not possible for anyone to buy their way onto these pages. Nor is it possible for the owner to write their own description. We will say if the bedrooms are small, or if a main road is near. We do our best to avoid misleading people.

## Disclaimer

We make no claims to pure objectivity in choosing these places. They are here simply because we like them. Our opinions and tastes are ours alone and this book is a statement of them; we hope you will share them. We have done our utmost to get our facts right but apologise unreservedly for any mistakes that may have crept in.

You should know that we don't check such things as fire regulations, swimming pool security or any other laws with which owners of properties receiving paying guests should comply. This is the responsibility of the owners.

Photo: Nonsuch House, entry 112

### Finding the right place for you

All these places are special in one way or another. All have been visited and then written about honestly so that you can take what you like and leave the rest. Those of you who swear by Sawday's books trust our write-ups precisely because we don't have a blanket standard; we include places simply because we like them. But we all have different priorities, so do read the descriptions carefully and pick out the places where you will be comfortable. If something is particularly important to you then do check when you book: a simple question or two can avoid misunderstandings.

### Maps

Each property is flagged with its entry number on the maps at the front. These maps are a great starting point for planning your trip, but please don't use them as anything other than a general guide – use a decent road map for real navigation. Most places will send you detailed instructions once you have booked your stay.

### Ethical Collection

We're always keen to draw attention to owners who are striving to have a positive impact on the world, so you'll notice that some entries are flagged as being part of our "Ethical Collection". These places are working hard to reduce their environmental footprint, making significant contributions to their local community, or are passionate about serving local or organic food. Owners have had to fill in a very detailed questionnaire before becoming part of this Collection – read more on page 412. This doesn't mean that other places in the guide are not taking similar initiatives – many are – but we may not yet know about them.

### Sawday's Travel Club

We've recently launched a Travel Club, based around the Special Places to Stay series; you'll see a 💼 symbol on those places offering something extra to Club members, so to find out how to join see page 414.

### Symbols

Below each entry you will see some symbols, which are explained at the very back of the book. They are based on the information given to us by the owners. However, things do change: bikes may be under repair or a new pool may have been put in. Please use the symbols as a guide rather than an absolute statement of fact and double-check anything that is important to you – owners occasionally bend their own rules, so it's worth asking if you may take your child or dog even if they don't have the symbol.

Children – The 🏃 symbol shows places which are happy to accept children of all ages. This does not mean that they will necessarily have cots, high chairs, etc. If an owner welcomes children but only those above a certain age, we have put these details at the end of their write-up. These houses do not have the child symbol, but even these folk may accept your younger child if you are the only guests. Many who say no to children do so not because they don't like them but because they may have a steep stair, an unfenced pond or they find balancing the needs of mixed age groups too challenging.

Pets – Our 🐕 symbol shows places which are happy to accept pets. It means they can sleep in the bedroom with you, but not on the bed. Be realistic about your pet – if it is nervous or excitable or doesn't like the company of other dogs, people, chickens, children, then say so. Do let the owners know when booking that you intend to bring your pet – particularly if it is not the usual dog!

Owners' pets – The 🐈 symbol is given when the owners have their own pet on the premises. It may not be a cat! But it is there to warn you that you may be greeted by a dog, serenaded by a parrot, or indeed sat upon by a cat.

## Quick reference indices

At the back of the book you'll find a number of quick-reference indices showing those places that offer a particular service, perhaps a room for under £70 a night, or owners who are happy for you to stay all day. They are worth flicking through if you are looking for something specific.

A further listing refers to houses within two miles of a Sustrans National Cycle Network route. Take your own bike or check if you can hire or borrow one from the owners before you travel, and enjoy a cycle ride on your break.

Photo left: Church Gate, entry 511
Photo right: Sarum College, entry 547

others like to have the house empty between, say, 10am and 4pm. If you would prefer not to wander far during the day then look for the places that have the 'Stay all day' quick reference at the back of the book.

## Rooms

**Bedrooms** – We tell you if a room is a double, twin/double (ie with zip and link beds), suite (with a sitting area), family or single. Most owners are flexible and can juggle beds or bedrooms; talk to them about what you need before you book. It is rare to be given your own room key in a B&B.

**Bathrooms** – Most bedrooms in this book have an en suite bath or shower room; we only mention bathroom details when they do not. So, you may get a 'separate' bathroom (yours alone but not in your room) or a shared bathroom. Under certain entries we mention that two rooms share a bathroom and are 'let to same party only'. Please do not assume this means you must be a group of friends to apply; it simply means that if you book one of these rooms you will not be sharing a bathroom with strangers. If these things are important to you, please check when booking. Bath/shower means a bath with shower over; bath and shower means there is a separate shower unit.

**Sitting rooms** – Most B&B owners offer guests the family sitting room to share, or they provide a sitting room specially

## Types of places

Some houses have rooms in annexes or stables, barns or garden 'wings', some of which feel part of the house, some of which don't. If you have a strong preference for being in the throng or for being apart, check those details. Consider your surroundings when you are packing: large, ancient country houses may be cooler than you are used to; city places and working farms may be noisy at times; and that peacock or cockerel we mention may disturb you. Light sleepers should pack ear plugs, and take a dressing gown if there's a separate bathroom (though these are sometimes provided).

Some owners give you a front door key so you may come and go as you please;

Photo: Larchdown Farm, entry 399

for guests. If neither option is available we generally say so, but do check. And do not assume that every bedroom or sitting room has a TV.

## Meals

Unless we say otherwise, a full cooked breakfast is included. Some owners – particularly in London – will give you a good continental breakfast instead. Often you will feast on local sausage and bacon, eggs from resident hens, homemade breads and jams. In some you may have organic yogurts and beautifully presented fruit compotes. Some owners are fairly unbending about breakfast times, others are happy to just wait until you want it, or even bring it to you in bed.

Apart from breakfast, no meals should be expected unless you have arranged them in advance. Although we don't say so on each entry – the repetition a few hundred times would be tedious – all owners who provide packed lunch, lunch or dinner need ADVANCE NOTICE. And they want to get things right for you so, when booking, please discuss your diet and meal times. Meal prices are quoted per person, and dinner is often a social occasion shared with your hosts and other guests.

Do eat in if you can – this book is teeming with good cooks. And how much more relaxing after a day out to have to move no further than the dining room for an excellent dinner, and to eat

and drink knowing there's only a flight of stairs between you and your bed. Very few of our houses are licensed, but most are happy for you to bring your own drink.

## Prices and minimum stays

Each entry gives a price PER ROOM for two people. We also include prices for single rooms, and let you know if there is a supplement to pay should you choose to loll in a double bed on your own.

The price range for each B&B covers a one-night stay in the cheapest room in low season to the most expensive in high

Photo: 14 Westgate Grove, entry 260

season. Some owners charge more at certain times (during regattas or festivals, for example) and some charge less for stays of more than one night. Some owners ask for a two-night minimum stay at weekends and we mention this where possible. Most of our houses could fill many times over on peak weekends and during the summer; book early, especially if you have specific needs.

## Booking and cancellation

Do be clear about the room booked and the price for B&B and for meals. Requests for deposits vary; some are non-refundable, especially in our London homes, and some owners may charge you for the whole of the booked stay in advance.

Some cancellation policies are more stringent than others. It is also worth noting that some owners will take the money directly from your credit/debit card without contacting you to discuss it. So ask them to explain their cancellation policy clearly before booking so you understand exactly where you stand; it may well avoid a nasty surprise.

## Payment

All our owners take cash and UK cheques with a cheque card. Few take credit cards but if they do, we have given them the appropriate symbol. Check that your particular credit card is acceptable.

Photo: Shakespeare House, entry 19

## Tipping

Owners do not expect tips. If you have been treated with extraordinary kindness, write to them, or leave a small gift. Please tell us, too – we love to hear, and we do note, all feedback.

## Arrivals and departures

Say roughly what time you will arrive (normally after 4pm), as most hosts like to welcome you personally. Be on time if you have booked dinner; if, despite best efforts, you are delayed, phone to give warning.

## Closed

When given in months this means the whole of the month stated.

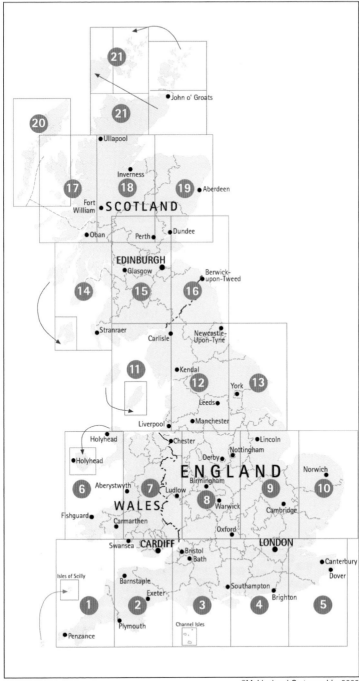

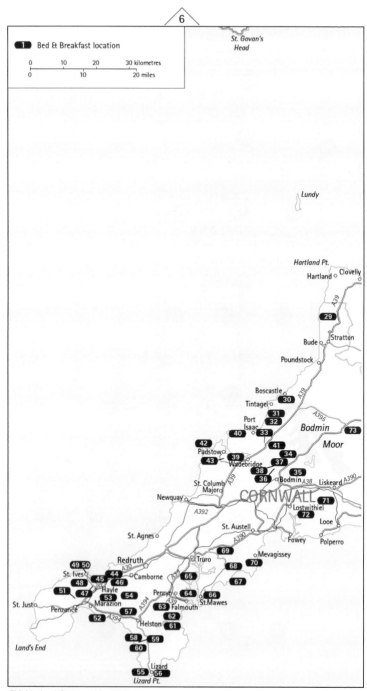

©Maidenhead Cartographic, 2009

Map 2    23

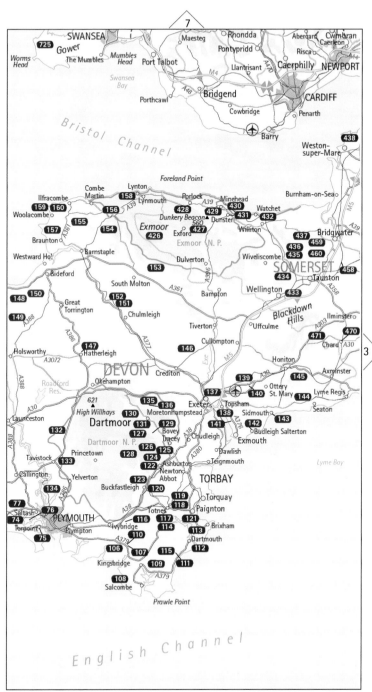

©Maidenhead Cartographic, 2009

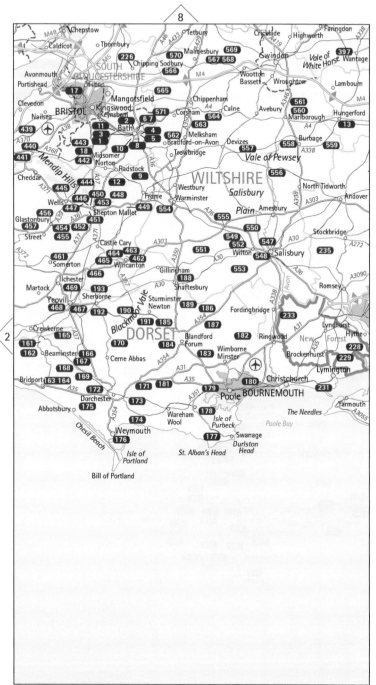

Map 4                                                            25

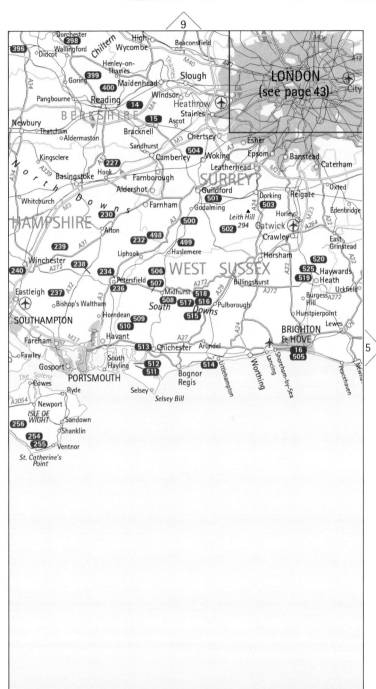

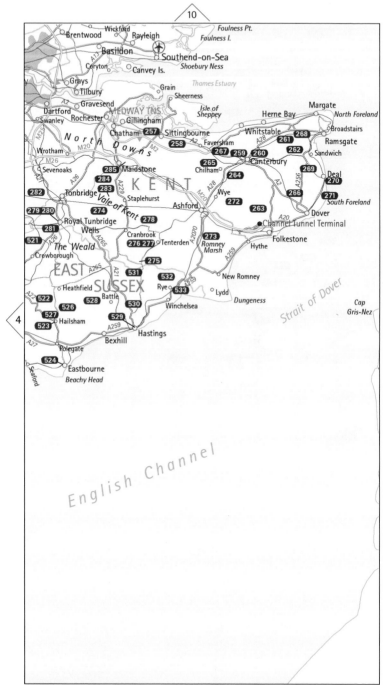

# Map 6

27

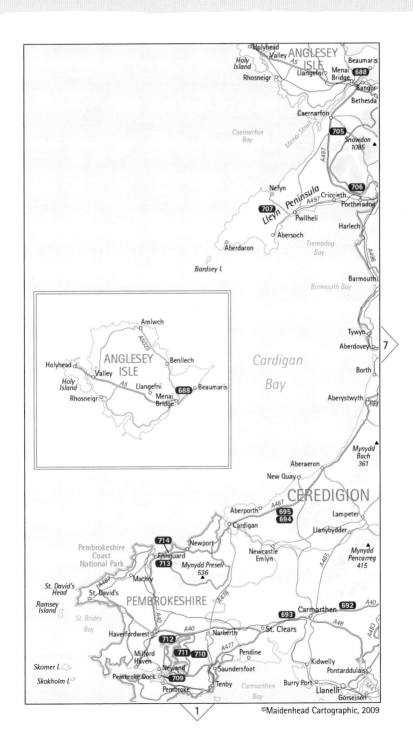

©Maidenhead Cartographic, 2009

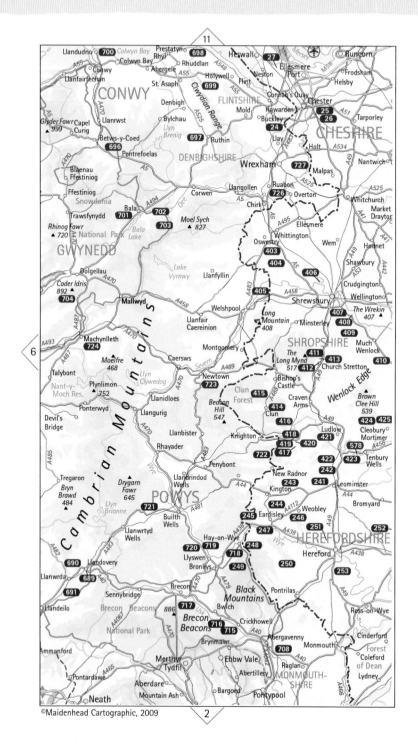

©Maidenhead Cartographic, 2009

# Map 8

29

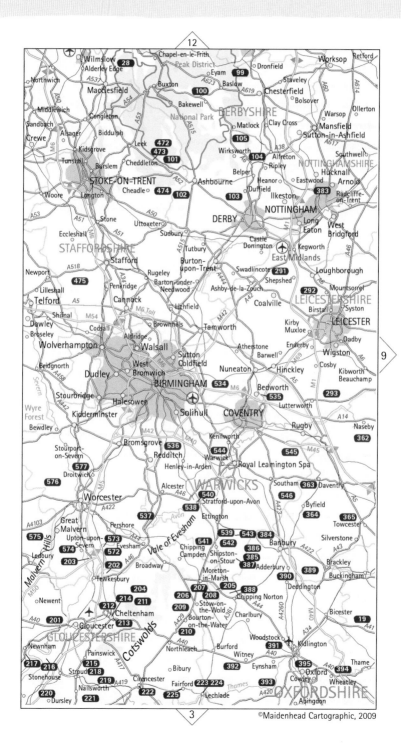

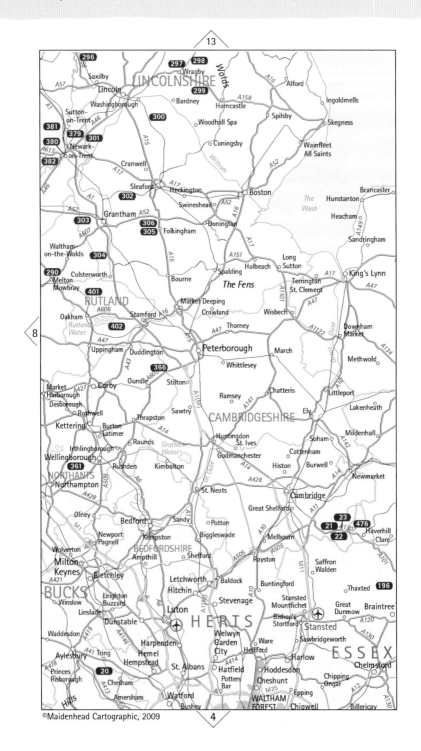

Map 10

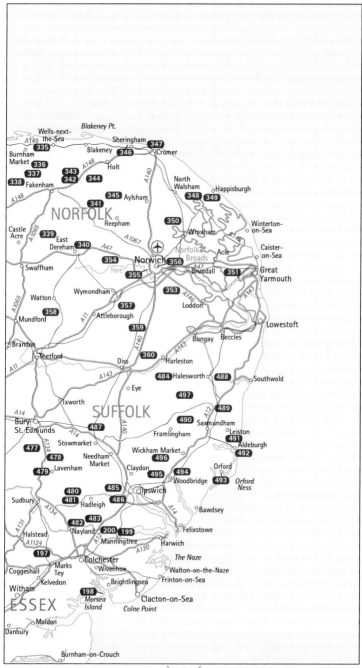

©Maidenhead Cartographic, 2009

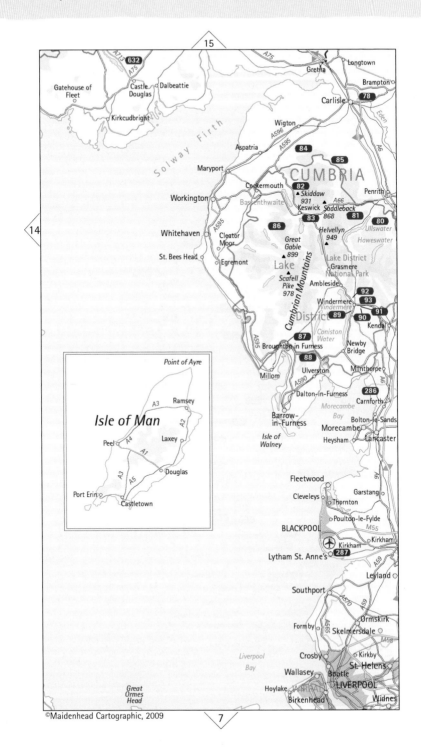

# Map 12

33

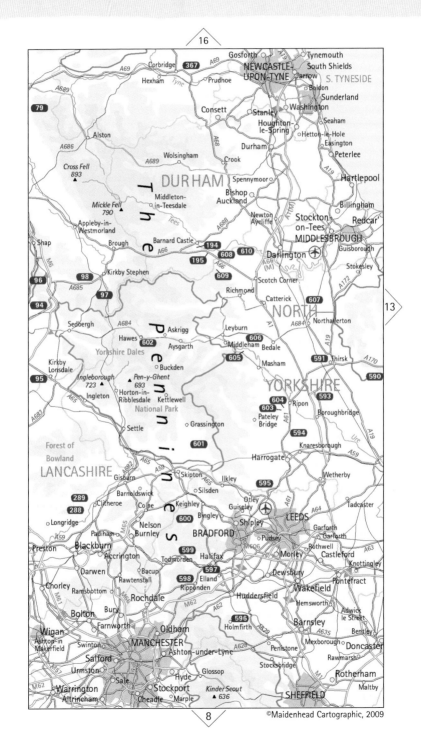

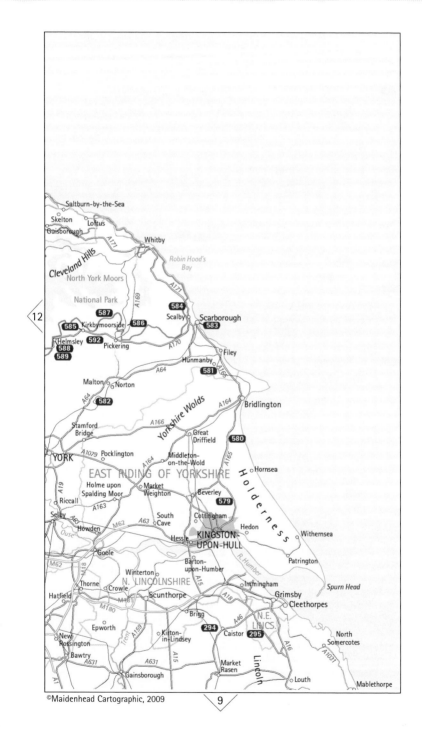

# Map 14

35

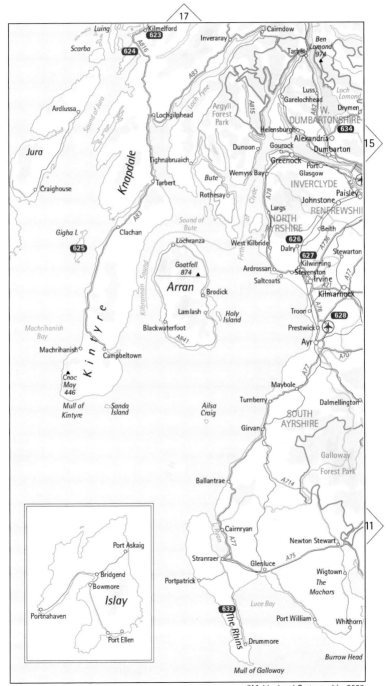

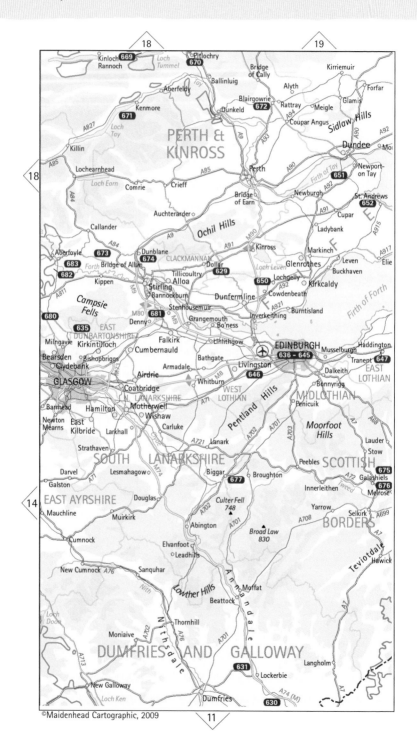

Map 16                                                                37

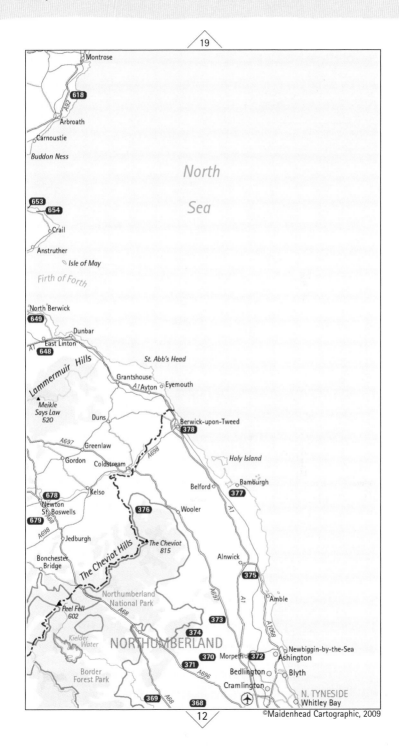

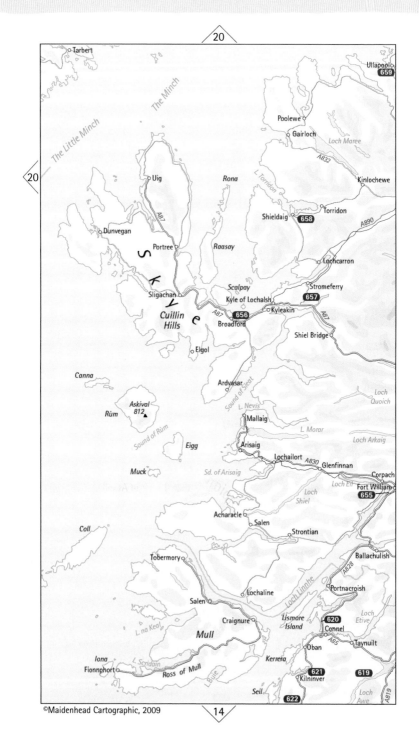

Map 18                                                                                                              39

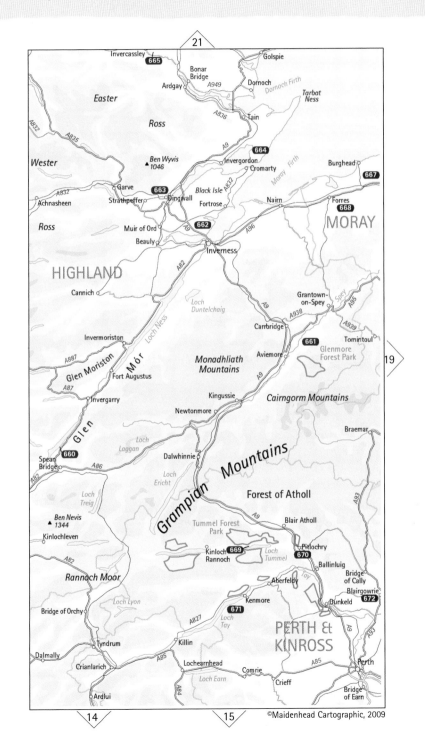

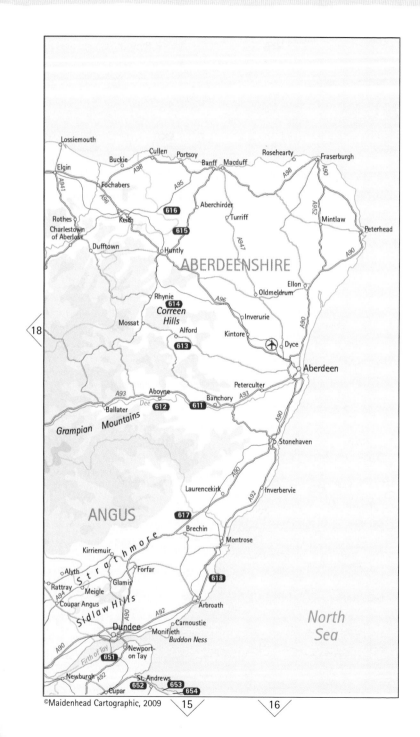

Map 20                                                                    41

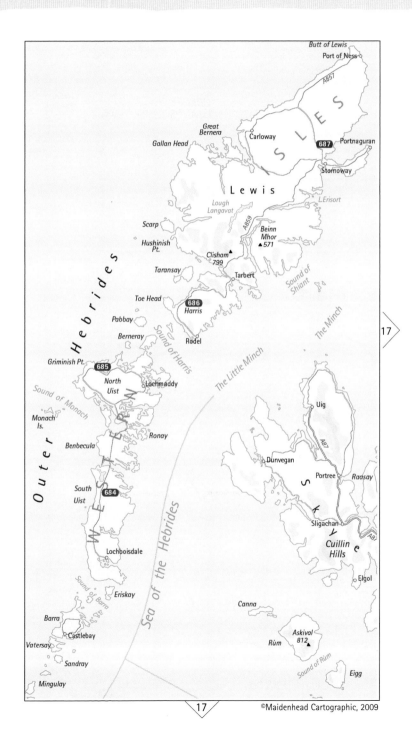

©Maidenhead Cartographic, 2009

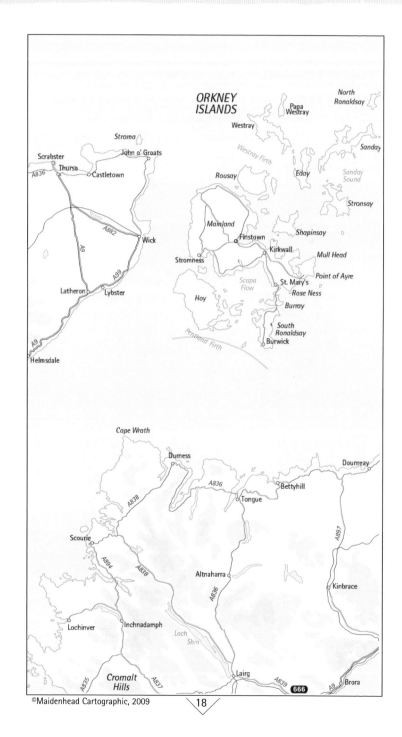

ORKNEY
ISLANDS

North
Ronaldsay

Papa
Westray

Westray

Sanday

Stroma

John o' Groats

Westray Firth

Eday

Sanday
Sound

Scrabster

Thurso

Castletown

A836

Rousay

Stronsay

Mainland

Finstown

Shapinsay

A882

Wick

Kirkwall

Mull Head

A9

Stromness

Point of Ayre

A99

Scapa
Flow

St. Mary's

Rose Ness

Latheron

Lybster

Hoy

Burray

A9

South
Ronaldsay

Pentland Firth

Burwick

Helmsdale

Cape Wrath

Durness

Dounreay

A836

Bettyhill

A838

Tongue

A897

Scourie

A894

A838

Altnaharra

Kinbrace

A836

Lochinver

Inchnadamph

Loch
Shin

Cromalt
Hills

A835

A837

Lairg

A839

666

A9

Brora

18

# Map 22

43

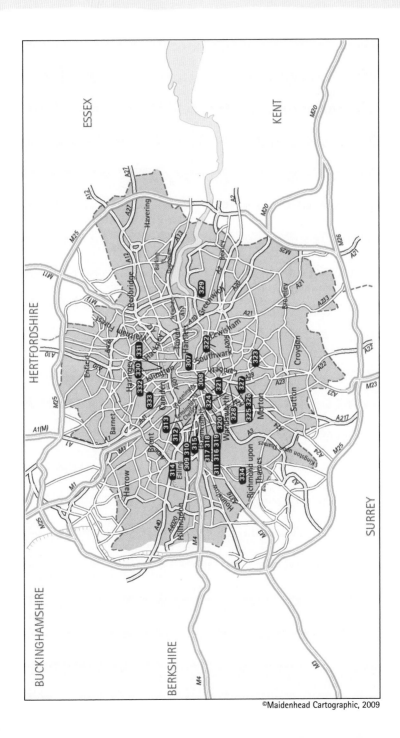

England

## Bath & N.E. Somerset

### 4 Brock Street

You'll be in clover here. Clever Minnie has performed a miracle at this natty Georgian townhouse tucked quietly behind The Circus and Royal Crescent. On either side of a sleek black door are box hedges with smart haircuts; walk in to a vast, elegant hallway, and up many curved stairs to two softly coloured bedrooms. Find plump beds covered in soft woollen rug or baby blue quilt, painted furniture and a view from each. Loll in a roll top or blast yourself in the swish wet room, enjoy breakfast at the long dining table (or the garden on warm days), then go and have fun in town. A fabulous place to stay.

| | |
|---|---|
| Price | From £95. |
| Rooms | 2: 1 double, 1 twin sharing bath & wet room (let to same party only). |
| Meals | Pubs/restaurants within walking distance. |
| Closed | Christmas & Easter. |
| Directions | In centre of Bath. Parking free between 6.00pm and 8.00am and all day Sunday. |

|  | Minnie Tatham |
|---|---|
| | 4 Brock Street, |
| | Bath, |
| | Bath & N.E. Somerset BA1 2LN |
| Tel | +44 (0)1225 460536 |
| Email | enquiries@no4brockstreet.co.uk |
| Web | www.no4brockstreet.co.uk |

Entry 1   Map 3

## Bath & N.E. Somerset

### 77 Great Pulteney Street

Tea and cakes await down the elegant stone steps to a garden flat in this broad street of immaculate Georgian houses. Inside all is pale wood, modern art, bergère chairs and palms. Downstairs is a comfortable bedroom with loads of books and its own door to a small but delightfully well-designed garden. On fine days you breakfast here without haste, on fruit from Ian and Henry's allotment, and gorgeous bacon and sausage butties; Ian is a fanatic foodie and dinner will also be special, but there are lots of good places to eat – and shop – nearby. Henry may play the Northumbrian pipes for you if you ask nicely...

| | |
|---|---|
| Price | £75–£95. Singles from £55. |
| Rooms | 1 double. |
| Meals | Dinner from £20. Packed lunch from £5. |
| Closed | Rarely. |
| Directions | A4 into centre of Bath. Last house before Laura Place on south side of Great Pulteney St. Parking by arrangement; 7-minute walk from station. |

|  | Ian Critchley & Henry Ford |
|---|---|
| | 77 Great Pulteney Street, |
| | Bath, |
| | Bath & N.E. Somerset BA2 4DL |
| Tel | +44 (0)1225 466659 |
| Email | critchford@77pulteneyst.co.uk |
| Web | www.77pulteneyst.co.uk |

Entry 2   Map 3

## Bath & N.E. Somerset

### 14 Raby Place

A listed Regency house within walking distance of one of Europe's most beautiful cities. Muriel likes modern art and has filled the elegant rooms with stunning pictures and objects, antique chairs and lovely fabrics. Beautifully proportioned double bedrooms are graceful and spotless with laundered linen; one on the top (third) floor has fabulous views over the city to the Abbey, the small single has a piano in case you get the urge. Breakfast is organic, delicious, and eaten at a communal table in the dining room; chat to Muriel or bury your head in a paper. *Free parking permit for road outside.*

| Price | £65–£70. Singles £35. |
|---|---|
| Rooms | 5: 2 doubles, 1 family room; 1 twin with separate shower; 1 single with separate bath. (Cot available.) |
| Meals | Restaurants 8-minute walk. |
| Closed | Rarely. |
| Directions | Bathwick Hill is turning off the A36 towards Bristol; look for signs to university. No. 14 on left-hand side as you go uphill, before left turn into Raby Mews. |

**Muriel Guy**
14 Raby Place,
Bathwick,
Bath,
Bath & N.E. Somerset BA2 4EH

Tel   +44 (0)1225 465120

## Bath & N.E. Somerset

### Tolley Cottage

Breakfast on the patio on fine days and watch the barges pass the bottom of the gorgeous garden; raise your eyes to Bath Abbey on the skyline. This Victorian house is a ten-minute walk from the city centre, the spa and the fine old theatre. Sunny and bright, rooms are a comfortable mix of contemporary and classical; books, art and interesting glass pieces catch the eye. Bedrooms are small, calming and charming with toile de Jouy and elegant furniture; bathrooms sparkle. Judy cooks special breakfasts; James, Master of Wine, can arrange tastings. Both are warm and relaxed, and love sharing their home.

Ethical Collection: Food. See page 412.

Travel Club offer. See page 414.

| Price | From £95. Singles from £85. |
|---|---|
| Rooms | 2: 1 double, 1 twin. |
| Meals | Pubs/restaurants 10-minute walk. |
| Closed | Christmas. |
| Directions | Follow signs for American Museum & University up Bathwick Hill. Take 1st turn right to Sydney Buildings. House 200 yds on right. Free parking. |

**Judy & James John**
Tolley Cottage,
23 Sydney Buildings,
Bath,
Bath & N.E. Somerset BA2 6BZ

Tel   +44 (0)1225 463365
Email   jj@judyj.plus.com
Web   www.tolleycottage.co.uk

## Bath & N.E. Somerset

### Alexis House

Dazzling Simone has a natural sense of fun and a great deal of Franco-Caribbean colour: breakfasts of fruit, yogurt and cereals, or full English (much organic), are served on Limoges china overlooking the garden's box parterre and rambling roses. Immaculate bedrooms have a touch of 18th-century boudoir with their embroidered sheets, antique brass beds, frou-frou chairs and sumptuous drapes; views sail over the charming garden to the floodlit Abbey. Simone is wonderfully attentive and the delights of Bath, with its Thermae Spa, are a short walk along the canal.

| | |
|---|---|
| Price | From £95. Singles £75. |
| Rooms | 2: 1 double with separate bath; 1 twin/double with separate shower & wc. |
| Meals | Pubs/restaurants 10-minute walk. |
| Closed | Christmas. |
| Directions | From Bath centre, signs to American Museum. At A36 r'about 1st exit onto Bathwick Hill. Sydney Buildings 1st road on right, house 300 yds on right. All-day parking. |

|  | Mrs Simone Johnson |
|---|---|
|  | Alexis House, |
|  | 47 Sydney Buildings, |
|  | Bath, |
|  | Bath & N.E. Somerset BA2 6DB |
| Tel | +44 (0)1225 463033 |
| Fax | +44 (0)1225 461054 |
| Web | www.alexishousebath.co.uk |

Entry 5   Map 3

## Bath & N.E. Somerset

### Bathwick Gardens

The period, hand-printed wallpaper is just one of the remarkable features of this elegant Grade I-listed house: Julian is an expert. The house, in one of Bath's finest Regency terraces, has been so beautifully restored that the BBC used its rooms for Jane Austen's *Persuasion*. Bedrooms are flooded with light and views are stunning; one stylish bathroom has marquina marble, cherrywood and ebony. Breakfast is taken in the family kitchen, or in the conservatory. For the adventurous, Mechthild serves up an Austrian alternative of cold meats and cheeses, fresh rye breads and homemade cakes. Herrlich!

 Travel Club offer. See page 414.

| | |
|---|---|
| Price | £95-£120. Singles £85. |
| Rooms | 3 twins/doubles. |
| Meals | Pub/restaurant 300 yds. |
| Closed | Rarely. |
| Directions | A46 to Bath, then A4 for city centre. Left onto A36 over Cleveland Bridge; follow signs to Holburne Museum. Directly after museum, left. House is two thirds along on right. Parking available by prior arrangement. |

|  | Mechthild Self von Hippel |
|---|---|
|  | Bathwick Gardens, |
|  | 95 Sydney Place, |
|  | Bath, |
|  | Bath & N.E. Somerset BA2 6NE |
| Tel | +44 (0)1225 469435 |
| Email | mechthild.svh@virgin.net |
| Web | www.bathwickgardens.co.uk |

Entry 6   Map 3

## Bath & N.E. Somerset

### The Bath Courtyard

You are a brisk ten-minute walk from the centre, but all is hushed in this Bath stone cottage, neatly tucked down a back lane. Shoes must be removed at the door; pad through to a dining room with a big mahogany table and interesting paintings, a large conservatory for breakfasts (fresh fruit salad, smoked salmon and scrambled eggs) and a long, rose-filled garden. Bedrooms are perfectly presented in pale yellows, with silk curtains, pocket-sprung mattresses and well-lit, ultra-modern bathrooms. Borrow bikes from Michael and his partner, and head for the tow path, or pedal into town for the shops and sights.

 Travel Club offer. See page 414.

| | |
|---|---|
| Price | £90–£110. Singles £75. |
| Rooms | 2 doubles. |
| Meals | Pubs/restaurants 0.25 miles. |
| Closed | Rarely. |
| Directions | M4, Bath signs; London Road, over river (Cleveland Bridge), past fire station. Right at next lights; left into Sydney Place; Vellore Lane 200 yds on right. Private parking is available. |

**Michael Wilson**
The Bath Courtyard,
38 Vellore Lane, Bath,
Bath & N.E. Somerset BA2 6JQ
Tel    +44 (0)1225 424741
Email  michaelnwilson@gmail.com
Web    www.thebathcourtyard.co.uk

✗ 🚂 📶 🐾 🚲

Entry 7  Map 3

## Bath & N.E. Somerset

### Grey Lodge

In a conservation area, yet only a short drive from the centre of Bath, the views are breathtaking from wherever you stand. The steep valley rolls out ahead of you from most of the rooms, and from the garden comes a confusion and a profusion of scents and colours – a glory in its own right. The friendly and likeable Sticklands are conservationists as well as gardeners and have a Green Certificate to prove it. Breakfasts are a feast: bacon and eggs, cereals, home-grown jam, smoked fish and much more. Jane will tell you all about wonderful local gardens to visit.

 Travel Club offer. See page 414.

| | |
|---|---|
| Price | £80–£90. Singles £50–£55. |
| Rooms | 3: 2 twins/doubles, 1 family room. |
| Meals | Pubs/restaurants 2 miles. |
| Closed | Rarely. |
| Directions | From A36, 3 miles out of Bath on Warminster road, take uphill road by lights & viaduct. 1st left, 100 yds, signed Monkton Combe. After village, house 1st on left; 0.5 miles on. |

**Jane & Anthony Stickland**
Grey Lodge,
Summer Lane, Combe Down, Bath,
Bath & N.E. Somerset BA2 7EU
Tel    +44 (0)1225 832069
Fax    +44 (0)1225 830161
Email  greylodge@surfree.co.uk
Web    www.greylodge.co.uk

🕊 ✗ 📖 🚂 🐾

Entry 8  Map 3

# Bath & N.E. Somerset

## Hollytree Cottage

Meandering lanes lead to this 16th-century cottage, with roses round the door, a grandfather clock in the hall and an air of genteel tranquillity. The cottage charm has been updated with Regency mahogany and sumptuous sofas. There's even a four-poster bed and the bedrooms have long views over farmland and undulating countryside. Behind is a sloping, south-facing garden with a pond and some rare trees and shrubs. A place to come for absolute peace and quiet, birdsong and walks and the joys of elegant Bath 20 minutes away. Julia knows the city well so can help you plan trips.

Travel Club offer. See page 414.

| | |
|---|---|
| Price | £80–£90. Singles £45–£50. |
| Rooms | 3: 1 double, 1 twin, 1 four-poster. |
| Meals | Pub/restaurant 0.5 miles. |
| Closed | Rarely. |
| Directions | From Bath, A36 to Wolverton. Just past Red Lion, turn for Laverton. 1 mile to x-roads; towards Faukland; downhill for 80 yds. On left, just above farm entrance on right. |

|   |   |
|---|---|
| | **Mrs Julia Naismith** |
| | Hollytree Cottage, |
| | Laverton, Bath, |
| | Bath & N.E. Somerset BA2 7QZ |
| Tel | +44 (0)1373 830786 |
| Fax | +44 (0)1373 830786 |
| Email | jnaismith@toucansurf.com |
| Web | www.hollytreecottagebath.co.uk |

Entry 9   Map 3

# Bath & N.E. Somerset

## Manor Farm Barn

Duchy of Cornwall farmland stretches as far as the eye can see; the views from this converted barn – with light open-plan spaces – are splendid by any standards, but remarkable considering you are so close to Bath. There's much wildlife, too: sparrowhawks nest in the gable end, buzzards circle above the valley, and deer may gaze at you eating your breakfast. Giles, who pots, and Sue, who paints, are gentle and easy-going hosts; spruce guest rooms have built-in wardrobes, houseplants and excellent beds. For those in search of birdsong and country peace after a day on the hoof in Bath.

| | |
|---|---|
| Price | £60–£70. Singles £40–£42.50. |
| Rooms | 2: 1 twin/double; 1 double with separate shower. |
| Meals | Pubs/restaurants 2.5 miles. |
| Closed | Christmas & New Year. |
| Directions | From Bath, A367 (Wells Rd). At Red Lion r'bout right (Bristol A4). Straight on, pass Culverhay School on left. After 100 yds left to Englishcombe. There, right after postbox to church, fork right, follow road; last on right. |

|   |   |
|---|---|
| | **Sue & Giles Barber** |
| | Manor Farm Barn, |
| | Englishcombe, Bath, |
| | Bath & N.E. Somerset BA2 9DU |
| Tel | +44 (0)1225 424195 |
| Email | info@manorfarmbarn.com |
| Web | www.manorfarmbarn.com |

Entry 10   Map 3

## Corston Fields Farm

In rolling agricultural land, a short hop from Bath with its new Thermea spa, the Addicotts have given over swathes of their farm to natural habitat for indigenous wildlife – and have a Gold Award under the Duke of Cornwall's Habitat Award scheme to boot. Gerald and Rosaline, both keen rugby supporters, are utterly committed to the environment, and flax from the vibrant blue linseed crops is used to heat their stone-mullioned, listed house. Large bedrooms – the best is in the house – have all mod cons. Come for the setting, the views, a wildflower meadow and the wonderful hosts. *Minimum stay two nights at weekends.*

## Melon Cottage Vineyard

Interesting, child-friendly hosts who are entirely natural and unbusinesslike make this place special; it's excellent value, too. The ancient Mendip-style 'long cottage' with mullioned windows and beams made of ships' timbers, fronted by a small vineyard, is temptingly close to Babington House, the treasures of Bath and Wells, the gardens and concerts at Stourhead, and Gregorian chant in Downside Abbey. Rooms are cosy, the jams are homemade and the hosts the kindest you may meet. No sitting room, but tea in the walled garden is rich compensation. *Children over five welcome. Minimum stay two nights.*

| | |
|---|---|
| Price | From £94. Singles £60. |
| Rooms | 4: 1 double; 1 double, 1 twin sharing bath (2nd room let to same party only). Annexe: 1 double. |
| Meals | Pub 300 yds. |
| Closed | Christmas & New Year. |
| Directions | From A4 west of Bath, A39 through Corston. 1 mile on, just before Wheatsheaf Pub (on right), right. Signed 200 yds along lane on right. |

| | |
|---|---|
| Price | £50–£65. Singles £25. |
| Rooms | 1 double/family. |
| Meals | Pubs 2 miles. |
| Closed | Rarely. |
| Directions | From Bath A367, Wells road, through Radstock. After 3 miles, at large r'bout, B3139 for Trowbridge. After 1.1 miles, and Charlton sign, right up 2nd driveway on right. Pink house at top, visible from road. |

| | |
|---|---|
| | **Gerald & Rosaline Addicott** |
| | Corston Fields Farm, |
| | Corston, Bath, |
| | Bath & N.E. Somerset BA2 9EZ |
| Tel | +44 (0)1225 873305 |
| Email | corston.fields@btinternet.com |
| Web | www.corstonfields.com |

| | |
|---|---|
| | **Virginia & Hugh Pountney** |
| | Melon Cottage Vineyard, |
| | Charlton, Radstock, Bath, |
| | Bath & N.E. Somerset BA3 5TN |
| Tel | +44 (0)1761 435090 |
| Email | meloncottage@hotmail.co.uk |
| Web | www.meloncottage.co.uk |

Entry 11   Map 3

Entry 12   Map 3

## Berkshire

### Wilton House

With its handsome Queen Anne frontage, "the most ambitious house in Hungerford" (Pevsner) conceals medieval origins – and the roofline is pure Dickens. A classic townhouse in a charming market town, its interior is a panelled, soft-painted delight. Light floods through sash windows onto paintings and prints, books, antiques and wide, inviting sofas; bedrooms are understatedly elegant and relaxing; bathrooms are a good size. So is your (almost all local or organic) breakfast in the 18th-century dining room: the Welfares, and their labradors, look after you perfectly. *Children over eight welcome.*

| Price | From £76. Singles from £62. |
| --- | --- |
| Rooms | 2: 1 double, 1 twin/double. |
| Meals | Packed lunch £5. Pub 100 yds. |
| Closed | Christmas. |
| Directions | M4 exit 14; A338 to A4; right for Marlborough, turning at Bear Hotel onto Salisbury road (A338). Over canal bridge into High St. House 200 yds past Town Hall on right. |

**Deborah & Jonathan Welfare**
Wilton House,
33 High Street, Hungerford,
Berkshire RG17 0NF

| Tel | +44 (0)1488 684228 |
| --- | --- |
| Fax | +44 (0)1488 685037 |
| Email | welfares@hotmail.com |
| Web | www.wiltonhouse-hungerford.co.uk |

Entry 13   Map 3

## Berkshire

### Eastmere

Opposite the duck pond in a pretty, tucked-away village, this Victorian redbrick house is near to Windsor, Ascot and Henley: Heathrow is an easy drive. Get a friendly welcome and homemade biscuits from Catherine, a successful artist who loves to cook: rare breed bacon from the village, eggs from the chickens who roam the garden. Your simple ground floor bedroom has its own entrance, lovely linen sheets, white painted Edwardian furniture. Settle on the sofa with a book from the library in the comfortable conservatory by a log burning stove. Stroll the commons or along the Thames. *French & Italian spoken.*

| Price | £75. Singles £55. |
| --- | --- |
| Rooms | 1 double. |
| Meals | Dinner, 4 courses, £25. Pub 5-minute walk. |
| Closed | Christmas & New Year. |
| Directions | Leave M4 at junction 8/9. A404 towards High Wycombe, then left onto A4 towards Reading. After 3 miles, left to Waltham St Lawrence, then over staggered x-road. On right opposite pond. |

**Catherine & Peter Turner**
Eastmere,
Shurlock Row,
Berkshire RG10 0PS

| Tel | +44 (0)1189 340946 |
| --- | --- |
| Email | mrspturner@hotmail.co.uk |

Entry 14   Map 4

## Berkshire

### Whitehouse Farm Cottage

Once you get past the housing estates of Bracknell, this is a fabulous find. A 17th-century farmhouse with a delightful garden, and two charmingly converted buildings with their own entrances. Garden Cottage has a beamed drawing room downstairs and a gallery bedroom with creamy walls and a cast-iron bed. The Forge has the blacksmith's fireplace and lovely views onto the courtyard garden and its pebble mosaics. The single is in the house with its own comfortable sitting room. Locally sourced breakfasts with fresh bread are served in the house by friendly Keir and Louise, who are film prop makers.

| | |
|---|---|
| Price | £75–£95. Singles £65–£85. |
| Rooms | 3: 1 single & sitting room. The Forge: 1 double. Garden Cottage: 1 double & sitting room. |
| Meals | Picnics by arrangement. Pubs/restaurants within 1 mile. |
| Closed | Christmas & occasionally. |
| Directions | From A329, B3408 to Binfield. Left at r'bout, left at traffic lights, into St Marks Road. Then 2nd left Foxley Lane, 1st left Murrell Hill Lane. House is 1st on right. |

| | |
|---|---|
| | **Keir Lusby** |
| | Whitehouse Farm Cottage, |
| | Murrell Hill Lane, |
| | Binfield, Bracknell, |
| | Berkshire RG42 4BY |
| Tel | +44 (0)1344 423688 |
| Email | garden.cottages@ntlworld.com |

Entry 15   Map 4

## Brighton & Hove

### Lansdowne Guest House

Fun, refreshing and bang in the middle of Pimlico-by-Sea. This is Hove: grand white Regency villas and the promenade a hop away. In this 1920s mansion built for a lord's mistress, the Bundys occupy the first floor. Enter a big friendly living room with a fire for winter nights, a sprinkling of modern art and a superb spread for the morning: Asian or English. Your hosts are attentive, interesting, well-travelled and love meeting their guests. Up under the roof are low-ceilinged, stylish bedrooms and a landing with a comfortable sofa; bathrooms, cleverly compact, have lotions and bubbles. Brighton lies at your feet.

Travel Club offer. See page 414.

| | |
|---|---|
| Price | £75–£85. Singles from £65. |
| Rooms | 2: 1 double, 1 twin/double. |
| Meals | Dinner from £20. Packed lunch from £7.50. Picnic hampers from £10. |
| Closed | Christmas & occasionally. |
| Directions | A23 to seafront, then right towards Hove. 2nd right after Brunswick Square into Holland Rd; right at 2nd lights. House 2nd left behind red brick wall. Street parking with visitor's voucher. |

| | |
|---|---|
| | **Diana & Michael Bundy** |
| | Lansdowne Guest House, |
| | 21 Lansdowne Road, Hove, |
| | Brighton & Hove BN3 1FE |
| Tel | +44 (0)1273 773700 |
| Fax | +44 (0)1273 773718 |
| Email | lansdowneguesthouse@hotmail.co.uk |
| Web | www.lansdowneguesthouse.synthasite.com |

Entry 15a   Map 4

# Brighton & Hove

## 5 Palmeira Square

Drift along Brighton seafront, and emerge into the Regency splendour of Palmeira Square. Susie with the twinkling eyes welcomes you into a fun, bohemian, ground-floor flat in Hove. Rooms are flooded with light, ceilings are high, furnishings have pizzazz (kilims on bamboo floors, funky chandeliers). Your bedroom is deep lilac and lovely, your bathroom (big shower, stylish toiletries) is Susie's. She has lived in Portugal, Brazil, Bordeaux, works from home and delivers a delicious breakfast to your door. Or, at a pretty seat in the window bay; turn your head and you'll catch the sea. *Minimum stay two nights.*

 Travel Club offer. See page 414.

| | |
|---|---|
| Price | £75-£85. |
| Rooms | 1 double with shared bath. |
| Meals | Continental breakfast.<br>Pub/restaurant 500 yds. |
| Closed | Rarely. |
| Directions | Seafront towards Hove. Right onto Adelaide Crescent (white Regency buildings) then immediate right, following road up into Palmeira Square. No 5 is just after Crescent becomes Square. |

|  | Susie de Castilho |
|---|---|
| | Flat 1, 5 Palmeira Square,<br>Hove,<br>Brighton & Hove BN3 2JA |
| Tel | +44 (0)1273 719087 |
| Email | stay@2staybrighton.co.uk |
| Web | www.2staybrighton.co.uk |

Entry 16   Map 4

# Bristol

## 9 Princes Buildings

A super city base with jolly comfortable beds, charming owners and, without a doubt, the best views in Clifton. You are a short hop from the elegant Suspension Bridge, good restaurants, shops and pubs of the village and a ferry to whisk you to town or the station; yet all is quiet, green and leafy. Walk in to a big square hall, a drawing room with a peaceful feel and a veranda for gazing in fine weather. Your bedroom is fresh, light and traditional, one downstairs overlooks the garden and has a quirky 70s bathroom. Best of all, Simon and Joanna are easy-going and give you a breakfast cooked to order with homemade jams.

| | |
|---|---|
| Price | From £80. Singles £50. |
| Rooms | 4: 2 doubles, 1 twin/double;<br>1 twin/double with separate bath. |
| Meals | Pub/restaurant 100 yds. |
| Closed | Never. |
| Directions | In Bristol follow signs to Clifton and Clifton Suspension Bridge, just before bridge take left down Sion Hill, past Avon Gorge hotel on right. House is next to hotel with double red front doors. |

|  | Simon & Joanna Fuller |
|---|---|
| | 9 Princes Buildings,<br>Clifton,<br>Bristol BS8 4LB |
| Tel | +44 (0)117 973 4615 |
| Email | info@9pb.co.uk |
| Web | www.9pb.co.uk |

Entry 17   Map 3

# Bristol

## Folly Farm

You may fall asleep listening to the hoot of an owl and the wind in the trees; this lovely 250 acre organic farm is also open as an educational resource. Apartments in a converted farm building have ancient beams, thick stone walls and a sitting room with a sofa and TV. Bedrooms are plain and simple, softened by pictures and piles of fluffy white towels: all have either twin beds, so good for a family holiday or groups of friends; shower rooms are spick and span. Breakfast is left for you in the kitchen: Dorset cereal, fruit, cheese, yogurt, muffins. Wonderful walks through open fields and mixed woodland.

| | |
|---|---|
| Price | £60. Singles £45. |
| Rooms | 9 twins (3 with bath/shower; 6 with shower). |
| Meals | Dinner, £10 (for groups of 8 or more). Breakfast from £5. Pub 1.5 miles. |
| Closed | Never. |
| Directions | A37 south from Bristol for 8 miles. After Pensford right at Chelwood r'bout, A368 for Weston-s-M. After 2 miles pass right turn Chew Magna; turning to house next left, small track marked as a dead end. |

|  | **Philip Niemand** |
|---|---|
| | Folly Farm, |
| | Stowey, Bishop Sutton, |
| | Bristol BS39 4DW |
| Tel | +44 (0)1275 331590 |
| Email | enquiries@follyfarm.org |
| Web | www.follyfarm.org |

Entry 18  Map 3

# Buckinghamshire

## Shakespeare House

If you love dramatic décor, you'll adore what Nick and Roy have done with this Tudor coaching inn. Through a heavy oak door lies a whirl of patterned sofas, fringed cushions, masks, tall candles among leaded windows and elegant beams. Tasteful flamboyance, restrained extravagance… Savour Roy's gourmet creations in a blue-gold dining room, then pounce up an ancient staircase to the suite, revelling in glitzy throws, shiny fabrics, feathery shades; up steep stairs to smaller rooms, just as enticing. Bucolic to the back and smart at the front with its clipped evergreens and gravel drive, the house allegedly hosted Shakespeare. Full-on and fabulous.

Travel Club offer. See page 414.

| | |
|---|---|
| Price | £85-£210. Singles from £65. |
| Rooms | 5: 2 doubles; 3 doubles with separate bathrooms. |
| Meals | Dinner £25. Pub 500 yds. Restaurant 3 miles. |
| Closed | 20 December-2 January. |
| Directions | From Bicester, A41 east towards Aylesbury & Waddesdon. Follow sign to left for Edgcott, Calvert & Grendon Underwood. Into village, at church turn right. House is 200 yds on right. |

|  | **Nickolas Hunter & Roy Elsbury** |
|---|---|
| | Shakespeare House, |
| | Main Street, Grendon Underwood, |
| | Buckinghamshire HP18 0ST |
| Tel | +44 (0)1296 770776 |
| Email | shakespearehouse@msn.com |
| Web | www.shakespeare-house.co.uk |

Entry 19  Map 8

# Buckinghamshire

## Field Cottage

Sue, relaxed and friendly, is the consummate professional: the fitted bedrooms are immaculate, chintzy and filled with treats, and the bathrooms pristine. She has also created a horticultural haven amid open fields (old-fashioned roses, a willow tunnel, colourful clematis). The peachy guest sitting room is neat and comfortable – doors swing open onto the garden and a patio suntrap – and you tuck into breakfast in the conservatory surrounded by peaceful pastoral views. It's walking distance across fields to the pub and to the Ridgeway National Trail, Britain's oldest road. *Children over 12 welcome.*

| | |
|---|---|
| Price | £70–£75. Singles £45–£50. |
| Rooms | 3: 1 double; 1 twin with separate shower; 1 single with separate bath/shower. |
| Meals | Pub 0.5 miles. |
| Closed | Christmas & New Year. |
| Directions | South on A413 from Wendover. Pass Jet station, left to Kings Ash; 2 miles on, left at x-roads, past pub; 0.5 miles on, sharp left onto bridlepath; 2nd gate along. |

Mike & Sue Jepson
Field Cottage,
St Leonards, Tring, Buckinghamshire
HP23 6NS

| | |
|---|---|
| Tel | +44 (0)1494 837602 |
| Fax | +44 (0)1494 837137 |
| Email | michael.jepson@lineone.net |
| Web | www.fieldcottagebandb.co.uk |

Entry 20　Map 9

# Cambridgeshire

## Springfield House

A fine mix of town and country: you are in a rural village yet wonderfully close to Cambridge. The former school house hugs the bend of a river, its French windows opening to rambling, delightful gardens with scented roses in June and July and a yew garden in the spring. The conservatory, draped with a huge mimosa, is an exceptional spot for summer breakfasts. Beds and bedrooms are large and comfortable, with thick curtains, interesting books, fresh flowers and garden or river views. This is an old-fashioned, elegant home and Judith is a quietly nurturing, ever-thoughtful hostess. Good value.

| | |
|---|---|
| Price | £65–£70. Singles £45–£50. |
| Rooms | 2 doubles. |
| Meals | Pubs 150 yds. |
| Closed | Rarely. |
| Directions | A1307 from Cambridge, left into High St. 1st right after The Crown (on left) into Horn Lane. House on right next to chapel, before ford. Or bus no. 13 and 13A from Cambridge. |

Judith Rossiter
Springfield House,
14–16 Horn Lane, Linton,
Cambridgeshire CB21 4HT

| | |
|---|---|
| Tel | +44 (0)1223 891383 |
| Fax | +44 (0)1223 890335 |
| Email | fredrossiter@tiscali.co.uk |
| Web | www.springfieldhouse.org |

Entry 21　Map 9

# Cambridgeshire

## Westoe Farm

Immerse yourself in miles of waving wheat, woodlands and sugar beet. The house is a flint-knapped oasis of deep comfort: you will find traditionally comfortable bedrooms and a large and attractive hall with a huge sitting-room that is yours; you may not want to go out if the stove is seductive and the weather not so. Generous Tim and Henrietta are a capable pair and you are well looked after: meats are local, the eggs are theirs, jams and honey are homemade. There's a fine, rose-filled garden and woods and fields; stroll around to your heart's content before a delicious dinner of home-grown vegetables and local game in season.

Travel Club offer. See page 414.

| | |
|---|---|
| Price | £100. Singles £65. |
| Rooms | 2 twins/doubles. |
| Meals | Dinner, 2 courses, £25. BYO. Pub/restaurant 1 mile. |
| Closed | Christmas & New Year. |
| Directions | A1307 to Linton, right at Bartlow crossroads through Bartlow, then 1 mile from village house is signed, 3rd farm track on right. |

Mrs Henrietta Breitmeyer
Westoe Farm,
Bartlow,
Cambridgeshire CB21 4PR

| | |
|---|---|
| Tel | +44 (0)1223 892731 |
| Fax | +44 (0)1223 892731 |
| Email | enquire@bartlow.u-net.com |
| Web | www.westoefarm.co.uk |

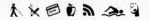

Entry 22   Map 9

# Cambridgeshire

## The Old Chapel

Tardis-like, this 1823 converted chapel opens out to a series of lovely light rooms and a gorgeous garden with cows peeping over the fence. You have a large drawing room with a wood-burner, a dining room with a grand piano, a verdant conservatory, a fabulous library, even a sauna. Bedrooms are beautifully dressed with cream bedspreads, pale carpets, fine antiques and heaps of cushions; bathrooms have gleaming tiles and fresh flowers. Alex and Ian are both keen cooks and love entertaining; the vast kitchen, with arched chapel windows, has a huge table and food is sourced as locally as possible. Good fun.

Ethical Collection: Environment; Food. See page 412.

Travel Club offer. See page 414.

| | |
|---|---|
| Price | £70–£75. Singles £45. |
| Rooms | 2: 1 double; 1 single with separate bath. |
| Meals | Dinner £25. Pubs easy walking distance. Restaurants 7 miles. |
| Closed | Rarely. |
| Directions | A1307 dir. Haverhill. through Linton; after dual carriageway, left slip road into village. Left at sign of horse on green towards West Wickham. House 200 yds on left opposite thatched cottage. |

Alexandra & Ian Rose
The Old Chapel,
West Wickham Road,
Horseheath,
Cambridge, Cambridgeshire CB21 4QA

| | |
|---|---|
| Tel | +44 (0)1223 894027 |
| Email | alexchapel@btinternet.com |
| Web | www.theoldchapelbandb.co.uk |

Entry 23   Map 9

# Cheshire

## The Mount

Britain at its best: rare trees planted in 1860, bountiful flowers, a pond, a vegetable garden and Rachel – delightful, warm and friendly. The Victorian house, built for a Chester corn merchant and furnished in a traditional style, has garden views from every light-filled window. You get an airy drawing room, a high-ceilinged dining room and comfortable, spacious, country-house bedrooms with attractive paintings and soft furnishings. A haven for garden buffs and walkers – and there's a tennis court too. Chester, North Wales and two airports are conveniently close. *Arrivals after 5pm.*

| Price | £60. Singles £40. |
|---|---|
| Rooms | 3: 2 doubles, 1 twin. |
| Meals | Pub/restaurant 5-minute walk. |
| Closed | Christmas & New Year. |
| Directions | From A55 signed North Wales. A5104 Broughton; at 2nd r'bout left to Pennyfordd. Through village, cross over A55 then left Lesters Lane, signed Higher Kinnerton 1.25 miles. House 0.75 miles on right, on the bend. |

Jonathan & Rachel Major
The Mount,
Higher Kinnerton, Chester,
Cheshire CH4 9BQ
Tel       +44 (0)1244 660275
Email    themount@higherkinnerton.com
Web      www.bandbchester.com

Entry 24   Map 7

# Cheshire

## Cotton Farm

Only a four-mile hop from Roman Chester and its 900-year-old cathedral is this sprawling, red-brick farmhouse. Elegant chickens peck in hedges, ponies graze, lambs frisk and cats doze. The farm, run by conservationists Nigel and Clare, is under the Countryside Stewardship Scheme – there are wildflower meadows, summer swallows and 250 acres to roam. Bedrooms are large, stylish farmhouse with lovely fabrics and touches of luxury (bath towels are huge), but best of all is the relaxed family atmosphere. Breakfasts are delicious and beautifully presented. *Stabling available. Children over ten welcome.*

| Price | £72. Singles £52. |
|---|---|
| Rooms | 3: 2 doubles, 1 twin. |
| Meals | Pub 1.5 miles. |
| Closed | Rarely. |
| Directions | A51 Chester-Nantwich. 1.5 miles from outskirts, after golf course on left, right, down Cotton Lane, signed Cotton Edmunds; 1.5 miles, left on sharp right-hand bend; 2nd drive on right. |

Clare & Nigel Hill
Cotton Farm,
Cotton Edmunds, Chester,
Cheshire CH3 7PG
Tel       +44 (0)1244 336616
Email    echill@btinternet.com
Web      www.cottonfarm.co.uk

Entry 25   Map 7

## Cheshire

### Greenlooms Cottage

This pretty cottage was where the estate's chief hedger and ditcher lived. The smallholding has gone but the walnuts, quinces and garden pump remain – and the views still reach to the Peckforton Hills. Now it is a stylishly simple and fun place to stay, thanks to Deborah – traveller, ex-potter, fabulous cook – and Peter, furniture-maker and restorer. Follow your nose to the Aga-cosy kitchen where the best black pudding and bacon are waiting to fuel you for a day on the Cheshire cycle route. Return to two sweet bedrooms, one up one down: crisp white duvets, Floris soaps in simple walk-in showers, ethnic touches.

| | |
|---|---|
| Price | £70. Singles from £45. |
| Rooms | 2: 1 double, 1 twin. |
| Meals | Dinner, £25 with wine. Pub 3 miles. |
| Closed | Never. |
| Directions | A41 Whitchurch; south from Chester. After petrol station, 2nd left at antiques shop. On for 1.5 miles through village, right into Martins Lane; 1 mile on right. |

**Deborah Newman**
Greenlooms Cottage,
Martins Lane, Hargrave,
Chester, Cheshire CH3 7RX
Tel +44 (0)1829 781475
Email dnewman@greenlooms.com
Web www.greenlooms.com

Entry 26   Map 7

## Cheshire

### Goss Moor

Crunch up the gravelled drive to a big, but not imposing, white mansion house – this is still very much Chris and Sarah's family home. You are a short drive (or take the ferry) from the capital of culture or the wilds of north Wales; return to an open fireplace, comfy sofas and a kind welcome from Sarah. Sleep peacefully in sunny bedrooms painted white, with elegant antiques, squishy pillows and views to the front; bathrooms are spotless and warm. Tuck in to a generous breakfast – or delicious supper – in the huge, open-plan kitchen with its steam-engine red Aga and views over the back garden. On hot days cool off in the pool.

Travel Club offer. See page 414.

| | |
|---|---|
| Price | £80-£85. Singles £50-£55. |
| Rooms | 2: 1 twin/double; 1 double with separate bath. |
| Meals | Dinner £25 including wine. Pub/restaurant 2 miles. |
| Closed | Christmas. |
| Directions | From Chester, A540 north. After about 7 miles right to Willaston. Right at T-junction, then first left into Mill Lane. House is 9th on left. |

**Chris & Sarah White**
Goss Moor,
Willaston,
Cheshire CH64 1RG
Tel +44 (0)1513 274000
Email sarahcmwhite@aol.com
Web www.gossmoor.co.uk

Entry 27   Map 7

# Cheshire

## Harrop Fold Farm

Artists, foodies and walkers adore this antique-filled farmhouse with soul-lifting views. On the edge of the Peak District, the oldest building on the farm dates from 1694 (Bonnie Prince Charlie visited here!). The B&B part has a warm, peaceful breakfast room, a stone-flagged sitting room, a spectacular studio. Fresh flowers, antique beds, fine fabrics, hot water bottles with chic covers, bathrooms with fluffy robes: you get the best. Gregarious Sue and daughter Leah hold art and cookery courses so the food too is special. Bedrooms have stupendous views – and flat-screen TV and DVD just in case they pall.

Ethical Collection: Food; Community.
See page 412.

Travel Club offer. See page 414.

| Price | £85. Singles £55. |
|---|---|
| Rooms | 2 doubles. |
| Meals | Cookery demonstration and dine, £40. Dinner, 5 courses, £30. Supper £15. Packed lunch available. Pub 0.25 miles. |
| Closed | Never. |
| Directions | B470 Macclesfield to Whaley Bridge. On for 4 miles to Highwayman pub; 0.25 miles further down track (rutted at top); on left, immed. before sharp right-hand bend. |

|  | Sue Stevenson |
|---|---|
|  | Harrop Fold Farm, |
|  | Rainow, Macclesfield, |
|  | Cheshire SK10 5UU |
| Tel | +44 (0)1625 560085 |
| Email | stay@harropfoldfarm.co.uk |
| Web | www.harropfoldfarm.co.uk |

Entry 28   Map 8

# Cornwall

## The Old Vicarage

The first sight of quirky chimneys – the spires of former owner Reverend Hawker's parish churches – sets the scene for a huge house packed with interest and steeped in Victoriana. Jill and Richard, both delightful, know the local history – and the clifftop walks, which are glorious. Rooms are casually grand, dotted with *objets* – brass gramophone, magic lantern, eccentric Hawker memorabilia. Browse books in the study, play the grand piano, sip brandy over billiards. Bedrooms are country-house pretty, with most bathrooms refurbished, lawns well tended and views to the sea. Blissfully, mobiles don't work.

| Price | £80. Singles £40. |
|---|---|
| Rooms | 3: 1 double, 1 twin, 1 single. |
| Meals | Pub/tea rooms 5-10-minute walk. |
| Closed | December & January. |
| Directions | From A39 at Morwenstow, follow signs for church. Small turning on right, just before church, marked 'public footpath'. Drive down to house. |

|  | Jill & Richard Wellby |
|---|---|
|  | The Old Vicarage, |
|  | Morwenstow, |
|  | Cornwall EX23 9SR |
| Tel | +44 (0)1288 331369 |
| Fax | +44 (0)1288 356077 |
| Web | www.rshawker.co.uk |

Entry 29   Map 1

# Cornwall

## The Old Parsonage

A spellbinding coastline, secret coves, spectacular walks. All this and a supremely comfortable Georgian rectory – with a drying room for wet togs to return to. Morag and Margaret have transformed the interior. Superb pitch pine floors and original woodwork add warmth and a fresh glow, the big engaging bedrooms (including one on the ground floor) have a quirky, upbeat mix of furniture and furnishings, and the bathrooms are pampering. In front of the house the land slopes away to the Atlantic, just a five-minute walk across a SSSI. There are plans afoot for the garden, which already has some pleasant corners.

Ethical Collection: Environment; Food. See page 412.

🧳 Travel Club offer. See page 414.

| | |
|---|---|
| Price | From £80. Singles from £55. |
| Rooms | 5 twins/doubles. |
| Meals | Dinner, by arrangement, £20. Packed lunch £5.95. Pub/restaurant 600 yds. |
| Closed | Rarely. |
| Directions | In Boscastle head towards Tintagel on B3263. 500 yds after garage on left, turn right into Green Lane. After bend, house 3rd on right. |

|   | Morag Reeve & Margaret Pickering |
|---|---|
|   | The Old Parsonage, |
|   | Forrabury, Boscastle, |
|   | Cornwall PL35 0DJ |
| Tel | +44 (0)1840 250339 |
| Email | morag@old-parsonage.com |
| Web | www.old-parsonage.com |

🚶 ✗ 🖃 🌰 🔊 🍶

Entry 30   Map 1

# Cornwall

## Upton Farm

A restored farmhouse set back from the rugged coastline with unrivalled views, from Tintagel to Port Isaac and beyond… sunsets are sublime. Bedrooms are traditional and smart, there's a games room and safe storage for surfers. Slate slabs in the hall, gentle colours throughout; from the depths of the sea-green sofa in your drawing room, breathe in those AONB views. Such seclusion! Yet ten minutes across fields is the coastal path and, nearby, serious surfing, great pub, restaurant and more. Kick-start your day with Ricardo's signature muesli. *Minimum stay two nights. Children over eight welcome.*

🧳 Travel Club offer. See page 414.

| | |
|---|---|
| Price | From £90. |
| Rooms | 4: 2 doubles, 1 twin, 1 family. |
| Meals | Pub/restaurant 1 mile. |
| Closed | Rarely. |
| Directions | South through Delabole, near end of village right into Treligga Downs Rd; 0.5 miles to T-junc.; turn right. 1 mile on, pass Trecarne Farm on left; 100 yds, house on right. |

|   | Elizabeth & Ricardo Dorich |
|---|---|
|   | Upton Farm, |
|   | Trebarwith, |
|   | Cornwall PL33 9DG |
| Tel | +44 (0)1840 770225 |
| Email | ricardo@dorich.co.uk |
| Web | www.upton-farm.co.uk |

✗ 🐈

Entry 31   Map 1

# Cornwall

## Caradoc of Tregardock

A 300-acre farm with hens, sheep and wheeling gulls; lush fields roll down to a tidal beach. Children love it, artists come to paint, you can take the whole place and cook for yourself (the kitchen is super) or dig into something delicious, perhaps fresh lobster, roast lamb, lemon meringue pie. Janet lives in the farmhouse, you get a converted listed barn. Expect a warm country feel, the odd beam, seascapes on the wall, comfy bedrooms. There's a vast first-floor sitting room that's open to the rafters and a deck for glorious sunsets. Total peace is guaranteed, the night sky can be amazing. *Cream teas.*

# Cornwall

## Tremoren

Views stretch sleepily over the Cornish countryside. You might feel inclined to do nothing more than snooze over your book on the terrace, but the surfing beaches, the Camel Trail and the Eden Project are all close by. The stone and slate former farmhouse has been smartly updated with a light and airy ground-floor bedroom – all soft colours, pretty china and crisp bed linen – and a swish, power-shower bathroom. Your red-walled sitting room, full of books and interesting maps, leads out onto the flower-filled terrace: perfect for that evening drink. Lanie is bubbly and engaging, and food is her passion.

Travel Club offer. See page 414.

| | |
|---|---|
| Price | £90-£130. Singles £45-£65. Whole house self-catering £475-£2,000 per week. |
| Rooms | 4 twins/doubles. |
| Meals | Dinner with wine, £35, by arrangement. Private chef available. Pub/restaurant 2 miles. |
| Closed | Never. |
| Directions | Take turn to Treligga off B3314; 2nd farm road, signed. |

| | |
|---|---|
| Price | £80. |
| Rooms | 1 double & sitting room. |
| Meals | Dinner, 4 courses, £25. Inn 0.5 miles. |
| Closed | Rarely. |
| Directions | A39 to St Kew Highway through village; left at Red Lion. Down lane, 1st left round sharp right-hand bend. 2nd drive on right; signed. |

| | |
|---|---|
| | **Janet Cant** |
| | Caradoc of Tregardock, |
| | Treligga, |
| | Delabole, Cornwall PL33 9ED |
| Tel | +44 (0)1840 213300 |
| Email | info@tregardock.com |
| Web | www.tregardock.com |

| | |
|---|---|
| | **Philip & Lanie Calvert** |
| | Tremoren, |
| | St Kew, Bodmin, |
| | Cornwall PL30 3HA |
| Tel | +44 (0)1208 841790 |
| Fax | +44 (0)1208 841031 |
| Email | la.calvert@btopenworld.com |

Entry 32   Map 1

Entry 33   Map 1

# Cornwall

### Higher Lank Farm

Families rejoice: you can only come if you have a child under five! Celtic crosses in the garden and original panelling hint at the house's 500-year history; bedrooms, newly decorated, have pocket sprung mattresses and large TVs. Nursery teas begin at 5pm, grown-up suppers are later and energetic Lucy will cheerfully babysit while the rest of you slink off to the pub. Farm-themed playgrounds are covered in safety matting and grass, there are piglets and chicks, a pony to ride, eggs to collect, a nursery rhyme trail, a sand barn for little ones and cream teas in the garden. Oh, and real nappies are provided!

| | |
|---|---|
| Price | From £95. Singles by arrangement. |
| Rooms | 3 family rooms. |
| Meals | Supper £20. Nursery tea £6.50. Pub 1.5 miles. |
| Closed | November-Easter. |
| Directions | A30 past Launceston. Right to St Brevard 4 miles. Across moor through Bradford, then first right. Hump back bridge and crossroads, turn left (no sign & not straight on to St Brevard). Follow road to bottom of hill; signed opposite. |

**Lucy Finnemore**
Higher Lank Farm,
St Breward, Bodmin, Cornwall
PL30 4NB
Tel +44 (0)1208 850716
Email higherlankfarm@waitrose.com
Web www.higherlankfarm.co.uk

Entry 34   Map 1

# Cornwall

### Cabilla Manor

There's a treasure round every corner and an opera house in one of the barns. Instant seduction as you enter the old manor house out on the moor, brimful of interest and colour. Rich exotic rugs and cushions, artefacts from around the world, Louella's sumptuous hand-stencilled quilts, huge beds, coir carpets, garden flowers. There's a dining room crammed floor to ceiling with books, many of them Robin's (a writer and explorer) and a lofty conservatory for meals overlooking a semi-wild garden – with tennis and elegant lawns. The views are heavenly, the hosts wonderful and the final mile thrillingly wild.

| | |
|---|---|
| Price | £80. Singles £40. |
| Rooms | 4: 1 double; 1 double with separate bath; 1 double, 1 twin, sharing bath (let to same party only). |
| Meals | Dinner, 3 courses, £30. Pub 4 miles. Restaurant 8-10 miles. |
| Closed | Christmas & New Year. |
| Directions | 6 miles after Jamaica Inn on A30, left for Cardinham. Through Millpool & straight on, ignoring further signs to Cardinham. After 2.5 miles, left to Manor 0.75 miles; on right down drive. |

**Robin & Louella Hanbury-Tenison**
Cabilla Manor,
Mount, Bodmin, Cornwall PL30 4DW
Tel +44 (0)1208 821224
Fax +44 (0)1208 821267
Email louella@cabilla.co.uk
Web www.cabilla.co.uk

Entry 35   Map 1

# Cornwall

## Park Farmhouse

A gorgeous slate-roofed farmhouse on the north Cornish coast, near to surfing, coastal path, Camel trail. Flop in the guests' sitting room with a wood-burner and comfortable brocade sofa; bedrooms (one on the ground floor) are sumptuous with antique beds, fresh striped curtains and crisp linen (any road noise is muffled by mature trees). Justin and Sarah are passionate and knowledgeable about food, so you eat really well (home smoked chicken and duck, the freshest local fish) and you dine surrounded by antlers at a gleaming table. Afterwards take a turn round the well-planned garden. *Gourmet food and pilates weekends.*

Ethical Collection: Food. See page 412.

 Travel Club offer. See page 414.

| Price | £70–£80. Singles £50. |
|---|---|
| Rooms | 4: 2 doubles; 1 double, 1 single sharing bath. |
| Meals | Dinner, 3 courses, £30. Children's teas £15. Hotel 0.5 miles; pub 2 miles. |
| Closed | Never. |
| Directions | From Bodmin, A389 for Wadebridge. Cross river, pass signs for Camelford & Pencarrow; through Washaway; for 1 mile, down long hill. At bottom, blue sign on right. |

| | Justin & Sarah Mason |
|---|---|
| | Park Farmhouse, Washaway, Bodmin, Cornwall PL30 3AG |
| Tel | +44 (0)1208 841277 |
| Email | parkfarmhouse@googlemail.com |
| Web | www.park-farmhouse.com |

Entry 36  Map 1

# Cornwall

## Lavethan

A glorious house in the most glorious of settings: views sail down to the valley. It rambles on many levels and is part 15th-century: walls are stone, floors are flagged, stairs are oak. The sunny bedroom in the house is best, with its panelled walls and smart bathroom; bedrooms across the courtyard are very private with their own entrances and have pretty quilted bedspreads. Catherine, a warm hostess, has decorated in country style; the guest sitting room is hugely welcoming with books, flowers and piano. All this and acres of ancient woods, Celtic crosses and a heated pool in the old walled garden. *Children over ten welcome.*

| Price | £90. Singles £50. |
|---|---|
| Rooms | 3: 2 twins/doubles, 1 double. |
| Meals | Pub 0.25 miles. |
| Closed | Rarely. |
| Directions | From A30, turn for Blisland. There, past church on left & pub on right. Take lane at bottom left of village green. 0.25 miles on, drive on left (granite pillars & cattle grid). |

| | Christopher & Catherine Hartley |
|---|---|
| | Lavethan, Blisland, Bodmin, Cornwall PL30 4QG |
| Tel | +44 (0)1208 850487 |
| Fax | +44 (0)1208 851387 |
| Email | chrishartley@btconnect.com |
| Web | www.lavethan.com |

Entry 37  Map 1

# Cornwall

## Menkee

From this handsome Georgian farmhouse there are long views towards the sea; you're 20 minutes away from the coastal path and wild surf but you may not want to budge. Gage and Liz are deliciously unstuffy and look after you well: newspapers and a weather forecast appear with a scrumptious breakfast, your gorgeously comfortable bed is turned down in the evening and walkers can be dropped off and collected. The elegant house is filled with beautiful things, gleaming furniture, fresh flowers, roaring fires and pretty fabrics – all you have to do is slacken your pace and wind down. *Minimum stay two nights in high season.*

Ethical Collection: Food. See page 412.

Travel Club offer. See page 414.

| | |
|---|---|
| Price | £80-£90. Singles from £40. |
| Rooms | 2 doubles. |
| Meals | Pub/restaurant 1.3 miles. |
| Closed | Rarely. |
| Directions | A389 Bodmin-Wadebridge; 2.5 miles, then fork right on B3266; on for 2 miles for Camelford; 600 yds after St Mabyn turn-off, left down drive. |

**Gage & Liz Williams**
Menkee,
St Maybn, Wadebridge,
Cornwall PL30 3DD

| | |
|---|---|
| Tel | +44 (0)1208 841378 |
| Email | gagewillms@aol.com |
| Web | www.cornwall-online.co.uk/menkee |

Entry 38   Map 1

# Cornwall

## Roskear

Drive down the fields to this 17th-century working farmhouse, a blissfully peaceful escape. A large sitting room with log fire, a warm and smiling hostess, happy dogs, a comfortable bedroom, a cheerful Aga, fabulous estuary views – country life at its most charming. Delicious breakfasts are served on blue china, doors open to the garden on sunny days and there are acres of woodland and grassland to explore. Good restaurants include Rick Stein's, the ferry takes you to Rock, surfing is a short drive and the Camel cycle trail is nearby (hire bikes locally). Uncomplicated, good value B&B.

| | |
|---|---|
| Price | From £70. Singles £35. |
| Rooms | 2: 1 double with separate bath; 1 twin/double sharing bath (let to same party only). |
| Meals | Pubs/restaurants 0.5-6 miles. |
| Closed | Rarely. |
| Directions | Bypass Wadebridge on A39 for Redruth. Over bridge, pass garage on left, straight over roundabout, filter 1st right to Edmonton. By modern houses immed. right to Roskear over cattle grid. |

**Rosina Messer-Bennetts**
Roskear,
St Breock, Wadebridge,
Cornwall PL27 7HU

| | |
|---|---|
| Tel | +44 (0)1208 812805 |
| Email | rosina@roskear.com |
| Web | www.roskear.com |

Entry 39   Map 1

# Cornwall

## Porteath Barn

What a spot! This upside-down house is elegantly uncluttered and cool with seagrass flooring and a wood-burner in the sitting room. Bedrooms – not vast – have fresh flowers, quilted bedspreads and there's an Italian marble shower room; the feel is private with your own doors to the lovely, large garden. Walks from here down a path with ponds will take you to Epphaven Cove and the beach at the bottom of the valley or to a good pub for supper if you're feeling hearty. The Bloors have perfected the art of B&B-ing, being kind and helpful without being intrusive. *Children over 12 by arrangement.*

| Price | From £80. Singles by arrangement. |
|---|---|
| Rooms | 3: 2 twins/doubles, each with separate bath or shower; 1 double let to same party only. |
| Meals | Pub 1.5 miles. |
| Closed | Rarely. |
| Directions | A39 to Wadebridge. At r'bout follow signs to Polzeath, then to Porteath Bee Centre. Through Bee Centre shop car park, down farm track; house signed on right after 150 yds. |

**Jo & Michael Bloor**
Porteath Barn,
St Minver,
Wadebridge,
Cornwall PL27 6RA
Tel   +44 (0)1208 863605
Email   m.bloor17@btinternet.com

Entry 40    Map 1

# Cornwall

## Polrode Mill Cottage

A lovely, beamy, 17th-century cottage in a birdsung valley. Inside, flagged floors, Chesterfields, a wood-burner and a light, open feel. Your friendly young hosts live next door; they are working hard on the informal flower and vegetable garden, much of the produce is used in David's delicious homemade dinners, there's pumpkin marmalade and eggs from the hens. Bedrooms are cottage-cosy with stripped floors, comfy wrought-iron beds and silver cast-iron radiators; fresh bathrooms have double-ended roll tops. A slight hum of traffic can be heard outside, but inside is blissfully peaceful. *Minimum stay two nights in high season.*

 Travel Club offer. See page 414.

| Price | £81–£90. Singles £60. |
|---|---|
| Rooms | 3: 2 doubles; 1 double with separate bath. |
| Meals | Dinner, 3 courses, £30. Pub/restaurant 3 miles. |
| Closed | Rarely. |
| Directions | From A395 A39 towards Camelford. Through Camelford; continue on A39 to Knightsmill. From there, 1.8 miles on left-hand side. |

**Deborah Hilborne & David Edwards**
Polrode Mill Cottage,
Allen Valley, St Kew, Wadebridge,
Cornwall PL30 3NS
Tel   +44 (0)1208 850203
Email   polrode@tesco.net
Web   www.polrodeguesthouse.co.uk

Entry 41    Map 1

# Cornwall

## Mother Ivey Cottage

So close to the sea that there are salt splashes on the windows! Exceptionally lovely hosts here and a simple refuge from crashing surf and Atlantic winds. The house was once a fish cellar for processing catches, and recently a location for a TV film. Look out of the window to the big blue below, swim to the lifeboat launch, barbecue on the beach. The coastal path is stunning and you can walk to surfing beaches or just drop down to the quiet bay beneath your window. Cultured, kind hosts and a relaxed atmosphere; bedrooms and bathrooms are not frilly or smart but come for the views. Families love it.

| | |
|---|---|
| Price | From £70. Singles by arrangement. |
| Rooms | 2 twins. Extra single bed. |
| Meals | Dinner from £25. Packed lunch from £5. Pub/restaurant 5 miles. |
| Closed | Rarely. |
| Directions | From St Merryn, right for Trevose Head. Over sleeping policemen. After tollgate ticket machine, right through 2nd farm gate. On towards sea; cottage gate at end of track, on right. |

Phyllida & Antony Woosnam-Mills
Mother Ivey Cottage,
Trevose Head,
Padstow,
Cornwall PL28 8SL
Tel    +44 (0)1841 520329
Email  antony@trevosehead.co.uk

Entry 42   Map 1

# Cornwall

## Molesworth Manor

It's a splendid old place, big enough to swallow hoards of people, peppered with art and interesting antiques. There are palms and a play area in the garden, a drawing room with an honesty bar and an open fire for cosy nights, a carved staircase leading to bedrooms that vary in style and size – His Lordship's at the front, the Maid's in the eaves – and bathrooms that are lovely and pampering. The whiff of homemade muffins lures you downstairs in the morning, the Cornish Riviera and its food scene will ravish you later – you're in the heart of it all. A superb bolthole run by Geoff and Jessica, youthful and fun.

Travel Club offer. See page 414.

| | |
|---|---|
| Price | £58–£100. Singles from £45. |
| Rooms | 9: 7 doubles, 1 twin/double; 1 twin with separate shower. |
| Meals | Pubs/restaurants 2 miles. |
| Closed | November-January. Open off-season by arrangement for larger parties. |
| Directions | Off A389 between Wadebridge & Padstow. Entrance clearly signed; 300 yds from bridge in Little Petherick. |

Geoff French & Jessica Clarke
Molesworth Manor,
Little Petherick, Padstow, Cornwall
PL27 7QT
Tel    +44 (0)1841 540292
Email  molesworthmanor@aol.com
Web    www.molesworthmanor.co.uk

Entry 43   Map 1

# Cornwall

## Calize Country House

Beneath wheeling gulls and close to blond beaches, the big square 1870 house has amazing views of skies and sea. Virginia Woolf's lighthouse is in the bay and winter seals cavort at the colony nearby. A fresh, uncomplicated décor brings the tang of the sea to every room. Artworks recall a world of surf; deckchair stripes clothe the dining table and dress the window; traditional sofas call for quiet times with a book. Upstairs, patterned or pale walls, practical bath or shower rooms, perhaps a sea view. Jilly and Nigel are testament to the benefits of sea air and look after you beautifully.

Ethical Collection: Environment; Food. See page 412.

Travel Club offer. See page 414.

| | |
|---|---|
| Price | £80–£90. Singles £55. |
| Rooms | 4: 2 doubles, 1 twin, 1 single. |
| Meals | Packed lunch £5. Pub 350 yds. |
| Closed | Rarely. |
| Directions | Exit A30 at Camborne (west) A3047. Left, then right at r'bout. Right on entering Connor Downs, then on for 2 miles. House on right after sign for Gwithian. |

Jilly Whitaker
Calize Country House,
Gwithian,
Hayle, Cornwall TR27 5BW
Tel    +44 (0)1736 753268
Fax    +44 (0)1736 753268
Email  jilly@calize.co.uk
Web    www.calize.co.uk

Entry 44   Map 1

# Cornwall

## Treglisson

A short drive from St Ives, the glorious bay and some nifty surfing beaches. Inside the old farmhouse, all is calm and peaceful. Stephen and Heather are thoughtful, fun, easy-going and filled with enthusiasm for looking after you: large light bedrooms in soft colours, generous beds with lovely linen, modern white bathrooms, good art on the walls, a beautiful antique-marble hall floor. Cornish Aga-cooked breakfasts can be relished late if you prefer; in the evening, take a sundowner to the garden in summer or relax by the log fire in winter. There's a heated indoor pool too in the summer.

Travel Club offer. See page 414.

| | |
|---|---|
| Price | £55–£75. Singles from £35. |
| Rooms | 4: 1 double, 1 twin, 2 family rooms. |
| Meals | Pubs/restaurants 2-5 miles. |
| Closed | Christmas & New Year. |
| Directions | A30 to Hayle; 4th exit on r'bout into Hayle. Left at mini r'bout into Guildford Rd; up hill for 1 mile. Turn left at green sign into lane. |

Stephen & Heather Reeves
Treglisson,
Wheal Alfred Road,
Hayle,
Cornwall TR27 5JT
Tel    +44 (0)1736 753141
Email  steve@treglisson.co.uk
Web    www.treglisson.co.uk

Entry 45   Map 1

# Cornwall

### House at Gwinear

An island of calm – it sits, as it has for 500 years, in its own bird-trilled acres a short drive from St Ives. The Halls are devoted to the encouragement of the arts and crafts which is reflected in their lifestyle. There's no stuffiness – just fresh flowers on the breakfast table, a piano in the corner, rugs on polished floors and masses of books. In a separate wing you have a cosy bedroom and sitting room and a fine view of the church from the bath. The big lawn-filled gardens are there for bare-footed solace, and you can have breakfast in the Italianate courtyard on sunny days.

Travel Club offer. See page 414.

| | |
|---|---|
| Price | From £75. |
| Rooms | 1 twin/double & sitting room with separate bath. |
| Meals | Dinner, 3 courses including wines, from £29. Supper, 2 courses and glass of wine, £20. Pub 1.5 miles. |
| Closed | Rarely. |
| Directions | From A30 exit Hayle (Loggans Moor r'bout); 100 yds left at mini r'bout; 400 yds left for Gwinear; 1.5 miles, top of hill, driveway on right, just before 30mph Gwinear sign. |

**Charles & Diana Hall**
House at Gwinear,
Gwinear,
St Ives,
Cornwall TR27 5JZ

| | |
|---|---|
| Tel | +44 (0)1736 850444 |
| Fax | +44 (0)1736 850444 |
| Email | charleshall@btinternet.com |

Entry 46   Map 1

# Cornwall

### The Old Vicarage

Artists will be inspired, not just with the proximity to St Ives but with Jackie's dazzling collection of her own and other artists' work. This is a light, airy, welcoming house whose big sash windows overlook a subtropical garden; wander at will after a grand breakfast of fresh fruit and local bacon and sausages. Bedrooms have soft coloured walls, deeply comfortable beds, period furniture and more lovely artwork adding spots of colour; bathrooms are gleaming and fresh. There's a sandy beach 20-minutes' walk away and you can join the coastal path just up the road. Wonderful house, lovely owners.

Travel Club offer. See page 414.

| | |
|---|---|
| Price | £70-£75. Singles £40. |
| Rooms | 3: 1 twin; 1 double with separate bath, 1 single sharing bath (let to same party only). |
| Meals | Pubs 5-8 minute walk. Restaurants in St Ives 2.5 miles. |
| Closed | 1 November-30 March. |
| Directions | A30 dir. Penzance. At 2nd Hayle r'bout, A3074 St Ives. After Wyvale Garden Centre, over mini r'bout; right at next one & into Lelant. Brush End is lane on left after sign for Elm Farm. House at end. |

**Jackie & Howard Hollingsbee**
The Old Vicarage,
Brush End,
Lelant,
St Ives, Cornwall TR26 3EF

| | |
|---|---|
| Tel | +44 (0)1736 753324 |
| Email | bookings@oldvicaragelelant.co.uk |
| Web | www.oldvicaragelelant.co.uk |

Entry 47   Map 1

## Cornwall

### Jamies

Breathe in the ocean views from this stylish 1920s villa. Airy bedrooms are hotel-smart with white bed linen, striped and checked curtains, fresh new bathrooms, a feeling of space and sea views; two have proper sitting areas. Crisp linen and silver at the breakfast table create an elegant mood – relish an exotic fruit salad in a perfect white room overlooking the bay, or admire some of artist Felicity's inspiring work. Generous, easy-going Felicity and Jamie are ex-hoteliers with a great sense of fun, the white sands of Carbis Bay are a five-minute walk, and St Ives lies just beyond. *Children over 12 welcome.*

| | |
|---|---|
| Price | From £100. Singles £80. |
| Rooms | 4: 3 twins/doubles, 1 suite. |
| Meals | Pub 3-minute walk. Restaurants 1.5 miles. |
| Closed | Rarely. |
| Directions | A30, then A3074 for St Ives. At Carbis Bay, Marshalls estate agents & Methodist church on left. Next right down Pannier Lane; 2nd right is Wheal Whidden; 1st house on left. |

Felicity & Jamie Robertson
Jamies,
Wheal Whidden, Carbis Bay,
St Ives, Cornwall TR26 2QX
Tel       +44 (0)1736 794718
Email    info@jamiesstives.co.uk
Web      www.jamiesstives.co.uk

Entry 48   Map 1

## Cornwall

### Organic Panda B&B & Gallery

A five-minute walk from busy St Ives, with a panoramic view of the bay, boutique B&B in perfect harmony with this artistic spot; come for a bold scattering of modern art and a ten-seater rustic table. Spacious contemporary bedrooms have a laid-back style with organic linen, bamboo towels, chunky beds, white walls and raw-silk cushions. Shower rooms are small but perfectly formed. Andrea is an artist and theatre designer, Peter a photographer and organic chef; the food is delicious and bread home baked. The most beautiful coastal road in all England leads to St Just. *Minimum stay three nights Christmas, Easter, July & August.*

Ethical Collection: Environment; Food.
See page 412.

Travel Club offer. See page 414.

| | |
|---|---|
| Price | £75–£120. |
| Rooms | 3: 2 doubles, 1 twin. |
| Meals | Packed lunch £10. Restaurants nearby. |
| Closed | Rarely. |
| Directions | A3074 to St Ives. Signs to leisure centre; house behind 3rd sign, on left-hand bend. |

Peter Williams & Andrea Carr
Organic Panda B&B & Gallery,
1 Pednolver Terrace,
St Ives, Cornwall TR26 2EL
Tel       +44 (0)1736 793890
Email    info@organicpanda.co.uk
Web      www.organicpanda.co.uk

Entry 49   Map 1

# Cornwall

## 11 Sea View Terrace

In a smart row of Edwardian villas, with views over harbour, island and sea, is a delectable retreat. Sleek, softy coloured interiors are light and gentle on the eye – an Italian circular glass table here, a painted seascape there – deeply civilised. Bedrooms are perfect with crisp linen, vistas of whirling gulls, your own terrace; bathrooms are state-of-the-art. Rejoice in softly boiled eggs with anchovy and chive-butter soldiers for breakfast – or continental in bed if you prefer. Grahame looks after you impeccably and design aficionados will be happy. *Free admission to Tate Gallery & Barbara Hepworth Museum.*

| Price | £95–£125. Singles from £70. |
| --- | --- |
| Rooms | 3 suites. |
| Meals | Dinner, with wine, from £25 (groups only). Packed lunch £10. Pubs/restaurants 5-minute walk. |
| Closed | Rarely. |
| Directions | At Porthminster Hotel, signs for Tate; down Albert Rd, right just before Longships Hotel. Limited parking. |

Grahame Wheelband
11 Sea View Terrace,
St Ives,
Cornwall TR26 2DH
Tel +44 (0)1736 798440
Email elevenseaviewterrace@btinternet.com
Web www.11stives.co.uk

Entry 50  Map 1

# Cornwall

## Trezelah Farmhouse

You'll feel high here, on the moor between Penzance and St Ives. The humble manor farmhouse with solid stone walls and huge chimney breast at one end has a light and fresh interior of waxed floors, limed walls, Indian scatter rugs, books, a wood-burner and soft white sofas. Small bedrooms with fine antiques and gentle lighting will calm you, as will the unusually pretty bathrooms – and the lovely Caro who painted many of the pictures here. Stride out round the north coastal path, then take a breather at the Tinners Arms in Zennor and go all Lawrencian; this is a wonderful part of Cornwall.

Travel Club offer. See page 414.

| Price | From £80. |
| --- | --- |
| Rooms | 3: 2 doubles; 1 twin with separate bath. |
| Meals | Pub 3 miles. |
| Closed | October–March. |
| Directions | After Tesco r'bout heading into Penzance on A30, B3311 towards St Ives. Through Gulval, left at Badgers Cross towards Chysauster; left to Trezelah. |

Caro Woods
Trezelah Farmhouse,
Trezelah, Badgers Cross,
Penzance, Cornwall TR20 8XD
Tel +44 (0)1736 874388
Email info@trezelah.co.uk
Web www.trezelah.co.uk

Entry 51  Map 1

# Cornwall

## Ednovean Farm

There's a terrace for each immaculate bedroom (one truly private) with views to the wild blue yonder and St Michael's Mount Bay – an enchanting outlook that changes with the passage of the day. Come for peace, space and the best of eclectic fabrics and colours, pretty lamps, gleaming copper, fluffy bathrobes and handmade soaps. The beamed, open-plan sitting/dining area is an absorbing mix of exotic, rustic and elegant; have full breakfast here, strictly on time, or continental in your room. A footpath through the field leads to the village; walk to glorious Prussia Cove and Cudden Point, or head west to Marazion.

# Cornwall

## Ennys

Prepare to be spoiled. A fire smoulders in the sumptuous sitting room, tea is laid out in the Aga-warm kitchen, and bedrooms are luxurious: a king-size bed or an elegant modern four-poster, powerful showers and crisp white linen. The stylishness continues into the family suites and everywhere there are fascinating artefacts from Gill's travels, designer fabrics and original art. The road ends at Ennys, so it is utterly peaceful; walk down to the river and along the old towpath to St Ives Bay. Or stay put: play tennis (on grass!) and swim in the heated pool sunk deep into the tropical gardens.

 Travel Club offer. See page 414.

| | |
|---|---|
| Price | £85–£105. |
| Rooms | 3: 2 doubles, 1 four-poster. |
| Meals | Pub 5-minute walk. |
| Closed | Christmas & rarely. |
| Directions | From A30 after Crowlas r'bout, A394 to Helston. 0.25 miles after next r'bout, 1st right for Perranuthnoe. Drive on left, signed. |

| | |
|---|---|
| Price | £90–£125. Singles from £65. |
| Rooms | 5: 3 doubles. Barn: 2 family suites. |
| Meals | Pub 3 miles. |
| Closed | 1 November–25 March. |
| Directions | 2 miles east of Marazion on B3280, look for sign & turn left leading down Trewhella Lane between St Hilary & Relubbus. On to Ennys. |

|  | **Christine & Charles Taylor** |
|---|---|
| | Ednovean Farm, |
| | Perranuthnoe, Penzance, |
| | Cornwall TR20 9LZ |
| Tel | +44 (0)1736 711883 |
| Email | info@ednoveanfarm.co.uk |
| Web | www.ednoveanfarm.co.uk |

|  | **Gill Charlton** |
|---|---|
| | Ennys, St Hilary, |
| | Penzance, Cornwall TR20 9BZ |
| Tel | +44 (0)1736 740262 |
| Fax | +44 (0)1736 740055 |
| Email | ennys@ennys.co.uk |
| Web | www.ennys.co.uk |

Entry 52   Map 1

Entry 53   Map 1

## Cornwall

### Drym Farm

Rural, but not too deeply: the Tate at St Ives is a 15-minute drive. The 1705 farmhouse, beautifully revived, is surrounded by ancient barns, a dairy and a forge, fascinating to Cornish historians. Jan arrived in 2002, with an enthusiasm for authenticity and simple, stylish good taste. French limestone floors in the hall, striking art on the walls, a roll top bath, a *bateau lit*, an antique brass bed. Paintwork is fresh cream and taupe. There are old fruit trees and young camellias, a TV-free sitting room with two plump sofas and organic treats at breakfast. Charming and utterly peaceful.

## Cornwall

### Carmelin

The setting of this bungalow is sensational, looking straight out to sea from the Lizard, England's most southerly point. Breakfasts – a feast of breads and pastries, fruits, freshly made yogurt, homemade preserves – have to fight for your attention, so spectacular are the views. The bedroom has them too – and the sun room – making a private suite with its own entrance, sitting and dining area; a gorgeous spot to sit and watch sparkling waves and sunsets. John and Jane are gentle, relaxed people who enjoy their guests, and are happy to advise on the best local walks. *French & German spoken.*

 Travel Club offer. See page 414.

| | |
|---|---|
| Price | £70-£90. Singles from £55. |
| Rooms | 2 doubles. |
| Meals | Pubs/restaurants within 1-4 miles. |
| Closed | Rarely. |
| Directions | From A30 to Hayle; through Hayle to r'bout, left to Helston. At Leedstown, left for Drym. Follow road until right turn to Drym. Farm 4th on lane, on right after Drym House. |

Travel Club offer. See page 414.

| | |
|---|---|
| Price | From £78. Singles by arrangement. |
| Rooms | 1 suite for 2 with separate bath/shower. |
| Meals | Dinner by arrangement. Pub within walking distance. |
| Closed | Rarely. |
| Directions | From Helston to the Lizard; at Lizard Green, right, opp. Regent Café (head for Smugglers Fish & Chips); immed. right, pass wc on left. Road unmade; on for 500 yds; double bend; 2nd on right. |

| | |
|---|---|
| | **Jan Bright** |
| | Drym Farm, |
| | Drym, Praze-an-Beeble, |
| | Camborne, Cornwall TR14 0NU |
| Tel | +44 (0)1209 831039 |
| Email | drymfarm@hotmail.co.uk |
| Web | www.drymfarm.co.uk |

| | |
|---|---|
| | **Jane & John Grierson** |
| | Carmelin, |
| | Pentreath Lane, |
| | The Lizard, Cornwall TR12 7NY |
| Tel | +44 (0)1326 290677 |
| Email | pjcarmelin@gmail.com |
| Web | www.bedandbreakfastcornwall.co.uk |

Entry 54   Map 1

Entry 55   Map 1

# Cornwall

## Landewednack House

Susan and her pug dogs will greet you enthusiastically with tea and biscuits in the drawing room of this immaculate house. Antony the chef keeps the wheels oiled and the food coming – treat yourself to green crab soup or succulent lobster; the wine cellar holds over 2.000 bottles so there's plenty of choice. Upstairs to bedrooms that are not huge and not all with sea views, but everything you could possibly need is there, from robes to brandy. The pool area is stunning with a French feel, the garden is filled with interest and it's just a three-minute walk to the sea. *Minimum stay two nights July & August.*

| Price | From £110. Singles £55-£85. |
|---|---|
| Rooms | 3: 2 doubles, 1 twin. |
| Meals | Dinner, 4 courses, £33-£38. |
| Closed | Open all year. |
| Directions | From Helston, A3083 south. Just before Lizard, left to Church Cove. Follow signs for about 0.75 miles. House on left behind sage green gates. |

| | |
|---|---|
| | Susan Thorbek |
| | Landewednack House, |
| | Church Cove, |
| | The Lizard, Cornwall TR12 7PQ |
| Tel | +44 (0)1326 290877 |
| Email | luxurybandb@landewednackhouse.com |
| Web | www.landewednackhouse.com |

# Cornwall

## The Gardens

Two old miners' cottages combine to create this small, modest, pretty home. Irish Moira, a retired midwife, adores flowers and her posies brighten every corner; Goff, a potter and painter, tends the vegetables. Both are charming and kind. Sweet snug bedrooms have patchwork quilts, cotton sheets, antique linen runners and plenty of books. One is on the ground floor overlooking the pretty cottage garden, two are up a narrow stair. Aga-cooked breakfasts and homemade jams are brought to the sun-streamed conservatory and there's homemade cake in the sitting room by the wood-burner. Great value.

| Price | From £65. Singles £32.50-£36. |
|---|---|
| Rooms | 3: 2 doubles; 1 twin/double with separate bath. |
| Meals | Packed lunch from £7.50. Pubs & restaurants 10-minute drive. |
| Closed | Christmas & New Year. |
| Directions | A394 Helston to Penzance, 2nd right after Ashton Post Office for Tresowes Green. After 0.25 miles, sign for house on right. |

| | |
|---|---|
| | Moira & Goff Cattell |
| | The Gardens, |
| | Tresowes, Ashton, |
| | Helston, |
| | Cornwall TR13 9SY |
| Tel | +44 (0)1736 763299 |
| Email | moira.cattell@gmail.com |

# Cornwall

## Chydane

All that separates you from the sand and sea is the coastal path. At the far end of the marvellous, three-mile beach is Porthleven; beyond, West Penwith stretches into the distance. All this, and lighthouses, basking sharks, dolphins. No guest sitting room, but the elegant double has gorgeous linen, a superb bed and a chesterfield, and opens onto a French balcony overlooking the waves. The bathrooms, too, are warm and you get thick white bathrobes, lovely candles, big showers. Upstairs is a second room with a porthole window and a new bathroom. Close to the spectacular Mullion links golf course. *Children over 12 welcome.*

Ethical Collection: Food. See page 412.

Travel Club offer. See page 414.

| | |
|---|---|
| Price | From £100. |
| Rooms | 2 doubles. |
| Meals | Meals by arrangement. Pub 200 yds. |
| Closed | Christmas. |
| Directions | From Helston A3083 to the Lizard. After 2 miles right to Gunwalloe. Right before Halzephron Inn. Chydane on right immediately above beach. |

Carla Caslin
Chydane,
Gunwalloe, Helston,
Cornwall TR12 7QB
Tel      +44 (0)1326 241232
Email    carla.caslin@btinternet.com
Web      www.chydane.co.uk

Entry 58   Map 1

# Cornwall

## Halzephron House

A rambling white seaside cottage with a crenellated roof and the whiff of a gentleman's folly about it. Step in to a contemporary interior of thick wood floors, original paintings, velvet sofas and lots of fresh flowers: the Tower room in the house has its own white-walled sitting room overlooking the bay and, upstairs, a beautiful French bed. Peace seekers and lovers will choose to stay in the Cabin – a white painted wooden shack with roll top bath and porthole overlooking the garden – or the Observatory, a carefully designed funky space for two. Lucy and Roger give you super local breakfasts too. *Dogs welcome in Observatory & Cabin only.*

Travel Club offer. See page 414.

| | |
|---|---|
| Price | £100–£120. |
| Rooms | 3: Tower: 1 suite. Cabin: 1 suite. Observatory: 1 double. |
| Meals | Pub 0.25 miles. |
| Closed | Rarely. |
| Directions | From Helston head towards The Lizard. After 2 miles, right signed Gunwalloe. Once in village take lane towards Church Cove passing Halzephron Inn on left. House is at top of hill overlooking the sea. |

Lucy & Roger Thorp
Halzephron House,
Gunwalloe, Helston,
Cornwall TR12 7QD
Tel      +44 (0)1326 241719
Email    lucy@halzephronhouse.co.uk
Web      www.halzephronhouse.co.uk

Entry 59   Map 1

# Cornwall

## Halftides

Hugely enjoyable and special, surrounded by three acres with a private path down to the beach. Funky bedrooms, not huge but filled with light, have gorgeous fabrics, crisp bedding, dreamy views; bathrooms (one a pod-shower in the room) are sleek in glass and chrome. Susie is an artist and chef and gives you a delicious organic breakfast and a dinner of seasonal food – perhaps a barbecue in the garden in summer. Take the coastal path north or south, visit the working harbour in the village – or snaffle a packed lunch from Susie and head for the beach. This is the perfect place to relax and unwind. *Minimum stay two nights.*

| | |
|---|---|
| Price | £80-£110. Singles £60-£70. |
| Rooms | 3: 1 double; 1 double, 1 single sharing separate bath. |
| Meals | Dinner £25-£30. Packed lunch £10. Pub 0.5 miles. |
| Closed | January & February. |
| Directions | A3083 to Lizard, right to Cury, 5 miles; pass Poldhu beach & enter Mullion. Right into Laflouder Lane, follow bumpy track to very end, past sign 'Private Road'. House 1st on right. |

| | |
|---|---|
| | Charles & Susie Holdsworth Hunt |
| | Halftides, |
| | Laflouder Lane, |
| | Mullion, Helston, |
| | Cornwall TR12 7HU |
| Tel | +44 (0)1326 241935 |
| Email | halftides@btinternet.com |
| Web | www.halftides.co.uk |

Entry 60   Map 1

# Cornwall

## The Hen House

Greenies will explode with delight: Sandy and Gary, truly welcoming, are passionately committed to sustainability and love guiding you to the best places to eat, to visit and to walk; there are even OS maps on loan for hikers. Enlightened souls will adore the spacious, colourful rooms, the bright fabrics, the wildflower meadow with inviting sun loungers, the pond, the tai chi, the fairy-lit courtyard at night, the scrumptious local food, the birdsong. There's even a sanctuary room for reiki and reflexology set deep into the earth. Join in or flounder. *Minimum stay two nights. Children over 12 welcome.*

Ethical Collection: Environment; Food. See page 412.

Travel Club offer. See page 414.

| | |
|---|---|
| Price | £70-£85. Singles £60. Barn self-catering £200-£450 per week. |
| Rooms | 2+1: 2 doubles. Barn: 1 double. |
| Meals | Pub/restaurant 1 mile. |
| Closed | Rarely. |
| Directions | A3083 from Helston; B3293 to St Keverne; left to Newtown-in-St Martin. After 2 miles, right at T-junc. Follow road for 2.3 miles then left fork. Round 7 bends then right at triangulation stone for Tregarne. |

| | |
|---|---|
| | Sandy & Gary Pulfrey |
| | The Hen House, |
| | Tregarne, |
| | Manaccan, |
| | Helston, Cornwall TR12 6EW |
| Tel | +44 (0)1326 280236 |
| Email | henhouseuk@aol.com |
| Web | www.thehenhouse-cornwall.co.uk |

Entry 61   Map 1

# Cornwall

## Trerose Manor

Follow winding lanes through glorious countryside to find the prettiest, listed manor house, a warm family atmosphere and welcoming tea in the beamed kitchen. Large, light bedrooms, one with floor-to-ceiling windows, sit peacefully in your own wing and have views over the stunning garden. Both are dressed in pretty colours, have comfy seats for gazing and smartly tiled bathrooms. A sumptuous breakfast can be taken outside in summer, there are lovely walks over fields to river or beach, stacks of interesting places to visit and a warming gas wood-burner in the library for the lazy. Lovely. *French, German & Italian spoken.*

| | |
|---|---|
| Price | £80–£100. Singles £70. |
| Rooms | 2 doubles. |
| Meals | Pubs/restaurants within walking distance. |
| Closed | Rarely. |
| Directions | Left at Red Lion in Mawnan Smith. After 0.5 miles right down Old Church Road. 0.5 miles further on through white gate on right immediately after Trerose Farm. |

**Tessa Phipps**
Trerose Manor,
Mawnan Smith,
Falmouth,
Cornwall TR11 5HX

| | |
|---|---|
| Tel | +44 (0)1326 250784 |
| Email | info@trerosemanor.co.uk |
| Web | www.trerosemanor.co.uk |

# Cornwall

## Bosvathick

A huge old Cornish house that has been in Kate's family since 1760 along with all the pictures, books, heavy furniture, Indian rugs, ornate plasterwork, pianos and even a harp. Historians and garden lovers will be in their element: pass three Celtic crosses dating from the 7th century before the long drive finds the imposing house (all granite gate posts and lions) and a magnificent garden with grotto, lake, pasture and woodland. Bedrooms are peaceful and traditional, full of books and antiques; bathrooms are plain, functional and clean. Come then to experience a 'time warp' and Kate's good breakfasts.

| | |
|---|---|
| Price | £80. Singles £40–£60. |
| Rooms | 4: 1 twin/double, 1 twin, 2 singles with 2 bathrooms (let to same party only). |
| Meals | Packed lunch on request. Pubs 2 miles. |
| Closed | Usually Christmas, New Year & Easter. |
| Directions | From Constantine, signs to Falmouth. 2 miles, pass Bosvathick Riding Stables, next entrance on left. Drive through gateposts & green gate. A map can be sent to visitors. |

**Kate & Stephen Tyrrell**
Bosvathick,
Constantine,
Falmouth, Cornwall TR11 5RD

| | |
|---|---|
| Tel | +44 (0)1326 340103 |
| Fax | +44 (0)1326 340426 |
| Email | kate@forgottenhouses.co.uk |
| Web | www.pasticcio.co.uk/bosvathick |

## Cornwall

### Tregew Vean

Once the home of a packet skipper, this pretty Georgian slate-hung house stands in a sunny spot above Flushing. From the garden with its palms, agapanthus, olive and fig trees, you glimpse the Fal estuary. The house is fresh and elegant, with tenderly cared-for antiques and an entertaining straw hat collection in the hall; Sandra and Rodney – both chatty and charming – give you comfortable bedrooms in your own part of the house. Flushing is a ten-minute walk and in the village there are two pubs that do food and a restaurant on the quay. There's plenty to do and you can catch the passenger ferry to Falmouth.

[🧳] Travel Club offer. See page 414.

| Price | From £90. Singles £50. |
|---|---|
| Rooms | 2 doubles, sharing bath (same party only). |
| Meals | Pubs/restaurants 0.25 miles. |
| Closed | Christmas. |
| Directions | From Penryn towards Mylor. After 1 mile right to Flushing. Entrance 1 mile down road on right, 40 yds before T-junction, opposite 'Give Way 40 yds' sign. |

|  | Sandra & Rodney Myers |
|---|---|
|  | Tregew Vean, |
|  | Flushing, Falmouth, |
|  | Cornwall TR11 5TF |
| Tel | +44 (0)1326 379462 |
| Email | tregewvean@aol.com |
| Web | www.tregewvean.co.uk |

🕴 ✕ �train 🔊 🐕

Entry 64   Map 1

## Cornwall

### Trevilla House

Come for the position: the sea and Fal estuary wrap around you, and the King Harry ferry gives you an easy reach into the glorious Roseland peninsula. Inside, find frog stencils in the bathroom, and old-fashioned, comfortable bedrooms – the twin with garden views and a sofa, the double with sea views. Jinty is warm and welcoming and rustles up delicious locally-sourced breakfasts with homemade jams in the sunny conservatory that looks south over the sea. Trelissick Gardens and the Copeland China Collection are just next door, and the Maritime Museum, Eden, Tate, cycling, watersports and coastal walks are close by.

| Price | From £80. Singles £50. |
|---|---|
| Rooms | 3: 1 twin; 1 double with separate bath/shower & sitting room. Extra single for same party, sharing bath. |
| Meals | Restaurants/pubs 1-2 miles. |
| Closed | Christmas & New Year. |
| Directions | A390 to Truro; A39 to Falmouth. At double r'bout with garage, left off 2nd r'bout (B3289); pass pub on left; at x-roads, left (B3289); 200 yds on, fork right to Feock. On to T-junc., then left; 1st on right. |

|  | Jinty & Peter Copeland |
|---|---|
|  | Trevilla House, |
|  | Feock, Truro, |
|  | Cornwall TR3 6QG |
| Tel | +44 (0)1872 862369 |
| Email | jinty@trevilla.com |
| Web | www.trevilla.com |

🕴 ✕ 🔊 🐕

Entry 65   Map 1

# Cornwall

## Pelyn

Sheep on the hillside driveway remain curiously unmoved by the view that sweeps so lushly down to the creek. Sheltered in its own green acres, minutes from golden beaches, this traditional house built around an 11th-century dwelling, is a peaceful, yet accessible hideaway. Fresh flowers are some of the personal touches in light, airy bedrooms (one cosy with sofa) and charming country bathrooms. Tuck into French toast, fresh fruit, home eggs (from lilac hens!) and local bacon in the warm, relaxing conservatory as you gaze out on rabbits and birds. The coastal path is minutes away for fabulous walking.

| Price | From £80. Singles by arrangement. |
|---|---|
| Rooms | 2: 1 twin/double; 1 double with separate bathroom. |
| Meals | Lobster & wine dinner from £40, by arrangement. Packed lunch £7.50. Pubs 5-minute drive. |
| Closed | Rarely. |
| Directions | Through Gerrans, road to St Anthony Head. Just after Percuil turning, next drive right at 150 yds in dip in road & sharp bend (mirrored). Signed. |

| | **Graham & Bridget Reid** |
|---|---|
| | Pelyn, |
| | Gerrans, Portscatho, |
| | Truro, Cornwall TR2 5ET |
| Tel | +44 (0)1872 580837 |
| Email | pelyncreek@aol.com |
| Web | www.pelyncreek.com |

Entry 66   Map 1

# Cornwall

## Pine Cottage

The Cornish sea laps the steep quay of this narrow inlet's port, its blue horizon just visible from the window of the elegant bedroom high up on the coveside. A perfect spot to wake on a summer's morn. The house is as sunny as its owner, the guest bedroom charmingly informal with its hand-painted violet-strewn wallpaper, super big bed and shelves brimming with books. A handful of small open-top fishing boats slips out at dawn to bring back catches of crab and lobster. Clare will give you a splendid breakfast of warm fruit salad and organic or local produce whenever possible.

| Price | £85. |
|---|---|
| Rooms | 1 double. |
| Meals | Pub 100 yds. Restaurants within 5 miles. |
| Closed | Rarely. |
| Directions | From Tregony, A3078 to St Mawes. After 2 miles, at garage, left to Portloe. through village to Ship Inn. Right fork after pub car park. Cottage immed. on left between white gateposts up drive. |

| | **Clare Holdsworth** |
|---|---|
| | Pine Cottage, |
| | Portloe, |
| | Truro, |
| | Cornwall TR2 5RB |
| Tel | +44 (0)1872 501385 |
| Web | www.pine-cottage.net |

Entry 67   Map 1

# Cornwall

## Hay Barton

Giant windows overlook many acres of farmland, well-stocked with South Devon cows and their calves. Jill and Blair look after you well with lovely homemade cake, granola and yogurt, sausages and bacon from the village; later, retire to the guest sitting room with log fire. Bedrooms are fresh and pretty with garden flowers, soft white linen on big beds, floral green walls and stripped floors. Gloriously large panelled bathrooms have long roll top baths and are painted in earthy colours. Guests can use the tennis court; you are near to good gardens and plenty of places to eat. *Minimum stay two nights in summer.*

# Cornwall

## Creed House

A light-filled Georgian former rectory surrounded by one of Cornwall's loveliest gardens. Complete independence is yours in a guest wing: two elegant bedrooms have antique furniture and gleaming bathrooms. Your fridge is filled with delicious local produce ready for a continental breakfast, taken in a beautifully decorated sitting room. Gardeners will be happy: you are close to Heligan and the Eden Project and the beaches of the beautiful Roseland peninsular are wonderful. Nicely private: ideal for one couple, or two sets of friends together.

🧳 Travel Club offer. See page 414.

| | | | |
|---|---|---|---|
| Price | £80. Singles £50. | Price | £90. |
| Rooms | 2 twins/doubles. | Rooms | 2: 1 double, 1 twin. |
| Meals | Pubs 1-2 miles. | Meals | Pub/restaurant 1 mile. |
| Closed | Rarely. | Closed | Christmas & New Year. |
| Directions | A3078 from Tregony village towards St Mawes. After 1 mile, house on left, 100 yds down lane. | Directions | From St Austell, A390 to Grampound. Just beyond clock tower, left into Creed Lane. After 1 mile, left at grass triangle opp. church. House behind 2nd white gates on left. |

|  | **Jill & Blair Jobson** | | **Jonathon & Annabel Croggon** |
|---|---|---|---|
| | Hay Barton, | | Creed House, |
| | Tregony, | | Creed, |
| | Truro, Cornwall TR2 5TF | | Grampound, Truro, |
| Tel | +44 (0)1872 530288 | | Cornwall TR2 4SL |
| Email | jill@haybarton.com | Tel | +44 (0)1872 530372 |
| Web | www.haybarton.com | Email | jrcroggon@btinternet.com |

Entry 68   Map 1

Entry 69   Map 1

# Cornwall

## Bodrugan Barton

Everything's lovely – the setting, the winding lanes, the gentle activity of the farm, the charming family who look after you with such enthusiasm. You get a freshly-painted, pretty bedroom on the end of the house with a good bathroom, a super big living room (red walls, wood-burner, piano), family antiques and a fine breakfast. An ancient lane leads to Colona Bay: small, secluded and full of rock pools. There are an indoor pool and sauna here (shared by self-catering guests) and Heligan and the Eden Project nearby. A delightfully relaxing home. *Children over 12 welcome. Guided walks by arrangement. Painting courses.*

| Price | £90. |
|---|---|
| Rooms | 1 double with shower room. |
| Meals | Pubs within 2 miles. |
| Closed | Never. |
| Directions | St Austell B3273 for Mevagissey. At x-roads on hill, right to Heligan, avoiding bottleneck in Mevagissey. Through Gorran, bend left to Portmellon. After 1.5 miles, right at grass triangle into farm, before hill. |

|  | **Sally & Tim Kendall** |
|---|---|
|  | Bodrugan Barton, |
|  | Mevagissey, |
|  | Cornwall PL26 6PT |
| Tel | +44 (0)1726 842094 |
| Email | stay@bodrugan.co.uk |
| Web | www.bodrugan.co.uk |

🍴 📷 🚂 📶 🐈 🚜 🏊

Entry 70  Map 1

# Cornwall

## Trussel Barn

Jo and Mike look after you beautifully: large, light bedrooms with super views, squashy pillows, state-of-the-art bathrooms, fancy dressing gowns, your own hidden-away fridge. But they're dead keen on reducing their carbon footprint, too. View Mike's experimental straw wall in the garden, drink water from their borehole, enjoy a locally sourced breakfast cooked in an eco-Aga, ask about their plans for off-grid electricity – it's all fascinating stuff. Explore acres of garden running down to a wildlife pond, or hike the five miles to the coast; come home to a roaring fire in the guest sitting room.

| Price | £75–£80. Singles £55. |
|---|---|
| Rooms | 2: 1 double; 1 double with separate bath. |
| Meals | Pubs/restaurants within 2 miles. |
| Closed | Rarely. |
| Directions | A38 Plymouth–Liskeard, then B3254 to St Keyne for 1.5 miles. Climb steep hill; at bend, 1st left into Trussel Barn. Or train to Liskeard, 2 miles. |

|  | **Jo Lawrence** |
|---|---|
|  | Trussel Barn, |
|  | St Keyne, |
|  | Liskeard, Cornwall PL14 4QL |
| Tel | +44 (0)1579 340450 |
| Email | jo@trusselbarn.co.uk |
| Web | www.trusselbarn.co.uk |

🚶 🍴 📷 🚂 📶 🐈

Entry 71  Map 1

# Cornwall

### Collon Barton

Come for the lofty position on a grassy hillside, the heartlifting views over unspoiled countryside and the pretty creekside village of Lerryn. This 18th-century house is a working sheep farm and an artistic household (sculptures galore). Interesting and generous Anne and Iain give you eggs from their free-range chickens, a traditional bedroom with an Edwardian painted bed on the second floor, and an elegant drawing room. Anne sells huge dried hydrangeas and, on sunny days, welcomes you with tea in the summer house. Wonderful riverside and coastal walks and good gardens; the Eden Project 20 minutes away. *Children & pets by arrangement.*

| | |
|---|---|
| Price | £80. Singles £40. |
| Rooms | 1 twin/double (with dressing room & extra beds). |
| Meals | Pub 10-minute walk. |
| Closed | Rarely. |
| Directions | A390 to Lostwithiel. After Lostwithiel sign 1st left, signed Lerryn. 200 yds, left at 1st x-roads for Lerryn. After 2 miles, at top of hill, hard left signed Bodmin & Liskeard. Immed. right by 5-bar gate, stone farm lane. |

| | |
|---|---|
| | **Anne & Iain Mackie** |
| | Collon Barton, |
| | Lerryn, |
| | Lostwithiel, |
| | Cornwall PL22 0NX |
| Tel | +44 (0)1208 872908 |
| Email | i.mackie@btconnect.com |

🐾 🐕 🚜

Entry 72   Map 1

# Cornwall

### Hornacott

The garden, in its lovely valley setting, has seats in little corners poised to catch the evening sun — perfect for a pre-dinner drink. The peaceful house is named after the hill and you have a private entrance to your wonderfully fresh and airy suite: a room with twin beds plus a large, square, high sitting room with windows that look down onto the wooded valley. With CD player, music, chocolates and magazines you'll feel beautifully self-contained. Jos, a kitchen designer, and Mary-Anne clearly enjoy having guests, and give you fresh local produce and free-range eggs for breakfast.

 Travel Club offer. See page 414.

| | |
|---|---|
| Price | From £80. Singles £50. |
| Rooms | 2: 1 suite; 1 single with separate shower. |
| Meals | Dinner, 3 courses, £20. BYO. Pubs/restaurants 4.5 miles. |
| Closed | Christmas. |
| Directions | B3254 Launceston-Liskeard. Through South Petherwin, down steep hill, last left before little bridge. House 1st on left. |

| | |
|---|---|
| | **Jos & Mary-Anne Otway-Ruthven** |
| | Hornacott, |
| | South Petherwin, |
| | Launceston, Cornwall PL15 7LH |
| Tel | +44 (0)1566 782461 |
| Fax | +44 (0)1566 782461 |
| Email | stay@hornacott.co.uk |
| Web | www.hornacott.co.uk |

🐾 ✗ 🐕 🚲

Entry 73   Map 1

# Cornwall

## Buttervilla Farm

Gill and Robert are so good at growing vegetables (organically) they supply the local restaurants. They're pretty good at looking after you too, in a totally relaxed fashion, delivering breakfasts of superb rare-breed bacon and modern Cornish suppers; fish and Red Ruby steak are specialities. No sitting room but bedrooms are big, colourful, comfortable and cared for; bathrooms are smart with solar-powered showers. Explore these 15 beautiful eco acres, stride the coastal path or head for the surf. Young and fun – with soul. *Soil Association certified organic smallholding.*

Ethical Collection: Environment; Food. See page 412.

Travel Club offer. See page 414.

| | |
|---|---|
| Price | £85-£105. |
| Rooms | 3 doubles. |
| Meals | Dinner, 3 courses, £30. Light dinners £10. Restaurants 3 miles. |
| Closed | Rarely. |
| Directions | Turn by Halfway House at Polbathic for Downderry. House 400 yds up hill from inn, on left; signed before lane. |

Gill & Robert Hocking
Buttervilla Farm,
Polbathic,
St Germans, Torpoint,
Cornwall PL11 3EY
Tel      +44 (0)1503 230315
Email    info@buttervilla.com
Web      www.buttervilla.com

Entry 74   Map 2

# Cornwall

## Bulland House

Whether you come to this unspoiled part of Cornwall by ferry or road you will find welcoming hosts and a 300-year-old chocolate-box farmhouse. Elke and Clive give you fresh and uncluttered bedrooms with plenty of sunshine, deliciious biscuits, pretty pink quilts, gleaming bathrooms and views to daffodil-strewn fields in spring. There's a guest sitting room with roaring wood-burner, maps and books; plan your day over a lazy breakfast of local bacon, farm eggs, homemade bread and honey from up the road. Snooze on a bench in the pretty garden or strike out for the coastal path and the most stunning walks.

Ethical Collection: Food. See page 412.

Travel Club offer. See page 414.

| | |
|---|---|
| Price | From £70. Singles £45. |
| Rooms | 2: 1 double; 1 twin/double with separate bath. |
| Meals | Packed lunch £5. Pub/restaurant 1.5 miles. |
| Closed | Christmas & Boxing Day. |
| Directions | From the west, exactly 2.3 miles from Torpoint ferry on main road A374, sign on right. From the east, 1 mile from Antony village main road A374, sign on left. |

Elke & Clive Owen
Bulland House,
Antony,
Torpoint,
Cornwall PL11 2PE
Tel      +44 (0)1752 813823
Email    info@averywarmwelcome.co.uk
Web      www.averywarmwelcome.co.uk

Entry 75   Map 2

# Cornwall

## Erth Barton

Everyone is bowled over by this house; open to three tidal estuaries, it makes your heart leap. The manor house was once owned by the National Trust and is casually grand, with its own derelict chapel; a 14th-century fresco still clings to the walls. Relaxed Jenny and Nicholas, its privileged trustees, keep hens and two young retrievers, and, in spite of the rabbits, grow their own salads and veg. You mostly get the run of the house – up the brown stair carpet lie no-nonsense bedrooms with floral fabrics and peaceful views. You can pick quiet spots in the large garden, and enjoy stunning walks. *Residential gardening courses.*

| | |
|---|---|
| Price | £60–£90. Singles £60. |
| Rooms | 5: 3 doubles; 1 double, 1 twin with shared bath. |
| Meals | Packed lunch from £5. Dinner from £20. Pubs/restaurants 2 miles. |
| Closed | Rarely. |
| Directions | Plymouth, Tamar Bridge (A38); at 1st r'bout take exit Liskeard. Turn left Trematon, left Elmgate then right Elmgate. Right at White Cottage signed Erth Barton, keep straight on until the end. |

|  | **Nicholas & Jenny Foster** Erth Barton, Elmgate, Saltash, Cornwall PL12 4QY |
|---|---|
| Tel | +44 (0)1752 841560 |
| Email | nicholasfoster@btopenworld.com |
| Web | www.erthbarton.co.uk |

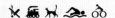

Entry 76   Map 2

# Cornwall

## Lantallack Farm

You will be inspired here: a heart-warming old Georgian farmhouse and Nicky runs courses in landscape painting and sculpture. Find a straw-yellow sitting room with a log fire, books to read, a grand piano and bedrooms with deliciously comfortable beds: views are breathtaking across countryside, streams and wooded valleys. Breakfast in the walled garden on fine days; apple juice from the hugely-productive orchard through which hens potter, bacon and sausages from their own pigs. There are 40 acres to explore, a leat-side trail and a heated outdoor pool; marvellous. *Minimum stay two nights at weekends.*

Ethical Collection: Environment; Community; Food. See page 412.

Travel Club offer. See page 414.

| | |
|---|---|
| Price | From £100. Singles by arrangement. |
| Rooms | 2 doubles. |
| Meals | Pubs/restaurants 1 mile. |
| Closed | Rarely. |
| Directions | A38 through Saltash & on for 3 miles. At Landrake 2nd right at West Lane. After 1 mile, left at white cottage for Tideford. House 150 yds on, on right. |

|  | **Nicky Walker** Lantallack Farm, Landrake, Saltash, Cornwall PL12 5AE |
|---|---|
| Tel | +44 (0)1752 851281 |
| Fax | +44 (0)1752 851281 |
| Email | enquiries@lantallack.co.uk |
| Web | www.lantallack.co.uk |

Entry 77   Map 2

# Cumbria

## Warwick Hall

Warwick Hall stands on the River Eden facing east towards the hills, and owning one of the best salmon beats in the country. Basil Hume used to fish here, Bonnie Prince Charlie once stayed, though not in the comfort you can expect. Vast windows flood the house with light, breakfast is taken in a cavernous dining room, a beautiful sitting room opens onto a terrace. Bedrooms – some entered through a lovely rod room – are excellent (super beds, candles in the bathroom, lots of books, fine views). The house stands in 270 acres, a two-mile walk spins you round. There's yoga, too, and delicious home cooking. *Minimum stay two nights at weekends.*

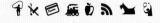 Travel Club offer. See page 414.

| | |
|---|---|
| Price | £100–£150. Singles from £85. |
| Rooms | 6: 1 double, 3 twins/doubles, 2 suites. |
| Meals | Dinner, 4 courses, £25 by arrangement. |
| Closed | Rarely. |
| Directions | M6, junc. 43, then A69 east. After 2 miles, pass town sign and on left down hill before bridge. |

|  | |
|---|---|
| | Val & Nick Marriner |
| | Warwick Hall, |
| | Warwick-on-Eden, |
| | Carlisle, Cumbria CA4 8PG |
| Tel | +44 (0)1228 561 546 |
| Email | info@warwickhall.org |
| Web | www.warwickhall.org |

Entry 78   Map 11

# Cumbria

## Sirelands

Sirelands, once a gardener's cottage, stands among rhododendrons and spreading trees on a sunny slope, a stream trickling by. The Carrs have lived here for years and the house has a reassuringly relaxed, homely feel. Enjoy home-grown produce at dinner on a polished table, then retire to the sitting room, delightful with log basket, honesty bar, flowers and lots of books. Sash windows overlook the wooded garden, visited by roe deer, red squirrels and various birds. Bedrooms and bathrooms are pleasant, peaceful and spotless; one loo has an amazing view! Friendly Angela loves cooking and treats you to tea and homemade cake. Stunning spot.

| | |
|---|---|
| Price | £80. |
| Rooms | 2: 1 twin; 1 double with separate bath/shower. |
| Meals | Dinner, 2-3 courses, £22–£27.50. Pubs within 4 miles. |
| Closed | Christmas & New Year. |
| Directions | M6 north to junc. 43; A69 Newcastle; 3 miles to traffic lights. Right, on to Heads Nook; house 2 miles after village. |

| | |
|---|---|
| | David & Angela Carr |
| | Sirelands, |
| | Heads Nook, |
| | Brampton, |
| | Carlisle, Cumbria CA8 9BT |
| Tel | +44 (0)1228 670389 |
| Email | carr_sirelands@btconnect.com |

Entry 79   Map 12

## Whitbysteads

Swing into the yard of a gentleman's farmhouse at the end of a drive lined with gorse, stone walls and sheep. It's a working farm, so lots going on with four-wheel drives, dogs, busy hens and relaxed bustle. Victoria does styles and periods well: warm rugs, flowery sofas with plain linen armchairs, modern family paintings. The main bedroom is sumptuous and stylish, the smaller room simpler; bathrooms are wonderfully vintage, eclectic and big. Great hosts who make you feel instantly at home here; enjoy the breathtaking views over the fells – easy for the M6 too. Dress up in the evening for dinner at Sharrow Bay. *Garden open for NGS.*

## Greenah

Tucked into the hillside off a narrow lane, this 1750s smallholding is surrounded by fells, so is perfect for walkers. Absolute privacy for four friends or family with your own entrance to a beamed and stone-flagged sitting room with wood-burning stove, creamy walls and cheery floral curtains. Warm bedrooms have original paintings, good beds, hot water bottles, bathrobes and a sparkling bathroom – which has a loo with a remarkable view. Malcolm is a climber; Marjorie is totally committed to organic food so you get a fabulous breakfast and good advice about the local area. Fell walking is not compulsory!

Ethical Collection: Food. See page 412.

| Price | £100–£110. |
|---|---|
| Rooms | 3: 1 double; 1 double, 1 twin with shared bath. |
| Meals | Children's tea available £5. Pub 0.5 miles. |
| Closed | Rarely. |
| Directions | Exit 39 M6. A6 north, through Askham village, left up hill past postbox, over cattle grid and fork left. House is about 1 mile up here – on the top of the hill to the left. |

| Price | £76–£84. Singles £48. |
|---|---|
| Rooms | 2: 1 double, 1 twin sharing shower (let to same party only). |
| Meals | Pubs/restaurants 3 miles. |
| Closed | Rarely. |
| Directions | M6 junc. 40 follow A66 west. Left for Matterdale; after 1.5 miles, left signed Dacre. Up hill, right fork to Lowthwaite, house 100 yds on right. |

| | Mrs Victoria Lowther |
|---|---|
| | Whitbysteads, |
| | Askham, |
| | Penrith, Cumbria CA10 2PG |
| Tel | +44 (0)1931 712284 |
| Fax | +44 (0)1931 712211 |
| Email | info@gnap.fsnet.co.uk |
| Web | www.whitbysteads.org |

| | Marjorie & Malcolm Emery |
|---|---|
| | Greenah, |
| | Mattterdale, |
| | Penrith, |
| | Cumbria CA11 0SA |
| Tel | +44 (0)1768 483387 |
| Email | info@greenah.co.uk |
| Web | www.greenah.co.uk |

Entry 80  Map 11

Entry 81  Map 11

# Cumbria

## Willow Cottage

Gaze across rooftops through tiny windows towards the towering mass of Skiddaw, the Lakes' third highest mountain. Here is a miniature cottage garden with sweet peas, herbs, vegetables and flowers... all suitably rambling. Roy and Chris have kept most of the old barn's features: wooden floorboards, wonderful beams. Dried flowers, pretty china, antique linen, glowing lamps and patchwork quilts, a collection of christening gowns... dear little bedrooms have panelled bathrooms and old pine furniture. TV is delightfully absent, classical music plays and you are in the heart of a farming village.

| | |
|---|---|
| Price | £65–£70. Singles £50. |
| Rooms | 2: 1 double, 1 twin. |
| Meals | Packed lunch £5. Pub 300 yds. |
| Closed | December & January. |
| Directions | From Keswick A591 towards Carlisle (6.5 miles) right for Bassenthwaite village (0.5 miles). Straight on at village green, house on right. |

**Roy & Chris Beaty**
Willow Cottage,
Bassenthwaite,
Keswick,
Cumbria CA12 4QP

Tel +44 (0)1768 776440
Email chriswillowbarn@googlemail.com
Web www.willowbarncottage.co.uk

Entry 82   Map 11

# Cumbria

## Howe Keld

Dismiss all thoughts of the chintzy Keswick guest house: David and Val have swept through with carpets made of Herdwick sheep wool, bedroom furniture made by a local craftsman, gorgeous fabrics, striking wallpaper and smart bathrooms with green slate. It's luxurious but not flashy, and there's a cosy sitting room in primary colours crammed with local info; theatre, shops and restaurants are all strolling distance (choose rooms at the front if you need total quiet). Fill up at breakfast on home baked bread, freshly made smoothies or a jolly good fry-up. *Minimum stay two nights at weekends, three on bank holidays.*

Ethical Collection: Environment. See page 412.

 Travel Club offer. See page 414.

| | |
|---|---|
| Price | £80–£110. Singles £45-60. |
| Rooms | 14: 13 doubles, 1 single. |
| Meals | Pub/restaurant 300 yds. |
| Closed | Part December including Christmas. Most of January excl. New Year. |
| Directions | From Penrith (junc. 40 on M6) west on A66, 18 miles until r'bout with A591. Left for Keswick. After 800 yds left at junction. On to mini r'bout in high street (600 yds), then right. After 600 yds right into The Heads. |

**David Fisher**
Howe Keld,
5/7 The Heads,
Keswick, Cumbria CA12 5ES

Tel +44 (0)17687 72417
Fax +44 (0)17687 80378
Email david@howekeld.co.uk
Web www.howekeld.co.uk

Entry 83   Map 11

# Cumbria

## The Old Rectory

The setting of this lovely old house could hardly be more pastoral. Many of its rooms face south and have superb views, with mountains and fells beyond. History has created an intriguing house full of unexpected corners; the old rectory dates from around 1360 but bedrooms are freshly contemporary and have super big beds. Gill cooks in imaginative 'bistro' style, David knows his wines and you eat by candlelight in a 16th-century room. They're relaxed and charming and, when the place is full, create a fabulous house-party feel. Outside, red squirrels and well-fed rabbits, a croquet lawn and stunning Skiddaw.

Ethical Collection: Environment; Community; Food. See page 412.

| Price | From £100. Singles from £70. |
|---|---|
| Rooms | 3: 1 double, 1 twin/double; 1 double with separate bath. |
| Meals | Dinner, 3 courses, £33. Pub 10-minute drive. |
| Closed | Christmas & New Year. |
| Directions | B5305 to Wigton; at A595, left. After 5 miles, left to Boltongate. Left at T-junc.; in village, signs for Ireby; down hill, last driveway on left. |

**Gill & David Taylor**
The Old Rectory,
Boltongate,
Ireby, Cumbria CA7 1DA
Tel +44 (0)1697 371647
Email boltongate@talk21.com
Web www.boltongateoldrectory.com

🍴 📺 🚂 🐾 📶 🍶

Entry 84 Map 11

# Cumbria

## Daffodil

Who wouldn't love it here? Teen and David, young and friendly, live in a bright-white-and-pale-green farmhouse in soaring countryside with the waggiest dog, wandering hens, ducks and geese, their own pigs. They also care about feeding you well: homemade cakes, mouth watering breakfasts, delicious suppers, or a lift to the local pub. Through your own entrance find a surprisingly sexy bedroom with an enormous, pillow-filled bed, fresh flowers, pink bubbly, fruit and cosy robes; opposite is a spanking new bathroom and a kitchen with an honesty fridge. Generous and fun. *£10 discount if you come without a car.*

💼 Travel Club offer. See page 414.

| Price | £110. Singles £90. |
|---|---|
| Rooms | 1 double. |
| Meals | Packed lunch from £7.50. Supper from £10. Pub within 1 mile. |
| Closed | Rarely. |
| Directions | M6 exit 41, B5305 to Wigton. After 7 miles left Hesket Newmarket, 2nd right Hallfield. Pass farm in dip, at brow of hill turn right in front of dry stone wall into lane to house. |

**David & Teen Fisher**
Daffodil,
Banks Farm, Hesket Newmarket,
Wigton, Cumbria CA7 8HR
Tel +44 (0)1697 478137
Email banksfarm@mac.com
Web www.daffodilbanksfarm.co.uk

🚶 🦆 🍴 🐾 📶 🐕 🐴 🚲

Entry 85 Map 11

# Cumbria

### New House Farm

The large, comfortable beds, the linen, the fabrics, the pillows – comfort par excellence. You'll be impressed by the renovation, too – the plasterwork stops here and there to reveal old beam, slate or stone. A trio of the bedrooms are named after the mountain each faces; Swinside brings the 1650s house its own spring water. The breakfast room has a wood-burner, hunting prints and polished tables for Hazel's breakfasts which will fuel your adventures, the sitting room sports fireplaces and brocade sofas, and walkers will fall gratefully into the hot spring spa. *Children over six welcome.*

 Travel Club offer. See page 414.

| | |
|---|---|
| Price | £140-£170. Singles £70-£120. |
| Rooms | 5: 2 doubles, 1 twin/double. Stables: 2 four-posters. |
| Meals | Lunch from £6 (April-November). Dinner, 3-5 courses, £26-£36. Pubs 2.5 miles. |
| Closed | Never. |
| Directions | A66 to Cockermouth, then B5289 for Buttermere. Signed left 2.5 miles south of Lorton. |

| | |
|---|---|
| | Hazel Thompson |
| | New House Farm, |
| | Lorton, Cockermouth, |
| | Cumbria CA13 9UU |
| Mobile | +44 (0)7841 159818 |
| Email | hazel@newhouse-farm.co.uk |
| Web | www.newhouse-farm.com |

Entry 86   Map 11

# Cumbria

### Cockenskell Farm

Sara loves her house and hill farm garden with its wild rhododendrons and damson orchard; it sits at the southern end of Lake Coniston. Inside are beamed bathrooms and faded lemon quilts, old pine, patterned walls and idiosyncratic touches of colour. Relax with a book in the conservatory, stroll through the magical garden or tackle a bit of the Cumbrian Way which meanders through the fields to the back. On sunny days lovely Sara will give you breakfast in the garden with the birds. History seeps from every pore, the place glows with loving care and to stay here is a treat. *Children over 12 welcome.*

 Travel Club offer. See page 414.

| | |
|---|---|
| Price | £80. Singles from £40. |
| Rooms | 3: 1 twin; 1 twin with separate bath; 1 single sharing bath. |
| Meals | Packed lunch £5. Pubs 2-4 miles. |
| Closed | November-February. |
| Directions | In Blawith, opp. church up narrow lane, through farmyard. Right after cattle grid, over fell, right at fork through gates & up drive. |

| | |
|---|---|
| | Sara Keegan |
| | Cockenskell Farm, |
| | Blawith, |
| | Ulverston, Cumbria LA12 8EL |
| Tel | +44 (0)1229 885217 |
| Email | keegan@cockenskell.fsnet.co.uk |
| Web | www.cockenskell.co.uk |

Entry 87   Map 11

## Cumbria

### Howe Foot

A cluster of buildings in a dell, tall hill above and trees along the trout beck. In a former centre for swill basket making, a miracle of restoration has taken place – and this dear little cottage for two. A patterned rug and a sofa on a new slate floor, a cream bedspread on a pine bed, fern-green towels in a spic and span shower. An immaculate wood pile fuels your wood-burner and the garden slips seamlessly into the nature that surrounds it. Roses and honeysuckle scent the air, pied wagtails nest in the wall and Sue and Martin, talented and full of life, are the warmest hosts; tasty breakfast brought to you on wicker trays.

| Price | £85-£95. Singles £55. |
|---|---|
| Rooms | Cottage: 1 double, sitting room & kitchen. |
| Meals | Pub 0.7 miles. |
| Closed | Rarely. |
| Directions | Through Greenodd on A5092, 2 miles to Farmer's Arms Pub. After 0.5 miles, left at crossroads up narrow fell road; 0.2 miles, 1st used track on left to house. |

Sue & Martin Hawkard
Howe Foot,
Low Beck Bottom, Lowick, Ulverston,
Cumbria LA12 8EA
Tel    +44 (0)1229 885007
Fax    +44 (0)1229 885007
Email  info@howe-foot.co.uk
Web    www.howe-foot.co.uk

Entry 88   Map 11

## Cumbria

### Low Fell

The family is great fun, their warmth is infectious and their well-orchestrated house is packed with maps, lists, books and guides. Bedrooms are bright, sunny, pretty, with elegant patterned or checked fabrics, heavenly big beds, plump pillows, warm towels; the suite up in the loft is a super hideaway and you overlook trees animated with birds. Tuck into warm homemade bread and Aga pancakes at breakfast, warm your toes by the fire in winter, relax in the lovely secluded garden with a glass of wine in summer. The house is a five-minute stroll from the lake and bustling Bowness. *Children over ten welcome.*

 Travel Club offer. See page 414.

| Price | £78-£104. Half-price for children. |
|---|---|
| Rooms | 2: 1 double, 1 family suite (1 double, 1 twin). |
| Meals | Pubs/restaurants 200 yds. |
| Closed | Christmas. |
| Directions | Directions sent on confirmation of booking. |

Louise & Stephen Broughton
Low Fell, Ferney Green,
Bowness-on-Windermere,
Windermere,
Cumbria LA23 3EW
Tel    +44 (0)1539 445612
Email  louisebroughton@btinternet.com
Web    www.low-fell.co.uk

Entry 89   Map 11

# Cumbria

## Low House

A mile from the bustle of Windermere and Kendal, but you are quietly tucked down a lane; the 17th-century house is set in woodland and rolling fields. New managers, Bernie and Danny, welcome you in to a bright drawing room, with well chosen antiques and a twinkling fire on chilly days; dip into a book, take tea, pour yourself a sherry. The bedrooms are lovely, with grand beds and thick towels; spotless bathrooms have opulent mirrors. Breakfast can be taken downstairs, or tired souls can have continental in their room. Walkers can stride off straight from the door; return to delicious Aga-cooked dinners.

 Travel Club offer. See page 414.

| | |
|---|---|
| Price | £60–£130. Singles £50–£80. |
| Rooms | 3: 1 double, 1 twin/double; 1 double with separate bath. |
| Meals | Dinner £30. Pubs/restaurants 1 mile. |
| Closed | Christmas. |
| Directions | M6 exit 36; A590/591, past Kendal; 1st left at r'bout onto B5284 to Crook; 5 miles (past Windermere golf course); right signed Heathwaite; 100 yds on right. |

Johnnie & Heather Curwen
Low House,
Windermere,
Cumbria LA23 3NA

| | |
|---|---|
| Tel | +44 (0)1539 443156 |
| Email | info@lowhouse.co.uk |
| Web | www.lowhouse.co.uk |

Entry 90   Map 11

# Cumbria

## Gillthwaite Rigg

All is calm and ordered in this light, airy and tranquil Arts and Crafts house. Come for nature and to be surrounded by countryside – you may spot a badger or deer. Find panelled window seats, gleaming oak floors, leaded windows, wooden latched doors and motifs moulded into white plaster. Homely bedrooms, reached via a spiral staircase, have an uncluttered simplicity and mountain and lake views. Interesting antiques abound; banks of books, fresh flowers, a wood-burner for cold nights and kind, affable hosts add cheer. Rhoda and Tony are passionate about conservation and wildlife in their 14 acres. *Babies & children over six welcome.*

 Travel Club offer. See page 414.

| | |
|---|---|
| Price | £70–£80. Singles £55. |
| Rooms | 2: 1 double, 1 twin/double. |
| Meals | Pubs/restaurants 1 mile. |
| Closed | Christmas & New Year. |
| Directions | M6 junc. 36; A590 & A591 to r'bout; B5284 (signed 'Hawkshead via ferry') for 6 miles. After golf club, right for Heathwaite. Bear right up hill past nursery. Next drive on right; central part of manor. |

Rhoda M & Tony Graham
Gillthwaite Rigg,
Heathwaite Manor,
Lickbarrow Road,
Windermere, Cumbria LA23 2NQ

| | |
|---|---|
| Tel | +44 (0)1539 446212 |
| Fax | +44 (0)1539 446212 |
| Email | tony_rhodagraham@hotmail.com |

Entry 91   Map 11

## Cumbria

### Fellside Studios

Off the beaten tourist track, a piece of paradise in the Troutbeck valley: seclusion, stylishness and breathtaking views. Prepare your own candlelit dinners, rise when the mood takes you, come and go as you please. The flowerbeds spill with heathers, hens cluck, and there's a decked terrace for continental breakfast in the sun – delivered the night before for early risers; your gently hospitable hosts live in the attached house. You get oak floors, slate shower rooms, immaculate kitchenettes with designer touches, DVD players, comfy chairs, luxurious towels. Wonderful. *Minimum stay two nights.*

## Cumbria

### Middle Reston

A proper Edwardian summer house in the heart of the Lakes (Windermere is the nearest) set high and with mature rhododendrons. Inside is crammed with beautiful dark furniture, Turkish rugs, gorgeous paintings and oak overmantles; there is a comfortable drawing room which you may use. Two traditional bedrooms have claret walls and dark carpets; the yellow attic room is more modern; all are a good size and entirely quiet. Ginny and Simon are great fun and give you a stylish breakfast by a blazing fire with the newspapers; then explore the magic outside – woods, gardens, fabulous views of the mountains.

| | |
|---|---|
| Price | £70–£90. Singles from £45. |
| Rooms | 2 studios: each with 1 double, 1 twin/double & kitchen. |
| Meals | Pub/restaurant 0.5 miles. |
| Closed | Rarely. |
| Directions | From Windermere, A592 north for 3 miles; after bridge, immed. before church, left signed Troutbeck; 300 yds, 1st house on right. |

| | |
|---|---|
| Price | £90–£110. |
| Rooms | 3: 1 double with shower; 2 twins sharing bath. |
| Meals | Pub 1 mile. |
| Closed | Christmas & occasionally. |
| Directions | A591 Kendal-Windermere; 500 yds past 2nd Staveley turning, turn right by small blue bicycle sign, then immediately hard left up drive. |

|  | |
|---|---|
| | **Monica & Brian Liddell** |
| | Fellside Studios, |
| | Troutbeck, Windemere, |
| | Cumbria LA23 1PE |
| Tel | +44 (0)1539 434000 |
| Email | enquiry@fellsidestudios.co.uk |
| Web | www.fellsidestudios.co.uk |

|  | |
|---|---|
| | **Simon & Ginny Johnson** |
| | Middle Reston, |
| | Staveley, Kendal, |
| | Cumbria LA8 9PT |
| Tel | +44 (0)1539 821246 |
| Email | simonhj@btinternet.com |
| Web | www.lake-district-accomodation.com |

# Cumbria

## Howestone Barn

In the back of most-beautiful-beyond, down narrow lanes, this converted barn is a gorgeous retreat for two or four. Rick and Gillian give you privacy and an upstairs sitting room with log stove, comfy sofa, exposed beams and a balcony with views.Bedrooms are plain and elegantly rustic with sweeping beams and modern, stone-tiled bathrooms. Breakfast is delivered: sausages and bacon from their Saddlebacks, eggs from their hens, homemade organic bread. Stroll along lowland tracks, watch curlews and lapwings, puff to the top of Whinfell. Windermere, Ambleside and Beatrix Potter's house are near.

Ethical Collection: Food. See page 412.

![] Travel Club offer. See page 414.

| | |
|---|---|
| Price | £50-£90. Singles from £35. |
| Rooms | Barn: 2 twins/doubles & sitting room. |
| Meals | Packed lunch £5. Pub/restaurant 3.5 miles. |
| Closed | Rarely. |
| Directions | A685 Kendal-Appleby. 500 yds after Morrison's petrol station, left for Mealbank; over long hill after Mealbank, after 2nd bridge at Patton, take middle road of 3. After Borrans Farm, left fork; 0.25 miles on left. |

**Rick & Gillian Rodriguez**
Howestone Barn,
Whinfell, Kendal,
Cumbria LA8 9EQ

| | |
|---|---|
| Tel | +44 (0)1539 824373 |
| Email | stay@lapwingsbarn.co.uk |
| Web | www.lapwingsbarn.co.uk |

Entry 94   Map 12

# Cumbria

## Lavender House

An 1850s house – the local vet's for many years – a comfortable stroll away from the centre of the bustling little market town with its interesting shops and pubs; John can collect you if you come by train. Tea and homemade cake are served in the yellow sitting room – admire Diana's lovely paintings on the walls – with comfy chairs and a fire on chilly days. Bedrooms are bright, with vibrant cushions and antique furniture; bathrooms have big mirrors, thick towels and plenty of soaps and bubbles. On sunny mornings try a Manx kipper on the roof terrace with its 'Mary Poppins' views and smart potted plants.

![] Travel Club offer. See page 414.

| | |
|---|---|
| Price | £70-£80. Singles from £35. |
| Rooms | 2: 1 double; 1 twin/double with separate bath. |
| Meals | Packed lunch £6. Pub/restaurant 150 yds. |
| Closed | Rarely. |
| Directions | M6 junc. 36; A65 Kirkby Lonsdale. After 6.5 miles, left at roundabout. Pass Booth's supermarket. Right at junction. House 50 yds on left; park in drive. |

**John & Diana Craven**
Lavender House,
17 New Road, Kirkby Lonsdale,
Cumbria LA6 2AB

| | |
|---|---|
| Tel | +44 (0)1524 272086 |
| Email | info@lavenderhousebnb.co.uk |
| Web | www.lavenderhousebnb.co.uk |

Entry 95   Map 12

## Cumbria

### Low Jock Scar

Those who like to be made a bit of a fuss of will settle in well here: a cheerful greeting from John and Roslyn comes with homemade cake in the garden, or the guest sitting room with its books and maps, and wood-burning stove for chilly days. Roslyn is a keen cook and spoils you with seasonal and local produce in the sun room with its lovely garden views. Gloriously peaceful and comfortable bedrooms have pine furniture and pretty fabrics; all are a good size and filled with light. Stride those hills, explore Kendal with its interesting shops and theatre, or just find a seat in the garden by the river, watch the wildlife go by and unruffle yourself.

| | |
|---|---|
| Price | £70–£90. Singles from £45–£55. |
| Rooms | 5: 3 doubles, 2 twins. |
| Meals | Dinner £23. |
| | Pubs/restaurants 6-8 miles. |
| Closed | Rarely. |
| Directions | From Kendal, A6 to Penrith. After 6 miles, sign on left for Low Jock Scar. From north M6 junction 37 to A6 south; after 9 miles sign on right for Low Jock Scar. |

| | |
|---|---|
| | John & Roslyn Flackett |
| | Low Jock Scar, |
| | Selside, Kendal, |
| | Cumbria LA8 9LE |
| Tel | +44 (0)1539 823259 |
| Email | info@lowjockscar.co.uk |
| Web | www.lowjockscar.co.uk |

Entry 96　Map 12

## Cumbria

### A Corner of Eden

In the listed farmhouse surrounded by Cumbrian hills and infinite sky, tradition and comfort luxuriously combine. The sitting room has a cosy log fire; the dining room is red and gold; bedrooms glow with designer fireplaces and wooden floors; in one is a contemporary four-poster. Ochres, golds and rich fabrics embellish all, along with robes and slippers for shared bathrooms. Engaging Richard and Debbie live in the barn and show a passion for detail: sloe gin in the rooms, barbours by the door, an honesty bar and home-bakes in the dairy. Offset any indulgence by a walk to the pub – across three glorious fields.

Ethical Collection: Environment. See page 412.

Travel Club offer. See page 414.

| | |
|---|---|
| Price | £130. |
| Rooms | 4: 3 doubles, 1 twin, all sharing 2 bathrooms. |
| Meals | Supper, 2 courses, £21. |
| | Dinner, 3 courses, £26. Pub 3 miles. |
| Closed | Christmas. |
| Directions | M6 junc. 38, signs for Brough on A685. Right into Ravenstonedale; through village until The Fat Lamb, then right. After 0.5 miles left to Stennerskeugh, keep bearing left. |

| | |
|---|---|
| | Debbie Temple & Richard Greaves |
| | A Corner of Eden, |
| | Low Stennerskeugh, Ravenstonedale, |
| | Kirkby Stephen, Cumbria CA17 4LL |
| Tel | +44 (0)1539 623370 |
| Email | enquiries@acornerofeden.co.uk |
| Web | www.acornerofeden.co.uk |

Entry 97　Map 12

# Cumbria

## Coldbeck House

An old mill leat runs through the garden – elegant with trees, populated by woodpeckers and red squirrels; at breakfast they feed by the window. Belle's forte is her cooking and Richard assists with walks; both are natural hosts. The dignified 1820s house with Victorian additions has sanded and polished floors, antiques and splendid stained glass, a guest sitting room with a log-burning stove and a country-house feel. Bedrooms are delightful: fresh flowers, homemade biscuits, towels to match colourful walls. It's peaceful here, on the edge of a village with a green, and you are in unsurpassed walking country.

# Derbyshire

## Horsleygate Hall

Hens and guinea fowl animate the charming old stable yard, and the gardens are vibrant and fascinating, with stone terraces and streams, hidden patios, modern sculptures and seats in every corner... the Fords, attentive and kind, encourage you to explore. Inside the 1783 house, Margaret has created yet more charm. There is a warm, timeless, harmonious feel, with worn kilims on pine boards, striped and floral wallpapers, deep sofas and pools of light. Breakfast is served round a big table in the old schoolroom – homemade jams and oatcakes, garden fruit, eggs from the hens. Special. *Children over five welcome.*

 Travel Club offer. See page 414.

| | | | | |
|---|---|---|---|---|
| Price | £80-£90. Singles £50-£55. | | Price | £65-£75. Singles from £40. |
| Rooms | 3: 2 doubles, 1 twin. | | Rooms | 3: 1 double; |
| Meals | Dinner for groups, 2-4 courses, £18.50-£30. Pubs 5-minute walk. | | | 1 family room, 1 twin sharing bath. |
| | | | Meals | Pub 1 mile. |
| Closed | Christmas. | | Closed | 23 December-4 January. |
| Directions | M6 exit 38; A685 to Kirkby Stephen; 6 miles, then right to Ravenstonedale. 1st left opp. Kings Head pub; drive immed. on left. | | Directions | M1 exit 29; A617 to Chesterfield; B6051 to Millthorpe; Horsleygate Lane 1 mile on, on right at bottom of lane. House 25 yds on left. |

|  | | | |
|---|---|---|---|
| | Belle Hepworth | | Robert & Margaret Ford |
| | Coldbeck House, | | Horsleygate Hall, |
| | Ravenstonedale, Kirkby Stephen, | | Horsleygate Lane, |
| | Cumbria CA17 4LW | | Holmesfield, |
| Tel | +44 (0)1539 623407 | | Derbyshire S18 7WD |
| Email | belle@coldbeckhouse.co.uk | Tel | +44 (0)1142 890333 |
| Web | www.coldbeckhouse.co.uk | Fax | +44 (0)1142 890333 |

Entry 98   Map 12

Entry 99   Map 8

# Derbyshire

## River Cottage

Well-travelled Gilly and John have restored their large house – built in the 1740s – and given it a fresh modern twist. Interiors are light and airy; modern wallpapers, soft furnishings, mirrors and antiques give each room a charm of its own. There's the little village to explore and a lovely, tiered garden with the duck-and-trout-filled river Wye idling past; easy to forget the busy A6 when settled here with a cup of tea or glass of wine. Fishing can be arranged and you are ten minutes from Chatsworth. Many guests come by bus: it stops outside the house. *Minimum stay two nights at weekends Easter-October.*

 Travel Club offer. See page 414.

| | |
|---|---|
| Price | £88-£125. Singles from £69. |
| Rooms | 4 doubles. |
| Meals | Pubs 600 yds. |
| Closed | 10 December-10 February. |
| Directions | On northern edge of Ashford village, 1.5 miles north of Bakewell on A6. Buses from Nottingham, Matlock, Manchester & Buxton stop outside the door. |

| | |
|---|---|
| | Gilly & John Deacon |
| | River Cottage, |
| | The Duke's Drive, |
| | Ashford-in-the-Water, Bakewell, |
| | Derbyshire DE45 1QP |
| Tel | +44 (0)1629 813327 |
| Email | info@rivercottageashford.co.uk |
| Web | www.rivercottageashford.co.uk |

Entry 100   Map 8

# Derbyshire

## Alstonefield Manor

Country manor house definitely, but delightfully understated and cleverly designed to look natural. Local girl Jo spoils you with warm, homemade scones and tea when you arrive, on the lawns overlooking the rolling hills, or in the elegant drawing room with its soft pale tones and warming fire. The bedroom soothes the soul with a painted wooden floor, antique iron bed, vintage linen, huge fluffy towels and a cool, quirky bathroom. Wake to birdsong – and a candlelit breakfast with local bacon and Staffordshire oatcakes. After a game or two of badminton or croquet, take supper at The George in the village. A joy.

 Travel Club offer. See page 414.

| | |
|---|---|
| Price | £80-£120. Singles £50-£70. |
| Rooms | 1 double. |
| Meals | Pub 100 yds. |
| Closed | Christmas & occasionally. |
| Directions | A515 north out of Ashbourne; 6 miles, left into Alstonefield. Over the bridge (river Dove) and up hill. 1st left on entering village, go towards church. House on right. |

| | |
|---|---|
| | Robert & Jo Wood |
| | Alstonefield Manor, |
| | Alstonefield, |
| | Ashbourne, |
| | Derbyshire DE6 2FX |
| Tel | +44 (0)1335 310393 |
| Email | stay@alstonefieldmanor.com |
| Web | www.alstonefieldmanor.com |

Entry 101   Map 8

# Derbyshire

## Rose Cottage

Peaceful Rose Cottage lies up a tiny country lane – brighter and airier than 'cottage' would suggest. The hall sets the tone: Indian rugs on a tiled floor, a grandfather clock and ancestral paintings (there's one of Lord Byron!). Bedrooms are traditional and you may gaze on dreamy views across the Dove valley and the Dales. Although elegant, the house is nevertheless a home and guests are treated as friends. No off-limits: a small book-lined sitting room for guests and a big informal garden. Cynthia (Australian) and Peter are the most delightful couple for whom nothing is too much trouble.

| | |
|---|---|
| Price | £70-£76. |
| Rooms | 2: 1 double; 1 twin with separate bath. |
| Meals | Pub 2 miles. |
| Closed | Christmas. |
| Directions | From Ashbourne, A515 Lichfield road. After 4 miles, right onto B5033. After 1 mile, 2nd lane on right; 0.5 miles on, on right. |

|  |  |
|---|---|
| | Peter & Cynthia Moore |
| | Rose Cottage, |
| | Snelston, Ashbourne, |
| | Derbyshire DE6 2DL |
| Tel | +44 (0)1335 324230 |
| Fax | +44 (0)1335 324651 |
| Email | peter.moore.1@btinternet.com |
| Web | www.rose-cottage-ashbourne.co.uk |

Entry 102   Map 8

# Derbyshire

## Park View Farm

An amazing farm stay, run by hospitable hosts. Daringly decadent, every inch of this plush Victorian farmhouse brims with flowers, sparkling trinkets, polished brass, plump cushions and swathes of chintz. The rooms dance in swirls of colour, frills, gleaming wood, lustrous glass, buttons and bows – it is an extravagant refuge after a long journey. New-laid eggs from the hens for breakfast, fresh fruits and homemade breads accompany the grand performance. The solid brick farmhouse sits in 370 organic acres and Kedleston Hall Park provides a stunning backdrop. *Children over eight welcome.*

Ethical Collection: Food. See page 412.

Travel Club offer. See page 414.

| | |
|---|---|
| Price | £80-£90. Singles £50-£60. |
| Rooms | 3: 2 doubles; 1 double with separate bath. |
| Meals | Pub/restaurant 1 mile. |
| Closed | Christmas. |
| Directions | From A52 & A38 r'bout west of Derby, A38 north, 1st left for Kedleston Hall. 1.5 miles past park on x-roads in Weston Underwood. |

|  |  |
|---|---|
| | Linda Adams |
| | Park View Farm, |
| | Weston Underwood, |
| | Ashbourne, |
| | Derbyshire DE6 4PA |
| Tel | +44 (0)1335 360352 |
| Email | enquiries@parkviewfarm.co.uk |
| Web | www.parkviewfarm.co.uk |

Entry 103   Map 8

## Derbyshire

### Mount Tabor House

On a steep hillside between the Peaks and the Dales, a chapel with a peaceful aura and great views. Enter a hall where light streams through stained-glass windows – this is a relaxed, easy place to stay with a distinctive and original interior. Breakfast, served in a dining room with open stone walls, is mainly from the village shops, and as organic as possible; you can eat on the balcony in summer. Enjoy a delicious dinner in or walk to the pub, then retire to a luxurious bed. Rooms, thanks to charming Fay, are as inviting as can be, and bathrooms a treat. *Usually minimum stay two nights at weekends.*

Travel Club offer. See page 414.

| | |
|---|---|
| Price | £80. Singles £60. |
| Rooms | 2: 1 double, 1 twin/double. |
| Meals | Occasional dinner, £25. Pubs 100 yds. |
| Closed | Rarely. |
| Directions | M1 exit 26; A610 towards Ripley. At Sawmills, right under r'way bridge, signed Crich. Right at marketplace onto Bowns Hill. Chapel 200 yds on right. Can collect from local stations. |

Fay Whitehead
Mount Tabor House,
Bowns Hill, Crich,
Matlock,
Derbyshire DE4 5DG
Tel    +44 (0)1773 857008
Email  mountabor@msn.com
Web    www.mountabor.co.uk

Entry 104   Map 8

## Derbyshire

### Manor Farm

Between two small dales, close to great houses (Chatsworth), lies this cluster of ancient farms and church, designated a World Heritage Site; step into the 16th century! Simon and Gilly, warm, delightful and fascinated by the history, have great green plans for the romantic old wing. The Elizabethan kitchen, arched and atmospheric, is where you are served breakfast, scrumptious and organic. There's a 'book exchange' in the old milking parlour, one bedroom, cosy and quaint, overlooks the church, another has a super big bathroom. The pretty garden swoops to fields and distant river. *Children over six welcome.*

Ethical Collection: Environment; Community; Food. See page 412.

| | |
|---|---|
| Price | £65-£75. Singles £40-£55. |
| Rooms | 3: 1 double, 1 twin/double; 1 double with separate bath. |
| Meals | Pubs 5-10 minute drive. |
| Closed | Rarely. |
| Directions | From M1 exit 28. A38 then A615 following Matlock signs all the way. Left 3 miles before Matlock, signed Dethick Lane. Down lane 1 mile. |

Simon & Gilly Groom
Manor Farm,
Dethick, Matlock,
Derbyshire DE4 5GG
Tel    +44 (0)1629 534302
Fax    +44 (0)1629 534008
Email  gilly.groom@virgin.net
Web    www.manorfarmdethick.co.uk

Entry 105   Map 8

# Devon

## Orchard Cottage

Tucked into a quiet village corner, this is the last cottage in a row of three. Walk through the pretty garden, past seats that (sometimes!) bask in the sun and down to your own entrance and terrace... you may come and go as you please. Your bedroom is L-shaped and large, with a comfortable brass bed and a super en suite shower; it is spotless yet rustic. The Ewens are friendly and fun, their two spaniels equally so and you are brilliantly sited for Dartmoor, Plymouth, the sand and the sea. Breakfasts in the beamed dining room are generous and delicious; this is excellent value B&B.

| | |
|---|---|
| Price | From £55. Singles £40. |
| Rooms | 1 double. |
| Meals | Pubs 300 yds. |
| Closed | Christmas. |
| Directions | A379 from Plymouth for Modbury. On reaching Church St at top of hill, before Modbury, fork left at Palm Cross, then 1st right by school into Back St. Cottage 3rd on left, past village hall. |

Maureen Ewen
Orchard Cottage,
Back Street,
Palm Cross Green,
Modbury,
Devon PL21 0RF
Tel +44 (0)1548 830633
Email moewen@talktalk.net

Entry 106 Map 2

# Devon

## Annapurna

Rural bliss: the garden of this pretty, cream-painted longhouse surrounded by munching cows and happy hens looks down the folded valley to the steeple of Modbury Church. Inside, Carol and Peter spoil you with blueberry pancakes, organic home-baked bread, home-laid eggs and charming bedrooms with a fresh, country feel. Choose independence in the annexe with your own sitting room, or sleep in the main house; each room is lovely with garden flowers, good beds and sparkling bath or shower rooms. Fabulous walking starts from the door and you are close to the watery delights of Salcombe and Dartmouth.

Ethical Collection: Food. See page 412.

Travel Club offer. See page 414.

| | |
|---|---|
| Price | £65-£75. Singles £30-£40. |
| Rooms | 3: 1 twin/double; 1 single with separate bath. Annexe: 1 double & sitting room (small single room let to same party only). |
| Meals | Pubs/restaurants 1 mile. |
| Closed | Rarely. |
| Directions | A38 Modbury/Ermington, After 1.5 miles approx. Kittaford Cross straight on, through California Cross. After 2.4 miles left down unmarked lane. 300 yds on right. |

Carol Farrand & Peter Foster
Annapurna,
Mary Cross,
Modbury,
Devon PL21 0SA
Tel +44 (0)1548 831299
Email carolfarrand@tiscali.co.uk
Web www.annapurna-devon.co.uk

Entry 107 Map 2

## Devon

### Rafters Barn

A delightful and peaceful 300-year-old barn along the narrowest of lanes and with soaring views from the valley to the sea. This is big sailing country but mostly agricultural so you will avoid the madding crowds. You have a comfy guest sitting room with big sofas and a wood-burner that belts out the heat, neat bedrooms in bright colours with pretty touches, tiled bathrooms that gleam and a great big breakfast in the open hallway. Elizabeth is thoughtful and smiley and will point you to the best beaches and places to eat in Salcombe. Or let her cook for you – with produce fresh from farmers' markets.

Travel Club offer. See page 414.

| | |
|---|---|
| Price | From £75. Singles £50. |
| Rooms | 3: 1 double, 1 twin; 1 single with separate bath. |
| Meals | Dinner £20 by arrangement. Pubs/restaurants 4 miles. |
| Closed | Christmas & New Year. |
| Directions | A381 for Salcombe. Just before Hope Cove sign, right to Bagton & S. Huish. Follow lane for 1 mile; 30 yds past saw mill, right up farm lane; at bottom on left. |

| | |
|---|---|
| | Elizabeth Hanson |
| | Rafters Barn, |
| | Holwell Farm, |
| | South Huish, Kingsbridge, Devon |
| | TQ7 3EQ |
| Tel | +44 (0)1548 560460 |
| Email | raftersdevon@yahoo.co.uk |
| Web | www.raftersdevon.co.uk |

Entry 108   Map 2

## Devon

### Washbrook Barn

Hard not to feel happy here – even the blue-painted windows on rosy stone walls make you want to smile. Inside is equally sunny. The barn – decrepit until Penny bought it six years ago – rests at the bottom of a quiet valley. She has transformed it into a series of big light-filled rooms with polished wooden floors, pale beams and richly coloured walls lined with fabulous watercolours: the effect is one of gaiety and panache. No sitting room as such, but armchairs in impeccable bedrooms from which one can admire the rural outlook. The beds are divinely comfortable and the fresh bathrooms sparkle.

Travel Club offer. See page 414.

| | |
|---|---|
| Price | From £75. Singles £50. |
| Rooms | 3: 1 double; 1 double, 1 twin, each with separate bath/shower. |
| Meals | Dinner occasionally available in winter. Pubs/restaurants 10-min walk. |
| Closed | Christmas & New Year. |
| Directions | From Kingsbridge quay to top of Fore St; right into Duncombe St; on to T-junc.; left to Church St. Right into Belle Cross Rd; 150 yds, right into Washbrook Lane; 250 yds left; at bottom on right. |

| | |
|---|---|
| | Penny Cadogan |
| | Washbrook Barn, |
| | Washbrook Lane, |
| | Kingsbridge, |
| | Devon TQ7 1NN |
| Tel | +44 (0)1548 856901 |
| Email | penny.cadogan@homecall.co.uk |
| Web | www.washbrookbarn.co.uk |

Entry 109   Map 2

# Devon

## High Barn

A quiet spot among rolling hills with artist Nick, cook Jill, two pointers, an inquisitive cat and some roaming chickens. This is a warm, generous household with an easy-going atmosphere: three large sofas round a wood-burner, big art, a snooker table, comfy bedrooms, patchwork quilts and one extremely pink bathroom. At breakfast you get freshly squeezed juice, homemade yogurt and bacon from the farm next door; suppers can be simple or elaborate, or a barbecue in the garden. Explore Dartmoor, walk the coastal paths or head for the beaches; there's plenty of space for storing boats, boards and sandy wetsuits.

| Price | From £60. |
|---|---|
| Rooms | 2: 1 twin/double, 1 family. |
| Meals | Dinner, 2 courses, £15.<br>Pubs within 2 miles. |
| Closed | Rarely. |
| Directions | A379 west from Kingsbridge to Aveton Gifford. through village, then right past church. Continue 2 miles to Chillaton Cross, then left (after Lixton turning). House 1st on left. |

**Nick & Jill Bremer**
High Barn,
Chillaton,
Loddiswell, Kingsbridge,
Devon TQ7 4EG
Tel     +44 (0)1548 550838
Email   stay@highbarndevon.co.uk
Web    www.highbarndevon.co.uk

Entry 110    Map 2

# Devon

## Strete Barton House

Contemporary, friendly, passionately green. There's much to love, and the coastal path runs outside the door. Your caring hosts live their dream running immaculate B&B by the sea. The old Manor House at the top end of the village has French sleigh beds and Asian art, white basins and black chandeliers – and the garden has sofas for the views. Breakfasts are exuberantly local (village eggs, sausages from Dartmouth, honey from the bay), there's a wood-burner in the sitting room and Kevin and Stuart know just which beach, walk or pub is perfect for you. *Minimum stay two nights in summer. Pets in cottage only.*

Ethical Collection: Community; Food
See page 412.

 Travel Club offer. See page 414.

| Price | £80–£120. Singles £70. |
|---|---|
| Rooms | 6: 3 doubles, 1 twin; 1 twin with separate shower.<br>Cottage: 1 suite & sitting room. |
| Meals | Pub & restaurant 50 yds. |
| Closed | Rarely. |
| Directions | From Dartmouth, A379 to Kingsbridge. At mini roundabout, left onto A379 signed Stoke Fleming. Follow A379 to Strete, then right into Totnes Road. House 20 yds up hill on right. |

**Stuart Litster & Kevin Hooper**
Strete Barton House,
Totnes Road, Strete,
Dartmouth, Devon TQ6 0RU
Tel     +44 (0)1803 770364
Fax     +44 (0)1803 771182
Email   info@stretebarton.co.uk
Web    www.stretebarton.co.uk

Entry 111    Map 2

# Devon

## Nonsuch House

The photo says it all! You are in your own crow's nest, perched above the flotillas of yachts zipping in and out of the estuary mouth: stunning. Kit and Penny are great fun and look after you well; Kit is an ex-hotelier, smokes his own fish fresh from the quay and knocks out brilliant dinners. Further pleasures lie across the water: a five-minute walk brings you to the ferry that transports you and your car to the other side. Breakfasts in the conservatory are a delight, bedrooms are big and comfortable and fresh bathrooms sparkle. *Children over ten welcome. Minimum stay two nights at weekends.*

Ethical Collection: Food. See page 412.

 Travel Club offer. See page 414.

| | |
|---|---|
| Price | £105–£145. Singles £80–£120. |
| Rooms | 4: 3 twins/doubles, 1 double. |
| Meals | Dinner, 3 courses, £35. (Not Tues/Wed/Sat.) Pub/restaurant 5-minute walk & short boat trip. |
| Closed | Rarely. |
| Directions | 2 miles before Brixham on A3022, A379. After r'bout, fork left (B3205) downhill, through woods, left up Higher Contour Rd, down Ridley Hill. At hairpin bend. |

**Kit & Penny Noble**
Nonsuch House,
Church Hill, Kingswear,
Dartmouth, Devon TQ6 0BX
Tel    +44 (0)1803 752829
Fax    +44 (0)1803 752357
Email  enquiries@nonsuch-house.co.uk
Web    www.nonsuch-house.co.uk

Entry 112   Map 2

# Devon

## The White House

Gaze on the sparkling estuary from the comfort of your bed in this very friendly, very relaxing house at the top of the hill – filled with books and art. There's classical music and Hugh's homemade bread at breakfast, and a real fire for your sitting room in winter. Fresh, pretty bedrooms have sherry, chocolates, bathrobes and opera glasses for views; more village and estuary views from the garden terrace. A ferryman transports you to Agatha Christie's house just across the river: shake the bell opposite the Inn! Another ferry takes you to Dartmouth – catch the river boat on to Totnes. *Children by arrangement.*

| | |
|---|---|
| Price | £85. Singles £55. |
| Rooms | 2 doubles. |
| Meals | Pubs a short walk. |
| Closed | Christmas. |
| Directions | Off A3122 at Sportsman's Arms. After approx. 3 miles down hill into Dittisham, sharp right immed. before Red Lion. Along The Level, up narrow hill & house entrance opp. at junc. of Manor St & Rectory Lane. |

**Hugh & Jill Treseder**
The White House,
Manor Street,
Dittisham,
Devon TQ6 0EX
Tel    +44 (0)1803 722355
Fax    +44 (0)1803 722355
Email  jilltreseder@btinternet.com

Entry 113   Map 2

# Devon

## Riverside House

The loveliest 17th-century cottage with wisteria and honeysuckle growing up its walls and the tidal river estuary bobbing past with boats and birds; in summer you can dip your toes in the water while sitting in the garden. Felicity, an artist, and Roger, a passionate sailor, give you beautiful bedrooms, fresh flowers, thick towels and pretty china. No need to stir from your fine linen-and-down nest to use the binoculars: bedrooms have long views over the water and wide windows. Wander up to the pub for dinner – in fine weather they have quayside barbecues and live music. *Minimum stay two nights at weekends.*

| | |
|---|---|
| Price | From £75. Singles from £60. |
| Rooms | 2: 1 double; 1 double with separate shower. |
| Meals | Packed lunch £6. Pubs 100 yds. |
| Closed | Rarely. |
| Directions | In Tuckenhay, pass Maltsters Arms on left to 2nd thatched house on left, at right angle to road. Drive past, turn at bridge and return to slip lane. |

**Felicity & Roger Jobson**
Riverside House,
Tuckenhay,
Totnes,
Devon TQ9 7EQ
Tel    +44 (0)1803 732837
Email    felicity@riverside-house.co.uk
Web    www.riverside-house.co.uk

Entry 114    Map 2

# Devon

## Lower Norton Farmhouse

Hard to believe the downstairs bedroom was a calving pen and its smart bathroom the dairy. Now it has a seagrass floor and a French walnut bed. All Glynis's rooms are freshly decorated, and she and Peter are the most amenable hosts, genuinely happy for you to potter around all day should you wish to do so. For the more active, a yacht on the Dart and a cream Bentley are to hand, with Peter as navigator and chauffeur – rare treats. Return to gardens, paddocks, peaceful views, super dinners and a big log fire. Off the beaten track, a tremendous find. *Children over ten welcome.*

 Travel Club offer. See page 414.

| | |
|---|---|
| Price | From £70. Singles £60. |
| Rooms | 3: 2 doubles, 1 twin. |
| Meals | Dinner, 2 courses, £25. Lunch £9. Packed lunch £7. Pub/restaurant 1.5 miles. |
| Closed | Rarely. |
| Directions | From A381 at Halwell, 3rd left signed Slapton; 4th right after 2.3 miles signed Sherford, Kingsbridge at Wallaton Cross. House down 3rd drive on left. |

**Peter & Glynis Bidwell**
Lower Norton Farmhouse,
Coles Cross,
East Allington,
Totnes, Devon TQ9 7RL
Tel    +44 (0)1548 521246
Email    peter@lowernortonfarmhouse.co.uk
Web    www.lowernortonfarmhouse.co.uk

Entry 115    Map 2

## Devon

### The Old Rectory

Fresh flowers and spacious elegance... Jill and John's Regency rectory, on the edge of Diptford, was once the home of William Gregor, a vicar who discovered titanium! (There are still some titanium bowls in the large and lovely hall with its fine staircase.) You'll enjoy eating here, in the splendour of the dining room, for vivacious Jill is a superb Leith-trained cook who is happy to do weddings too. Bedrooms are large and light; one has three huge windows with views over the garden to the moors – and a chesterfield so you can appreciate them in comfort. *Minimum stay two nights. Dogs welcome by arrangement.*

 Travel Club offer. See page 414.

| | |
|---|---|
| Price | £95-£110. Singles £60. |
| Rooms | 5: 3 doubles, 1 twin, 1 family suite for 4. |
| Meals | Dinner £27.50. Supper £18. Packed lunch available. Pubs 2 miles. |
| Closed | November-January. |
| Directions | Avonwick to Diptford road. First house on right after village sign. |

**Jill Hitchins**
The Old Rectory,
Diptford,
Totnes, Devon TQ9 7NY
Tel +44 (0)1548 821575
Email hitchins@oldrectorydiptford.co.uk
Web www.oldrectorydiptford.co.uk

Entry 116  Map 2

## Devon

### Avenue Cottage

The tree-lined approach is steep and spectacular; the cottage sits in 11 wondrous acres of rhododendron, magnolia and wild flowers with a lily-strewn pond, grassy paths and lovely views over the river. Find a quiet spot in which to read or simply sit and absorb the tranquillity. Richard is a gifted gardener, and the archetypal gardener's modesty and calm have penetrated the house itself – it is uncluttered, comfortable and warmed by a log fire. The old-fashioned twin room has a big, faded bathroom with a faux-marble basin and a balcony with sweeping valley views; the pretty village and pub are a short walk away.

| | |
|---|---|
| Price | £60-£80. Singles £40-£50. |
| Rooms | 2: 1 twin/double; 1 double sharing shower. |
| Meals | Pub 0.5 miles. |
| Closed | Rarely. |
| Directions | A381 Totnes-Kingsbridge for 1 mile; left for Ashprington; into village, then left by pub ('Dead End' sign). House 0.25 miles on right. |

**Richard Pitts**
Avenue Cottage,
Ashprington,
Totnes, Devon TQ9 7UT
Tel +44 (0)1803 732769
Email richard.pitts@btinternet.com
Web www.avenuecottage.com

Entry 117  Map 2

# Devon

## Parliament House

The ancient rambling house (where William of Orange held his first Parliament) is on the road at the bottom of the valley, and has been beautifully restored by two designers. This is a fresh, stylish and charming cottage where wallpapers, napkins and toile de Jouy are to Carole's own design. White walls and serene colours form a lovely backdrop for pretty touches. Breakfasts are feasts – creamy mushrooms on a toasted muffin, three sorts of bread – and bedrooms are low-ceilinged and cosy with cast-iron fireplaces and hand-stencilled paper. There's a sitting room and a library with a piano – and the garden is a joy.

 Travel Club offer. See page 414.

| | |
|---|---|
| Price | From £75. |
| Rooms | 2: 1 double; 1 twin/double with separate bath/shower. |
| Meals | Pubs/restaurants within 2 miles. |
| Closed | Rarely. |
| Directions | From Totnes, A385 Paignton road; 2 miles on, right at Riviera Sports Cars. House 1st on right. Just past house to parking area on right. |

Carole & Harry Grimley
Parliament House,
Longcombe,
Totnes,
Devon TQ9 6PR
Tel    +44 (0)1803 840288
Email  parliamenthouse@btopenworld.com

※ 🚂 🐾

Entry 118   Map 2

# Devon

## Manor Farm

Capable Sarah is a keen gardener, and produces vegetables that will find their way into your (excellent) dinner, and raspberries for your muesli. She keeps bees and hens too, so you can have honey and eggs for breakfast, served in a smart red dining room. The farmhouse twists and turns around unexpected corners thanks to ancient origins, and the good-sized bedrooms, one with its own bathroom, both painted light yellow, are reached via two separate stairs – nicely private. The lovely village is surrounded by apple orchards and has two good pubs for eating out.

| | |
|---|---|
| Price | £70. Singles £45–£50. |
| Rooms | 2: 1 double; 1 twin with separate bath/shower. |
| Meals | Dinner £15–£21. Packed lunch £4–£5. Pubs 500 yds. |
| Closed | Rarely. |
| Directions | From Newton Abbot, A381 for Totnes. After approx. 2.5 miles, right for Broadhempston. Past village sign, down hill & 2nd left. Pass pub on right & left 170 yds on into courtyard. |

Sarah Clapp
Manor Farm,
Broadhempston, Totnes,
Devon TQ9 6BD
Tel    +44 (0)1803 813260
Fax    +44 (0)1803 813260
Email  mandsclapp@btinternet.com

♟ ※ 🐕 🐾

Entry 119   Map 2

Devon

### Kilbury Manor

You can stroll down to the Dart from the garden and onto their little island, when the river's not in spate! Back at the Manor – a listed longhouse from the 1700s – are four super-comfortable bedrooms, the most private in the stone barn. Your genuinely welcoming hosts (with dogs Dillon and Buster) moved to Devon to renovate a big handsome house and open it to guests. Julia does everything beautifully so there's organic smoked salmon for breakfast, baskets of toiletries by the bath, the best linen on the best beds and a drying room for wet gear – most handy if you've come to walk the Moor. Spot-on B&B.

Travel Club offer. See page 414.

| | |
|---|---|
| Price | £67-£80. Singles from £45. |
| Rooms | 4: 2 doubles. Barn: 1 twin/double; 1 double with separate bath. |
| Meals | Pubs/restaurants 1.5-4 miles. |
| Closed | Rarely. |
| Directions | Leaving A38, left for Totnes. After 0.5 miles, right over river on narrow bridge; follow lane over railway bridge then immed. left into Colston Rd. 0.25 miles on left. |

Julia & Martin Blundell
Kilbury Manor,
Colston Road,
Buckfastleigh,
Devon TQ11 0LN
Tel +44 (0)1364 644079
Email info@kilburymanor.co.uk
Web www.kilburymanor.co.uk

Entry 120   Map 2

Devon

### Old Mill Farm

Position, position, position. Dazzling sunsets, resident kingfisher, the occasional seal, total seclusion; painters and birdwatchers will think they have died and gone to heaven. The approach is stunning: from the top of the hill you descend to the estuary's edge, and find a hugely refitted house with Elizabethan origins and glamorous Robert and Kate. Bedrooms are spacious, plush, stylish; bathrooms have thick fluffy towels and one has a bath with the best-ever view. Breakfast is posh (eggs benedict, home baked croissants, kippers) and eaten in the river room with slate floor, French windows and… views. A treat.

Travel Club offer. See page 414.

| | |
|---|---|
| Price | £100-£135. |
| Rooms | 3 doubles. |
| Meals | Pub less than a mile. |
| Closed | January & February. |
| Directions | From Brixham road into Galmpton, straight through (Greenway Road), with primary school on right. Up hill out of village, right at 'No Through Road' sign, down lane. Entrance on left. |

Robert & Kate Chaston
Old Mill Farm,
Greenway,
Galmpton, Devon TQ5 0ER
Tel +44 (0)1803 842344
Fax +44 (0)1803 843750
Email enquiries@oldmillfarm-dart.co.uk
Web www.oldmillfarm-dart.co.uk

Entry 121   Map 2

# Devon

## Tudor House

A merchant's townhouse now happily given over to rooms for the Agaric Restaurant. Sophie and Nick are young, fun and very clever: in these mostly large, individually styled rooms, fabrics are plush, colours innovative and bathrooms have roll tops. A breakfast room is cool with leather and palms; full English or anything else you want is delivered here. Don't come without booking into the restaurant for fabulous modern British cooking – then stagger two steps down the street to your well-earned bed. Ashburton bustles with good food shops, antiques and books.

 Travel Club offer. See page 414.

| | |
|---|---|
| Price | £100-£125. Singles £50. |
| Rooms | 4: 2 doubles, 1 family, 1 single. |
| Meals | Owners' restaurant next door. Packed lunch from £10 for 2. |
| Closed | Rarely. |
| Directions | From A38 follow signs to Ashburton. North Street is main street, house is on right after Town Hall. |

| | |
|---|---|
| | **Sophie & Nick Coiley** |
| | Tudor House, |
| | 36 North Street, |
| | Ashburton, |
| | Devon TQ13 7QD |
| Tel | +44 (0)1364 654478 |
| Email | eat@agaricrestaurant.co.uk |
| Web | www.agaricrestaurant.co.uk |

Entry 122   Map 2

# Devon

## Golden Lion House

Antiques, vintage clothes, real food shops: you are in a handsome, cream-painted Georgian house on the main road of this lively old stannary town. Uncluttered bedrooms are all on the first floor: find pale colours, comfortable spaces to sit, large televisions, oil paintings, and tiled bathrooms with plenty of good white towels. Friendly, outgoing Phil and Muriel bake their own bread and will cook your breakfast: start with fresh fruit salad and organic yogurt; you eat at separate tables in a light, spacious room with more artwork. Fabulous moorland walks are a short drive, or just mooch about the village.

 Travel Club offer. See page 414.

| | |
|---|---|
| Price | £75. Singles £55-£60. |
| Rooms | 4: 3 doubles, 1 twin/double. |
| Meals | Pub/restaurant 200 yds. |
| Closed | Christmas Day & Boxing Day. |
| Directions | At southern end of M5, take A38. From Ashburton turn off follow signs to town centre. House on left with large golden lion above porch. |

| | |
|---|---|
| | **Phil & Muriel Carrodus** |
| | Golden Lion House, |
| | 58 East Street, |
| | Ashburton, Devon TQ13 7AX |
| Mobile | +44 (0)7831 787837 |
| Fax | +33 (0)8719 005232 |
| Email | phil.carrodus@goldenlionhouse.com |
| Web | www.goldenlionhouse.com |

Entry 123   Map 2

Devon

## Penpark

Clough Williams-Ellis of Portmeirion fame did more than design an elegant house; he made sure it communed with nature. Light pours in from every window and the views are long, across rolling farmland to Dartmoor and Hay Tor. The big double has a comfy sofa and its own balcony; the private suite has arched French doors to the garden and an extra room for young children. Antiques and heirlooms, African carvings, silk and fresh flowers – it is deeply traditional and comforting. Your generous hosts have been doing B&B for years; they and their two springer spaniels look after you well.

 Travel Club offer. See page 414.

| | |
|---|---|
| Price | £70–£76. Singles by arrangement. |
| Rooms | 3: 1 family suite; 1 twin/double with separate bath; 1 double with separate shower. |
| Meals | Pub 1 mile. |
| Closed | Rarely. |
| Directions | A38 west to Plymouth; A382 turn off; 3rd turning off r'bout, signed Bickington. There, right at junc. (to Plymouth), right again (to Sigford & Widecombe). Over top of A38 & up hill; 1st entrance on right. |

Madeleine & Michael Gregson
Penpark,
Bickington, Ashburton,
Devon TQ12 6LH
Tel +44 (0)1626 821314
Email maddy@penpark.co.uk
Web www.penpark.co.uk

Entry 124   Map 2

---

Devon

## Hooks Cottage

At the end of a long bumpy track, the hideaway mine captain's house may have few original features but the woodland setting is gorgeous. Mary and Dick have a finely judged sense of humour; labradors Archie and Cobble will charm you. It is simple, rural, close to the Moors, with woodland birds and a gentle river to unwind stressed souls. Carpeted bedrooms have a faded floral charm and pretty stream views; bathrooms are plain. Enjoy local sausages and Mary's marmalade for breakfast, a lovely garden and amazing bluebells in spring; walks from the house are sublime. Your horse is welcome too.

| | |
|---|---|
| Price | £55–£60. Singles £40. |
| Rooms | 2: 1 double en suite (wc across landing); 1 twin with separate bath. |
| Meals | Pub/restaurant 2 miles. |
| Closed | Rarely. |
| Directions | From A38, A382 at Drumbridges for Newton Abbot; 3rd left at r'bout for Bickington. 2.7 miles on, down hill, right for Haytor. Under bridge, 1st left & down long, bumpy track, past thatched cottage to house. |

Mary & Dick Lloyd–Williams
Hooks Cottage,
Bickington,
Ashburton,
Devon TQ12 6JS
Tel +44 (0)1626 821312
Email hookscottage@yahoo.com

Entry 125   Map 2

# Devon

## Bagtor House

What a setting! A ten-minute walk and you're on the moor. Enfolded by garden, green fields and sheep, the 15th-century house with the Georgian façade is the last remaining manor in the parish. Find ancient beauty in granite flagstones, oak-panelled walls, great fireplaces glowing with logs and country dressers brimming with china. Sue looks after hens, geese, labradors, guests, grows everything and makes her own bread. She offers you a large and elegant double room with an antique brass bed and, steeply up the stairs, a big attic-cosy suite perfect for families. Warm, homely, spacious, civilised.

Travel Club offer. See page 414.

| Price | £76. Singles by arrangement. |
|---|---|
| Rooms | 2: 1 double, 1 family room, each with separate bath/shower. |
| Meals | Restaurants/pubs 1 mile. |
| Closed | Never. |
| Directions | From A38 to Plymouth, A382 turn off at r'bout, 3rd exit to Ilsington; up through village, 2nd left after hotel (to Bickington), 1st crossroads right to Bagtor, 0.5 miles, on right next to Farm. |

|  | Sue Cookson |
|---|---|
|  | Bagtor House, |
|  | Ilsington, Bovey Tracey, |
|  | Devon TQ13 9RT |
| Tel | +44 (0)1364 661538 |
| Fax | +44 (0)1364 661538 |
| Email | sawreysue@hotmail.com |
| Web | www.bagtormanor.co.uk |

Entry 126   Map 2

# Devon

## Easdon Cottage

Replenish your soul in this newly decorated, light and beautifully proportioned cottage; if the charming big double in the house is taken, you may stay in the nearby barn. Both have tranquillity and delightful moor views. Inside are wood-burners in the dining and drawing rooms, and an enchanting mix of good pictures, oriental rugs, books, plants and some handsome Victorian finds. You are in a classic Devon valley, Dartmoor lies beyond, and the sweet cottage garden is filled with birds. Liza and Hugh's veggie and vegan breakfasts are imaginative and delicious. *Children & pets by arrangement.*

Ethical Collection: Environment; Food. See page 412.

| Price | From £65. Singles from £40. |
|---|---|
| Rooms | 1 twin/double. |
| Meals | Occasional supper £10-£20. Pub/restaurant 3 miles. |
| Closed | Rarely. |
| Directions | A38 from Exeter; A382 for Bovey Tracey. There, left at 2nd r'bout for Manaton; 2 miles beyond Manaton, right at x-roads for M'hampstead. 0.5 miles on, right, signed Easdon. On left up track. |

|  | Liza & Hugh Dagnall |
|---|---|
|  | Easdon Cottage, |
|  | Long Lane, Manaton, |
|  | Devon TQ13 9XB |
| Tel | +44 (0)1647 221389 |
| Fax | +44 (0)1647 221389 |
| Email | easdondown@btopenworld.com |
| Web | www.easdoncottage.co.uk. |

Entry 127   Map 2

# Devon

## Corndonford Farm

An ancient Devon longhouse and an engagingly chaotic haven run by warm and friendly Ann and Will, along with their Shire horses and Dartmoor ponies. Steep, stone circular stairs lead to bedrooms; bright lemon walls, a four poster with lacy curtains, gorgeous views over the cottage garden and a bathroom with a beam to duck. A place for those who want to get into the spirit of it all – maybe help catch an escaped foal, chatter to the farm workers around the table; not for fussy types or Mr and Mrs Tickety Boo. Good for walkers too – the Two Moors Way footpath is on the doorstep. *Children over ten by arrangement.*

Ethical Collection: Food. See page 412.

Travel Club offer. See page 414.

| | |
|---|---|
| Price | £60–£70. Singles £35. |
| Rooms | 2: 1 twin, 1 four-poster sharing bath. |
| Meals | Pub 2 miles. |
| Closed | Rarely. |
| Directions | From A38 2nd Ashburton turn for Dartmeet & Princetown. In Poundsgate pass pub on left; 3rd right on bad bend signed Corndon. Straight over x-roads, 0.5 miles, farm on left. |

Ann & Will Williams
Corndonford Farm,
Poundsgate,
Newton Abbot,
Devon TQ13 7PP
Tel    +44 (0)1364 631595
Email  corndonford@btinternet.com

Entry 128   Map 2

# Devon

## Hammerslake Cottage

Be seduced by narrow lanes and high hedges before you arrive at this smartly painted 16th-century farm worker's cottage on the edge of Dartmoor. You are surrounded by a tranquil garden with twittering birds, a trickling stream and dramatic views; breakfast out here in summer, on eggs from Caroline's hens, local bacon, kedgeree. Two bedrooms (one with a balcony) are smartly dressed with big beds, goosey pillows, fresh flowers and chocolate, the third is a frill-free space for kids with bunks, comics and games. Tents can be put up in the garden, trees can be climbed; this is an affable place with a lovely owner.

| | |
|---|---|
| Price | £65–£75. |
| Rooms | 3: 2 doubles, 1 bunk room. |
| Meals | Pub 1 mile. |
| Closed | Rarely. |
| Directions | From Lustleigh, with church on right & shop opposite, turn left down lane to steep T-junc.; right for North Bovey, Pethybridge & Cleave. On for 1 mile, to blind bend with thatched cottage on right. Next house on right, set back from road, signed 'B&B'. |

Caroline Byng
Hammerslake Cottage,
Ellimore Road, Lustleigh,
Newton Abbot, Devon TQ13 9SQ
Tel    +44 (0)1647 277547
Email  caroline.byng@btinternet.com
Web    www.lustleighbedandbreakfast.co.uk

Entry 129   Map 2

# Devon

## Cyprian's Cot

A charming terraced cottage of 16th-century nooks and crannies and beams worth ducking. The setting is exquisite: the garden leads into fields of sheep, the Dartmoor Way goes through the town and the Two Moors Way skirts it. Shelagh, a lovely lady, gives guests their own sitting room with a fire, lit on cool nights; breakfasts, served in the cosy dining room, are fresh, free-range and tasty. Up the narrow stairs and into simple bedrooms – a small double and a tiny twin. A perfect house and hostess, and a perfect little town to discover, with its pubs, fine restaurant and delicatessen, organic shop and tearoom.

# Devon

## The Gate House

An idyllic house in an idyllic village, lost on the edge of the moor. The medieval longhouse (1460) has all the low beams and wonky walls you could hope for, and is beautifully looked after. Rose-print curtains and spruce quilts in the bedrooms, a wood-burner and flowers in the sitting room, robes, good soaps and soft towels in pretty bathrooms – and John and Sheila, delightful, attentive, serving you delicious Aga-side meals on white linen with candles. You will feel well and truly spoiled. A small pool in the lush garden overlooks beautiful woodland and moors... what more could you ask?

Travel Club offer. See page 414.

| | |
|---|---|
| Price | £60. Singles from £30. |
| Rooms | 2: 1 twin; 1 double with separate bath. |
| Meals | Pubs/restaurants 4-minute walk. |
| Closed | Rarely. |
| Directions | In Chagford pass church on left; 1st right beyond Globe Inn opposite. House 150 yds on right. |

| | |
|---|---|
| Price | £76–£80. Singles £50. |
| Rooms | 3: 2 twins/doubles; 1 double with separate bath/shower. |
| Meals | Supper trays £12.50. BYO. Packed lunch available. Pub/restaurant 50 yds. |
| Closed | Rarely. |
| Directions | From Moretonhampstead via Pound St to North Bovey (1.5 miles). House 25 yds off village green, down Lower Hill past inn on left. |

| | |
|---|---|
| | **Shelagh Weeden** |
| | Cyprian's Cot, |
| | 47 New Street, Chagford, |
| | Newton Abbot, Devon TQ13 8BB |
| Tel | +44 (0)1647 432256 |
| Email | shelaghweeden@btinternet.com |
| Web | www.cyprianscot.co.uk |

| | |
|---|---|
| | **John & Sheila Williams** |
| | The Gate House, |
| | North Bovey, Devon TQ13 8RB |
| Tel | +44 (0)1647 440479 |
| Fax | +44 (0)1647 440479 |
| Email | srw.gatehouse@btinternet.com |
| Web | www.gatehouseondartmoor.co.uk |

Entry 130 Map 2

Entry 131 Map 2

## Devon

### Burnville House

Granite gateposts, Georgian house, rhododendrons, beechwoods and rolling fields of sheep: that's the setting. But there's more. Beautifully proportioned rooms reveal subtle colours, elegant antiques, squishy sofas and bucolic views, stylish bathrooms are sprinkled with candles, there are sumptuous dinners and pancakes at breakfast. Your hosts left busy jobs in London to settle here, and their place breathes life – space, smiles, energy. Swim, play tennis, walk to Dartmoor from the door, take a trip to Eden or the sea. Or... just gaze at the moors and the church on the Tor and listen to the silence, and the sheep.

| | |
|---|---|
| Price | From £75. Singles £50. |
| Rooms | 2 doubles. |
| Meals | Dinner from £19. Pub 2 miles. |
| Closed | Rarely. |
| Directions | A30 Exeter-Okehampton; A386 for Tavistock. Right for Lydford opp. Dartmoor Inn; after 4 miles (through Lydford), Burnville Farm on left (convex traffic mirror on right). |

| | |
|---|---|
| | Victoria Cunningham |
| | Burnville House, |
| | Brentor, Tavistock, |
| | Devon PL19 0NE |
| Tel | +44 (0)1822 820443 |
| Email | burnvillef@aol.com |
| Web | www.burnville.co.uk |

Entry 132   Map 2

## Devon

### Mount Tavy Cottage

Joanna and Graham, a lovely Devon couple, have worked hard to restore this former gardener's bothy, Graham making much of the furniture himself. Pretty bedrooms in the house have stripped floorboards, a four-poster or half-tester bed, and deep, free-standing baths. Two other, simpler rooms are across the courtyard in the old potting shed; here you can be completely independent, or trot over to the house for a delicious breakfast. Outside are ponds – one with a breezy pagoda for summer suppers – and a walled Victorian garden. Tavistock is just a short walk. *Arrivals after 5pm, unless previously arranged.*

| | |
|---|---|
| Price | From £70. Singles from £35. |
| Rooms | 4: 1 double, 1 four-poster each with separate bath. Houses in garden: 2 twins/doubles, each with separate bath. |
| Meals | Dinner, 3 courses, £20. Pub 2 miles. |
| Closed | Rarely. |
| Directions | From Tavistock B3357 towards Princetown; 0.25 miles on, after Mount House School, left. Drive past lake to house. |

| | |
|---|---|
| | Mr & Mrs G H Moule |
| | Mount Tavy Cottage, |
| | Tavistock, |
| | Devon PL19 9JL |
| Tel | +44 (0)1822 614253 |
| Email | mounttavy@btinternet.com |
| Web | www.mounttavy.co.uk |

Entry 133   Map 2

# Devon

## South Hooe Count House

It's lovely here, so peaceful in your own private cottage perched above the river; steep steps lead to canoes for the intrepid. Delightful Trish leaves you homemade bread and marmalade, deep-yellow yolked eggs from her chickens and local bacon for you to cook. Choose a spot on the cushioned window seat or write your novel on the sheltered terrace which catches the sun; Martha the aged donkey may drop in for tea. There's a soft sofa and a wood-burner in the sitting room, and a large double bed in the light-filled bedroom. Live by the tide and emerge refreshed. *Babes in arms & children over eight welcome.*

🧳 Travel Club offer. See page 414.

| Price | £70–£85. Singles from £35. |
|---|---|
| Rooms | 1 double/twin. |
| Meals | Supper rarely. Pub 3 miles. |
| Closed | Rarely. |
| Directions | Into Bere Alston on B3257, left for Weir Quay. Over x-roads. Follow Hole's Hole sign, right for Hooe. Fork left for South Hooe Farm; 300 yds on, turn sharply back to your left (signed South Hooe Mine) & down track. |

Trish Dugmore
South Hooe Count House,
South Hooe Mine,
Hole's Hole, Bere Alston,
Yelverton, Devon PL20 7BW

| Tel | +44 (0)1822 840329 |
| Email | southhooe@aol.com |

Entry 134   Map 2

# Devon

## Higher Eggbeer Farm

Over 900 years old and still humming with life: pigs, cows, ponies, rabbits, and chickens share the rambling gardens. Sally Anne and William are artistic, fun, slightly wacky and charming. It's an adventure to stay, so keep an open mind: the house is a historic gem and undeniably rustic. Huge inglenook fireplaces, interesting art, books, piano, wellies, muddle and charm. Your lovely hosts will take children to feed animals and collect eggs, and will babysit. Be wrapped in peace in your own half of the house (with beautiful drawing room), immersed in a magnificent panorama of forest, hills and fields of waving wheat.

| Price | £65–£75. Singles £42. |
|---|---|
| Rooms | 3: 2 twins/doubles sharing bath (2nd room let to same party); 1 double sharing owners' bath. Self-catering option. |
| Meals | Restaurants 5-minute walk. |
| Closed | Rarely. |
| Directions | A30 to Okehampton. After 10 miles left exit into Cheriton Bishop; 1st left after Old Thatch pub, signed Woodbrooke. Down & up hill; road turns sharp left but you don't. Turn right down private lane. |

Sally Anne & William Selwyn
Higher Eggbeer Farm,
Cheriton Bishop,
Exeter,
Devon EX6 6JQ

| Tel | +44 (0)1647 24427 |

Entry 135   Map 2

# Devon

## The Old Inn

This lovely, rambling building sits happily in the village square: walk straight in to a warm, creamy-walled sitting/dining room with deep red sofas and a huge wood-burner for gazing. Bedrooms are stylish, with soft furnishings made by clever Charlotte, smooth linen and great mattresses; bathrooms spoil with organic soaps and lotions. Breakfasts are sublime: try yogurt with local honey, eggs from their hens, Dartmoor sausages, locally baked bread, or (if you are lucky) buttery homemade kedgeree. Stride out for fabulous walking, or hit trendy Chagford with its music and arts festivals. Bliss.

# Devon

## The Garden House

Refulgent! An extraordinary restoration of a 1930s house, carried out with passion. Bedrooms are sumptuous; beds plump with cushions, fabrics smooth, colours vibrant, scents divine. The exuberance reaches the garden; Jane's energy among the pots, quirky topiary and tulips is almost palpable. A huge collection of books are stacked hither and thither, the chandeliers sparkle, homemade cakes abound, candles flicker and there's a vast choice of locally-sourced breakfasts, beautifully served. It may not be minimalist but it is deeply comfortable, good-humoured and an easy walk into the city.

Travel Club offer. See page 414.

| | |
|---|---|
| Price | £75-£95. Singles £50-£60. |
| Rooms | 5: 3 doubles; 1 single with separate shower; 1 family room for 3 with separate bath. |
| Meals | Pub 100 yds. |
| Closed | 22 December-1 March. |
| Directions | A30 south from Exeter to Whiddon Down. Left off r'bout towards Mortonhampstead (A382); 400 yds, left to Drewsteignton. Enter village, house on right. |

| | |
|---|---|
| Price | £85-£90. Singles £50-£60. |
| Rooms | 2: 1 double; 1 twin. |
| Meals | Restaurant 8-minute walk. Pubs nearby. |
| Closed | Rarely. |
| Directions | M5 junc. 30 for city centre & university. Behind old Debenhams, Longbrook St into Pennsylvania Rd. Through lights, 2nd left into Hoopern Ave; house at end on left. |

|  |  |
|---|---|
| | Charlotte Hammick |
| | The Old Inn, |
| | Drewsteignton, |
| | Exeter, |
| | Devon EX6 6QR |
| Tel | +44 (0)1647 281276 |
| Email | charlotte.hammick@gmail.com |
| Web | www.old-inn.co.uk |

|  |  |
|---|---|
| | David & Jane Woolcock |
| | The Garden House, |
| | 4 Hoopern Avenue, Pennsylvania, |
| | Exeter, Devon EX4 6DN |
| Tel | +44 (0)1392 256255 |
| Fax | +44 (0)1392 256255 |
| Email | david.woolcock1@virgin.net |
| Web | www.exeterbedandbreakfast.co.uk |

Entry 136   Map 2

Entry 137   Map 2

# Devon

## Beach House

Lapping at the riverside garden is the Exe estuary, wide and serene. Birds and boats, the soft hills beyond, a gorgeous Georgian house on the river and kind hosts who have been here for years. The garden is pretty with quirky rooster-shaped topiary and old apple trees; you may have a locally sourced breakfast in the conservatory or in the dining room, with raspberries and blackberries in season. Relax on comfy chairs in the bedrooms, which are soft and chintzy, with antique white bedspreads, charmingly old-fashioned bathrooms and estuary views. Cycle into Exeter, for culture and Cathedral.

| Price | From £80. Singles £50. |
|---|---|
| Rooms | 2: 1 twin, 1 double. |
| Meals | Pubs/restaurants 8-minute walk. |
| Closed | Christmas & New Year. |
| Directions | M5 exit 30; signs to Exmouth. Right at George & Dragon. After 1 mile, immed. left after level crossing. At mini r'bout, left down The Strand. Last on left by beach. |

Trevor & Jane Coleman
Beach House,
45 The Strand,
Topsham,
Exeter, Devon EX3 0BB

| Tel | +44 (0)1392 876456 |
|---|---|
| Fax | +44 (0)1392 873159 |
| Email | janecoleman45@hotmail.com |

Entry 138   Map 2

# Devon

## Larkbeare Grange

Expectations rise as you follow the new, tree-lined drive to the immaculate Georgian house... and are met, the second you enter. The upkeep is perfect, the feel is chic and the whole place exudes well-being. Sparkling sash windows fill big rooms with light, floors shine and the grandfather clock ticks away the hours. Expect the best: good lighting, goose down duvets, contemporary luxury in fabric and fitting, the fabulous suite – perfect for a small family, flexible breakfasts and lovely views from the bedrooms at the front. Charlie, Savoy-trained, and Julia are charming and fun: you are in perfect hands.

Ethical Collection: Environment.
See page 412.

Travel Club offer. See page 414.

| Price | £90–£140. Singles from £75. |
|---|---|
| Rooms | 4: 2 doubles, 1 twin/double, 1 suite. |
| Meals | Pub 1.5 miles. |
| Closed | Rarely. |
| Directions | From A30 Exmouth & Ottery St Mary junc. At r'bouts follow Whimple signs. 0.25 miles, right; 0.5 miles, left signed Larkbeare. House 1 mile on left. |

Charlie & Julia Hutchings
Larkbeare Grange,
Larkbeare,
Talaton,
Exeter, Devon EX5 2RY

| Tel | +44 (0)1404 822069 |
|---|---|
| Email | stay@larkbeare.net |
| Web | www.larkbeare.net |

Entry 139   Map 2

Devon

### Lower Allercombe Farm

Horses in the paddock and no-frills bedrooms at this down-to-earth, very friendly B&B. Don't expect twinsets and pearls; Susie, ex-eventer, may greet you in two-tone jodphurs instead. She and Lizzie (her terrier) live at one end of the listed longhouse, guests at the other. There's a sitting room with horsey pictures and cosy wood-burner, and bedrooms upstairs that reflect the fair price. You'll feast on home eggs and tomatoes in the morning, and rashers from award-winning pigs. Very handy for Exeter, the south coast and Dartmoor; the airport is ten minutes away, the A30 is 350 yards. *Stabling available.*

| | |
|---|---|
| Price | £55–£70. Singles £35–£45. |
| Rooms | 3: 1 double, 1 twin; 1 double with separate bath. |
| Meals | Pub/restaurant 2 miles. |
| Closed | Rarely. |
| Directions | From Exeter junction 29, M5. A30 towards Honiton. At Daisymount exit to Ottery St Mary, take B3180 off roundabout. Go 200 yds, then right to Allercombe. 1 mile until crossroads, then right. House is 50 yds on right. |

Susie Holroyd
Lower Allercombe Farm,
Rockbeare,
Exeter, Devon EX5 2HD
Tel +44 (0)1404 822519
Email holroyd.s@gmail.com
Web www.lowerallercombefarm.co.uk

Entry 140   Map 2

Devon

### Varnes

Catch the train to this tidy village on the estuary, with its winding streets and picture book cottages; there are super walks and a cycle path from here. You stay in a long, white-painted house, hunkered in a dip with a large, pretty garden: well-travelled Prim gives you comfortable, bright, uncluttered bedrooms (one has its own sitting room) with lots of pictures, hot water bottles, fresh milk, feather duvets, modern bathrooms and a feeling of independence in your own wing. All is peaceful and quiet; breakfast is mainly locally sourced and is taken in the sunny conservatory. *Well-behaved dogs by arrangement.*

| | |
|---|---|
| Price | £60–£65. Singles £45. |
| Rooms | 2: 1 double, 1 twin. |
| Meals | Pub/restaurant 30 yds. |
| Closed | Christmas. |
| Directions | From junction 30 M5, take A376 towards Exmouth. After 5 miles, right at traffic lights by Saddlers Arms, on outskirts of Lympstone. After 0.75 miles, right into first open gateway after the parish church. |

Chris & Prim Finney
Varnes,
Church Road, Lympstone,
Devon EX8 5JT
Tel +44 (0)1395 276999
Email chris@varnes16.freeserve.co.uk
Web www.varnes.co.uk

Entry 141   Map 2

# Devon

## Simcoe House

A gem of a setting, this gracious 18th-century house was the summer home of General Simcoe in 1790 and is within strolling distance of the beach and town. There are stunning views from wide windows in the lovely guest sitting room, so find a book and settle in a comfy chair while the sun streams in. Jane gives you breakfast in the pretty conservatory or the dining room. Bedrooms are sunny and charming with fresh flowers and fabulous vistas. Laze on the terrace, look up the house history in the local museum or relish the Jurassic coast. A unique house with a beachy feel and delightful owners. *Children over ten welcome.*

| Price | From £80. Singles from £60. |
|---|---|
| Rooms | 2: 1 double, 1 twin. |
| Meals | Pubs/restaurants 5 minute walk. |
| Closed | Christmas. |
| Directions | M5 junc. 30 onto A376. Then B3179 to Budleigh Salterton (approx. 8 miles). Into town centre then left opposite The Creamery, onto Fore Street Hill. 150 yds on right and through white gates into car park. Steps lead to front door. |

|  | Jane Crosse |
|---|---|
|  | Simcoe House, |
|  | 8 Fore Street Hill, |
|  | Budleigh Salterton, Devon EX9 6PE |
| Tel | +44 (0)1395 446013 |
| Email | simcoehouse@hotmail.co.uk |
| Web | www.simcoehouse.co.uk |

Entry 142   Map 2

# Devon

## Rose Cottage

Seaside fun in this 1824 house right on the front in sleepy Sidmouth, this is a quick hop to the beach – why not rent the family's beach hut? – or onto the coastal path for bracing walks. With stripped pine floorboards, stained-glass features and pretty cushions, Jackie has created a jolly place. Bedrooms are small with sunny walls and quilted covers, two have tiny showers, another has a slipper bath. There's homemade muesli and organic bacon for breakfast in a room with a seaside tea shop feel; no sitting room but a pretty cottage garden with seats for fine weather days. *Children by arrangement.*

Ethical Collection: Food. See page 412.

Travel Club offer. See page 414.

| Price | From £70. Singles from £60. |
|---|---|
| Rooms | 4: 2 doubles, 1 twin; 1 double with separate bath. |
| Meals | Pubs/restaurants 300 yds. |
| Closed | Christmas, New Year & occasionally. |
| Directions | From Exeter A3052 to Sidmouth. Over r'bout at Woodlands Hotel. House is 100 yds on left just before zebra crossing. |

|  | Jacalyn & Neil Cole |
|---|---|
|  | Rose Cottage, |
|  | Coburg Road, |
|  | Sidmouth, Devon EX10 8NF |
| Tel | +44 (0)1395 577179 |
| Email | neilsurf@tesco.net |
| Web | www.rosecottage-sidmouth.co.uk |

Entry 143   Map 2

# Devon

## Glebe House

Set on a hillside with fabulous views over the Coly valley, this late-Georgian vicarage has become a heart-warming B&B. The views will entice you, the hosts will delight you and the house is filled with interesting things. Chuck and Emma spent many years at sea – he a Master Mariner, she a chef – and have filled these big light rooms with cushions, kilims and treasured family pieces. There's a sitting room for guests, a lovely conservatory with a vintage vine, peaceful bedrooms with blissful views and bathrooms that sparkle. All this, a lone goat, wildlife beyond the ha-ha and the fabulous coast a hike away.

# Devon

## West Colwell Farm

Devon lanes, pheasants, bluebell walks *and* sparkling B&B. The Hayes clearly love what they do; ex-TV producers, they have converted this 18th-century farmhouse and barns into a cosy, warm and stylish place to stay. Be charmed by original beams and pine doors, heritage colours and clean lines. Bedrooms feel self-contained, two have terraces overlooking the wooded valley and the most cosy is tucked under the roof. Linen is luxurious, showers are huge and breakfasts (Frank's pancakes, lovely bacon, eggs from next door) are totally flexible. A pretty garden in front, beaches nearby, peace all around. Bliss.

Travel Club offer. See page 414.

| Price | From £70. Singles £45. |
|---|---|
| Rooms | 3: 1 double, 1 twin/double, 1 family. |
| Meals | Pubs/restaurants 2.5 miles. |
| Closed | Christmas & New Year. |
| Directions | A375 from Honiton; left opposite Hare & Hounds on B3174 to Seaton. 2nd left to Southleigh, 1.5 miles. In village 1st left to Northleigh; 600 yds, drive on left. |

| Price | From £75. Singles £55. |
|---|---|
| Rooms | 3 doubles. |
| Meals | Restaurants 3 miles. |
| Closed | December & January. |
| Directions | 3 miles from Honiton; Offwell signed off A35 Honiton-Axminster road. In centre of village, at church, down hill. Farm 0.5 miles on. |

|  | Emma & Chuck Guest |
|---|---|
|  | Glebe House, |
|  | Southleigh, |
|  | Colyton, Devon EX24 6SD |
| Tel | +44 (0)1404 871276 |
| Fax | +44 (0)1404 871276 |
| Email | emma_guest@talktalk.net |
| Web | www.guestsatglebe.com |

|  | Frank & Carol Hayes |
|---|---|
|  | West Colwell Farm, |
|  | Offwell, |
|  | Honiton, |
|  | Devon EX14 9SL |
| Tel | +44 (0)1404 831130 |
| Email | stay@westcolwell.co.uk |
| Web | www.westcolwell.co.uk |

Entry 144   Map 2

Entry 145   Map 2

## Devon

### The Devon Wine School

Alastair and Carol run their wine school from this delightfully rural spot where the night sky still twinkles, and look after you to perfection. Chill out in an open-plan sitting/dining room with wooden floors, smart chesterfields, Xian terracotta warriors, claret walls. Choose from bedrooms in the house, or brand new ones in a separate building; all are light, unfussy and elegant with swish bathrooms. Work up an appetite on the hard tennis court: food is taken seriously and sourced locally, the wine is a joy and reasonably priced, the atmosphere is house party style; relaxed and friendly. *Children over eight welcome.*

## Devon

### Raymont House

Delightful to be in the heart of a historic little town with a Tuesday market, good pubs and new bistro, yet close to the wilds of Dartmoor. This is civilised B&B: your charming hosts give you one bedroom (or, if you're a party, three), peaceful, pretty and serene, and a wow of a bathroom that mixes period features with beautiful modern fittings. No guest sitting room but TVs, homemade biscuits, delicious breakfasts, dressing gowns and fresh flowers... The breakfast room is warmed by a wood-burner, there's a drying room for wet gear, you're on the Tarka Trail and near to RHS Rosemoor. Great value.

Travel Club offer. See page 414.

| | |
|---|---|
| Price | From £75. Singles by arrangement. |
| Rooms | 5: 1 double, 1 twin. Old Milking Parlour: 3 doubles. |
| Meals | Dinner, 3 courses, from £29.50. Occasional lunch. Pub 1 mile. |
| Closed | Rarely. |
| Directions | From Cadeleigh, 1.5 miles to Postbox Cross, turn left to Cheriton Fitzpaine. Follow road to Redyeates Cross x-roads, then right, house is 150 yds on left down track. |

| | |
|---|---|
| Price | From £65. Singles £45. |
| Rooms | 3: 2 doubles, 1 single all sharing bathroom (for one party only). |
| Meals | Pub/restaurant 50 yds. |
| Closed | Christmas to New Year. |
| Directions | From Okehampton, signs to Hatherleigh for 6 miles. At roundabout, right through Hatherleigh to top of Market Street. On left. |

Alastair & Carol Peebles
The Devon Wine School,
Redyeates Farm,
Cheriton Fitzpaine,
Crediton, Devon EX17 4HG
Tel       +44 (0)1363 866742
Email    alastair@devonwineschool.co.uk
Web      www.devonwineschool.co.uk

Jan & Alan Toogood
Raymont House,
49 Market Street,
Hatherleigh,
Okehampton, Devon EX20 3JP
Tel       +44 (0)1837 810850
Email    alan.toogood@yahoo.co.uk
Web      www.raymonthouse.co.uk

Entry 146   Map 2

Entry 147   Map 2

## Devon

### Leworthy Barton

Biscuits, scones, fresh flowers. Breakfasts are courtesy of their own Tamworth pigs with homemade bread, jams and marmalade, eggs from their hens; wellies and waxed jackets on tap. Rupert and Kim are busy farmers and artist/designers who choose to give guests what they would most like themselves. So... you have the whole of the stables, tranquil, beautifully restored and with field and sky views. Downstairs is open-plan plus kitchen; upstairs, sloping ceilings, warm wood floors, big bed, soft towels. It's cosy yet spacious, stylish yet homely, and the Atlantic coast is the shortest drive.

Ethical Collection: Food. See page 412.

| | |
|---|---|
| Price | £80. Singles £60. |
| Rooms | Barn: 1 double, sitting room & kitchen. |
| Meals | Pub 3 miles. |
| Closed | Never. |
| Directions | A39 to Woolfardisworthy. At T-junc. in village, left. 0.5 miles left to Stibb Cross. Over bridge bear right, then left. Uphill, right towards Leworthy & Mill; 0.5 miles; on left. |

| | |
|---|---|
| | Rupert & Kim Ashmore |
| | Leworthy Barton, |
| | Woolsery, |
| | Bideford, |
| | Devon EX39 5PY |
| Tel | +44 (0)1237 431140 |
| Email | kim@westcountrylife.co.uk |

Entry 148   Map 2

## Devon

### South Worden

Come for the lovely, quiet setting, the rose-filled garden and rousing breakfasts of sausages and bacon from the Cornish Bacon Company. Michael and Shirley look after you impeccably: relax in the low-beamed sitting room with a wood-burning stove and doors to the garden, sleep soundly (one bedroom up, one down) on good mattresses with white cotton sheets, splash about in warm, spotless bathrooms – one snazzier than the other. There are books to read, good walks from the house and dinner is a treat if you wish to stay in. You are near Dartmoor, Exmoor and good public gardens to visit.

 Travel Club offer. See page 414.

| | |
|---|---|
| Price | £80–£90. Singles £50–£60. |
| Rooms | 2: 1 double; 1 double with separate bath/shower. |
| Meals | Dinner, 3 courses, £20. Pub/restaurant 2 miles. |
| Closed | December & January. |
| Directions | From Bideford towards Gt Torrington, after 2 miles right to Holsworthy. On till Stibb Cross x-roads, then right, A388 Milton Damerel. At Venn Green x-roads, right for Bradworthy. Left at Five Lanes x-roads for Bradworthy. 1st turn on right; on left. |

| | |
|---|---|
| | Michael French |
| | South Worden, West Putford, |
| | Holsworthy, Devon EX22 7LG |
| Tel | +44 (0)1409 261448 |
| Fax | +44 (0)5602 042699 |
| Email | mike@southworden.co.uk |
| Web | www.southworden.co.uk |

Entry 149   Map 2

## Devon

### Beara Farmhouse

The moment you arrive at the whitewashed farmhouse you feel the affection your hosts have for the place. Richard is a lover of wood and a fine craftsman – every room echoes his talent; he also created the pond that's home to mallards and geese. Ann has laid brick paths, stencilled, stitched and painted, all with an eye for colour; bedrooms and guest sitting room are delectable and snug. Open farmland all around, sheep, pigs and hens in the yard, the Tarka Trail on your doorstep and hosts happy to give you 6.30am breakfast should you plan a day on Lundy Island. Readers love this place. *Min. stay two nights June-September.*

Travel Club offer. See page 414.

| | |
|---|---|
| Price | £70. Singles by arrangement. |
| Rooms | 2: 1 double, 1 twin. |
| Meals | Pub 1.5 miles. |
| Closed | 20 December–5 January. |
| Directions | From A39, left into Bideford, round quay, past old bridge on left. Signs to Torrington; 1.5 miles, right for Buckland Brewer; 2.5 miles, left; 0.5 miles, right over cattle grid & down track. |

**Ann & Richard Dorsett**
Beara Farmhouse,
Buckland Brewer,
Bideford,
Devon EX39 5EH
Tel       +44 (0)1237 451666
Web      www.bearafarmhouse.co.uk

Entry 150   Map 2

## Devon

### Hillbrow House

You could be forgiven for thinking this 'house on the hill' is genuine Georgian – but it's mostly new, with a deep veranda and glorious views over the golf course (and, on a clear day, to distant Dartmoor). The light, uncluttered rooms are neat as a pin with coordinated colours, thick fabrics, antiques and your own upstairs studio sitting room; bedrooms have feather pillows, proper blankets and luxurious bathrooms. Golfers and walkers will be in paradise, surfers can reach Croyde easily and a plethora of gentler beaches lie in the other direction. Stoke up on delicious homemade granola for breakfast.

Travel Club offer. See page 414.

| | |
|---|---|
| Price | From £80. Singles £45. |
| Rooms | 2: 1 double; 1 double with separate bath. |
| Meals | Dinner, 3 courses, £25. Pubs/restaurants within walking distance. |
| Closed | Christmas. |
| Directions | B3226 from S. Molton for 5 miles. Turn right for Chittlehamholt, left at T-junc., then through village. House last on right. |

**Clarissa Roe**
Hillbrow House,
Chittlehamholt,
Umberleigh, Devon EX37 9NS
Tel       +44 (0)1769 540214
Email    clarissaroe@btinternet.com
Web      www.hillbrowhouse.com

Entry 151   Map 2

# Devon

## Lower Hummacott

Bright clear colours, antique furniture, charming decorative touches. There are fresh fruit and flowers in the bedrooms (one with a king-size bed) and two guest sitting rooms. Delicious, organic and traditionally reared meat, veg and eggs, fresh fish, homemade cakes... As if that were not enough, the Georgian farmhouse has a stunning formal garden created from scratch – spring-fed pools, lime walk, pergola, arches, herbaceous beds and a new gazebo. Liz, a weaver, and Tony, an award-winning artist (he has a large gallery by the house) are charming and friendly and look after you beautifully.

| | |
|---|---|
| Price | £68. |
| Rooms | 2 doubles. |
| Meals | Dinner £27 (Sunday & Monday only). Pub/restaurant 1.5 miles. |
| Closed | Rarely. |
| Directions | 0.5 miles east of Kings Nympton village is Beara Cross; straight over towards Romansleigh for 0.75 miles; Hummacott is 1st entrance on left by iron wheel. |

| | |
|---|---|
| | Tony & Liz Williams |
| | Lower Hummacott, |
| | Kings Nympton, |
| | Umberleigh, Devon EX37 9TU |
| Tel | +44 (0)1769 581177 |
| Fax | +44 (0)1769 581177 |

Entry 152   Map 2

# Devon

## Sannacott

On the southern fringes of Exmoor you're in peaceful countryside with hidden valleys. The Trickeys breed national hunt racehorses from their Georgian style farmhouse: downstairs is a happy mix of casual countryside living, antiques, open fires and family pictures. Bedrooms are traditional, clean and comfortable, some have lovely long views across rolling hills and trees. Clare bakes her own bread, most produce is organic or local and there's a pretty bird-filled garden to wander through. Great for walkers with the North Devon coastal path nearby: riders, birdwatchers and nature lovers will be happy too.

Travel Club offer. See page 414.

| | |
|---|---|
| Price | £70–£80. Singles £45. |
| Rooms | 3: 1 double; 1 twin/double sharing bath. Annexe: 1 twin with separate bath/shower. |
| Meals | Occasional dinner, 3 courses, £20. Pub 5 miles. |
| Closed | Rarely. |
| Directions | M5 J27; A361 for Barnstaple, past Tiverton, 15.5 miles; right at r'bout (small sign Whitechapel). 1.5 miles to junc., right for N. Molton; 1.5m to 3rd on left, black gates. |

| | |
|---|---|
| | Mrs Clare Trickey |
| | Sannacott, |
| | North Molton, Devon EX36 3JS |
| Tel | +44 (0)1598 740203 |
| Email | mctrickey@hotmail.com |
| Web | www.sannacott-exmoor.co.uk |

Entry 153   Map 2

## Devon

### Bratton Mill

Breakfast is locally sourced and superb; in summer, eat by the Exmoor trout stream to almost deafening birdsong. Absolute privacy down the long track to a thickly wooded and beautifully secluded valley: watch for dragonflies, red deer, buzzards and the flash of the kingfisher. To the backdrop of the rushing stream is the house, painted white and filled with treasure – including Marilyn who spoils you: elegant china, fresh flowers, warm bathrooms, crisp linen and a comforting decanter of port. There are strolls or hikes straight from the door. Wonderful. *Self-catering cottage & folly available.*

Travel Club offer. See page 414.

| | |
|---|---|
| Price | £75–£95. Singles from £45. |
| Rooms | 2: 1 twin/double, 1 four-poster. Children's rooms available. |
| Meals | Dinner/supper available. Pub close walking distance. |
| Closed | Rarely. |
| Directions | From Bratton Fleming High Street right into Mill Lane. Down road for 0.5 miles through railway cutting; turn right. |

|  |  |
|---|---|
| | Marilyn Holloway |
| | Bratton Mill, |
| | Bratton Fleming, |
| | Barnstaple, Devon EX31 4RU |
| Tel | +44 (0)1598 710026 |
| Email | contact@brattonmill.co.uk |
| Web | www.brattonmill.co.uk |

Entry 154   Map 2

## Devon

### Hewish Barton

The second you arrive you're 'away from it all'. In the majestic Georgian house framed by green hills and a garden bouncing with birds, Maggi gives you delicious homemade cake for tea. You get a kitchen, too, and a lovely log-fired sitting room full of artefacts and books. Bedrooms have big sash windows, generous wardrobes and amazing views; baths encourage long soaks. Come for home comforts and cooking, breakfasts by the Aga, woodland paths... and Woolacombe and Ilfracombe (the next Padstow?) down the road. Good value, great for couples *and* house parties, and the loveliest hosts.

| | |
|---|---|
| Price | From £70. Singles from £40. |
| Rooms | 3 doubles. Guest kitchen. |
| Meals | Pub 2 miles. |
| Closed | Rarely. |
| Directions | A361 to Barnstaple. Follow A39 past hospital, left onto B3230 to Ilfracombe. Through Muddiford; 1 mile, quarry on left, right into drive. |

|  |  |
|---|---|
| | Maggi & Keith Wase |
| | Hewish Barton, |
| | Muddiford, Barnstaple, Devon EX31 4HH |
| Tel | +44 (0)1271 850245 |
| Email | hewish_barton@mwase.freeserve.co.uk |
| Web | www.hewish-barton.co.uk |

Entry 155   Map 2

## Devon

### Beachborough Country House

A gracious 18th-century rectory with stone-flagged floors, lofty windows, wooden shutters, charming gardens. Viviane is vivacious and she spoils you with seemingly effortless food straight from the Aga, either in the kitchen or in the elegant dining room with twinkling fire. Chickens cluck, horses whinny but otherwise the peace is deep; this is perfect walking or cycling country. Ease any aches and pains in a steaming roll top; bathrooms are awash with fluffy towels, large bedrooms are fresh as a daisy with great views – admire them from the window seats. Combe Martin is a short hop for a grand beach day. *Dogs £5.*

Ethical Collection: Community; Food. See page 412.

 Travel Club offer. See page 414.

| Price | From £70. Singles £45. |
|---|---|
| Rooms | 3: 1 twin/double, 2 doubles. |
| Meals | Dinner, 2-3 courses, from £19. Pub 3 miles. |
| Closed | Rarely. |
| Directions | From A361, A399 for 12 miles. At Blackmoor Gate, left onto A39. House 1.5 miles on right. |

|  | Viviane Clout Beachborough Country House, Kentisbury, Barnstaple, Devon EX31 4NH |
|---|---|
| Tel | +44 (0)1271 882487 |
| Email | viviane@beachborough.freeserve.co.uk |
| Web | www.beachboroughcountryhouse.co.uk |

Entry 156   Map 2

## Devon

### Long Cottage

Surfers are near to fabulous beaches, and Simon can inspire all beginners! He and Karine have transformed this old farm worker's cottage into an uncluttered, gorgeous home: you have your own entrance, a ground-floor space with piles of books, photographs on the walls, maps and a piano; bring a bottle of wine and a takeaway here in the evenings. Bedrooms are softly coloured, with good mattresses, crisp sheets and light oak furniture, some made by Simon; bathrooms are spanking new with deep baths, cool basins. Locally sourced breakfasts are flexible feasts: walk it off on the coastal path. *Beauty & massage treatments.*

| Price | From £70. Singles from £45. |
|---|---|
| Rooms | 3: 1 double, 1 family room. 1 double with separate bath. |
| Meals | Pub 1.2 miles. |
| Closed | Rarely. |
| Directions | From Barnstaple A361 for Ilfracombe, through Braunton & Knowle. Left signed Upcott. House approximately 1 mile on right. |

|  | Simon Swallow Long Cottage, Upcott, Braunton, Devon EX33 1HT |
|---|---|
| Tel | +44 (0)1271 817533 |
| Email | simon@simonswallow.co.uk |
| Web | www.longcottage.co.uk |

Entry 157   Map 2

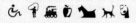

# Devon

## North Walk House

Come for the organic, local food: jazz-enthusiasts Kelvin and Liz are passionate cooks, serving candlelit dinners in the large bistro-style dining room at one convivial table; try Appledore sea bass or braised Exmoor beef. Bedrooms, all with sea views, have brass beds, stripped floors, local art, modern pine and TVs; bathrooms are brand new with tiles from Provence – all is clean, comfortable and informal but not state of the art. A paved terrace at the front is fine for a cup of coffee, or a glass of wine, and a look at the view. Great for coastal path walkers and foodies. *Minimum stay two nights.*

Ethical Collection: Food. See page 412.

Travel Club offer. See page 414.

| | |
|---|---|
| Price | £78. Singles £44.10. |
| Rooms | 5: 4 doubles, 1 twin. |
| Meals | Packed lunch £7. Dinner, 4 courses, from £24.95. Pub/restaurant 0.25 miles. |
| Closed | January. |
| Directions | A39 from Barnstaple to Lynton Town Hall. From there, left turn at the church down North Walk. Third hotel on left. |

**Kelvin Jacobs & Liz Hallum**
North Walk House,
North Walk,
Lynton, Devon EX35 6HJ
Tel +44 (0)1598 753372
Email walk@northwalkhouse.co.uk
Web www.northwalkhouse.co.uk

Entry 158  Map 2

---

# Devon

## Victoria House

Beachcombers, surfers and walkers will be in their element in this Edwardian seaside villa where all of the bedrooms have magnificent views. Choose between two in the main house with state-of-the-art bathrooms and one in the annexe with a beach-hut feel and a private deck. Heather is lively and fun, she and David are ex-RAF and clearly enjoy looking after you; breakfast is a main meal of nuts, fresh fruits, yogurts, eggs benedict, smoked salmon or the full Monty. You are on the coastal road to Woolacombe for International Surf and Kite Surfing competitions; Lundy is always in view. Bucket and spade bliss.

Ethical Collection: Food. See page 412.

Travel Club offer. See page 414.

| | |
|---|---|
| Price | £90-£140. |
| Rooms | 3 doubles. |
| Meals | Packed lunch £8. Pubs/restaurants 200 yds. |
| Closed | Rarely. |
| Directions | From B3343, right for Mortehoe. Through village & past the old chapel. Down steep hill, with the bay ahead; house 3rd on left. |

**Heather & David Burke**
Victoria House,
Chapel Hill, Mortehoe,
Woolacombe, Devon EX34 7DZ
Tel +44 (0)1271 871302
Email heatherburke59@fsmail.net
Web www.victoriahousebandb.co.uk

Entry 159  Map 2

# Devon

## Southcliffe Hall

An Argentinian chandelier, antique French radiators, a rediscovered Victorian garden. Eccentric owners have left their mark on what was originally the Manor House, a grandly idiosyncratic home overlooking the sea. The owners give you vast bedrooms with rich carpets, big beds, antique flourishes. Bathrooms are one-offs – roll top baths to Victorian high-level cisterns – and each floor resounds with history. Dinner is in the panelled dining room; for breakfast there's local produce. Spot deer in the woodland, walk to the beach, hike along the coast, listen to the sea: the setting is fabulous.

Ethical Collection: Food. See page 412.

Travel Club offer. See page 414.

| | |
|---|---|
| Price | £100. Singles by arrangement. |
| Rooms | 2 twins/doubles. |
| Meals | Dinner, 3 courses, £30. Pub 5-minute walk. |
| Closed | Rarely. |
| Directions | From A361, B3343 for Woolacombe. Turn right, through Lincombe, into Lee. Drive to house on left, between village hall & red 'phone box. |

|  | Kate Seekings & Barry Jenkinson |
|---|---|
| | Southcliffe Hall, |
| | Lee, Devon EX34 8LW |
| Tel | +44 (0)1271 867068 |
| Fax | +44 (0)1271 867068 |
| Email | stay@southcliffehall.co.uk |
| Web | www.southcliffehall.co.uk |

Entry 160   Map 2

# Dorset

## Bowes House

A great place to blow the cobwebs away. The light, airy and spacious 1980s house with wide country views is at the end of a track, just where it peters out into a bridleway. With a gorgeous big garden and an orchard It's a great place for families... Lisa and Jeremy have two young sons, a dog, cats, geese and a clutch of hens. No traffic – just the occasional passing horse – and walking from the door. Lisa is seriously eco-minded, so a wood has been planted to fuel the fires and the Rayburn; breakfast is local, homemade and often organic. Super comfy bedrooms, too; the twin has Spanish bedheads.

Ethical Collection: Environment. See page 412.

Travel Club offer. See page 414.

| | |
|---|---|
| Price | From £60. |
| Rooms | 3: 1 double; 1 twin, 1 single sharing bathroom (let to same party only). |
| Meals | Pub 2.5 miles. |
| Closed | Rarely. |
| Directions | A3066 from Beaminster to Mosterton. Having entered village from south, turn right immediately before Eeles Pottery into Bowes Lane. House is last on left. |

|  | Lisa & Jeremy Purkiss |
|---|---|
| | Bowes House, |
| | Bowes Lane, Mosterton, |
| | Beaminster, Dorset DT8 3HN |
| Tel | +44 (0)1308 868862 |
| Email | info@boweshousebandb.com |
| Web | www.boweshousebandb.com |

Entry 161   Map 3

# Dorset

## Crosskeys House

In previous lives a pub, a cobbler's shop and a smithy, this listed stone house, right on the village crossroads, is well settled into its B&B role. Robin and Liz offer you a fabulous breakfast menu and happily advise you on the glories of west Dorset (walks, pubs, stately homes): nothing is too much trouble. Their sitting room is softly traditional – plump sofas, family portraits and antiques, garden flowers, glossy magazines – while lovely cosy bedrooms have king-size beds and interesting books. The house is near the road but there's a courtyard garden for breakfast and water fresh from the well.

Travel Club offer. See page 414.

| Price | From £85. Singles from £60. |
|---|---|
| Rooms | 2: 1 double, 1 twin/double. |
| Meals | Pub 200 yds. |
| Closed | Rarely. |
| Directions | A35 to Bridport then A3066 to Beaminster. B3163 to Broadwindsor. House at end of one-way system, last on right (just before crossroads). |

**Robin & Liz Adeney**
Crosskeys House,
High Street, Broadwindsor,
Beaminster, Dorset DT8 3QP
Tel       +44 (0)1308 868063
Fax       +44 (0)1308 868063
Email     robin.adeney@care4free.net
Web       www.crosskeyshouse.com

Entry 162   Map 3

# Dorset

## Knowle Farm

Find a classic Dorset Long House, fragrant with wisteria in May, and hosts with a passion for rare and special plants. Alison and John's garden is a peaceful place of gentle colours and careful structure; it's open for the National Gardens Scheme but all are welcome to stroll around the old cider orchard, rose walk, wildlife garden and greenhouse. Bedrooms are pretty in pinks and lilacs, one in a converted barn with private entrance; bathrooms are swish. Stroll past thatched cottages to the pub for a meal, wake to an Aga-cooked breakfast, browse gardening books, lounge in a lofty sitting room, savour the loveliness of it all.

| Price | £80. Singles £45. |
|---|---|
| Rooms | 2: 1 double; 1 twin with separate bath. |
| Meals | Pub 200 yds. |
| Closed | Christmas week & occasionally. |
| Directions | Exit A35 two miles east of Bridport, following signs to Uploders. Left at Crown Inn, in village. House on right opposite white chapel. |

**Alison & John Halliday**
Knowle Farm,
Uploders, Bridport,
Dorset DT6 4NS
Tel       +44 (0)1308 485492
Email     info@knowlefarmbandb.com
Web       www.knowlefarmbandb.com

Entry 163   Map 3

# Dorset

## Orchard Barn

Immerse yourself in huge chalk cliffs, fabulous sea scapes and secret villages hiding in green folds. This is 'River Cottage' country and you will eat like kings – from the dazzling breakfast menu (try Jersey cream on your porridge) to delicious light suppers, all as local and organic as possible. Inside your own barn-like sitting room a fire burns brightly all day, bedrooms are nurturing and fresh, bathrooms awash with perfumed oils and fluffy towels. Nigel and Margaret are old hands at making everything very relaxing indeed. Sit on the terrace in summer and admire the lovely garden.

Travel Club offer. See page 414.

| Price | £115–£135. Singles from £75. |
|---|---|
| Rooms | 2 twins/doubles. |
| Meals | Light supper £6.50–£15.50. Pubs/restaurants within 1 mile. |
| Closed | Rarely. |
| Directions | From A35 east of Bridport within 30mph limit, left into Lee Lane (with 6' 6" width restriction) & follow to bottom. Over bridge, round bend & into Dead End Lane. On right. |

Nigel & Margaret Corbett
Orchard Barn,
Bradpole, Bridport, Dorset DT6 4AR
Tel +44 (0)1308 455655
Fax +44 (0)1308 455655
Email corbett@lodgeatorchardbarn.co.uk
Web www.lodgeatorchardbarn.co.uk

Entry 164  Map 3

# Dorset

## Wooden Cabbage House

Down a private driveway with stunning views across the unspoilt, secluded valley, is a smartly restored keeper's cottage. This is a spacious, stylish home: fresh flowers, crisp linen and fine antiques upstairs and a verdant garden room down, with a long oak table for breakfasts and a comfy sofa for magical views. Or, in winter, breakfast by the Aga on the finest of local produce and Susie's own preserves; you can stay in for delicious home-cooked suppers too. Pictures celebrate the country life, Martyn and Susie look after you brilliantly, and there are great walks straight from the door. *Children over ten welcome.*

Travel Club offer. See page 414.

| Price | £90. Singles £60. |
|---|---|
| Rooms | 3: 2 doubles, 1 twin. |
| Meals | Dinner, 3 courses, £30. Pub/restaurants 3 miles. |
| Closed | Rarely. |
| Directions | 3 miles S of Yeovil on A37, turn west to Closworth. Continue on this road, past turn to Halstock; 200 yds on right, over cattle grid. House 1st on left. |

Martyn & Susie Lee
Wooden Cabbage House,
East Chelborough,
Dorchester, Dorset DT2 0QA
Tel +44 (0)1935 83362
Email relax@woodencabbage.co.uk
Web www.woodencabbage.co.uk

Entry 165  Map 3

# Dorset

## Higher Holway Farm

Heaven to walk here rather than drive. Hop over the cattle grid and amble down the quilted valley to find a listed, deliciously renovated farmhouse with a distinct 'designer-style' interior. Downstairs has chunky beams, soft colours, fresh flowers and a light, airy sitting room; ample bedrooms are deeply smart with the best linen, floaty goose down and restful views. Food is taken seriously; try a Beaminster banger for breakfast (on the elegant terrace in summer) or one of Sarah's Cordon Bleu dinners. The MacMillan Way is on the doorstep; for walkers who demand solace, this is perfect

 Travel Club offer. See page 414.

| | |
|---|---|
| Price | £90. Singles £60. |
| Rooms | 2 twins/doubles. |
| Meals | Dinner with wine, £30. Pubs/restaurants 5-10 minute drive. |
| Closed | Christmas. |
| Directions | A37 Yeovil-Dorchester. Turn right to Evershot, left towards Cattistock. Left at x-roads to Cattistock. 1.5 miles; where telegraph poles finish on right, farm is on left. |

**Nigel & Sarah Hadden-Paton**
Higher Holway Farm,
Cattistock, Dorchester, Dorset DT2 OHH
Tel +44 (0)1935 83822
Fax +44 (0)1935 83820
Email bumble@hadden-paton.com
Web www.higherholwayfarm.co.uk

Entry 166   Map 3

# Dorset

## Fullers Earth

Such an English feel: the village with pub, post office and stores, the walled garden with fruit trees beyond (source of perfect compotes and breakfast jams), the gentle church view. This listed house – its late-Georgian face added in 1820 – was where the Cattistock huntsmen lived; the unusual thatched stables alongside housed their steeds. Guests share a large and lovely sitting room in sand, cream and dove-blue; carpeted bedrooms have a lofty feel; the resplendent coastline – at times dramatic, at other times softly serene – is yours to discover, and Wendy and Ian will always plan your walks with you.

| | |
|---|---|
| Price | £75-£85. Singles from £60. |
| Rooms | 2 doubles. |
| Meals | Pub 500 yds. |
| Closed | Christmas. |
| Directions | From A37 take Cattistock turning downhill to T-junc. Left through village. Pub on left. After 90 degree right-hand bend, 5th house on right. |

**Wendy Gregory**
Fullers Earth,
Cattistock,
Dorchester, Dorset DT2 0JL
Tel +44 (0)1300 320190
Email stay@fullersearth.co.uk
Web www.fullersearth.co.uk

Entry 167   Map 3

## Gray's Farmhouse

Rosie greets you with tea and cake — in the lovely garden on warm days. This former shooting lodge has flagstones and vibrant art on aqua walls; Rosie paints, Roger writes poetry. Light, peaceful bedrooms have goose down, crisp cotton sheets (and blankets if you prefer); a cosy 'snug' is filled with music, books, maps, treats and a fridge; you can picnic here too. Breakfast well on homemade or local produce, sometimes in the conservatory with its long views over the valleys of Hardy county. Walk the Jurassic coast or wander the bird-rich woods and wonderful footpaths from the house. *Minimum stay two nights.*

## Frampton House

A grand Grade II*-listed house in parkland landscaped by Capability Brown... and two labradors, Potter and Dumble, to greet you as you scrunch up the gravel. Beyond the Georgian façade lies a delicious mix of English and Gallic styles. Bedrooms combine comfort with outstanding views, a magnificent four-poster in one, everywhere fine linen and plump pillows. Georgina is a portrait painter and a food and arts writer. Breakfasts, served in the conservatory, are true-blue English, with spectacular bangers. Log fires in the drawing room in winter, tea on the terrace in summer, dinners accompanied by French wines.

 Travel Club offer. See page 414.

| | | | |
|---|---|---|---|
| Price | £70–£95. Singles from £60. | Price | £90. |
| Rooms | 2: 1 double, 1 double/family. | Rooms | 3: 2 twins/doubles, 1 four-poster. |
| Meals | Pub 3 miles. | Meals | Dinner, 3 courses with wine, £25. Pub 2 miles. |
| Closed | Rarely. | Closed | Rarely. |
| Directions | A356 from Dorchester, left at 1st sign for T. Porcorum. Through, & up hill 1 mile. Ignore right turn, continue through village; on 1 mile, right for Powerstock & Hooke. Under bridge, 0.3 miles, left at unmarked crossroads. | Directions | A37 Dorchester-Yeovil; A356 for Crewkerne & Maiden Newton. In Frampton, left at green; over white bridge; left, opp. Frampton Roses. 'Private' track to house, signed 3rd on left. |

| | | | |
|---|---|---|---|
| | Rosie & Roger Britton | | Georgina & Nicholas Maynard |
| | Gray's Farmhouse, | | Frampton House, |
| | Toller Porcorum, | | Frampton, |
| | Dorchester, Dorset DT2 0EJ | | Dorchester, Dorset DT2 9NH |
| Tel | +44 (0)1308 485574 | Tel | +44 (0)1300 320308 |
| Email | rosieroger@farmhousebnb.co.uk | Email | maynardryder@btconnect.com |
| Web | www.farmhousebnb.co.uk | Web | www.frampton-house.co.uk |

Entry 168   Map 3

Entry 169   Map 3

## Dorset

### Holyleas House

This is a fabulous house, comfortable and easy; Tia and her two friendly dogs are genuinely welcoming. You breakfast by a log fire in the elegant dining room in winter: free-range eggs, bacon and sausages from the farmers' market, homemade jams and marmalade. Sleep in light, softly-coloured bedrooms with lovely views across the well-tended gardens, and spotless bathrooms. Walkers and explorers will be happy: return to a roaring fire and a good book in the drawing room. It's a short hop to the pub for supper and Tia is happy to babysit too. *Minimum stay two nights in high season & at weekends.*

Travel Club offer. See page 414.

| Price | £80–£90. Singles £40. |
|---|---|
| Rooms | 3: 1 double, 1 family room; 1 single with separate bath. |
| Meals | Pub a short walk. |
| Closed | Christmas & New Year. |
| Directions | From Dorchester, B3143 into Buckland Newton over x-roads; Holyleas on right opp. village cricket pitch. |

Tia Bunkall
Holyleas House,
Buckland Newton,
Dorchester, Dorset DT2 7DP
Tel +44 (0)1300 345214
Email tiabunkall@holyleas.fsnet.co.uk
Web www.holyleashouse.co.uk

Entry 170   Map 3

## Dorset

### The White Cottage

Strolling distance from magnificent Athelhampton House and its stunning gardens is this thatched cottage which Lindsay and Mark, escapees from London, have been renovating madly. It's a bright and sunny house with gorgeous bedrooms, super linen, fresh flowers, plump pillows, chocolates; generous bathrooms have thick white towels and lovely bottles of lotions. The suite has its own entrance, large sitting room, comfortable sofas and soft pink and cream bedroom. The river Piddle runs through the garden – fish for brown trout but put them back! You will be well fed – Lindsay's passion is cooking.

Travel Club offer. See page 414.

| Price | £70–£120. |
|---|---|
| Rooms | 3: 1 double, 1 suite for 2-4 (with sofa bed); 1 twin with separate bath. |
| Meals | Dinner £16–£18. Pub 1 mile. |
| Closed | Open all year. |
| Directions | A35 exit Puddletown & Athelhampton; signs for Athelhampton House. Left at lights in Puddletown; house 200 yds on right, after Athelhampton House. |

Lindsay & Mark Piper
The White Cottage,
Athelhampton,
Dorchester, Dorset DT2 7LG
Tel +44 (0)1305 848622
Email bookings@white-cottage-bandb.co.uk
Web www.white-cottage-bandb.co.uk

Entry 171   Map 3

# Dorset

## Whitfield Farm Cottage

Jackie and David make light of the practicalities of B&B; they and their 200-year-old cottage have much character and charm. Breakfast in the large, stone-tiled, beamed kitchen, or in the walled courtyard in summer. The twin with garden access and its own shower is immaculate in its fresh white and blue checks; the sitting room is cosy with comfy sofas and pretty coral-checked cushions, inglenook fireplace and window seats. Minutes from the main road but with a rural feel; the Frome – beloved by local fishermen – is 150 yards away and you can fish here for £30 a day. *Minimum stay two nights.*

| Price | From £75–£80. Singles £50. |
|---|---|
| Rooms | 1 twin/double. |
| Meals | Pubs/restaurants 1.25 miles. |
| Closed | Christmas & Easter. |
| Directions | From r'bout at top of Dorchester, west on B3150 for 100 yds. Right onto Poundbury Rd (before museum); 1 mile; over another road; 2nd track on right by house sign. Cottage set back from road. |

|  | Jackie & David Charles |
|---|---|
|  | Whitfield Farm Cottage, |
|  | Poundbury Road, |
|  | Dorchester, Dorset DT2 9SL |
| Tel | +44 (0)1305 260233 |
| Email | dcharles@gotadsl.co.uk |
| Web | www.whitfieldfarmcottage.co.uk |

Entry 172   Map 3

# Dorset

## Higher Came Farmhouse

A listed, handsome farmhouse dating from 1640, with honeysuckle and clematis clambering over the local stone front. Inside, winding corridors, sloping floors and the odd wonky wall. Bedrooms are a good size, particularly the cream triple, which has its own dressing room and good views. All are comfortable with good mattresses, thick bathrobes and a melée of patterns on walls and bed covers. Lisa and Tim, B&B pros, are terrific with guests and deliver great, locally-sourced breakfasts; delicious dry cured bacon and sausages from their own happy pigs. It's secluded and quiet here but Weymouth Bay is a short drive.

| Price | £70–£80. Singles £45–£50. |
|---|---|
| Rooms | 4: 1 triple; 1 double; 1 twin/double, 1 triple, each with separate bath. |
| Meals | Packed lunch £4.50. Pub/restaurant 2.5 miles. |
| Closed | Rarely. |
| Directions | From Dorchester bypass A354 to Weymouth. 1st left to Winterbourne Herringston; at T-junc. right, on for 1 mile; look out for golf course, next left to house. |

|  | Lisa Bowden |
|---|---|
|  | Higher Came Farmhouse, |
|  | Higher Came, |
|  | Dorchester, Dorset DT2 8NR |
| Tel | +44 (0)1305 268908 |
| Email | enquiries@highercame.co.uk |
| Web | www.highercame.co.uk |

Entry 173   Map 3

# Dorset

## Marren

On the Dorset coastal path, with spectacular views of Portland, a blissfully tranquil and bird-rich spot. Designers Peter and Wendy have transformed their 1920s house and the interiors sing with good taste; antique pine floors softened with kilims, colours contemporary. From six acres of terraced and wooded garden, step into your airy room, perfect with its own entrance, deep-mattressed bed, crisp sheets and luxurious bathroom. Breakfasts of farm produce and homemade bread will set you up for clifftop hikes – leave the low-slung Morgan at home: the track here is adventurously steep!

| | |
|---|---|
| Price | £90. |
| Rooms | 2 doubles. |
| Meals | Pub 1 mile. |
| Closed | Rarely. |
| Directions | On A353 after Poxwell, left at Ringstead sign; up hill (not to Ringstead), over cattle grid into NT car park; cross & drive through gate 'No Cars'; 2 more gates; 100 yds after 3rd gate, sharp right down steep track. |

| | |
|---|---|
| | Peter Cartwright |
| | Marren, |
| | Holworth, |
| | Dorchester, Dorset DT2 8NJ |
| Tel | +44 (0)1305 851503 |
| Email | marren@lineone.net |
| Web | www.marren.info |

🎣 🕯 🔊 🐈

Entry 174   Map 3

# Dorset

## Waddon House

Don't be daunted when this magnificent Dorset manor house swings into view: it's grand yet gracious and Suzie is lovely. The house breathes 500 years of history and at every turn you'll discover a fine artefact or period feature, from white hounds at the courtyard entrance to silver tureens in a handsome oak dining room. Bedrooms are in the east wing, one a vision of fine yellow silk and antique pieces, the other a raftered art deco dream with stained glass windows and furniture from the Queen Mary. Formal gardens envelop the house, a maze of balustrades, finials, statues and steps, with stunning views to the Jurassic coast. Unique.

| | |
|---|---|
| Price | £80–£130. Singles £75–£95. |
| Rooms | 2: 1 twin/double; 1 four-poster with separate bath. |
| Meals | Dinner, 3 courses, £25. Pub/restaurant 2 miles. |
| Closed | Occasionally. |
| Directions | A30 from Dorchester; at Winterbourne Abbas take left towards Portesham. In Portesham take the left turning to Upwey. House 1 mile. |

| | |
|---|---|
| | Suzie Chaffyn-Grove |
| | Waddon House, |
| | Waddon, Portesham, |
| | Weymouth, Dorset DT3 4ER |
| Tel | +44 (0)1305 871241 |
| Fax | +44 (0)1305 871041 |
| Email | suzie@waddonhouse.co.uk |
| Web | www.waddonhouse.co.uk |

🕯 🚂 🐕 🔊 🐈 🚜

Entry 175   Map 3

# Dorset

### Glenthorne

From the garden (where you may trip over a fossil or two) there are wide boat-spotted sea views all the way to Portland and Chesil; you'll also find a heated pool, and a path to a secret sandy beach – store and launch your own boat here. A Victorian former rectory with turn-of-the-century tiles and staircase, vibrant colours, stuffed foxes, elephant tusks and ornate mahogany; character, too, in the drawing room with log fire and the roomy bedrooms – your hosts both paint and their work hangs on the walls. Weymouth is bustling with life, has the best sunshine record on the south coast and its own jazz and kite festivals.

 Travel Club offer. See page 414.

| Price | From £80. Singles £40-£60. |
| --- | --- |
| Rooms | 3: 1 twin, 1 family for 4; 1 family for 3 with separate bath/shower. |
| Meals | Pub/restaurant 50 yds. Restaurants 10-min walk. |
| Closed | Rarely. |
| Directions | A354 Weymouth to Portland, 0.5 miles to top of hill. As road bears right, turn left into Old Castle Road. Follow signs to house. |

**Mrs Olivia Nurrish**
Glenthorne,
15 Old Castle Road,
Weymouth,
Dorset DT4 8QB

| Tel | +44 (0)1305 777281 |
| Email | info@glenthorne-holidays.co.uk |
| Web | www.glenthorne-holidays.co.uk |

Entry 176   Map 3

# Dorset

### Lower Lynch House

On the glorious Isle of Purbeck, between the old stone village of Corfe Castle and Kingston atop a hill, this wisteria-strewn house sits at the end of a long woodland track. Aga-cooked breakfast is served at tables overlooking courtyard and garden; cosy, old-fashioned bedrooms with pale colours and florals are as peaceful as can be. No sitting room, but a small sofa in the double. You are a five-minute drive from the coastal path: a great spot for walkers and peace-seekers. Warm, clean, comfortable B&B – and if you spot wild deer munching on the roses, tell Bron. *Minimum stay two nights.*

| Price | From £75. |
| --- | --- |
| Rooms | 2: 1 twin; 1 double with separate bath. |
| Meals | Inn 0.75 miles. |
| Closed | Christmas & New Year. |
| Directions | A351 from Wareham to Corfe Castle. At end of village fork right on B3069 for Kingston. Left 0.5 miles down track (sign on roadside). |

**Bron & Nick Burt**
Lower Lynch House,
Kingston Hill,
Corfe Castle,
Dorset BH20 5LG

| Tel | +44 (0)1929 480089 |
| Email | bronburt@tiscali.co.uk |

Entry 177   Map 3

## Dorset

### Gold Court House

Anthea and Michael have created a mood of restrained luxury and uncluttered, often beautiful, good taste in their Georgian townhouse. Bedrooms are restful in cream with mahogany furniture, sloping ceilings, beams, armchairs and radios. There's a large drawing room and good paintings. Your hosts are delightful – "they do everything to perfection," says a reader; both house and garden are a refuge. Views are soft and lush yet you are in the small square of this attractive town; the house was rebuilt in 1762 after a great fire, and the Hipwells added their creative spin seven years ago. *Children over ten welcome.*

## Dorset

### Bering House

Fabulous in every way. Renate's attention to detail reveals a love of running B&B: the fluffy dressing gowns and bathroom treats, the biscuits, fruit and sherry. She and John are welcoming, enthusiastic, delightful. Expect pretty little sofas, golden bath taps, a gleaming breakfast table, a big sumptuous suite with fine views across sparkling Poole harbour, Brownsea Island and the Purbeck Hills. Breakfasts are served on blue and white Spode china, among the birds and the breezes on summery days. Fresh fruit, Parma ham, smoked salmon, kedgeree: the choice is superb. An immaculate harbourside retreat.

| | |
|---|---|
| Price | £75. Singles from £45. |
| Rooms | 3: 1 double; 2 twins/doubles, each with separate bath. |
| Meals | Dinner £20, available in winter. Restaurants 50 yds. |
| Closed | Rarely. |
| Directions | From A35, A351 to Wareham. Follow signs to town centre. In North St, over lights into South St. 1st left into St John's Hill; house on far right-hand corner of square. |

**Anthea & Michael Hipwell**
Gold Court House,
St John's Hill, Wareham,
Dorset BH20 4LZ

| | |
|---|---|
| Tel | +44 (0)1929 553320 |
| Fax | +44 (0)1929 553320 |
| Email | info@goldcourthouse.co.uk |
| Web | www.goldcourthouse.co.uk |

Entry 178   Map 3

| | |
|---|---|
| Price | £75-£90. Singles by arrangement. |
| Rooms | 2: 1 twin/double; 1 suite & kitchenette. |
| Meals | Pub 400 yds. |
| Closed | Rarely. |
| Directions | From A35 & A350 at Upton, take Blandford road B3068 south to Hamworthy & Rockley Park. 1.5 miles on at Red Lion pub on left, turn right into Lake Rd; under bridge past Yachtsman pub; 2nd left down Branksea Ave. House last on left. |

**Renate & John Wadham**
Bering House,
53 Branksea Avenue,
Hamworthy,
Poole, Dorset BH15 4DP

| | |
|---|---|
| Tel | +44 (0)1202 673419 |
| Fax | +44 (0)1202 673419 |
| Email | johnandrenate1@tiscali.co.uk |

Entry 179   Map 3

# Dorset

## 7 Smithfield Place

Valerie adores large mirrors – which she paints and distresses herself – rich fabrics, real wood, dainty antiques. She also delights in looking after guests, so no detail is missed in her elegant home, from heated floors in the gorgeous bathroom to a 'full works' breakfast – taken in the spanking new breakfast room or on a sunny patio. Built in 1880 as a worker's cottage, the house sits on a quiet cul-de-sac off Winton's thriving high street, two miles from Bournemouth town centre with easy public transport. The garden is lit up in spring by blooming camellias and cherry blossom, and the whole house sparkles – as does your charming hostess.

| | |
|---|---|
| Price | £70. Singles £50. |
| Rooms | 1 double. |
| Meals | Packed lunch £15. Pub/restaurant 100 yds. |
| Closed | Christmas. |
| Directions | M27 to New Forest, on to A31, 11.5 miles exit left A338 Bournemouth. 8 miles exit on to A3049, up to roundabout, 3rd exit still on A3049. 1.5 miles, right into Wimborne Road, 0.4 miles left into Smithfield Place. |

| | |
|---|---|
| | Valerie Johns |
| | 7 Smithfield Place, |
| | Winton, |
| | Bournemouth, Dorset BH9 2QJ |
| Tel | +44 (0)1202 520722 |
| Email | valeriejohns@btinternet.com |
| Web | www.smithfieldplace.co.uk |

Entry 180   Map 3

# Dorset

## Honeycombe Cottage

As dreamy as its name, the 16th-century cottage in the village, with deep walls, open fireplaces and flagged floors houses two dogs, one cat and gentle, generous Heather. Now her children have flown the nest, she gives you a garden that blooms as wonderfully as the house and, up under the eaves, soft curtains, soothing colours, aromatic oils and a delicious bed. Have breakfast (pancakes with maple syrup, bacon from up the road) in the homely kitchen, or outside on fine days, where lawns and borders drift effortlessly into orchard, fields and hills. An all-year-round delight. *Children over five welcome.*

| | |
|---|---|
| Price | From £75. |
| Rooms | 2 twins/doubles. |
| Meals | Pubs/restaurant 1.5 miles. |
| Closed | Rarely. |
| Directions | From A31 to Bere Regis on West Street. At end of village, left down 'No Through Road', over bridge. Thatched wall on left, cottage at end. |

| | |
|---|---|
| | Heather Loxton |
| | Honeycombe Cottage, |
| | Shitterton, |
| | Bere Regis, Dorset BH20 7HU |
| Tel | +44 (0)1929 471660 |
| Email | heather.loxton@virgin.net |
| Web | www.honeycombecottage.com |

Entry 181   Map 3

## Dorset

### Thornhill

Here is a pretty Thirties' thatched house, with peaceful views from every window... of fields, woods and two landscaped acres. Sara and John encourage the wildlife on their patch; you may spot a deer on the lawn. Inside are patterned fabrics and old-fashioned candlewick covers, pastel walls and polished antiques. All is neat, tidy, spacious and spotless, and Sara pays attention to detail: a toothbrush for the forgetful, fruit and chocolates in the rooms, a choice of teas. Walkers can stride out straight from the door, gardeners will be happy here – and bridge players, if they come on a Thursday!

| | |
|---|---|
| Price | From £60. Singles from £30. |
| Rooms | 3: 1 double, 1 twin, 1 single, all sharing 2 baths. Possible use of separate bath. |
| Meals | Pub/restaurant 400 yds. |
| Closed | Rarely. |
| Directions | From Wimborne B3078 towards Cranborne. Right to Holt. After 2 miles Thornhill on right, 200 yds beyond Old Inn. |

**John & Sara Turnbull**
Thornhill,
Holt,
Wimborne,
Dorset BH21 7DJ
Tel +44 (0)1202 889434
Email scturnbull@lineone.net

Entry 182   Map 3

## Dorset

### Crawford House

Below, the river Stour winds through the valley and under the medieval, nine-arched bridge. Above, an Iron Age hill fort; between is Crawford House. It's an elegant Georgian house in an acre of walled garden, soft and pretty inside with an easy, relaxed atmosphere. Carpeted bedrooms are homely and warm, with long curtains; one room has four-poster twin beds with chintz drapes. The sun streams through the floor-to-ceiling windows of the downstairs rooms, and charming 18th- and 19th-century oil paintings hang in the dining room. Visit the Isle of Purbeck coastline – a World Heritage Site.

Travel Club offer. See page 414.

| | |
|---|---|
| Price | From £60. Singles £30. |
| Rooms | 3: 1 twin/double; 1 twin with separate bath; 1 twin with separate shower. |
| Meals | Pub in village 0.5 miles. |
| Closed | Mid-October to mid-April. |
| Directions | A350 north; after entering Spetisbury, 1st gateway immed. on left after crossroads (B3075). |

**Andrea Lea**
Crawford House,
Spetisbury,
Blandford Forum, Dorset DT11 9DP
Tel +44 (0)1258 857338
Fax +44 (0)1258 858152
Email andrea@lea8.wanadoo.co.uk

Entry 183   Map 3

## Dorset

### Stickland Farmhouse

Charming Dorset... and a soft, delightful thatched cottage in an enviably rural setting. Sandy and Paul have poured love into this listed farmhouse and garden, the latter bursting with lupins, poppies, foxgloves, clematis, delphiniums. Sandy gives you delicious breakfasts with homemade soda bread from the Aga. Cottagey bedrooms have crisp white dressing gowns and lots of books and pictures – one room opens onto your own seating area in the garden. You are in a village with a good pub, and Cranbourne Chase, rich in barrows and hill forts, is close by. *Children over ten welcome. Minimum stay two nights at weekends in summer.*

| | |
|---|---|
| Price | £65-£70. Singles £50. |
| Rooms | 3: 2 doubles, 1 twin. |
| Meals | Pub 3-minute walk. |
| Closed | Never. |
| Directions | Leave Blandford for SW, cross river Stour. Hard right after Bryanston school for W. Stickland (4.5 miles). Down North St, right signed W. Houghton. House 150 yds on left with 5-bar gate. |

Sandy & Paul Crofton-Atkins
Stickland Farmhouse,
9 West Street, Winterborne Stickland,
Blandford Forum, Dorset DT11 0NT
Tel      +44 (0)1258 880119
Email    sandysticklandfarm@tiscali.co.uk
Web      www.sticklandfarmhouse.co.uk

🚶 🐾 🐕

Entry 184   Map 3

## Dorset

### Manor Barn

What was once an L-shaped cow shed is now a rather smart self-contained barn – attached to the main house and with views to an Iron Age hill. Relax in a roomy and beamed sitting room with squashy sofas, white walls, a wood-burning stove; down a corridor are two restful bedrooms with delightful linen and huge fluffy pillows. It is all very rustic-contemporary. A huge breakfast is brought to you, and kind Carolyn will cook a delicious, locally sourced supper if you want a night in with a DVD. Perfect for friends or families and you have complete independence. *Children over eight welcome.*

🧳 Travel Club offer. See page 414.

| | |
|---|---|
| Price | £90. Singles £60. |
| Rooms | 2 twins/doubles. |
| Meals | Dinner £20-£30. Light supper £10-£15. Pub in village & more within 3 miles. |
| Closed | Rarely. |
| Directions | South on A350 from Shaftesbury; right at sign 'Child Okeford 3 miles'. Just before village, drive is on left, opposite 30 ft high hedge. |

Carolyn Sorby
Manor Barn,
Upper Street, Child Okeford,
Blandford Forum, Dorset DT11 8EF
Tel      +44 (0)1258 860638
Email    carisorby@btinternet.com
Web      www.manorbarnbedandbreakfast.co.uk

♿ 🍴 📖 🐕 📶 🐕

Entry 185   Map 3

# Dorset

## The Old Rectory

Walk all day on Cranborne Chase, return for tea at The Old Rectory, then stroll off for a meal at the much-fêted pub down the road... What could be nicer? Vicky's brick-and-flint Victorian house is in the middle of the village, yet feels wonderfully peaceful in its ten-acre grounds. Bedrooms are simple, comfortable and restful; bathrooms clean and functional. The drawing and dining rooms have the warm, gracious air of a much-loved and lived-in home, family portraits hang on the walls, the furniture is polished, the spaniel is friendly and big windows overlook sweeping lawns and summer terrace.

![] Travel Club offer. See page 414.

| | |
|---|---|
| Price | £80. |
| Rooms | 2: 1 double, 1 twin. |
| Meals | Pub within walking distance. |
| Closed | Christmas. |
| Directions | 16 miles south west of Salisbury on A354 Blandford Forum road. Farnham is signed off main road; house in Farnham opposite Museum pub. |

Vicky Forbes
The Old Rectory,
Farnham,
Blandford Forum,
Dorset DT11 8DE
Tel       +44 (0)1725 516474
Email     forbescopper@compuserve.com

Entry 186   Map 3

# Dorset

## Launceston Farmhouse

Farmhouse chic in the most glorious of surroundings: Sarah has created beautiful, themed bedrooms in her Georgian family home, all with deep mattresses, crisp cotton, feather pillows and a great deal of style – two have roll tops in the room – and bathrooms are super. Downstairs is an open-plan room with a mishmash of comfy chairs and sofas, an open fire and views over the new parterre; in the evenings you dine well here by candlelight, perhaps tagine of kid goat and lemon posset. Farm tours are a must, and this would be perfect for a house party – there's even a swimming pool. *Children over 12 welcome.*

![] Travel Club offer. See page 414.

| | |
|---|---|
| Price | £70-£95. Singles £45-£95. |
| Rooms | 6: 5 doubles, 1 twin. |
| Meals | Dinner, 2 courses, £20; 3 courses £25 (Monday & Friday only by arrangement). |
| Closed | Rarely. |
| Directions | From Salisbury, A354 to Blandford Forum. Left at Tarrant Hinton. First village is Tarrant Launceston; house is on right. |

Mrs Sarah Worrall
Launceston Farmhouse,
Tarrant Launceston,
Blandford Forum, Dorset DT11 8BY
Tel       +44 (0)1258 830528
Email     info@launcestonfarm.co.uk
Web       www.launcestonfarm.co.uk

Entry 187   Map 3

## Dorset

### Rose Cottage

You are buried deep in a quiet corner here, just perfect for long walks: return to a wood-burner and a cup of tea in a beamed sitting room with plenty of sofas and books – no dull TV. Your bedroom is long, low-ceilinged and light with chintzy curtains and views over the pretty garden; loll in a big bed with duck-egg blue cushions and crisp white sheets – you have a choice of pillows. Breakfast is a fairly flexible, mostly organic treat and served in an elegant yellow-walled dining room, with gleaming furniture and dollops of morning sunshine. Amanda, warm and welcoming, looks after you very well indeed.

Travel Club offer. See page 414.

| | |
|---|---|
| Price | £70. Singles £40. Child £15. |
| Rooms | 1 twin/double. |
| Meals | Dinner, 3 courses, £20. Pub/restaurant 1 mile. |
| Closed | Christmas. |
| Directions | From Shaftesbury on A350 north. Right signed Wincombe/Donhead St. Mary. After 2 miles take second right. Watery Lane is 100 yds on left, house is then 400 yds on right. |

Giles & Amanda Vardey
Rose Cottage,
Watery Lane,
Donhead St. Mary, Shaftesbury,
Dorset SP7 9DF
Tel      +44 (0)1747 828449
Email   amanda@rosecottage.uk.com
Web     www.rosecottage.uk.com

Entry 188    Map 3

## Dorset

### The Old Forge, Fanners Yard

Tim and Lucy are tangibly happy in this beautifully restored forge. It was built in the 1700s; the wheelwright and carriage-builder from the local estate used to work here. Tim has beautifully restored the cosy gypsy caravan which has super views and a picnic table outside. The attic bedrooms are snug, with Lucy's quilts, country antiques and sparkling bathrooms. Delicious Aga-cooked breakfasts include eggs from their own free-strutting hens, organic sausages and bacon, home-grown jams, apple juice straight from the orchard. The Downs beckon walkers; warm corners invite readers. Utterly genuine.

Travel Club offer. See page 414.

| | |
|---|---|
| Price | From £75. |
| Rooms | 3: 1 double, 1 family. Gypsy caravan: 1 double with separate shower & wc (20 yds). |
| Meals | Pub/restaurant 1 mile. |
| Closed | Rarely. |
| Directions | From Shaftesbury, A350 to Compton Abbas. House 1st on left before Compton Abbas sign. Left; entrance on left. |

Tim & Lucy Kerridge
The Old Forge, Fanners Yard,
Compton Abbas, Shaftesbury,
Dorset SP7 0NQ
Tel      +44 (0)1747 811881
Fax     +44 (0)1747 811881
Email   theoldforge@hotmail.com
Web     www.theoldforgedorset.co.uk

Entry 189    Map 3

## Dorset

### Golden Hill Cottage

Deep in the countryside lies Stourton Caundle and this charming thatched cottage. The sitting room, traditionally furnished with antiques, paintings and coal fire, is all yours if you stay, along with a carpeted twin room and small shower up a private stair. Anna, courteous and kind, brings you splendid platefuls of local bacon and sausage, homemade jams and Dorset honey for breakfast; nothing is too much trouble for these owners. There are glorious walks from the village, a good pub that serves food and real ales, and Sherborne, Montacute and Stourhead for landscape, culture and history. *Babes in arms welcome.*

Travel Club offer. See page 414.

| Price | £66–£80. Singles £40. |
|---|---|
| Rooms | 1 twin & sitting room. |
| Meals | Pubs/restaurants within 3 miles. |
| Closed | Rarely. |
| Directions | From Sherborne, A352 to Dorchester; after 1 mile, left onto A3030; on to far end of Bishops Caundle, left to Stourton Caundle; after sharp left into village street, house 200 yds on right. |

author block
Anna & Andrew Oliver
Golden Hill Cottage,
Stourton Caundle,
Sturminster Newton,
Dorset DT10 2JW
Tel      +44 (0)1963 362109
Email    anna@goldenhillcottage.co.uk
Web      www.goldenhillcottage.co.uk

Entry 190   Map 3

## Dorset

### Gorse Farm House

Wendy is a generous soul and throws open her lovely house; you are free to wander the garden, grab a book and laze in the sunny conservatory or settle into the snug and watch TV. Upstairs find a light-filled, peaceful bedroom with dreamy views over fields, a bowl of sweets, dainty china and more books; a shiny new bathroom is just across the landing. Lee is a sculptor and his work peeps out from clever planting around the garden: find a seat on the veranda or near the natural pond and listen to the birds. Breakfast on local sausages, bacon and free-range farm eggs then tackle some fabulous walks and cycles straight from the door.

Travel Club offer. See page 414.

| Price | From £60. Singles £40. |
|---|---|
| Rooms | 1 twin/double with separate bath. |
| Meals | Pub/restaurant 2 miles. |
| Closed | Christmas. |
| Directions | West of Sturminster Newton, turn south off A357 signed Hazlebury Bryan. 0.5 miles Rivers Corner, turn left signed Fifehead St Quinton. 0.5 miles bear right at sign for Fifeheads. House 0.25 miles on left. |

Wendy Dickenson
Gorse Farm House,
Fifehead St Quintin,
Sturminster Newton,
Dorset DT10 2AW
Tel      +44 (0)1258 475343
Email    contactus@gorsefarmhousebb.co.uk
Web      www.gorsefarmhousebb.co.uk

Entry 191   Map 3

# Dorset

## Holt Cottage

The house stands on high ground and the views are amazing – enough to seduce Richard and Annabel from the west country. She is a whizz in the kitchen, he loves classic cars, both give you a big welcome and two super bedrooms in the cottage a step away. One is upstairs, with a sitting space and views, the other, perfect for children, is down. Both are fresh, light and inviting, with elegant prints on the walls, white towels on the rails, fabulous mattresses. Breakfast on homemade bread and croisssants, local bacon and sausages. In the garden: dogs romp, hens hatch, and orchard and pergola are on their way.

Ethical Collection: Food. See page 412.

 Travel Club offer. See page 414.

| Price | From £75-£85. Singles £55-£65. |
|---|---|
| Rooms | Cottage: 1 double & sitting room; 1 twin/double with separate bath (let to same party only). |
| Meals | Packed lunch from £5. Dinner, 3 courses, £25. Pub/restaurant 1 mile. |
| Closed | Christmas & occasionally. |
| Directions | From Sherborne, A352 south. After 1 mile, left onto A3030 Blandford road. In Bishops Caundle, left at Murco garage. House 1 mile on left. |

Richard & Annabel Buxton
Holt Cottage,
Alweston,
Sherborne, Dorset DT9 5JF
Tel +44 (0)1963 23014
Email annabelbuxton@hotmail.com
Web www.holtcottagedorset.com

Entry 192　Map 3

# Dorset

## Windrush Farm

Fun to breakfast in the farmhouse kitchen with its polished oak table and rag-rolled dresser full of colourful plates. Upstairs, too, is delightful – creaky carpeted floors, sloping ceilings, a maze of corridors and cubby holes. Well-furnished bedrooms are in soft yellows and blues, pinks and creams; paintings, prints and books catch your eye. On colder evenings, your charming hosts will light a fire for you in the sitting room, traditional and snug, while for summer there's a scented, rambler-strewn garden and a terrace with the loveliest views. Bustling Sherborne is a ten-minute drive.

| Price | From £75. Singles from £45. |
|---|---|
| Rooms | 2: 1 double with separate bath; 1 twin sharing bath (2nd room let to same party only). |
| Meals | Dinner £20. Pub/restaurant 1 mile. |
| Closed | Christmas. |
| Directions | A357 Wincanton-Templecombe; 2nd turn Stowell, on right opp. entrance to Horsington House. Down hill past church for 0.5 miles; house on left. |

Richard & Jenny Gold
Windrush Farm,
Stowell,
Sherborne, Dorset DT9 4PD
Tel +44 (0)1963 370799
Email jennygold@hotmail.co.uk
Web www.windrushfarmbedandbreakfast.com

Entry 193　Map 3

# Durham

### 34 The Bank

In this impressive Georgian townhouse live Eva, Ian and Otto the wire-haired Hungarian vizsla. Ian cooks the breakfasts and Eva arranges them artistically because that's her thing – the house if filled with interesting art from their travels. They love their guests and provide beautiful, newly-refurbished rooms – all different, but with enormous beds, lovely views, easy chairs and spoiling bathrooms; there's much comfort in the sitting room too, with its open fire. Sally forth to see the rest of bonny Barney on the Tees: the castle, the antique shops and the restaurant next door where Cromwell really stayed.

| | |
|---|---|
| Price | £65-£85. Singles from £45. |
| Rooms | 3: 1 four-poster; 1 double, 1 twin both with separate bath. |
| Meals | Pubs/restaurants within 50 yds. |
| Closed | Rarely. |
| Directions | At A1 Scotch Corner, A66 west for 14 miles. Then 1st dual carriageway; right for Barnard Castle. At lights right over bridge, left at T-junc. to Market Cross. Left down The Bank, house on left. |

Ian & Eva Reid
34 The Bank,
Barnard Castle,
Durham DL12 8PN

Tel +44 (0)1833 631304
Email evasreid@aol.com
Web www.number34.com

Entry 194   Map 12

# Durham

### The Coach House

There's so much to gladden your heart – the cobbled courtyard that evokes memories of its days as a coaching inn, the river running through the estate, the drawing room's log fire, the delicious breakfasts, the blackberry crumbles with cream... and Peter and Mary, your kind, unstuffy, dog-adoring hosts (they have three well-behaved ones). All your creature comforts are attended to in this small, perfect, English country house: lined chintz, starched linen, cushioned window seats, cut flowers, heated towel rails. Friendly, delightful, and the perfect stepping stone to Scotland or the south.

| | |
|---|---|
| Price | £80. Singles £50. |
| Rooms | 2: 1 twin/double; 1 twin/double with separate bath. |
| Meals | Dinner, 3 courses, £25. Pub/restaurants within 3 miles. |
| Closed | Rarely. |
| Directions | A1(M) to Scotch Corner. A66 west for 8 miles until Greta Bridge turn-off. House on left just before bridge. Front door is near right hand corner of courtyard. |

Peter & Mary Gilbertson
The Coach House,
Greta Bridge,
Barnard Castle, Durham DL12 9SD

Tel +44 (0)1833 627201
Email info@coachhousegreta.co.uk
Web www.coachhousegreta.co.uk

Entry 195   Map 12

# Essex

## Brook Farm

Large low Georgian windows fill the house with light, unpretentious family pieces warm the bedrooms and the stunning carved crossbeam in the largest is late-medieval. Anne, country lover and B&B-er, has farmed here for over 30 years; outbuildings dot the yard, sheep and horses roam the acres. In Anne's sitting room logs fill the copper and hunting prints line the walls – no TV, but magazines and books aplenty – and you breakfast (deliciously) at a long table with fine antique benches. The handsome bright farmhouse oozes history and a faded country charm – yet is 30 minutes from Stansted.

| | |
|---|---|
| Price | £70–£80. Singles £35–£45. |
| Rooms | 3: 1 twin; 1 double, 1 family room, both with separate bath. |
| Meals | Packed lunch £3–£5. Pubs within 2 miles. |
| Closed | Rarely. |
| Directions | House on B1053, 500 yds south of Wethersfield. |

**Mrs Anne Butler**
Brook Farm,
Wethersfield,
Braintree, Essex CM7 4BX
Tel +44 (0)1371 850284
Fax +44 (0)1371 850284
Email abutlerbrookfarm@aol.com

Entry 196   Map 9

# Essex

## Caterpillar Cottage

Traditional brick and clapboard, dormer windows, tall chimneys – this looks like the real thing. But the 'converted farm building' in the grounds of Patricia's former grand house is brand new! Filled with fine furniture, family photographs and *objets* from far-flung travels, it invites relaxation. The double-height, vaulted sitting room brims with sofas and books, logs crackle on chilly nights and bedrooms are simple and comfortable with decent-sized bathrooms. Patricia, a lively grandmother, adores children while her big garden promises home-grown fruit and tranquillity.

Travel Club offer. See page 414.

| | |
|---|---|
| Price | From £65. Singles from £35. |
| Rooms | 2: 1 triple; 1 double with separate bath/shower. |
| Meals | Packed lunch available. Pubs 50 yds. |
| Closed | Rarely. |
| Directions | A12 to A1124. In Fordstreet, cottage through gateway shared with Old House, opposite Old Queens Head pub. 88 bus stops at the gate. |

**Patricia Mitchell**
Caterpillar Cottage,
Fordstreet, Aldham,
Colchester, Essex CO6 3PH
Tel +44 (0)1206 240456
Fax +44 (0)1206 240456
Email bandbcaterpillar@tiscali.co.uk

Entry 197   Map 10

# Essex

## Bromans Farm

The island of Mersea is surprisingly secluded, and Bromans Farm is in the most tranquil corner; the sea murmurs across the Saltings where the Brent geese wheel and the great Constable skies stretch. The house began in 1343 – nearly as old as the exquisite church. The Georgians added their bit, but the venerable beams and uneven old construction shine through. Ruth and Martin are charming and this is a sunny, comfortable house, with good linen in the bedroom and a warm bathroom, a snug book-filled sitting room and a beautiful Welsh oak dresser in the breakfast room. Wild walks beckon.

| | |
|---|---|
| Price | £70–£80. Singles £40. |
| Rooms | 1 twin/double with separate bath. |
| Meals | Pub 0.5 miles. |
| Closed | Rarely. |
| Directions | From Colchester B1025, over causeway, bear left. After 3 miles, pass Dog & Pheasant pub; 3rd right into Bromans Lane. 1st on left. |

| | |
|---|---|
| | **Mrs Ruth Dence** |
| | Bromans Farm, |
| | East Mersea, Essex CO5 8UE |
| Tel | +44 (0)1206 383235 |
| Fax | +44 (0)1206 383235 |
| Email | ruth.dence@homecall.co.uk |
| Web | www.bromansfarm.co.uk |

Entry 198    Map 10

# Essex

## Emsworth House

Unexpectedly tranquil, this 1937 vicarage – with wide views over the Stour and some wonderful light for painting – will both energise and calm you. Penny, an artist, is a generous host and looks after you well. This is Constable country so great for walking, you are near to Frinton beach and good golf, sailing and riding. Return to comfy sofas and chairs, open fires and good books, fairly basic bedrooms with a country feel and the odd African throw or splash of colour, lots of lovely paintings and a garden filled with birds. Perfect for families too – Penny has camp beds and a can-do attitude.

Travel Club offer. See page 414.

| | |
|---|---|
| Price | From £55. Singles from £45. |
| Rooms | 3: 1 double, 1 twin; 1 double with separate bath. |
| Meals | Pub/restaurant 0.5 miles. |
| Closed | Rarely. |
| Directions | A12-A120 (to Harwich) & left to B1035; right at TV mast to Bradfield, 2 miles; house on right. Manningtree Station 5 miles. A14-A137-B1352, house on left. |

| | |
|---|---|
| | **Penny Linton** |
| | Emsworth House, |
| | Ship Hill, Station Road, Bradfield, |
| | Manningtree, Essex CO11 2UP |
| Tel | +44 (0)1255 870860 |
| Email | emsworthhouse@hotmail.com |
| Web | www.emsworthhouse.co.uk |

Entry 199    Map 10

## Essex

### West Lodge

This beautifully mellowed brick 1600s coach house has the original huge front door and stunning views from the garden over Dedham Vale. There's a comfortable snug for guests with pinky, terracotta walls and a red sofa; go up your own staircase to simple, light and airy bedrooms and old-fashioned, compact bathrooms. Friendly Penny, and ex-chef Paul, will give you local bacon and sausages and very good dinners in a colourful dining room stuffed full of gleaming antiques and silver – or on balmy evenings in the summer house, maybe with a cocktail up in the trees first. *Babes in arms & children over eight welcome. French & Spanish spoken.*

Travel Club offer. See page 414.

| | |
|---|---|
| Price | £60–£65. Singles £45. |
| Rooms | 3: 2 doubles, 1 family suite. |
| Meals | Dinner, 3 courses, £18.50; 2 courses, £15. Packed lunch from £8. Pub/restaurant 140 yds. |
| Closed | Rarely. |
| Directions | From A12 exit for B1070, at junc. left towards East Bergholt. At Carriers Arms pub (0.8 miles) turn right. At post office (0.4 miles), right into Cemetery Lane. Entrance to house 80 yds on left. |

Paul & Penny Lewis
West Lodge,
The Street,
East Bergholt,
Essex CO7 6TF
Tel +44 (0)1206 299808
Email westlodgebandb@talktalk.net
Web www.westlodge.uk.com

Entry 200   Map 10

## Gloucestershire

### The Pinetum Lodge

A year-round Gloucestershire retreat. Come for sheets of snowdrops in January, the nightingale's song in spring, stunning foliage in autumn – and delightful hosts. Their home is a hunting lodge with views over the rolling Cotswold Hills from homely bedrooms with new beds and bathrooms. Enter an enchanted wood surrounded by a RSPB sanctuary and an arboretum planted by Thomas Gambier Parry in 1844 – the scent of pine wafts into the house. Carol and David give you home-grown veg for dinner, there are 13 acres and a fabulous treehouse to explore, and it truly is secluded and peaceful here – rediscover your soul.

Travel Club offer. See page 414.

| | |
|---|---|
| Price | £70–£80. Singles £45. |
| Rooms | 3 doubles. |
| Meals | Dinner £22.50. Pub/restaurant 3 miles. |
| Closed | Rarely. |
| Directions | After r'bout with A48, follow A40 (Ross) for 0.7 miles. Right where white line goes double into drive of black & white cottage at speed camera sign on left; track into woods; through gates; drive round to front door. |

David & Carol Wilkin
The Pinetum Lodge,
Churcham,
Gloucestershire GL2 8AD
Tel +44 (0)1452 750554
Email carol@igeek.co.uk
Web www.pinetumlodge.ik.com

Entry 201   Map 8

# Gloucestershire

## Upper Court

A splendid Georgian manor in acres of landscaped grounds – all you'd want from a glorious country house. Bring friends for a party, get married, or come for a weekend of romantic indulgence – you are looked after by family, or lovely staff. Antique furniture, floral flourishes, sumptuous four-poster beds, swish new bathrooms, consummate hosts – and there's heaps to do: tennis, croquet, billiards, an outdoor pool, hill-walking, riding or clay-pigeon shooting. Groups can book dinner, there are art and pottery classes in the stables and a good pub in the village. *Minimum stay two nights at weekends, unless late booking. Self-catering available for large parties.*

| | |
|---|---|
| Price | £95–£120. Singles £75. |
| Rooms | 3: 2 doubles, 1 twin. |
| Meals | Dinner, for parties only, £35. Pubs/restaurants 3-minute walk. |
| Closed | Christmas. |
| Directions | M5 junc. 9, A46 to Teddington Hands; left & follow signs for Kemerton. Left at War Memorial. House directly behind parish church (not Catholic church). |

**Bill & Diana Herford**
Upper Court,
Kemerton, Tewkesbury,
Gloucestershire GL20 7HY
Tel     +44 (0)1386 725351
Fax     +44 (0)1386 725472
Email    herfords@uppercourt.co.uk
Web     www.uppercourt.co.uk

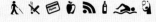

Entry 202   Map 8

# Gloucestershire

## Astalleigh House

The views from here to the Malvern Hills are worth the journey alone, but you also get bright, softly-coloured bedrooms with outrageously snuggly beds, the floatiest goose down, and compact bathrooms with generous towels and Body Shop goodies. There's a sitting room with pale walls, lots of books and magazines, jazzy striped cushions on a comfy sofa and interesting paintings of Northumberland – you can flop here happily. Affable Harriet gives you eggs from their hens and delicious sausages and bacon from the local butcher to set you up for grand walks; this is a good romantic escape for those with outdoor tastes.

| | |
|---|---|
| Price | From £75. Singles £50. (Child £15.) |
| Rooms | 2: 1 double, 1 family. |
| Meals | Pub/restaurant 0.5 miles. |
| Closed | Christmas & New Year. |
| Directions | M5, junc. 8, M50 junc. 1 north A38. Then 2nd left Ripple, Uckinghall, Equine Hospital, left at crossroads. House first on left. Train to Cheltenham, Gloucester or Pershore. |

**Harriet & Keith Jewers**
Astalleigh House,
School Lane,
Ripple, Tewkesbury,
Gloucestershire GL20 6EU
Tel     +44 (0)1684 593740
Email    jewers@jewers.freeserve.co.uk
Web     www.astalleighhouse.co.uk

Entry 203   Map 8

# Gloucestershire

## Isbourne Manor House

The part-Tudor, part Georgian house is named after the river flowing through its garden. Sudeley Castle is next door – just nip through the kissing gate into the glorious grounds. David, a retired organic grain merchant, and Felicity are gentle-mannered and easy, and treat you to breakfasts of homemade and local produce. One bedroom has an ornately carved, comfortable four-poster; the twin, under the eaves, has its own sun terrace. In the drawing room: oils on walls, antiques, an honesty bar and open fire. Winchcombe is a satisfying little town, with useful shops, buzzing inns and a real sense of community.

| Price | £80–£100. Singles from £60. |
|---|---|
| Rooms | 3: 1 double, 1 four-poster; 1 twin with separate shower. |
| Meals | Pubs/restaurants 2–5 minute walk. |
| Closed | Christmas & possibly Easter. |
| Directions | On B4632 between Cheltenham & Broadway. Turn into Castle St by White Hart in village centre. On left at bottom of steep hill. |

|  | Felicity & David King |
|---|---|
|  | Isbourne Manor House, |
|  | Castle Street, |
|  | Winchcombe, |
|  | Gloucestershire GL54 5JA |
| Tel | +44 (0)1242 602281 |
| Email | felicity@isbourne-manor.co.uk |
| Web | www.isbourne-manor.co.uk |

Entry 204   Map 8

# Gloucestershire

## The Old School

Comfortable, warm and filled with understated style is this 1854 Cotswold stone house. Wendy and John are generous, beds are enormous, linen is laundered, towels and robes are thick and fluffy. Your own mini fridge is carefully hidden and lighting is well thought-out. Best of all is the upstairs sitting room: a chic, open-plan space with church style windows letting the light flood in and super sofas, good art, lovely fabrics. A wood-burner keeps you toasty, Wendy is a grand cook and all is flexible. A gorgeous, relaxing place to stay – on the A44 but peaceful at night – where absolutely nothing is too much trouble.

Travel Club offer. See page 414.

| Price | £90. Singles £60. |
|---|---|
| Rooms | 4: 3 doubles, 1 twin/double. |
| Meals | Dinner, 4 courses, £32. Supper, 2 courses, £18. Supper tray £12. Pub 0.5 miles. |
| Closed | Rarely. |
| Directions | From Moreton, A44 for Chipping Norton & Oxford. Little Compton 3.5 miles; stay on main road, then right for Chastleton village. House on corner, immed. left into drive. |

|  | Wendy Veale & John Scott-Lee |
|---|---|
|  | The Old School, |
|  | Little Compton, |
|  | Moreton-in-Marsh, |
|  | Gloucestershire GL56 0SL |
| Tel | +44 (0)1608 674588 |
| Email | wendy@theoldschoolbedandbreakfast.com |
| Web | www.theoldschoolbedandbreakfast.com |

Entry 205   Map 8

# Gloucestershire

## Windy Ridge House

Astonishing! Find mullioned windows, gables, roofs of stone slate and thatch, winding staircases and unexpected corners. The bonhomie starts on arrival: Nick and Jennifer are the second generation to own this family home and they are delighted to throw open house, arboretum and prize-winning gardens to guests. All is polished to perfection, there's a grand country-house feel; bedrooms are warm, carpeted and cosy. Take a book to the pine-panelled drawing room, help yourself from the honesty bar, or fling yourself into tennis, croquet and a swim in the summer heated pool. Sumptuous, generous, great fun.

| | |
|---|---|
| Price | From £90. Singles from £70. |
| Rooms | 4: 2 doubles; 1 double, 1 twin, each with separate bath. |
| Meals | Pub 100 yds. |
| Closed | Rarely. |
| Directions | From Stow, north for Broadway on A424 for 2 miles to Coach & Horses pub on left. Opposite, turn right by postbox & 30mph signs down single-track lane. Entrance 100 yds down on left, bear left up drive. |

Nick & Jennifer Williams
Windy Ridge House,
Longborough, Moreton-in-Marsh,
Gloucestershire GL56 0QY
Tel    +44 (0)1451 830465
Fax    +44 (0)1451 831489
Email  nick@windy-ridge.co.uk
Web    www.windy-ridge.co.uk

Entry 206   Map 8

# Gloucestershire

## Wren House

Barely two miles from Stow-on-the-Wold, the peaceful house sits charmingly in a tiny hamlet. The stylish stone house was built before the English Civil War and Kiloran spent two years renovating it; the results are a joy. Downstairs, light-filled, elegant rooms with glowing rugs on pale Cotswold stone; upstairs, delicious bedrooms, spotless bathrooms and a doorway to duck. Breakfast can include cream from the Jerseys over the wall, and the well-planted garden, in which you are encouraged to sit, has far-reaching views. Explore rolling valleys and glorious gardens; Kiloran can advise. *Children over six welcome.*

Ethical Collection: Food. See page 412.

 Travel Club offer. See page 414.

| | |
|---|---|
| Price | £90–£100. Singles from £70. |
| Rooms | 2: 1 twin/double; 1 twin/double with separate bath/shower. |
| Meals | Pubs/restaurants 2 miles. |
| Closed | Rarely. |
| Directions | A429 between Stow & Moreton; turn to Donnington; 400 yds, bear left uphill; 100 yds, sign on right in wall beside The Granary Cottage with parking at rear through 5-bar gate. |

Kiloran McGrigor
Wren House,
Donnington,
Stow-on-the-Wold,
Gloucestershire GL56 0XZ
Tel    +44 (0)1451 831 787
Email  enquiries@wrenhouse.net
Web    www.wrenhouse.net

Entry 207   Map 8

# Gloucestershire

## Lower Farm House

Nicholas and Zelie are charming and articulate hosts who love entertaining and nurturing their guests: nothing is too much trouble. In peaceful little Aldestrop, a perfect Georgian house – high ceilings, sash windows, elegant proportions, gracious furnishings. The bedrooms are generous in size (as are the sumptuous double beds) and have restful views over the garden – a joy to wander through or sit out in. Meals – everything as organic and locally sourced as possible – sound superb: cooking and gardening are Zelie's passions. Bustling little Stow-on-the-Wold is a hop and a skip away. Guests are full of praise.

 Travel Club offer. See page 414.

| Price | £96–£104. Singles £68. |
|---|---|
| Rooms | 3: 1 double, 2 twins/doubles. |
| Meals | Dinner, 3 courses, £30. Pubs/restaurants 1.5 miles. |
| Closed | Rarely. |
| Directions | A436 from Stow; after 3 miles, left to Adlestrop; right at T-junc.; after double bend drive 50 yds on right; sign at end of drive. Map on website. |

|  | Nicholas & Zelie Mason Lower Farm House, Adlestrop, Stow-on-the-Wold, Gloucestershire GL56 0YR |
|---|---|
| Tel | +44 (0)1608 658756 |
| Fax | +44 (0)1608 659458 |
| Email | info@adlestrop-lowerfarm.com |
| Web | www.adlestrop-lowerfarm.com |

Entry 208   Map 8

# Gloucestershire

## Rectory Farmhouse

Once a monastery, now a farmhouse with style. Passing a development of converted farm buildings to reach the Rectory's warm Cotswold stones makes the discovery doubly exciting. More glory within: Sybil, a talented designer, has created something immaculate, fresh and uplifting. A woodburner glows in the sitting room, bed linen is white, walls cream; beds are superb, bathrooms sport cast-iron slipper baths and power showers and views are to the church. Sybil used to own a restaurant and her breakfasts – by the Aga or in the conservatory under a rampant vine – are a further treat.

| Price | From £90. Singles £60. |
|---|---|
| Rooms | 2 doubles. |
| Meals | Pubs/restaurants 1 mile. |
| Closed | Christmas & New Year. |
| Directions | B4068 from Stow to Lower Swell, left just before Golden Ball Inn. Far end of gravel drive on right. |

|  | Sybil Gisby Rectory Farmhouse, Lower Swell, Stow-on-the-Wold, Gloucestershire GL54 1LH |
|---|---|
| Tel | +44 (0)1451 832351 |
| Email | rectoryfarmhouse@yahoo.com |

Entry 209   Map 8

## Gloucestershire

### Clapton Manor

Karin and James's 16th-century manor is as all homes should be: loved and lived-in. And, with three-foot-thick walls, flagstoned floors, sit-in fireplaces and stone-mullioned windows, it's gorgeous. The enclosed garden, full of birdsong and roses, wraps itself around the house. One bedroom has a secret door that leads to a fuchsia-pink bathroom; the other room, smaller, is wallpapered in a honeysuckle trellis and has wonderful garden views. Wellies, dogs, barbours, log fires... and breakfast by a vast Tudor fireplace on homemade bread and jams and eggs from the hens. A happy, charming family home.

| | |
|---|---|
| Price | From £95. Singles £85. |
| Rooms | 2: 1 double, 1 twin/double. |
| Meals | Pub/restaurants within 15-minute drive. |
| Closed | Rarely. |
| Directions | A429 Cirencester-Stow. Right signed Sherborne & Clapton. In village, pass grassy area to left, postbox in one corner; house straight ahead on left on corner, facing down hill. |

Karin & James Bolton
Clapton Manor,
Clapton-on-the-Hill,
Gloucestershire GL54 2LG
Tel     +44 (0)1451 810202
Email   bandb@claptonmanor.co.uk
Web     www.claptonmanor.co.uk

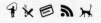

Entry 210   Map 8

## Gloucestershire

### Westward

Susie and Jim are highly organised and efficient, juggling farm, horses and B&B. She's also a great cook (Leith trained). The grand, but cosy, house sits above Sudeley Castle surrounded by its own 600 acres; all bedrooms look west to long views. Colours, fabrics and furniture are in perfect harmony, beds and linen are inviting, and the easy mix of elegant living and family bustle is delightful. There's tea on the terrace in summer and by a log fire in winter... your hosts delight in sharing this very English home. Wonderful walks, Cheltenham, Cotswold villages, fabulous restaurants and pubs are near.

| | |
|---|---|
| Price | From £80. Singles from £55. |
| Rooms | 3: 1 double, 2 twins/doubles. |
| Meals | Pubs/restaurants 1 mile. |
| Closed | December & January. |
| Directions | From Abbey Sq., Winchcombe, go north; after 50 yds, right into Castle St. Follow for 1 mile; after farm buildings, right for Sudeley Lodge; follow for 600 yds. House on right; first oak door. |

Susie & Jim Wilson
Westward,
Sudeley Lodge, Winchcombe,
Cheltenham, Gloucestershire GL54 5JB
Tel     +44 (0)1242 604372
Fax     +44 (0)1242 609198
Email   westward@haldon.co.uk
Web     www.westward-sudeley.co.uk

Entry 211   Map 8

## Gloucestershire

### 5 Ewlyn Road

In a bustling suburb of Cheltenham, Barbara's red-brick villa remains firmly unmodernised. The whiff of beeswax fills the air and Barbara looks after you with old-fashioned ease; the front room has an open fire where you can read a book or chat. Your bedroom is peaceful, the bed is firm, and the white cotton sheets robustly pressed; the clean and purposeful bathroom is shared but not noticeably. In the warm parlour Barbara gives you freshly squeezed orange juice, best Gloucester Old Spot bacon, sausage and free-range eggs – have it outside the sunny back door in summer. Authentic, great value B&B.

| | |
|---|---|
| Price | £50. Singles £25. |
| Rooms | 1 twin sharing bath (& separate shower). |
| Meals | Pubs/restaurants 5-minute walk. |
| Closed | Rarely. |
| Directions | From A40, signs to Stroud. Up Bath Road past shops; at mini roundabout bear left, then left signed Emmanuel Church. House 2nd on right; front door to side. |

| | |
|---|---|
| | Barbara Jameson |
| | 5 Ewlyn Road, |
| | Cheltenham, |
| | Gloucestershire GL53 7PB |
| Tel | +44 (0)1242 261243 |

Entry 212  Map 8

## Gloucestershire

### Hanover House

The former home of Elgar's wife, set in an early-Victorian terrace in Cheltenham's heart, is warm, elegant, inviting – and surprisingly peaceful. There are big trees all around and the river Chelt laps at the foot of the garden. Inside, a graceful period décor is enlivened by Bracken and Sophie (the dogs!) and exuberant splashes of colour; the delectable drawing room, with pale walls and trio of arched windows, is the perfect foil for paintings, books and rugs. Bedrooms have vivid Indian throws, bathrooms are simple and stylish. But best of all are Veronica and James: musical, well-travelled, irresistible.

| | |
|---|---|
| Price | £80-£100. Singles £60-£70. |
| Rooms | 3: 1 double; 1 double, 1 twin each with separate bath. |
| Meals | Pubs/restaurants 500 yds. |
| Closed | Rarely. |
| Directions | In Cheltenham town centre, 200 yds from bus/coach station; 600 yds from railway station. Parking available. |

| | |
|---|---|
| | Veronica & James Ritchie |
| | Hanover House, |
| | 65 St George's Road, Cheltenham, |
| | Gloucestershire GL50 3DU |
| Tel | +44 (0)1242 541297 |
| Email | hanoverhouse@tiscali.co.uk |
| Web | www.hanoverhouse.org |

Entry 213  Map 8

# Gloucestershire

### The Courtyard Studio

This new first-floor studio, attractive in reclaimed red brick, is reached via its own wrought-iron staircase; you are beautifully private. The friendly owners live next door, and will cook you a delicious breakfast in the house, or leave you a continental one in your own fridge. Find a clever, compact, contemporary space with a light and uncluttered living area, a mini window seat opposite two very comfortable boutique hotel style beds, fine linen, wicker armchair, and a patio area for balmy days. A 20-minute walk will take you to the centre of Cheltenham and you're a two-minute canter from the races. *Minimum stay two nights.*

Travel Club offer. See page 414.

| Price | £75. |
|---|---|
| Rooms | 1 twin. |
| Meals | Restaurants/pubs within 1 mile. |
| Closed | Rarely. |
| Directions | From racecourse roundabout on A435 towards town centre, turn right on to Cleevelands Drive (telephone and old postbox), 300 metres on left, through brick portal gateway. No 1 in left corner. |

John & Annette Gill
The Courtyard Studio,
1 The Cleevelands Courtyard,
Cleevelands Drive, Cheltenham,
Gloucestershire GL50 4QF
Tel      +44 (0)1242 573125
Email   courtyardstudio@aol.com

Entry 214   Map 8

# Gloucestershire

### St Annes

Step straight off the narrow pavement into a sunny hall – and a welcome to match. Iris worked in tourism for years and lives here with antique restorer Greg, two smiling children and Rollo the dog. They've also made this pretty 17th-century house in the centre of a captivating village (some road noise) as eco-friendly as possible. The biggest and most beautiful bedroom has a four-poster and a bathroom down the hall; the smallish double and the twin rooms will charm you. Farmer's market breakfasts are a warm, cosy, stylish feast. Brilliant all-round B&B. *Minimum stay two nights at weekends April-September.*

Ethical Collection: Environment; Food.
See page 412.

| Price | £65. Singles £40. |
|---|---|
| Rooms | 3: 1 double, 1 twin; 1 four-poster with separate bathroom. |
| Meals | Packed lunch £5. Restaurants/pubs in village. |
| Closed | Rarely. |
| Directions | A46 Stroud-Painswick; in Painswick, left after lights; house 3rd door on right. Bus: from Cheltenham & Stroud. |

Iris McCormick
St Annes,
Gloucester Street, Painswick,
Gloucestershire GL6 6QN
Tel      +44 (0)1452 812879
Email   greg.iris@btinternet.com
Web     www.st-annes-painswick.co.uk

Entry 215   Map 8

# Gloucestershire

## Frampton Court

Deep authenticity in this magnificent Grade I-listed house. The manor of Frampton-on-Severn has been in the family since the 11th century and although Rollo and Janie look after the estate, it is Gillian who greets you on behalf of the family and looks after you (very well). Exquisite examples of decorative woodwork and, in the hall, a cheerful log fire; perch on the mouseman fire seat. Bedrooms are traditional with antiques, panelling and long views. Beds have fine linen, one with embroidered Jacobean hangings. Stroll around the ornamental canal, soak up the old-master views. An architectural masterpiece.

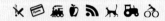

Travel Club offer. See page 414.

| | |
|---|---|
| Price | £110–£150. |
| Rooms | 3: 1 twin/double, 1 double, 1 four-poster. |
| Meals | Dinner £29. Pub across the green. Restaurant 3 miles. |
| Closed | Rarely. |
| Directions | From M5 junc. 13 west, then B4071. Left down village green, 400 yds, then look to left! 2nd turning left, between two chestnut trees & through ornamental gates in wall. |

| | |
|---|---|
| | Rollo & Janie Clifford |
| | Frampton Court, |
| | Frampton-on-Severn, |
| | Gloucestershire GL2 7EQ |
| Tel | +44 (0)1452 740267 |
| Fax | +44 (0)1452 740698 |
| Email | framptoncourt@framptoncourtestate.co.uk |
| Web | www.framptoncourtestate.co.uk |

Entry 216   Map 8

# Gloucestershire

## Grove Farm

Boards creak and you duck, in a farmhouse of the best kind: simple, small-roomed, stone-flagged, beamed, delightful. The walls are white, the furniture is good and there are pictures everywhere. In spite of great age (16th century), it's light, with lots of windows. You'll be fed well, too; the 400 acres are farmed organically and Penny makes a grand breakfast – continental at busy times. Stupendous views across the Severn estuary to the Cotswolds, the Forest of Dean on the doorstep and woodland walks, carpeted with spring flowers. And there is simply no noise – unless the guinea fowl are in voice.

| | |
|---|---|
| Price | £60–£70. Singles £35. |
| Rooms | 2: 1 double; 1 twin/double with separate bath. |
| Meals | Packed lunch £4. Pub 2 miles. |
| Closed | Rarely. |
| Directions | 2 miles south of Newnham on A48, opp. turn for Bullo Pill, large 'pull-in' with phone box on right; turn here; follow farm track to end. |

| | |
|---|---|
| | Penny & David Hill |
| | Grove Farm, |
| | Bullo Pill, Newnham, |
| | Gloucestershire GL14 1DZ |
| Tel | +44 (0)1594 516304 |
| Fax | +44 (0)1594 516304 |
| Email | davidandpennyhill@btopenworld.com |
| Web | www.grovefarm-uk.com |

Entry 217   Map 8

# Gloucestershire

## Nation House

Three cottages were knocked together to create this wisteria-clad, listed village house, now a terrific B&B. Beams are exposed, walls are pale and hung with prints, floors are close-carpeted, the sitting room is formally cosy and quiet. Smart, comfortable bedrooms have patchwork quilts, low beams and padded seats at lattice windows; the bathroom is spotless and the shower room compact. In summer, breakfast in the conservatory on still-warm homemade bread, local bacon and sausages, Brenda's preserves. The village is a Cotswold treasure, with two good eating places and with many walks from the door.

🧳 Travel Club offer. See page 414.

| | |
|---|---|
| Price | £70–£85. Singles £50. |
| Rooms | 3: 1 family; 2 doubles sharing bath (let to same party only). |
| Meals | Pubs 50 yds. |
| Closed | Rarely. |
| Directions | From Cirencester A419 for Stroud. After 7 miles right to Bisley. Left at village shop. House 50 yds on right. |

**Brenda & Mike Hammond**
Nation House,
George Street,
Bisley,
Gloucestershire GL6 7BB
Tel    +44 (0)1452 770197
Email  nation.house@homecall.co.uk

🎣 🍴 🚂

Entry 218   Map 8

# Gloucestershire

## Well Farm

Perhaps it's the gentle, unstuffy attitude of Kate and Edward. Or the great position of the house with its glorious views across the valley. Whatever, you'll feel comforted and invigorated by your stay here. It's a real family home and guests have a fresh, pretty bedroom that feels very private, and the use of a comfortable, book-filled sitting room that opens to a courtyard – Kate is an inspired gardener. Sleep soundly on the softest of pillows, wake to the deep peace of the countryside and tuck in to eggs from their own hens, local sausages, good bacon. The area teems with great walks.

| | |
|---|---|
| Price | From £80. |
| Rooms | 1 twin/double & sitting room. |
| Meals | Dinner from £20. Pubs nearby. |
| Closed | Rarely. |
| Directions | Directions on booking. |

**Kate & Edward Gordon Lennox**
Well Farm,
Frampton Mansell, Stroud,
Gloucestershire GL6 8JB
Tel    +44 (0)1285 760651
Email  kategl@btinternet.com
Web    www.well-farm.co.uk

🍴 🐾 🐕 🍽 🚲

Entry 219   Map 8

# Gloucestershire

## Drakestone House

A treat by anyone's reckoning. Utterly delightful people with wide-ranging interests (ex British Council and college lecturing; arts, travel, gardening) in a manor-type house full of beautiful furniture. The house was born of the Arts and Crafts movement: wooden panels painted green, a log-fired drawing room for guests, handsome old furniture, comfortable proportions, good beds with proper blankets. The garden's massive clipped hedges, Monterey Pines and smooth, great lawn are impressive, as is the whole place – and the views stretch to the Severn Estuary and Wales.

# Gloucestershire

## Lodge Farm

A plum Cotswolds position, a striking garden, a rolling programme of improvements, exceptional linen – there are plenty of reasons to stay here. Then there are your flexible hosts, who can help wedding groups, give you supper en famille next to the Aga or something smart and candlelit round the dining-room table: perfect for a house party. The sitting room has flowers, family photographs and lots of magazines; sometimes home-produced lamb for dinner, always excellent coffee at breakfast and their own free-range eggs. Peace and quiet lovers will delight, yet you are a short walk from Tetbury.

Travel Club offer. See page 414.

| Price | £78. Singles £49. |
|---|---|
| Rooms | 3: 1 twin/double, 1 double, 1 twin, all with separate bath/shower. |
| Meals | Dinner £32. BYO. Pub/restaurant under 1 mile. |
| Closed | Christmas. |
| Directions | B4060 from Stinchcombe to Wotton-under-Edge. 0.25 miles out of Stinchcombe village. Driveway on left marked, before long bend. |

| Price | £65–£75. Singles from £55. Family room £85. |
|---|---|
| Rooms | 4: 2 twins/doubles; 1 twin/double, 1 family room sharing bath. |
| Meals | Dinner, 2-3 courses, £15–£25. Pub/bistro 2.5 miles. |
| Closed | Rarely. |
| Directions | From Cirencester A433 to Tetbury, right B4014 to Avening. After 250 yds, left onto Chavenage Lane. Lodge Farm 1.3 miles on right; left of barn on drive. |

|  | Hugh & Crystal Mildmay |
|---|---|
|  | Drakestone House, |
|  | Stinchcombe, |
|  | Dursley, |
|  | Gloucestershire GL11 6AS |
| Tel | +44 (0)1453 542140 |
| Fax | +44 (0)1453 542140 |

|  | Robin & Nicky Salmon |
|---|---|
|  | Lodge Farm, |
|  | Chavenage, Tetbury, |
|  | Gloucestershire GL8 8XW |
| Tel | +44 (0)1666 505339 |
| Fax | +44 (0)1666 505346 |
| Email | rsalmon.lodgefarm@btinternet.com |
| Web | www.lodgefarm.co.uk |

Entry 220   Map 8

Entry 221   Map 8

## Gloucestershire

### 107 Gloucester Street

Slip through gates into a narrow courtyard of potted shrubs and honey-coloured Cotswold stone. This modest Georgian merchant's house is three minutes from the charming town centre yet blissfully quiet. Inside: buttery colours, well-loved antiques, soft uncluttered spaces. Restful, understated bedrooms are small, chic and spotless. Kitchen breakfasts overlook the sheltered garden – a verdant spot for relaxing in summer. For evenings, a creamy first-floor sitting room with a small log fire. Ethne and her ex-army husband are full of fun and good humour – very special. *Children over ten welcome.*

| | |
|---|---|
| Price | £70. Singles £50. |
| Rooms | 2: 1 double, 1 twin. |
| Meals | Hotel 300 yds & restaurants 8-minute walk. |
| Closed | Christmas & Easter. |
| Directions | Directions on booking. |

Ethne McGuinness
107 Gloucester Street,
Cirencester,
Gloucestershire GL7 2DW

Tel     +44 (0)1285 657861
Email   ethnemcg@onetel.com

Entry 222   Map 8

## Gloucestershire

### Lady Lamb Farm

Light pours into perfectly proportioned rooms through windows hung with velvet and chintz; soft sofas entice; china sits in alcoves on both sides of the fireplace. Jeanie and James, farmers, inventors, built the honey-stone house years ago and have kept their Cotswold dream ship-shape. You can play tennis and swim in the pool, bedrooms are a good size and have dreamy views, Aga breakfasts are scrumptious; locally cured bacon and eggs from the chickens that strut on the manicured lawn. Fishing, cycling and golf can all be organised for you and Kelmscott Manor (the country home of William Morris) is close.

| | |
|---|---|
| Price | From £70. Singles £45. |
| Rooms | 2: 1 twin; 1 twin/double with separate bath. |
| Meals | Pubs/restaurants 1-4 miles. |
| Closed | Christmas & New Year. |
| Directions | From Fairford on A417. After 0.5 miles look for sign for Waitenhill and Cherry Tree House. Entrance directly opposite on left. |

Jeanie Keyser
Lady Lamb Farm,
Meysey Hampton, Cirencester,
Gloucestershire GL7 5LH

Tel     +44 (0)1285 712206
Fax     +44 (0)1285 712206
Email   jeanie@jameskeyser.co.uk

Entry 223   Map 8

# Gloucestershire

## The Old Rectory

English to the core – and to the bottom of its lovely garden, with a new woodland walk and plenty of quiet places to sit. You sweep into the circular driveway to a yellow labrador welcome. The house, despite its magnificent age, throbs with family energy and warmth – Caroline is calmly competent and amiable, with a talent for understated interior décor. The two large, airy bedrooms are furnished with antiques, very good beds, a chaise longue or an easy chair, even a bottle opener and wine glasses. Elsewhere, old furniture and creaky floorboards complete the sense of well-being in a very special place.

| | |
|---|---|
| Price | £80–£95. Singles from £50. |
| Rooms | 2: 1 double, 1 twin. |
| Meals | Pub 200 yds. |
| Closed | December & January. |
| Directions | South through village from A417. Right after Masons Arms. 200 yds on left, through stone pillars. |

**Roger & Caroline Carne**
The Old Rectory,
Meysey Hampton, Cirencester,
Gloucestershire GL7 5JX

| | |
|---|---|
| Tel | +44 (0)1285 851200 |
| Fax | +44 (0)1285 850602 |
| Email | carolinecarne@cotswoldwireless.co.uk |
| Web | www.meyseyoldrectory.co.uk |

Entry 224  Map 8

# Gloucestershire

## Kempsford Manor

On the edge of the Cotswolds, this 17th-century village house is surrounded by large hedges and mature trees. Crunch up the gravelled drive to find floor-to-ceiling bay windows, dark pine floors with patterned rugs, wood panelling and built-in bookcases. Bedrooms vary hugely – one has a Chinese theme – but all are a good size and have super garden views; bathrooms are functional and old-fashioned. Two acres of beautifully tended gardens (snowdrops are special here) lead to an orchard and a canal walk; stoke up on Zehra's homemade muesli and come back for dinner – vegetables are homegrown.

Travel Club offer. See page 414.

| | |
|---|---|
| Price | £60–£70. Singles £40. |
| Rooms | 3: 2 doubles, 1 single sharing 2 bathrooms. |
| Meals | Dinner available by arrangement. Pub 200 yds. |
| Closed | Open all year. |
| Directions | A419 Cirencester-Swindon; Kempsford is signed with Fairford. Right into village, past small village green; on right, through stone columns. Glass front door, by a fountain. |

**Mrs Zehra I Williamson**
Kempsford Manor,
High Street,
Kempsford, Fairford,
Gloucestershire GL7 4EQ

| | |
|---|---|
| Tel | +44 (0)1285 810131 |
| Email | info@kempsfordmanor.com |
| Web | www.kempsfordmanor.com |

Entry 225  Map 8

# Gloucestershire

## The Moda House

A fine house and a big B&B, but one that retains a deeply homely feel; Duncan and Jo are hugely well-travelled and have filled it with pictures and artefacts from all over the world. Bedrooms differ (three are in a neat annexe) but all are cosy and well decorated with lovely colours, good fabrics, pocket sprung mattresses and bright bathrooms with thick towels. Breakfast is a truly local feast and will set you up for fabulous walks (you are a mile from the Cotswold Way), there's a basement sitting room with comfy armchairs and lots of books, and you have the bustling town to explore with its shops and restaurants.

| Price | £82–£95. Singles £65. |
|---|---|
| Rooms | 10: 6 doubles, 1 family, 3 singles. |
| Meals | Pubs/restaurants within 0.25 miles. |
| Closed | Never. |
| Directions | Exit M4 at junction 18. Follow A46 northbound. Turn left and follow A432 into town centre. House is at top of High Street. |

Duncan & Jo MacArthur
The Moda House,
1 High Street, Chipping Sodbury,
Gloucestershire BS37 6BA

| Tel | +44 (0)1454 312135 |
|---|---|
| Fax | +44 (0)1454 850090 |
| Email | enquiries@modahouse.co.uk |
| Web | www.modahouse.co.uk |

Entry 226   Map 3

# Hampshire

## Little Cottage

Just 45 minutes from Heathrow but the peace is deep, the views are long and the wildlife thrives – watch fox and deer, hear the rare nightjar. Chris and Therese grow many of their own vegetables and fruit, source meat locally and give you superb home cooking; guests have a lovely sitting room with an eclectic mix of modern and antique furniture, and a pretty terrace overlooks the garden. Bedrooms are all ground-floor, fresh and light, the double has distant views; perfect for walkers and those who seek solace from urban life but don't want to go too far. *Minimum stay two nights at weekends. Children over 12 welcome.*

Ethical Collection: Food. See page 412.

Travel Club offer. See page 414.

| Price | £70–£80. Singles £50. |
|---|---|
| Rooms | 3: 1 twin/double, 1 double, 1 single. |
| Meals | Dinner from £15. Pub 1.5 miles. |
| Closed | Between Christmas & New Year & occasionally. |
| Directions | B3011 from A30 in Hartley Wintney for 1.5 miles. Cottage just before the continuous double white line down the middle of road becomes a single line. |

Chris & Therese Abbott
Little Cottage,
Hazeley Heath,
Hartley Wintney,
Hook, Hampshire RG27 8LY

| Tel | +44 (0)1252 845050 |
|---|---|
| Email | info@little-cottage.co.uk |
| Web | www.little-cottage.co.uk |

Entry 227   Map 4

## Hampshire

### Home Close

The setting is gorgeous, surrounded by the New Forest – walks start from the gate. The house, once a farm belonging to the Beaulieu estate, is now home to friendly Sally and Bob. You sleep in a sunshine-yellow bedroom overlooking the lovely garden, there are Lloyd Loom chairs for reading or TV, bottled water, proper milk, homemade shortbread. A generous breakfast, sometimes with home-baked bread, is taken in the pretty blue dining room at a solid oak table, from where you can watch the comings and goings of the birds beneath the arbour. Perfect for exploring the New Forest or a day trip to the Isle of Wight.

| | |
|---|---|
| Price | From £80. |
| Rooms | 1 double. |
| Meals | Packed lunch £6. Pubs/restaurants within 7 miles. |
| Closed | Christmas, New Year & occasionally. |
| Directions | M27 junc. 2. A326, then B3054 signed Beaulieu 1.1 miles from New Forest cattle grid, down gravel track signed Home Close & Vanguard. Left past cottage to gate. |

| | |
|---|---|
| | Sally Brearley |
| | Home Close, |
| | Hill Top, Beaulieu, |
| | Hampshire SO42 7YR |
| Tel | +44 (0)1590 612287 |
| Email | homeclose@talktalk.net |
| Web | www.homeclosebedandbreakfast.co.uk |

Entry 228   Map 3

## Hampshire

### Pepperbox House

Expect charming British hospitality in this quaint 1650s brick house on Beaulieu's high street, a perfect base for exploring the New Forest. Thick oak beams from the shipyard at nearby Buckler's Hard support a low ceiling in the dining room, cosy with its polished table and oil painting; step through an original wood door to a winding staircase which curls up to an airy twin and sweet double under the eaves. Jane's garden is brimming with honeysuckle, clematis, climbing roses, a lovely place to relax after a day spent stomping the park's myriad trails. End with a traditional English meal and a sound sleep: homely, well cared-for, a treat.

| | |
|---|---|
| Price | £70-£80. Singles £45-£60. |
| Rooms | 2: 1 double, 1 twin with separate shared bathroom. |
| Meals | Dinner, 2 courses, £17.50; 3 courses £22. Picnic lunch £7.50-£10. Pub/restaurant 0.25 miles. |
| Closed | Rarely. |
| Directions | B3056 from Lyndhurst. Left into Beaulieu, then right into High St. House about 500 yds on left. |

| | |
|---|---|
| | Mrs Jane Skinner |
| | Pepperbox House, |
| | 54 High Street, Beaulieu, |
| | Hampshire SO42 7YD |
| Tel | +44 (0)1590 612728 |
| Email | jane@pepperboxhouse.co.uk |
| Web | www.pepperboxhouse.co.uk |

Entry 229   Map 3

# Hampshire

### The Manor House

Gracious yet informal, a crisp Regency house in this little corner of Hampshire where Jane Austen wrote most of her books. Clare will spoil you, even collect you from the station if you come without a car. Bedrooms are airy and light with space for chairs, knick-knacks and family pictures; bathrooms are smart. Eat a delicious home-cooked breakfast in the elegant dining room whose French windows overlook glorious lawns, impressive herbaceous borders and mature trees. Clare has a good knowledge of places to visit locally – especially gardens; she even organises garden tours to Normandy.

Travel Club offer. See page 414.

| | |
|---|---|
| Price | £80. Singles £55. |
| Rooms | 2: 1 double; 1 twin with separate bath. |
| Meals | Pub 0.25 miles. |
| Closed | Never. |
| Directions | Turn West at r'bout on A31 north of Alton, signed for Alton & Holybourne. Over railway; 1st right into Holybourne. After 300 yds road dips; up hill and at top left into Church Lane; 100 yds on left up 2nd gravel drive without gate. |

Clare Whately
The Manor House,
Holybourne, Alton,
Hampshire GU34 4HD
Tel      +44 (0)1420 541321
Email   clare@whately.net
Web     www.manor-house-holybourne.co.uk

Entry 230   Map 4

# Hampshire

### Bay Trees

Step in from the village street and you find yourself in a striking hall where the guest book perches on the music stand! Comfortable bedrooms have just been refurbished, the double with French windows opening to a lush suntrap of a garden – a wonderful surprise – full of arbours and weeping willow and a brook at the end with a seat for two. Breakfasts are gourmet here, served in the conservatory overlooking the magnolia. Robert, humorous and down-to-earth, makes you feel at ease the moment you arrive. The shingle beach with views to the Isle of Wight is a sprint away. *Minimum stay two nights at weekends.*

Travel Club offer. See page 414.

| | |
|---|---|
| Price | £80-£130. Singles from £50. |
| Rooms | 4: 1 double, 1 four-poster; 1 triple, 1 single sharing bath (2nd room let to same party only). |
| Meals | Restaurants/pubs 100 yds. |
| Closed | Rarely. |
| Directions | From Lymington follow signs for Milford-on-Sea (B3058). On left, just past village green. |

Robert Fry
Bay Trees,
8 High Street, Milford-on-Sea,
Lymington, Hampshire SO41 0QD
Tel      +44 (0)1590 642186
Email   rp.fry@virgin.net
Web     www.baytreebedandbreakfast.co.uk

Entry 231   Map 3

# Hampshire

## Land of Nod

A 1939 house of character with hosts to match and one of the greatest gardens in the book... seven tended acres within 100 acres of woodland. There are azaleas and camellias, specimen trees, croquet, tennis, a white wisteria 40 years old – and orchids: Jeremy's passion. Breakfast in the chinoiserie dining room – the allegorical tableau is charming, the needlework on the walls dates from 1901. No sitting room, but bedrooms are spacious, with views over the garden; original baths have vast taps. Flexible breakfasts are locally sourced, with seasonal fruit and preserves from the garden. *Children over ten welcome.*

 Travel Club offer. See page 414.

| | |
|---|---|
| Price | From £80. Singles from £50. |
| Rooms | 2: 1 twin; 1 twin with separate bath. |
| Meals | Restaurants 5-minute drive. |
| Closed | Rarely. |
| Directions | South on A3 to lights at Hindhead. Straight across & after 400 yds, right onto B3002. On for 3 miles. Entrance (signed) on right in a wood. |

| | |
|---|---|
| | **Jeremy & Philippa Whitaker** |
| | Land of Nod, |
| | Headley, Bordon, Hampshire GU35 8SJ |
| Tel | +44 (0)1428 713609 |
| Fax | +44 (0)1428 717698 |
| Email | pwhitaker100@hotmail.com |

Entry 232　Map 4

# Hampshire

## Sandy Corner

Stride straight onto open moorland from this smallholding on the edge of the New Forest – a great place for anyone who loves walking, cycling, riding, wildlife and the great outdoors. And there's plenty of room for wet clothes and muddy boots. Cattle graze within ten feet of the window, you may hear the call of a nightjar in June, Dartford warblers nest nearby, happy hens cluck around the yard. Sue also keeps a horse, two cats, a few sheep. You have a little guest sitting room, lovely fresh bedrooms, your own spot in the garden and a marvellous, away-from-it-all feel. You can walk to one pub; others are nearby.

| | |
|---|---|
| Price | From £75. Singles from £50. |
| Rooms | 2 doubles. |
| Meals | Packed lunch £8. Pub within walking distance, restaurant 2.5 miles. |
| Closed | Rarely. |
| Directions | On A338, 1 mile S of Fordingbridge, at small x-roads, turn for Hyde & Hungerford. Up hill & right at school for Ogdens; left at next x-roads for Ogdens North; on right at bottom of hill. |

| | |
|---|---|
| | **Sue Browne** |
| | Sandy Corner, |
| | Ogdens North, |
| | Fordingbridge, |
| | Hampshire SP6 2QD |
| Tel | +44 (0)1425 657295 |

Entry 233　Map 3

# Hampshire

## Little Shackles

Gaze upon the pretty Arts and Crafts house from the comfort of the hammock or solar-heated pool: this is a charming place to stay. Rosemary advises on local gardens to visit (her own two acres are also special) and is the loveliest of hosts. Your bedroom has an elegant country air – homemade quilts on firm beds, new armchairs and a new TV – and a spring-like bathroom with fluffy bathrobes and views to fresh green fields. Breakfast is plentiful; dinner, at the lovely old drover's pub down the sleepy lane, is a simple treat. Goodwood and Portsmouth are close, and the walks on the South Downs are marvellous.

| | |
|---|---|
| Price | £68. Singles from £30. |
| Rooms | 2: 1 twin/double, 1 single sharing bath (2nd room let to same party only). |
| Meals | Packed lunch £7. Pub 0.5 miles. |
| Closed | Rarely. |
| Directions | From London A3 take A272 junc. Petersfield, right at r'bout. 1st right into Kingsfernsden Lane, over level crossing into Reservoir Lane. Right into Harrow Lane. House 2nd driveway on right. |

**Rosemary & Martin Griffiths**
Little Shackles,
Harrow Lane, Petersfield,
Hampshire GU32 2BZ
Tel +44 (0)1730 263464
Email martgriff@freenet.co.uk

Entry 234  Map 4

# Hampshire

## Yew Tree House

A charming papier-mâché cat welcomes you at the front door, setting the tone for this artistic, tranquil house. The views, the house and the villagers are said to have inspired Dickens, who escaped London for the peace of the valley. The exquisite red brick was there 200 years before him; the rare dovecote, to which you may have the key, 300 years before that. Thoughtful hosts, interesting to talk to, have created a house of understated elegance: a yellow-ochre bedroom with Descamps bed linen, cashmere/silk curtains designed by their son, a view onto an enchanting garden, a profusion of flowers. Great value.

| | |
|---|---|
| Price | £65. Singles by arrangement. |
| Rooms | 2: 1 twin; 1 double with separate bath. |
| Meals | Pub in village. |
| Closed | Rarely. |
| Directions | From A30 west of Stockbridge for 1.5 miles, left at minor x-roads. After 2 miles left at T-junc. House on left at next junc. opposite Greyhound. |

**Philip & Janet Mutton**
Yew Tree House,
Broughton, Stockbridge,
Hampshire SO20 8AA
Tel +44 (0)1794 301227
Email pandjmutton@onetel.com

Entry 235  Map 3

# Hampshire

## Mizzards Farm

Wow! The central hall is three storeys high, its vaulted roof open to the rafters. This is the oldest part of this rambling, mostly 16th-century farmhouse: kilims and fine antiques look splendid with the ancient flagstones. There's a drawing room for musical evenings and an upstairs conservatory from which you can see the garden with its lake, swimming pool, outdoor chess and sculptures. The four-poster is extraordinarily kitsch with electric curtains, the other bedrooms traditional and fresh. Come in the summer for mini Glyndebourne on the lawn. *Children over eight welcome. Minimum stay two nights.*

| | |
|---|---|
| Price | £80–£90. Singles by arrangement. |
| Rooms | 3: 1 double, 1 twin, 1 four-poster. |
| Meals | Pubs 0.5 miles. |
| Closed | Christmas & New Year. |
| Directions | From A272 at Rogate, turn for Harting & Nyewood. Cross humpback bridge; drive signed to right after 300 yds. |

Harriet & Julian Francis
Mizzards Farm,
Rogate,
Petersfield,
Hampshire GU31 5HS

| | |
|---|---|
| Tel | +44 (0)1730 821656 |
| Fax | +44 (0)1730 821655 |
| Email | francis@mizzards.co.uk |

Entry 236  Map 4

# Hampshire

## Little Ashton Farm

Part 18th-century farm cottage, part extended Victorian extension; this is a laid-back, friendly house, full of jolly clutter and muddle. Felicity is a keen cook with a burgeoning kitchen garden: plums, figs for bottling and jamming. You eat in the dining room or conservatory; delicious "everything's local" breakfasts and irresistible dinners. The charming, small double has garden views, good linen and furniture, books and paintings; there's a downstairs sitting room and the garden terraces are filled with pots and deep borders. Country walks from the doorstep, yet close to the M27, M3 and Winchester.

Travel Club offer. See page 414.

| | |
|---|---|
| Price | £70. Singles £45. |
| Rooms | 1 double. |
| Meals | Dinner, 3 courses, £25; 2 courses £20. Pubs/restaurants nearby. |
| Closed | Mid-December to 28 March. |
| Directions | B2177 Winchester to Portsmouth. Just after 40mph sign into Bishop's Waltham, left into Ashton Lane. 0.75 miles up on left, black wrought-iron gates into drive. |

Felicity & David Webb-Carter
Little Ashton Farm,
Ashton Lane, Bishop's Waltham,
Hampshire SO32 1FR

| | |
|---|---|
| Tel | +44 (0)1489 894055 |
| Fax | +44 (0)1489 894055 |
| Email | flossywebb@hotmail.com |
| Web | www.littleashtonfarm.20m.com |

Entry 237  Map 4

# Hampshire

## The Threshing Barn

You are on the edge of the rolling Meon valley, the approach through hedge-lined lanes is bucolic and the beautifully restored barn sits on a conservation award-winning farm run by John. Choose between a colourful and homely double in the main house or independence in the glorious bothy – a beamed and light space with a double walk-in shower. Find fresh flowers, good mattresses and feather and down pillows. All guests are greeted with tea and scones, breakfast is a local or homegrown extravaganza (check out Emma's borage honey) and views are to one of the tallest village church spires in Hampshire.

Travel Club offer. See page 414.

| | |
|---|---|
| Price | £75–£85. Singles £55. |
| Rooms | 3: 1 double, 1 single with shared bath (let to same party only). Bothy: 1 twin/double. |
| Meals | Packed lunch £7–£8. Pub 2 miles. |
| Closed | Rarely. |
| Directions | A272 Winchester to Petersfield. After A32/A272 crossing, continue 0.8 miles for Petersfield. Left up Stocks Lane, 0.5 miles to house. |

| | |
|---|---|
| | **Emma Bird** |
| | The Threshing Barn, |
| | Stocks Lane, |
| | Privett, |
| | Hampshire GU34 3NZ |
| Tel | +44 (0)1730 828382 |
| Email | emmacbird@stocksfarmprivett.co.uk |
| Web | www.thethreshingbarn.co.uk |

Entry 238  Map 4

# Hampshire

## Mulberry House

Deep into Jane Austen country, among ancient apple trees and rose bushes, is Mulberry House – the red-brick stable block of Old Alresford House. Peter and Sue are charming, and so is their home, filled with interesting pictures, fresh flowers and family photos. Private, quietly elegant guest rooms share a sitting room and kitchenette; the one in the eaves overlooks a pretty courtyard where a fountain plays. The dining room is elegant, but in fine weather you breakfast beneath the wisteria and vine-hung pergola on home-laid eggs and homemade jams. Comfortably English with a lovely garden.

Ethical Collection: Food. See page 412.

Travel Club offer. See page 414.

| | |
|---|---|
| Price | £75. Singles £55. |
| Rooms | 2: 1 double, 1 twin/double. |
| Meals | Pubs/restaurants within 10-minute walk. |
| Closed | Rarely. |
| Directions | M3 exit 9, signs to Alresford. In town centre, left onto B3046 to church on right. Then right into Colden Lane. House is 3rd on right through field gate. |

| | |
|---|---|
| | **Sue & Peter Paice** |
| | Mulberry House, |
| | Colden Lane, Old Alresford, |
| | Alresford, Hampshire SO24 9DY |
| Tel | +44 (0)1962 735518 |
| Fax | +44 (0)1962 736155 |
| Email | suepaice@btinternet.com |
| Web | www.mulberryhousebnb.com |

Entry 239  Map 4

# Hampshire

## Brymer House

Complete privacy in a B&B is rare. Here you have it, a 12-minute walk from town, cathedral and water meadows. Relax in your own half of a Victorian townhouse immaculately furnished and decorated and with a garden to match – all roses and lilac in the spring. Fizzy serves sumptuous breakfasts, there's a log fire in the guests' sitting room and fresh flowers abound – guests have been delighted. You are also left with an 'honesty box' so you may help yourselves to drinks. Bedrooms are small and elegant, with antique mirrors, furniture and bedspreads; bathrooms are warm and spotless. *Children over seven welcome.*

| Price | £70-£80. Singles £54-£60. |
|---|---|
| Rooms | 2: 1 double, 1 twin. |
| Meals | Pubs/restaurants nearby. |
| Closed | Christmas. |
| Directions | M3 junc. 9; A272 Winchester exit, then signs for Winchester Park & Ride. Under m'way, straight on at r'bout signed St Cross. Left at T-junc. St Faith's Rd veers off 100 yds ahead to the left on reaching bend. |

|  | Guy & Fizzy Warren |
|---|---|
|  | Brymer House, |
|  | 29-30 St Faith's Road, St Cross, |
|  | Winchester, Hampshire SO23 9QD |
| Tel | +44 (0)1962 867428 |
| Email | brymerhouse@aol.com |
| Web | www.brymerhouse.co.uk |

Entry 240   Map 4

# Herefordshire

## Eyton Old Hall

Quintessentially English but with wonderful views to the Welsh hills. This is country house living at its most delightful – grand yet cosy; it is relaxed and without pretence. Set in parkland, high above the River Lugg, the fine Regency house is James and Henrietta's lovely family home, full of light, colour, lots of interesting pictures and prints, log fires, and some unusual touches. Traditional bedrooms are large, with good beds and proper linen sheets; bathrooms are old-fashioned but gloriously warm, and showers are energetic. Breakfast is special, and there are acres of glorious walks straight from the house.

| Price | £75. Singles £40. |
|---|---|
| Rooms | 3: 2 doubles, 1 twin. |
| Meals | Dinner, 3 courses, £20. Pubs 2-4 miles. |
| Closed | Christmas & Easter. |
| Directions | From Leominster B4361 north; 0.5 miles on, left for Eyton; 1.5 miles on, left for Kingsland. House 0.5 miles on right. |

|  | James & Henrietta Varley |
|---|---|
|  | Eyton Old Hall, |
|  | Eyton, Leominster, |
|  | Herefordshire HR6 0AQ |
| Tel | +44 (0)1568 612551 |
| Email | varleyeoh@hotmail.com |
| Web | www.eytonoldhall.com |

Entry 241   Map 7

## Herefordshire

### Bunns Croft

The timbers of the medieval house are probably 1,000 years old. Little of the structure has ever been altered and it is an absolute delight: stone floors, rich colours, a piano, dogs, books and cosy chairs – all give a homely, warm feel. Cruck-beamed bedrooms are snugly small, the stairs are steep – this was a yeoman's house – and the twin's bathroom has its own sweet fireplace. The countryside is 'pure', too, with 1,500 acres of National Trust land five miles away. Anita is charming, loves to look after her guests, grows her own fruit and vegetables and makes fabulous dinners. Just mind your head.

| | |
|---|---|
| Price | £70-£80. Singles £35. |
| Rooms | 4: 1 twin; 1 double, 2 singles, sharing bath (let to same party only). |
| Meals | Dinner, 3 courses, £20. Pub 3 miles. |
| Closed | Rarely. |
| Directions | From Leominster, A49 towards Ludlow; 4 miles to village of Ashton, then left. House on right behind postbox after 1 mile. |

|  |  |
|---|---|
| | Mrs Anita Syers-Gibson |
| | Bunns Croft, |
| | Moreton Eye, |
| | Leominster, |
| | Herefordshire HR6 0DP |
| Tel | +44 (0)1568 615836 |

✗ 🐕 🐾

Entry 242   Map 7

## Herefordshire

### Staunton House

The Georgian rectory's well-proportioned rooms, painstakingly restored, brim with beautiful furnishings, interesting pictures and fine furniture. The original oak staircase leads to peaceful bedrooms with comfortable beds; the blue room looks onto garden and pond. It's a house that matches its owners – quiet, traditional and country-loving. Wander through the lovely garden, drive to Hay or Ludlow, stride some ravishing countryside, play golf near Offa's Dyke; return to Rosie and Richard's delicious dinner in the elegant dining room or in the large kitchen if you prefer. You will be well tended here.

| | |
|---|---|
| Price | From £75. Singles from £45. |
| Rooms | 2: 1 double, 1 twin/double. |
| Meals | Dinner, 2-3 courses, £20-£25. Pub/restaurant 2.5 miles. |
| Closed | Rarely. |
| Directions | A44 Leominster-Pembridge; right to Shobdon. After 0.5 miles, left to Staunton-on-Arrow; at x-roads, over into village. Opp. church, with black wrought-iron gates. |

|  |  |
|---|---|
| | Rosie & Richard Bowen |
| | Staunton House, |
| | Staunton-on-Arrow, Pembridge, |
| | Leominster, Herefordshire HR6 9HR |
| Tel | +44 (0)1544 388313 |
| Email | rosbown@aol.com |
| Web | www.stauntonhouse.co.uk |

🕊 ✗ 🚂 🐕 🐦 🐾 🏊 🍷

Entry 243   Map 7

# Herefordshire

## Bollingham House

The views alone might earn the house a place in this book. But there's more... a beautifully furnished interior and an interesting four-acre garden with a perfumed rose walk. Stephanie and John, working unobtrusively to make your stay enjoyable, are natural hosts. Bedrooms are large, bright and comfortable, and Stephanie has cleverly brought vibrant colours, fine furniture and paintings together with a dash of elegance. Gaze from your windows across the Wye Valley to the Malvern Hills, or west to the Black Mountains. Stephanie's cooking is worth a detour.

| | |
|---|---|
| Price | From £75. Singles from £40. |
| Rooms | 2: 1 twin; 1 double with separate bath. |
| Meals | Dinner from £25. Packed lunch £6. Pub 2 miles. |
| Closed | Occasionally. |
| Directions | A438 Hereford to Brecon road, towards Kington on A4111; through Eardisley; house 2 miles up hill on left, behind long line of conifers. |

|  | Stephanie & John Grant |
|---|---|
| | Bollingham House, |
| | Eardisley, Herefordshire HR5 3LE |
| Tel | +44 (0)1544 327326 |
| Email | grant@bollinghamhouse.com |
| Web | www.bollinghamhouse.com |

Entry 244   Map 7

# Herefordshire

## Hall's Mill House

Quiet lanes bring you to this most idyllic spot – a stone cottage in a light and open valley. The sitting room is snug with wood-burner and sofas but the kitchen is the hub of the place – delicious breakfasts and dinners are cooked on the Aga. Grace, chatty and easy-going, obviously enjoys living in her modernised mill house. Rooms are small, fresh, with exposed beams and slate sills; only the old mill interrupts the far-reaching, all-green views. Drift off to sleep to the sound of the Arrow burbling by – a blissful tonic for walkers and nature lovers. Great value, too. *Children over four welcome.*

| | |
|---|---|
| Price | £50–£55. Singles £25–£27.50. |
| Rooms | 3: 1 double; 1 double, 1 twin, sharing bath. |
| Meals | Dinner from £15. Pub/restaurant 3 miles. |
| Closed | Christmas. |
| Directions | A438 from Hereford. After Winforton, Whitney-on-Wye & toll bridge, sharp right for Brilley. Left fork to Huntington, over x-roads & next right to Huntington. Next right into 'No Through Road', then 1st right. |

|  | Grace Watson |
|---|---|
| | Hall's Mill House, |
| | Huntington, |
| | Kington, |
| | Herefordshire HR5 3QA |
| Tel | +44 (0)1497 831409 |

Entry 245   Map 7

## Herefordshire

### Garnstone House

Come for peace and quiet in the Welsh Marches, good food and lovely, humorous, down-to-earth hosts. The atmosphere is easy, and the furniture a lifetime's accumulation of eclectic pieces and pictures and prints of horses, hounds and country scenes. After dinner and good conversation, climb the picture-lined stairs to a comfortably carpeted bedroom – either a twin or a double – and a bathroom that is properly old-fashioned. Delicious breakfasts, good dinners and a stunning garden to explore – the variety and colour of the springtime flowers are astonishing and the clematis is a glory.

Travel Club offer. See page 414.

| | |
|---|---|
| Price | From £80. Singles from £40. |
| Rooms | 1 twin or double with separate bath. |
| Meals | Dinner from £22.50. Pub/restaurant 1 mile. |
| Closed | Rarely. |
| Directions | A480 from Hereford; after 10 miles, right onto B4230 for Weobley. After 1.75 miles, right onto level tarmac private road; 2nd on left over cattle grid. |

**Dawn & Michael MacLeod**
Garnstone House,
Weobley, Herefordshire HR4 8QP

Tel +44 (0)1544 318943
Email macleod@garnstonehouse.co.uk
Web www.garnstonehouse.co.uk

Entry 246　Map 7

## Herefordshire

### Winforton Court

Dating from 1500, the Court is dignified in its old age – undulating floors, great oak beams, thick walls. It is a dramatic, colourful home with exceptional timber-framed bedrooms; one room has an Indian-style bathroom and huge roll top bath, the suite a sitting area with two sofas. You also have a roomy guest sitting room and a small library for restful evenings. Your hosts are delightful and spoil you with decanters of sherry and bedside chocolates; the long room gallery seats up to 25 – great for family get-togethers. Visit Hay, walk down to the Wye or relax in the splendid garden. *Fishing can be arranged.*

Travel Club offer. See page 414.

| | |
|---|---|
| Price | £85-£115. Singles from £70. |
| Rooms | 3: 1 double, 1 four-poster, 1 four-poster suite. |
| Meals | Pub/restaurant 2-minute walk. |
| Closed | 20 December-30 December. |
| Directions | From Hereford, A438 into village. House on left with a green sign & iron gates. |

**Jackie Kingdon**
Winforton Court,
Winforton, Herefordshire HR3 6EA

Tel +44 (0)1544 328498
Fax +44 (0)1544 328498
Web www.winfortoncourt.co.uk

Entry 247　Map 7

## Lower House

I was in the equatorial forest, surely. The view reached over a pattern of tree tops to a distant hill, whose mist hovered as it awaited the day's heat. The house, itself a forest of old timber, is almost lost within the beautiful garden. It is old, but restored with affection. Stairs twist and creak, the unexpected awaits you. Bedrooms are panelled or timber-clad, bathrooms are neat, there is a handsome room where you eat breakfast, read or play the piano. Nicky and Pete are unpretentious and easy, steeped in good taste and this exquisite project, next to Offa's Dyke path and on the Welsh border. *Minimum stay two nights.*

Ethical Collection: Environment; Food.
See page 412.

| Price | From £80. |
|---|---|
| Rooms | 2: 1 double; 1 double with separate bath. |
| Meals | Pubs/restaurants 1 mile. |
| Closed | Rarely. |
| Directions | East through Hay on B4348 for Bredwardine. On edge of Hay, right into Cusop Dingle; 0.75 miles, old mill house on left; drive on right, across stone bridge over stream. |

Nicky & Peter Daw
Lower House,
Cusop Dingle, Hay-on-Wye,
Herefordshire HR3 5RQ
Tel       +44 (0)1497 820773
Email    nicky.daw@btinternet.com
Web      www.lowerhousegardenhay.co.uk

Entry 248   Map 7

---

## Ty-Mynydd

Six miles over open heathland from Hay-on-Wye, it is a remote, precipitous approach up the mountainside to Ty-Mynydd, and this renovated, stone-flagged farmhouse is absolutely gorgeous. Sheep graze the hillside, the views are simply the best and the garden is colourful, informal, delightful. Turn on the taps and taste water straight from your hosts' own mountain stream; awake to bacon and eggs produced in the fields around you (this is a working organic farm). The lovely young family give you two sweetly restful rooms on the ground floor, one with 'that view', and a simple country bathroom. The sunsets are magical.

Ethical Collection: Environment; Food.
See page 412.

| Price | From £80. Singles £60. |
|---|---|
| Rooms | 2 doubles sharing bath (2nd room let to same party only). |
| Meals | Pubs 6-8 miles. |
| Closed | Rarely except Christmas & New Year. |
| Directions | From Hay on A438, 1st left after Swan Hotel; 6 miles uphill to open heath under Hay Bluff; 2nd right signed Capel Y Ffin; 1 mile, signed. |

Miss N Spenceley
Ty-Mynydd,
Llanigon, Hay-on-Wye,
Herefordshire HR3 5RJ
Tel       +44 (0)1497 821593
Email    nikibarber@tiscali.co.uk
Web      www.tymynydd.co.uk

Entry 249   Map 7

## Herefordshire

### Ladywell House

Snuggling in the Golden Valley, wrapped by ancient oaks and a deep peacefulness, you will relax here. The whitewashed, Edwardian dower house is welcoming and informal with understated good taste: soft colours, family paintings and antiques. The four-poster bedroom is regal, the twin is fresh in blues and creams, and bathrooms are stylish and spoiling – one has a corner spa bath. Breakfast in the light conservatory, take drinks to the new Breeze House in the garden, dine well by candlelight at a rustic oak table. Sarah and Charles are warm and generous – this is very much 'open house'.

Ethical Collection: Environment; Food.
See page 412.

| | |
|---|---|
| Price | From £60. Singles from £50. |
| Rooms | 2: 1 four-poster; 1 twin with separate bath. |
| Meals | Dinner, 3 courses, from £25. Bistro 10-minute drive. Pub 15-minute drive. |
| Closed | Rarely. |
| Directions | From A465 Hereford-Abergavenny, B4348 for Hay-on-Wye. In Vowchurch, left for Michaelchurch. Through hamlet of Turnastone, house 0.5 miles on right. |

Charles & Sarah Drury
Ladywell House,
Turnastone, Vowchurch,
Herefordshire HR2 0RE
Tel +44 (0)1981 550235
Email sarah@ladywellhouse.com
Web www.ladywellhouse.com

Entry 250 Map 7

## Herefordshire

### Burghill Grange

A big, happy, friendly, family house. Harriet and John have sandblasted beams, waxed elm floors, uncovered some fine 18th-century ceilings and put in three smart bathrooms. Your sitting room is cosy – bright with fire, bold fabrics and interesting books; enjoy home-laid eggs, fresh bread, delicious coffee and sausages from Ludlow while looking over the peaceful garden and pond. A first-floor double is calm and uncluttered, the others beamed and large with great views to church tower and orchards; bathrooms have chunky roll tops, big towels and organic bubbles and creams. Handy for Hay, golf, antiques and the Brecons.

Travel Club offer. See page 414.

| | |
|---|---|
| Price | £90. Singles £55. |
| Rooms | 3: 1 double; 1 twin/double with separate shower; 1 twin with separate bath. |
| Meals | Occasional dinner £20. Pubs/restaurants 1-4 miles. |
| Closed | Rarely. |
| Directions | A4103 north of Hereford, then A4100 north to Cannon Pyon. After 2 miles, after Portway sign, left to Burghill. After Burghill sign, house 1st on left. |

Harriet Gordon
Burghill Grange,
Burghill, Hereford,
Herefordshire HR4 7SE
Tel +44 (0)1432 761016
Email enquiries@burghillgrange.com
Web www.burghillgrange.com

Entry 251 Map 7

# Herefordshire

## Moor Court Farm

The buildings, about 500 years old, ramble and enfold both gardens and guests. This is an honest, authentic farmhouse in a deeply rural position. Elizabeth, a busy farmer's wife, manages it all efficiently with husband Peter; they were lambing when we were there. They also dry their own hops and in September you can watch the lovely old oast house (with resident owls and bats) at work. Elizabeth is an excellent, traditional cook – make the most of the home-produced meat, preserves and vegetables. Cottagey bedrooms have plump pillows and goose down duvets; one has views to the Malvern Hills.

| | |
|---|---|
| Price | From £60. Singles £35. |
| Rooms | 3: 1 double, 2 twins. |
| Meals | Dinner, 3 courses, from £19. |
| Closed | Rarely. |
| Directions | From Hereford, east on A438. A417 into Stretton Grandison; 1st right past village sign, through Holmend Park. Bear left past phone box. House on left. |

**Elizabeth & Peter Godsall**
Moor Court Farm,
Stretton Grandison, Ledbury,
Herefordshire HR8 2TP
Tel       +44 (0)1531 670408
Fax       +44 (0)1531 670408
Email     elizabeth@moorcourtfarm.co.uk
Web       www.moorcourtfarm.co.uk

Entry 252   Map 7

# Herefordshire

## Pullastone

Find a quiet, secluded corner in the two acres of garden hugging this ancient black and white farmhouse: watch the Indian Runner Ducks on their pond, spot deer, buzzards and shy hedgehogs. Inside is lovely: soaring beams, sculptures, turned wood chairs, prints, pictures and photos, all interesting, all beautiful. Two bedrooms on the ground floor have good beds, quilted covers, fresh flowers; one upstairs has a high vaulted ceiling and abstract art. Breakfast comes with a weather forecast and duck eggs; in season you get asparagus soldiers. Alison just wants you to be comfortable, to relax and feel at home. You will.

Travel Club offer. See page 414.

| | |
|---|---|
| Price | £70–£80. Singles from £35. |
| Rooms | 3: 2 doubles, 1 family room for 3. |
| Meals | Pubs within 2 miles. |
| Closed | Christmas. |
| Directions | A49 from Hereford towards Ross. Past car show rooms, then up hill. Where road narrows take turning on left to Aconbury, then 2nd drive on left. |

**Alison Davies**
Pullastone,
Kingsthorn,
Herefordshire HR2 8AQ
Tel       +44 (0)1981 540450
Fax       +44 (0)1981 540450
Email     info@pullastone.com
Web       www.pullastone.com

Entry 253   Map 7

# Isle of Wight

## Gotten Manor

Such character, such style — miles from the beaten track, bordered by beautiful stone barns. There's a refreshing simplicity to this unique Saxon house where living space was above, downstairs was for storage. Romantic bedrooms, one hidden up a steep open stair, have limewashed walls, wooden floors, A-frame beams, sofas. You sleep on a French rosewood bed, you bathe in a roll top tub in the room! Wallow by candlelight with a glass of wine. The garden bursts with magnificent fruit trees; Caroline's breakfasts include smoked salmon and smoothies. Rustic perfection, ancient peace. *Minimum stay two nights at weekends.*

Ethical Collection: Environment; Food.
See page 412.

| | |
|---|---|
| Price | £70–£95. Singles by arrangement. |
| Rooms | 2 doubles. |
| Meals | Pub 1.5 miles. |
| Closed | Rarely. |
| Directions | 0.5 miles south of Chale Green on B3399. After village, left at Gotten Lane. House at end of lane. |

Caroline Gurney-Champion
Gotten Manor,
Gotten Lane,
Chale,
Isle of Wight PO38 2HQ
Tel      +44 (0)1983 551368
Email   as@gottenmanor.co.uk
Web     www.gottenmanor.co.uk

✗ 🔊 ♿

Entry 254   Map 4

# Isle of Wight

## The Old Rectory

This old rectory dates to 1868: it comes in Gothic style with arched windows and was influenced by the work of Ruskin and Pugin. Selina and Jon are perfect foils to the grandeur of their refurbished home. Both were teachers — he art, she music — and Jon's paintings cover the walls. Elsewhere, you'll find a tiled entrance hall, French windows that open onto a lawned garden and a red dining room for delicious communal breakfasts. Bedrooms upstairs are just the ticket with lots of books, fresh fruit and lovely linen; bathrooms are a little dated but spotless. The coast is close for cliff-top walks.

| | |
|---|---|
| Price | £90–£110. Singles from £60. |
| Rooms | 3: 2 doubles, 1 twin/double. |
| Meals | Dinner £25–£30. Packed lunch £10. Pubs a few hundred yds. |
| Closed | Never. |
| Directions | From Ventnor take the Whitwell road. 1 mile. Pass Whitwell village hall on right; house is on left immediately before church. |

Jon & Selina Hepworth
The Old Rectory,
Ashknowle Lane,
Whitwell,
Isle of Wight PO38 2PP
Tel      +44 (0)1983 731242
Email   info@oldrectory1868.co.uk
Web     www.oldrectory1868.co.uk

✗ 📧 🐕 🔊

Entry 255   Map 4

# Isle of Wight

## North Court

A glorious Jacobean house with matchless grounds: 15 acres of pathed terraced gardens, exotica and subtropical flowers. The house, too, is magnificent, with 80 rooms, its big, comfortable guest bedrooms in two wings. The library houses a full-size snooker table (yes, you may use it), there's a chamber organ in the hall, and in the vast music room a grand piano (yours to play). The dining room has separate tables and delightful Nina Campbell wallpaper. Step back in time – in a quiet, untouristy village in lovely downland, this large house is very much a family home, and the perfect base for walkers and garden lovers.

| Price | £65–£100. Singles £40–£50. |
| --- | --- |
| Rooms | 6 twins/doubles. |
| Meals | Occasional light meals. Pub 3-minute walk through gardens. |
| Closed | Rarely. |
| Directions | From Newport, drive into Shorwell; down a steep hill, under a rustic bridge & right opposite thatched cottage. Signed. |

|  | John & Christine Harrison |
| --- | --- |
|  | North Court, |
|  | Shorwell, |
|  | Isle of Wight PO30 3JG |
| Tel | +44 (0)1983 740415 |
| Email | christine@northcourt.info |
| Web | www.northcourt.info |

Entry 256  Map 4

# Kent

## Hartlip Place

The house resonates with a faded, funky grandeur. Family portraits and mahogany pieces, a drawing room to die for, an antique table shimmering with hyacinths, sash windows with sweeping views, happy dogs, chirpy peacocks, a garden intricate and special. After a candlelit dinner, up the circular stair to a colonial-style bedroom (or delightful four-poster) with garden views, decanter for sherry, old-fashioned bathroom and – big treat – real winter fire. John is unflappable and a touch mischievous, Gillian cooks, daughter Sophie greets – you'll like the whole family. *Children over 12 welcome.*

Travel Club offer. See page 414.

| Price | From £90. Singles £50. |
| --- | --- |
| Rooms | 2: 1 four-poster; 1 twin/double with separate bath. |
| Meals | Dinner £25. Pub 1 mile. |
| Closed | Christmas & New Year. |
| Directions | From Dover, M2 to Medway Services. Into station, on past pumps. Ignore no exit signs. Left at T-junc., 1st left & on for 2 miles. Left at next T-junc. House 3rd on left. |

|  | Gillian & John Yerburgh |
| --- | --- |
|  | & Sophie & Richard Ratcliffe |
|  | Hartlip Place, |
|  | Place Lane, |
|  | Sittingbourne, Kent ME9 7TR |
| Tel | +44 (0)1795 842323 |
| Email | hartlipplace@btinternet.com |
| Web | www.hartlipplace.co.uk |

Entry 257  Map 5

# Kent

## Dadmans

Once the dower house to Lynsted Park, Dadmans sits in a parkland setting with nearby orchards and grazing cattle and sheep. Amanda's rare-breed hens provide your breakfast eggs and there is good local produce for dinner too, served in the dining room on gleaming mahogany or in the Aga-warmed kitchen. Bedrooms have patterned fabrics, indulgent beds, fresh flowers and good bathrooms. Outside there are ancient trees around the walled gardens and lots of newly planted species including a nuttery; Doddington Place with its gardens (and summer opera) is a 5-minute drive. *Children over four welcome.*

 Travel Club offer. See page 414.

| Price | £80. Singles by arrangement. |
|---|---|
| Rooms | 2: 1 twin; 1 double with separate bath. |
| Meals | Dinner, 4 courses, £30. Supper from £15. Pubs/restaurants nearby. |
| Closed | Rarely. |
| Directions | M20 junc. 8, then east on A20; left in Lenham towards Doddington. At The Chequers in Doddington, left; house 1.7 miles on left before Lynsted. |

Amanda Strevens
Dadmans,
Lynsted,
Sittingbourne,
Kent ME9 0JJ
Tel    +44 (0)1795 521293
Email    amanda.strevens@btopenworld.com
Web    www.dadmans.co.uk

Entry 258   Map 5

# Kent

## 7 Longport

A delightful, unexpected hideaway bang opposite the site of St Augustine's Abbey and a five-minute walk to the Cathedral. You pass through Ursula and Christopher's elegant Georgian house to emerge in a pretty courtyard, on the other side of which is the self-contained cottage. Downstairs is a cosy sitting room with pale walls, tiled floors and plenty of books, and a clever, compact wet room with mosaic tiles. Then up steep stairs to a swish bedroom with crisp cotton sheets on a handmade bed and views of magnolia and ancient wisteria. You breakfast in the main house or in the courtyard on sunny days. Perfect.

Ethical Collection: Food. See page 412.

Travel Club offer. See page 414.

| Price | £80. Singles £60. |
|---|---|
| Rooms | Cottage: 1 double & sitting room. |
| Meals | Restaurant 30 yds (closed Mondays). |
| Closed | Rarely. |
| Directions | Follow ring road around Canterbury. Signs for Sandwich A257, at St George's r'bout turn for Dover. After 300 yds left for Sandwich. At mini r'bout, left; house on left just before corner. |

Ursula & Christopher Wacher
7 Longport,
Canterbury,
Kent CT1 1PE
Tel    +44 (0)1227 455367
Email    ursula.wacher@btopenworld.com

Entry 259   Map 5

# Kent

## 14 Westgate Grove

Slap bang in the city, overlooking the river Stour and within strolling distance of the cathedral... step through the understated door and you will be astonished. Pippa is an interior designer, her husband an architect, and bedrooms are cool, smooth and fresh with good lighting, smart fabrics and pretty flowers. Bathrooms dazzle with rain showers, Brazilian black slate and the fluffiest of towels; don't feel guilty – it's rainwater heated by solar panels. On warm days you breakfast in the rosy-walled garden with its ancient vines, olives, lemons, mimosa; for cooler evenings there is an outdoor fireplace. Lovely.

| Price | £80–£100. |
|---|---|
| Rooms | 2: 1 double; |
| | 1 double with separate bath. |
| Meals | Pub/restaurant 50 yds. |
| Closed | Rarely. |
| Directions | Centre of Canterbury, on river by the Westgate Towers. |

|  | Pippa Clague |
|---|---|
| | 14 Westgate Grove, |
| | Canterbury, |
| | Kent CT2 8AA |
| Tel | +44 (0)1227 769624 |
| Email | pippa@clague.plus.com |

Entry 260   Map 5

# Kent

## Forstal House

Where to begin – the house or the garden? Both are a rare delight. The interiors are beautiful, lived-in, quietly traditional: muted colours in a sunlit drawing room; a riot of paintings; masses of books. Cosy, welcoming bedrooms (it feels like staying with friends), one up, one down, look onto the gardens – graceful, formal, tantalising; Duncan, a painter, sculptor and printmaker, redesigned much after the 1987 storm. Your hosts love their 17th- and 18th-century home and look after you well; fruit from the orchards ends up in crumbles, pies and delicious breakfast jams. *Children over seven welcome.*

| Price | £75–£50. Singles from £50. |
|---|---|
| Rooms | 2: 1 twin/double, 1 double. |
| Meals | Dinner, 3 courses, £25. |
| | Pub/restaurant 2 miles. |
| Closed | Christmas. |
| Directions | From A257, Canterbury to Sandwich; left at Wingham, north towards Preston. In Preston, The Forstal is 2nd left; 500 yds to house. |

|  | Elizabeth Scott |
|---|---|
| | Forstal House, |
| | The Forstal, Preston, |
| | Canterbury, Kent CT3 1DT |
| Tel | +44 (0)1227 722282 |
| Email | emscott@forstal.fsnet.co.uk |

Entry 261   Map 5

# Kent

## Great Weddington

The listed house of perfect proportions was built by a Sandwich brewer of ginger beer. The décor is delicious, the bedrooms desirable and cosy, the bathrooms snug and spotless, and Katie fills the rooms with flowers; she also arranges the flowers for Canterbury Cathedral. Dinner is followed by coffee and chocolates in the drawing room – rich fabrics, shelves of books, fine watercolours, much-loved antiques. Outside, stunning hedges and lawns and a terrace for tea in the summer. An enchanting home in a farmland setting, and the area hums with history. *Minimum stay two nights at weekends April-September. Pets by arrangement.*

| | |
|---|---|
| Price | £95-£115. Singles £75-£85. |
| Rooms | 2 twins/doubles. |
| Meals | Dinner, 4 courses, £35 (excluding Sunday). |
| Closed | Christmas & New Year. |
| Directions | From Canterbury, A257 for Sandwich. On approach to Ash, stay on A257 (do not enter village), then 3rd left at sign to Weddington. House 200 yds down on left. |

| | |
|---|---|
| | **Katie & Neil Gunn** |
| | Great Weddington, |
| | Ash, Canterbury, Kent CT3 2AR |
| Tel | +44 (0)1304 813407 |
| Fax | +44 (0)1304 812531 |
| Email | greatweddington@hotmail.com |
| Web | www.greatweddington.co.uk |

Entry 262　Map 5

# Kent

## Park Gate

Peter and Mary are a generous team and their conversation is informed and easy. Behind the wisteria-clad façade are two sitting rooms (one with chesterfield, one with wood-burner), ancient beams and polished wood. Bedrooms are freshly comfortable with gorgeous views over the garden to the fields beyond; bathrooms gleam, meals are delicious. More magic outside: croquet, tennis and thatched pavilions, wildlife and roses and a sprinkling of sheep to mow the paddock. The house has a noble history: Sir Anthony Eden lived here and Churchill visited during the war. Great value, and convenient for the Channel Tunnel.

Travel Club offer. See page 414.

| | |
|---|---|
| Price | £80. Singles £40. |
| Rooms | 3: 2 twins/doubles; 1 single with separate shower. |
| Meals | Dinner, 3 courses, £25. Pubs/restaurants 1 mile. |
| Closed | Christmas & New Year. |
| Directions | A2 Canterbury to Dover road; Barham exit. Through Barham to Elham. After Elham sign 1st right signed Park Gate 0.75 miles. Over brow of hill; house on left. |

| | |
|---|---|
| | **Peter & Mary Morgan** |
| | Park Gate, |
| | Elham, |
| | Canterbury, Kent CT4 6NE |
| Tel | +44 (0)1303 840304 |
| Email | marylmorgan@hotmail.co.uk |

Entry 263　Map 5

# Kent

## Little Mystole

All is reassuringly traditional and peaceful in this corner of Kent. The small Georgian house and delightful garden is run with the lightest of touches by your well-travelled, charming hosts. Cosy, comfortable bedrooms have a touch of chintz, inviting beds and glorious views. Tuck into a delicious breakfast in the handsome dining room, relax in the beamed sitting room filled with antiques, plump sofas, gilt-framed portraits and pretty flower arrangements. Golf at Royal St George's can be arranged and there are walks through rolling downland, hop fields and orchards. *10 mins from Canterbury, 30 mins from ferry & tunnel.*

# Kent

## Pond Cottage

A rural exterior and rolling countryside – but inside is cool, funky and fabulously colourful. Off the garden: a bedroom with an Indian theme – hot pink rubber floor, electric blue shiny bedcover, sixties chair and eastern wall hanging. You have your own walk-in shower and the use of a gorgeous roll top upstairs. Try Jude's juices at breakfast (celery, ginger, cucumber) or tuck into kippers, smoked salmon, eggs from the hens, enjoyed outside on your own terrace on fine days; suppers are delicious too. Wander the Italianate herb garden, splash about in a cedar wood hot tub, slow down with an aromatherapy massage.

 Travel Club offer. See page 414.

| | |
|---|---|
| Price | £85. Singles £20-£50. |
| Rooms | 2: 1 double with extra single bed, 1 twin. |
| Meals | Pubs/restaurants 1.5 miles. |
| Closed | Christmas & Easter. |
| Directions | A28 Canterbury-Ashford. Left to Shalmsford Street; right immed. after post office at Bobbin Lodge Hill. Road bends left, then right at T-junc.; 2nd drive on left at junc. with Pickelden Lane. |

| | |
|---|---|
| Price | From £95. |
| Rooms | 1 double. |
| Meals | Dinner from £15. Packed lunch £8. Pub 2 miles. |
| Closed | Rarely. |
| Directions | A28 Canterbury to Ashford. At junction with A252, turn up Cobbs Hill to Old Wives Lees. Past Star Inn, then continue on Selling Road. House 0.5 miles on left. |

|  | **Hugh & Patricia Tennent** |
|---|---|
| | Little Mystole, |
| | Mystole Park, Canterbury, Kent CT4 7DB |
| Tel | +44 (0)1227 738210 |
| Email | little_mystole@yahoo.co.uk |
| Web | www.littlemystole.co.uk |

|  | **Jude Adams** |
|---|---|
| | Pond Cottage, |
| | Selling Road, Old Wives Lees, Canterbury, Kent CT4 8BD |
| Mobile | +44 (0)7795 424570 |
| Email | jude@pondstays.com |
| Web | www.pondstays.com |

Entry 264   Map 5

Entry 265   Map 5

# Kent

## West End House

The very smart red-bricked Georgian house, formerly the village surgery, is now a gorgeous retreat; there's a deeply peaceful and rural feel, yet you are near to Dover and Canterbury. Choose between complete independence in the spacious suite at the 'North End' of the house, or the Tulip room in the main house. Lovely easy-going Lynne gives you homemade cake when you arrive, and delicious breakfasts (including smoked salmon and scrambled eggs) in an elegant family dining room with garden views. Bedrooms are crisp and pretty in shades of blue and green, mattresses are excellent and bathrooms have scented goodies.

 Travel Club offer. See page 414.

| | |
|---|---|
| Price | £65-£95. Singles £40-£55. |
| Rooms | 2: 1 double & sitting room; 1 suite for 2 with sitting room & kitchen. |
| Meals | Dinner on request. Pub 800 yds. |
| Closed | Christmas & New Year. |
| Directions | A2 towards Dover. Follow signs for Coldred. With the green on left, take right fork for Eythorne. House is on left after village sign. |

Lynne Backhouse
West End House,
Coldred Road,
Eythorne, Canterbury, Kent CT15 4BE
Tel      +44 (0)1304 830594
Email   lynne_backhouse@yahoo.co.uk
Web     www.westendhousekent.co.uk

Entry 266   Map 5

# Kent

## The Linen Shed

A weatherboard house with a winding footpath to the front door and a pot-covered veranda out the back: sit here and nibble something delicious and homemade while you contemplate the pretty garden with its gypsy caravan. Vickie, wreathed in smiles, has created a 'vintage' interior: find wooden flooring, reclaimed architectural pieces, big old roll tops, a mahogany loo seat. Bedrooms (one up, one down) are painted in the softest colours, firm mattresses are covered in fine linen, cotton or linen dressing gowns wait patiently in the smart bathrooms. Food is seriously good here, and adventurous – try a seaside picnic hamper!

Travel Club offer. See page 414.

| | |
|---|---|
| Price | From £65. Singles from £55. |
| Rooms | 2: 1 double with separate bath; 1 double with separate shared bath. |
| Meals | Dinner from £20. Picnic hamper from £15. Pub/restaurant 300 yds. |
| Closed | Rarely. |
| Directions | M2, junc. 7 for Canterbury; A2 for Canterbury. 1st immediate turnoff (100 yds) for Boughton, after 1 mile at the T-junc. turn left. After 1 mile, left at 'phone box up an elevated lane. House further along. |

Vickie Hassan
The Linen Shed,
104 The Street, Boughton under Blean,
Faversham, Kent ME13 9AP
Tel      +44 (0)1227 752271
Email   vixmiles@hotmail.com
Web     www.thelinenshed.com

Entry 267   Map 5

# Kent

## Hoo Farmhouse

Jane and Nicolas are keen shrimpers – let them take you to Minnis Bay and cook your catch for supper! Passionate about the coastline and the area, Jane is also a generous hostess, baking cakes for your arrival and giving you greengages and flowers from the garden. Bedrooms are big and sunny and have Georgian skirting boards and elegant sash windows; new bathrooms have soaps from Provence. The large Georgian-fronted house, surrounded on three sides by garden and rosy-brick outbuildings, has pale classic colours within, a breakfast conservatory, a drawing room with a fire – and a cathedral down the road.

Ethical Collection: Food. See page 412.

| Price | £90. Singles £65. |
|---|---|
| Rooms | 2 twins/doubles. |
| Meals | Supper, 2 courses, £12.50. Dinner, 3 courses, £25. Pub 1 mile. |
| Closed | Rarely. |
| Directions | A28 from Canterbury to Sarre, then A253 to Ramsgate. 4th exit at Monkton r'bout onto Willets Hill. Left at mini r'bout. House 0.75 miles on left. |

| | Jane Irwin |
|---|---|
| | Hoo Farmhouse, |
| | Monkton Road, Minster, |
| | Ramsgate, Kent CT12 4JB |
| Tel | +44 (0)1843 821322 |
| Email | stay@hoofarmhouse.com |
| Web | www.hoofarmhouse.com |

Entry 268   Map 5

# Kent

## Orchard Barn

Alison knows how to spoil (big beds, bread from the mill, home-grown soft fruit, homemade jams), David knows the wildlife, and they both love doing B&B. The big beautiful barn has been sympathetically restored, its middle section left open to create a stunning covered courtyard: find soaring beams, a comfortable leather sofa, fresh flowers. You get two snug, carpeted bedrooms up in the eaves – pale beams, bright colours, and a sweet bath (or shower) room. A delightful village, the ancient port of Sandwich nearby and egrets, kingfishers, swallows and squirrels a walk away. *Children over seven welcome.*

Travel Club offer. See page 414.

| Price | £65-£75. Singles from £45. |
|---|---|
| Rooms | 2: 1 double, 1 twin/double. |
| Meals | Pubs/restaurants within 1.5 miles. |
| Closed | 20 December-3 January. |
| Directions | A258 Sandwich to Deal. 1st right after Worth sign into Federland Lane; 0.5 miles concealed entrance on left, opp. black barn. |

| | David & Alison Ross |
|---|---|
| | Orchard Barn, |
| | Felderland Lane, |
| | Worth, |
| | Kent CT14 0BT |
| Tel | +44 (0)1304 615045 |
| Web | www.orchardbarn-worth.co.uk |

Entry 269   Map 5

# Kent

## Beaches

A proper seaside townhouse on The Strand, facing Walmer Green and the sea. But no fierce landlady inside – just cheery Rosie and two sleek, cool bedrooms, one on the ground floor, one on the first. Both are light, bright and fresh, dressed mainly in pale colours but with colourful headboards and cushions, and with comfy chairs for admiring views. Bathrooms are funky in a nautical way, there's a super little garden for breakfast on sunny days, and good restaurants close by. Start your day with eggs Benedict, cinnamon brioche, fresh croissants, good coffee. The perfect English seaside treat. *Minimum stay two nights for singles.*

| | |
|---|---|
| Price | £80–£90. Singles £65–£75. |
| Rooms | 2 doubles. |
| Meals | Breakfast or picnic brunch for the beach. Pubs/restaurants 0.5 miles. |
| Closed | Last 2 weeks in July. |
| Directions | From Deal station or town centre, south along Victoria Road passing Deal Castle. Then on to The Strand which opens onto Walmer Green. House opposite bandstand. |

Rosanna Lillycrop
Beaches,
34 The Strand,
Walmer, Deal, Kent CT14 7DX

| | |
|---|---|
| Tel | +44 (0)1304 369692 |
| Email | enquiries@beaches.uk.com |
| Web | www.beaches.uk.com |

Entry 270  Map 5

# Kent

## Kingsdown Place

Wow. A huge white villa set in stunning terraced gardens running down to the sea; on clear days you can see France! Tan has renovated the house and garden with panache: works of modern art festoon the walls, statues lurk and all is contemporary inside. Upstairs find neat bedrooms – one four poster with long views, and up a spiral staircase in the loft, is a fabulous, very private bedroom with a sitting room and terrace; all have Conran mattresses and white linen. Breakfast on scrambled eggs and smoked salmon or the full works; take it outside on the terrace in good weather. Seaside chic.

Travel Club offer. See page 414.

| | |
|---|---|
| Price | £85–£100. Singles £70. |
| Rooms | 3: 1 double with sitting room and terrace; 1 double, 1 four-poster each with separate bath and sitting room. |
| Meals | Packed lunch £10. Dinner £25. Restaurant 500 yds. Pub 0.5 miles. |
| Closed | Christmas & New Year. |
| Directions | Through Kingsdown village towards sea; at high flint wall turn right, through gateway, then 3rd gateway on left. |

Tan Harrington
Kingsdown Place,
Upper Street,
Kingsdown, Kent CT14 8BT

| | |
|---|---|
| Tel | +44 (0)1304 380510 |
| Fax | +44 (0)1304 380510 |
| Email | tan@tanharrington.com |

Entry 271  Map 5

## Kent

### Woodmans

No traffic noise, just blissful peace – and you're no more than a short hop to Canterbury. Your cosy ground-floor bedroom has its own entrance via the glorious garden where there are plenty of places to sit when its sunny. Tuck into local bacon and eggs (from Sarah's own rescued hens) in the breakfast room with its old pine table, dresser and flowers – or decide to be lazy and let Sarah bring it to your room. You can eat delicious dinner here too, perhaps after some hearty walking on the Wye Downs with its magnificent Chalk Crown and far-reaching views to Dungeness and the coast. *Babies welcome but cot not available.*

🧳 Travel Club offer. See page 414.

| Price | £70. Singles £35. |
|---|---|
| Rooms | 1 double. |
| Meals | Dinner, 3 courses, £22.50. Packed lunch £6.50. Pub/restaurant 1 mile. |
| Closed | Rarely. |
| Directions | From M20, junc. 9 Ashford. Follow signs to Wye/Kennington A28. Right for Wye, follow road over level crossing & through village. Up onto downs, then at x-roads left to Canterbury. Hassell Street is 2nd turn on left; house is 4th on left with signed gate. |

| | Sarah Rainbird |
|---|---|
| | Woodmans, |
| | Hassell Street, |
| | Hastingleigh, |
| | Ashford, Kent TN25 5JE |
| Tel | +44 (0)1233 750250 |
| Email | sarah.rainbird@googlemail.com |

👟 🍴 🐾 🐕

Entry 272   Map 5

## Kent

### The Old Rectory

On a really good day (about once every five years) you can see France. But you'll be more than happy to settle for the superb views over Romney Marsh, the Channel in the distance. The big, friendly house, built in 1850, has impeccable, elegant bedrooms and good bathrooms; the large, many-windowed sitting room is full of books, pictures and flowers from the south-facing garden. Marion and David are both charming and can organise transport to Ashford International for you. It's remarkably peaceful – perfect for walking (right on the Saxon Shore path), cycling and birdwatching. *Children over ten welcome.*

| Price | £65–£75. Singles £45. |
|---|---|
| Rooms | 2: 1 twin; 1 twin with separate bath/shower. |
| Meals | Pubs within 4 miles. |
| Closed | Christmas & New Year. |
| Directions | M20, exit 10 for Brenzett & Hastings on A2070. After 6 miles, right for Hamstreet; immed. left; in Hamstreet, left B2067. After 1.5 miles, left (Ash Hill); 700 yds on right. |

| | Marion & David Hanbury |
|---|---|
| | The Old Rectory, |
| | Ruckinge, |
| | Ashford, Kent TN26 2PE |
| Tel | +44 (0)1233 732328 |
| Email | oldrectory@hotmail.com |
| Web | www.oldrectoryruckinge.co.uk |

🍴 🚂 📶 🐕 🌂

Entry 273   Map 5

# Kent

## West Winchet

Annie has got hospitality down to a fine art: homemade compotes and scrumptious rashers at breakfast, the run of the gardens, treats in your room. The house is spotless but infectiously informal, the Parkers are great company and Annie is a treasure. Light, bright, ground-floor bedrooms are in the post-Edwardian wing, one opening to the terraced lawns; all is polished, nothing looks out of place: floral fabrics, soft carpeting, fresh flowers. Breakfast in the splendid drawing room with huge windows – or in bed. Beautifully, traditionally English. *Children over five welcome. Minimum stay two nights at weekends in summer.*

| | |
|---|---|
| Price | From £80. Singles from £55. |
| Rooms | 2: 1 double, 1 twin. |
| Meals | Pubs 2 miles. |
| Closed | Christmas & New Year. |
| Directions | A262 to Goudhurst. There, B2079 to Marden. House 2.5 miles from village, on left. |

Annie Parker
West Winchet,
Winchet Hill, Goudhurst,
Cranbrook, Kent TN17 1JX
Tel    +44 (0)1580 212024
Fax    +44 (0)1580 212250
Email    annieparker@jpa-ltd.co.uk
Web    www.westwinchet.co.uk

Entry 274   Map 5

# Kent

## Lamberden Cottage

Down a farm track find two 1780 cottages knocked into one, with flagstone floors, a cheery wood-burner in the guest sitting room and welcoming Beverley and Branton. There's a traditional country cottage feel with pale walls, thick oak beams, soft carpeting and very comfortable bedrooms (the twin has a child's bedroom adjoining); views from all are across the Weald of Kent. Wander the lovely gardens to find your own private spot, sip a sundowner on the terrace, eat well in the family dining room on home-grown vegetables and fruit. Near to Sissinghurst, Great Dixter and many historic places.

| | |
|---|---|
| Price | From £65. Singles from £50. |
| Rooms | 2: 1 double, 1 twin (twin has adjoining room for children). |
| Meals | Dinner, 2 courses, £20. Pub/restaurant 0.75 miles. |
| Closed | Christmas & New Year. |
| Directions | From Tenterden A28 to Hastings. 2.5 miles Rolvenden. 2.5 miles to junction. Å268 right to Sandhurst. 300 yds Sandhurst sign on left. 20 yds right down farm track. House 80 yds on left. |

Beverley & Branton Screeton
Lamberden Cottage,
Rye Road,
Sandhurst,
Cranbrook, Kent TN18 5PH
Tel    +44 (0)1580 850743
Email    thewalledgarden@lamberdencottage.co.uk
Web    www.lamberdencottage.co.uk

Entry 275   Map 5

# Kent

## Ramsden Farm

A truly interesting, calm and comfortable house, with south-facing views across the Wealds; charming Sally has renovated these former farm buildings with flair. Unhurried breakfasts are eaten in the huge kitchen with a lemon-coloured Aga and floor to ceiling glass doors opening on to a wooden deck; spill outside on jolly days. After a hearty walk you can doze in front of a tree-devouring inglenook, but your bedroom is lovely too: find sunny, bright rooms with more of that view from each, tip-top mattresses, hand embroidered duvet covers and sparkling bathrooms with Travertine marble and underfloor heating. Spoiling.

 Travel Club offer. See page 414.

| | |
|---|---|
| Price | From £75. |
| Rooms | 3: 1 double, 1 twin; 1 double with separate bath. |
| Meals | Pub 1 mile. |
| Closed | Rarely. |
| Directions | From Benenden on B2086 towards Rolvenden, Dingleden Lane on right after 1 mile. House is 3rd on left. |

Sally Harrington
Ramsden Farm,
Dingleden Lane,
Beneden, Kent TN17 4JT
Tel     +44 (0)1580 240203
Email   sally@ramsdenfarmcottage.co.uk
Web    www.ramsdenfarmcottage.co.uk

Entry 276   Map 5

# Kent

## Pullington Barn

Up a private drive and straight in to a vast, beamed expanse of bright light, warm colours, beautiful pictures and a cheery welcome from Gavin and Anne in their converted barn. There are endless books to choose: settle in the comfortable drawing room with its grand piano. Or sit in the pretty south-facing garden on a fine day; on the other side, views from the orchard spread over oast houses and church spires. Bedrooms (one on the ground floor) are both a good size with comfortable mattresses, co-ordinated bed linen and feather pillows. You breakfast soundly on local goodies; stride out for lovely country walks from the door.

| | |
|---|---|
| Price | From £72. Singles £45. |
| Rooms | 2: 1 double, 1 twin. |
| Meals | Pub/restaurant 0.5 miles. |
| Closed | Christmas. |
| Directions | A228 out of Tunbridge Wells. A21 to The Weald Garden of England roundabout. A262 to Sissinghurst. Right to Benenden |

Gavin & Anne Wetton
Pullington Barn,
Benenden,
Kent TN17 4EH
Tel     +44 (0)1580 240246
Email   anne@wetton.info
Web    www.wetton.info/bandb

Entry 277   Map 5

# Kent

## Barclay Farmhouse

Lynn's breakfasts are fabulous: fresh fruits, warm croissants, banana bread, eggs en cocotte. The weatherboarded guest barn may be in perfect trim but has a been-here-forever feel; you have a country-cosy dining room for breakfast or playing cards, a patio for summer, a big peaceful garden, a bird-happy pond. Gleaming bedrooms have brocade bedspreads, French oak furniture, chocolates, slippers, flat-screen TVs; shower rooms are in perfect order. Couples, honeymooners, garden lovers – many would love it here (but no children: the pond is deep). Warm-hearted B&B, and glorious Sissinghurst nearby. *Minimum stay two nights at weekends in high season.*

Travel Club offer. See page 414.

| | |
|---|---|
| Price | £80. Singles from £60. |
| Rooms | Barn: 3 doubles. |
| Meals | Pubs/restaurants 1 mile. |
| Closed | Rarely. |
| Directions | From Biddenden centre, south on A262: Tenterden road. 0.7 miles, bear right (signed Par3 Golf, Vineyard & Benenden). Immed. on right. |

|  | Lynn Ruse |
|---|---|
| | Barclay Farmhouse, |
| | Woolpack Corner, |
| | Biddenden, Kent TN27 8BQ |
| Tel | +44 (0)1580 292626 |
| Fax | +44 (0)1580 292288 |
| Email | info@barclayfarmhouse.co.uk |
| Web | www.barclayfarmhouse.co.uk |

Entry 278   Map 5

# Kent

## 22 Lansdowne Road

Built in 1861, the house in leafy Tunbridge Wells "has never been as Victorian as it is now". So says Harold, whose devotion to Victoriana knows no bounds. Deep colours, rich velvets, marble tables, authentic wallpapers, tasselled lamps, portraits of Queen Vic, tea and scones by the fire... be prepared to take a serious step back in time. Bedrooms are simple in comparison: ruched chintz in the ground-floor double, damask in the twin below – and a door to the conservatory. Bathrooms have large mirrors and brand new fittings, breakfast is a locally sourced spread. Those in search of heritage will marvel. *Off-road parking.*

Travel Club offer. See page 414.

| | |
|---|---|
| Price | £80–£120. Singles £80. |
| Rooms | 3: 1 double, 1 twin/double; 1 studio with separate wc. |
| Meals | Dinner, 2 courses, £20. Pubs/restaurants within 5-minute walk. |
| Closed | January. |
| Directions | From A21 to Tonbridge A26 to T. Wells centre. Grosvenor Rd one way system turn left onto Victoria Rd. Onto Garden Rd turn right onto Lansdowne Rd. |

|  | Harold Brown |
|---|---|
| | 22 Lansdowne Road, |
| | Tunbridge Wells, |
| | Kent TN1 2NJ |
| Tel | +44 (0)1892 533633 |
| Email | haroldmbrown@hotmail.com |

Entry 279   Map 5

# Kent

## Swan Cottage

A delightful Georgian townhouse in Tunbridge Wells, just near the Pantiles with its covered walkways between shops, coffee houses and spas. Your genial host is an artist, his studio can be seen through the glass wall in the open-plan dining room and his engaging pen and ink drawings dot every wall. Bedrooms have plenty of space, are comfortable and contemporary with big sash windows and fresh flowers; bathrooms are roomy, light and white, one with rooftop views. In summer there's a little patio for local sausages and eggs at a pink table under the magnolia tree. And the High Street is at the bottom of the road.

Travel Club offer. See page 414.

| | |
|---|---|
| Price | £80. Singles £50. |
| Rooms | 2: 1 twin/double; 1 single with separate bath. |
| Meals | Pubs/restaurants 200 yds. |
| Closed | Rarely. |
| Directions | From railway station follow High Street for 300 yds, left up Little Mt Sion. House faces you at top of hill. Parking to left of house. |

David Gurdon
Swan Cottage,
17 Warwick Road, Tunbridge Wells,
Kent TN1 1YL

| | |
|---|---|
| Tel | +44 (0)1892 525910 |
| Email | swancot@btinternet.com |
| Web | www.swancottage.co.uk |

Entry 280    Map 5

# Kent

## 40 York Road

A smart Regency townhouse, slap bang in the centre of Royal Tunbridge Wells and a five-minute walk from the delightfully preserved Pantiles. Patricia will enjoy cooking for you – in another life she served up delights for hungry skiers coming off the French mountains. She is a gentle presence and leaves you to come and go as you please; guests have a comfortable sitting room and bright, spotless bedrooms that are quieter than you may think. In the summer you may breakfast outside in the pretty courtyard garden before wandering into town for the cluster of great little shops and restaurants. *Children over 12 welcome.*

Travel Club offer. See page 414.

| | |
|---|---|
| Price | From £70. Singles from £40. |
| Rooms | 2 twins/doubles. |
| Meals | Dinner, 4 courses with wine, £25. Picnic available. Pub/restaurant nearby. |
| Closed | 23 December–2 January. |
| Directions | From M25 junc. 5 onto A21, then A26 through Southborough to Tunbridge Wells. Take sign for Lewes, incline left taking 4th road left. Halfway along, on left. Car parks nearby, from £3.50 per 24 hours. |

Patricia Lobo
40 York Road,
Tunbridge Wells,
Kent TN1 1JY

| | |
|---|---|
| Tel | +44 (0)1892 531342 |
| Email | yorkrd@uwclub.net |
| Web | www.yorkroad.co.uk |

Entry 281    Map 5

# Kent

## Charcott Farmhouse

The 1750 tile-hung brick farmhouse is very much a family home, so don't come expecting a sterile, immaculate environment and you should love it here. You share a pretty sitting room in the old bakehouse with the original beams and bread oven, and bedrooms are simple and fresh, with traditional fabrics and country views. Ginny is charming and Nicholas – a tad eccentric for some – is highly knowledgeable about the area and a brilliant chef. Breakfast is an unrushed, happy affair with heaps of homemade bread and marmalade and free-range eggs from the family flock. Best of all, you can come and go as you please.

Travel Club offer. See page 414.

| | |
|---|---|
| Price | From £65. Singles from £50. |
| Rooms | 3: 2 twins; 1 twin with separate bath. |
| Meals | Pub 5-minute walk. |
| Closed | Rarely. |
| Directions | B2027 0.5 miles north of Chiddingstone Causeway. Equidistant between Tonbridge & Edenbridge. Look for signs to Greyhound pub. |

Nicholas & Ginny Morris
Charcott Farmhouse,
Charcott, Leigh,
Tonbridge,
Kent TN11 8LG
Tel      +44 (0)1892 870024
Email   charcottfarmhouse@btinternet.com

Entry 282   Map 5

# Kent

## Merzie Meadows

You get your own suite in this modern, ranch-style house with huge windows, pergolas groaning with climbers, and a mediterranean-style swimming pool in the twittering garden. Pamela is just as light and bright: she keeps horses and hens and gives you locally sourced breakfasts. Your bedroom has a contemporary, uncluttered feel and is beautifully dressed in pale colours with pretty fabrics and a super bed, your own sitting room looks out onto the garden and the bathroom is sleek with Italian marble and plump towels. All is quiet and calm; garden and nature lovers will adore it here. *Minimum stay two nights April-September.*

Travel Club offer. See page 414.

| | |
|---|---|
| Price | £85-£95. |
| Rooms | 1 suite. |
| Meals | Pub 2.5 miles. |
| Closed | Mid-December to mid-February. |
| Directions | A229 Maidstone to Hastings road, then B2079 for Marden. 1st right into Underlyn Lane, 2.5 miles, large Chainhurst sign, right onto drive. |

Pamela Mumford
Merzie Meadows,
Hunton Road, Marden,
Maidstone, Kent TN12 9SL
Tel      +44 (0)1622 820500
Fax      +44 (0)1622 820500
Email   pamela@merziemeadows.co.uk
Web      www.merziemeadows.co.uk

Entry 283   Map 5

## Reason Hill

Brian and Antonia's 200-acre fruit farm is perched on the edge of the Weald of Kent, with stunning views over orchards and oast houses. The farmhouse has 17th-century origins (low ceilings, wonky floors, stone flags) and a conservatory for sunny breakfasts; colours are soft, antiques gleam and the mood is relaxed. The roomy double has a bay window and armchairs, the pretty twin looks over the garden. Come in spring for the blossom, summer for the fresh fruit and veg from the garden and anytime for a break – the Greensand Way runs along the bottom of the farm, you are close to Sissinghurst Castle and 45 minutes from the Channel Tunnel.

| | |
|---|---|
| Price | £75. |
| Rooms | 3: 1 double; 1 twin with separate shower, 1 single sharing shower (let to same party only). |
| Meals | Pubs within 3 miles. |
| Closed | Christmas & New Year. |
| Directions | From Maidstone A229 for Hastings. After 4.5 miles, right at lights on B2163. In Coxheath, left up Westerhill Rd, 0.2 miles then right into private road. Leave large white house on left, follow road through fruit trees to Reason Hill. |

| | |
|---|---|
| | Brian & Antonia Allfrey |
| | Reason Hill, |
| | Linton, |
| | Maidstone, Kent ME17 4BT |
| Tel | +44 (0)1622 743679 |
| Email | antonia@allfrey.net |
| Web | www.reasonhill.co.uk |

Entry 284   Map 5

## The Limes

A three-minute motor from 'the loveliest castle in the world' (magnificent Leeds, on two islands) is a well-renovated, oak-beamed, inglenook'd and thoroughly refurbished Wealdon hall house overlooking the village green. Your hostess greets you with a lovely bright smile and ushers you in to an immaculate interior traditionally decorated with a crisp, modern slant – and bedrooms that delight in fine fabrics and bedding. (Sonia has her own bed linen business so you are assured of the best.) The breakfast buffet is equally splendid: fresh, organic, and served, on warm days, on the sun-trap terrace.

Travel Club offer. See page 414.

| | |
|---|---|
| Price | From £90. Singles from £75. |
| Rooms | 2 doubles. |
| Meals | Pubs/restaurant a short walk. |
| Closed | Christmas & New Year. |
| Directions | M20 exit 7 for Maidstone. At 2nd r'bout, signs for Bearsted. Past railway station on left, past shops. 50 yds on left overlooking green. |

| | |
|---|---|
| | Sonia Ashdown |
| | The Limes, |
| | The Green, Bearsted, |
| | Maidstone, Kent ME14 4DR |
| Tel | +44 (0)1622 730908 |
| Email | info@limesonthegreen.co.uk |
| Web | www.limesonthegreen.co.uk |

Entry 285   Map 5

# Lancashire

## Challan Hall

The wind in the trees, the boom of a bittern and birdsong. That's about as noisy as it gets. On the edge of the village, the Victorian former farmhouse overlooks fields, woods and Lake Haweswater. Deer, squirrels and Leighton Moss Nature Reserve are your neighbours. The Cassons are well-travelled and the house is filled with a colourful mish-mash of mementos. Comfortably traditional, there's a sofa-strewn sitting room, a smart red and polished-wood dining room and two cosily floral bedrooms. Morecambe Bay and the Lakes are on the doorstep – come back for peaceful views and stunning sunsets.

| | |
|---|---|
| Price | £70. Singles from £40. |
| Rooms | 2: 1 twin/double; 1 twin/double with separate bath. |
| Meals | Packed lunch available. Pubs 1 mile. |
| Closed | Rarely. |
| Directions | M6 exit 35 to Carnforth, past railway station to Warton. Turn left signed Silverdale. After 2.5 miles T-junction, turn right, past golf club on left. Further 1 mile, house on right. |

**Mrs Charlotte Casson**
Challan Hall,
Silverdale, Lancashire LA5 0UH
Tel      +44 (0)1524 701054
Fax      +44 (0)1524 701054
Email    cassons@btopenworld.com
Web      www.challanhall.co.uk

Entry 286   Map 11

# Lancashire

## Northwood

A super stretch of golden beach with sand dunes is just across the road and delightful Lytham is a couple of miles away. The Victorian façade conceals light, lofty rooms mixing vintage and modern; bold wallpaper on odd walls, huge displays of flowers, original artwork. Your hosts happily find babysitters, advise on restaurants (then drive you there) and offer you maple syrup pancakes at breakfast, along with other treats. Bedrooms are generous: find coir carpets, baskets of plump blankets and towels, lovely colours and DVDs to watch on wet days. The whole place has an informal, warm and happy family vibe.

 Travel Club offer. See page 414.

| | |
|---|---|
| Price | £80. Family £90. Singles from £75. |
| Rooms | 2: 1 double, 1 double/family room. |
| Meals | Restaurants 5-minute walk. |
| Closed | Christmas & New Year. |
| Directions | M6 exit 32 then M55 to Blackpool. Follow signs for Lytham St Annes then St Annes. Head for the promenade. |

**Shannon Kuspira**
Northwood,
24 North Promenade, St Annes on Sea,
Lancashire FY8 2NQ
Tel      +44 (0)1253 782356
Email    skuspira@hotmail.com
Web      www.24northwood.co.uk

Entry 287   Map 11

# Lancashire

## Sagar Fold House

Helen transformed this 17th-century dairy and created two perfect studio apartments, self contained, all mod cons, very here and now. Your own entrance leads to large, beamed spaces that bring together comfort, immaculate efficiency and unusual beauty. There are books, DVDs, and comfortable sofas to curl up on; continental breakfast is supplied, using homemade, organic or local produce whenever possible. Now gaze over the Italian knot garden, which ties in lines of a lovely landscape. Take wonderful walks in deeply peaceful countryside, and it's not far to top-notch places to eat.

# Lancashire

## Peter Barn Country House

Wild deer roam – this is the Ribble Valley, an AONB that feels like a time-locked land. In this former 18th-century tithe barn, where old church rafters support the big yet cosy guest sitting room, you settle in among plump sofas, log fire and flat-screen TV. Bedrooms, too, are on the top floor – nicely private. The Smiths couldn't be more helpful and breakfast is a feast: jams and muesli are homemade, stewed fruits are from the gardens. Step outside: Jean has transformed a field into a riot of colour and scent, there are pretty corners, a meandering stream and water lilies bask in still pools. *Minimum stay two nights.*

 Travel Club offer. See page 414.

| | |
|---|---|
| Price | £80. |
| Rooms | 2: 1 double, 1 studio both with kitchenette. |
| Meals | Continental breakfast in fridge. Pubs/restaurants 1-2 miles. |
| Closed | Rarely. |
| Directions | A59 through centre of Whalley. At 2nd mini r'bout left to Mitton; 3 miles, Three Fishes pub on left. Right to Whitewell Chaigely; 1 mile, left to Whitewell Chaigely; 0.5 miles, 3rd drive left to house. |

Helen & John Cook
Sagar Fold House,
Higher Hodder,
Clitheroe,
Lancashire BB7 3LW
Tel +44 (0)1254 826844
Email cookj@thomas-cook.co.uk

Entry 288  Map 12

| | |
|---|---|
| Price | £64-£68. Singles £38. |
| Rooms | 3: 1 double, 1 twin/double; 1 double with separate bath. |
| Meals | Restaurants/pubs 1.5 miles. |
| Closed | Christmas & New Year. |
| Directions | M6 junc. 31, A59 to Clitheroe. Through Clitheroe to Waddington. Through village 0.5 miles, left on Cross Lane for 0.75 miles, past Colthurst Hall, house on left. |

Jean & Gordon Smith
Peter Barn Country House,
Cross Lane/Rabbit Lane,
Waddington, Clitheroe,
Lancashire BB7 3JH
Tel +44 (0)1200 428585
Email jean@peterbarn.co.uk
Web www.peterbarn.co.uk

Entry 289  Map 12

## Leicestershire

### The Gorse House

Passing cars are less frequent than passing horses – this is a peaceful spot in a pretty village. The lasting impression of this 17th-century cottage is of lightness, brightness and space. There's a fine collection of paintings and furniture, everything gleams and oak doors lead from dining room to guest sitting room. Country style bedrooms are fresh, the largest with three views. The garden was designed by Bunny Guinness, the stables accommodate up to six horses and it's strolling distance to a good pub dinner. The house is filled with laughter and the Cowdells are terrific hosts who absolutely love having guests to stay.

## Leicestershire

### White House Fields Farm

A house with a very pretty front – Georgian with a leaded porch and sash windows – but you arrive at the back, past rather modern farm buildings. You have your own entrance from the courtyard garden into a light, beamed bedroom – painted a cheerful yellow, brightened with fresh flowers and soothing with linen and goose down. This is a comfortable, lived-in farm with no pretensions – but Charlotte gives you very special food indeed, either a smart affair in the dining room or a kitchen supper with her young family. Very convenient for Donington race track and East Midlands Airport, yet peaceful.

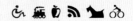 Travel Club offer. See page 414.

| Price | From £60. Singles £32.50. |
|---|---|
| Rooms | 3: 1 double, 1 family for 3. Stable: 1 triple & kitchenette. |
| Meals | Packed lunch £5. Pub 75 yds. |
| Closed | Rarely. |
| Directions | From A46 Newark-Leicester; B676 for Melton. At x-roads, straight for 1 mile; right to Grimston. There, up hill, past church. House on left, just after right-hand bend at top. |

| Price | £85-£90. Singles £60-£65. |
|---|---|
| Rooms | 1 double. |
| Meals | Dinner, 3 courses with coffee & wine, £25. Pub/restaurant 0.5 miles. |
| Closed | Christmas & New Year. |
| Directions | M1 junc. 23a. Head towards East Midlands Airport, follow signs to Breedon on the Hill. Left signed Worthington. House 0.5 miles on right. |

Mr & Mrs R L Cowdell
The Gorse House,
33 Main Street, Grimston,
Melton Mowbray,
Leicestershire LE14 3BZ

| Tel | +44 (0)1664 813537 |
| Email | cowdell@gorsehouse.co.uk |
| Web | www.gorsehouse.co.uk |

Mrs Charlotte Meynell
White House Fields Farm,
Worthington, Ashby de la Zouch,
Leicestershire LE65 1RA

| Tel | +44 (0)1332 862312 |
| Fax | +44 (0)1332 863827 |
| Email | charlottemeynell@btinternet.com |
| Web | www.whff.co.uk |

Entry 290  Map 9

Entry 291  Map 8

# Leicestershire

## Curtain Cottage

A pretty village setting for this cottage on the main street, next door to Sarah's interior design shop. You have your own entrance by the side and through a large garden, which backs onto fields with horses and the National Forest beyond. A conservatory is your sitting room: wicker armchairs, wooden floors, a contemporary take on the country look. Bedrooms are light and fresh, linen from The White Company on sumptuous beds, a slate-tiled bathroom, stunning fabrics. Breakfast is anything, anytime, full English or fresh fruit and croissants from the local shop – all is delivered to you. Perfect privacy.

# Leicestershire

## The Grange

Behind the mellow brick exterior (Queen Anne in front, Georgian at the back) is a warm family home. Log fires brighten chilly days and you are greeted with kindness and generosity by Mary and Shaun, whose young family includes two sweet dogs. Big, beautifully quiet bedrooms, one in the attic, are hung with strikingly unusual wallpapers and furnished with excellent beds and pretty antiques, bathrooms are simple yet impeccable and there's a fireplace in the big, flagstoned hall decorated with sporting prints and deeds. The garden has a treehouse and is large enough to roam.

 Travel Club offer. See page 414.

| | |
|---|---|
| Price | £80. Singles £55. |
| Rooms | 2: 1 double, 1 twin. |
| Meals | Pubs/restaurants 150 yds. |
| Closed | Rarely. |
| Directions | Gravel driveway to left of Barkers Interiors Design Showroom on Main Street. From car park, access to cottage via gate into garden at rear of showroom. |

| | |
|---|---|
| Price | £70. Singles £45. |
| Rooms | 2: 1 twin, 1 double. |
| Meals | Pubs/restaurants 0.5-1.5 miles. |
| Closed | Christmas & New Year. |
| Directions | M1 exit 20; A4304 towards Market Harborough. First left after Walcote marked 'Gt Central Cycle Ride'; 2 miles, then right into Kimcote, pass church on left. On right after Poultney Lane. |

| | |
|---|---|
| | Sarah Barker |
| | Curtain Cottage, |
| | 92-94 Main Street, Woodhouse Eaves, |
| | Leicestershire LE12 8RZ |
| Tel | +44 (0)1509 891361 |
| Fax | +44 (0)1509 890100 |
| Email | sarah@curtaincottage.co.uk |
| Web | www.curtaincottage.co.uk |

| | |
|---|---|
| | Shaun & Mary Mackaness |
| | The Grange, |
| | Kimcote, |
| | Leicestershire LE17 5RU |
| Tel | +44 (0)1455 203155 |
| Email | shaunandmarymac@hotmail.com |
| Web | www.thegrangekimcote.co.uk |

Entry 292  Map 8

Entry 293  Map 8

# Lincolnshire

## 1 Waterhills Court

Follow a lane from Caistor's marketplace to this contemporary townhouse, a haven of comfort for those trekking the Viking Way. Built into the eaves on the second floor, your suite is a seductively large and airy space with crisp white walls, wooden blinds and clever plays on lighting – with power jets in the bathroom to invigorate aching limbs. Vivacious Suzy, a therapist and yoga teacher, treats you to an organic English breakfast in the wood-floored kitchen, bright with the works of her art student daughter. Restorative B&B in the Lincolnshire Wolds – yet minutes from Humberside airport. Great value, too.

| | |
|---|---|
| Price | £60-£70. Singles £45-£50. |
| Rooms | 1 suite for 2-4. |
| Meals | Pub/restaurant 170 yds. |
| Closed | Occasionally. |
| Directions | From A46, turn into Caistor sign. In Caistor go through market place, left towards Brigg. Then 1st right into North Street. House 150 yds on left. |

|  | Suzy Walgate |
|---|---|
| | 1 Waterhills Court, |
| | North Street, |
| | Caistor, |
| | Lincolnshire LN7 6QW |
| Mobile | +44 (0)7876 466989 |
| Email | suzy@waterhills.org |

✗ 🚂 📶 🐈

Entry 294   Map 13

# Lincolnshire

## The Old Farm House

Hidden in the Lincolnshire Wolds, an 18th-century, ivy-covered house – and Nicola's father still farms the fields beyond the ha-ha. The stone-flagged, terracotta-washed hall gives a hint of warm colours to come; creamy walls show off tawny fabrics, prints and antiques; the beamed sitting/breakfast room has a big, rosy brick inglenook fireplace and tranquil views. Such a welcoming, tucked-away place, hopping with pheasant but just a 10-15-minute drive from shops, golf and racing in the nearby towns. Excellent value, and perfect if you fancy privacy and space. *Children over eight welcome.*

| | |
|---|---|
| Price | £70. Singles £50. |
| Rooms | 2: 1 double; 1 triple with separate bath. |
| Meals | Pub 2 miles. |
| Closed | Christmas, New Year & occasionally. |
| Directions | M180 exit 5; A18 signed Louth. Past airport; 2.5 miles after junction of A46 take right signed Hatcliffe. House is third on right, before village. |

|  | Nicola Clarke |
|---|---|
| | The Old Farm House, |
| | Low Road, Hatcliffe, |
| | Lincolnshire DN37 0SH |
| Tel | +44 (0)1472 824455 |
| Email | clarky.hatcliffe@btinternet.com |
| Web | www.oldfarmhousebandbgrimsby.co.uk |

✗ 🐈 ♿

Entry 295   Map 13

## Lincolnshire

### Knaith Hall

This intriguing place, medieval church at its gate, dates from the 16th century. Lawns slope down to the river Trent, daffodils, lambs, a passing barge and waterfowl pattern the serenity. And the skyscapes are terrific! At night, a distant power station shines, actually enhancing that 'great rurality of taste' referred to in Pevsner. Indoors, diamond-paned windows, a domed dining room and fine furniture are softened by easy décor and a log fire. An appealing family house, with a relaxed atmosphere. Your own room is comfortable and restful with the very best of old-fashioned bedding.

 Travel Club offer. See page 414.

| Price | From £70. Singles £40. |
|---|---|
| Rooms | 2: 1 double with separate shower, 1 twin with separate bath. |
| Meals | Dinner, 3 courses with wine, £20. Pub 4 miles. |
| Closed | Rarely. |
| Directions | Knaith 3 miles south of Gainsborough on A156 Lincoln to Gainsborough road. After Knaith signs, look for white gateposts on west side with sign for St Mary's Church. |

**John & Rosie Burke**
Knaith Hall,
Knaith, Gainsborough,
Lincolnshire DN21 5PE

Tel     +44 (0)1427 613005
Fax    +44 (0)1427 613005
Email   jandrburke@aol.com

Entry 296   Map 9

## Lincolnshire

### The Manor House

One guest's summing up reads: "Absolutely perfect – hostess, house, garden and marmalade." Delightful Ann – interested in horses, food, photography, people – makes you feel immediately at home. You have the run of downstairs: all family antiques, fresh flowers and space. Chintzy, carpeted bedrooms have dreamy views of the lovely sweeping gardens and duck-dabbled lake; dinners are adventurous and delicious: game casserole, ginger meringue bombe… Perfect stillness at the base of the Wolds and a pretty one-mile walk along the route of the old railway that starts from the front door. Very special, great value.

| Price | From £70. Singles £50. |
|---|---|
| Rooms | 2: 1 double, 1 twin. |
| Meals | Dinner from £18. BYO. Pub/restaurant 2 miles. |
| Closed | Christmas. |
| Directions | From Wragby A157 for Louth. After approx. 2 miles, at triple road sign, right. Red postbox & bus shelter at drive entrance, before graveyard. |

**Ann Hobbins**
The Manor House,
West Barkwith,
Lincolnshire LN8 5LF

Tel     +44 (0)1673 858253
Fax    +44 (0)1673 858253

Entry 297   Map 9

## Lincolnshire

### The Grange

Wide open Lincolnshire farmland on the edge of the Wolds. This immaculately kept farm has been in the family for five generations; their award-winning farm trail helps you explore. Listen to birdsong, catch the sun setting by the trout lake, have supper before the fire in a dining room whose elegant Georgian windows are generously draped. Sarah is a young and energetic host and offers you delicious homemade cake on arrival. Comfortable bedrooms have spick and span bath or shower rooms and fabulous views that stretch to Lincoln Cathedral. A delightful couple running good farmhouse B&B.

Travel Club offer. See page 414.

| | |
|---|---|
| Price | From £60. Singles £40. |
| Rooms | 2 doubles. |
| Meals | Supper from £15. Dinner, 3 courses, from £18. BYO. (No meals at harvest time.) Pub/restaurant 1 mile. |
| Closed | Christmas & New Year. |
| Directions | Exit A157 in East Barkwith at War Memorial, into Torrington Lane. House 0.75 miles on right after sharp right-hand bend. |

Sarah & Jonathan Stamp
The Grange,
Torrington Lane, East Barkwith,
Lincolnshire LN8 5RY

| | |
|---|---|
| Tel | +44 (0)1673 858670 |
| Email | sarahstamp@farmersweekly.net |
| Web | www.thegrange-lincolnshire.co.uk |

Entry 298   Map 9

## Lincolnshire

### Baumber Park

Lincoln red cows and Longwool sheep surround this attractive rosy-brick farmhouse – once a stud that bred a Derby winner. The old watering pond is now a haven for frogs, newts and toads; birds sing lustily. Maran hens conjure delicious eggs and charming Clare, a botanist, is hugely knowledgeable about the area. Bedrooms are light and traditional, not swish, with mahogany furniture; two have heart-stopping views. Guests have their own wisteria covered entrance, sitting room with a log fire, dining room with local books and the lovely garden to roam. This is good walking, riding and cycling country; seals and rare birds on the coast.

Travel Club offer. See page 414.

| | |
|---|---|
| Price | £62-£66. Singles from £35. |
| Rooms | 3: 2 doubles; 1 twin with separate bath. |
| Meals | Pubs/restaurants 4 miles. |
| Closed | Christmas & New Year. |
| Directions | From A158 in Baumber take road towards Wispington & Bardney. House 300 yds down on right. |

Mike & Clare Harrison
Baumber Park,
Baumber, Horncastle,
Lincolnshire LN9 5NE

| | |
|---|---|
| Tel | +44 (0)1507 578235 |
| Fax | +44 (0)1507 578417 |
| Email | mail@baumberpark.com |
| Web | www.baumberpark.com |

Entry 299   Map 9

## Lincolnshire

### Ryelands House

Farmer Mike and charming Caroline built this large red-brick and slate house on their land and are much committed to the Countryside Stewardship programme; hang out of your bedroom window to watch waders, even deer, round the nearby pond. Inside is warm with underfloor heating, and spacious. Your bedroom has a boutique hotel feel in shades of cream and brown, while two beautifully-lit sitting rooms are smoothly uncluttered and have comfortable armchairs. Pedal along those lovely flat lanes after breakfast, head to Lincoln and its cathedral or Horncastle for antiques; walk to the local pub for excellent bar food.

| | |
|---|---|
| Price | From £65. Singles from £40. |
| Rooms | 1 twin/double & sitting room. |
| Meals | Packed lunch from £2.50. Restaurant 0.5 miles. |
| Closed | Christmas, New Year & occasionally. |
| Directions | A15 Lincoln for Sleaford. Left at Mere onto B1178 for 3 miles; over staggered x-roads into Potterhanworth. At T-junc. right for 100 yds to War Memorial; left onto Barff Rd, 0.5 miles, driveway on left. |

Michael & Caroline Norcross
Ryelands House,
Barff Road,
Potterhanworth,
Lincoln, Lincolnshire LN4 2DU
Tel      +44 (0)1522 793563
Email    norcross@ukfarming.co.uk
Web      www.ryelands-house.co.uk

Entry 300    Map 9

## Lincolnshire

### Brills Farm

There aren't many hills in Lincolnshire, but Sophie and Charlie's early Georgian farmhouse is at the top of one of them. Built of warm brick, near a Roman settlement site, it shines with country elegance and charm, subtle colours and antique furniture. The drawing and dining rooms, filled with fresh flowers, overlook the valley, the beautiful, airy bedrooms have goose down duvets and lovely linen. The Whites are a delightful, young couple with a flourishing family (Sophie is a professional cook and event rider), enthusiastic and hospitable they will give you innovative dinners, and bacon from their own pigs. *Children over 12 welcome.*

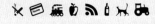
Travel Club offer. See page 414.

| | |
|---|---|
| Price | £82. Singles £51. |
| Rooms | 3: 2 doubles, 1 twin/double. |
| Meals | Supper £15.50. Dinner £25. Packed lunches £8. Pubs 5-minute drive. |
| Closed | Christmas & New Year. |
| Directions | A46 Newark-Lincoln. Exit Brough, Norton Disney & Stapleford. Right at T-junc.; 0.5 miles; 1st left onto lane; 0.75 miles; wide gravel entrance, on right before hill (unsigned). |

Charles & Sophie White
Brills Farm,
Brills Hill,
Norton Disney,
Lincoln, Lincolnshire LN6 9JN
Tel      +44 (0)1636 892311
Email    admin@brillsfarm-bedandbreakfast.co.uk
Web      www.brillsfarm-bedandbreakfast.co.uk

Entry 301    Map 9

## Lincolnshire

### Churchfield House

The little house was built in the sixties; inside glows with character and charm. Bridget is an interior decorator whose eye for detail and sense of fun will delight you. A snug bedroom sports fresh checks in creams and greens, firm mattress, down pillows, interesting pictures, even a gilt-trimmed copy of a Louis XIV chair. The bathroom is small but spotless, and there's a conservatory mood to the warm red, stone-tiled dining room, where glass doors open to a large, lush garden in summer. You're close to a good golf course, Bridget cooks and chats with warmth and humour – this is a gem.

| | |
|---|---|
| Price | £55. Singles £35. |
| Rooms | 1 twin with separate bath. |
| Meals | Dinner from £15. Pubs/restaurants 3 miles. |
| Closed | Christmas & New Year. |
| Directions | A607 Grantham to Lincoln road. On reaching Carlton Scroop, 1st left for Hough Lane. Last house on left. |

**Mrs Bridget Hankinson**
Churchfield House,
Carlton Scroop,
Grantham, Lincolnshire NG32 3BA
Tel    +44 (0)1400 250387
Fax    +44 (0)1400 250241
Email   info@churchfield-house.co.uk
Web    www.churchfield-house.co.uk

Entry 302   Map 9

## Lincolnshire

### Belvoir Vale Cottage

The Vale of Belvoir is gloriously quiet and you are just 200 yards from the Viking Way. Kindly Norman and Suzie have restored two old roadside cottages, charmingly; the emphasis is on warmth, lovely colours, beautifully arranged fresh flowers, good food and gorgeous views over the pretty garden to Belvoir Castle. Bedrooms and bathrooms are a good size and have thick carpets and new windows to let in the sunshine; expect big, comfortable beds, fluffy towels, crisp white linen. Start the day with a full English or undyed haddock with poached eggs; you'll be truly spoiled. *Children welcome if rooms let to one party.*

Travel Club offer. See page 414.

| | |
|---|---|
| Price | £70-£90. Singles from £50. |
| Rooms | 3: 1 twin/double & sitting room; 1 twin/double, 1 double. |
| Meals | Dinner from £25. Packed lunch available. Pubs/restaurants 1.2 miles. |
| Closed | Rarely. |
| Directions | A52 Nottingham-Grantham. At Sedgebrook x-roads, turn for Stenwith & Woolsthorpe. After 1.5 miles cross double bridges - private car park 300 yds. |

**Suzie & Norman Davis**
Belvoir Vale Cottage,
Stenwith,
Woolsthorpe-by-Belvoir, Grantham,
Lincolnshire NG32 2HE
Tel    +44 (0)1949 842434
Email   reservations@belvoirvale-cottage.co.uk
Web    www.belvoirvale-cottage.co.uk

Entry 303   Map 9

# Lincolnshire

### Tanyard House

This 1643 tanner's house is listed and the Knights Templar convened in the cellar. Sloping ceilings, twisting stairs – a completely refurbished house of immense history; enter through a huge oak door into a book and flower filled hall. Claire, full of enthusiasm for guests, gives you a sunny room, overlooking a maturing garden and terrace, with mahogany dining table and generous sofas. One bedroom is in the old part (mullion windows, copse views), one (big and beautiful) in the new. Linen is white and crisp; bathrooms are modern with good soaps. Glamorous chickens roam and provide delicious eggs; expect to be stylishly spoiled.

 Travel Club offer. See page 414.

| | |
|---|---|
| Price | £70. Singles £45. |
| Rooms | 2 twins, each with separate bath/shower. |
| Meals | Occasional dinner, 3 courses, £25; supper, 2 courses, £15. Pubs 0.75 miles. |
| Closed | Rarely. |
| Directions | North on A1, exit after Ram Jam Inn to S. Witham. Or: going south on A1, exit after Fox Inn to S. Witham; enter village, 1st right into Church Lane; 2nd drive on right. |

|  |  |
|---|---|
| | Alex & Claire van Straubenzee |
| | Tanyard House, |
| | South Witham, |
| | Grantham, Lincolnshire NG33 5PL |
| Tel | +44 (0)1572 767976 |
| Fax | +44 (0)1572 767603 |
| Email | tanyardhouse@btinternet.com |
| Web | www.tanyardhouse.co.uk |

Entry 304   Map 9

# Lincolnshire

### The Barn

Simon and Jane, the nicest people, have farmed for 30 years and love having guests to stay. Breakfasts are entirely local or homemade, home-grown and delicious; there are endless extras and nothing is too much trouble. In this light-filled barn conversion find old beams, new walls and good antiques; a brick-flanked fireplace glows and heated floors keep toes warm. Above the high-raftered main living/dining room is a comfy, good-sized double; in the adjoining stables, two further rooms, a crisp feel, sparkling showers, restful privacy. Views are to sheep-dotted fields and the village is on a 25-mile cycle trail.

 Travel Club offer. See page 414.

| | |
|---|---|
| Price | £70. Singles £40. |
| Rooms | 3: 1 double, 1 twin/double; 1 single with separate bath/shower. |
| Meals | Supper, 2 courses, £15. Dinner, 3 courses, £20. BYO. Pub in village & 2 miles. |
| Closed | Rarely. |
| Directions | Midway between Lincoln & Peterborough. From A15, in Folkingham, turn west into Spring Lane next to village hall; 200 yds on right. |

|  |  |
|---|---|
| | **Simon & Jane Wright** |
| | The Barn, |
| | Spring Lane, |
| | Folkingham, Sleaford, |
| | Lincolnshire NG34 0SJ |
| Tel | +44 (0)1529 497199 |
| Email | sjwright@farming.co.uk |
| Web | www.thebarnspringlane.co.uk |

Entry 305   Map 9

# Lincolnshire

## The White House

The wisteria-clad, smart Georgian house is right by the village green in this conservation village. Victoria and David, understandably passionate about the place, have filled the rooms with gorgeous things. Feel free to discover interesting books in the library; admire the fine moulded fireplace and the etchings, the watercolours and the English and Chinese porcelain. The bedrooms, too, are striking, one with an antique four-poster canopied in green silk; bathrooms are fresh and appealing. Your friendly hosts give you afternoon tea in the pretty walled garden in summer, by a roaring fire in winter.

# London

## 6 Oakfield Street

This district dates from the mid-1660s and local historian Simon has maps to prove it; their road is the second smallest in London. Language, art and Egypt lovers, hospitable Margaret and Simon's stylish 1860s house has her beautiful roof mural, and a marble-topped table, in the dining room and a collection of Egyptian prints. There's an open-plan feel to the kitchen, and a roof terrace where you can sit in summer. Bedrooms are at the top of the house: the twin is little but, being at the back, is silent at night; the double has a big wooden bed and an antique armoire. Stroll to restaurants on Hollywood Road.

Travel Club offer. See page 414.

| Price | £70. Singles £45. |
|---|---|
| Rooms | 2: 1 twin/double; 1 four-poster (with adjoining room if required) with separate bath. |
| Meals | Pub/restaurant in village. |
| Closed | Rarely. |
| Directions | A15 to Folkingham; on village green. |

| Price | £80. Singles £60. |
|---|---|
| Rooms | 2: 1 double, 1 twin. |
| Meals | Restaurants nearby. |
| Closed | Occasionally. |
| Directions | Tube: Earl's Court 15-minute walk. Nearest car park £25 for 24 hrs. South Kensington 20-minute walk. |

Victoria & David Strauss
The White House,
25 Market Place,
Folkingham,
Sleaford, Lincolnshire NG34 0SE
Tel     +44 (0)1529 497298
Email   victoria.strauss@btinternet.com
Web     www.bedandbreakfastfolkinghamlincolnshire.co.uk

Margaret & Simon de Maré
6 Oakfield Street,
Little Chelsea,
London SW10 9JB
Tel     +44 (0)20 7352 2970
Email   demare@easynet.co.uk
Web     www.athomeinnchelsea.com

Entry 306   Map 9

Entry 307   Map 22

# London

## 37 Trevor Square

A fabulous find, luxury in the middle of Knightsbridge. The square is impossibly pretty, unexpectedly peaceful and a three-minute walk from Hyde Park or Harrods. Margaret runs an interior design company – rather successfully, by the look of things. You breakfast in the kitchen/diner, by the twinkling fire in winter, and there's a small conservatory you are welcome to use. Bedrooms (one downstairs has an enormous bed and a little patio) have lovely cotton sheets, goose down pillows, cashmere duvets, electric blankets and a mini fridge; slip on your robe, listen to some music or watch a DVD – it's all here.

# London

## 20 Bywater Street

In a quiet, pretty cul-de-sac off the fashionable King's Road, a delightful pastel-coloured house and a welcoming B&B. Caroline and Richard give you a light, quiet bedroom downstairs, with a deep green carpet and a wicker chair, fresh flowers, lots of magazines and books and a digital radio. The private shower room is next door with fluffy towels and good toiletries. Breakfast on freshly squeezed juice, fruit, muesli, croissants, muffins and more across the hall in the kitchen/conservatory, a cheery room that swims in morning sun, with doors opening onto a flower filled Yorkstone patio garden. The best of London laps at the door.

Travel Club offer. See page 414.

| | |
|---|---|
| Price | From £160. Singles £100. |
| Rooms | 3: 1 twin/double; 1 double, 1 twin sharing bath & shower (let to same party only). |
| Meals | Restaurants 200 yds. |
| Closed | Occasionally. |
| Directions | Tube: Knightsbridge. Nearest car park £25 for 24 hrs (closed overnight). |

| | |
|---|---|
| Price | From £99. |
| Rooms | 1 double with separate shower. |
| Meals | Continental breakfast. Pubs/restaurants/cafes nearby. |
| Closed | Occasionally. |
| Directions | Tube: Sloane Square 5-minute walk (down King's Road, 6th street on right). Parking available locally. |

|  | Margaret & Holly Palmer |
|---|---|
| | 37 Trevor Square, |
| | Knightsbridge, London SW7 1DY |
| Tel | +44 (0)20 7823 8186 |
| Fax | +44 (0)20 7823 9801 |
| Email | margaret@37trevorsquare.co.uk |
| Web | www.37trevorsquare.co.uk |

|  | Caroline & Richard Heaton-Watson |
|---|---|
| | 20 Bywater Street, |
| | Chelsea, |
| | London SW3 4XD |
| Tel | +44 (0)20 7581 2222 |
| Email | caheatonw@aol.com |
| Web | www.20bywaterstreet.com |

Entry 308   Map 22

Entry 309   Map 22

# London

## 90 Old Church Street

In a quiet street facing the Chelsea Arts Club, an enticing, contemporary haven. Softly spoken Nina is passionate about the arts, knows Chelsea inside out and takes real pleasure in looking after her guests. Antique shop spoils stand alongside more modern delights, the attention to detail is amazing and there are plentiful bunches of flowers. A lush carpet takes you up to the second floor and your super-private, surprisingly peaceful and deliciously designed bedroom. Breakfast – an array of fresh fruit, yogurts and croissants – is shared with Nina in the kitchen. We love this place.

| Price | From £95. Singles from £80. |
|---|---|
| Rooms | 1 double. |
| Meals | Continental breakfast. Restaurants/coffee shops/pubs nearby. |
| Closed | Occasionally. |
| Directions | Tube: South Kensington. |

Nina Holland
90 Old Church Street,
Chelsea,
London SW3 6EP
Tel  +44 (0)20 7352 4758
Email  ninastcharles@btinternet.com

# London

## 12A Evelyn Mansions

Your passport to Pimlico – one of the last 'villages' left in London with proper shops and a good choice of restaurants. Find comfort and elegance in this Edwardian mansion flat, its lovely drawing room sprinkled with interesting objects from Moranna's travels as the wife of a diplomat – she is a charming hostess. Your bedroom (double glazed) has a great view of the junction between Victoria Street and the station – a people-watcher's paradise – and is spoiling: goose down, easy chairs, good books, a shining white bathroom. It is the perfect city bolthole and good value too.

| Price | £90. Singles £50. |
|---|---|
| Rooms | 1 twin/double with separate bath. |
| Meals | Pubs/restaurants nearby. |
| Closed | Rarely. |
| Directions | 3-minute walk to Victoria bus & tube; 5-minute walk to coach station. Carlisle Place is just off Victoria Street. |

Moranna Colvin
12A Evelyn Mansions,
Carlisle Place,
London SW1P 1NH
Tel  +44 (0)20 7834 1889

# London

## 101 Abbotsbury Road

The area is one of London's most desirable and Sunny's family home is opposite the borough's loveliest park, with open-air opera in summer. The whole top floor is generally given over to visitors. Cosy, spotless bedrooms are in gentle yellows and greens, with pale carpets, white duvets, pelmeted windows and a dressing table in the double. The bathroom, marble-tiled and sky-lit, shines. You are well placed for Kensington High Street, Olympia, Notting Hill, Portobello Market, Kensington Gardens, the Albert Hall, Knightsbridge and Piccadilly. Feel free to come and go. *Children over ten welcome.*

| | |
|---|---|
| Price | From £100. Singles from £55. |
| Rooms | 2: 1 double, 1 single, sharing bath. |
| Meals | Continental breakfast. Pubs/restaurants 5-minute walk. |
| Closed | Occasionally. |
| Directions | Tube: Holland Park 7-minute walk. Off-street parking sometimes available. |

Sunny Murray
101 Abbotsbury Road,
Holland Park,
London W14 8EP
Tel    +44 (0)20 7602 0179
Email  sunny.murray@googlemail.com

Entry 312   Map 22

# London

## 26 Hillgate Place

You are in luxurious, bohemian Notting Hill: a movie at the Coronet, a pint at the Windsor Castle, the best Thai at the Churchill and the chic-est shops. Whatever you do, roll back to Hilary and Maryo's easy-going home for a bit of eastern spice; Indian textiles, old teak dressers, the odd wooden elephant, wildly colourful art (Hilary paints). The bigger double has a Indo-Caribbean influence and shares a bathroom up a flight of stairs; the smaller is smarter – immaculate, actually – with a sofa and a claw-foot bath. Both rooms come with bathrobes and small fridge, and there are two gardens to look out on, one on a roof.

Travel Club offer. See page 414.

| | |
|---|---|
| Price | £80- £98  Singles £70-£80. |
| Rooms | 2: 1 double; 1 double with guest bed sharing family bathroom. |
| Meals | Pubs/restaurants nearby. |
| Closed | Occasionally. |
| Directions | Tube: Notting Hill Gate 5-minute walk. |

Hilary Dunne & Maryo Josef
26 Hillgate Place,
Notting Hill Gate, London W8 7ST
Tel    +44 (0)20 7727 7717
Email  hilary.dunne@virgin.net
Web    www.26hillgateplace.co.uk

Entry 313   Map 22

# London

## 31 Rowan Road

Terrific value for money in Brook Green: two private studios — one under the eaves with a big comfy bed, a window seat, and a bathroom with a deep cast-iron bath from which you can gaze out at the birds — the other (larger, more contemporary in style) on the lower ground floor, with its own wisteria-clad entrance. Continental breakfast is popped into your fridge the night before. Or join in with family life in a pink bedroom with books and hats, and a teenager's bedroom — and take breakfast in the pretty conservatory with Vicky and Edmund. There's a garden full of blossom and super restaurants close by.

| Price | £40-£95. Extra person £10. |
| --- | --- |
| Rooms | 4: 2 doubles with shared bath. Studios: 2 for 2-3, with twin or twin/double & kitchen or kitchenette. |
| Meals | Continental breakfast. Pubs/restaurants 2 minutes. |
| Closed | Occasionally. |
| Directions | Tube: Hammersmith. Off-street parking £15 a day. |

**Vicky & Edmund Sixsmith**
31 Rowan Road,
Brook Green,
Hammersmith, London W6 7DT
Tel        +44 (0)20 8748 0930
Email    vickysixsmith@btconnect.com
Web      www.abetterwaytostay.co.uk

Entry 314   Map 22

# London

## 50a Penywern Road

In a super-central London street, strolling distance from the tube, a luxurious slice of peace. Past pots and down steps to warm, smiling, Irish Breege, who ushers you into a light lower ground-floor space zinging with art and good taste. Off her kitchen is your guest bedroom, roomy, well-lit and inviting. Find a beautifully dressed bed, chrome chairs, a mini fridge, fresh walls splashed with art and a gorgeous shower room, a symphony in white. Steps ascend to a grassy garden where statues peep out of bushes and seats beckon. Boutique B&B that's relaxing and fun — readers sing its praises. *Minimum stay two nights.*

| Price | £85. Singles £70. |
| --- | --- |
| Rooms | 1 double. |
| Meals | Continental breakfast. |
| Closed | Rarely. |
| Directions | Tube: Earl's Court 2-minute walk. Pay & Display parking 8.30-6.30 Mon-Sat. Free at other times in P&D bays & on yellow lines. |

**Breege Collins**
50a Penywern Road,
Earl's Court,
London SW5 9SX
Tel        +44 (0)20 7244 7178
Email    info@breegecollins.com

Entry 315   Map 22

# London

## 21 Barclay Road

The grand piano is a magnet for conductors and music professors from around the world; delightful Charlotte and Adrian host lively social music evenings. Charlotte, who does something unspeakably high-powered by day, happily advises on the best London sites. You pretty much get the run of the house: a large sitting room with an open fire, two tiny but beautifully laid out bedrooms with waffle bathrobes and a decanter of sherry. Breakfast is a feast of homemade apple fritters, fresh fruit salad, the best coffee – eat on the tree-top terrace in summer. Bring your instrument, a great city find. *Use of grand piano by arrangement.*

 Travel Club offer. See page 414.

| | |
|---|---|
| Price | £88. Singles £68. |
| Rooms | 2 doubles sharing guest bathroom. |
| Meals | Food & music evenings occasionally. Restaurants 2-minute walk. |
| Closed | Occasionally. |
| Directions | Tube: Fulham Broadway 2-minute walk. Parking free 8pm-9am & all Sunday. 9am-8pm pay & display. |

|  | **Charlotte Dexter** |
|---|---|
| | 21 Barclay Road, |
| | Fulham, London SW6 1EJ |
| Tel | +44 (0)20 7384 3390 |
| Email | info@barclayhouselondon.com |
| Web | www.barclayhouselondon.com |

Entry 316   Map 22

# London

## 22 Marville Road

Smart railings help a pink rose climb, orange lilies add a touch of colour, and breakfast is in the pretty back garden in good weather. Tess, the spaniel, and Christine – music lover, traveller, rowing coach – make you feel at home. A single on the first floor shares the main bathroom (claw-foot bath, huge shower) with the owner. The spacious room in the eaves comes in elegant French grey and has a chaise longue; it was tested and vacated with regret. Treasures from Christine's travels, gentle music at (continental) breakfast, crisp linen, restaurants and shops a stroll away – and the Boat Race down the river.

 Travel Club offer. See page 414.

| | |
|---|---|
| Price | From £90. Singles from £50. |
| Rooms | 2: 1 twin/double; 1 single with pull-out truckle bed sharing bath/shower. |
| Meals | Occasional dinner. Pubs/restaurants nearby. |
| Closed | Rarely. |
| Directions | At Fulham Rd junc. with Parson's Green Lane, turn down Kelvedon Rd. Cross Bishop Rd into Homestead Rd; 1st left into Marville Rd. |

|  | **Christine Drake** |
|---|---|
| | 22 Marville Road, |
| | Fulham, London SW6 7BD |
| Tel | +44 (0)20 7381 3205 |
| Email | christine.drake@btinternet.com |
| Web | www.londonguestsathome.com |

Entry 317   Map 22

# London

## 15 Delaford Street

A pretty Victorian terraced home, unassuming from the front but with space and charm inside. In a tiny, sun-trapping courtyard you can have continental breakfast in good weather – tropical fruits are a favourite; a second miniature garden bursts with life at the back. The bedroom, up a spiral staircase, looks down on it all. Expect perfectly ironed sheets, a quilted throw, books in the alcove, a sunny bathroom and fluffy white towels. The tennis at Queen's is in June and on your doorstep. Tim and Margot – she's from Melbourne – are fun, helpful and happy to pick you up from the nearest tube.

Travel Club offer. See page 414.

| | |
|---|---|
| Price | £85. Singles £60. |
| Rooms | 1 double. |
| Meals | Restaurants nearby. |
| Closed | Occasionally. |
| Directions | Tube: West Brompton. Parking free eves & weekends; otherwise pay & display. 74 bus to West End nearby. |

**Margot & Tim Woods**
15 Delaford Street,
Fulham,
London SW6 7LT
Tel +44 (0)20 7385 9671
Email woodsmargot@hotmail.co.uk

Entry 318   Map 22

# London

## 8 Parthenia Road

Caroline, an interior designer, mixes the sophistication of the city with the feel of the countryside and her handsome big kitchen is clearly the engine-room of the house. It leads through to a light breakfast room with doors onto a pretty brick garden with chairs and table – hope for fine days. The house is long and thin, Fulham style, and reaches up to a large, sloping-ceilinged bedroom in the eaves that is sunny and bright. A surprisingly quiet place to stay in an accessible part of town, near the King's Road with its antique and designer shops and Chelsea Football ground.

| | |
|---|---|
| Price | £80–£100. Singles from £75. |
| Rooms | 1 twin/double. |
| Meals | Continental breakfast. Restaurants nearby. |
| Closed | Rarely. |
| Directions | Tube: Parsons Green 4-minute walk. Parking £14.40 per day in street. Bus: no. 22, 2-minute walk. |

**Caroline & George Docker**
8 Parthenia Road,
Fulham, London SW6 4BD
Tel +44 (0)20 7384 1165
Fax +44 (0)20 7371 8819
Email carolined@angelwings.co.uk

Entry 319   Map 22

# London

## 39 Brookville Road

You are in the throng of vibrant Fulham with its quirky boutiques and antique shops, and a short walk to the King's Road, but these pretty pastel-coloured terraced houses are remarkably quiet inside. Musical Leah enjoys having guests: you breakfast on a sweet roof terrace with views, or at a long wooden table in the peachy dining room with tapestry chairs. Bedrooms are filled with lovely things: a buddha lamp, an antique walnut table, thick woven bedspreads and original art; beds are dressed well and duvets are duck down. One bathroom has a church arch mirror and the other a large, ornately framed, mirror. Super restaurants are a stroll away. *Children over six welcome.*

| | |
|---|---|
| Price | £80-£90. |
| Rooms | 3: 1 double; 1 double, 1 twin sharing shower. |
| Meals | Pubs/restaurants within 0.25 miles. |
| Closed | Rarely. |
| Directions | Within 5-minute walk of Parsons Green tube station. |

| | |
|---|---|
| | Leah Shellim |
| | 39 Brookville Road, |
| | Parsons Green, London SW6 7BH |
| Tel | +44 (0)20 7381 2093 |
| Email | leah492@btinternet.com |
| Web | www.thevillesbedandbreakfast.co.uk |

Entry 320   Map 22

---

# London

## 20 St Philip Street

Come for peace and undemanding luxury: the 1890 Victorian cottage with delightful courtyard garden protects you from the frenzy of city life. You breakfast in the pretty dining room – the full English works (unusual for London). Across the hall is the sitting room, with gilt-framed mirrors, wooden blinds, plump-cushioned sofas and a piano you are welcome to play. Upstairs is a bright and restful bedroom with pretty linen and a cloud of goose down to snuggle into. Your bathroom next door is fabulous with its porthole windows and huge mirror. Nothing has been overlooked.

| | |
|---|---|
| Price | £100. Singles £75. |
| Rooms | 1 double with separate bath & shower. |
| Meals | Pubs/restaurants 200 yds. |
| Closed | Occasionally. |
| Directions | Nearby r'way stations (6-min ride Waterloo, 3-min ride Victoria). Or 137 & 452 bus (Sloane Sq) & 156 (Vauxhall). Tubes 10 mins. Parking limited to 4 hrs (£1.80 per hr) or £10 day ticket, 9.30-5.30 Mon-Fri. Otherwise free. |

| | |
|---|---|
| | Barbara Graham |
| | 20 St Philip Street, |
| | Battersea, London SW8 3SL |
| Tel | +44 (0)20 7498 9967 |
| Email | stay@bed-breakfast-battersea.co.uk |
| Web | www.bed-breakfast-battersea.co.uk |

Entry 321   Map 22

# London

## 113 Pepys Road

Anne is Chinese, well-travelled, loves this house, loves her guests, and is a trained Cordon Bleu cook; convivial breakfast can be English or oriental. The house overlooks the first landscaped park of its kind in south-east London; at night you see a carpet of lights. There are hats on the hat stand, batiks on the walls, orchids (Anne's passion). The downstairs room has a huge bed, bamboo blinds, a kimono for the bathroom; our favourites are upstairs, airy, bright, overlooking the garden (the magnolias are majestic). It's a ten-minute walk downhill to buses, tubes and trains... and blissfully quiet for London.

Travel Club offer. See page 414.

| | |
|---|---|
| Price | From £100. Singles from £75. |
| Rooms | 3: 1 double, 1 twin/double; 1 twin with separate bath. |
| Meals | Dinner from £35. BYO. Restaurant 0.5 miles. |
| Closed | Rarely. |
| Directions | Directions on booking. |

Anne Marten
113 Pepys Road,
New Cross, London SE14 5SE
Tel    +44 (0)20 7639 1060
Fax    +44 (0)20 7639 8780
Email  annemarten@pepysroad.com
Web    www.pepysroad.com

Entry 322   Map 22

# London

## 24 Fox Hill

This part of London is full of sky, trees and wildlife; Pissarro captured on canvas the view up the hill in 1870 (the painting is in the National Gallery). There's good stuff everywhere – things hang off walls and peep over the tops of dressers; bedrooms are stunning, with antiques, textiles, paintings and big, firm beds. Sue, a graduate from Chelsea Art College, employs humour and intelligence to put guests at ease and has created a special garden, too. Tim often helps with breakfasts. Frogs sing at night, woodpeckers wake you in the morning, in this lofty, peaceful retreat. *Victoria is 20 minutes by train.*

Travel Club offer. See page 414.

| | |
|---|---|
| Price | £90-£100. Singles £50. |
| Rooms | 3: 1 twin/double; 1 double, 1 twin sharing shower. |
| Meals | Dinner £30-£35. Pubs/restaurants 5-minute walk. |
| Closed | Rarely. |
| Directions | Train: Crystal Palace (7-min. walk). Collection possible. Good buses to West End & Westminster. |

Sue & Tim Haigh
24 Fox Hill,
Crystal Palace, London SE19 2XE
Tel    +44 (0)20 8768 0059
Email  suehaigh@hotmail.co.uk
Web    www.foxhill-bandb.co.uk

Entry 323   Map 22

# London

### 28 Old Devonshire Road

Keen gardeners will love it here, in a surprisingly quiet part of Balham close to the leafy common: Georgina's award-winning rectangular plot is brimming with colour and scent. You can take breakfast out here on sunny days, or in the orange dining room with its long wooden table, marble fireplace, and original watercolours. Your bedroom is peaceful and cosy with a brand new bed, fresh flowers from the garden and books about gardening and wildlife – but you also get a flat-screen TV. A very spacious bathroom has a good shower, dressing gowns from Singapore and more interesting art. You are near to a plethora of restaurants. *French & Italian spoken.*

# London

### 108 Streathbourne Road

It's a handsome house in a conservation area that manages to be both elegant and cosy. The cream-coloured double bedroom has an armchair, a writing desk, pretty curtains and a big, comfy walnut bed; the twin is light and airy. The dining room overlooks a secluded terrace and garden and there are newspapers at breakfast. Dine in – David, who works in the wine trade, always puts a bottle on the table – or eat out at one of the trendy new restaurants in Balham. A friendly city base on a quiet, tree-lined street – maximum comfort and good value for London. Delightful. *Minimum stay two nights.*

🧳 Travel Club offer. See page 414.

| | |
|---|---|
| Price | £90. Singles £65. |
| Rooms | 1 double. |
| Meals | Pubs/restaurants 500 yds. |
| Closed | Rarely. |
| Directions | Old Devonshire Road off Balham High Road, which is part of the A24 London to Dorking road. 5-min walk from Balham mainline and tube stations. Visitors' parking permits available £5 per day. |

| | |
|---|---|
| Price | £85–£95. Singles £70–£80. |
| Rooms | 2: 1 double with separate bath; 1 twin sharing bath (let to same party only). |
| Meals | Dinner £30. Restaurants 5-minute walk. |
| Closed | Occasionally. |
| Directions | Tube: Tooting Bec 7-minute walk. 319 bus to Sloane Square. Free parking weekends, otherwise meters or £6 daily. |

|  |  |
|---|---|
| | **Georgina Ivor** |
| | 28 Old Devonshire Road, |
| | Balham, London SW12 9RB |
| Tel | +44 (0)20 8673 7179 |
| Fax | +44 (0)20 8675 8058 |
| Email | georgina@balhambandb.co.uk |
| Web | www.balhambandb.co.uk |

|  |  |
|---|---|
| | **Mary & David Hodges** |
| | 108 Streathbourne Road, |
| | Balham, London SW17 8QY |
| Tel | +44 (0)20 8767 6931 |
| Fax | +44 (0)20 8672 8839 |
| Email | mary.hodges@virgin.net |
| Web | www.streathbourneroad.com |

Entry 324   Map 22

Entry 325   Map 22

# London

## The Coach House

A rare privacy: you have your own coach house, separated from the Notts' home by a stylish terracotta-potted courtyard with Indian sandstone paving and various fruit trees (peach, pear, nectarine). Breakfast in your own sunny kitchen, or let Meena treat you to a full English in hers (she makes fine porridge, too). The big main attic bedroom has toile de Jouy bedcovers, cream curtains, rugs on polished wood floors; the brick-walled ground-floor twin is pleasant, light and airy, and both look over the peaceful garden. *Minimum stay three nights; two nights January & February.*

# London

## 52 Becmead Avenue

The house has an Arts and Crafts hall and brims with beautiful pictures, exquisite maps, gorgeous prints: more than just a little style. Peaceful bedrooms have books, original tiled fireplaces, rugs on floors, crisp linen and garden views; this is very much a family home and you breakfast well around a long oak farmhouse table in a big open-plan kitchen/dining room (have a peek at the Italian library on the way). Katherine will cook the full works or you can go continental and have cheese and ham. She also makes her own marmalade, but you'll have to beat Michael to it. A very friendly place with good restaurants nearby.

| | | | |
|---|---|---|---|
| Price | £85–£175. | Price | £80–£90. Singles £40–£50. |
| Rooms | Coach House for 2-5: 1 family room; 1 twin with separate shower. Same-party bookings only. | Rooms | 3: 1 double with separate bath; 1 double, 1 single with separate shared shower. |
| Meals | Pub/restaurant 200 yds. | Meals | Pubs/restaurants within walking distance. |
| Closed | Occasionally. | | |
| Directions | From r'bout on south side of Wandsworth Bridge, south down Trinity Rd on A214. At 3rd set of lights, 1.7 miles on, left into Upper Tooting Park. 4th left into Marius Rd, then 3rd left. | Closed | Occasionally. |
| | | Directions | Train: Streatham (to London Bridge); Streatham Hill (to Victoria).Tube: Brixton (10 minutes by bus).Bus: 57, 133, 159, 319. |

**Meena & Harley Nott**
The Coach House,
2 Tunley Road, Balham,
London SW17 7QJ
Tel       +44 (0)20 8772 1939
Fax       +44 (0)8701 334957
Email     coachhouse@chslondon.com
Web       www.coachhouse.chslondon.com

**Katherine & Michael Thomson-Glover**
52 Becmead Avenue,
Streatham,
London SW16 1UQ
Tel       +44 (0)20 8696 0107
Email     katherinetg@tiscali.co.uk
Web       www.52becmeadavenue.co.uk

# London

## 39 Telford Avenue

A very pretty Edwardian home, a family enclave, with logs piled high at the front door and a fire in the hall on cold afternoons. Warm interiors come with stripped floors, bright colours, fresh flowers and a piano in the dining room. There's a sofa in the homely double bedroom, a wall of good books and an electric pink bathroom two paces across the landing. Breakfast is a treat: homemade bread and yogurt, the full cooked works, a good selection of teas. Richard, an architect, loves his cricket; prints of Lords hang on the walls. You can be in Victoria in 15 minutes, and there's off-street parking, too.

Ethical Collection: Food. See page 412.

| | |
|---|---|
| Price | From £70. Singles from £35. |
| Rooms | 2: 1 twin/double, 1 single each with separate bath. |
| Meals | Restaurants 2-minute walk. |
| Closed | Occasionally. |
| Directions | Train: Streatham Hill (to Victoria) 5-minute walk. Bus from Brixton tube (Victorian line). Or ring on arrival at Clapham South tube (Northern line) & you will be collected. |

Katharine & Richard Wolstenholme
39 Telford Avenue,
Streatham Hill,
London SW2 4XL
Tel      +44 (0)20 8674 4343
Email    rwolstenholme@aol.com

Entry 328   Map 22

# London

## 16 St Alfege Passage

The approach is along the passage between the Hawksmoor church and its graveyard, away from the village's hubbub. At the end of the lane is a 'cottage' set about with greenery, lamp posts and benches. Inside, a cup of tea and flapjack await you in the eccentrically furnished (stuffed cat on dentist chair, huge parasol) sitting room. Bedrooms are cosy and colourful, with double beds (not huge) that positively encourage intimacy. Breakfast is in the basement, another engagingly furnished room awash with character. Robert, an actor, is easy, funny, chatty – and has created an unusual and attractive place.

| | |
|---|---|
| Price | From £90. Singles from £60. |
| Rooms | 3: 1 four-poster, 1 double, 1 single. |
| Meals | Pubs/restaurants 2-minute walk. |
| Closed | Rarely. |
| Directions | 3-minute walk from Greenwich train & Docklands Light Railway station or Cutty Sark DLR station. Parking free from 5pm (6pm Sundays) to 9am. |

Nicholas Mesure & Robert Gray
16 St Alfege Passage,
Greenwich, London SE10 9JS
Tel      +44 (0)20 8853 4337
Email    info@st-alfeges.co.uk
Web      www.st-alfeges.co.uk

Entry 329   Map 22

# London

### 26 Florence Street

There's a dramatic vibrancy to Valerie's home, just off Upper Street with its restaurants, and right by the Almeida and Sadler's Wells theatres. The Victorian house is stuffed with oriental, French and Italian pieces; your basement bedroom is filled with light and character. A feast of beautiful scenes and stories, every angle of Valerie's interior design merits applause: walls, doors and much of the furniture are ragged, sponged and stencilled in the colourful style of the Bloomsbury set; the conservatory has John Soane perspectives and Arabian Nights lanterns, screens and exotic plants. *Children over 12 welcome.*

| Price | From £105. Singles £75. |
|---|---|
| Rooms | 1 double with separate shower (extra single available, so occasional share). |
| Meals | Pubs/restaurants nearby. |
| Closed | Occasionally. |
| Directions | From Highbury & Islington tube, right out of station. Down Upper Street, past Town Hall. Left immed. before Shell garage. Free overnight & weekend parking (Sat 6.30pm); otherwise meters & car parks. |

|  | Valerie Rossmore |
|---|---|
|  | 26 Florence Street, |
|  | Islington, London N1 2FW |
| Tel | +44 (0)20 7359 5293 |
| Email | valerie.rossmore@googlemail.com |
| Web | www.valerierossmore.co.uk |

Entry 330   Map 22

# London

### Arlington Avenue

This 1848 townhouse is a real find – from here you can follow the canal up to Islington. Inside you find a world of books and art: bedrooms are simply furnished and a tad bohemian for some, but filled with pictures, etchings and character, with views over several gardens to the back. The grey marble bathroom might be shared now and then, and is two flights down, but if you don't mind that, you've struck gold. Shop locally, eat picnic suppers in the red and gold dining room, chill drinks in the fridge. You help yourself to breakfast in a lemon coloured country style kitchen; this is laissez-faire B&B and fantastic value.

Travel Club offer. See page 414.

| Price | £45–£55. Singles £40–£45. |
|---|---|
| Rooms | 2: 1 double, 1 single with shared bath. |
| Meals | Pubs/restaurants 100 yds. |
| Closed | Rarely. |
| Directions | Equal distance from Angel and Old Street tubes (15-minute walk). 2 minutes for bus stop to City, St Pauls, Tate Modern (City 5 minutes). 7 minutes to bus stop for West End (West End 20 minutes). Limited parking (by arrangement). |

|  | Thomas Blaikie |
|---|---|
|  | Arlington Avenue, |
|  | Islington, London N1 7AX |
| Mobile | +44 (0)7711 265183 |
| Email | thomas@arlingtonavenue.co.uk |
| Web | www.arlingtonavenue.co.uk |

Entry 331   Map 22

# London

## 66 Camden Square

A modern, architect designed house made of African teak, brick and glass. Climb wooden stairs under a glazed pyramid to light-filled, Japanese-style bedrooms with low platform beds, modern chairs and adjacent sitting room/study. Sue and Rodger have travelled widely so there are pictures, photographs and ethnic pieces everywhere – and a parrot called Peckham. Share their lovely open-plan dining space at breakfast overlooking a bird-filled courtyard or eat outside on warmer days. Camden's bustling market and the zoo are near, and a huge choice of places to eat. *Children by arrangement.*

| | |
|---|---|
| Price | £100–£110. Singles £50–£55. |
| Rooms | 2: 1 double, 1 single sharing bath (2nd room let to same party only). |
| Meals | Pubs/restaurants nearby. |
| Closed | Occasionally. |
| Directions | Tube: Camden Town or Kentish Town. Parking free at weekends; meters during week. 10 minutes by taxi from St Pancras Eurostar Terminal. |

Sue & Rodger Davis
66 Camden Square,
Camden Town,
London NW1 9XD
Tel +44 (0)20 7485 4622
Email rodgerdavis@btopenworld.com

Entry 332   Map 22

# London

## 30 King Henry's Road

Shops, restaurants and sublime views of Primrose Hill are a five-minute stroll from this homely 1860s house; walls are covered in a lifetime collection of watercolours, drawings and maps. Your room on the top floor has a comfortable brass bed, a sisal floor, fine pieces of furniture, a wall of books and digital TV. Breakfast on homemade bread and jams, bagels, croissants, yogurts and fresh fruit salad in the large kitchen/dining room with a big open fire and garden views. There's open-air theatre in Regent's Park in summer; Carole and Ted know London well and will happily advise.

| | |
|---|---|
| Price | £100. Singles £80. |
| Rooms | 1 double. |
| Meals | Pubs/restaurants 2-minute walk. |
| Closed | Occasionally. |
| Directions | Tube: Chalk Farm 5-minute walk. Free parking weekends, ticket parking nearby. |

Carole & Ted Cox
30 King Henry's Road,
Primrose Hill,
London NW3 3RP
Tel +44 (0)20 7483 2871
Fax +44 (0)20 7483 2871
Email carole.l.cox@googlemail.com

Entry 333   Map 22

## Middlesex

### Middle Cottage

What a find! A terrific spot right next to the Thames: Jonathan and Sarah have an eye for detail and do things well; you have your own, very private space in one half of their early Victorian cottages, Your light, upstairs sitting room has a dazzling collection of art and sculpture, chunky glass shelves full of design magazines and a soft grey sofa for reading. Your bedroom (not huge) is crisp and uncluttered with excellent lighting and blindingly white sheets; the funky bathroom is toasty with underfloor heating. Browse the newspapers over a robust breakfast; you can stroll to great shops and restaurants.

## Norfolk

### The Merchants House

The oak four-poster – a beauty – came with the house. Part of the building (1400) is the oldest in Wells; in those days, the merchant could bring his boats up to the door. Liz and Dennis know the history, and happily share it. Inside is warm, friendly, inviting: the mahogany shines, the bathrooms sparkle, there are papers for breakfast, books to borrow and pretty sash windows overlooking salt marshes. As for Wells, it is on the famous Coastal Path, has a quay bustling with sailing boats and 16 miles of sands. Birdwatch by day, dine out at night – easy when you're in the centre. Breakfasts are a treat.

🧳 Travel Club offer. See page 414.

| | |
|---|---|
| Price | £95. |
| Rooms | 1 double. |
| | (Sofa bed in sitting room.) |
| Meals | Pub/restaurant 20 yds. |
| Closed | Never. |
| Directions | Follow Teddington High Street towards river. Middle Cottage sits within a terrace of 3, beside the footbridge near Teddington Lock. |

| | |
|---|---|
| Price | £70. Singles £45. |
| Rooms | 2: 1 four-poster, 1 double. |
| Meals | Pubs/restaurants 300 yds. |
| Closed | Christmas & Boxing Day. |
| Directions | B1105 from Fakenham to Wells-next-the-Sea, then follow signs to beach/quay. House is 150 yds west of the quay. |

|  | Jonathan & Sarah Barker |
|---|---|
| | Middle Cottage, |
| | 12 Ferry Road, Teddington, |
| | Middlesex TW11 9NN |
| Tel | +44 (0)20 8973 0707 |
| Email | sarah@middlecottage.org |
| Web | www.middlecottage.org |

|  | Elizabeth & Dennis Woods |
|---|---|
| | The Merchants House, |
| | 47 Freeman Street, |
| | Wells-next-the-Sea, Norfolk NR23 1BQ |
| Tel | +44 (0)1328 711877 |
| Email | denniswoods@talktalk.net |
| Web | www.the-merchants-house.co.uk |

🎣 ✗ 📖 🚂 🔊 🚴

Entry 334  Map 22

✗ 🚂 🔊 🐱

Entry 335  Map 10

# Norfolk

## Glebe Farmhouse

After a wild walk on Holkham Beach, return to a house filled with warmth and colour. Life revolves around the big, square farmhouse kitchen: a painted dresser brimming with bright china, well-cushioned sofas, books, paintings, gentle fabrics, wooden floors and French windows to the garden. Mary, a painter, designer and thoughtful host, gives you a delicious breakfast here, or on the terrace in summer. TV-free bedrooms are peaceful and cosy, with views to garden or fields; old-fashioned bathrooms are perfectly functional. Mary and Jeremy have been doing B&B since renovating their traditional Norfolk farmhouse back in 1991.

| Price | From £75. Singles from £40. |
|---|---|
| Rooms | 2: 1 double, 1 twin/double. Extra fold-up bed for child & cot. |
| Meals | Pub 5-minute walk. |
| Closed | Rarely. |
| Directions | A148 King's Lynn to Cromer, north onto B1355 just west of Fakenham. 6.5 miles to North Creake. Right after red phone box, then 300 yds. On right. |

|  | **Mary & Jeremy Brettingham Smith** Glebe Farmhouse, Wells Road, North Creake, Fakenham, Norfolk NR21 9LG |
|---|---|
| Tel | +44 (0)1328 730133 |
| Fax | +44 (0)1328 730444 |
| Email | enquiries@glebe-farmhouse.co.uk |
| Web | www.glebe-farmhouse.co.uk |

Entry 336   Map 10

# Norfolk

## 1 Leicester Meadows

Up among 13 acres of wild meadow and woodland – not another building in sight. It's all so relaxed and unhurried: barn owls roosting in the outhouse, hens strutting the garden, geese pottering up from the pond. The 19th-century cottages, once the home of workers on the Holkham estate, have been imaginatively restored and enlarged. (Bob was an architect, Sara an art teacher; both are immensely friendly and helpful.) Polished wood and old brick are topped with bright rugs; paintings and ceramics engage the eye; steep stairs take you up to the bedrooms – one large, contemporary and elegant, the other cosy and fun.

| Price | From £60. Singles from £45. |
|---|---|
| Rooms | 2: 1 double; 1 double with separate bath. |
| Meals | Supper from £15. Pub 1 mile. |
| Closed | Rarely. |
| Directions | Off A148 near Fakenham; B1355 dir. Burnham Market. In S. Creake, left by flint bus shelter, right into Avondale Rd; 1 mile, taking left fork. At bottom of hill, house set back 100 yds on left. |

|  | **Bob & Sara Freakley** 1 Leicester Meadows, South Creake, Fakenham, Norfolk NR21 9NZ |
|---|---|
| Tel | +44 (0)1328 823533 |
| Email | rf@freakley.com |
| Web | www.leicestermeadows.com |

Entry 337   Map 10

## Bagthorpe Hall

Close to bustling Burnham Market, yet here you are immersed in peaceful countryside. Tid is a pioneer of organic farming and good things from his 700 acres wing their way monthly to the farmers' market. Gina's passions are music, dance and gardens and she organises open days and concerts for charity. Theirs is a large, elegant house with a mural in the hall chronicling their family life. It's fascinating, and beautiful. Wonderful colours, good beds, generous curtains, excellent food – maybe fresh raspberries for breakfast. Birdwatching, boats, salt marshes and crab nets are a 15-minute drive. *Stabling available.*

| | |
|---|---|
| Price | £45-£80. Singles £50. |
| Rooms | 3: 1 double; 1 double with separate shower; 1 twin with separate bath. |
| Meals | Pubs/restaurants 2 miles. |
| Closed | Rarely. |
| Directions | From King's Lynn for A148 to Fakenham. Left at East Rudham by Cat & Fiddle pub. 3.5 miles to Bagthorpe. Past farm on left, wood on right, white gates set back from trees. At top of drive. |

**Gina Morton**
Bagthorpe Hall,
Bagthorpe, Bircham, King's Lynn,
Norfolk PE31 6QY

| | |
|---|---|
| Tel | +44 (0)1485 578528 |
| Fax | +44 (0)1485 578151 |
| Email | dgmorton@hotmail.com |
| Web | www.bagthorpehall.co.uk |

Entry 338   Map 10

---

## Litcham Hall

For the whole of the 19th century this was Litcham's doctor's house; the red-brick Hall is still at the centre of the community. The big-windowed guest bedrooms look onto the stunning gardens with yew hedges, a lily pond and herbaceous borders. This is a thoroughly English home with elegant proportions – the hall, drawing room and dining room are gracious and beautifully furnished. The hens lay the breakfast eggs, the garden fills the table with soft fruit in season and John and Hermione are friendly and most helpful. There's a sitting room for guests. *Children & pets by arrangement.*

| | |
|---|---|
| Price | £70-£90. Singles by arrangement. |
| Rooms | 3: 1 double, 1 twin; 1 twin with separate bath. |
| Meals | Pub/restaurant 3 miles. |
| Closed | Christmas. |
| Directions | From Swaffham, A1065 north for 5 miles, then right to Litcham on B1145. House on left on entering village. Georgian red-brick with stone balls on gatepost. |

**John & Hermione Birkbeck**
Litcham Hall,
Litcham,
King's Lynn,
Norfolk PE32 2QQ

| | |
|---|---|
| Tel | +44 (0)1328 701389 |
| Fax | +44 (0)1328 701164 |
| Email | hermionebirkbeck@hotmail.com |

Entry 339   Map 10

# Norfolk

## Carrick's at Castle Farm

A comfortable, and jolly, mix of farmhouse B&B — rare-breed cattle, tractors, a large, warm-bricked house — and a rather swish interior. Both Jean and John are passionate about conservation and the protection of wildlife, and here you have absolute quiet for birdwatching, fishing, shooting or walking; recover in the drawing room with its books and lovely river views from long windows. Bedrooms are large, light and well thought-out with great bathrooms and binoculars, food is home grown or local, and there is coffee and cake, or wine, when you arrive. The pretty garden leads down to the River Wensum and a footpath.

Ethical Collection: Environment; Community; Food. See page 412.

| | |
|---|---|
| Price | From £85. Singles £55. |
| Rooms | 4: 2 doubles; 1 double, 1 twin each with separate bath (let to same party only). |
| Meals | Dinner, 3 courses, £20. BYO. Pub 0.5 miles. |
| Closed | Never. |
| Directions | From Norwich A47 to Dereham (don't go into Dereham). B1147 to Swanton Morley. In village, take Elsing Road at Darby's pub; farm drive 0.5 miles on left. |

|  |  |
|---|---|
| | Jean Wright |
| | Carrick's at Castle Farm, |
| | Castle Farm, Swanton Morley, |
| | Dereham, Norfolk NR20 4JT |
| Tel | +44 (0)1362 638302 |
| Email | jean@castlefarm-swanton.co.uk |
| Web | www.carricksatcastlefarm.co.uk |

# Norfolk

## The Courtyard

Walk straight in through French doors to your own, underfloor-heated room in the courtyard; privacy from the main house where young and friendly Simon and Catherine live. The rooms are decorated in soft colours, mattresses are perfect, cotton sheets are smooth and your handsome bathroom has limestone tiles — all rather luxurious. A table in the corner is beautifully laid for your continental breakfast (take it outside on good days) and you have a fridge to cool a bottle. There is a big attic room in one barn where you can play table tennis or read a book. Stunning walks await on the coast. *Minimum stay two nights.*

Travel Club offer. See page 414.

| | |
|---|---|
| Price | £75. Singles from £45. |
| Rooms | 4: 3 doubles, 1 twin. |
| Meals | Pub/restaurant 6 miles. |
| Closed | Never. |
| Directions | From Fakenham take Norwich road for 10 minutes. Take Foulsham turning at the large water tower. House is first on left. |

|  |  |
|---|---|
| | Simon & Catherine Davis |
| | The Courtyard, |
| | Westfield Farm, Foxley Road, Foulsham, |
| | Dereham, Norfolk NR20 5RH |
| Tel | +44 (0)1362 683333 |
| Email | westfieldfarm1@btopenworld.com |
| Web | www.norfolkcourtyard.co.uk |

# Norfolk

## Holly Lodge

The whole place radiates a lavish attention to detail, from the spoilingly comfortable beds to the complementary bottle of wine. It's perfect for those who love their privacy: these three snug guest 'cottages' have their own entrances as well as smart iron bedsteads and rugs on stone tiles, neat little shower rooms and tapestry-seat chairs, and books, music and TVs. Enjoy the Mediterranean garden with pond and decking in summer, the handsome conservatory and the utter peace. Your hosts are delightful: ex restaurateur Jeremy who cooks enthusiastically, ethically and with panache, and Canadian-raised Gill.

 Travel Club offer. See page 414.

| | |
|---|---|
| Price | £90–£120. Singles £70–£100. |
| Rooms | 3 cottages for 2. |
| Meals | Dinner, 3 courses with wine, £19.50. Pubs/restaurants 1 mile. |
| Closed | January. |
| Directions | From Fakenham A148, Fakenham-Cromer road; 6 miles; left at Crawfish pub. Signs to Thursford Collection, past village green; 2nd drive on left. |

Jeremy Bolam
Holly Lodge,
Thursford Green,
Norfolk NR21 0AS
Tel       +44 (0)1328 878465
Email    info@hollylodgeguesthouse.co.uk
Web      www.hollylodgeguesthouse.co.uk

Entry 342   Map 10

# Norfolk

## The Old Vicarage

Norfolk at its best in this fine Georgian vicarage....huge skies, views that stretch forever, absolute peace. A curved staircase springs from the flagstoned inner hall lit by a cupola high above. Two traditional bedrooms (one much larger and with spectacular views) have comfy beds and fine furniture, pretty china, fresh flowers. Enjoy hearty, home-produced breakfast in the sunlit dining room; wander through French windows to the garden. Sandy beaches, marsh walks and the seal colony are near; on your return a log fire and the lure of Rosie's scrumptious candlelit dinner will tempt you to stay put. *French spoken.*

 Travel Club offer. See page 414.

| | |
|---|---|
| Price | From £65. Singles from £45. |
| Rooms | 2: 1 twin/double; 1 double with separate bath. |
| Meals | Dinner, 3 courses, £22. BYO. Pub 2 miles. |
| Closed | Christmas & New Year. |
| Directions | A148 Fakenham to Cromer for 6 miles. Left at Crawfish Inn into Hindringham, down hill & left before church, into Blacksmith's Lane. After 0.5 miles, first entrance on left beyond 30mph sign. |

Rosie & Robin Waters
The Old Vicarage,
Blacksmith's Lane, Hindringham,
Norfolk NR21 0QA
Tel       +44 (0)1328 878223
Fax      +44 (0)1328 878223
Email    watersrobin@hotmail.com

Entry 343   Map 10

## Norfolk

### Burgh Parva Hall

Sunlight bathes the Norfolk longhouse on summer afternoons; the welcome from the Heals is as warm. The listed house is all that remains of the old village of Burgh Parva, deserted after the Great Plague. It's a handsome house and warmly inviting... old furniture, rugs, books, pictures and Magnet the terrier-daschund. Large guest bedrooms face the sunsets and the garden annexe makes a sweet hideaway, especially in the summer. Breakfast eggs are from the garden hens, vegetables are home-grown, fish comes fresh from Holt and the game may have been shot by William. Settle down by the fire and tuck in.

| | |
|---|---|
| Price | £60-£80. Singles from £35. |
| Rooms | 3: 1 double, 1 twin; 1 twin with separate bath. |
| Meals | Dinner £22. BYO. Pub/restaurant 4 miles. |
| Closed | Rarely. |
| Directions | Fakenham A148 for Cromer. At Thursford B1354 for Aylsham. Just before Melton, speed bumps, left immed. before bus shelter; 1st house on right after farmyard. |

Judy & William Heal
Burgh Parva Hall,
Melton Constable,
Norfolk NR24 2PU
Tel +44 (0)1263 862569
Email judyheal@dsl.pipex.com

Entry 344  Map 10

## Norfolk

### Stable Cottage

In the park of a privately owned village, one of Norfolk's finest Elizabethan houses, Heydon Hall. In the Dutch-gabled stable block, fronted by Cromwell's Oak, is this cottage – fresh, sunny and enchanting. Each room is touched by Sarah's warm personality and love of beautiful things; seagrass floors and crisp linen, toile de Jouy walls and pretty china. Bedrooms are cottagey and immaculate, there are fresh fabrics, baskets of treats in the bathrooms (one has a roll top bath) and delicious food on your plate (golden yolked eggs from Sarah's own hens and fruit from the kitchen garden). 20 minutes from the coast.

| | |
|---|---|
| Price | £80. Singles £45. |
| Rooms | 2 twins/doubles. |
| Meals | Occasional dinner, 3 courses, £20. BYO. Pub 1 mile. |
| Closed | Christmas. |
| Directions | From Norwich, B1149 for 10 miles. 2nd left after bridge, for Heydon. 1.5 miles, right into village, over cattle grid, into park. Pass Hall on left, cottage in front of you; left over cattle grid & into stable yard. |

Sarah Bulwer-Long
Stable Cottage,
Heydon Hall,
Heydon,
Norfolk NR11 6RE
Tel +44 (0)1263 587343

Entry 345  Map 10

# Norfolk

## Cleat House

In a quiet, residential area, but with all the bustle of town a short walk away, this is an attractive brick and mock-timber Edwardian seaside villa built by a wealthy London merchant. Sumptuous bedrooms have original fireplaces, sash windows, upbeat fabrics, original art, and an eclectic mix of antique and vintage furniture. Your own, comfortable, sitting room has an honesty bar and lots of local information to help plan trips. Rob and Linda greet you with homemade treats and serve a tasty breakfast at separate tables – try Linda's dish of the day. You will feel very well cared for. *Minimum stay two nights at weekends.*

| | |
|---|---|
| Price | £80–£100. Singles £65–£80. |
| Rooms | 3: 2 doubles with sitting area; 1 double with sitting area and separate bath. |
| Meals | Pubs/restaurants within 0.5 miles. |
| Closed | Occasionally. |
| Directions | Off A148 onto A1082, at roundabout left, then right into Church Street. First left into The Boulevard, 2nd left into North Street. Montague Road is at the end of North Street. |

**Rob & Linda Ownsworth**
Cleat House,
7 Montague Road, Sheringham,
Norfolk NR26 8LN
Tel +44 (0)1263 822765
Email roblinda@cleathouse.co.uk
Web www.cleathouse.co.uk

Entry 346  Map 10

# Norfolk

## Incleborough House

A listed, mellow-bricked 17th-century house which faces a pretty, bird-filled, walled garden. Nick and Barbara have done a terrific restoration job and give you sumptuous bedrooms with huge beds, beautiful linen, super views, shining contemporary bathrooms, chocolates and wine. There's an elegant sitting room for tea and cakes, with an open fire and books to read. Breakfast at white linen-topped tables in the conservatory is a treat – try slow-baked marmalade ham with poached eggs. You are only 300 yards from the sea and the local walks are fabulous. *Minimum stay two nights at weekends; check for late availability.*

Travel Club offer. See page 414.

| | |
|---|---|
| Price | £150–£185. Singles £112.50–£123.75. |
| Rooms | 4: 3 doubles, 1 twin/double. |
| Meals | Occasional dinner, with wine, £22.50. Restaurant 100 yds. |
| Closed | Never. |
| Directions | From Sheringham head for Cromer. In East Runton, 1st right into Felbrigg Road. House 200 yds on left behind oak trees. |

**Nick & Barbara Davies**
Incleborough House,
Lower Common, East Runton,
Cromer, Norfolk NR27 9PG
Tel +44 (0)1263 515939
Email enquiries@incleboroughhouse.co.uk
Web www.incleboroughhouse.co.uk

Entry 347  Map 10

# Norfolk

## The Old Rectory

Conservation farmland all around; acres of wild heathland busy with woodpeckers and owls; the coast two miles away. Relax in the spacious drawing room of this handsome 17th-century rectory and friendly family home, set in four acres of grounds. Fiona loves to cook and bakes her bread daily, food is delicious, seasonal and locally sourced, jams are homemade. Comfortable bedrooms have *objets* from diplomatic postings and the spacious suite comes with mahogany furniture and armchairs so you can settle in with a book. Super views, friendly dogs, tennis in the garden and masses of space.

Travel Club offer. See page 414.

| | |
|---|---|
| Price | From £55. Singles £35. |
| Rooms | 2: 1 suite; 1 double with separate bath & shower. |
| Meals | Dinner from £15. Pubs 2 miles. |
| Closed | Rarely. |
| Directions | From Norwich A1151 for Stalham. Just before Stalham, left to Happisburgh. Left at T-junc.; 3 miles; 2nd left after E. Ruston church, signed byway to Foxhill. Right at x-roads; 1 mile on right. |

|  | Peter & Fiona Black |
|---|---|
| | The Old Rectory, |
| | Ridlington, |
| | Norfolk NR28 9NZ |
| Tel | +44 (0)1692 650247 |
| Email | blacks7@email.com |
| Web | www.oldrectory.northnorfolk.co.uk |

Entry 348  Map 10

# Norfolk

## Manor Farmhouse

A family buzz and candlelight in the farmhouse where you eat, peace in the 17th-century barn where you stay. All rooms lead off its charming, stylish, vaulted sitting room with cosy winter fire. You have a four-poster and a tiny shower on the ground floor, then two narrow staircases to two beautifully-dressed bedrooms upstairs – small, quirky, fun, with a tucked-up-in-the-roof feel. Come for a sunny courtyard garden, billiards in the stable, fresh flowers, lovely hosts, gorgeous food – and you may come and go as you please. Great value, a perfect rural retreat. *Children over seven welcome.*

Travel Club offer. See page 414.

| | |
|---|---|
| Price | From £50. Singles from £40. |
| Rooms | 3: 1 double, 1 twin/double, 1 four-poster. |
| Meals | Dinner, 3 courses, £17.50. BYO. Pubs 1 mile. |
| Closed | Christmas & New Year. |
| Directions | From Norwich, A1151 & A149 almost to Stalham. Left for Walcott. At T-junc. left again. 1 mile on, right for H'burgh. Next T-junc., right. Next T-junc., left. Road bends right, look for house sign by wall. |

|  | David & Rosie Eldridge |
|---|---|
| | Manor Farmhouse, |
| | Happisburgh, Norfolk NR12 0SA |
| Tel | +44 (0)1692 651262 |
| Fax | +44 (0)1692 650220 |
| Email | manorathappisburgh@hotmail.com |
| Web | www.northnorfolk.co.uk/manorbarn |

Entry 349  Map 10

## Norfolk

### Sloley Hall

A grand and gracious yellow-brick Georgian house with formal gardens, tree-studded parkland and glorious views from every window. It has also been beautifully renovated, with flagstoned floors, Persian rugs, gleaming circular tables and vases of garden-grown flowers. Your hosts are delightful – Barbara and Simon were married here and are charmingly easy-going and helpful. A huge light-flooded dining room is perfect for breakfast; the drawing room is comfy but uncluttered in pinks, with a marble fireplace and long views. Bedrooms are large and elegant with sumptuous bed linen, and generous bathrooms glow with warmth.

Travel Club offer. See page 414.

| | |
|---|---|
| Price | £70–£90. Singles from £50. |
| Rooms | 3: 1 suite; 1 double with separate shower; 1 twin with separate bath. Extra child bed available. |
| Meals | Pub/restaurant 2-4 miles. |
| Closed | Rarely. |
| Directions | From Norwich ring road, B1150 through Coltishall & Scottow. Right after Three Horseshoes pub (byway to Sloley); across staggered junc., 1st drive on right. |

Mrs Barbara Gorton
Sloley Hall,
Sloley, Norwich,
Norfolk NR12 8HA
Tel +44 (0)1692 538582
Email babsgorton@hotmail.com
Web www.sloleyhall.com

Entry 350  Map 10

## Norfolk

### Manor House

Sally looks after you beautifully in this elegant house on the edge of Halvergate marshes. Excellent walking – the Weavers Way runs past the farmhouse door – and there is good birdwatching; spot pink-footed geese in winter. Your sitting room is an open landing outside the bedroom with comfortable chairs, TV, books, guides and fresh flowers. Bedrooms are traditional and spotless with soft colours, splashes of colour from cushions and curtains and touches of luxury; mattresses are firm, bathrooms sparkle. Breakfast bacon and sausages are from the farm shop – wonderful – and jams and marmalades are homemade. *Children over seven welcome.*

Travel Club offer. See page 414.

| | |
|---|---|
| Price | £80–£90. Singles £40. |
| Rooms | 2: 1 double with separate bath; 1 twin sharing bath (let to same party only). |
| Meals | Packed lunch £6.50. Pub 3 miles. |
| Closed | Christmas, New Year & February. |
| Directions | A47 towards Great Yarmouth. After Acle, right signed Halvergate. Into village, past Red Lion pub on right, take 3rd right signed Tunstall only. After 0.5 miles, farmhouse on left before the ruined church. |

Sally More
Manor House,
Tunstall Road, Halvergate, Acle,
Norwich, Norfolk NR13 3PS
Tel +44 (0)1493 700279
Fax +44 (0)1493 700279
Email smore@fsmail.net
Web www.manorhousenorfolk.co.uk

Entry 351  Map 10

## Norfolk

### Buck House

A bijou pad in town is how the owners like to describe their London B&B. Faced with a surfeit of rooms after their four children flew the nest, not to mention a hefty tax bill, owners Liz and Greek husband Phil have fixed up the old place for paying guests. Liz isn't your typical hands on hostess, in fact she rarely even changes the sheets. Bacon comes from their hippy son's pig farm in Gloucestershire. Gardens are on the small side – 42 acres – and if you do bump into your hostess walking her pack of Corgis, just be sure not to turn your back on her – she won't be amused.

| | |
|---|---|
| Price | A king's ransom. |
| Rooms | 750: all four-posters. |
| Meals | State banquets. |
| Closed | Always. |
| Directions | Follow the fleet of open-top red buses. |

Liz & Phil Windsor
Buck House,
London ER11 0N0
Web   www.heirsandgraces.guv

## Norfolk

### Washingford House

Tall octagonal chimney stacks and a Georgian façade give the house a stately air. In fact, it's the friendliest of places to stay and Paris gives you a delicious, locally sourced breakfast including plenty of fresh fruit. The house, originally Tudor, is a delightful mix of old and new. Large light-filled bedrooms have loads of good books and views over the four-acre garden, a favourite haunt for local birds. Bergh Apton is a conservation village seven miles from Norwich and you are in the heart of it; perfect for cycling and the twelve Wherryman's Way circular walks are close by. *Children over 12 welcome.*

Travel Club offer. See page 414.

| | |
|---|---|
| Price | £65–£75. Singles £35–£45. |
| Rooms | 2: 1 twin/double; 1 single with separate bath. |
| Meals | Pubs/restaurants 4–6 miles. |
| Closed | Rarely. |
| Directions | A146 from Norwich to Lowestoft for 4 miles. Right after Gull Pub, signed Slade Lane. First left, then left at T-junc. for 1 mile. Straight over x-roads; house on left past post office. |

Paris & Nigel Back
Washingford House,
Cookes Road, Bergh Apton,
Norwich,
Norfolk NR15 1AA
Tel   +44 (0)1508 550924
Email   parisb@waitrose.com
Web   www.washingford.com

# Norfolk

## The Buttery

Down a farm track, a treasure: a thatch-and-flint octagonal dairy house perfectly restored by local craftsmen and as neat as a new pin. You get a jacuzzi bath, a little kitchen and a fridge stocked with delicious bacon and ground coffee so you can breakfast when you want – and take it onto the sun terrace in good weather. The sitting room is terracotta-tiled and has a music system, a warming fire and a sofabed for those who don't want to tackle the steep wooden stairs to the snuggly mezzanine bedroom. You may walk from the door into parkland and woods, or try your hand at tennis or fishing.

🧳 Travel Club offer. See page 414.

| | |
|---|---|
| Price | £80-£95. |
| Rooms | Cottage: 1 double, sitting room & small kitchen. |
| Meals | Pub 10-minute walk. |
| Closed | Rarely. |
| Directions | From A47 Barnham Broom & Weston Longville x-roads, south towards Barnham Broom. After 150 yds, 1st farm track on right. Left at T-junc., left again, on left. |

Deborah Meynell
The Buttery,
Berry Hall, Honingham,
Norwich, Norfolk NR9 5AX
Tel     +44 (0)1603 880541
Fax     +44 (0)1603 880887
Email   thebuttery@paston.co.uk
Web     www.thebuttery.thesiliconworkshop.com

Entry 354   Map 10

# Norfolk

## 175 Newmarket Road

You can walk to the centre of town, but this Edwardian villa is rather grandly set back from the road in its large garden with mature shrubs and trees. Sit quietly in the guest sitting room with local art, books and papers to read; there's a sunny conservatory with bright sofas overlooking a well-tended garden and a heated indoor pool. Charming Dawn gives you extremely elegant, well-dressed bedrooms with an interesting mix of modern and antique furniture, sumptuous linen and quiet views; bathrooms are large, warm and well lit. Breakfast is generous and there's lots to explore on the doorstep. *Minimum stay two nights at weekends.*

🧳 Travel Club offer. See page 414.

| | |
|---|---|
| Price | £60-£75. Singles £35-£50. |
| Rooms | 3 doubles. |
| Meals | Pubs 0.25 miles. |
| Closed | Christmas. |
| Directions | 1.5 miles from city centre. Newmarket road leads from the main shopping and commercial district; easily accessible by bus. |

Dawn & Peter Thompson
175 Newmarket Road,
Norwich,
Norfolk NR4 6AP
Tel     +44 (0)1603 506160
Fax     +44 (0)845 8338990
Email   enquiries@bedandbreakfastinnorwich.co.uk
Web     www.bedandbreakfastinnorwich.co.uk

Entry 355   Map 10

# Norfolk

## 38 St Giles

No expense spared here in this high-ceilinged, elegantly windowed town house: silk curtains in ravishing colours, handmade mattresses, plump goose down pillows and duvets, sumptuous linen, bathrobes, smart gadgetry, and thick towels in gorgeous bathrooms with L'Occitane treats. Breakfast on freshly baked croissants, porridge with caramelised apples, fruit and yogurt, or the full works – much will be locally sourced by Jeanette and William. Leave the car behind: you are slap bang in the right place here for languid strolls to the theatre, cathedral, historic market, interesting shops and good restaurants.

# Norfolk

## Sallowfield Cottage

In the drawing room find gorgeous prints and paintings, unusual furniture and decorative lamps: Caroline's cottage is so crammed with family treasures it takes time to absorb the splendour. One bedroom, not huge but handsome, has a Regency-style canopied bed and decoration to suit the house (1850); other ground floor bedrooms are gloriously quiet with shower rooms. Drift into the fascinating garden to find hedged rooms and a jungly pond that slinks between the trees. Caroline – and pets – loves having guests and if you have friends locally she can do lunch for up to ten. *Children over nine welcome.*

 Travel Club offer. See page 414.

| | |
|---|---|
| Price | £120–£150. Singles £80–£110. |
| Rooms | 5: 3 doubles, 1 suite, 1 single. |
| Meals | Packed lunch £5. Light supper from £5. Pub/restaurant 50 yds. |
| Closed | 23–27 December. |
| Directions | From inner ring road in Norwich, up Grape's Hill and at roundabout turn left onto St Giles Street. House is 200 yds down hill on right. |

| | |
|---|---|
| Price | From £60. Singles £35. |
| Rooms | 4: 1 double, 1 twin; 1 double with separate bath; 1 single with separate shower. |
| Meals | Lunch £12.50. Dinner from £20. Pub 2 miles. |
| Closed | Christmas & New Year. |
| Directions | A11 Attleborough-Wymondham. Take Spooner Row sign. Over x-roads by Three Boars pub. 1 mile; left at T-junc. to Wymondham for 1 mile. Look for rusty barrel on left, turn into farm track. |

| | |
|---|---|
| | **Jeanette Bennett &**<br>**William Cheeseman**<br>38 St Giles, St Giles Street,<br>Norwich, Norfolk NR2 1LL |
| Tel | +44 (0)1603 662944 |
| Email | booking@38stgiles.co.uk |
| Web | www.38stgiles.co.uk |

| | |
|---|---|
| | **Caroline Musker**<br>Sallowfield Cottage,<br>Wattlefield, Wymondham,<br>Norwich, Norfolk NR18 9NX |
| Tel | +44 (0)1953 605086 |
| Email | caroline.musker@tesco.net |
| Web | www.sallowfieldcottage.co.uk |

Entry 356  Map 10

Entry 357  Map 10

# Norfolk

## College Farm

Lavender has done B&B for years and looks after her stupendous listed house single-handedly. Over afternoon tea, she tells colourful stories of the house and her family's local history: from 1349 until the Dissolution of the Monasteries the house was a college of priests and there's stunning Jacobean panelling in the dining room. Bedrooms are big and lived-in, two of the bathrooms are tiny, all have lovely views over the garden with its pingos (ice age ponds). Come for history and architecture and friendly Lavender, and breakfast from the farm shop down the road. *Children over seven welcome.*

# Norfolk

## Le Grys Barn

Light pours into this 17th-century threshing barn – a jewel of a conversion in peaceful Norfolk. Julie lived in Hong Kong and sells jewellery from Bali. Her house glows with warmth and colour. Glass-topped tables increase the sense of space, Persian carpets beautify beech floors, golden buddhas rest in quiet corners. Across a courtyard, two private beamed and raftered bedrooms are stunningly equipped: guidebooks and glossies, easy chairs and Thai silk, music, flowers and mini fridge. Bathrooms have Italian tiles and breakfast, served on a Chinese altar table, is as delicious as all the rest.

| | |
|---|---|
| Price | From £60. Singles £30. |
| Rooms | 3: 1 twin, 1 twin/double; 1 double with separate bath. Extra shower available. |
| Meals | Afternoon tea included. Pub 1 mile. |
| Closed | Rarely. |
| Directions | From Thetford, A1075 north for Watton. After 9 miles, left to Thompson at 'Light Vehicles Only' sign. After 0.5 miles, 2nd left at red postbox on corner. Left again, house at end. |

| | |
|---|---|
| | Lavender Garnier |
| | College Farm, |
| | Thompson, Thetford, |
| | Norfolk IP24 1QG |
| Tel | +44 (0)1953 483318 |
| Fax | +44 (0)1953 483318 |
| Email | collegefarm83@amserve.net |

| | |
|---|---|
| Price | £70-£75. Singles from £45. |
| Rooms | 2: 1 double, 1 twin/double. |
| Meals | Dinner, 3 courses, £20. BYO. Packed lunch available. Pub 5-minute drive. |
| Closed | Christmas & New Year. |
| Directions | From A140 at Long Stratton, take Flowerpot Lane (opp. Shell garage) to Wacton; at x-roads left by phone box, past swings; 500 yds to telegraph pole with sign: left turn up 'Private Rd', over cattle grid to end of lane. |

| | |
|---|---|
| | Mrs Julie Franklin |
| | Le Grys Barn, |
| | Wacton Common, Long Stratton, |
| | Norfolk NR15 2UR |
| Tel | +44 (0)1508 531576 |
| Email | jm.franklin@virgin.net |
| Web | www.legrys-barn.co.uk |

Entry 358   Map 10

Entry 359   Map 10

# Norfolk

## Rushall House

Plenty of treats to be had in this light and bright Victorian rectory: blue-shelled eggs for breakfast, homemade cake for tea, and radios, books and sofas in the double bedrooms. The wood-burner warm sitting room is classically decorated with a contemporary touch, airy bedrooms have pale walls, rich fabrics and a grand mix of colours and textiles (Jane's vintage furniture and fabrics are for sale in the courtyard studio). Walk or cycle after breakfast – it's good flat countryside and there are plenty of restorative pubs. Jane and Martin are relaxed hosts, and children will love collecting the eggs.

Ethical Collection: Food. See page 412.

| | |
|---|---|
| Price | From £65. Singles £40. |
| Rooms | 3: 1 double; 1 double, 1 twin sharing bath/shower. |
| Meals | Dinner £23. BYO. Pubs/restaurants 0.5-3 miles. |
| Closed | Rarely. |
| Directions | Turn off A140 at r'bout to Dickleburgh; right at village store. After two miles pass Lakes Rd & Vaunces Lane, on right. Shortly after z-bend sign, house on right. |

Martin Hubner & Jane Gardiner
Rushall House,
Dickleburgh Road, Rushall, Diss,
Norfolk IP21 4RX
Tel    +44 (0)1379 741557
Email  janegardineruk@aol.com
Web    www.rushallhouse.co.uk

Entry 360  Map 10

# Northamptonshire

## Mears Ashby Hall

Treat yourself to a slice of elegant living here among the old stone hounds, rich textiles, English furniture and objects from all over the world – even a yawning tiger rug – but this is very much Clive and Pamela's family home and there's not a hint of stuffiness. Bedrooms are blissfully indulgent and generous (the four-poster the larger) with best feather pillows, stone mullioned windows with cushioned seats for serious gazing, and tactile bathrooms with deep baths and chunky towels. Explore acres of garden: regiments of cutting flowers, rose-tumbled walls, pootling pigs and hens that give you your breakfast egg. Lovely.

Travel Club offer. See page 414.

| | |
|---|---|
| Price | £100–£120. |
| Rooms | 2: 1 double; 1 double with separate bath. |
| Meals | Pubs/restaurants within 5 miles. |
| Closed | Christmas & New Year. |
| Directions | A45 east from Northampton. Exit at Earls Barton. Over lights after 1.5 miles, then further 1.5 miles to Mears Ashby. Right at small crossroads, then follow lane for 400 yds. Entrance on right. |

Clive & Pamela Hilton
Mears Ashby Hall,
Mears Ashby,
Northamptonshire NN6 0DY
Tel    +44 (0)1604 810341
Fax    +44 (0)1604 810099
Email  clive@mc.uk.com

Entry 361  Map 9

## Northamptonshire

## Northamptonshire

### Coton Lodge

Hidden at the end of a mile-long drive, a handsome, wisteria-clad farmhouse surrounded by enchanting gardens and mature trees. On the farm Joanne and Peter raise rare-breed sheep in the pastures, bantams patrol the orchard and miscanthus grass (an alternative energy crop) grows in the distance. The elegant rooms are filled with light and overlook a gentle valley. Bedrooms are traditional, utterly comfortable and immaculate. Breakfast on the best of local produce and homemade jams – in the conservatory on sunny days. *Children over 12 welcome. Minimum stay two nights at weekends March-September.*

### Colledges House

Huge attention to comfort here, and a house full of laughter. Liz clearly derives pleasure from sharing her 300-year-old stone thatched cottage, immaculate garden, conservatory and converted barn with guests. Sumptuous bedrooms have deep mattresses with fine linen, sparkling bathrooms are a good size. The house is full of interesting things: a Jacobean trunk, a Bechstein piano, mirrors and pictures, pretty china, bright fabrics, a beautiful bureau. Cordon Bleu dinners are elegant affairs – and great fun. Stroll around the conservation village of Staverton – delightful. *Children over eight & babes in arms welcome.*

 Travel Club offer. See page 414.

| | |
|---|---|
| Price | From £90. Singles from £70. |
| Rooms | 3: 2 doubles, 1 twin/double. |
| Meals | Packed lunch £5. Pub 3 miles. |
| Closed | Rarely. |
| Directions | From M1 junc. 18 follow signs for Crick & W. Haddon. Bypass W. Haddon following signs to Guilsborough. After 0.5 miles fork right to Guilsborough, Coton Lodge 0.75 miles on right. |

| | |
|---|---|
| Price | £102-£106. Singles £67.50-£69.50. |
| Rooms | 4: 1 single; 1 double with separate bath. Cottage: 1 double, 1 twin. |
| Meals | Dinner, 3 courses, £32. Pub 4-minute walk. |
| Closed | Rarely. |
| Directions | From Daventry, A425 to Leamington Spa. 100 yds past Staverton Park Conference Centre, right into village, then 1st right. Keep left, & at 'Give Way' sign, sharp left. House immed. on right. |

Joanne de Nobriga
Coton Lodge,
West Haddon Road, Guilsborough,
Northampton,
Northamptonshire NN6 8QE
Tel     +44 (0)1604 740215
Email   jo@cotonlodge.co.uk
Web    www.cotonlodge.co.uk

Liz Jarrett
Colledges House,
Oakham Lane,
Staverton, Daventry,
Northamptonshire NN11 6JQ
Tel     +44 (0)1327 702737
Email   liz@colledgeshouse.co.uk
Web    www.colledgeshouse.co.uk

Entry 362   Map 8

Entry 363   Map 8

# Northamptonshire

## The Vyne

Weighed down by wisteria, this 16th-century cottage rests in a honey-hued conservation village on the cusp of Oxfordshire. Beams and wonky lines abound; rooms are filled with good antiques and eclectic art. The spacious twin is enchanting, tucked under the rafters, its beds decorated in willow-pattern chintz, its walls glinting with gilded frames; the double has a Georgian four-poster and a sampler-decorated bathroom that's a quick flit next door. Warm and charming, Imogen not only works in publishing but is a dedicated gardener and Cordon Bleu cook – enjoy supper in her sunny secluded garden. *Babies welcome.*

Travel Club offer. See page 414.

| | |
|---|---|
| Price | £75. Singles from £45. |
| Rooms | 2: 1 twin; 1 four-poster with separate bath. |
| Meals | Supper £20. Dinner £30. BYO. Pub 2-minute walk. |
| Closed | Christmas & New Year. |
| Directions | M40 exit 11. A422 to Northampton, left onto B4525. 2 miles, left to Thorpe Mandeville. 3 miles, left to Culworth. After Culworth, right to Eydon. |

Imogen Butler
The Vyne,
High Street, Eydon,
Daventry, Northamptonshire NN11 3PP
Tel    +44 (0)1327 264886
Fax    +44 (0)1327 260735
Email  Imogen@ibutler2.wanadoo.co.uk

Entry 364    Map 8

# Northamptonshire

## The Coach House

Sunlight and flower-scent fill this sprawling, rosy-brick home. Originally a coach house and stabling, it's now a series of elegant, light-filled ground-floor rooms around a central courtyard: on sunny days you can breakfast here – bread is homemade. Sarah's eye for colour and design shows in the clever mix of modern and traditional, gingham curtains, pretty fabrics and striking lampshades. Bedrooms ooze country-house luxury with fine cotton bed linen, fluffy towels, glossy magazines and doors to garden or courtyard. Relax here – or on the tennis court – after a day out at Silverstone or Towcester Racecourse.

Travel Club offer. See page 414.

| | |
|---|---|
| Price | £70. Singles £45. |
| Rooms | 2: 1 double, 1 twin. |
| Meals | Packed lunch on request. Pub/restaurant within 5 miles. |
| Closed | Rarely. |
| Directions | From A43 dual carriageway, A5 North for Hinckley. After 1.1 miles sharp left to Duncote. 1st house on left, 300 yds, 2nd gate. |

Sarah Baker Baker
The Coach House,
Duncote,
Towcester,
Northamptonshire NN12 8AQ
Tel    +44 (0)1327 352855
Email  sarahbb@3disp.co.uk

Entry 365    Map 8

# Northamptonshire

## Bridge Cottage

A truly restful place: sip a glass of wine on the decking down by the Willowbrook; rolling green countryside envelops you, the cattle are drinking peacefully, kingfishers flash by and you may see a red kite (borrow some binoculars). Inside find beautiful bedrooms with sloping ceilings, the purest cotton sheets and proper blankets; bathrooms are thickly towelled and full of lovely lotions and bubbles. Rules are few, breakfast is local and scrumptious and served in the friendliest kitchen facing that heavenly view, there's a tranquil conservatory for a quiet read, and Judy and Rod look after you very well indeed.

| Price | From £80. Singles from £40. |
|---|---|
| Rooms | 4: 1 double, 2 twins; 1 double with separate bath. |
| Meals | Pub/restaurant 2 miles. |
| Closed | Rarely. |
| Directions | From south A1 to Peterborough junction. A605 signed Oundle & Northampton for 4 miles. At 1st r'bout right through Fotheringhay, then Woodnewton. House is first on left on bridge. |

Judy Colebrook
Bridge Cottage, Oundle Road,
Woodnewton, Peterborough,
Northamptonshire PE8 5EG
Tel +44 (0)1780 470779
Email enquiries@bridgecottage.net
Web www.bridgecottage.net

Entry 366  Map 9

# Northumberland

## Matfen High House

Bring the wellies! You are 25 miles from the border and the walking is a joy. Struan and Jenny are amusing company, love sporting pursuits and will drive you to Matfen Hall for dinner. The sturdy stone house of 1735 is a pleasant, pretty place to stay: the en suite bedrooms have fine fabrics and good pictures, the bathrooms are stocked with fluffy towels and the drawing room promises books and choice pieces. Breakfasts are superb (bacon and sausages from the farmer; bread, mustards and jams all Jenny's) and the countryside is stunning. Hadrian's Wall and the great castles (Alnwick, Bamburgh) beckon.

Travel Club offer. See page 414.

| Price | £60-£75. Singles £30-£40. |
|---|---|
| Rooms | 4: 1 double, 1 twin; 1 double, 1 twin sharing bath. |
| Meals | Packed lunch £4.50. Restaurant 2 miles. |
| Closed | Rarely. |
| Directions | A69 at Heddon on the Wall, onto B6318 past Robin Hood Inn; 500 yds, right to Moorhouse; right at next junction signed High House Brewery; past Hadrian Pet Hotel; 300 yds, right, opp. cottages. |

Struan & Jenny Wilson
Matfen High House,
Matfen, Corbridge,
Northumberland NE20 0RG
Tel +44 (0)1661 886592
Fax +44 (0)1661 886847
Email struan@struan.enterprise-plc.com

Entry 367  Map 12

## Northumberland

### Bog House

It's too quiet for some townies – and thank goodness! If you've had it with bustle, bury yourself in the depths of Northumberland, two miles from Hadrian's Wall. Here is an immaculate barn conversion that's mercifully free from the usual modern furniture; what you have is a contemporary, airy feel and an open-raftered space stuffed with antiques. Rosemary has created a stunning place. Breakfast is later at weekends and sausages are local, bread is freshly baked. The peace here is total; you have your own entrance and may come and go as you please. An indulgent, wonderful retreat. *Children over 12 welcome.*

## Northumberland

### The Hermitage

A magical setting, only three miles from Hadrian's wall. Through ancient woodland, up the long drive and over the burn to this beautiful Georgian house. Inside is supremely comfortable and elegant but still homely. Large, carpeted and delightful bedrooms are furnished with antiques, prints and superb beds; bathrooms have large roll top baths. There's a walled garden, and breakfasts (delicious) can be served on the terrace. Katie grew up in this lovely house, looks after you brilliantly and knows all there is to know about the area. *Guests back please by 11pm. Children over seven & babes in arms welcome.*

Travel Club offer. See page 414.

| | |
|---|---|
| Price | £80-£90. Singles £45-£50. |
| Rooms | 2: 1 twin, 1 double. |
| Meals | Dinner, 2 courses, £17-£20. Pubs/restaurants 15-minute drive. |
| Closed | Rarely. |
| Directions | A68; 5 miles north of Corbridge, right onto B6318. After 3.5 miles, left signed Moorhouse. On for 1 mile, right; left to Bog House after 1 mile. Last farm on left. |

Travel Club offer. See page 414.

| | |
|---|---|
| Price | From £80. Singles from £45. |
| Rooms | 3: 1 double, 1 twin; 1 twin with separate bath. |
| Meals | Pub 2 miles. |
| Closed | October-February. |
| Directions | 7 miles north of Corbridge on A68. Left on A6079 for 1 mile, then right through lodge gates with arch. House 0.5 miles down drive. |

| | |
|---|---|
| | Rosemary Stobart |
| | Bog House, |
| | Matfen, |
| | Northumberland NE20 0RF |
| Tel | +44 (0)1661 886776 |
| Email | rosemary.stobart@btinternet.com |
| Web | www.boghouse-matfen.co.uk |

| | |
|---|---|
| | Simon & Katie Stewart |
| | The Hermitage, |
| | Swinburne, Hexham, |
| | Northumberland NE48 4DG |
| Tel | +44 (0)1434 681248 |
| Fax | +44 (0)1434 681110 |
| Email | katie.stewart@themeet.co.uk |

Entry 368  Map 16

Entry 369  Map 16

## Northumberland

### The Old Vicarage

Come for the tiny village, the ancient church, and a gentler way of life in this stone built, wisteria-covered former vicarage. Light pours in to an elegant drawing room with large open fire, chintzy chairs and sofa, softly-coloured rugs, beautiful antique furniture and pictures. Bedrooms are comfortably traditional, with crisp white sheets, squishy pillows, thick curtains and white bathrooms. Margaret gives you a grand breakfast in a toasty warm conservatory overlooking the garden; wander down to the river or to have a peek at the church, which dates from 1080! Newcastle, Alnwick Garden and stunning beaches are all a short drive away.

Travel Club offer. See page 414.

| | |
|---|---|
| Price | £75. Singles £50. |
| Rooms | 3: 1 double; 1 twin, 1 single sharing bathroom. |
| Meals | Supper £20. Pub 1 mile. |
| Closed | Christmas, New Year & Easter Day. |
| Directions | 6 miles west of Morpeth on B6343, towards Scots Gap and Cambo. |

Margaret Smart
The Old Vicarage,
Hartburn,
Morpeth,
Northumberland NE61 4JB
Tel       +44 (0)1670 772562
Email   margiecook2001@yahoo.co.uk

Entry 370   Map 16

## Northumberland

### Shieldhall

The guest rooms are in the charming 18th-century farm buildings, each with its own entrance. Stephen and his sons make and restore antique furniture and rooms are named after the wood used within: Elm, Oak, Mahogany, Pine. Bathrooms are spacious, there's a cosy sitting room/library and you pop across the courtyard for meals in the main house – once home to the family of Capability Brown. Celia is friendly and attentive and loves cooking, so ingredients are often organic or locally sourced; there's also a secret bar and a small but interesting wine list. Peaceful, hospitable B&B – with fine views.

Travel Club offer. See page 414.

| | |
|---|---|
| Price | £80. Singles £50. |
| Rooms | 3: 1 double, 1 twin, 1 four-poster. |
| Meals | Dinner, 4 courses, £25. Pub 7 miles. |
| Closed | Rarely. |
| Directions | From Newcastle A696 for Jedburgh. 5 miles north of Belsay, right onto B6342. On left after 500 yds (turn into front courtyard). |

Celia & Stephen Robinson-Gay
Shieldhall,
Wallington, Morpeth,
Northumberland NE61 4AQ
Tel       +44 (0)1830 540387
Fax      +44 (0)1830 540490
Email   stay@shieldhallguesthouse.co.uk
Web     www.shieldhallguesthouse.co.uk

Entry 371   Map 16

# Northumberland

## Lansdown House

The arched coach house doors to this 1600s house are still right on the pavement on the busy market town street. But nip down a side corridor and you could be in deep countryside; a delightfully long town garden and your own entrance give you independence, and bubbly Lesley is on hand to make sure you have all you need. Fab breakfasts (in bed if you want) set you up for miles of sandy beaches, cycling, shooting, riding, fly fishing and Alnwick Castle. Lazy lumps can just loll in a sumptuous bed admiring the Designers Guild wallpaper, the TV (flat-screen, naturally) and the fine pieces of furniture.

# Northumberland

## Thistleyhaugh

Enid thrives on hard work and humour, her passions are pictures, cooking and people and if she's not the perfect B&B hostess, she's a close contender. Certainly you eat well – local farm eggs at breakfast and their own beef at dinner. Choose any of the five large, lovely bedrooms and stay the week; they are awash with old paintings, silk fabrics and crisp white linen. But if you do stray downstairs, past the log fire and the groaning table, there are 720 acres of organic farmland to discover and a few million more of the Cheviots beyond that. Wonderful hosts, house and region.

Travel Club offer. See page 414.

| | | | |
|---|---|---|---|
| Price | £70–£80. Singles from £48. | Price | £80. Singles £52.50–£75. |
| Rooms | 2: 1 double, 1 twin. | Rooms | 5: 3 doubles, 1 twin, 1 single. |
| Meals | Packed lunch £5. Pubs/restaurants walking distance. | Meals | Dinner, 3 courses, £20. Pub/restaurant 2 miles. |
| Closed | Rarely. | Closed | Christmas, New Year & January. |
| Directions | The house is on the main thoroughfare through Morpeth, on right heading north, next to Sour Grapes wine bar. Easy free parking. | Directions | Leave A1 for A697 for Coldstream & Longhorsley; 2 miles past Longhorsley, left at Todburn sign; 1 mile to x-roads, then right; on 1 mile over white bridge; 1st right, right again, over cattle grid. |

| | | | |
|---|---|---|---|
| | Lesley Mantel | | Henry & Enid Nelless |
| | Lansdown House, | | Thistleyhaugh, |
| | 90 Newgate Street, | | Longhorsley, Morpeth, |
| | Morpeth, | | Northumberland NE65 8RG |
| | Northumberland NE61 1BU | Tel | +44 (0)1665 570629 |
| Tel | +44 (0)1670 511129 | Fax | +44 (0)1665 570629 |
| Email | kitchendiva@gmail.com | Email | thistleyhaugh@hotmail.com |
| Web | www.lansdownhouse.co.uk | Web | www.thistleyhaugh.co.uk |

Entry 372   Map 16

Entry 373   Map 16

## Northumberland

### East Hepple Farmhouse

In the farmhouse sitting room, a wood-burner blazes away in winter. The double, too, has a sitting room, with an original cast-iron range and shelves groaning with books – bibliophile heaven. The peace is so deep in the Coquet valley that you may sleep until the whiff of sizzling local bacon hits your nostrils. Beds are firm, old pine pieces pretty, pillows feathery soft and views over the river to the Simonside hills abundant. Joan and Brian are expert at looking after you, will drive you to dinner and guide you the next day to the beaches, Cragside, Alnwick Castle and fabulous walking. To stay is a treat. *Fishing can be arranged nearby.*

## Northumberland

### Bilton Barns

A solidly good farmhouse B&B whose lifeblood is still farming. The Jacksons know every inch of the countryside and coast that surrounds their 1715 home; it's a pretty spot. They farm 400 acres of mixed arable land that sweeps down to the coast yet always have time for guests. Dorothy takes pride in creating an easy and sociable atmosphere – three couples who were introduced to each other one weekend now return for reunions! Bedrooms are big, carpeted, fresh and comfortable, a conservatory leads onto the garden and there's an airy guests' sitting room with an open fire and views to the sea.

 Travel Club offer. See page 414.

| | | | | |
|---|---|---|---|---|
| Price | £65-£70. Singles from £45. | | Price | £68-£78. Singles £31-£55. |
| Rooms | 2: 1 double & sitting room; 1 twin (let to same party only). | | Rooms | 3: 1 double, 1 twin, 1 four-poster. |
| Meals | Packed lunch £5. Pubs/restaurants 2.5 miles. | | Meals | Packed lunch from £5. Pub/restaurant 1.5 miles. |
| Closed | Rarely. | | Closed | Christmas & New Year. |
| Directions | West from Rothbury on B6341. In Hepple, pass church on left; next right, then immediate hard right into driveway. | | Directions | From Alnwick, A1068 to Alnmouth. At Hipsburn r'bout follow signs to station & cross bridge. 1st lane to left, 0.3 miles down drive. |

| | | | |
|---|---|---|---|
| | Joan & Brian Storey East Hepple Farmhouse, Hepple, Rothbury, Northumberland NE65 7LH | | Brian & Dorothy Jackson Bilton Barns, Alnmouth, Alnwick, Northumberland NE66 2TB |
| | | Tel | +44 (0)1665 830427 |
| Tel | +44 (0)1669 640221 | Fax | +44 (0)1665 833909 |
| Email | joanstorey@coquetdale.net | Email | dorothy@biltonbarns.com |
| Web | www.easthepplefarmhouse.co.uk | Web | www.biltonbarns.com |

Entry 374   Map 16

Entry 375   Map 16

# Northumberland

## Hethpool

Come for the location: it's remote, rugged and breathtakingly beautiful; private roads are virtually car-free (vehicles are restricted). Inside, old family pieces, honeysuckle chintz, hunting gear, milling dogs – and Martin and Eildon who have lived here for years. Bedrooms, old-fashioned and definitely not swish, share a sitting room; after one of Eildon's fine dinners, settle in front of the fire. Walkers will be happy, and those who prefer a bit of character in a home; there's a 16th-century pele tower in the garden and the National Park beyond. Bring your horse and let your hosts be your guide!

Ethical Collection: Food. See page 412.

Travel Club offer. See page 414.

| | |
|---|---|
| Price | From £70. |
| Rooms | 2: 1 twin; 1 double with separate bath. |
| Meals | Dinner, 2-3 courses, £18.50-£25. Pub 8 miles. |
| Closed | Rarely. |
| Directions | From Wooler A697 for Coldstream; 2 miles left onto B6351. After 4 miles left to Hethpool; 1.5 miles, left at 'Private Drive' sign; 2nd on right. |

|  | Eildon & Martin Letts<br>Hethpool,<br>Wooler,<br>Northumberland NE71 6TW |
|---|---|
| Tel | +44 (0)1668 216232 |
| Email | eildon@hethpoolhouse.co.uk |
| Web | www.hethpoolhouse.co.uk |

Entry 376   Map 16

# Northumberland

## Broome

A totally surprising one-storey house, full of beautiful things. It is an Aladdin's cave and sits in the middle of a coastal village with access to miles of sandy beaches. The garden/breakfast room is its hub and has a country cottage feel; enjoy locally smoked kippers here, award-winning 'Bamburgh Bangers' and home-cured bacon from the village butcher. There's also a sun-trapping courtyard full of colourful pots for breakfasts in the sun. Guests have a cheerful sitting/dining room and bedrooms with fresh flowers and good books. Mary is welcoming and amusing and has stacks of local knowledge.

| | |
|---|---|
| Price | £80-£100. Singles £55-£65. |
| Rooms | 2: 1 double, 1 twin, sharing separate bath/shower (2nd room let to same party only). |
| Meals | Pubs/restaurants 2-minute walk. |
| Closed | 1 November-4 March. |
| Directions | From Newcastle north on A1; right for Bamburgh on B1341. To village, pass 30mph sign & hotel; 1st right at Victoria Hotel. 400 yds on right. |

|  | Mary Dixon<br>Broome,<br>22 Ingram Road,<br>amburgh,<br>Northumberland NE69 7BT |
|---|---|
| Tel | +44 (0)1668 214287 |
| Email | mdixon4394@aol.com |

Entry 377   Map 16

## Northumberland

### West Coates

Slip through the gates of this Victorian townhouse and you're in the country. Two acres of leafy gardens, with shady or sunny spots to relax, belie the closeness of Berwick's centre. As surprising are the indoor pool and hot tub tucked in the corner. From the lofty ceilings and sash windows to the soft colours, paintings and gleaming furniture, the house has a calm, ordered elegance. Bedrooms have antiques and garden views; two have roll top baths; fruit, homemade cakes, flowers welcome you. Warm, friendly Karen is a stunning cook, inventively using local produce and spoiling you.

| Price | £90–£120. Singles from £60. |
|---|---|
| Rooms | 3: 1 double, 1 twin/double; 1 twin/double with separate bath/shower. |
| Meals | Dinner £35. Pub/restaurant 10-minute walk. |
| Closed | Christmas & New Year. |
| Directions | From A1 take A6105 into Berwick. House 300 yds on left. Stone pillars at end of drive. Train station 20-minute walk. |

Karen Brown
West Coates, 30 Castle Terrace,
Berwick-upon-Tweed,
Northumberland TD15 1NZ
Tel     +44 (0)1289 309666
Email   karenbrownwestcoates@yahoo.com
Web    www.westcoates.co.uk

Entry 378   Map 16

## Nottinghamshire

### The Old Vicarage

Jillie's grandmother studied at the Slade and her paintings line the walls; glass and china adorn every surface. This wisteria-clad Victorian vicarage next to the 12th-century church was falling down when the Steeles bought it; now it's an elegant, traditional country home and popular with honeymoon couples. Long windows are generously draped, two of the bedrooms are spacious, baths have claw feet and a number of friendly cats and dogs wait to welcome you. Jerry bakes the bread and all the vegetables come from the garden. Mary Queen of Scots is reputed to have stayed at Langford as guest of the Earl of Shrewsbury!

Travel Club offer. See page 414.

| Price | £75–£85. Singles £50–£55. |
|---|---|
| Rooms | 3: 2 doubles, 1 twin. |
| Meals | Dinner, for special occasions, £25. Pub/restaurant 1.5 miles. |
| Closed | Rarely. |
| Directions | From A1, A46 to Lincoln & left onto A1133 for Gainsborough. Through Langford, 0.5 miles on, then left for Holme. House 100 yds on, on right, by church. |

Jerry & Jillie Steele
The Old Vicarage,
Holme Lane, Langford, Newark,
Nottinghamshire NG23 7RT
Tel     +44 (0)1636 705031
Email   jillie.steele@virgin.net
Web    www.langfordoldvicarage.co.uk

Entry 379   Map 9

## Nottinghamshire

### Compton House

Two minutes from Newark's antique shops and ancient market, seek out this terraced Georgian townhouse where the mayor once lived. Naturally elegant, and overlooking Fountain Gardens, the sunny drawing room has a marble fireplace; Lisa and Mark have embellished the place with lovely personal touches. Rooms are named after friends, from plush red-gold Judy's room to Harry's bijou single; the best is Cooper's, with a four-poster bed, a roll top bath through a draped archway and a wall hand painted by a local artist. Pad down to the sunny basement for Mark's feast of a breakfast. Hotel comforts but a wonderfully personal feel.

 Travel Club offer. See page 414.

| | |
|---|---|
| Price | £85. Singles from £58. |
| Rooms | 7: 2 doubles, 1 twin/double, 2 twins, 1 four-poster; 1 single with separate shower. |
| Meals | Packed lunch £6. Buffet lunch £10. Dinner, 2 courses, from £20. Pub/restaurant 0.5 miles. |
| Closed | Occasionally Christmas. |
| Directions | From Nottingham take A52, join A46 north to Newark. At roundabout take 2nd exit. Right at lights, left at next lights then 1st right. House is on left. |

**Mark & Lisa Holloway**
Compton House,
117 Baldertongate, Newark,
Nottinghamshire NG24 1RY
Tel +44 (0)1636 708670
Email info@comptonhousenewark.com
Web www.comptonhousenewark.com

Entry 380  Map 9

## Nottinghamshire

### Willoughby House

Past the village pub, through a gate, this three-storey brick farmhouse reflects its owners' skilful interior design. The house brims with tokens of its 18th century past, like meat hooks in the scullery-turned-sitting room, but feels ever so smart. Climb up to Harry's room with its brass bed and toy soldiers over the fireplace; Edward's and George's share raftered loft space and a swish bathroom. Sarah rustles up meals – and cheeses from her market stall – in a dining room embraced by poppy red walls and shutters. Get out on hikes or bikes; round the little village, or Southwell and Newark are close.

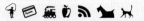 Travel Club offer. See page 414.

| | |
|---|---|
| Price | £60–£75. Singles £45–£55. |
| Rooms | 3: 1 double, 1 twin (let to same party only). 1 double with separate bath. |
| Meals | Dinner, 2 courses, from £10. Packed lunch £7.50. Pub 3-minute walk; pubs/restaurants within 5 miles. |
| Closed | Christmas & occaaionally. |
| Directions | 1.5 miles off A1, 5 miles N of Newark, Cromwell/Norwell exit (signed 'Doll Museum'). At Cromwell left to Norwell 1.5 miles. House in village opp. school lane on corner of Willoughby Court. |

**Andrew & Sarah Nesbitt**
Willoughby House,
Main Street, Norwell, Newark,
Nottinghamshire NG23 6JN
Tel +44 (0)1636 636266
Email willoughbybandb@aol.com
Web www.willoughbyhousebandb.co.uk

Entry 381  Map 9

# Nottinghamshire

## Wisteria Court

A listed, terraced cottage in Georgian Southwell – ideal for visiting the Minster. On the road but quiet at night, the modest cottage with a big-house feel is crisply elegant inside. Bedrooms, one with a cast-iron fireplace, another with a beautifully upholstered armchair, are small but charming with pillows to die for; the sitting room has rich rugs and cushions. Friendly Lynn treats you to fruit salads, organic eggs, bacon and honeycomb from the farm shop – in the coutyard garden on sunny days. The town is pretty; numerous castles and antique shops are close by. *Children over 12 welcome.*

Ethical Collection: Food. See page 412.

| | |
|---|---|
| Price | £75. Singles £37.50. |
| Rooms | 2: 1 double, 1 twin. |
| Meals | Pubs/restaurants 300 yds. |
| Closed | Rarely. |
| Directions | From A1 at Newark A617 towards Southwell. Left after Averham; 3 miles on, approach town, 'Minster spires' in view; sharp right turn, house 200 yds on left. |

Lynn McKay
Wisteria Court,
58 Church Street,
Southwell,
Nottinghamshire NG25 0HG
Tel      +44 (0)1636 815509
Email   susan_lynn@btinternet.com

Entry 382   Map 9

# Nottinghamshire

## The Yellow House

A butter-yellow 30s semi in a quiet, tree-lined street. Suzanne, a well-travelled ex-model, and Misza her lovely dog, welcome you in. Colour schemes are cool, peaceful, with the occasional oriental touch. Your bedroom in the eaves – a charming, cossetting little eyrie, with a good big bed – is crisply decorated in bold cream-and-olive florals, and has an armchair with books and a good shower. Suzanne offers breakfast on the terrace in fine weather and has loads of info on walks. Nottingham's attractions are three miles away, the great oaks of Sherwood Forest are 12 miles north.

| | |
|---|---|
| Price | £65. Singles £45. |
| Rooms | 1 double. |
| Meals | Pubs 0.5 miles, restaurants 1 mile. |
| Closed | Christmas & New Year. |
| Directions | From A60 main Mansfield road going north, at junc. with Vale Pub right onto Thackerey's Lane; at r'bout straight on; after 100 yds right into Whernside Rd. Left at x-roads into Littlegreen Rd; house on left. |

Mrs Suzanne Prew-Smith
The Yellow House,
7 Littlegreen Road, Woodthorpe,
Nottingham, Nottinghamshire NG5 4LE
Tel      +44 (0)1159 262280
Email   suzanne.prewsmith1@btinternet.com
Web     www.bandb-nottingham.co.uk

Entry 383   Map 8

# Oxfordshire

## Uplands House

Come to be spoiled at this 'farmhouse' built in 1875 for the Earl of Jersey's son and completely renovated by this talented couple. It's elegant and sumptuously furnished with large, light bedrooms, crisp linen, thick towels, spoiling bathrooms and long bucolic views from the Orangery where you have tea and cake. Relax here with a book as the sounds and smells of the garden waft by, or chat to charming Poppy while she creates a delicious dinner. Breakfast is Graham's domain – try smoked salmon with scrambled eggs and red caviar. You're well placed for exploring but you may find it hard to leave.

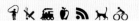 Travel Club offer. See page 414.

| | |
|---|---|
| Price | £90–£150. Singles £60–£90. |
| Rooms | 3: 1 double, 1 twin/double, 1 four-poster. |
| Meals | Dinner, 2-4 courses, £20–£30. Pub 1.25 miles. |
| Closed | Rarely. |
| Directions | M40 junc.11; through Banbury, A422 through Wroxton, pass 'Warwickshire' & 'Upton House 200 yds' signs. Turn right after 10 yds down drive signed Uplands Farm; 1st entrance on right. |

Poppy Cooksey & Graham Paul
Uplands House,
Upton, Banbury,
Oxfordshire OX15 6HJ

| | |
|---|---|
| Tel | +44 (0)1295 678663 |
| Email | poppy@cotswolds-uplands.co.uk |
| Web | www.cotswolds-uplands.co.uk |

Entry 384   Map 8

# Oxfordshire

## Buttslade House

Choose between a gorgeous ground-floor retreat across the courtyard, or a very pretty room in the 17th-century farmhouse with its barns and stables. Both have their own sitting rooms with a clever melody of ancient and contemporary styles; Spanish art, antique sofas, bright cushions. Beds have seriously good mattresses, feather and down pillows and crisp white linen; bathrooms are smart and sparkling – one with a Victorian roll top. Diana is lovely, and will pamper you or leave you, there's a blissful garden to stroll through, food is fresh and local and it's a hop to the village pub. A fun and stylish treat.

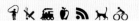 Travel Club offer. See page 414.

| | |
|---|---|
| Price | £75. Singles £50. |
| Rooms | 2: 1 double & sitting room; 1 twin & sitting room with separate bath. |
| Meals | Dinner, 3 courses, £25. Lunch £7. Pub 100 yds. |
| Closed | Rarely. |
| Directions | From B4035 look for signs to Wykham Arms. Buttslade is 2nd house beyond pub, going down hill. |

Diana Thompson
Buttslade House,
Temple Mill Road, Sibford Gower,
Banbury, Oxfordshire OX15 5RX

| | |
|---|---|
| Tel | +44 (0)1295 788818 |
| Email | janthompson50@hotmail.com |
| Web | www.buttsladehouse.co.uk |

Entry 385   Map 8

# Oxfordshire

## Gower's Close

All the nooks, crannies and beams you'd expect from an ancient thatched cottage in a Cotswold village... and more besides: good food, lively conversation and lots of inside information about gardens to visit. Judith is a keen gardener who writes books on the subject (her passion for plants is evident from her own glorious garden) and her style and intelligence are reflected in her home. Pretty, south-facing and full of sunlight, the sitting room opens onto the garden and terrace. Bedrooms are light, charming and cottagey – the twin is at garden level. A thoroughly relaxing place to stay.

| | |
|---|---|
| Price | £75. Singles £50. |
| Rooms | 2: 1 double, 1 twin. |
| Meals | Dinner, 4 courses, £28 (min. 4 people). Pub/restaurant 100 yds. |
| Closed | Christmas & New Year. |
| Directions | In Sibford Gower, 0.5 miles south off B4035 between Banbury & Chipping Campden. On Main Street, same side as church & school. |

|  | Judith Hitching & John Marshall |
|---|---|
| | Gower's Close, |
| | Sibford Gower, Banbury, |
| | Oxfordshire OX15 5RW |
| Tel | +44 (0)1295 780348 |
| Email | judith@gowersclose.co.uk |
| Web | www.gowersclose.co.uk |

✕ 🐾 🐈

Entry 386   Map 8

# Oxfordshire

## Minehill House

Bump your way up the track (mind the car!) to the top of a wild and windswept hill and a gorgeous family farmhouse with views for miles and young, energetic Hester to care for you. Children will adore the ping-pong table and the trampoline; their parents will enjoy the gleaming old flagstones, vibrant contemporary oils, wood-burning stove and seriously sophisticated food. Rest well in the big double room with its verdant leafy wallpaper and stunning views, and a cubbyhole door to extra twin beds; bathrooms are sparklingly clean and spacious. Bracing walks straight from the door.

| | |
|---|---|
| Price | £90. Singles from £50. |
| Rooms | 1 double/family. |
| Meals | Dinner, 3 courses, £30. Supper £15. BYO. Packed lunch available. Pubs 1-5 miles. |
| Closed | Christmas & New Year. |
| Directions | From Banbury B4035 to Brailes; after 10 miles left for Hook Norton; 0.5 miles, right onto unmarked uphill farm track to house. |

|  | Hester & Ed Sale |
|---|---|
| | Minehill House, |
| | Lower Brailes, |
| | Banbury, |
| | Oxfordshire OX15 5BJ |
| Tel | +44 (0)1608 685594 |
| Email | ed_and_hester@lineone.net |

🏃 🐾 🐈

Entry 387   Map 8

# Oxfordshire

## Rectory Farm

A general sense of peaceful order pervades at this solid, big house set in a manicured lawn. Inside find large, light bedrooms, floral and feminine, with bold chintz bed covers, draped kidney-shaped dressing tables, thick mattresses; some have garden views, others face the farm buildings. Sink into comfy sofas flanking a huge fireplace in the drawing room, breakfast on local bacon and sausage with free-range eggs, stroll the pretty garden, or grab a rod and try your luck on one of the trout lakes. Elizabeth knows her patch well; walkers can borrow maps, and she can point the way to lovely shops for the dedicated.

| Price | £80–£90. Singles £50–£65. |
|---|---|
| Rooms | 3: 1 double, 1 twin/double; 1 twin/double with separate bath. |
| Meals | Pub/restaurant 1.5 miles. |
| Closed | December & January. |
| Directions | A44 out of Chipping Norton towards Moreton-in-the-Marsh. After 1.5 miles right into Salford. Right at pub, then immediate left uphill past green on right. Left into drive for Rectory Farm, continue 200 yds then left. |

Elizabeth Colston
Rectory Farm,
Salford,
Chipping Norton,
Oxfordshire OX7 5YZ

| Tel | +44 (0)1608 643209 |
|---|---|
| Email | colston@rectoryfarm75.freeserve.co.uk |
| Web | www.rectoryfarm.info |

Entry 388   Map 8

# Oxfordshire

## Home Farmhouse

The house is charming, with low, wobbly ceilings, exposed beams, Inglenook fireplaces and winding stairs; the bedrooms, perched above their own staircases like crows' nests, are decorated with extravagant swathes of rich floral chintz. All rooms are unusual, old and full of character, but luxurious; lavish curtains embellish one bath. The family's history and travels are evident all over, the barn room has its own entrance and the Grove-Whites – who are super – run their B&B as a team. Two delightful dogs, too – Samson and Goliath. It's all so laid-back you'll find it hard to leave.

Travel Club offer. See page 414.

| Price | £80. Singles £52. |
|---|---|
| Rooms | 3: 2 twins/doubles, 1 double. |
| Meals | Dinner £27. Supper £20. Pub 100 yds. |
| Closed | Christmas. |
| Directions | M40 junc. 10, A43 for Northampton. After 5 miles, left to Charlton. There, left & house on left, 100 yds past Rose & Crown. |

Rosemary & Nigel Grove-White
Home Farmhouse,
Charlton, Banbury,
Oxfordshire OX17 3DR

| Tel | +44 (0)1295 811683 |
|---|---|
| Fax | +44 (0)1295 811683 |
| Email | grovewhite@lineone.net |
| Web | www.homefarmhouse.co.uk |

Entry 389   Map 8

# Oxfordshire

## The Old Post House

Great natural charm in the 17th-century Old Post House: shiny flagstones, rich dark wood and mullion windows combine with warm fabrics, deep sofas and handsome furniture. Bedrooms are big, with antique wardrobes, oak headboards and a comforting old-fashioned feel. The walled gardens are lovely – rich with espaliered fruit trees and there's a pool for sunny evenings. Christine, a well-travelled ex-pat, has an innate sense of hospitality – as do her two Springer spaniels – and breakfasts are delicious. There's village traffic but your sleep should be sound, and Deddington is delightful. *Children over 12 welcome.*

| | |
|---|---|
| Price | £80. Singles £52. |
| Rooms | 3: 1 twin/double; 1 double with separate bath, 1 four-poster with separate shower. |
| Meals | Occasional dinner. Pubs/restaurants in village. |
| Closed | Rarely. |
| Directions | A4260 Oxford–Banbury. In Deddington, on right next to cream Georgian house. Park opposite. |

Christine Blenntoft
The Old Post House,
New Street,
Deddington,
Oxfordshire OX15 0SP
Tel +44 (0)1869 338978
Email kblenntoft@aol.com
Web www.oldposthouse.co.uk

Entry 390   Map 8

# Oxfordshire

## Manor Farmhouse

Helen and John radiate pleasure and good humour. Blenheim Park is a short walk down the lane and this soft old stone house is perfect for any delusions of grandeur: good prints and paintings, venerable furniture, gentle fabrics, nothing cluttered or overdone. Shallow, curvy, 18th-century stairs lead past grandfather's bronze bust to the splendid double; the other small bedroom has its own challenging spiral stair to a cobbled courtyard. Breakfast is by the rough-hewn fireplace and the ancient dresser. Wander through the lovely garden in spring and summer; the village is palpably quiet.

| | |
|---|---|
| Price | £70-£78. Singles from £60. |
| Rooms | 2 doubles, sharing shower room. |
| Meals | Pub within walking distance. |
| Closed | Christmas. |
| Directions | A44 north from Oxford's ring road. At r'bout, 1 mile before Woodstock, left onto A4095 into Bladon. Last left in village; house on 2nd bend in road, with iron railings. |

Helen Stevenson
Manor Farmhouse,
Manor Road, Bladon, Woodstock,
Oxfordshire OX20 1RU
Tel +44 (0)1993 812168
Fax +44 (0)1993 812168
Email helstevenson@hotmail.com
Web www.oxtowns.co.uk/woodstock/manor-farmhouse/

Entry 391   Map 8

## Oxfordshire

### Caswell House

A handsome 15th-century manor house with an ancient orchard, walled gardens, smooth lawns and a moat brimming with trout. A flagstoned hall leads to a warm sitting room with vast fireplaces and squishy sofas. Spoil yourself in comfortable bedrooms, most with new shower rooms, thick towels, lovely bathroom treats and gorgeous views of the garden through leaded windows. Amanda and Richard are generous and easy-going – a game of snooker is a must! – and seasonal produce is sourced from the farm shop and cooked on the Aga. A great place to relax; for heartier souls there are 450 acres of rolling farmland.

 Travel Club offer. See page 414.

| | |
|---|---|
| Price | £85. Singles £65. |
| Rooms | 3: 2 doubles, 1 twin/double. |
| Meals | Pubs/restaurants nearby. |
| Closed | Rarely. |
| Directions | A40 Burford to Oxford. Right after 1.8 miles to Brize Norton, left at staggered x-roads. Right at r'bout, left at mini r'bout for Curbridge; on for 1.2 miles, house on right. |

|  | Amanda Matthews |
|---|---|
| | Caswell House, |
| | Caswell Lane, Brize Norton, |
| | Oxfordshire OX18 3NJ |
| Tel | +44 (0)1993 701064 |
| Fax | +44 (0)1993 774901 |
| Email | stay@caswell-house.co.uk |
| Web | www.caswell-house.co.uk |

Entry 392   Map 8

## Oxfordshire

### Rectory Farm

Come for the happy buzz of family life. It's relaxed and informal and you are welcomed with tea and homemade shortbread by Mary Anne. The date above the entrance stone reads 1629 and bedrooms, light and spotless, have beautiful stone-arched and mullioned windows. The huge twin has ornate plasterwork and views over the garden and church; the double is cosier with a carved pine headboard; both have good showers and large fluffy towels. The pedigree North Devon cattle are Robert's pride and joy and his family has farmed here for three generations. It's a treat to stay. *Minimum stay two nights at weekends & high season.*

 Travel Club offer. See page 414.

| | |
|---|---|
| Price | £75-£80. Singles £55. |
| Rooms | 2: 1 double, 1 twin. |
| Meals | Pub 2-minute walk. |
| Closed | Mid-December to mid-January. |
| Directions | From Oxford, A420 for Swindon for 8 miles & right at r'bout, for Witney (A415). Over 2 bridges, immed. right by pub car park. Right at T-junc.; drive on right, past church. |

|  | Mary Anne Florey |
|---|---|
| | Rectory Farm, |
| | Northmoor, |
| | Witney, |
| | Oxfordshire OX29 5SX |
| Tel | +44 (0)1865 300207 |
| Email | pj.florey@farmline.com |
| Web | www.oxtowns.co.uk/rectoryfarm |

Entry 393   Map 8

# Oxfordshire

## Langsmeade House

This 1920s house is irresistibly comfortable and perfect for house parties. There are two sitting rooms, velvet and tapestry sofas, wooden floors, panelling, excellent beds in flouncy bedrooms, some lovely Dutch furniture and swathes of lawn to loll on in the summer. Big-hearted Marianne imposes few rules, prepares terrific breakfasts and gives lifts in her London cab to Oxford's Park & Ride, the Ridgeway, restaurants and Garsington Opera; she will collect you up until midnight! Traffic noise from the nearby M40 is constant – loud outside, audible inside – but we defy you not to be charmed.

| | |
|---|---|
| Price | £85. Singles £50. |
| Rooms | 3: 1 double; 2 doubles sharing bath/shower (let to same party only). |
| Meals | Lunch £5. Dinner £17.50. Packed lunch £3.50. Pub 2 miles. |
| Closed | Rarely. |
| Directions | From London exit 8 M40, A418 to Thame. Cross over motorway. 1st right to Wallingford. Almost immediately house signed on right. |

**Mrs M Aben**
Langsmeade House,
Milton Common, Thame,
Oxfordshire OX9 2JY

| | |
|---|---|
| Tel | +44 (0)1844 278727 |
| Fax | +44 (0)1844 279256 |
| Email | enquiries@langsmeadehouse.co.uk |
| Web | www.langsmeadehouse.co.uk |

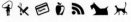

Entry 394   Map 8

# Oxfordshire

## 71 Charlbury Road

An excellent Oxford address, frequent buses or a 25-minute walk to town, traditionally comfortable, utterly peaceful. Jacqueline, talented needlewoman, pianist and ex-stewardess, pays gentle attention to housekeeping and guests, yet never intrudes. Up carpeted stairs are comfy-cosy bedrooms with Vi-Spring mattresses and, in the double, a hand-made patchwork quilt. Spotless bathrooms are stocked with towels and bedroom windows face the garden; college playing fields stretch beyond. The sitting room has pale sofas, velvet armchairs, a harpsichord, a grand piano – let Jacqueline treat you to a little Chopin!

| | |
|---|---|
| Price | £70. Singles £40. |
| Rooms | 2: 1 single; 1 double with separate bathroom. |
| Meals | Pubs/restaurants 0.5 miles. |
| Closed | Christmas, New Year & February. |
| Directions | North out of Oxford on A4165, Banbury Road, take 6th exit on right, Belbroughton Road. Left at the end into Charlbury Road; 2nd turning on right, first house on left. |

**Mrs Jacqueline Burgess**
71 Charlbury Road,
Oxford,
Oxfordshire OX2 6UX

| | |
|---|---|
| Tel | +44 (0)1865 511752 |
| Email | jackiebjoyful@yahoo.com |

Entry 395   Map 8

# Oxfordshire

## Cowdrays

Walkers will be happy here and Margaret keeps a much-used stock of plasters. The house is down a quiet lane, there are chickens, geese, dogs and, in the lovely garden – a corner of which is Gertrude Jekyll-inspired – a tennis court. This is a homely, endearingly timeworn sort of place, neither smart nor stylish, but with good furniture, masses of books, clean bathrooms, a little sitting room… even a kitchen area in which to prepare a snack if you prefer not to walk to the historic village's pubs. Birdsong and sunlight find their way into every room: the downstairs room is perfect for wheelchair-users.

| | |
|---|---|
| Price | £70–£80. Singles £35. |
| Rooms | 5: 2 doubles; 1 twin with separate shower; 1 twin, 1 single sharing bath/shower. |
| Meals | Packed lunch £7.50. Pubs within 10-minute walk. |
| Closed | Rarely. |
| Directions | Off A417, 3 miles from Wantage. Into East Hendred, 3rd right into Orchard Lane; past Plough pub on left; left into Cat St. House behind wall & gates (immediately on right). Good map on website. |

|  | Margaret Bateman |
|---|---|
| | Cowdrays, |
| | Cat Street, |
| | East Hendred, Wantage, |
| | Oxford, Oxfordshire OX12 8JT |
| Tel | +44 (0)1235 833313 |
| Email | enquiries@cowdrays.co.uk |
| Web | www.cowdrays.co.uk |

# Oxfordshire

## Brook Barn

Not your average country B&B, but a swish interior of light oak, soaring rafters, lots of light and space, and well-travelled charming owners. Bedrooms are of the boutique-hotel breed: good lighting, lots of space for sitting, and beds that you want to climb into there and then; bathrooms vary in size but all have enormous towels and lovely lotions and potions. Breakfast at a time to suit you, either in your room, on your terrace, or in the beamed dining room; all is sourced locally and the mushrooms are home grown. Grab a book, stroll round the garden, or find a sofa to flop into downstairs – this is a place to relax.

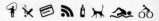

Travel Club offer. See page 414.

| | |
|---|---|
| Price | £75–£125. Singles £55–£95. |
| Rooms | 3: 2 doubles; 1 twin/double with separate bath/shower. |
| Meals | Dinner £28.50. Supper, 2 courses, £15. Late supper, soup & sandwich, £5. Packed lunch £10.50–£19.50. (Dinner/supper prices may vary.) Pub/restaurant 2 miles. |
| Closed | Christmas. |
| Directions | Ashbury road out of Wantage. Left turn to Letcombe Regis, round right hand bend, 400 yds after cream house, drive on left. |

|  | Sarah-Jane & Mark Ashman |
|---|---|
| | Brook Barn, |
| | Letcombe Regis, Wantage, |
| | Oxfordshire OX12 9JD |
| Tel | +44 (0)1235 766502 |
| Fax | +44 (0)1183 290452 |
| Email | info@brookbarn.com |
| Web | www.brookbarn.com |

## Oxfordshire

### Fyfield Manor

One of the most fabulous houses in Oxfordshire (once owned by Simon de Montfort) with vast water gardens created by the Browns. Through the grand wood-panelled hall enter a beamed dining room with high-backed chairs and brass rubbings; you breakfast (local, free-range, organic) through the 12th-century arch... or al fresco. Bedrooms are large, warm and light with snowy bed covers and views. Oxford Park & Ride is nearby, there's walking from the door and delightful Christine has wangled you a free glass of wine in the local pub if you walk or cycle. Superb. *Children over ten welcome.*

Ethical Collection: Environment.
See page 412.

Travel Club offer. See page 414.

| | |
|---|---|
| Price | From £70. Singles from £50. |
| Rooms | 2: 1 twin/double; 1 twin/double/family with separate bath. |
| Meals | Pubs within 1 mile. |
| Closed | Rarely. |
| Directions | M4 junc. 8/9; A4130 through Henley to Wallingford. Turn off for Benson; continue through village 1 mile. Last house on right, behind 6 foot-high brick wall. |

|  | **Christine Brown** |
|---|---|
| | Fyfield Manor, |
| | Benson, Wallingford, |
| | Oxfordshire OX10 6HA |
| Tel | +44 (0)1491 835184 |
| Fax | +44 (0)1491 825635 |
| Email | chris_fyfield@hotmail.co.uk |
| Web | www.fyfieldmanor.co.uk |

Entry 398  Map 4

## Oxfordshire

### Larchdown Farm

There's a huge wow factor here: the sight of honey-coloured rafters to the ceiling and the polished ash floor and balusters along the gallery in the entrance hall is breathtaking. This open space connects the two ends of the house: visitors have the right-hand end to themselves with their own drawing room. An extremely comfortable family home with lovely pictures, old rugs, books, pretty furniture and lots of flowers; the traditional, large ground-floor bedroom leads out to a wild area of the garden. Have the Horton mega-breakfast in the kitchen with its wonderful pool and garden views: watch the endless stream of visiting birds.

Travel Club offer. See page 414.

| | |
|---|---|
| Price | From £80. Singles £45–£75. |
| Rooms | 2 twins/doubles. |
| Meals | Pub/restaurant 1 mile. |
| Closed | Christmas & New Year. |
| Directions | A4074 to Oxford; right to Checkendon. In village pass pub, church & cricket pitch; right after red phone box. Whitehall Lane out of Checkendon, Larchdown 400 yards on right. |

|  | **David & Cally Horton** |
|---|---|
| | Larchdown Farm, |
| | Whitehall Lane, |
| | Checkendon, Reading, |
| | Oxfordshire RG8 0TT |
| Tel | +44 (0)1491 682282 |
| Email | larchdown@onetel.com |
| Web | www.larchdown.com |

Entry 399  Map 4

# Oxfordshire

## Hernes

The lovely rambling farmhouse has been in the family for over a century and has a warmly individual flavour. Pre-Raphaelite Aunt Connie looks down on you in the dimly-lit hall, the billiard room, with log-burning stove and comfortable chairs, is vast, and more ancestors keep an eye on you at breakfast. High-ceilinged bedrooms come without the usual arctic chill and have long views and country-house charm. The garden is wonderful, the surroundings peacefully rural and there's home-produced honey and marmalade for breakfast. Perfect for exploring Henley and some gorgeous *Vicar of Dibley* countryside.

Travel Club offer. See page 414.

| | |
|---|---|
| Price | From £99. Singles from £67.50. Single-night bank holiday surcharge. |
| Rooms | 3: 1 twin/double, 1 four-poster; 1 double with separate bath. |
| Meals | Pub/restaurants 1 mile. |
| Closed | December to mid-January & occasionally. |
| Directions | Over lights in centre of Henley as far as Town Hall. Left through car park; right onto Greys Rd for 2 miles; 300 yds after 30mph zone, 2nd drive on right; signed drive to main house. |

| | |
|---|---|
| | **Richard & Gillian Ovey** |
| | Hernes, |
| | Henley-on-Thames, |
| | Oxfordshire RG9 4NT |
| Tel | +44 (0)1491 573245 |
| Email | governor@herneshenley.com |
| Web | www.herneshenley.com |

Entry 400   Map 4

# Rutland

## Old Rectory

Jane Austen fans will swoon. This elegant 1740s village house was used as Mr Collins's 'humble abode' by the BBC: you breakfast in the beautiful dining room that was 'Mr Collins's hall', and you can sleep in 'Miss Bennett's bedroom'. Victoria is the archetypal English woman – feisty, fun and gregarious – and looks after you beautifully with White Company linen in chintzy old-fashioned bedrooms and (not swish) bathrooms, fruit from the lovely garden and Aga-cooked bacon and eggs. You are near to some pleasant market towns and lovely walking and riding country. Don't forget the smelling salts!

Travel Club offer. See page 414.

| | |
|---|---|
| Price | £80. |
| Rooms | 2: 1 twin; 1 double with separate bath. |
| Meals | Pubs within 3 miles. |
| Closed | Rarely. |
| Directions | 5 miles NE of Oakham, through Ashwell. Or 7 miles west of A1 from Stretton. |

| | |
|---|---|
| | **Victoria Owen** |
| | Old Rectory, |
| | Teigh, |
| | Oakham, |
| | Rutland LE15 7RT |
| Tel | +44 (0)1572 787681 |
| Email | torowen@btinternet.com |
| Web | www.teighbedandbreakfast.co.uk |

Entry 401   Map 9

# Rutland

## Old Hall Coach House

A rare and special setting; the grounds of the house meet the edge of Rutland Water, with far-reaching lake and church views. Inside: high ceilings, stone archways, antiques and a conservatory overlooking a year-round stunning garden and croquet lawn. Bedrooms are traditional with modern touches and comfortable; the double and single have super new bathrooms. Rutland is a mini-Cotswolds of stone villages and gentle hills, the lake encourages you to sail, fish, walk or ride, and Georgian Stamford, Burghley House and Belvoir Castle are nearby. Cecilie is a well-travelled, interesting host. *Minimum stay two nights at weekends.*

| | |
|---|---|
| Price | From £90. Singles from £40. |
| Rooms | 3: 1 double; 1 twin, 1 single, each with separate bath. |
| Meals | Dinner £30. Pub/restaurant 5-minute walk. |
| Closed | Occasionally. |
| Directions | From A1 Stamford bypass A606 for Oakham for 3 miles. Fork left for Edith Weston; past village sign; 1st right, Church Lane; past church, right down hill; on right on left bend. |

Cecilie Ingoldby
Old Hall Coach House,
Edith Weston, Oakham,
Rutland LE15 8HQ

| | |
|---|---|
| Tel | +44 (0)1780 721504 |
| Email | cecilieingoldby@aol.com |
| Web | www.oldhallcoachhouse.co.uk |

Entry 402   Map 9

# Shropshire

## Pinfold Cottage

Heart-warming B&B in a beautiful spot with lots of books, a parrot called Polly and vintage games and toys to add to the merry clutter. Walls are covered in illustrations and some lovely paintings, bedrooms are calm, simple and charming, but the biggest treat is Sue. Generous with her time, spirit and home cooking, she makes her own muesli with fruits and nuts from the garden. Natural sounds are provided by the well-fed birdlife and the trickle of the stream that meanders through the enchanting garden. Breakfasts are healthy and delicious and you'll revel in the peace. Superb value.

| | |
|---|---|
| Price | £50. Singles £30. |
| Rooms | 2: 1 double, 1 single, each with separate shower. Extra bath available. |
| Meals | Dinner, 3 courses, from £15. Packed lunch £7. Restaurant 0.5 miles. |
| Closed | Rarely. |
| Directions | From Oswestry, A483 from A5 for Welshpool. 1st left to Maesbury; 3rd right at x-roads with school on corner; 1st house on right. |

Mrs Sue Barr
Pinfold Cottage,
Newbridge,
Maesbury, Oswestry,
Shropshire SY10 8AY

| | |
|---|---|
| Tel | +44 (0)1691 661192 |
| Email | suebarr100@hotmail.com |

Entry 403   Map 7

## Shropshire

### Top Farmhouse

The charming roadside house in little Knockin is 16th-century, magpie-gabled and rambling, the church and pound are 800 years old and Pam is theatrical and fun. Downstairs is attractive, warm and cosy, a lattice of beams dividing the dining room from the sitting room where wine and conversation flow. Upstairs, floors rise, fall and creak, and all is in apple-pie order: beds are of brass, oak and varnished pine, tea trays are filled with treats. A place with a huge heart to which the loyal return – and Pam's breakfasts are as generous as her spirit. Chirk and Powys castles are near. *Children over 11 welcome.*

| Price | £65–£75. Singles from £35. |
|---|---|
| Rooms | 3: 1 double, 1 twin, 1 double/family room. |
| Meals | Packed lunch available. Pub walking distance. |
| Closed | Rarely. |
| Directions | From Shrewsbury, A5 north. Through Nesscliffe & after 2 miles, left to Knockin. Through Knockin, past Bradford Arms. 250 yds on left. |

|  | Pam Morrissey |
|---|---|
|  | Top Farmhouse, |
|  | Knockin, Oswestry, |
|  | Shropshire SY10 8HN |
| Tel | +44 (0)1691 682582 |
| Email | p.a.m@knockin.freeserve.co.uk |
| Web | www.topfarmknockin.co.uk |

Entry 404   Map 7

## Shropshire

### Brimford House

Tucked under the Breidden Hills, farm and Georgian farmhouse have been in David's family for four generations. Views stretch all the way to the Severn; the simple garden does not try to compete. Bedrooms are spotless and fresh: a half-tester with rope-twist columns and Sanderson fabrics, a twin with Victorian wrought-iron bedsteads, a double with a brass bed and huge bathroom with roll top bath. Liz, friendly and helpful, serves you breakfast round the tulip-legged table: tuck into fresh farm eggs and homemade preserves. Farmhouse comfort, great value and walks from the door.

 Travel Club offer. See page 414.

| Price | £55–£70. Singles £40–£60. |
|---|---|
| Rooms | 3: 2 doubles, 1 twin. |
| Meals | Packed lunch £4.50. Pub 3-minute walk. |
| Closed | Rarely. |
| Directions | From Shrewsbury A458 Welshpool road. After Ford, right onto B4393. Just after Crew Green, left for Criggion. House 1st on left after Admiral Rodney pub. |

|  | Liz & David Dawson |
|---|---|
|  | Brimford House, |
|  | Criggion, Shrewsbury, |
|  | Shropshire SY5 9AU |
| Tel | +44 (0)1938 570235 |
| Email | info@brimford.co.uk |
| Web | www.brimford.co.uk |

Entry 405   Map 7

# Shropshire

## The Isle

History buffs and nature lovers will delight: these 800 acres are almost enfolded by the River Severn; drive through lion-topped stone pillars to the house, built in about 1682 and extended later. Charming Ros and Edward are truly hands-on: all wood for fires is grown on the estate which also provides eggs, bacon, ham and vegetables – so you eat well! Flop in front of a huge fire in the drawing room with Chinese rug, family antiques and sublime views. Peaceful bedrooms are large and light with pocket-sprung memory mattresses and snazzy, upmarket bathrooms. Super walks, rides and fishing on the estate.

Travel Club offer. See page 414.

| Price | £75–£90. Singles £50–£60. |
|---|---|
| Rooms | 3: 2 doubles; |
| | 1 twin with separate bath. |
| Meals | Packed lunch £5. Dinner £20. |
| | Pub/restaurant 4.3 miles. |
| Closed | Never. |
| Directions | From Shrewsbury follow signs for |
| | Oswestry/Bicton (B4380). At Four |
| | Crosses pub turn right into Isle |
| | Lane. After 0.5 mile drive through |
| | pillars with lions. Follow B&B signs. |

Ros & Edward Tate
The Isle,
Bicton,
Shrewsbury,
Shropshire SY3 8EE
Tel      +44 (0)1743 851218
Email  enandrstate@lineone.net

Entry 406    Map 7

# Shropshire

## Meole Brace Hall

The Hathaways take B&B to a new state of excellence and love having guests in their heavenly house: Georgian and listed, with manicured gardens. It is the quintessence of English period elegance. Joan is a terrific cook who radiates courtesy and charm; Charles cheerfully assumes the role of 'mine host'. Their sumptuous home is rich with antiques, polished mahogany and eye-catching wallpapers and fabrics, and the Blue Room has an elegant half-tester bed. Summer breakfasts are taken in the conservatory, as is afternoon tea. A 20-minute stroll from Abbey and town, but it feels a million miles away.

| Price | From £79. Singles from £59. |
|---|---|
| Rooms | 3: 2 doubles, 1 twin. |
| Meals | Restaurants 1 mile. |
| Closed | Rarely. |
| Directions | A5 & A49 junc. (south of bypass), |
| | follow signs to centre. Over 1st mini |
| | r'bout, 2nd exit at next; 2nd left |
| | into Upper Rd; 150 yds on at bend, |
| | left & immed. right into Church |
| | Lane. Drive at bottom on left. |

Joan Hathaway
Meole Brace Hall,
Shrewsbury, Shropshire SY3 9HF
Tel      +44 (0)1743 235566
Fax     +44 (0)1743 236886
Email  hathaway@meolebracehall.co.uk
Web    www.meolebracehall.co.uk

Entry 407    Map 7

## Shropshire

### Brompton Farmhouse

Surround yourself with calming caramels, creams, beiges and golds in this Georgian farmhouse with a contemporary twist. Phillipa, an interior designer, has worked her magic here and it's all delightfully understated: a large comfortable sitting room with open fire and squishy sofas, bright bathrooms with thick towels, spoiling beds and linen, fresh flowers and gleaming furniture. Outside are acres of National Trust land, beautifully looked after, for walks, ambles and picnics. Food is scrumptious and generous; smoked kippers, scrambled eggs and homemade damson jam at breakfast, and farmhouse cooking for supper. *Brompton cookery school in converted barn; courses to suit all.*

## Shropshire

### Acton Pigot

Elegance abounds and yet there's a family farmhouse feel. The fine old house sits well on its ancient piece of ground, its sash windows looking across to the site of England's first parliament. The delightful Owens spoil you with afternoon tea before a log fire in the sitting room (and in the lovely garden in summer). Come for deep beds, soft lights, fine linen, hand-printed wallpaper and English oak in stair, beam and floor. Bedrooms are inviting and cosy. The two-acre garden hugs the house – a treat with rare plants, croquet lawn, shady spots and pool for summer. A restorative place run by special people.

Travel Club offer. See page 414.

| | |
|---|---|
| Price | £75–£95. Singles from £55. |
| Rooms | 3 twins/doubles. |
| Meals | Packed lunch £5. Dinner £25. Restaurants 1.5 miles. |
| Closed | Christmas & New Year. |
| Directions | 4 miles south of Shrewsbury on A458. In Cross Houses, left after petrol station, signed Atcham. Down lane & right to Brompton; follow to farm. |

| | |
|---|---|
| Price | From £75. Singles £50. |
| Rooms | 3: 1 double, 1 twin/double, 1 family room. |
| Meals | Pub 3 miles. |
| Closed | Christmas. |
| Directions | From A5 & Shrewsbury, onto A458 for Bridgnorth; 200 yds on, right to Acton Burnell. Entering Acton Burnell, left to Kenley; 0.5 miles, left to Acton Pigot; house 1st on left. |

|  |  |
|---|---|
| | **Philippa Home** |
| | Brompton Farmhouse, |
| | Cross Houses, |
| | Shrewsbury, |
| | Shropshire SY5 6LE |
| Tel | +44 (0)1743 761629 |
| Email | info@bromptonfarmhouse.co.uk |
| Web | www.bromptonfarmhouse.co.uk |

|  |  |
|---|---|
| | **John & Hildegard Owen** |
| | Acton Pigot, |
| | Acton Burnell, |
| | Shrewsbury, |
| | Shropshire SY5 7PH |
| Tel | +44 (0)1694 731209 |
| Email | actonpigot@farming.co.uk |
| Web | www.actonpigot.co.uk |

Entry 408   Map 7

Entry 409   Map 7

# Shropshire

## Hannigans Farm

High on the hillside, a mile up the drive, the views roll out before you – stunning. Privacy and peace are yours in the converted dairy and barn across the flower-filled yard. Big, carpeted, ground-floor rooms have comfy beds and sofas; one has views that roll towards the setting sun. In the morning Fiona and Alistair, delightful, easy-going and fun, serve you home eggs, sausages from their own pigs and honey from their bees in the book-lined dining room of their farmhouse. Feel free to take tea in the garden with its little hedges and manicured lawns; you'll feel restored in this quiet Shropshire corner.

 Travel Club offer. See page 414.

| | |
|---|---|
| Price | £70. Singles by arrangement. |
| Rooms | 2 twins. |
| Meals | Pub 1.25 miles. |
| Closed | Rarely. |
| Directions | From Bridgnorth, A458 to Shrewsbury. 0.5 miles after Morville, right onto stone road & follow signs for 1 mile, to farm. |

**Mrs Fiona Thompson**
Hannigans Farm,
Morville,
Bridgnorth,
Shropshire WV16 4RN
Tel       +44 (0)1746 714332
Email   hannigansfarm@btinternet.com
Web    www.hannigans-farm.co.uk

Entry 410   Map 7

# Shropshire

## Jinlye

*Wuthering Heights* in glorious Shropshire – and every room with a view. There's comfort too, in the raftered lounge with its huge open fire, the swish dining room for fun breakfasts, the conservatory scented in summer – and the spacious bedrooms with their deep-pile carpets, new mattresses and sumptuous touches... expect faux-marble reliefs, floral sinks, boudoir chairs and spotless *objets*. Sheltered Jinlye sits in lush landscaped gardens surrounded by hills, rare birds, wild ponies and windswept ridges. Kate, Jan and their little papillon dogs look after you professionally and with ease.

| | |
|---|---|
| Price | £74–£86. Singles £54–£62. |
| Rooms | 6: 3 doubles, 2 twins/doubles, 1 twin. |
| Meals | Packed lunch on request. Pubs 1 mile. |
| Closed | Christmas Day. |
| Directions | From Shrewsbury A49 to Church Stretton then right towards All Stretton. Once in All Stretton right, immed. past phone box, up a winding road, up the hill to Jinlye. |

**Jan & Kate Tory**
Jinlye,
Castle Hill, All Stretton,
Church Stretton, Shropshire SY6 6JP
Tel       +44 (0)1694 723243
Fax      +44 (0)1694 723243
Email   info@jinlye.co.uk
Web    www.jinlye.co.uk

Entry 411   Map 7

## Shropshire

### Victoria House

A lovely part of England, with great walking on the doorstep, but in this cosy town house you get a few urban treats like a good pub next door and a tea shop below. Breakfast is hearty with organic leanings, there's a little guest sitting room for flopping, and your bedroom is deeply comfortable: posh mattresses, lovely linen, fluffy towels, views over the town to the Longmynd hill range and a Victorian feel with the odd splosh of contemporary chic. Bathrooms are fairly modest and not state-of-the-art, but all are scrupulously fresh, and Linda – a Shropshire lass – looks after you impeccably.

Ethical Collection: Food; Community.
See page 412.

Travel Club offer. See page 414.

| Price | £55–£70. Singles £32.50–£40. |
|---|---|
| Rooms | 6: 4 doubles, 1 twin; 1 double with separate shower. |
| Meals | Packed lunch £5. Pub/restaurant 10 yds. |
| Closed | Never. |
| Directions | From Shrewsbury or Ludlow take A49 to Church Stretton. Turn off A49 into Sandford Avenue. Left onto High Street, past square, past Bucks Head pub on right. House is next door but one to Bucks Head. |

|  | Linda Smith Victoria House, 48 High Street, Church Stretton, Shropshire SY6 6BX |
|---|---|
| Tel | +44 (0)1694 723823 |
| Email | victoriahouse@fsmail.net |
| Web | www.bedandbreakfast-shropshire.co.uk |

Entry 412   Map 7

## Shropshire

### The Manor House

The house, garden and owner have bags of character: clever Caroline, an interior designer, gives you lots of space to roam. Find ancient beams and salvaged panels, the odd contemporary painting or ceramic, a twinkling wood-burner, and bright splashes of colour. Your bedroom is lovely, with a sloping ceiling, fresh white walls and a bang-up-to-date bathroom – all chubby towels and Jo Malone potions. Peaceful breakfasts overlooking the bird-filled garden will set you up for anything and there are plenty of hearty walks from the door, or nearby Ludlow and Church Stretton to explore. *Minimum stay two nights.*

Travel Club offer. See page 414.

| Price | £95. Singles £80. |
|---|---|
| Rooms | 1 double. |
| Meals | Packed lunch £10. Dinner, 2 courses, £15; 3 courses, £20. BYO. Pub/restaurant 100 yds. |
| Closed | Christmas & New Year. |
| Directions | From Ludlow, left off A49 into Church Stretton, up to staggered cross roads, then right. Past schools on right, into All Stretton. Past Yew Tree pub, next council road left, by phone box & postbox & immed. left into drive. |

|  | Caroline Montgomery The Manor House, All Stretton, Shropshire SY6 6JU |
|---|---|
| Tel | +44 (0)1694 724508 |
| Fax | +44 (0)1694 724447 |
| Email | caro@manorhouseallstretton.co.uk |
| Web | www.manorhouseallstretton.co.uk |

Entry 413   Map 7

## Shropshire

### Clun Farm House

These young owners make a great team. Susan gives you fabulous marmalade at breakfast and seasonal produce at dinner, Anthony helps you discover the secrets of the historic village and the heavenly hills. Both are enthusiastic collectors of country artefacts and have filled their listed, 15th-century farmhouse with eye-catching things; the cowboy's saddle by the old range echoes Susan's roots. Bedrooms have aged, oiled floorboards, fun florals and bold walls. Walk Offa's Dyke and the Shropshire Way; return to a cosy wood-burner, a warm smile and a delicious dinner. Brilliant value.

| | |
|---|---|
| Price | From £70. Singles by arrangement. |
| Rooms | 2: 1 double (with extra bunk-bed room); 1 twin/double with separate shower. |
| Meals | Dinner from £25. Packed lunch £3.50. Pubs/restaurants nearby. |
| Closed | Occasionally. |
| Directions | A49 from Ludlow & onto B4368 at Craven Arms, for Clun. In High St on left 0.5 miles from Clun sign. |

Anthony & Susan Whitfield
Clun Farm House,
High Street, Clun,
Craven Arms, Shropshire SY7 8JB
Tel      +44 (0)1588 640432
Fax      +44 (0)1588 640432
Web      www.clunfarmhouse.co.uk

Entry 414   Map 7

## Shropshire

### The Birches Mill

Just as a mill should be, tucked in the nook of a postcard valley. It ended Gill and Andrew's search for a refuge from the city; it is a treat to share its seclusion and natural beauty where the only sounds are watery ones from the river. The fresh, breezy rooms in the 17th-century part have elegant brass beds, goose down duvets, fine linen and one has an original, very long, roll top bath; the new stone and oak extension blends beautifully and has become a large, attractive twin. Gill and Andrew are affable hosts in their stunning valley of meadowland and woods. *Children over 12 welcome.*

Travel Club offer. See page 414.

| | |
|---|---|
| Price | £78-£88. Singles by arrangement. |
| Rooms | 3: 1 double, 1 twin; 1 double with separate bath. |
| Meals | Packed lunch £6. Pub 3 miles. |
| Closed | November-March. |
| Directions | From Clun A488 for Bishops Castle. 1st left, for Bicton. 2nd left for Mainstone, then narrow winding lane for 1.5 miles. Up bank to farm, then 1st right for Burlow. House at bottom of hill on left by river. |

Gill Della Casa & Andrew Farmer
The Birches Mill,
Clun,
Craven Arms, Shropshire SY7 8NL
Tel      +44 (0)1588 640409
Email    gill@birchesmill.fsnet.co.uk
Web      www.birchesmill.co.uk

Entry 415   Map 7

## Shropshire

### Hopton House

Karen looks after her guests with competence and care – she even runs courses on how to do B&B! Relax and enjoy the country views in this fresh, uplifting, converted granary with old beams, high ceilings and a new sun-filled dining/sitting room overlooking the hills. Bedrooms, warm, charming, just refurbished, have digital radio, good lighting and decanters of sherry; one has a balcony, another alder wood floors. Bathrooms are spoiling, breakfast promises Ludlow sausages, Hopton House hen eggs and homemade jams, dinner is local and home-grown. Perfect B&B.

Ethical Collection: Environment; Food. See page 412.

 Travel Club offer. See page 414.

| | |
|---|---|
| Price | £75–£95. Singles from £55. |
| Rooms | 3 doubles. |
| Meals | Light supper £12.50. Restaurant 3 miles. |
| Closed | 23 December–2 January & occasionally. |
| Directions | A49 Craven Arms exit, B4368 west. After 1 mile, left signed Hopton Heath. At Hopton Heath x-roads, right over bridge, follow road right. House 2nd on left. |

| | |
|---|---|
| | Karen Thorne |
| | Hopton House, |
| | Hopton Heath, Craven Arms, |
| | Shropshire SY7 0QD |
| Tel | +44 (0)1547 530885 |
| Email | info@shropshirebreakfast.co.uk |
| Web | www.shropshirebreakfast.co.uk |

Entry 416   Map 7

## Shropshire

### Brick House Farm

From the roadside this looks unexceptional, but once through the gates and into the farmyard with strutting chickens you can see the black and white checked side of this freshly-painted 16th-century longhouse. In the guest sitting room David has kept the walls simple white, restored beams and stone flags, and found a hidden fireplace mentioned in Pevsner; warm yourself here on a comfy sofa with a good book. Sleep soundly on smart mattresses, soak in a deep Villeroy & Boch bath, tuck into home-grown lamb for supper at a smart table. The garden seeps into unspoilt countryside with peaceful, grazing horses.

| | |
|---|---|
| Price | £75. |
| Rooms | 2: 1 double, 1 twin/double, each with separate bath. |
| Meals | Dinner, 4-5 courses, £25. BYO. Packed lunch £5. |
| Closed | Rarely. |
| Directions | On A4110, from Leintwardine; house 1st on left, with sandy coloured render, opposite church. |

| | |
|---|---|
| | David Watson |
| | Brick House Farm, |
| | Adforton, Leintwardine, Craven Arms, |
| | Shropshire SY7 0NF |
| Tel | +44 (0)1568 770870 |
| Email | info@adforton.com |
| Web | www.adforton.com |

Entry 417   Map 7

## Shropshire

### Upper Buckton

Hayden and Yvonne love their stunning location – which ensures a special stay. Bedrooms are large, with huge beds made to perfection, lovely linen and proper blankets; bathrooms sport robes and treats. Standing in lush gardens that slope peacefully down to millstream, meadows and river, the house has a motte and bailey castle site, a heronry, a point-to-point course and a ha-ha. Yvonne's cooking using local produce is upmarket and creative, Hayden's wine list is a treat – marvellous for walkers returning from a day in the glorious Welsh Borders. *Children by arrangement.*

Travel Club offer. See page 414.

| Price | £84–£100. Singles £57–£65. |
|---|---|
| Rooms | 3: 1 double; 2 twins/doubles each with separate bath. |
| Meals | Dinner, 4 courses, £28. Pub/restaurant 5 miles. |
| Closed | Rarely. |
| Directions | From Ludlow, A49 to Shrewsbury. At Bromfield, A4113. Right in Walford for Buckton, on to 2nd farm on left. Large sign on building. |

Hayden & Yvonne Lloyd
Upper Buckton,
Leintwardine, Craven Arms, Ludlow,
Shropshire SY7 0JU

| Tel | +44 (0)1547 540634 |
|---|---|
| Fax | +44 (0)1547 540634 |
| Email | ghlloydco@btconnect.com |

Entry 418   Map 7

## Shropshire

### Lower Buckton Country House

You are spoiled here in house party style; energetic Carolyn – passionate about Slow food – and Henry, are born entertainers. Kick off with homemade cake in the drawing room with its oil paintings, antique furniture and old rugs; return for delicious nibbles when the lamps and wood-burner are flickering. You dine well at a huge oak table (home-reared pork, local cheeses, dreamy puddings) then nestle into the best linen and the softest pillows in your deeply restful bedroom. This is laid-back B&B: play croquet on the lawn, admire stunning views, or just find a quiet spot with a good book. *Cookery courses. Stabling for horses.*

Travel Club offer. See page 414.

| Price | £90. |
|---|---|
| Rooms | 3: 2 doubles; 1 twin/double with separate bath. |
| Meals | Dinner, 4 courses, £30. BYO wine. Pub/restaurant 4 miles. |
| Closed | Rarely. |
| Directions | West through Leintwardine; after 0.25 miles right A4113. At Walford right at x-roads down narrow lane for Buckton. Over river, 2nd house on left, entrance by village green; white gate with postbox in wall. |

Henry & Carolyn Chesshire
Lower Buckton Country House,
Buckton, Leintwardine, Shropshire
SY7 0JU

| Tel | +44 (0)1547 540532 |
|---|---|
| Email | carolyn@lowerbuckton.co.uk |
| Web | www.lowerbuckton.co.uk |

Entry 419   Map 7

# Shropshire

## Walford Court

Come for a break from clock-watching and a spot of fresh air. Large bedrooms delight with feather and down on the comfiest mattresses, scented candles, books, games and double-end roll top baths – one under a west facing window. Aga-cooked breakfasts include eggs from 'the ladies of the orchard'; candlelit dinners may be served outside on fine evenings. Wander through apple, plum and pear trees, find a motte and bailey, strike out for a long hike. Craig and Debbie are thoughtful and hugely keen on wildlife (you get binoculars) and this is the perfect place to bring a special person – and a bottle of champagne.

Ethical Collection: Environment; Food.
See page 412.

 Travel Club offer. See page 414.

| Price | £70-£80. Singles £40. |
|---|---|
| Rooms | 3: 1 double; 2 doubles each with sitting room. |
| Meals | Dinner, 2-3 courses, £14-£22. Packed lunch £6. Lunch in the tea room. Pubs/restaurants 1-3 miles. |
| Closed | Christmas & Boxing Day. |
| Directions | A49 N of Ludlow; A4113 to Knighton. Through Leintwardine; right for Walford. There, left for Presteigne, then immed. left. Signs to Walford Court Tea Room. |

Debbie & Craig Fraser
Walford Court,
Walford,
Lentwardine,
Ludlow, Shropshire SY7 0JT
Tel       +44 (0)1547 540570
Email    info@romanticbreak.com
Web      www.romanticbreak.com

# Shropshire

## 35 Lower Broad Street

You're almost at the bottom of the town, near the river and the bridge. Elaine's terraced Georgian cottage is spotless and cosy; her office doubles as a sitting area for guests with leather armchairs and desk space for workaholics. Upstairs are two good-sized doubles with a country crisp feel, big beds and a pretty blue and white bathroom. Walkers, shoppers, antique- and book hunters can fill up on homemade potato scones, black pudding, organic eggs and good coffee before striding out to explore. This is excellent value B&B: comfortable, clean and can be enjoyed without a car. Perfect for two couples.

Ethical Collection: Environment; Food.
See page 412.

 Travel Club offer. See page 414.

| Price | £65. Singles £45. |
|---|---|
| Rooms | 2 doubles sharing bath & sitting room (let to same party only). |
| Meals | Pubs/restaurants 100 yds. |
| Closed | Rarely. |
| Directions | Right out of railway station, 200 yds to lights. Left onto Corve St, then up to top of hill. At lights, right & follow to Broad St; through arch into Lower Broad St. On right towards bottom. |

Elaine Downs
35 Lower Broad Street,
Ludlow,
Shropshire SY8 1PH
Tel       +44 (0)1584 876912
Email    a.downs@tesco.net
Web      www.ludlowbedandbreakfast.blogspot.com

## Shropshire

### Rosecroft

A pretty, quiet, traditional house with charming owners, well-proportioned rooms and an elegant sitting room. But there's not a trace of pomposity and breakfasts are huge enough to set you up for the day: Pimhill organic muesli, smoked or unsmoked local bacon, black pudding, delicious jams. The garden is a delight to stroll through – in summer you can picnic – and serious walkers are close to the Welsh borders. Bedrooms and bathrooms are polished to perfection, you have fresh flowers, homebaked cakes and biscuits when you arrive, the village has a super pub and Ludlow is five miles away. *Children over 12 welcome.*

## Shropshire

### Shortgrove

Not a straight line inside or out – on this stunning, Elizabethan, timber-framed house. The approach, too, is intriguing, across the gated common, away from all roads; revel in seclusion and peace. The old English feel continues inside, where there's spaciousness, comfort and calm: expect cool colours, soft fabrics, plump armchairs, an inglenook for chilly nights. Cottagey bedrooms sit cosily under the eaves, their lovely leaded windows gazing on the two-acre garden and Shropshire beyond. Beryl – a cookery tutor and kind, generous hostess – dispatches delicious breakfasts from her Aga.

Travel Club offer. See page 414.

| | |
|---|---|
| Price | £70–£75. Singles £45–£50. |
| Rooms | 2: 1 double; 1 double with separate bath. |
| Meals | Packed lunch £5. Pub 200 yds. |
| Closed | Rarely. |
| Directions | Between Ludlow & Leominster on A49, turn onto B4362 at Woofferton. After 1.5 miles, left into Orleton. Past school & small green, house on right, opp. vicarage. |

Travel Club offer. See page 414.

| | |
|---|---|
| Price | £80–£90. Singles from £65. |
| Rooms | 2: 1 twin; 1 double with separate bath. |
| Meals | Pub 1 mile. |
| Closed | October-Easter. |
| Directions | Off A49, 1 mile south of Woofferton into School Lane. Immed. left at 2nd School Lane sign. Through gate onto common. Fork left where track divides and cont. to end of track. |

|  | Mrs Gail Benson |
|---|---|
| | Rosecroft, |
| | Orleton, |
| | Ludlow, Shropshire SY8 4HN |
| Tel | +44 (0)1568 780565 |
| Fax | +44 (0)1568 780565 |
| Email | gailanddavid@rosecroftorleton.freeserve.co.uk |
| Web | www.stmem.com/rosecroft |

|  | Beryl Maxwell |
|---|---|
| | Shortgrove, |
| | Brimfield Common, |
| | Ludlow, |
| | Shropshire SY8 4NZ |
| Tel | +44 (0)1584 711418 |
| Web | www.shortgrove-ludlow-bb.co.uk |

Entry 422   Map 7

Entry 423   Map 7

# Shropshire

## Timberstone Bed & Breakfast

The house is young, engaging and fun – as are Tracey and Alex. She, once in catering, is a reflexologist and new generation B&Ber. Come for logs in winter, charming bedrooms under the eaves, a double ended or claw-foot bath, chunky beams with a modern feel, pale colours, white cotton… and the Bowen Technique (massage) in the garden studio or the relaxing sauna. In the warm guest sitting room – brimming with art – are books, kilims on oak boards, a wood-burner. Eggs come from their hens, breakfasts are special; have an excellent home-cooked supper or head for Ludlow and its clutch of Michelin stars.

Ethical Collection: Environment; Food.
See page 412.

Travel Club offer. See page 414.

| | |
|---|---|
| Price | £87.50–£100. Singles £45–£70. |
| Rooms | 4: 2 doubles, 1 twin, 1 family. Summerhouse: 1 double & kitchenette (summer only). |
| Meals | Dinner, 3 courses, £25. Pubs/restaurants 5 miles. |
| Closed | Rarely. |
| Directions | B4364 Ludlow-Bridgnorth. After 3 miles, right to Clee Stanton; on for 1.5 miles; left at signopst to Clee Stanton; 1st house on left. |

**Tracey Baylis & Alex Read**
Timberstone Bed & Breakfast,
Clee Stanton,
Ludlow,
Shropshire SY8 3EL
Tel      +44 (0)1584 823519
Email   enquiry@timberstoneludlow.co.uk
Web     www.timberstoneludlow.co.uk

Entry 424   Map 7

# Shropshire

## Cleeton Court

Rare peace: a tiny lane leads to this part 14th-century farmhouse, immersed in the countryside with views over meadows and heathland. You have your own entrance, and the use of the pretty drawing room, elegantly comfortable with sofas and a log fire. Beamed bedrooms are delightfully furnished, one with a magnificent, chintzy four-poster and a vast bathroom; recline in the cast-iron bath with a glass of wine, gaze on views from the window as you soak. Bring your boots: the walking is superb, and charming Ros gives you a smashing, locally-sourced breakfast to get you going. *Children over five welcome.*

Travel Club offer. See page 414.

| | |
|---|---|
| Price | From £75. Singles £45. |
| Rooms | 2: 1 twin/double, 1 four-poster. |
| Meals | Pubs/restaurants 4 miles. |
| Closed | Christmas & New Year. |
| Directions | From Ludlow, A4117 for Kidderminster for 1 mile; left on B4364 for Cleobury North; on for 5 miles. In Wheathill, right for Cleeton St Mary; on for 1.5 miles; house on left. |

**Rosamond Woodward**
Cleeton Court,
Cleeton St Mary,
Ludlow, Shropshire DY14 0QZ
Tel      +44 (0)1584 823379
Fax     +44 (0)1584 823379
Email   roswoodward@talktalk.net
Web     www.cleetoncourt.co.uk

Entry 425   Map 7

# Somerset

## Emmetts Grange

A superb landscape high on the moor with 900 acres of moorland asking to be discovered – the rugged real deal. This listed country house, at the end of a long drive, is well-loved and lived-in; be greeted by a fox head in the hall and a portrait of an ancestor in wig and ermine. Easy-going, kind Tom and Lucy have boys, dogs, ponies, hens, and raise Red Devon cattle; they are knowledgeable about the area and Lucy is keen on studying the family's genealogy. Bedrooms and bathrooms are large and comfortable with an old-fashioned but bright and colourful feel. Tom is the cook and, not surprisingly, is pretty keen on the local beef.

| Price | £80–£120. Singles from £50. |
|---|---|
| Rooms | 4: 2 twins/doubles, 1 twin, 1 four-poster. |
| Meals | Dinner, 3 courses, £30. Pub 2 miles. |
| Closed | Christmas, New Year & occasionally. |
| Directions | M5 exit 27. A361 towards South Molton. 25 miles then right to A399 Ilfracombe. 1 mile, right towards Simonsbath. 6 miles, entrance to Grange on right. |

Tom & Lucy Barlow
Emmetts Grange,
Simonsbath,
Minehead, Somerset TA24 7LD
Tel   +44 (0)1643 831138
Fax   +44 (0)1643 831093
Email   mail@emmettsgrange.co.uk
Web   www.emmettsgrange.co.uk

Entry 426    Map 2

# Somerset

## North Wheddon Farm

Pootle through the vibrant green patchwork of Exmoor National Park and bowl down a pitted track to land in Blyton-esque bliss – a classic Somerset farmyard, crackling with geese and hens, round which is the gentleman farmer's house. Bedrooms are airy and calming with grand views, books, fresh flowers and small, but neat-as-a-pin bathrooms. Bring children and they will be in heaven, with eggs to collect and pigs to pat, or come just for yourself and a bit of indulgence. Food is 'River Cottage' style and much is home reared, the walking is fabulous for miles and kind Rachael sends you off with a thermos of tea.

| Price | £70–£80. Singles £37.50. |
|---|---|
| Rooms | 3: 1 double, 1 twin/double; 1 single with separate bath. |
| Meals | Dinner, 3 courses, £20. Cold/hot packed lunch £6.75–£9.75. |
| Closed | Rarely. |
| Directions | From Minehead A396 to Wheddon Cross. Pass pub on right & Moorland Hall on left. North Wheddon is next driveway on right. |

Rachael Abraham
North Wheddon Farm,
Wheddon Cross,
Somerset TA24 7EX
Tel   +44 (0)1643 841791
Email   rachael@go-exmoor.co.uk
Web   www.northwheddonfarm.co.uk

Entry 427    Map 2

## Somerset

### Glen Lodge

High brick walls and tumbling gardens in the Victorian tanner's house give way to the warm embrace of a wood-burning stove and a giddy rush of intriguing artwork – one painting is by an elephant! Polished oak floors are dotted with oriental rugs, bedrooms are immaculate, bay windows gaze on the Bristol Channel. Meryl and David care about sustainable living – feast on American home baking and fruit from their 21 acres: all is recycled, composted and enjoyed. Surrounded by the woods and wilds of Exmoor National Park yet a short stroll from popular Porlock, you'll revel in comfort, warmth and their passion for life.

Travel Club offer. See page 414.

| | |
|---|---|
| Price | £80. Singles £55. |
| Rooms | 5: 1 double; 2 doubles sharing bath; 1 double, 1 twin both with separate bath. |
| Meals | Packed lunch £8. Dinner £28. Pub/restaurant 0.5 miles. |
| Closed | Christmas & New Year. |
| Directions | From Minehead, A39 to Porlock; on entering town, left at church into Parsons Street. At 'weak bridge' sign, left over bridge. Gate to house is in front. |

Meryl Salter
Glen Lodge,
Hawkcombe,
Porlock, Somerset TA24 8LN
Tel      +44 (0)1643 863371
Fax      +44 (0)1643 863016
Email    glenlodge@gmail.com
Web      www.glenlodge.net

Entry 428   Map 2

## Somerset

### Higher Orchard

A little lane tumbles down to the centre of lovely old Dunster (the village is a two minute-walk) yet here you have open views of fields, sheep and sea. Exmoor footpaths start behind the house and Janet encourages explorers, by bike or on foot; ever helpful and kind, she is a local who knows the patch well. The 1860s house keeps its Victorian features, bedrooms are quiet and simple and the double has a view to Blue Anchor Bay and Dunster castle and church. All is homely, with stripped pine, cream curtains, fresh flowers, garden fruit and home-laid eggs for breakfast. *Children & pets by arrangement.*

Ethical Collection: Environment; Food. See page 412.

Travel Club offer. See page 414.

| | |
|---|---|
| Price | £70. Singles from £35. |
| Rooms | 3: 1 double, 2 twins/doubles. |
| Meals | Packed lunch from £3.50. Restaurants 2-minute walk. |
| Closed | Christmas. |
| Directions | From Williton, A39 for Minehead for 8 miles. Left to Dunster. There, right fork into 'The Ball'. At T-junc. at end of road, right. House 75 yds on right. |

Mrs Janet Lamacraft
Higher Orchard,
30 St George's Street,
Dunster,
Somerset TA24 6RS
Tel      +44 (0)1643 821915
Email    lamacraft@higherorchard.fsnet.co.uk
Web      www.higherorchard-dunster.co.uk

Entry 429   Map 2

# Somerset

## The Old Priory

The 12th-century priory leans against its church, has a rustic gate, a walled garden, a tumble of flowers. Both house and hostess are dignified, unpretentious and friendly. Here are old oak tables, flagstones, panelled doors, higgledy-piggledy corridors and large bedrooms in the softest colours. But a perfect English house in a sweet Somerset village needs a touch of pepper and relaxed, cosmopolitan Jane adds her own special flair with artistic touches here and there, and books and dogs for company. Dunster Castle towers above on the hill, walks start from the door.

Ethical Collection: Food. See page 412.

 Travel Club offer. See page 414.

| | |
|---|---|
| Price | £80-£90. Singles by arrangement. |
| Rooms | 3: 1 twin, 1 four-poster; 1 double with separate shower. |
| Meals | Restaurants/pubs 5-minute walk. |
| Closed | Christmas. |
| Directions | From A39 into Dunster, right at blue sign 'Unsuitable for Goods Vehicles'. Follow until church; house adjoined. |

| | |
|---|---|
| | Jane Forshaw |
| | The Old Priory, |
| | Priory Green, |
| | Dunster, |
| | Somerset TA24 6RY |
| Tel | +44 (0)1643 821540 |
| Web | www.theoldpriory-dunster.co.uk |

✗ 🚂 🐕

Entry 430   Map 2

# Somerset

## No. 7

Feast on homemade biscuits, croissants and local whortleberry jam. Feast, too, on the views of the wooded valley. Then drink in the calm – TV-free! – of Lucy and Jean-Christophe's young, cosy, uncluttered 'cottage hotel': a peace punctuated only by the chimes of the ancient church. Bedrooms are light, not large, and airy, with goosefeather pillows, patchwork quilts and pretty iron beds – but mind your head on the beams. Bathrooms are immaculately white. Down the 17th-century spiralling wooden staircase to sofa and wood-burner below – or for a seat at a crisply white table for Jean-Christophe's delicious dinner.

| | |
|---|---|
| Price | £65-£85. Singles from £45. |
| Rooms | 3: 2 doubles; 1 double with separate shower. |
| Meals | Dinner, 3 courses, from £33 (including half bottle of wine). Afternoon tea from £5. Packed lunch from £5.50. |
| Closed | Christmas. |
| Directions | M5 exit 25. A358 for Minehead, then A39 to Dunster. through village past church, 200 yds; house on left. |

| | |
|---|---|
| | Lucy & Jean-Christophe Le Grand |
| | No. 7, |
| | 7 West Street, |
| | Dunster, Somerset TA24 6SN |
| Tel | +44 (0)1643 821064 |
| Email | info@no7weststreet.co.uk |
| Web | www.no7weststreet.co.uk |

✗ 📖 🌿 🛥 🐕

Entry 431   Map 2

# Somerset

## Wyndham House

A charming Georgian house tucked away in the unspoilt town of Watchet, with its interesting little shops. Susan and Roger will greet you with homemade cake and biscuits, either in their pretty dining room – or in the unexpectedly large and beautiful garden, which overlooks the harbour and small marina. Bedrooms are comfortable and traditional, one overlooking the pretty courtyard and the other with views to Wales. Delicious breakfasts are relaxed affairs accompanied by newspapers; walk it all off in the delightful Quantocks or Exmoor National Park – you are near to both. *Children & dogs by arrangement.*

Ethical Collection: Food. See page 412.

🧳 Travel Club offer. See page 414.

| | |
|---|---|
| Price | From £70. Singles from £35. |
| Rooms | 2: 1 twin/double, 1 double both with separate bath/shower. |
| Meals | Pub/restaurants a short walk. |
| Closed | Christmas. |
| Directions | From railway station & footbridge in Watchet, up South Rd (for Doniford). After 50 yds, left into Beverly Drive. House 50 yds on left with gravel parking area. |

| | |
|---|---|
| | Susan & Roger Vincent |
| | Wyndham House, |
| | 4 Sea View Terrace, |
| | Watchet, Somerset TA23 0DF |
| Tel | +44 (0)1984 631881 |
| Fax | +44 (0)1984 631881 |
| Email | info@wyndhamhousebb.co.uk |
| Web | www.wyndhamhousebb.co.uk |

Entry 432   Map 2

# Somerset

## Causeway Cottage

Robert and Lesley are ex-restaurateurs, so guests heap praise on their food, most of which is sourced from a local butcher and fishmonger; charming Lesley also runs cookery courses. This is the perfect Somerset cottage, with an apple orchard outside and views to a lofty church across a cottage garden and a field. The bedrooms are light, restful and have a country-style simplicity with their green check bedspreads, white walls and antique pine furniture. A great hideaway for food-lovers with easy access to the M5 and a quiet, rural feel. Very special. *Children over ten welcome.*

🧳 Travel Club offer. See page 414.

| | |
|---|---|
| Price | £70. Singles by arrangement. |
| Rooms | 3: 1 double, 2 twins. |
| Meals | Supper from £25. Pub/restaurant 0.75 miles. |
| Closed | Christmas. |
| Directions | From M5 junction 26, West Buckland road for 0.75 miles. 1st left just before stone building. Bear right; 3rd house at end of lane, below church. |

| | |
|---|---|
| | Lesley & Robert Orr |
| | Causeway Cottage, |
| | West Buckland, |
| | Taunton, |
| | Somerset TA21 9JZ |
| Tel | +44 (0)1823 663458 |
| Email | causewaybb@talktalk.net |
| Web | www.causewaycottage.co.uk |

Entry 433   Map 2

## Somerset

### Rock House

Tucked away in an AONB, near the Quantocks and Exmoor, this elegant Georgian house hides behind a tall hedge in a sleepy village. Deborah greets her guests with impeccable manners and scrumptious biscuits; take tea in the drawing room where fresh flowers are beautifully arranged and there are books to read. Bedrooms are well-presented and full of thoughtful touches like fresh milk and a torch; bathrooms have generous towels and Molton Brown lotions. The Rock House fry-up will set you up for miles of walking, or a quick stroll to the top of the pretty garden with its croquet lawn. *Children & pets by arrangement.*

## Somerset

### Bashfords Farmhouse

A feeling of warmth and happiness pervades the exquisite 17th-century farmhouse in the Quantock hills. The Ritchies love doing B&B even after 15 years, and there's a homely feel with splashes of style — well-framed prints, good fabrics, comfortable sofas. Rooms are pretty, fresh and large and look over the cobbled courtyard or open fields; the sitting room has an inglenook, sofas and books. Charles and Jane couldn't be nicer, know about local walks (the Macmillan Way runs past the door) and love to cook: local meat and game, tarte tatin, homemade bread and jams. A delightful garden rambles up the hill.

Travel Club offer. See page 414.

| | |
|---|---|
| Price | From £80. Singles from £40. |
| Rooms | 2: 1 twin/double; 1 double (extra single bed) with separate bathroom. |
| Meals | Pub in village. |
| Closed | Christmas. |
| Directions | M5 exit 25, signs to A358 Minehead. Left to Halse. Rock House in middle of village, 100 yds from pub. |

| | |
|---|---|
| Price | £65-£70. Singles £37.50-£40. |
| Rooms | 3: 1 double; 1 double with separate shower; 1 twin with separate bath. |
| Meals | Dinner £27.50. Supper £22.50. Pub 75 yds. |
| Closed | Rarely. |
| Directions | M5 junc. 25. A358 for Minehead. Leave A358 at West Bagborough turning. Through village for 1.5 miles. Farmhouse 3rd on left past pub. |

**Christopher & Deborah Wolverson**
Rock House,
Halse,
Taunton,
Somerset TA4 3AF
Tel    +44 (0)1823 432956
Email  dwolverson@rockhousesomerset.co.uk
Web    www.rockhousesomerset.co.uk

**Charles & Jane Ritchie**
Bashfords Farmhouse,
West Bagborough,
Taunton,
Somerset TA4 3EF
Tel    +44 (0)1823 432015
Email  info@bashfordsfarmhouse.co.uk
Web    www.bashfordsfarmhouse.co.uk

Entry 434   Map 2

Entry 435   Map 2

# Somerset

## Tilbury Farm

The highest B&B in Somerset – up with the buzzards and the wind. Renovation is the Smiths' business and their conversion is exemplary. Reclaimed flags and seasoned oak enhance the natural beauty of the old farmhouse and barns; Pamela is a perfectionist, full of life and plans. Antiques on seagrass floors, dusky pink walls and crisp linen, a sitting room cosy with log fires in winter, a wonderfully monastic dining room for delicious breakfasts. And the setting is spectacular: 20 acres of fields and woodland, wildlife lake and spring. On a clear day you can see for 30 miles. *Children over ten welcome.*

| Price | £60-£65. Singles £45-£50. |
|---|---|
| Rooms | 3: 2 doubles, 1 twin. |
| Meals | Pubs 0.5 miles. |
| Closed | Rarely. |
| Directions | From Taunton, A358 north for Williton. Approx. 7 miles on, right for West Bagborough. Through village, up hill for 0.5 miles. Farm on left. |

Mrs Pamela Smith
Tilbury Farm,
West Bagborough,
Taunton,
Somerset TA4 3DY
Tel    +44 (0)1823 432391

Entry 436   Map 2

# Somerset

## Parsonage Farm

Breakfast beside the open fire is a feast: homemade bread and jam, eggs from the hens, juices from the orchard, pancakes and porridge from the Aga. This is an organic smallholding and your enthusiastic hosts have added an easy comfort to their 17th-century rectory farmhouse – quarry floors, log fires, books, maps and piano in the cosy sitting room. Suki, from Vermont, has turned a stable into a studio, and her pots and paintings add charm to the décor. Big bedrooms have fresh flowers and tranquil views. Wonderful walking and cycling in the Quantock Hills, and the new Coleridge Way starts down the lane.

| Price | £55-£75. Singles £35-£50. |
|---|---|
| Rooms | 3: 1 double (extra sofa bed), 1 twin/double (extra pull-out bed); 1 double sharing bath. |
| Meals | Supper £10. Dinner, 2-3 courses, £20-£25. |
| Closed | Christmas Day. |
| Directions | A39 Bridgwater-Minehead. 7 miles on, left at Cottage Inn for Over Stowey; 1.8 miles; house on right after church. |

Susan Lilienthal
Parsonage Farm,
Over Stowey,
Nether Stowey,
Somerset TA5 1HA
Tel    +44 (0)1278 733237
Email   suki@parsonfarm.co.uk
Web    www.parsonfarm.co.uk

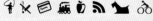

Entry 437   Map 2

# Somerset

## Church House

Feel happy in this warm Georgian rectory with sweeping views over gardens, seaside homes and the dramatic Bristol channel. Tony and Jane are great fun, enormously generous and love what they do. Bedrooms are large, pristine and indulgent with goose down duvets as soft as a cloud, swish modern bathrooms, huge towels and thoughtful extras like fluffy hot water bottles and scrumptious biscuits. Breakfasts are a grand feast of eggs from their hens, organic sausages and homemade preserves, all served on delightful china at a long mahogany table. Take the whole house and be cosseted – great for large gatherings.

| | |
|---|---|
| Price | From £80. Singles from £60. |
| Rooms | 5: 4 doubles, 1 twin. |
| Meals | Pubs 400 yds. |
| Closed | Rarely. |
| Directions | M5 junc. 21, follow signs for Kewstoke. After Old Manor Inn on right, left up Anson Rd. At T-junc. right into Kewstoke Rd. Follow road for 1 mile; church on right; drive between church & church hall. |

**Jane & Tony Chapman**
Church House,
27 Kewstoke Road, Kewstoke,
Weston-super-Mare,
Somerset BS22 9YD

| | |
|---|---|
| Tel/Fax | +44 (0)1934 633185 |
| Email | churchhouse@kewstoke.net |
| Web | www.churchhousekewstoke.co.uk |

Entry 438   Map 2

# Somerset

## Rolstone Court Barn

A converted Victorian grainstore, full of light, good family furniture, portraits and interesting finds. It's down a narrow lane on the Somerset Levels – fabulous walking country, with rabbits on the lawn and a productive potager. Two prettily decorated bedrooms are under the eaves, the other on the first floor, there's a lovely sitting room with open fire and a smart dining room for delicious breakfasts of organic bacon and sausages. Kathlyn, who extends her welcome to children and dogs, will collect from or deliver to Bristol airport, thus saving you airport parking. An attractive stopover for the Cornwall route.

🧳 Travel Club offer. See page 414.

| | |
|---|---|
| Price | £70. Singles £45. |
| Rooms | 3: 1 double; 1 double, 1 family room sharing bath/shower. |
| Meals | Pubs/restaurants 4 miles. |
| Closed | Rarely. |
| Directions | M5 junc. 21; north onto A370 towards Bristol. Take 2nd right to Rolstone, then 1st left into Balls Barn Lane. House 3rd & last. |

**Kathlyn Read**
Rolstone Court Barn,
Rolstone, Hewish,
Weston-super-Mare,
Somerset BS24 6UP

| | |
|---|---|
| Tel | +44 (0)1934 820129 |
| Email | read@rolstone-court.co.uk |
| Web | www.rolstone-court.co.uk |

Entry 439   Map 3

## Burrington Farm

Can this really be ten minutes from Bristol airport? High in the Mendips, it is blissfully quiet and rural, with fabulous views. A narrow lane takes you to Ros and Barry's 15th-century longhouse – and the kindest of welcomes. Inside are rugs and flagstones, books, paintings and fine old furniture. Guests have a cosy low-beamed snug and bedrooms are charming; you'll need to be nimble to negotiate ancient steps and stairs. For those who prefer a bit more privacy there's a lovely family room in a separate green oak barn – stunningly converted. The garden is enchanting and you are free to roam. *Airport pick-up offered.*

Travel Club offer. See page 414.

| | |
|---|---|
| Price | £75–£110. |
| Rooms | 4: 1 double, 1 family; 2 doubles sharing bath (let to same party only). |
| Meals | Pub 5-minute walk. |
| Closed | Christmas. |
| Directions | A368 Bath-Weston-super-Mare, between Blagdon and Churchill. Take Burrington village sign, on to square with school on right. House 4th on left after Parish Rooms, immed. after Stable Cottage. |

| | |
|---|---|
| | **Barry & Ros Smith** Burrington Farm, Burrington, Somerset BS40 7AD |
| Tel | +44 (0)1761 462127 |
| Fax | +44 (0)1761 462257 |
| Email | bookings@bedandburrington.co.uk |
| Web | www.bedandburrington.co.uk |

Entry 440   Map 3

## Barton Drove Cottage

Come for the views – on a clear day you can see the Black Mountains. The pretty cottage extension is tucked into the hill so the first-floor drawing room opens directly to the terrace. All is polished and spotless inside: pretty bedrooms have patterned rugs on soft carpets, goose down and crisp linen, fresh flowers, gleaming bathrooms and a loo with a view. Charming, child-friendly, Sarah gives you bacon and sausages from Mendip piggies, eggs from her hens, soft fruit from the garden and maybe pheasant casserole for supper. Roe deer in the field, primroses in the woods, wonderful walking on Wavering Down.

Ethical Collection: Food. See page 412.

Travel Club offer. See page 414.

| | |
|---|---|
| Price | £65. Singles £35. |
| Rooms | 2: 1 double; 1 twin with separate bath. |
| Meals | Dinner from £17.50. Packed lunch £5. Pub 1 mile. |
| Closed | Rarely. |
| Directions | From A38 0.5 miles up Winscombe Hill. When road begins to descend, left between houses onto unmade track. Cottage 100 yds on the left. |

| | |
|---|---|
| | **Sarah Gunn** Barton Drove Cottage, Winscombe Hill, Winscombe, Somerset BS25 1DJ |
| Tel | +44 (0)1934 842373 |
| Email | sarahgunn2000@hotmail.com |
| Web | www.bartondrovecottage.com |

Entry 441   Map 3

## Harptree Court

One condition of Linda's moving to her husband's family home was that she should be warm! She is, and you will be, too. Linda has softened the 1790 house and imbued the rambling rooms with an upbeat elegance – they're sunny and sparkling with beds and windows dressed in delicate fabrics in perfect contrast to solid antique pieces. On one side of the soaring Georgian windows, 17 acres of parkland with ponds, an ancient bridge and carpets of spring flowers; on the other, the log-fired guest sitting room and extravagant bedrooms. An excellent breakfast sets you up to walk the grounds. Relaxing and easy.

 Travel Club offer. See page 414.

| | |
|---|---|
| Price | £90–£110. Singles from £70. |
| Rooms | 3: 2 doubles; 1 twin with separate bath. |
| Meals | Dinner, 2-3 courses, £17.50–£25. Pub 300 yds. |
| Closed | January. |
| Directions | Turn off A368 onto B3114 towards Chewton Mendip. After approx. 0.5 miles, right into drive entrance, straight after 1st x-roads. Left at top of drive. |

Linda Hill
Harptree Court,
East Harptree,
Bristol,
Somerset BS40 6AA
Tel  +44 (0)1761 221729
Email  location.harptree@tiscali.co.uk
Web  www.harptreecourt.co.uk

Entry 442  Map 3

## The Tithe Barn

You are in a quiet, well-kept village surrounded by softly rolling hills, but the joys of Bath and Bristol are a short drive away. Down a narrow lane with lawns and orchard on either side, find Stephen and Pauline's soft pinky-red stone 15th-century tithe barn. You have your own cosy, rather old-fashioned sitting room with a wood-burning stove and a spiral staircase leading to a gallery and upstairs bedrooms, the twin a bit smaller, with views over the lovely garden and one bathroom with a jacuzzi. You breakfast well in the conservatory: smoked haddock, local bacon, home-grown toms in summer, delicious homemade jams and marmalade.

 Travel Club offer. See page 414.

| | |
|---|---|
| Price | £70–£90. Singles £60–£70. |
| Rooms | 3: 2 doubles; 1 twin with separate bath. |
| Meals | Pubs/restaurants 2 miles. |
| Closed | Never. |
| Directions | From Chew Magna on B3130, right after about 2 miles at little white cottage in middle of road. Right in village to Sandy Lane. House 200 yds on right. |

Stephen & Pauline Croucher
The Tithe Barn,
Sandy Lane,
Stanton Drew, Bristol,
Somerset BS39 4EL
Tel  +44 (0)1275 331887
Email  stephen.jcroucher@btinternet.com
Web  www.thetithebarnsomerset.co.uk

Entry 443  Map 3

## Somerset

### Beryl

A lofty, mullioned, low-windowed home — yet light, bright and devoid of Victorian gloom. Every bedroom has a talking point… an extravagantly draped four-poster here, a vintage cot there, an original bath clad in mahogany reached by a tiny private stair. The flowery rooms in the attic have a 'gothic revival' feel, thanks to arched doorways. Holly, her daughter and her devoted staff serve delicious breakfasts in the sunny dining room, and drinks in the richly elegant drawing room. The old walled garden is full of flowers, roses, ancient figs and espaliered apples: the wonders of Wells lie just below.

| | |
|---|---|
| Price | £75–£130. |
| Rooms | 10: 3 doubles, 2 twins, 1 twin/double, 2 four-posters, 2 family rooms (1 with four-poster). 1 double with separate shower. Kitchenette. |
| Meals | Pubs/restaurants within 1 mile. |
| Closed | Christmas. |
| Directions | From Wells B3139 for Radstock. Follow signs to Horringtons; after church left into Hawkers Lane, next to bus pull in. At top of lane, past Beryl sign; 500 yds to main gate. |

|  | Holly Nowell |
|---|---|
| | Beryl, |
| | Wells, |
| | Somerset BA5 3JP |
| Tel | +44 (0)1749 678738 |
| Fax | +44 (0)1749 670508 |
| Email | stay@beryl-wells.co.uk |
| Web | www.beryl-wells.co.uk |

Entry 444   Map 3

## Somerset

### Stoberry House

Super swish B&B in this old coach house surrounded by 26 acres of parkland, but within walking distance of Wells: Frances has thought of everything to soothe you: bedrooms are sumptuous and spoiling — all differently styled, and most are in the main house, but there's one little love nest in a cottage; bathrooms are vamped up and spacious. Breakfast is enormous: fresh fruit, porridge, boiled eggs with soldiers, prunes and berries, ham and salami, pancakes with grilled bacon, whatever you desire. Work it off with a stroll around the gorgeous gardens, and return to a choice of sitting rooms — one 40-foot long.

Ethical Collection: Community. See page 412.

Travel Club offer. See page 414.

| | |
|---|---|
| Price | £70–£100. Singles £60–£80. |
| Rooms | 3: 2 doubles,1 twin/double. |
| Meals | Dinner, 2 courses, £20; 3 courses, £25 (by arrangement). Pubs/restaurants 0.5 miles. |
| Closed | Christmas & New Year. |
| Directions | A39 from Bristol, enter Wells 30 mph limit, left into College Rd. Immed. left into Stoberry Park through wrought-iron railings at entrance to park. Follow track to Stoberry House at top of park. |

|  | Frances Young |
|---|---|
| | Stoberry House, |
| | Stoberry Park, |
| | Wells, Somerset BA5 3LD |
| Tel | +44 (0)1749 672906 |
| Fax | +44 (0)1749 674175 |
| Email | stay@stoberry-park.co.uk |
| Web | www.stoberry-park.co.uk |

Entry 445   Map 3

# Somerset

## Hillview Cottage

Don't tell too many of your friends about this place. It's an unpretentious ex-quarryman's cottage presided over by Catherine – a warm-spirited and cultured host who'll make fresh coffee, chat about the area, even show you around Wells Cathedral (she's an official guide). This is a comfy, tea-and-cakes family home with rugs on wooden floors, antique quilts, an old Welsh dresser in the kitchen and elevated views. The bedrooms have a French feel, the bathroom has an armchair for chatting, and there's a sitting room with open fire, books and magazines. Walk from the door, or play tennis (on grass!) or croquet. Wonderful value.

Travel Club offer. See page 414.

| | |
|---|---|
| Price | From £70. Singles from £35. |
| Rooms | 2: 1 twin/double, 1 twin sharing bathroom (2nd room let to same party only). |
| Meals | Pubs 0.25 miles. |
| Closed | Rarely. |
| Directions | From Wells A371 to middle of Croscombe. Right at red phone box & then immed. right into lane. House up on left after 0.25 miles. Straight ahead into signed drive. |

Michael & Catherine Hay
Hillview Cottage,
Paradise Lane,
Croscombe,
Wells,
Somerset BA5 3RN
Tel +44 (0)1749 343526
Email cathyhay@yahoo.co.uk

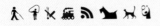

Entry 446  Map 3

# Somerset

## Manor Farm

Come for ducks, cats, hens, pet sheep... a charming rural feel. Also, a magical view of the cathedral: you can stride to Wells across the fields. Ros is a geologist and keen walker, who looks after guests with immense kindness and is happy for folk to linger. Her house is ancient and much loved (massive low beams, creaking floorboards), packed with books, pictures and a comfy mishmash of furniture; a log fire fills an inglenook in winter and the garden suite opens to a pretty corner of the garden (lit up in the evening). Delicious water comes from the spring, breakfast is a different treat each day – have it in the lovely new conservatory.

Travel Club offer. See page 414.

| | |
|---|---|
| Price | £70-£90. Singles from £40. |
| Rooms | 4: 2 doubles, 1 suite; 1 twin/double with separate bath & shower. |
| Meals | Packed lunch & light meals from £5. Pubs/restaurants 1 mile. |
| Closed | Rarely. |
| Directions | From Wells, A371 for Shepton Mallet for 1 mile; left onto B3139. In Dulcote, left at stone fountain. House on right after Manor Barn. |

Rosalind Bufton
Manor Farm,
Dulcote,
Wells, Somerset BA5 3PZ
Tel +44 (0)1749 672125
Fax +44 (0)1749 672125
Email rosalind.bufton@talktalk.net
Web www.wells-accommodation.co.uk

Entry 447  Map 3

## Somerset

### Claveys Farm

For the artistic seeker of inspiration: Fleur is a talented artist, Francis works for English Heritage, both have a passion for art, real food and lively conversation. Rugs are time-worn, panelling and walls are distempered with natural pigment, bedrooms are better than simple, beds have white linen. From the warm kitchen of this traditional farmhouse come delicious home-grown meals, breakfast eggs from the hens, oak-smoked bacon from Fleur's rare-breed pigs and homemade bread and jams. Acres of fields, footpaths and woodland await for long walks and Mells is a dream.

| Price | £70. Singles £40. |
|---|---|
| Rooms | 2: 1 double/family, 1 twin sharing separate bathroom. |
| Meals | Dinner, 3 courses, £25. BYO. Packed lunch £7. Pub in village. |
| Closed | Rarely. |
| Directions | At Mells Green on Leigh-on-Mendip road SW from Mells. Past phone box; house last on right before speed de-restriction signs. If lost, Mells PO, by pond, has map outside. |

|  | Fleur & Francis Kelly |
|---|---|
|  | Claveys Farm, |
|  | Mells, Frome, |
|  | Somerset BA11 3QP |
| Tel | +44 (0)1373 814651 |
| Email | bandb@fleurkelly.com |
| Web | www.fleurkelly.com/bandb |

🐦 🚂 🐾 🌾 🐈 🚜

Entry 448   Map 3

## Somerset

### Broadgrove House

Down a long, private lane with views towards Alfred's Tower and Longleat, tranquillity: a 17th-century stone house with a walled cottage garden. Inside is just as special. Beams, flagstones and inglenook fireplaces have been sensitively restored; rugs, pictures, comfy sofas and polished antiques add warmth and serenity. The twin, at the end of the house, has its own sitting room. Breakfast on homemade and farmers' market produce before exploring Stourhead, Wells, Longleat. Sarah, engaging, well-travelled and a great cook, looks after guests and horses with enthusiasm. *Shooting available. Children by arrangement.*

🧳 Travel Club offer. See page 414.

| Price | From £80. Singles £50. |
|---|---|
| Rooms | 2: 1 twin & sitting room; 1 double with separate bath. |
| Meals | Pub/restaurant 1 mile. |
| Closed | Christmas. |
| Directions | Directions on booking. |

|  | Sarah Voller |
|---|---|
|  | Broadgrove House, |
|  | Leighton, |
|  | Frome, Somerset BA11 4PP |
| Tel | +44 (0)1373 836296 |
| Email | broadgrove836@tiscali.co.uk |
| Web | www.broadgrovehouse.co.uk |

🐈

Entry 449   Map 3

## Somerset

### Burnt House Farm

Lovers of modern art, clean lines, pale wood and clever lighting will be thrilled, and nature lovers – you are in a deeply rural valley with no roads, and acres of ancient woodland to explore. David, an architect, and charming Elizabeth have transformed their farmhouse into a cool, clean space: tea and cake when you arrive, relaxed breakfasts in a light, slate-floored room with an ash table and contemporary fireplace, big bedrooms with fabulous views in the softest creams, thick mattresses, squishy pillows and a gleaming new bathroom. This feels remote but you are near to Bath, Wells and mystical Glastonbury.

Travel Club offer. See page 414.

| Price | £55-£70. |
|---|---|
| Rooms | 2: 1 double, 1 twin sharing bath (let to same party only). |
| Meals | Pub/restaurant 2 miles. |
| Closed | Christmas & Boxing Day. |
| Directions | From Bristol A37 to Shepton Mallet and Yeovil until after Gurney Slade. Down hill, then right at chevron posts. Right at Fern Cottage to Burnt House Farm. |

|  | David & Elizabeth Parry |
|---|---|
|  | Burnt House Farm, |
|  | Burnthouse Drove, Windsor Hill, |
|  | Shepton Mallet, Somerset BA4 4JQ |
| Tel | +44 (0)1749 840185 |
| Email | stay@burnthousedrove.co.uk |
| Web | www.burnthousedrove.co.uk |

Entry 450    Map 3

## Somerset

### The Manor House

Tucked into a hamlet, the house oozes tranquillity. Late medieval, owned by Glastonbury monks, an architectural flourish at every turn: plasterwork ceiling, Jacobean staircase, Tudor fireplace, English country-house furnishings are gorgeously mixed with Indian textiles and antiques. Three bedrooms in a private wing share a boldly stylish bathroom and are prettily feminine with hand-crafted bedheads, antiques and rich fabrics. The garden delights with rose pergola, knot garden and fish pond. Local bread and organic meats for breakfast, and Harriet and Bryan cultured and engaging.

| Price | £80. Singles £45. |
|---|---|
| Rooms | 3: 2 doubles, 1 single all sharing bath (let to same party only). |
| Meals | Pub 2 miles. |
| Closed | 15 December-15 January. |
| Directions | A361 Shepton Mallet-Glastonbury. At Pilton, turn between village stores and Crown Inn onto Totterdown Lane; 1 mile; right at T-junc. in W. Compton; next right 100 yds onto lane. On left. |

|  | Harriet Ray |
|---|---|
|  | The Manor House, |
|  | West Compton, Shepton Mallet, |
|  | Somerset BA4 4PB |
| Tel | +44 (0)1749 890582 |
| Fax | +44 (0)1749 890582 |
| Email | rayswestcompton@btinternet.com |

Entry 451    Map 3

## Somerset

### Pennard House

Pennard has been in Susie's family since the 17th century – the cellars date from then and the superstructure is stately, lofty and Georgian. Multi-lingual Martin runs an antiques business from here and he and Susie obviously enjoy having guests in their home. You have the run of the library, drawing room, magnificent billiard room, 60-acre orchard, meadows, woods, grass tennis court and six acres of garden with a spring-fed pool (swim with the newts). Bedrooms are large and have good views; one is oval with a corner bath in the room. Although this is a big house it still feels warm and comfortably lived in.

 Travel Club offer. See page 414.

| | |
|---|---|
| Price | £90. Singles from £45. |
| Rooms | 3: 1 double, 1 twin; 1 twin/double with separate bath/shower. |
| Meals | Pub 2 miles. |
| Closed | Rarely. |
| Directions | From Shepton Mallet south on A37, through Pylle, over hill & next right to East Pennard. After 500 yds, right & follow lane past church to T-junc. at very top. House on left. |

**Martin & Susie Dearden**
Pennard House,
East Pennard, Shepton Mallet,
Somerset BA4 6TP
Tel     +44 (0)1749 860266
Fax    +44 (0)1749 860700
Email  susie.d@ukonline.co.uk

Entry 452   Map 3

## Somerset

### Maplestone

You are in the oldest part of Shepton Mallet, with narrow lanes, tiny cottages and the Babycham factory. Through a charming, walled cottage garden, with views over parkland, find a thick front door and cheerful Donald and Gillian: you have one end of the weaver's cottages (one bedroom has a separate entrance and its own sitting room) so the feel is private. White walls, pale colours, lovely paintings by Gillian, and an eclectic mix of styles give a quirky feel; bedrooms are deeply comfortable and very quiet. Breakfast on local sausages and eggs from Wells market, explore the town or don your walking boots.

 Travel Club offer. See page 414.

| | |
|---|---|
| Price | £70–£80. Singles £55. |
| Rooms | 3: 1 double, 1 twin/double. Annexe: 1 double with separate shower & sitting room/kitchenette. |
| Meals | Pubs/restaurants within walking distance. |
| Closed | Christmas. |
| Directions | From Bristol A37. In Shepton Mallet, right at Gaymer's Cider down Town Lane. At bottom, right into Leg Square. House on left, 100 yds past the Dust Hole. |

**Donald & Gillian Sinclair**
Maplestone,
Quarr, Shepton Mallet,
Somerset BA4 5NP
Tel     +44 (0)1749 347979
Email  info@maplestonehall.co.uk
Web    www.maplestonehall.co.uk

Entry 453   Map 3

## Somerset

### Chalice Hill House

You can see St John's spire poking out over the treetops: vibrant Glastonbury buzzes just below. Fay's contemporary artistic flair mingles naturally with the classical frame of this Georgian house; grand mirrors, wooden floors, gentle colours and loads of books create an interesting feel. The bedrooms are enchanting, not at all understated; carved oak Slavic sleigh beds, embroidered Indian cotton bedspreads and views of the dovecote, wedding cake tree and Chalice Hill beyond. Weekend breakfasts are leisurely, served with panache (and optional chilli jam!). Exotic, comfortable elegance – and a lovely hostess.

## Somerset

### Westbrook House

David is an interior designer; Keith does gardens – hence this blend of good taste and style in a revamped 1870s house with generous, well-tended grounds. Wander through a young orchard, spot unusual plants, sit on stone benches or a sunny patio; a wildlife meadow contrasts with clipped lawns. Inside, every object has a story (your hosts are full of smiles and stories too): tapestries from India, a mirrored cabinet from an officer's mess, ornate brass lanterns. Light floods into the dining room as you breakfast on local treats – all the while absorbing the peace of this tranquil hamlet, where cows amble calmly down the lane.

| | |
|---|---|
| Price | £90. Singles £75. |
| Rooms | 2: 1 double, 1 twin. |
| Meals | Pubs/restaurants 5-minute walk. |
| Closed | Rarely. |
| Directions | From top of Glastonbury High Street, right; 2nd left into Dod Lane. Past Chalice Hill Close; right into driveway. |

| | |
|---|---|
| Price | £85. Singles £60. |
| Rooms | 3: 1 double, 1 twin. 1 double with separate bath (let to same party only). |
| Meals | Dinner by arrangement £25. Pub/restaurant 4 miles. |
| Closed | Never. |
| Directions | From Glastonbury A361 for Shepton Mallet. After 2 miles, right for W. Bradley. Follow signs for W. Bradley; at fork in road, right for Baltonsborough. House is immediately in front. |

**Fay Hutchcroft**
Chalice Hill House,
Dod Lane,
Glastonbury, Somerset BA6 8BZ
Tel +44 (0)1458 830828
Email mail@chalicehill.co.uk
Web www.chalicehill.co.uk

**Keith Anderson & David Mendel**
Westbrook House,
West Bradley,
Glastonbury, Somerset BA6 8LS
Tel +44 (0)1458 850604
Email mail@westbrook-bed-breakfast.co.uk
Web www.westbrook-bed-breakfast.co.uk

Entry 454   Map 3

Entry 455   Map 3

# Somerset

## Chindit House

Inside this light and elegant Edwardian mansion you will find fine architectural features, charming furniture, fresh flowers, vibrant paintings and compelling sculptures. There are long views over garden and town from the large, light sitting room; bedrooms have spoilingly serious mattresses, good art, thick curtains and sleek, contemporary bathrooms. Breakfast is enormous and locally sourced, cakes are home made. Peter, a sculptor, and Felicity, an art consultant, are easy going and fun. You are a short hop from the town with its lively mix of exotic shops and colourful characters.

Travel Club offer. See page 414.

| | |
|---|---|
| Price | £100-£125. Singles £70-£85. |
| Rooms | 4: 2 doubles; 2 singles with shared bath (let to same party only). |
| Meals | Pubs/restaurants 500 yds. |
| Closed | Never. |
| Directions | In the centre of Glastonbury. Left at top of High Street on to Wells Road. House about 200 yds along on left - just before corner with St Edmunds Road. |

**Peter Smith & Felicity Wright**
Chindit House,
23 Wells Road,
Glastonbury,
Somerset BA6 9DN
Tel     +44 (0)1458 830404
Email   enquiries@chindit-house.co.uk
Web    www.chindit-house.co.uk

Entry 456   Map 3

# Somerset

## Church Cottage

Partly clothed in English garden and with views to the church, this 400-year-old cottage has wooden beams, low ceilings and wonky walls. Ignore the modern house on the other side of the road and restore your senses with blue lias flagstones, neutral colours, soft cushions, a flash of Thompson gazelle skin, the whiff of woodsmoke and floppy roses on a scrubbed table. Caroline is artistic and rustles up a fine breakfast in her calm kitchen. Bedrooms are small and simple – pine furniture, cool colours; the Potting Shed is a private, generous nest for two. Miles of walking straight from the door.

Travel Club offer. See page 414.

| | |
|---|---|
| Price | £65-£80. |
| Rooms | 3: 2 doubles; 1 double with separate bath/shower. |
| Meals | Pubs 1 mile. |
| Closed | Rarely. |
| Directions | M5 exit 23 to A39. 7 miles; left to Shapwick. Cottage on left next to church. |

**Caroline Hanbury Bateman**
Church Cottage,
Station Road,
Shapwick, Bridgwater, Somerset
TA7 9NH
Tel     +44 (0)1458 210904
Email   caroline@shapwick.fsnet.co.uk
Web    www.profileskincare.co.uk/bnb/bnb.html

Entry 457   Map 3

## Somerset

### Saltmoor House

An abundance of Georgian elegance and comfort: fresh flowers, beautiful pictures and Italianate murals, an 18th-century French mirror and Empire chairs, checks, stripes and toile de Jouy... all exist in perfect harmony. Choose bedrooms in the house (gorgeous, light, with roll top baths) or in the Mill (a stylish and contemporary retreat with your own sitting room). Elizabeth's cooking is sublime and imaginative and she uses plenty of home-grown produce. You are in the heart of the Somerset Moors and Levels, surrounded by mystical views and countryside of huge environmental significance: wonderful.

| Price | From £110. Singles £55. |
|---|---|
| Rooms | 4: 1 twin/double with separate shower; 1 double with separate bath. Mill: 2 doubles. |
| Meals | Dinner, 3-4 courses, £30-£35. BYO. Pub 5 miles. |
| Closed | Rarely. |
| Directions | M5, junc. 24; 5 miles via Huntworth to Moorland; 2 miles after Moorland, house on right after sharp right-hand bend. |

|  | **Crispin & Elizabeth Deacon** |
|---|---|
|  | Saltmoor House, |
|  | Saltmoor, |
|  | Burrowbridge, |
|  | Bridgwater, Somerset TA7 0RL |
| Tel | +44 (0)1823 698092 |
| Email | saltmoorhouse@aol.com |
| Web | www.saltmoorhouse.co.uk |

✗ 🐾 🔊 🐈

Entry 458  Map 2

## Somerset

### Blackmore Farm

Come for atmosphere and architecture: the Grade I-listed manor-farmhouse is remarkable. Medieval stone walls, a ceiling open to a beamed roof, ecclesiastical windows, a fire blazing in the Great Hall. Ann and Ian look after guests and farm (900 acres plus dairy) with equal enthusiasm. Furnishings are comfortable not lavish, bedrooms are cavernous and the oak-panelled suite (with secret stairway intact) takes up an entire floor. Breakfast at a 20-foot polished table in the carpeted but baronial Great Hall, store your bikes in the chapel, visit the calves in the dairy. A rare place. *Farm shop on site.*

🧳 Travel Club offer. See page 414.

| Price | £75-£85. Singles £45-£55. |
|---|---|
| Rooms | 4: 1 double, 1 twin, 1 four-poster, 1 suite. |
| Meals | Pubs/restaurants 5-minute walk. |
| Closed | Rarely. |
| Directions | From Bridgwater, A39 west around Cannington. After 2nd r'bout, follow signs to Minehead; 1st left after Yeo Valley creamery; 1st house on right. |

|  | **Ann Dyer** |
|---|---|
|  | Blackmore Farm, |
|  | Cannington, Bridgwater, |
|  | Somerset TA5 2NE |
| Tel | +44 (0)1278 653442 |
| Fax | +44 (0)1278 653427 |
| Email | dyerfarm@aol.com |
| Web | www.dyerfarm.co.uk |

♿ 👤 ✗ 📖 🔊 🚜

Entry 459  Map 2

## Somerset

### Huntstile Organic Farm

Catapult yourself into country life in the foothills of the Quantocks, and make that connection between the rolling green hills, the idyllic munching animals and the delicious, organic food on your plate; here it is understood. Lizzie and John buzz with energy in this gorgeous old house with Jacobean pannelling and huge walk-in fireplaces, two sitting rooms, sweet and cosy rustic bedrooms, a café, and a restaurant serving their own meat, eggs and vegetables. House parties, weddings, team building, a stone circle for hand-fasting ceremonies – all come under Lizzie's happy and efficient umbrella, and there are woodlands to roam.

 Travel Club offer. See page 414.

| Price | From £85. Singles from £49. |
|---|---|
| Rooms | 5: 1 double; 1 double, 1 twin/double sharing bath. Apartment: 1 double, 1 twin with sitting room. |
| Meals | Dinner £12.50-£22. Packed lunch £5-£7.50. Pub/restaurant 3 miles. |
| Closed | 22 December-7 January. |
| Directions | M5 junction 24, left to North Petherton. Before entering village right to Goathurst & Broomfield. Second right to Goathurst. House 1 mile on right. |

Lizzie Myers
Huntstile Organic Farm,
Goathurst,
Bridgwater,
Somerset TA5 2DQ
Tel +44 (0)1278 662358
Email huntstile@live.co.uk
Web www.huntstileorganicfarm.co.uk

Entry 460 Map 2

## Somerset

### The Lynch Country House

Peace, seclusion and privacy at this immaculate Regency house in lush Somerset. First-floor bedrooms are traditionally grand, attic rooms are small but bright; those in the coach house have a more modern feel. Deep warm colours prevail, fabrics are flowery and carpets soft green. You'll feel as warm as toast and beautifully looked after. A stone stair goes right to the top where the observatory lets in a cascading light; the flagged hall, high ceilings, long windows and private tables at breakfast create a country-house hotel feel. A lovely garden has a pond, wildlife and a terrace to enjoy it from.

| Price | £70-£100. Singles £60-£70. |
|---|---|
| Rooms | 9: 1 double, 1 twin, 2 four-posters; 1 double (extra single bed) with separate bath. Coach house: 3 doubles, 1 twin. |
| Meals | Restaurants 5-minute walk. |
| Closed | Never. |
| Directions | From London, M3 junc. 8, A303. At Podimore r'bout A372 to Somerton. At junc. of North St & Behind Berry. |

Mr Roy Copeland
The Lynch Country House,
4 Behind Berry,
Somerton, Somerset TA11 7PD
Tel +44 (0)1458 272316
Fax +44 (0)1458 272590
Email the_lynch@talk21.com
Web www.thelynchcountryhouse.co.uk

Entry 461 Map 3

## Somerset

### Rectory Farm House

A mile off a fairly main road but as peaceful as can be. Lavinia has showered love and attention on her early Georgian house and garden in a landscape that has changed little since the 18th century. Beams, sash windows, wood fires and high ceilings are the backdrop for gleaming family furniture, paintings and delightfully arranged flowers. Good-sized bedrooms in restful colours have starched linen, fluffy bathrobes and binoculars for watching wildlife; spot deer, badgers, foxes, hares, buzzards. Breakfast is so local it could walk to the table – and includes homemade marmalade and jams.

| Price | From £90. Singles from £65. |
|---|---|
| Rooms | 3: 1 double;<br>1 twin/double, 1 double sharing bath (let to same party only). |
| Meals | Dinner £30. Pub 0.5 miles. |
| Closed | Rarely. |
| Directions | From the east, exit A303 on to B3081 for Bruton. After 1 mile, left into Rectory Lane. House 0.25 miles on right. |

Michael & Lavinia Dewar
Rectory Farm House,
Charlton Musgrove,
Wincanton,
Somerset BA9 8ET
Tel       +44 (0)1963 34599
Email   l.dewar@btconnect.com
Web    www.rectoryfarmhouse.com

Entry 462   Map 3

## Somerset

### Lower Farm

The Good Life in the depths of Somerset, and a delightful family. The Dowdings have converted an old stone barn into a self-contained apartment with lime-washed walls and lovely bedrooms with views across the garden to fields. Perfect for a larger party – the cosy oak-floored sitting room comes with a wood-burner and extra beds. The whole place has a charmingly French feel – hens strut around the orchard and you can sit at the breakfast table looking over a very smart 2-acre vegetable patch. Susie brings you homemade apple juice, local bacon, organic yogurt and home baked bread. A place to do your own thing.

Ethical Collection: Environment; Food.
See page 412.

| Price | From £90. |
|---|---|
| Rooms | 2: 1 double, 1 twin. Extra beds in shared sitting room; extra shower. |
| Meals | Pub 0.5 miles. |
| Closed | Rarely. |
| Directions | From junction of A371 and A359 towards Bruton. Right to Shepton Montague. At x-roads by pub follow sign to church and village hall. Sharp bend at church, house 100 yds on right. Park in yard behind house. |

Charles & Susie Dowding
Lower Farm,
Shepton Montague,
Wincanton,
Somerset BA9 8JG
Tel       +44 (0)1749 812253
Email   enquiries@lowerfarm.org.uk
Web    www.lowerfarm.org.uk

Entry 463   Map 3

# Somerset

## Bratton Farmhouse

A gorgeous old (1600) house around which strut hens and happy Jacob sheep. Intelligent and generous Suellen has created contemporary, warm interiors and the bedrooms are a joy. One, in the main house, has oak-panelled walls, bucolic views and a vast bed with old French embroidered linen. Another, in a newly converted studio across the courtyard, gives you complete independence with your own stylish sitting room made cosy with a wood-burner; lovers can laze till late in a huge nest of feather and down. Good books and art surround you, breakfasts are delicious and imaginative, and walks are from the door.

Travel Club offer. See page 414.

| | |
|---|---|
| Price | From £80. Singles from £50. |
| Rooms | 3: 1 twin/double & sitting room; 2 doubles, each with separate bath/shower. |
| Meals | Lunch £10. Dinner, 3 courses, £25. Packed lunch £5. Pub 2 miles. |
| Closed | Rarely. |
| Directions | A303 then A371 signed Wincanton & Castle Cary. Follow signs to Castle Cary. After approx. 2.5 miles, right to Bratton Seymour. House 0.4 miles on right. |

| | |
|---|---|
| | Suellen Dainty |
| | Bratton Farmhouse, |
| | Bratton Seymour, Wincanton, |
| | Somerset BA9 8BY |
| Tel | +44 (0)1963 32458 |
| Email | sdainty52@googlemail.com |
| Web | www.brattonfarmhouse.co.uk |

Entry 464  Map 3

# Somerset

## Yarlington House

A mellow Georgian manor surrounded by impressive parkland, formal gardens, rose garden, apple tree pergola and laburnum walk. Your hosts are friendly and flexible, artists with an eye for detail; her embroideries are everywhere. Something to astound at every turn: fine copies of 18th-century wallpapers, 18th-century fabric around the canopied bed and a bedroom whose Regency striped wallpaper extends across the entire ceiling creating the effect of a Napoleonic tent. There are elegant antiques, proper 50s bathrooms, log fires, a heated pool (summer only) and lovely local walks. Surprising, unique. *Children by arrangement.*

Travel Club offer. See page 414.

| | |
|---|---|
| Price | £120. Singles £60. |
| Rooms | 2: 1 double, 1 twin. |
| Meals | Pubs/restaurants nearby. |
| Closed | 1 July-20 August. |
| Directions | From Wincanton, 2nd left on A371, after Holbrook r'bout. Then 3rd right; 1st gateposts on left. |

| | |
|---|---|
| | Countess Charles de Salis |
| | Yarlington House, |
| | Wincanton, Somerset BA9 8DY |
| Tel | +44 (0)1963 440344 |
| Fax | +44 (0)1963 440335 |
| Email | carolyn.desalis@yarlingtonhouse.com |
| Web | www.yarlingtonhouse.com |

Entry 465  Map 3

## Somerset

### The Dairy House

A captivating place, tucked under Cadbury Hill. What were once 17th-century stables have been transformed by perfectionist Emma. Step through a smoky-blue stable door into a little cottage: the sitting room has a grey slate floor, pale walls, interesting art and smart seagrass-covered stairs winding up to an airy, sloping-ceilinged bedroom. It is subtle, understated and beautifully restful. The cottage stands in its own pretty orchard but you can also explore Emma's gorgeous walled garden. Wander over to the Dairy House for breakfast before you go for a scamper; there are super walks straight from the door. *Children over ten welcome.*

## Somerset

### Barwick Farm House

A proper old-fashioned smallholding with Dorset sheep, hens, horses and all the attendant wildlife. Angela and Robin (charming, and passionate about the soil) have saved ancient elm floorboards, exposed the sandstone linterns of the original fireplaces, stuck to traditional materials, then limewashed the walls in vibrant colours. Roomy bedrooms have ironed cotton sheets and a comforting mishmash of styles; one bathroom is painted bubble-gum pink and has a free-standing bath with views over fields. Wake to birdsong and the sizzle of bacon; good walking and cycling start from the door.

Travel Club offer. See page 414.

| | |
|---|---|
| Price | £85. Singles £50. |
| Rooms | Cottage: 1 twin/double; sofa bed, extra shower. |
| Meals | Pub/restaurant 1.5 miles. |
| Closed | Christmas, New Year & occasionally. |
| Directions | From Wincanton A303 west, exit Chapel Cross for Sparkford. Right for Sparkford, left for Little Weston. House 0.25 miles on left, sign on wooden gate. |

| | |
|---|---|
| Price | £60–£75. Singles from £35. |
| Rooms | 2: 1 double, 1 family room. |
| Meals | 'Early Bird' packed breakfasts also available. Restaurant 100 yds. |
| Closed | Rarely. |
| Directions | A37 to Dorchester; 0.25 miles outside Yeovil, 1st exit off r'bout (opp. Red House pub) following signs to Little Barwick House restaurant. House in fork of road. |

| | |
|---|---|
| | **Emma & Graham Barnett** |
| | The Dairy House, |
| | Little Weston, |
| | Sparkford, |
| | Somerset BA22 7HP |
| Tel | +44 (0)1963 440987 |
| Email | barnett1644@tiscali.co.uk |

| | |
|---|---|
| | **Angela Nicoll** |
| | Barwick Farm House, |
| | Barwick, |
| | Yeovil, Somerset BA22 9TD |
| Tel | +44 (0)1935 410779 |
| Email | info@barwickfarmhouse.co.uk |
| Web | www.barwickfarmhouse.co.uk |

Entry 466  Map 3

Entry 467  Map 3

# Somerset

## Number 29

Just a three-minute walk from the centre of town (so it's easy to leave the car behind), but this brick and hamstone Victorian house overlooks a leafy park with majestic trees and smooth lawns. You breakfast in a dining/sitting room with green views, a French oak table, original artwork and books to read. Angela loves cooking, so there's homemade cake, grand breakfasts and delicious suppers – try sweetcorn cakes with coriander chutney, corn fed chicken with feta, and pear and apple granola crumble. Bedrooms are light and large, beds high and inviting with pocket-sprung mattresses; bathrooms are pristine with handmade soaps.

Travel Club offer. See page 414.

| | |
|---|---|
| Price | £60–£75. Singles £40–£55. |
| Rooms | 3: 2 doubles, 1 twin/double each with separate bath. |
| Meals | Dinner, 2 courses & glass of wine, £15. Restaurant 0.5 miles, pub 2.7 miles. |
| Closed | Never. |
| Directions | From large roundabout by hospital follow A37 Bristol sign, left at next roundabout, first left then left again. House is 3rd on right, green door and gate. |

|  | Angela Hillier |
|---|---|
| | Number 29, |
| | The Park, |
| | Yeovil, |
| | Somerset BA20 1DG |
| Tel | +44 (0)1935 420046 |
| Email | info@number29.biz |
| Web | www.number29.biz |

# Somerset

## The Farmyard

A broad curve of zinc and glass, with stunning views over a lake (in which you may fish) and Glastonbury Tor. Find five apartments, all with studio-style kitchen/dining/living rooms and wide glass doors to terraces; eat outside or in. A black and white theme prevails, with odd splashes of colour and huge bright chandeliers; relax on white leather sofas, pad barefoot on grey slate heated from underneath. Bedrooms are luxurious and minimal: a glass screen behind the bed and floor to ceiling windows maximise that view. Breakfast is delivered and you can either cook for yourself in the evening, or nip into Yeovil.

Travel Club offer. See page 414.

| | |
|---|---|
| Price | £99–£110. Singles £85. |
| Rooms | 5 doubles. |
| Meals | Pubs/restaurants 2-10 miles. |
| Closed | Rarely. |
| Directions | From Yeovil Pen Mill station right onto Sherborne road. At r'bout, last exit onto Lyde Rd. At end of road (2 miles) left onto Mudford Rd. Pass Fleur de Lys pub on left, then next right onto Coombe St Lane. Immed. right onto Stone Lane. 2nd left (200 yds), signed. |

|  | Gemma Snell |
|---|---|
| | The Farmyard, |
| | Longcroft House, Stone Lane, |
| | Yeovil, Somerset BA21 4NU |
| Tel | +44 (0)1935 426426 |
| Fax | +44 (0)1935 314833 |
| Email | stay@farmyardretreat.co.uk |
| Web | www.farmyardretreat.co.uk |

# Somerset

## Bellplot House

This may not be the trendiest place in the book, but there are good Georgian features and Betty and Dennis to look after you. Step into a quirky interior of stripped floors, yellow walls, a pool table, and an honesty bar so you can help yourself to a drink before heading off to dinner. Bedrooms tend to be large and are furnished in a homely style: warm and spotless, lots of colour, crisp white linen, compact bathrooms, some have sofas, all have TVs. Wake to a delicious locally-sourced breakfast in the country-green dining room. You're on the high street, but it's quiet at night. Montacute House and Forde Abbey are both close.

 Travel Club offer. See page 414.

| | |
|---|---|
| Price | £89.50-£99.50. Singles £79.50. |
| Rooms | 7: 5 doubles, 1 family, 1 single. |
| Meals | Pubs/restaurants within 2 miles. |
| Closed | Never. |
| Directions | In centre of Chard, 500 yds from the Guildhall. Car park available. |

**Betty Jones**
Bellplot House,
High Street, Chard,
Somerset TA20 1QB
Tel     +44 (0)1460 62600
Fax     +44 (0)1460 62600
Email  info@bellplothouse.co.uk
Web    www.bellplothouse.co.uk

Entry 470   Map 2

---

# Somerset

## Pyle House

Swoop down onto a buttermilk yellow lodge with landscaped gardens hugged by rural Somerset's rolling green fields: it's so well renovated you'd never guess it was an 1800s hunting lodge for Whitestaunton Estate. Past the flagstoned hallway, discover a house of pristine paintwork, valley views, swish bathrooms and immaculate bedrooms. Madeleine loves to cook so expect a breakfast worthy of the fine china it comes on; Michael's pride and joy are his fossil finds – proof of the area's antiquity. It's perfect for walkers: kick boots into the drying room, browse through maps, stroll to the pub for a meal. *Children over ten welcome.*

 Travel Club offer. See page 414.

| | |
|---|---|
| Price | From £70. Singles £45. |
| Rooms | 3: 1 double, 1 twin/double, 1 suite all with separate shower rooms. |
| Meals | Pub/restaurant 0.5 miles. |
| Closed | Christmas & New Year. |
| Directions | From Chard A30 for Honiton. After 4 miles, right for Howley. 2nd right through stone pillars, signed Pyle, to cream house at end of drive. |

**Madeleine Berry**
Pyle House,
Whitestaunton,
Chard,
Somerset TA20 3DZ
Tel     +44 (0)1460 239268
Email  info@pylehouse.co.uk
Web    www.pylehouse.co.uk

Entry 471   Map 2

## Staffordshire

### Stoop House Farm

Step through a rosy arch from this enchanting 18th-century farmhouse: the view across garden, fields and valley will bowl you over. Inside, oak beams, heated flagged floors, a cast-iron range, a bedroom shot through with olive and gold. In this thriving conservation village (with lovely pub), the farm draws on the latest in green design, while two Andalusian horses share the grounds with sheep, pigs and poultry – expect superb eggs at breakfast! Your warm, lovely hosts, she a midwife, he a climber, share their passion for the outdoors with their guests – and the Peak District National Park lies at your feet.

Travel Club offer. See page 414.

| Price | £70. Singles £55. |
|---|---|
| Rooms | 1 suite & sitting room. |
| Meals | Pub 1-minute walk. |
| Closed | Rarely. |
| Directions | From Leek A523 towards Ashbourne. At crossroads left B5053. Through Onecote, up hill then 2nd right signed Butterton. Through village past shop on right, 200 yds, then right fork. House 2nd on right. |

|  | Andrea Evans |
|---|---|
|  | Stoop House Farm, |
|  | Butterton, |
|  | Leek, |
|  | Staffordshire ST13 7SY |
| Tel | +44 (0)1538 304486 |
| Email | bnfrench@yahoo.co.uk |

Entry 472  Map 8

## Staffordshire

### Martinslow Farm

High up in the Peaks, lost to the world, this listed 300-year-old farmhouse once sheltered donkeys... the accommodation has since stepped up a gear. The sitting room, as warm and engaging as Diana herself, is cosy with beams, log-burner and muted chintz. Peaceful bedrooms in the stable block (interconnecting for families) have a country feel: a rocking horse and equine curtains in the Stable (Diana and Richard love country pursuits, dogs and good company), mahogany beds in the Tack Room, carpets in both. Perfect tranquillity, a sheltered patio for great views, and delicious locally sourced food from Diana.

Travel Club offer. See page 414.

| Price | From £80. |
|---|---|
| Rooms | Stables: 1 double, 1 twin. |
| Meals | Dinner, 3 courses, £25. Supper £15. Pub 5-minute walk. |
| Closed | Rarely. |
| Directions | A523 Leek-Ashbourne. At Winkhill, signs to Grindon. Over x-roads, left at T-junction; 300 yds; house on right below lane. |

|  | Richard & Diana Bloor |
|---|---|
|  | Martinslow Farm, |
|  | Winkhill, Leek, |
|  | Staffordshire ST13 7PZ |
| Tel | +44 (0)1538 304500 |
| Email | richard.bloor@btclick.com |
| Web | www.dianabloor-apartments.co.uk |

Entry 473  Map 8

## Staffordshire

### Manor House

A working rare-breed farm in an area of great beauty, a Jacobean farmhouse with oodles of history. Behind mullioned windows is a glorious interior crammed with curios and family pieces, panelled walls and wonky floors... hurl a log on the fire and watch it roar. Rooms have four-posters; one bathroom flaunts rich red antique fabrics. Chris and Margaret are passionate hosts who serve perfect breakfasts (home-grown tomatoes, sausages and bacon from their pigs) and give you the run of a garden resplendent with plants, vistas, tennis, croquet, two springer spaniels and one purring cat. Heaven.

Ethical Collection: Food. See page 412.

Travel Club offer. See page 414.

| | |
|---|---|
| Price | £54–£65. Singles £34–£45. |
| Rooms | 4: 3 four-posters, 1 double. |
| Meals | Pub/restaurant 1.5 miles. |
| Closed | Christmas. |
| Directions | From Uttoxeter, B5030 for Rocester. Beyond JCB factory, left onto B5031. At T-junc. after church, right onto B5032. 1st left for Prestwood. Farm 0.75 miles on right over crest of hill, through arch. |

| | |
|---|---|
| | **Chris & Margaret Ball** |
| | Manor House, |
| | Prestwood, Denstone, |
| | Uttoxeter, Staffordshire ST14 5DD |
| Tel | +44 (0)1889 590415 |
| Fax | +44 (0)1335 342198 |
| Email | cm_ball@yahoo.co.uk |
| Web | www.4posteraccom.com |

Entry 474   Map 8

## Staffordshire

### Slab Bridge Cottage

A 19th-century cottage in a quiet setting beside the Shropshire Union Canal. Bedrooms have floral curtains and all is spotless and homely, with open fires, polished copper, silver and brass, old oak furniture, pretty bathrooms, fresh flowers. Eat outside on the terrace overlooking the canal, or on the narrowboat on an evening cruise – but do book! Diana makes her own bread, biscuits, cakes and jams and has four much-loved llamas (very therapeutic), including baby Scrumpy. David cuts fresh vegetables and salads from the garden. On a good day the hens lay fresh eggs too.

| | |
|---|---|
| Price | £65–£70. Singles £45–£50. |
| Rooms | 2: 1 double with separate bath; 1 double with separate shower. |
| Meals | Dinner £20. Packed lunch £5. Pub 2 miles. |
| Closed | Christmas & New Year. |
| Directions | M6 junc. 12; A5 west to r'bout; straight on. 1 mile to Stretton x-roads, right then 1st left (Lapley Lane); 3 miles to small x-roads at white house; left. Cottage 0.5 miles, on right. |

| | |
|---|---|
| | **Diana Walkerdine** |
| | Slab Bridge Cottage, |
| | Little Onn, |
| | Church Eaton, |
| | Staffordshire ST20 0AU |
| Tel | +44 (0)1785 840220 |
| Fax | +44 (0)1785 840220 |
| Email | ddwalkerdine@btinternet.com |

Entry 475   Map 8

# Suffolk

## The Old Vicarage

Up the avenue of fine old horse chestnut trees to find just what you'd expect from an old vicarage: a Pembroke table in the flagstoned hall, a log fire which warms the sitting room for tea and homemade cake, a refectory table sporting copies of *The Field*... an inviting sofa, a piano, hunting scenes and silver pheasants. Bedrooms are large, chintzy and handsomely furnished, and the double has hill views. Weave your way through the branches of the huge copper beech to the garden that Jane loves. She grows her own vegetables, and keeps hens and house with equal talent. *Children over seven welcome.*

# Suffolk

## The Manse

Unmissable in its coat of rich red paint, the beamed, 16th-century Manse overlooks a historic village green. The owners will present you with a superb breakfast each day, plus homemade cakes or scones for tea, and a fresh posy of garden flowers. Robin, ex diplomatic service, has a passion for opera; Bridget organises the church choir. The guest quarters are completely private and deliciously cosy; there are polished antiques, fine porcelain and a wood-burning stove, a rose-tumbled garden for breakfast on fine days, and a chivalrous black labrador called Tristan, always happy to take guests for a walk.

| | |
|---|---|
| Price | £75–£80. Singles £45. |
| Rooms | 2: 1 double; 1 twin with separate bath. Extra single room off twin. |
| Meals | Dinner £20. BYO. Packed lunch £6. Pub/restaurant 2 miles. |
| Closed | Christmas Day. |
| Directions | From Cambridge, A1307 for Haverhill. Left to Withersfield. At T-junc., left. Almost 3 miles on, high yew hedge; at 'Concealed Entrance' sign on left, sharp turn into drive. |

| | |
|---|---|
| Price | £65–£75. Singles from £40. |
| Rooms | 1 twin/double & sitting room. |
| Meals | Pub/restaurant 2-minute walk. |
| Closed | Rarely. |
| Directions | From Bury St. Edmunds, A143 to Haverhill; left on to B1066 for Glemsford. 6 miles to Hartest; house on far side of green, opp. phone box. From Long Melford A1092 for Clare, then 1st right on to B1066. |

|  |  |
|---|---|
| | Jane Sheppard |
| | The Old Vicarage, |
| | Great Thurlow, |
| | Newmarket, Suffolk CB9 7LE |
| Tel | +44 (0)1440 783209 |
| Fax | +44 (0)1638 667270 |
| Email | s.j.sheppard@hotmail.co.uk |

|  |  |
|---|---|
| | Bridget & Robin Oaten |
| | The Manse, |
| | The Green, |
| | Hartest, |
| | Suffolk IP29 4DH |
| Tel | +44 (0)1284 830226 |
| Email | robin@oatens.plus.com |

Entry 476   Map 9

Entry 477   Map 10

## Suffolk

### The Old Manse Barn

A large, lush loft apartment in sleepy Suffolk; this living/eating/sleeping space of blond wood, white walls and big windows has an urban feel yet overlooks glorious countryside. Secluded from the main house, in a timber-clad barn, the style is thrillingly modern: leather sofas, glass dining table, stainless steel kitchenette. Floor lights dance off the walls, CD surround-sound creates mood and you can watch the stars from your bed. Homemade granola, local bread and ham in the fridge – breakfast when you like. There's peace for romance, solitude for work, a garden to sit in and friendly Sue to suggest the best pubs.

## Suffolk

### 16 Bolton Street

The house is 15th century and rests on a quiet street in lovely, bustling Lavenham: part medieval, part Tudor, this is one of England's showpiece towns. Heavy beams, low doorways, books, magazines, fresh flowers and gentle hosts create a warm happy feel; steep oak stairs lead to fresh, cosy bedrooms where patchwork quilts, colourful cushions and handmade curtains abound. Gillian likes nothing better than to spoil her guests with breakfasts of local sausages and bacon, potato cakes, very special mushrooms and fresh fruit. A delightful, relaxed, generous place to stay.
*Minimum stay two nights at weekends.*

 Travel Club offer. See page 414.

| | |
|---|---|
| Price | From £70. |
| Rooms | Apartment: 1 double & kitchenette. |
| Meals | Pubs within walking distance. |
| Closed | Rarely. |
| Directions | A134 towards Bury St Edmunds & Sudbury; A1141 Lavenham, left after 1.4 miles towards Cockfield; house 1.2 miles on right. |

| | |
|---|---|
| Price | £80-£90. |
| Rooms | 2: 1 twin/double, 1 double. |
| Meals | Packed lunch £8. Pubs/restaurants in Lavenham. |
| Closed | Rarely. |
| Directions | From market square in Lavenham, pass The Great House Restaurant, then left into Bolton Street. Long pink house at bottom on right. Park outside to unload; Gillian will help with parking. |

| | |
|---|---|
| | **Sue & Ian Jones** |
| | The Old Manse Barn, |
| | Chapel Road, Cockfield, |
| | Bury St Edmunds, Suffolk IP30 0HE |
| Tel | +44 (0)1284 828120 |
| Email | bookings@theoldmansebarn.co.uk |
| Web | www.theoldmansebarn.co.uk |

| | |
|---|---|
| | **Bill & Gillian de Lucy** |
| | 16 Bolton Street, |
| | Lavenham, |
| | Suffolk CO10 9RG |
| Tel | +44 (0)1787 249046 |
| Email | gdelucy@aol.com |
| Web | www.guineahouse.co.uk |

Entry 478   Map 10

Entry 479   Map 10

## Suffolk

### Milden Hall

Over five generations of Hawkins have lived in this seemingly grand 16th-century hall farmhouse with its smooth wooden floors, enormous windows and vast fireplaces. Bedrooms range from big to huge, are elegantly old-fashioned and filled with interesting tapestries, wall hangings and lovely furniture; it's a bit of a trek to the loo from the family room so you need to be nimble. Juliet is a passionate conservationist, full of ideas for making the most of the surrounding countryside, on foot or by bicycle. Expect delicious home-grown bacon, sausages, bantam eggs and fruit compotes for breakfast.

Ethical Collection: Environment; Community; Food. See page 412.

| | |
|---|---|
| Price | £60-£90. Singles from £40. |
| Rooms | 3: 2 twins, 1 family room, all sharing bathroom. |
| Meals | Occasional light supper £15. BYO. Pubs/restaurants 2-3 miles. |
| Closed | Rarely. |
| Directions | From Lavenham, A1141 for Monks Eleigh. After 2 miles, right to Milden. At x-roads, right to Sudbury on B1115. Hall's long drive 0.25 miles on left. |

|  | Juliet & Christopher Hawkins |
|---|---|
| | Milden Hall, |
| | Milden, Lavenham, |
| | Suffolk CO10 9NY |
| Tel | +44 (0)1787 247235 |
| Email | hawkins@thehall-milden.co.uk |
| Web | www.thehall-milden.co.uk |

Entry 480  Map 10

## Suffolk

### Wood Hall

Susan greets you with the warmest of welcomes. Janus-like, her house looks both ways, Georgian to the front, and beamed Tudor behind. Breakfast on summer mornings on the terrace in the walled garden on homemade marmalade, jams and fruit compotes; in winter, settle beside the fire with a cup of tea. The bedrooms, one delicately floral, the other with cream walls, are elegant with padded headboards, thick curtains, armchairs, writing desks, candles, standard lamps, books and an ample tea tray. Wander through the garden to find a Victorian greenhouse with two types of vine. *Bridge classes offered to groups of four.*

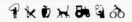 Travel Club offer. See page 414.

| | |
|---|---|
| Price | From £88. Singles £50 (Sun-Thurs only). |
| Rooms | 2: 1 double, 1 twin/double. |
| Meals | Pub 150 yds. |
| Closed | Christmas & New Year. |
| Directions | B1115 for Lavenham from Sudbury 3.5 miles; right to Little Waldingfield; house on left, 200 yds beyond The Swan. Parking at rear of house. |

|  | Mrs Susan Nisbett |
|---|---|
| | Wood Hall, |
| | Little Waldingfield, |
| | Lavenham, Suffolk CO10 0SY |
| Tel | +44 (0)1787 247362 |
| Email | susan@woodhallbnb.fsnet.co.uk |
| Web | www.thewoodhall.com |

Entry 481  Map 10

# Suffolk

## Hill House

Nayland is a charming village and this apricot-coloured, listed house sits on a quiet lane. Enter an unusual tunnel hall with flagstones, rugs and fresh flowers, to find a beamed drawing room and an elegant dining room. There are well-polished antiques, good art, and creamy colours dotted with bright chintz; smart, fresh bedrooms have good views over the pretty garden and you get a choice of pillows. Pauline happily shares her home with you and provides generous breakfasts – in the garden in summer. Good walks abound in Constable country; Beth Chatto gardens nearby. *Minimum stay two nights at weekends in summer.*

# Suffolk

## Nether Hall

The River Box borders the garden, you're welcome to use the hard tennis court and the garden cascades with old English roses in summer. This is a charming 16th-century home in a valley made famous by John Constable; make the most of this delightful area. Inside is warmly enticing. Find elegance and period charm in ancient doors and beams, massive open fireplaces in dining and drawing rooms, little windows, chintz and checks on the chairs. Bedrooms are simple and fresh; one is downstairs with its own entrance. Jennie and Patrick immediately put you at ease and the Aga breakfasts are plentiful and delicious.

Travel Club offer. See page 414.

| | | | |
|---|---|---|---|
| Price | From £72. Singles from £36. | Price | £80–£85. Singles £60. |
| Rooms | 2: 1 twin/double; 1 double with separate bath. | Rooms | 3: 1 double, 1 twin/double; 1 single with separate bath. |
| Meals | Pub/restaurant short walk. | Meals | Pubs 1 mile. |
| Closed | Christmas & New Year. | Closed | Rarely. |
| Directions | Enter village from A134 into Bear St. Past T-junction into Birch St. 100 yds turn left, house 70 yds uphill on right. | Directions | 3 miles from A12, on B1068 between Higham & Stoke-by-Nayland. On south side of road, 300 yds east of Thorington Street. |

|  | | | |
|---|---|---|---|
| | **Mrs Pauline Heigham** | | **Patrick & Jennie Jackson** |
| | Hill House, | | Nether Hall, |
| | Gravel Hill, Nayland, | | Thorington Street, |
| | Suffolk CO6 4JB | | Stoke-by-Nayland, |
| Tel | +44 (0)1206 262782 | | Suffolk CO6 4ST |
| Email | heighamhillhouse@hotmail.com | Tel | +44 (0)1206 337373 |
| Web | www.heighamhillhouse.co.uk | Email | patrick.jackson7@btopenworld.com |

Entry 482   Map 10

Entry 483   Map 10

# Suffolk

## Priory House

A soft, 16th-century Suffolk combination of bricks and beams; drink in the peace of house and garden all day if you wish. The house is friendly and informal, with antique furniture, gleaming brass and William Morris-style floral sofas and chairs; the fascinating, heavily timbered dining room was once a cheese room where 'Suffolk Bang' was made. Expect white walls in the bedrooms and a wood-burning stove in the guest sitting room, along with books and comfy chairs. Plan your days with friendly Rosemary – the Southwold coast is half an hour away. *Children over ten welcome. Minimum stay two nights July-October.*

| | |
|---|---|
| Price | From £80. Singles £40. |
| Rooms | 3: 1 double; 1 double, 1 twin, each with separate bath. |
| Meals | Pubs/restaurants 8-minute walk. |
| Closed | Christmas week. |
| Directions | From Scole, A140, right onto A143 for Gt Yarmouth. After 7 miles, right at Harleston. B1116 to Fressingfield. Pass church & Fox & Goose on left. At top of hill, right, then left into Priory Rd. |

Stephen & Rosemary Willis
Priory House,
Priory Road,
Fressingfield, Eye,
Suffolk IP21 5PH

| | |
|---|---|
| Tel | +44 (0)1379 586254 |
| Fax | +44 (0)1379 586254 |
| Email | willisbb@clara.co.uk |

Entry 484   Map 10

# Suffolk

## Mulberry Hall

Delight in the characterful architecture and uneven tread of this handsome hall house of 1523; it was owned by Cardinal Wolsey and has Henry VIII's coat of arms above the fire. It rambles round corners, is rich in beams and beloved family pieces, and has two winding stairs. Penny, gentle and well-travelled, gives you tea and cakes in the drawing room and lights a log fire on chillier days. In the garden: old roses, pear pergola and mulberry tree; in the bedrooms: leaded windows, beamed walls, good beds. Homemade jam on home-baked bread when you wake, soft robes for the bath before bed.

| | |
|---|---|
| Price | From £70. Singles from £40. |
| Rooms | 2: 1 twin; 1 double with separate shower. |
| Meals | Supper £8-£12. Pubs/restaurants 5-8 miles. |
| Closed | Christmas to New Year. |
| Directions | 5 miles west of Ipswich (off A1071). 300 yds into village on left next to farmyard but before phone box. |

Penny Debenham
Mulberry Hall,
Burstall,
Ipswich,
Suffolk IP8 3DP

| | |
|---|---|
| Tel | +44 (0)1473 652348 |
| Fax | +44 (0)1473 652110 |
| Email | pennydebenham@hotmail.com |

Entry 485   Map 10

## Suffolk

### Poplar Farm House

Only a few miles from Ipswich but down a green lane, this rambling farm house has a pretty, white-washed porch and higgledy-piggledy roof. All light, elegant and spacious with wonderful flowers, art, sumptuous soft furnishings (made by Sally) and quirky sculptures; expect comfortable beds, laundered linen and smart bathrooms. Sally and linguist Penton are relaxed and humorous; have tasty eggs from their handsome hens, homemade bread, veg from the garden on an artistically laid table. Play tennis, swim, steam in the sauna or book one of Sally's arts and crafts courses, then wander in the woods beyond with friendly collies Shale and Wizard.

Travel Club offer. See page 414.

| | |
|---|---|
| Price | £65. Singles £55. |
| Rooms | 3: 2 doubles, 1 twin with 2 shared bath/shower rooms. |
| Meals | Dinner, 3 courses, £15–£25. Packed lunch £7. Pub 1 mile. |
| Closed | Rarely. |
| Directions | From Ipswich A1214 for Colchester. After 2 miles at Holiday Inn right (at lights) onto A1071, for Hadleigh. Poplar Lane is immediately on left. House first on right. |

Penton Lewis & Sally Sparrow
Poplar Farm House,
Poplar Lane,
Sproughton,
Ipswich, Suffolk IP8 3HL
Tel    +44 (0)1473 601211
Email  sparrowsally@aol.com
Web    www.poplarfarmhousesuffolkbb.eu

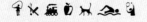

Entry 486   Map 10

## Suffolk

### Haughley House

A timber-framed, medieval manor in three acres of garden overlooking 30 acres of farmland. The attractive village is in a conservation area; your hosts: the Lord of the Manor and his wife. They also happen to be accomplished cooks and use the finest ingredients – their own beef, game and eggs, and vegetables and soft fruits from the kitchen garden. You'll find genuine country-house style here, tea and homemade cake on arrival, flowery wallpapers, much charm and sparkling shower rooms – there's even a stairlift. Ask Jeffrey to show you the manorial records and the priest hole. Aga-cooked breakfasts are a feast.

Travel Club offer. See page 414.

| | |
|---|---|
| Price | From £90. Singles from £60. |
| Rooms | 3: 2 doubles, 1 twin. |
| Meals | Dinner, 3 courses, £25. |
| Closed | Rarely. |
| Directions | From A14 exit 49, follow signs to Haughley. Fork left at village green, house 100 yds on left. |

Jeffrey & Caroline Bowden
Haughley House,
Haughley,
Suffolk IP14 3NS
Tel    +44 (0)1449 673398
Fax    +44 (0)1449 673170
Email  bowden@keme.co.uk
Web    www.haughleyhouse.co.uk

Entry 487   Map 10

## Suffolk

### Church Farmhouse

This lovely Elizabethan farmhouse is in a quiet hamlet by an ancient thatched church, but the bird sanctuary at Minsmere, Southwold, Snape Maltings, music and the coast are near for lovely days out. Characterful Sarah, well-travelled and entertaining, is also an excellent cook, so breakfast will be a treat, and occasional dinners are well worth staying in for. Bedrooms are restful and painted in soft colours; beds are supremely comfortable and well dressed in laundered white cotton. There are peaceful views, fresh flowers, lots of books and a calm atmosphere. *Children over 12 welcome. Minimum stay two nights at weekends in summer.*

| | |
|---|---|
| Price | From £75. Singles from £50. |
| Rooms | 3: 1 double, 1 twin; <br> 1 double with separate bath. |
| Meals | Dinner £25-£28. <br> Pub/restaurants within 4 miles. |
| Closed | Christmas. |
| Directions | A12 for Wangford; left signed Uggeshall; house 1 mile on left before church. |

Sarah Lentaigne
Church Farmhouse,
Uggeshall,
Southwold, Suffolk NR34 8BD
Tel      +44 (0)1502 578532
Email    uggeshalljupp@btinternet.com
Web      www.uggeshall.fsnet.co.uk

🍴 🐿 🐕 🚲

Entry 488   Map 10

## Suffolk

### The Old Methodist Chapel

Atmosphere and architecture – easy to see what seduced Jackum and David into converting this listed Victorian chapel into a home. Bedrooms have their own entrance and are charming – one, with access to conservatory and courtyard garden, has pale walls, oak floors and beams; the flag-floored Retreat Room sports bright rugs and bedcovers from far-flung places. The chapel is comfortably, cosily cluttered and the Browns are easy-going. Potions and lotions by your bath, videos, DVDs and music in your room, books and flowers in every corner, and famous bacon from Peasenhall. *Minimum stay two nights at weekends.*

 Travel Club offer. See page 414.

| | |
|---|---|
| Price | £75-£95. Singles £50-£65. |
| Rooms | 2: 1 twin, <br> 1 double with separate bath. |
| Meals | Nearest restaurant directly opposite. More pubs/restaurants within walking distance. |
| Closed | Rarely. |
| Directions | From A12 in Yoxford, A1120 signed Peasenhall & Stowmarket. Chapel 200 yds on right. |

Jackum & David Brown
The Old Methodist Chapel,
High Street,
Yoxford, Suffolk IP17 3EU
Tel      +44 (0)1728 668333
Email    browns@chapelsuffolk.co.uk
Web      www.chapelsuffolk.co.uk

🚶 ♟ 🚂 🐕

Entry 489   Map 10

# Suffolk

## Sandpit Farm

Idyllic views of the wide Alde valley from this deeply comfortable, listed farmhouse. The river borders their 20 acres of beautiful meadows, orchard, gardens, tennis court, ponds and remains of brick-lined moat. Be charmed by family antiques and portraits, easy colour schemes, some beams and open fires, and every cossetting thing in the pretty bedrooms, one with its own sitting room. Susie and her Aga will cook a scrumptious breakfast of homemade and local produce. Near the coast, Snape for concerts, great birdwatching, walks and cycling. Peaceful and so relaxing. *Painting classes possible.*

Travel Club offer. See page 414.

| | |
|---|---|
| Price | £65–£80. Singles from £50. |
| Rooms | 2: 1 double, 1 twin. |
| Meals | Pub/restaurant 1.5 miles. |
| Closed | Rarely. |
| Directions | From A1120, Yoxford to Stowmarket, east to Dennington; take B1120, Framlingham. First left; house 1.5 miles on left. |

Susie Marshall
Sandpit Farm,
Bruisyard,
Saxmundham, Suffolk IP17 2EB
Tel +44 (0)1728 663445
Email smarshall@aldevalleybreaks.co.uk
Web www.aldevalleybreaks.co.uk

Entry 490   Map 10

# Suffolk

## Arch House

Arch House stands in three acres of garden, meadow and woodland, in easy reach of the sea, Snape Maltings and Minsmere bird reserve. It is also home to the delightful and fun-loving Araminta and Hugh. He, a keen member of the Soil Association, shoots, fishes and grows his own veg; she offers complementary therapies. Both are fabulous cooks and you eat well in the farmhouse kitchen. The décor is traditional, the bedrooms colourful, and the elegant drawing/dining room has a boudoir grand piano. Trout, salmon or game for dinner; at breakfast, eggs from the hens. Wonderful value.

Ethical Collection: Food. See page 412.

Travel Club offer. See page 414.

| | |
|---|---|
| Price | £55–£70. Singles £35. |
| Rooms | 2: 1 double, 1 twin with separate bath. |
| Meals | Dinner from £15. BYO. Pub 200 yds. |
| Closed | Rarely. |
| Directions | From A12, A1094 into Aldeburgh. Left at r'bout onto B1122 to Leiston. On left, 0.5 miles after Aldringham sign. |

Araminta Stewart & Hugh Peacock
Arch House,
Aldeburgh Road,
Aldringham, Suffolk IP16 4QF
Tel +44 (0)1728 832615
Email amintys@aol.com
Web www.archhouse-aldeburgh.com

Entry 491   Map 10

## Suffolk

### Dunan House

You may get wild mushrooms for breakfast and new-laid eggs, homemade bread, jams and marmalade. This is a lovely place to stay, with an unusual, lively décor. Ann is a potter and her artistry is apparent everywhere: bedrooms are upbeat and attractive, with woven rugs and imaginative, decorative touches, and the double at the top has its own little sitting room and long views. Ann and Simon, an illustrator, are entertaining company. It is wonderfully close to town and sea with views over the marshes to the river Alde and beyond. *Minimum stay two nights at weekends; three on bank holidays. See website for availability calendar.*

| | |
|---|---|
| Price | From £75. Singles from £50. |
| Rooms | 3: 1 twin/double, 1 double, 1 double with single child's room. |
| Meals | Pubs & restaurants 7-minute walk. |
| Closed | Christmas & New Year. |
| Directions | From A1094 drive towards town from r'bout. First right towards hospital, through 'Private Road' gate. House 100 yds on left, opp. tennis courts. |

**Mr Simon Farr & Ms Ann Lee**
Dunan House,
41 Park Road,
Aldeburgh,
Suffolk IP15 5EN
Tel +44 (0)1728 452486
Email dunanhouse@btinternet.com
Web www.dunanhouse.co.uk

Entry 492   Map 10

## Suffolk

### The Old Butchers Shop

Artist Sarah has cleverly converted this old butcher's shop: you're right on the main street of an undisturbed brick and timber estuary village, a hop from the sea for birdwatching or walks, and Snape for music lovers. Bedrooms (the new ground floor one is the largest) are pretty and light with proper linen on supremely comfortable beds and views over the garden or a fine Norman church. Two happy cats lie comatose in the drawing room with its gay kilims and bright checks, books jostle for space with pictures. Sarah is laid-back and fun and cooks a mean breakfast: homemade yogurt and stewed fruits, local kippers.

Ethical Collection: Community; Food. See page 412.

Travel Club offer. See page 414.

| | |
|---|---|
| Price | £65-£75. Singles from £45. |
| Rooms | 3: 2 twins/doubles; 1 twin/double with separate bath/shower. |
| Meals | Pubs/restaurants within 5-min walk. |
| Closed | Rarely. |
| Directions | From A12, signs to Orford. Left-hand bend after King's Head pub towards quay. House on opposite side of road with blue door. Park in Market Square. |

**Mrs Sarah Holland**
The Old Butchers Shop,
111 Church Street, Orford,
Woodbridge, Suffolk IP12 2LL
Tel +44 (0)1394 450517
Fax +44 (0)1394 459436
Email sarah@oldbutchers-orford.co.uk
Web www.oldbutchers-orford.co.uk

Entry 493   Map 10

## Suffolk

### Melton Hall

There's more than a touch of theatre to this beautiful listed house. The dining room is opulent red; the drawing room, with its delicately carved mantelpiece and comfortable George Smith sofas, has French windows to the terrace. There's a four-poster in one bedroom, an antique French bed in another (occasional road noise) and masses of fresh flowers and books. The seven acres of garden include an orchid and wildflower meadow designated a County Wildlife Site. River walks, the coast and Sutton Hoo – the Saxon burial site – are close by. Generous Cindy, her delightful children, little dog, Snowball, and Bea the cat give a great welcome.

| Price | £100–£120. Singles from £55. |
|---|---|
| Rooms | 3: 1 double; 1 double, 1 single sharing bath. |
| Meals | Dinner, 1-3 courses, £18–£36. BYO. Pubs/restaurants nearby. |
| Closed | Rarely. |
| Directions | From A12 Woodbridge bypass, exit at r'bout for Melton. Follow for 1 mile to lights; there, right. Immediately on right. |

Mrs Lucinda de la Rue
Melton Hall,
Woodbridge,
Suffolk IP12 1PF
Tel +44 (0)1394 388138
Email cindy@meltonhall.co.uk
Web www.meltonhall.co.uk

Entry 494 Map 10

## Suffolk

### Bealings House

A picture postcard of a setting and a large, beautifully proportioned, Georgian house sitting high in mature parkland. Charming Selina and Jonathan give the whole thing an unpretentious feel and you are encouraged to make yourself at home, but it will be among family memorabilia, grand marble fireplaces, Irish linen, well-trodden floorboards under fading Persian rugs, first class antiques, gilt-framed landscape paintings and bursts of dried flowers. Bedrooms and bathrooms are fearfully old-fashioned and you may need to bring an extra jumper if you are a pampered city-dweller. Quirky, with wonderful grounds.

| Price | From £70. Singles from £50. |
|---|---|
| Rooms | 3: 1 double, 1 twin both with separate bath/shower. 1 double with separate bath, sitting room & kitchen. |
| Meals | Pub/restaurant 1 mile. |
| Closed | Rarely. |
| Directions | From Ipswich A12 N. At Woodbridge r'bout, N on A12; after 150 yds left at Seckford Hall Hotel sign. After 1 mile left at T-junc. at bottom of hill; then 1st right. Entrance immed. on right. |

Selina & Jonathan Peto
Bealings House,
Great Bealings, Woodbridge,
Suffolk IP13 6NP
Tel +44 (0)1394 382631
Email jonathanpeto@btinternet.com
Web www.bealingshouse.co.uk

Entry 495 Map 10

# Suffolk

## The Hayloft

Romantics, walkers, birdwatchers and those who need to get away from it all will be in heaven. In the old hayloft is a self-contained and stunningly stylish apartment: a raftered sitting room with a sweeping oak floor, cream sofas and a window to trumpet the view. The bedroom is uncluttered and cosy with a big leather bed, gorgeous linen and feathered bedside lights. Continental breakfast is in the fridge (homemade jams, local honey, their own fruits in summer, home-baked rolls), there are ten idyllic acres of gardens, meadows and wildlife, and bikes to borrow. Farmers' markets and festivals abound.

Travel Club offer. See page 414.

| | |
|---|---|
| Price | £120. Singles £80. |
| Rooms | Studio: 1 double & sitting room. |
| Meals | Restaurants 4 miles. |
| Closed | Christmas. |
| Directions | North of Woodbridge on A12, take road signed Bredfield. At T-junc. with B1078 (3 miles), left, then 1st right into Martins Lane. House on right, gravel parking on left. |

Adrian & Jane Stevensen
The Hayloft,
Valley Farm House, Clopton,
Woodbridge, Suffolk IP13 6QX
Tel       +44 (0)1473 737872
Fax      +44 (0)1473 737880
Email   info@thehayloftsuffolk.co.uk
Web     www.thehayloftsuffolk.co.uk

Entry 496   Map 10

# Suffolk

## Grange Farm

The tennis court and garden are surrounded by a 12th-century listed moat – this is a glorious old place. Ancient stairs rise and fall all over the 13th-century house, there are sloping floors and honey-coloured beams and a lovely dining room that was once the dairy. Bedrooms are large, comfortable and traditional; the sitting room is cosy with baby grand, log fire, fresh flowers, books, puzzles and games, and the views are to a garden full of birds. Delightful Elizabeth spoils you with homemade cake, local honey, own bread and homemade marmalade for breakfast. Good value, great fun.

Travel Club offer. See page 414.

| | |
|---|---|
| Price | £64. Singles £32. |
| Rooms | 2: 1 twin/double, 1 twin, sharing bath. |
| Meals | Pub 2-mile walk. |
| Closed | December-March. |
| Directions | A1120 (Yoxford to Stowmarket) to Dennington. B1116 north for approx. 3 miles. Farm on right 0.9 miles north of Owl's Green & red phone box. |

Elizabeth Hickson
Grange Farm,
Dennington,
Framlingham,
Woodbridge, Suffolk IP13 8BT
Tel       +44 (0)1986 798388
Web     www.grangefarm.biz

Entry 497   Map 10

## Surrey

### Hunters

Impossible to believe London is 45 minutes away! Surrounded by lawns, woodland and a palm-dotted terrace, the house feels buried deep in sunny countryside. Large and relaxed, it makes the most of the natural light: rugs on polished wood, flagstones, creamy colours, elegant furniture. Bedrooms (one with balcony) have a smooth, luscious, contemporary feel with bold shots of colour, Ros's vibrant paintings, an ethnic touch or a modern sculpture. Bathrooms are chic spaces of stone and natural wood. Take walks, play golf, relax over those woodland views, return to a delicious dinner.

| | |
|---|---|
| Price | From £80. Singles from £65. |
| Rooms | 3: 2 doubles sharing shower; 1 double with separate bath. |
| Meals | Dinner £25. Pub 4 miles. |
| Closed | Christmas. |
| Directions | From A3 onto B3002 for Bordon; 1 mile; through Grayshott; church on right, drive to house on left. |

|  | Mrs Ros Richards |
|---|---|
| | Hunters, |
| | Grayshott, |
| | Surrey GU26 6DL |
| Tel | +44 (0)1428 606623 |
| Email | rosrichards@hotmail.com |

Entry 498   Map 4

## Surrey

### Greenaway

An enchanting cottage. People return time and again – for the house, the dovecote, the garden, the countryside, and Sheila and John. The sitting room is vast with restful rich colours and textures. A sturdy, turning oak staircase leads to the sweet bedrooms – and newly decorated bathrooms with roll tops; a peek at them all will only confuse you: each one is gorgeous. There's an ornate bedstead in the Chinese room and, in another, an oak bedstead and beams. An exceptionally quiet place and a delightful village with glorious walks on the Greensand Way, yet so close to London and the airports.

| | |
|---|---|
| Price | £85-£95. Singles from £65. |
| Rooms | 3: 1 double; 1 double, 1 twin, sharing bath. |
| Meals | Hotel restaurant 0.25 miles. |
| Closed | Rarely. |
| Directions | A3 to Milford, then A283 for Petworth. At Chiddingfold, Pickhurst Road off green. House 3rd on left, with black dovecote. |

|  | Sheila & John Marsh |
|---|---|
| | Greenaway, |
| | Pickhurst Road, |
| | Chiddingfold, |
| | Surrey GU8 4TS |
| Tel | +44 (0)1428 682920 |
| Email | jfmarsh@gotadsl.co.uk |

Entry 499   Map 4

# Surrey

## Lower Easing Farmhouse

A homely place with a lovely walled garden and super hosts; Gillian, who speaks French, German and Spanish, enjoys welcoming people from all over the world. The house, 16th to 19th century, has exposed timbers, books and bold colours. The dining room is red; the guest sitting room – with open fire and decorated with fascinating artefacts from around the world – is big enough for a small company meeting, or a wedding group. Your hosts, who are great fun, run an efficient and caring ship. In the walled garden, sipping tea, the distant rumble of the A3 reminds you how well placed you are for Gatwick and Heathrow.

🧳 Travel Club offer. See page 414.

| Price | From £70. Singles from £45. |
|---|---|
| Rooms | 4: 1 twin/double; 1 twin/double with separate bath/shower; 2 singles sharing shower. |
| Meals | Pub 300 yds. |
| Closed | Occasionally. |
| Directions | A3 south. 5 miles after Guildford, Easing signed left at service station. House 150 yds on left behind white fence. |

**David & Gillian Swinburn**
Lower Easing Farmhouse,
Lower Easing,
Godalming,
Surrey GU7 2QF
Tel    +44 (0)1483 421436
Fax    +44 (0)1483 421436
Email  davidswinburn@hotmail.com

Entry 500   Map 4

# Surrey

## Old Great Halfpenny

It feels as rural as Devon, yet you are perfectly placed for airports and easy access to London, with Guildford a few minutes away. The 16th-century farmhouse sits on a country lane beneath the Pilgrim's Way; there are stunning views from every room and beyond Michael's immaculate gardens roll the Surrey Hills, with glorious walks right from the door. You have your own entrance up fairly steep steps to lovely bedrooms which Alison, an interior designer, has made beautiful with fine fabrics and antique French beds. Wake to the smell of home baked bread; in summer you breakfast on the terrace. Special.

| Price | £75-£85. Singles £65. |
|---|---|
| Rooms | 2 doubles, each with separate bath. |
| Meals | Pub 0.5 miles. |
| Closed | Rarely. |
| Directions | From London, exit A3 before Guildford, signed Burpham. From here 2 miles to house. Ring for detailed directions. |

**Michael & Alison Bennett**
Old Great Halfpenny,
Halfpenny Lane,
St Martha,
Guildford, Surrey GU4 8PY
Tel    +44 (0)1483 567835
Fax    +44 (0)1483 303037
Email  bennettbird@gmail.com

Entry 501   Map 4

## Surrey

### High Edser

Ancient wattle and daub, aged timbers and bags of character – it really does ramble. Built in 1532, High Edser sits in 2.5 acres of smooth lawns beyond which lie the village and the Surrey hills. But, unlike many houses of a certain age, this one is light and inviting and has the sort of family clutter that makes you feel at home. Bedrooms are full of character; kind Patrick and Carol leave you plenty of space to gently unfurl. The carved wooden fireplace in the stone-flagged dining room is spectacular, and there's a snug study just for guests. Very peaceful in an AONB, yet close to both airports.

## Surrey

### Blackbrook House

A large Victorian house sitting in lawns and garden and with a wide gravel drive; this has a rural feel but you are less than two miles from the centre of Dorking. Emma and Rae, both easy-going, give you a super little sitting room with a hidden TV and space to make a cup of tea; both bedrooms are spacious, smart and feminine with floral fabrics, deep pocket sprung mattresses and good linen, bathrooms are tip-top. Breakfast is beautifully presented with cereals, pancakes and maple syrup or the full Monty. Walk it off over lawns, shrubs and woods – or strike out further over National Trust land.

 Travel Club offer. See page 414.

| | | | |
|---|---|---|---|
| Price | £65–£70. Singles £30–£40. | Price | From £70. Singles from £45. |
| Rooms | 3: 2 doubles, 1 twin, all sharing bath. | Rooms | 2 doubles. |
| Meals | Pub/restaurant 300 yds. | Meals | Dinner, 2 courses, from £22. Pub at bottom of drive. |
| Closed | Rarely. | Closed | Christmas & New Year. |
| Directions | From A3, 1st exit after M25, for Ripley. Through Ripley & West Clandon, over dual c'way (A246) onto A25. 3rd right to Shere. There, right to Cranleigh. House 5 miles on left, 1 mile past The Windmill. | Directions | Roundabout outside Dorking A24 intersects A25. Follow A24 0.5 miles. Left into Blackbrook, signed. Follow road 1 mile until Plough pub. Turn into pub and up track. House 3rd on left. |

| | | | |
|---|---|---|---|
| | Patrick & Carol Franklin Adams | | Emma & Rae Burdon |
| | High Edser, | | Blackbrook House, |
| | Shere Road, Ewhurst, | | Blackbrook, |
| | Cranleigh, Surrey GU6 7PQ | | Dorking, |
| | | | Surrey RH5 4DS |
| Tel | +44 (0)1483 278214 | Tel | +44 (0)1306 888898 |
| Fax | +44 (0)1483 278200 | | |
| Email | carol@highedser.co.uk | Email | blackbrookbb@btinternet.com |
| Web | www.highedser.co.uk | Web | www.blackbrookhouse.org.uk |

Entry 502  Map 4

Entry 503  Map 4

# Surrey

### Swallow Barn

A squash court, coach house and stables, once belonging to next-door's manor, have become a home of old-fashioned charm. Full of family memories and run by a gentle and hospitable couple, the B&B is excellently placed for Windsor, Wisley and golf courses; close to both airports, too. Lovely trees in the garden, fields and woods beyond, a paddock and a summer pool... total tranquillity, and you can walk to the pub. None of the bedrooms is huge but the beds are firm, the garden views are pretty and the downstairs double has its own sitting room. Breakfasts are both generous and scrumptious. *Children over eight welcome.*

| Price | From £85. Singles from £55. |
|---|---|
| Rooms | 3: 1 double & sitting room; 1 twin with separate shower. Apple Store: 1 twin. |
| Meals | Pub/restaurant 0.75 miles. |
| Closed | Rarely. |
| Directions | From M25, exit 11, A319 into Chobham. Left at T-junc.; left at mini r'bout onto A3046. After 0.7 miles, right between street light & postbox. House 2nd on left. |

Joan & David Carey
Swallow Barn,
Milford Green, Chobham, Woking,
Surrey GU24 8AU
Tel +44 (0)1276 856030
Fax +44 (0)1276 856030
Email swallowbarn@web-hq.com
Web www.swallow-barn.co.uk

Entry 504  Map 4

# Sussex

### Redford Cottage

In a tiny village, a friendly home with much-loved books and very kind hosts. The immense inglenook dates back to 1510 and the garden suite opens to undulating lawns; it is cosy, old-worldly, floral and private, and its sitting room comes with a wood-burner. The barn has the woody spaciousness of a ski chalet and is perfect for friends... old rugs, new pine, games, views and (up steep open stairs) beds tucked under a sloped ceiling. The silence is filled with birdsong and you are surrounded by woodland, wildlife and the rolling South Downs. Breakfasts in the conservatory are a treat. *Minimum stay three nights during Goodwood.*

| Price | From £95. Singles from £65. |
|---|---|
| Rooms | 3: 1 suite. Barn: 2 twins/doubles & sitting room. |
| Meals | Pubs/restaurants 2.5-4 miles. |
| Closed | Christmas. |
| Directions | On old A3, north from Petersfield, at Hill Brow right for Rogate, left after 300 yds to Milland. Follow lane through woods for 6 miles; right for Midhurst & Redford. On right, 150 yds beyond Redford sign. |

Caroline & David Angela
Redford Cottage,
Redford,
Midhurst,
Sussex GU29 0QF
Tel +44 (0)1428 741242
Fax +44 (0)1428 741242

Entry 506  Map 4

## Sussex

### The Quag

Buried in a birchwood, The Quag feels remote, yet Midhurst – "the second most attractive town in England" – is only two miles away. Feel private in your own space with spanking new bedroom, striking bathroom with chequerboard floor, wooden-floored sitting room, useful fridge and separate stairs to garden and pool. You breakfast in the main house at a long wooden table. Views are to the lawns that run romantically down to the stream, then across to the South Downs, from which are a maze of footpaths across common land. Mark works for Christie's and Loveday looks after you. A happy, relaxed atmosphere.

| Price | From £80. Singles £50. |
|---|---|
| Rooms | 1 twin & sitting room. |
| Meals | Pubs/restaurants nearby. |
| Closed | Rarely. |
| Directions | A272 Midhurst-Petersfield; 2 miles from Midhurst, left signed Minsted. Count 7 telegraph poles, then 1st left. White house 1st on right. |

Loveday & Mark Wrey
The Quag,
Minsted,
Midhurst,
Sussex GU29 0JH
Tel +44 (0)1730 813623
Email beds@wrey.co.uk

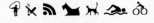

Entry 507 Map 4

## Sussex

### Amberfold

Down the secluded, wooded lane and through a stone archway to find a glorious terraced garden and a listed 17th-century house; the perfect hideaway. Bedrooms are in individual annexes so you can come and go as you please. Step in to vibrant colours and interesting art, large beds and fabulous linen, a refreshing lack of clutter and space for comfy armchairs; showers only do full pelt and towels are plentiful. Erling (who adores music and, clearly, gardening) is dedicated to your happiness, making this the perfect place to recharge the batteries in peace and quiet; breakfast on the terrace in summer.

| Price | £75-£100. Singles £55-£75. |
|---|---|
| Rooms | 2 doubles. |
| Meals | Pubs 1-4 miles. |
| Closed | Rarely. |
| Directions | From Midhurst, A286 for Chichester. After Royal Oak pub on left, Greyhound on right, on for 0.5 miles, left to Heyshott. On for 2 miles, do not turn off, look for house sign on left. |

Erling Sorensen
Amberfold,
Heyshott, Midhurst, Sussex GU29 0DA
Tel +44 (0)1730 812385
Fax +44 (0)1730 813559
Email erlingamberfold@aol.com
Web www.amberfold.co.uk

Entry 508 Map 4

## Sussex

### West Marden Farmhouse

Bowl down a gentle valley in the South Downs to find a 16th-century farmhouse with beautiful Sussex granaries and barn; the Edney family has farmed the land for generations. Your delightful, helpful hosts, committed to the environment, give you a sitting/dining room with a huge old fireplace, comfortable sofas, oak floor and French windows to the garden. Upstairs is a beamed bedroom with a luxurious feel and a fabulous bathroom (free-standing bath, swish shower) bursting with aromatic soaps and oils. Breakfasts are delicious, the walking is great, Goodwood is a 20-minute drive. *Minimum stay two nights at weekends.*

| | |
|---|---|
| Price | £95. |
| Rooms | 1 twin/double. |
| Meals | Pub 75 yds. |
| Closed | Christmas. |
| Directions | West Marden Farmhouse is in centre of village opposite Noredown Way. |

|  | Carole Edney |
|---|---|
| | West Marden Farmhouse, |
| | West Marden, Chichester, |
| | Sussex PO18 9ES |
| Tel | +44 (0)23 926 31761 |
| Email | carole.edney@btinternet.com |
| Web | www.westmardenfarmhousebandb.co.uk |

Entry 509   Map 4

## Sussex

### Lordington House

Croquet on the lawn in summer, big log fires and woolly jumpers in winter, brilliant food all year round. On a sunny slope of the Ems valley, life ticks by peacefully as it has always done… The house is vast and impressive and a lime avenue links the much-loved garden with the AONB beyond. The 17th-century staircase is a glory, the décor is engagingly old-fashioned: Edwardian beds with firm mattresses and floral bedspreads, carpeted Sixties-style bathrooms, shepherdess wallpapers up and over wardrobe doors. A privilege to stay in a house of this age and character! *Children over five welcome. Dogs by arrangement.*

 Travel Club offer. See page 414.

| | |
|---|---|
| Price | From £90. Singles from £45. |
| Rooms | 4: 1 double; 1 twin/double with separate bath/shower; 1 double, 1 single sharing bath/shower. |
| Meals | Dinner £20. Packed lunch from £5. Pub 1 mile. |
| Closed | Rarely. |
| Directions | Lordington (marked on some road maps) west side of B2146, 6 miles south of South Harting, 0.5 miles south of Walderton. Enter through white railings by letterbox; fork right after bridge. |

|  | Mr & Mrs John Hamilton |
|---|---|
| | Lordington House, |
| | Lordington, Chichester, |
| | Sussex PO18 9DX |
| Tel | +44 (0)1243 375862 |
| Fax | +44 (0)1243 375862 |
| Email | audreyhamilton@onetel.com |

Entry 510   Map 4

# Sussex

## Church Gate

Janie has added a conservatory and huge, sunny, Aga kitchen to her 1930s house; she greets with afternoon tea, rustles up tasty home eggs at breakfast, and may even treat guests to home-baked bread or croissants, served on the terrace in summer. The house is adorned with Nigerian musical instruments and Janie's photographs; the bedrooms are fresh with low windows looking onto the garden; lovely soaps in the bath and shower rooms, driftwood lamps in the flagstoned airy sitting room. Set off for nearby Chichester with its theatre and shops, or pretty Itchenor, a mecca for sailors.

Ethical Collection: Food. See page 412.

Travel Club offer. See page 414.

| | |
|---|---|
| Price | From £85. Singles from £65. |
| Rooms | Cottage: 1 double, 1 twin with sitting room. |
| Meals | Pub within 4 miles. |
| Closed | Most of the winter months. |
| Directions | From A27 at Chichester take A286 Witterings; 5 miles; at roundabout bear right onto B2179. 0.5 miles turn right to Itchenor. 1 mile, house opposite church. |

**Mrs Janie Impey**
Church Gate,
Itchenor, Chichester,
Sussex PO20 7DL
Tel     +44 (0)1243 514700
Email   janie.allen@btinternet.com
Web    www.chichesterbandb.co.uk

Entry 511    Map 4

# Sussex

## Itchenor Park House

The Duke of Richmond reportedly built Itchenor Park for his French mistress in 1783. If he was hoping to hide her away, he succeeded – the listed Georgian house sits in beautiful formal gardens on a vast 700-acre farmed estate. It is remote, wonderfully tranquil, and a field path brings you to Chichester harbour for boat trips and sailing bustle. More walks to the beach and around the village. You stay in a graceful self-contained apartment in the cricket pavilion wing with private sitting room and use of the walled garden (breakfast is in the fridge). Your hosts are gracious and energetic people.

| | |
|---|---|
| Price | £80. Singles from £40. |
| Rooms | 1 twin/double & sitting room with sofa bed & kitchenette. |
| Meals | Continental breakfast. Pub 5-minute walk. |
| Closed | Rarely. |
| Directions | From A27 at Chichester take A286 Witterings. At Birdham, right at garage onto B2179; 500 yds, right to Itchenor. Driveway on left past church, signed. |

**Susie Green**
Itchenor Park House,
Itchenor,
Chichester,
Sussex PO20 7DN
Tel     +44 (0)1243 512221
Email   susie.green@lineone.net

Entry 512    Map 4

## Sussex

### Crede Farmhouse

Walk through the characterful village of Bosham – for church, quay, history and boats. Lesley is vivacious and kind, Peter helps cook delectable Aga breakfasts. This flint house (1810) is fresh, peaceful and beautifully maintained: Farrow & Ball paints, elegant pictures, rococo-esque mirrors and lights. One bedroom is primrose, floral and white, with green views; the smaller double has a wrought-iron bed. An outdoor pool in summer, Chichester Theatre up the road and Portsmouth a 30-minute drive. A delightful place for harbour walks and Downland treks. *Minimum stay two nights in summer.*

 Travel Club offer. See page 414.

| | |
|---|---|
| Price | From £80. Singles from £65. |
| Rooms | 2: 1 double; 1 small double with separate bath. |
| Meals | Pubs/restaurants 5-minute walk. |
| Closed | Christmas. |
| Directions | From Chichester, A259 west for Bosham; through Fishbourne, past garden centre, left into Walton Lane. After sharp bend, right into Crede Lane; 200 yds to end of lane. On left, with white garage. |

Mrs Lesley Hankey
Crede Farmhouse,
Crede Lane,
Bosham,
Sussex PO18 8NX
Tel       +44 (0)1243 574929
Email    lesley@credefarmhouse.fsnet.co.uk

Entry 513   Map 4

## Sussex

### Baron's Hall Cottage

A delightful hideaway – your Normandy-styled annexe to a listed Georgian house leads into its own large garden and has a private entrance. In the 17th century it was a humble shelter but the thatch and beams are immaculate now. Marilyn's style reflects her warm personality – you have white bedding on a big brass bed, a rich rug on dark boards, small armchairs and an open stove, a hat stand for clothes and a fine chest of drawers. It's luxurious but cosy, with a shower room to match. An unspoilt beach, with dunes, is a seven-minute walk. Perfect. *Minimum stay two nights. Arrivals between 12 noon & 6pm.*

| | |
|---|---|
| Price | From £85. |
| Rooms | 1 double. |
| Meals | Pub/restaurants 2-10 minute walk. |
| Closed | Rarely. |
| Directions | A259 Littlehampton & Bognor. Left towards sea signed Climping Street & Beach. House 4th on right with private lay-by opposite. |

Marilyn Craine
Baron's Hall Cottage,
The Well House, Climping Street,
Climping, Littlehampton,
Sussex BN17 5RQ
Tel      +44 (0)1903 713314
Email   info@baronshall.co.uk
Web     www.baronshall.co.uk

Entry 514   Map 4

# Sussex

## Castle Cottage

However beautiful the countryside and the walks, you will be most enchanted by what your hosts have achieved. In birdsong woodland is a small house with a separate weather-boarded family barn and a cobbled conservatory. The barn's A-frame roof draws in the light and the front views, and there are perfect decorative touches: Persian carpets, dashing blue paints, a wrought-iron staircase, sculptures, handmade paper, superb lighting. The double in the house has the same magic. But the treehouse upstages all, high in a giant chestnut, with vast bed, veranda, sauna and shower room. Beautifully built… ineffable.

 Travel Club offer. See page 414.

| | |
|---|---|
| Price | £110–£135. |
| Rooms | 3: 1 double with separate bath/shower. Barn: 1 family suite. Treehouse: 1 double. |
| Meals | Pubs/restaurants 1.5 miles. |
| Closed | Rarely. |
| Directions | From Fittleworth, south on B2138. Right onto Coates Lane; 1 mile, then right onto 'private drive'. Right at castle, right again & immed. left. |

Alison Wyatt
Castle Cottage,
Coates Castle, Petworth,
Sussex RH20 1EU

| | |
|---|---|
| Tel | +44 (0)1798 865001 |
| Fax | +44 (0)1798 865032 |
| Email | alison@castlecottage.info |
| Web | www.castlecottage.info |

Entry 515  Map 4

# Sussex

## Riverhill Lodge

Views, views and more views over gorgeous National Park, from this handsome redbrick house with early Georgian origins. A sunny, airy sitting room with open fire and elegant cream and pink sofas, looks onto the well-planted garden; you breakfast copiously in a cosy terracotta-coloured dining room – cheerful Chris and Jenny serve up homemade bread, eggs from local hens and smoked bacon. Bedrooms are newly prettified in pale, neutral colours, with fresh fabrics and deep mattresses; bathrooms are sleekly up-to-date and toasty warm, with the thickest towels. Walk from the house for miles; the peace and quiet is palpable.

| | |
|---|---|
| Price | £85–£125. |
| Rooms | 2: 1 double, 1 twin/double. |
| Meals | Pub 0.75 miles. |
| Closed | Christmas & occasionally Easter. |
| Directions | From Petworth go east, past Welldiggers pub on right. 0.5 miles, then left. As road ceases to be a green 'tunnel' (before house on left) take right. Beech hedge on right. |

Christopher & Jenny Leaver
Riverhill Lodge,
Fittleworth,
Sussex RH20 1JY

| | |
|---|---|
| Tel | +44 (0)1798 343872 |
| Email | bookings@riverhilllodge.co.uk |
| Web | www.riverhilllodge.co.uk |

Entry 516  Map 4

## Sussex

### Fitzlea Farmhouse

A wooded track leads to the beautiful, mellow, 17th-century farmhouse with tall chimneys and a cluster of overgrown outbuildings. Wood-panelled walls and ancient oak beams, a vast open fireplace, mullioned windows and deep sofas create an atmosphere of relaxed country-house charm. Maggie welcomes you to a delicious breakfast in her Aga-warm farmhouse kitchen; in spring, the scent of bluebells wafts through open doors. A winding staircase leads to comfortable timbered bedrooms which overlook fields, rolling lawns and woodland where you can stroll in peace. Heavenly. *Children by arrangement.*

## Sussex

### Beauchamp Cottage

In the market town of Petworth, a tucked-away and very private retreat for two. The owners, who live nearby, have sensitively restored the little two-storey cottage with its brewery connections. Up the pine stair, under open rafters, is a light and airy sitting room with wooden floors and sofabed; downstairs, carved antique beds and fine linen, a super shower room and sweet garden views. Breakfast waits for you in the little kitchen with microwave and fridge; enjoy it on the patio. Petworth House (paintings, history, summer concerts in the park) is a mere stroll. *Off-street parking. Minimum stay two nights preferred.*

| | | | |
|---|---|---|---|
| Price | £50–£85. Singles by arrangement. | Price | £85–£105. |
| Rooms | 3: 1 family room; 1 double, 1 twin, sharing bath. | Rooms | Cottage: 1 twin/double, sitting room & kitchen area. |
| Meals | Packed lunch available. Pubs/restaurants 2 miles. | Meals | Pub/restaurant 180 yds. |
| Closed | Rarely. | Closed | Christmas. |
| Directions | Directions on booking. | Directions | In Petworth, follow one-way system to end of East St. Straight ahead onto Middle St; at T-junc. with High St, drive opp., through arch. |

|  | Maggie Paterson Fitzlea Farmhouse, Selham, Petworth, Sussex GU28 0PS |  | Dr David Parsons Beauchamp Cottage, c/o Fairfield House, High Street, Petworth, Sussex GU28 0AU |
|---|---|---|---|
| Tel | +44 (0)1798 861429 | Tel | +44 (0)1798 345110 |
|  |  | Fax | +44 (0)1798 345110 |
|  |  | Email | beauchampcottage@btinternet.com |

Entry 517  Map 4

Entry 518  Map 4

## Sussex

### Highbridge Mill

Many humorous touches here – a 'No Diving' mat by the bath, a life-size family of pigs on the back lawn – courtesy of Sue and Joffy, your mildly eccentric, extremely charming hosts. The old part of the house – attractive from the rear – was a flour mill (1810-1930) and there's a rusted wheel to prove it; the interiors are joyfully new. A red-Aga kitchen with wrought-iron chandelier, a bright sitting room with an open fire, bedrooms with quilts and happy colours. Gregarious Sue is a grand cook; walk off a very hearty breakfast in acres of garden, meadow and woodland. Huge fun. *Minimum stay two nights.*

| | |
|---|---|
| Price | £80. Singles £50. |
| Rooms | 2: 1 twin/double; 1 double with separate bath/shower. |
| Meals | Dinner, 3 courses, £40. Pubs within 10-minute drive. |
| Closed | 1 December-1 April. |
| Directions | A23, then A272 for Haywards Heath. Pass Ansty Cross pub, downhill towards Cuckfield Rd. Drive to house on right opposite the r'about sign. |

| | |
|---|---|
| | Sue Clarke |
| | Highbridge Mill, |
| | Cuckfield Road, Ansty, |
| | Haywards Heath, |
| | Sussex RH17 5AE |
| Tel | +44 (0)1444 450881 |
| Web | www.highbridgemill.com |

🗡 🚂 👤 🎣 🐈

Entry 519   Map 4

## Sussex

### Little Lywood

On the ground floor you feel nicely private; the bathroom is a couple of steps from your door. The softly-lit, unfussy room, which overlooks the drive and is well back from the road, has a pine dressing table, rattan chairs, matching curtains and duvet covers, and fresh flowers. You breakfast in the old part of this Elizabethan forester's cottage; a super dining room with small mullioned windows and ancient timbers – Jeannie and Nick will leave you to come and go as you please. Within easy reach of the Ashdown forest and Sussex's great gardens; the one here is lovely, too.

| | |
|---|---|
| Price | £70. Singles £50. |
| Rooms | 1 double with separate bath. |
| Meals | Pubs 2.5 miles. |
| Closed | Rarely. |
| Directions | From Haywards Heath, B2028 to Lindfield. House on left, 1.5 miles after passing church at north end of Lindfield. |

| | |
|---|---|
| | Jeannie & Nick Leadsom |
| | Little Lywood, |
| | Ardingly Road, |
| | Lindfield, |
| | Sussex RH16 2QX |
| Tel | +44 (0)1444 892571 |
| Email | nick@nleadsom.plus.com |

 🗡 🐈

Entry 520   Map 4

## Sussex

### The Grange

There's a time-worn feel to this dreamy home. Books are stuffed into shelves, walls are decorated with years of paintings and wooden African hippos guard the stairs. A mainly Queen Anne rectory in a secluded spot beside the church, the house is beautifully old-fashioned with oak stairs, antique swords, an ancient tapestry and your own comfortable sitting room. The bedroom is light and traditional with lovely views over the paddock; a single room is next door. Bunny will look after you perfectly and there's wonderful walking in Pooh Bear country.

| | |
|---|---|
| Price | From £70. Singles £40. |
| Rooms | 1 double & sitting room. |
| Meals | Pubs 200 yds. |
| Closed | Occasionally. |
| Directions | In centre of Hartfield, take road (Church Street) between The Haywagon & The Anchor pubs. Pass church on left; house beyond church, on left. |

Bunny & James Murray Willis
The Grange,
Hartfield,
Sussex TN7 4AG
Tel +44 (0)1892 770259
Email bunnymw@hotmail.co.uk

Entry 521   Map 5

## Sussex

### Old Whyly

Rich colours, lush fabrics, deep sofas, fine oils — there's an effortless elegance to this manor house, once home to one of King Charles's Cavaliers. Bedrooms are atmospheric, one in French style, and the treats continue outside to a beautiful flower garden annually replenished with 5,000 tulips, a lake and orchard, a stunning swimming pool and new tennis court — fabulous. Dine under the pergola in summer; food is a passion and Sarah's menus are adventurous with a modern slant. Glyndebourne is close so make a party of it and take a divine 'pink' hamper with blankets or a table and chairs included.

| | |
|---|---|
| Price | £90–£140. Singles by arrangement. |
| Rooms | 3: 2 twins/doubles; 1 twin/double with separate bath. |
| Meals | Dinner, 3 courses, £30. Hampers £35. Pub/restaurant 1 mile. |
| Closed | Rarely. |
| Directions | 0.5 miles past Halland on A22, south from Uckfield; 1st left off Shaw r'bout towards E. Hoathly; on for 0.5 miles. Drive on left with postbox; central gravel drive. |

Sarah Burgoyne
Old Whyly,
London Road,
East Hoathly, Sussex BN8 6EL
Tel +44 (0)1825 840216
Email stay@oldwhyly.co.uk
Web www.oldwhyly.co.uk

Entry 522   Map 5

# Sussex

## Hailsham Grange

Come for elegance and ease. Noel welcomes you into his lovely Queen 'Mary Anne' home (1701-1705) – set back from the road in a town where they still hold two cattle markets a week. No standing on ceremony here, despite the décor: classic English touched with chinoiserie in perfect keeping with the house. Busts on pillars, swathes of delicious chintz, books galore and bedrooms a treat: a sunny double and a romantic four-poster. Summery breakfasts are served on the flagged terrace, marmalades and jams on a silver salver. The town garden, with its box parterre and bank of cherry trees, is an equal joy.

 Travel Club offer. See page 414.

| | |
|---|---|
| Price | £95-£120. Singles from £65. |
| Rooms | 4: 1 double, 1 four-poster. Coach house: 2 suites. |
| Meals | Pub/restaurants 300 yds. |
| Closed | Rarely. |
| Directions | From Hailsham High St, left into Vicarage Rd. House 200 yds on left. Park in adjacent coach yard. |

| | |
|---|---|
| | **Mr Noel Thompson** Hailsham Grange, Hailsham, Sussex BN27 1BL |
| Tel | +44 (0)1323 844248 |
| Email | hgrange@4thenet.co.uk |
| Web | www.hailshamgrange.co.uk |

Entry 523   Map 5

# Sussex

## Ocklynge Manor

On top of a peaceful hill, a short stroll from Eastbourne, find tip-top B&B in an 18th-century house with an interesting history – ask Wendy! Now it is her home, and you will be treated to home-baked bread, delicious tea time cakes and scrummy jams – on fine days you can take it outside. Creamy carpeted, bright and sunny bedrooms, all with views over the lovely walled garden, create a mood of relaxed indulgence and are full of thoughtful touches: dressing gowns, DVDs, your own fridge. Breakfasts are superb and there's a chintzy, comfy sitting room just for guests: this is a very spoiling, nurturing place.

| | |
|---|---|
| Price | £80-£90. Singles from £50. |
| Rooms | 3: 1 twin, 1 suite for 3; 1 double with separate shower. |
| Meals | Pub 5-minute walk. |
| Closed | Rarely. |
| Directions | From Eastbourne General Hospital, over r'bout on A2021. 1st right to Kings Avenue; up hill to T-junction. Cream house faces you on right. |

| | |
|---|---|
| | **Wendy Dugdill** Ocklynge Manor, Mill Road, Eastbourne, Sussex BN21 2PG |
| Tel | +44 (0)1323 734121 |
| Email | ocklyngemanor@hotmail.com |
| Web | www.ocklyngemanor.co.uk |

Entry 524   Map 5

# Sussex

## Holy Well Barn

A sanctuary for those who wish to be alone in lush countryside, and who want a big TV too! A smartly converted old store house has a bedroom on the ground floor, all soaring beams and vaulted ceiling, with a coffee cream scheme, faux fur bed throw and a comfy sofa. Through a latched door find a sweet, snug bathroom, with robes and Harding soaps. Up the little stairs to a galleried space (not for giants!) for a hamper of goodies and a fridge. Breakfast is brought to you, the only sound is the little steam railway and birdsong, and you have your own terrace for sunny days. You are on 400 acres of organic farm. Romantic.

# Sussex

## Globe Place

A listed 17th-century house beside the church in a tiny village, ten minutes from Glyndebourne. Alison – a former chef to the Beatles – is a great cook and can provide you with a delicious and generous hamper, and tables and chairs too. Willie is a former rackets champion who gives tennis coaching; there's a court in the large, pretty garden, and a pool. Relax by the inglenook fire in the drawing room after a walk on the Cuckoo Trail or the South Downs, then settle down to a great supper – local fish, maybe, with home-grown vegetables. An easy-going, fun and informal household. *Children over 12 welcome.*

Travel Club offer. See page 414.

| | |
|---|---|
| Price | From £80. Singles from £60. |
| Rooms | 1 double. |
| Meals | Pub/restaurant 1.9 miles. |
| Closed | Rarely. |
| Directions | From Haywards Heath take B2028 to Lindfield. Drive out of Lindfield past church, take 2nd turning on right (Stonecross Lane). Left into Keysford Lane; driveway immediately on right. |

| | |
|---|---|
| Price | £80. Singles £45. |
| Rooms | 6: 2 doubles, 1 twin each with sep. bathroom; 2 singles sharing bathrooms (let to same party ). Cottage: 1 family suite for 3-4 with drawing room. |
| Meals | Dinner £25. BYO. Hamper £35. Pub 10-minute drive. |
| Closed | Christmas. |
| Directions | From Boship r'bout on A22, A267. 1st right to Horsebridge; immed. left to Hellingly. Pass church, left into Mill Lane. Next to church. |

|  | |
|---|---|
| | **Sophie Blaker** |
| | Holy Well Barn, |
| | Keysford Lane, Lindfield, |
| | Haywards Heath, Sussex RH16 2QT |
| Tel | +44 (0)1444 484438 |
| Email | info@holywellbarn.com |
| Web | www.holywellbarn.com |

|  | |
|---|---|
| | **Alison & Willie Boone** |
| | Globe Place, |
| | Hellingly, |
| | Sussex BN27 4EY |
| Tel | +44 (0)1323 844276 |
| Email | aliboone@globeplace.plus.com |

Entry 525   Map 4                    Entry 526   Map 5

# Sussex

## Netherwood Lodge

The whiff of the log fire, the scent of fresh flowers and a smattering of chintz over calm, uncluttered interiors will please you in this single storey coach house: engaging Margaret may give you homemade cake or scones in an elegant sitting room with views over the pretty garden. Cosy bedrooms are beautifully dressed and chic with wool carpets, silk and linen curtains, oak furniture and gloriously comfortable beds. You eat well, much is locally sourced and homemade for flexible breakfasts and delicious suppers. This is a quiet part of East Sussex, ideal for walking, National Trust properties and Glyndebourne.

| | |
|---|---|
| Price | From £90. Singles from £60. |
| Rooms | 2: 1 twin; 1 double with separate bath. |
| Meals | Dinner, 3 courses, £18. Pub/restaurant 1 mile. |
| Closed | Rarely. |
| Directions | A22 towards Eastbourne. Left at Golden Cross between BP garage and antique shop. 0.5 miles, right at T-junction then sharp right into unmade lane. House 2nd on left. |

Margaret Clarke
Netherwood Lodge,
Muddles Green, Chiddingly, Lewes,
Sussex BN8 6HS
Tel +44 (0)1825 872512
Email netherwoodlodge@hotmail.com
Web www.netherwoodlodge.co.uk

Entry 527  Map 5

# Sussex

## Fox Hole Farm

Whitewashed, carpeted and beamed, a wood-burner twinkling in its inglenook, the pretty tile-hung farmhouse is as cosy as can be. Come for stacks of woody character, a rolling hillside real farm setting and lovely hosts whose kindness goes beyond the call of duty. There are woodpeckers in the glorious cottage garden, nightingales in the wood and low-beamed bedrooms with latch cupboards, mellow boards and latticed windows that reveal sheep and hill views. Enjoy a really lovely breakfast (excellent bacon, eggs straight from the hens) after which you can set off for a two-mile woodland walk to Battle.

| | |
|---|---|
| Price | From £62. Singles from £45. |
| Rooms | 3: 2 doubles, 1 triple. |
| Meals | Restaurant 1.5 miles. |
| Closed | 24 December-1 February. |
| Directions | From Battle on A271, 1st right on B2096. After 0.75 miles, right into drive. |

Paul & Pauline Collins
Fox Hole Farm,
Kane Hythe Road,
Battle,
Sussex TN33 9QU
Tel +44 (0)1424 772053
Email foxholefarm@kanehythe.orangehome.co.uk

Entry 528  Map 5

# Sussex

## St Benedict

You can walk to town from here: the house, in a conservation area, has been restored by Stephen using the original 1880 floor plans. Lovers of Victoriana will swoon: find hand-printed wallpapers, gleaming mahogany, Persian rugs, Dutch marquetry furniture, coal fires in winter, decorative objects and artwork galore. Bedrooms are both extremely comfy with brass beds, eiderdowns and squishy pillows; wake to devilled kidneys, kedgeree, smoked haddock, all delivered by the working dumb waiter. Stephen will play the piano should you wish, or you can borrow a book from the lovely library and head for the summer house in the long garden.

Travel Club offer. See page 414.

| | |
|---|---|
| Price | £80. Singles £50. |
| Rooms | 2 doubles with separate bathrooms. |
| Meals | Dinner £25. Packed lunch £10. Pub/restaurant 0.5 miles. |
| Closed | Rarely. |
| Directions | From Hastings, west on A27 Marine Parade until London Rd, St Leonards. Turn right (signed London) away from sea. Pevensey Rd is 5th on left, just before disused church. At top of hill, over junc. beside St John's Church, house 100 yds further on left. |

|  | Stephen Groves |
|---|---|
| | St Benedict, |
| | 81 Pevensey Road, |
| | St Leonards on Sea, |
| | Sussex TN38 0LR |
| Tel | +44 (0)1424 434973 |
| Email | stephen.groves@zen.co.uk |
| Web | www.victorian-bed-and-breakfast.com |

Entry 529   Map 5

# Sussex

## Appletree Cottage

An enviable position facing south for this old hung-tile farmer's cottage, covered in roses, jasmine and wisteria; views are over farmland towards Fairlight Glen. Jane will treat you to tea and cake when you arrive – either before a warming fire in the drawing room, or in the garden in summer. Both bedrooms are sunny, spacious, quiet and traditional, one with gorgeous garden views. Breakfast well on apple juice from their own apples, homemade jams and marmalade, local bacon. Perfect for walkers with a footpath at the front gate, but birdwatchers will be happy too, and you are near the steam railway at Bodium.

Travel Club offer. See page 414.

| | |
|---|---|
| Price | £70. Singles £40. |
| Rooms | 2: 1 twin; 1 double with separate bath. |
| Meals | Pub/restaurant 0.5 miles. |
| Closed | Rarely. |
| Directions | A21 towards Hastings. Left at B2089 towards Rye. 0.25 miles beyond Cripps Corner left at Beacon Lane. Right at farm track at top of hill - house 1st on left (second drive). |

|  | Jane & Hugh Willing |
|---|---|
| | Appletree Cottage, |
| | Beacon Lane, |
| | Staplecross, Robertsbridge, |
| | Sussex TN32 5QP |
| Tel | +44 (0)1580 831724 |
| Email | appletree.cottage@hotmail.co.uk |
| Web | www.appletreecottagestaplex.com |

Entry 530   Map 5

## Sussex

### Wellington House

A stroll away from the gardens of Great Dixter is a warm, comfortable, charming B&B. Behind the Victorian red-brick façade the Brogdens have worked an informal magic, giving guests a cosy sitting room and two big peaceful bedrooms above. These are creamy-walled and carpeted, with comfy mattresses, antique bed linen, pristine shower rooms and good toiletries. Fanny is passionate about food, bakes her own bread, grows her own peaches – a treat; Vivian is a charmer. Visit Bodiam by river boat, comb Camber Sands, explore Rye, revel in Dixter... and return to tea and homemade cakes in the garden.

## Sussex

### Boonshill Farm

A glorious farmhouse down a cinder track with a duck pond, brick and weatherboard outbuildings, flouncing flower beds and charming Lisette, a garden designer from London who has achieved something different. Large bedrooms have original wide wood flooring, old garden gates for headboards, reclaimed windows as beautiful mirrors, comfortable chairs, pale colours and views across green fields. Outside are acres of lawns, a wildflower garden, chickens and handsome Berkshire pigs; breakfast here is special. You're ten minutes from the cobbled streets of Rye with its smart shops, and the walking's great, too.

Travel Club offer. See page 414.

| Price | From £75. Singles from £50. |
|---|---|
| Rooms | 2 doubles. |
| Meals | Supper, 2 courses, from £18; 3 courses, from £22 (min. 4). Pubs within 2 miles. |
| Closed | Christmas & New Year. |
| Directions | Follow brown tourist signs in Northiam village for Great Dixter House & Gardens to Dixter Rd. At main road end, next to opticians. |

| Price | £80–£100. Singles £50–£80. Child £20. |
|---|---|
| Rooms | 2: 1 double, 1 twin. Extra child bed. |
| Meals | Pub 1 mile. |
| Closed | Rarely. |
| Directions | Grove Lane opposite The Bell in Iden. Down lane for 1 mile, then left immediately before oast house, down track. Boonshill is at end of track, on left, white gate. |

|  | Fanny & Vivian Brogden |
|---|---|
|  | Wellington House, |
|  | Dixter Road, |
|  | Northiam, |
|  | Rye, |
|  | Sussex TN31 6LB |
| Tel | +44 (0)1797 253449 |
| Email | fanny@frances14.freeserve.co.uk |

|  | Lisette Pleasance |
|---|---|
|  | Boonshill Farm, |
|  | Grove Lane, |
|  | Iden, Rye, |
|  | Sussex TN31 7QA |
| Tel | +44 (0)1797 280533 |
| Email | boonshillfarm@yahoo.co.uk |
| Web | www.boonshillfarm.co.uk |

Entry 531   Map 5

Entry 532   Map 5

## Sussex

### Willow Tree House

A 500-yard trot from the centre, this is excellent town B&B. Simon and Wendy have overhauled a fine Georgian house and give you smart, spacious bedrooms – here and there an exposed brick wall or a rustic beam – with calm, neutral colours, comfy beds and snazzily tiled shower rooms. The breakfast room is like a small hotel with separate tables smartly dressed; there are homegrown tomatoes in the summer, homemade jams and all else is locally sourced. Free on-site parking, an honesty bar and a quiet garden at the back are welcome extras. *Minimum stay two nights bank holidays & Rye Fawkes Festival.*

## Warwickshire

### Hardingwood House

Close to Birmingham and the NEC and with a theatrical, Tudor feel. Denise, warm and delightful, spoils guests with big bedrooms, dressing rooms, good linen and deep gold-tapped baths. There are books, flowers, antique clocks and plush sofas; tapestry and velvet curtains frame leaded windows; dark timbers and reds and pinks abound. The 1737 barn is immaculate inside and out: the kitchen gives onto a stunning patio, while bedrooms have views to garden or fields. Much rural charm – and there's a self-catering cottage for two if you like your independence. *Advance booking essential.*

🧳 Travel Club offer. See page 414.

| | |
|---|---|
| Price | £80-£120. Singles £70-£85. |
| Rooms | 6: 5 doubles, 1 twin. (Extra child beds available.) |
| Meals | Pubs/restaurants 500 yds. |
| Closed | Rarely. |
| Directions | 500 yds from town centre; 1.5 miles from Rye Harbour. On-site parking. |

| | |
|---|---|
| Price | £80. Singles £55. |
| Rooms | 3: 1 double, 2 twins. |
| Meals | Pub 1 mile. |
| Closed | Rarely. |
| Directions | M6 junc. 4; A446 for Lichfield. Into right lane & 1st exit towards Coleshill. From High St, turn into Maxstoke Lane. After 4 miles, right. 1st drive on left. |

| | |
|---|---|
| | **Simon Crumpler** |
| | Willow Tree House, |
| | 113 Winchelsea Road, |
| | Rye, |
| | Sussex TN31 7EL |
| Tel | +44 (0)1797 227820 |
| Email | info@willow-tree-house.com |
| Web | www.willow-tree-house.com |

| | |
|---|---|
| | **Mrs Denise Owen** |
| | Hardingwood House, |
| | Hardingwood Lane, |
| | Fillongley, |
| | Coventry, |
| | Warwickshire CV7 8EL |
| Tel | +44 (0)1676 542579 |
| Email | denise@hardingwoodhouse.fsnet.co.uk |

Entry 533 Map 5

Entry 534 Map 8

## Warwickshire

### Park Farm House

Fronted by a circular drive, the warm red-brick farmhouse is listed and old – it dates from 1655. Linda is friendly and welcoming, a genuine B&B pro, giving you an immaculate guest sitting room filled with pretty family pieces. The bedrooms sport comfortable mattresses, mahogany or brass beds, blankets on request, bathrobes, flowers, magazines, DVDs. A haven of rest from the motorway (morning hum only) this is in the heart of a working farm yet hugely convenient for Birmingham, Warwick, Stratford, Coventry. You may get their own beef at dinner and the vegetables are home-grown.

| | |
|---|---|
| Price | £79. Singles from £48. |
| Rooms | 3: 2 doubles, 1 twin. |
| Meals | Dinner, 3 courses, from £25. Supper £18. Pub/restaurant 1.5 miles. |
| Closed | Rarely. |
| Directions | M6 & M69 exit 2; B4065 through Ansty to Shilton; left at lights then next left. Over small m'way bridge and right to Barnacle; through village. Left at brick wall signed Spring Road. House at end. |

Linda Grindal
Park Farm House,
Barnacle,
Shilton, Coventry,
Warwickshire CV7 9LG
Tel      +44 (0)2476 612628
Fax     +44 (0)247 6616010
Web    www.parkfarmguesthouse.co.uk

Entry 535   Map 8

## Warwickshire

### Mows Hill Farm

From the flagstoned kitchen, peep through the stable door at the cattle munching in their stalls – perfect for nature lovers! The place has been in the family for generations and the late-Victorian farmhouse has a warm, uplifting feel; Lynda and Edward give you an elegant and comfortable sitting and dining room. You get a proper farmhouse breakfast in the light, warm conservatory – homemade bread and jams, home-reared bacon, just-laid eggs – and field views reach out from every window. Bedrooms have cotton sheets, lots of books and magazines, armchairs for flopping and cosy bathrobes. *Children over ten welcome.*

| | |
|---|---|
| Price | £80-£90. Singles from £55. |
| Rooms | 2: 1 twin/double; 1 double with separate bath. |
| Meals | Pub/restaurant 3 miles. |
| Closed | Rarely. |
| Directions | A3400 Hockley Heath; B4101 (Spring Lane); left into Umberslade Rd. At 2nd triangle, keep right & onto Mows Hill Rd; 0.25 miles on right. |

Mrs Lynda Muntz
Mows Hill Farm,
Mows Hill Road, Kemps Green,
Tanworth in Arden,
Warwickshire B94 5PP
Tel      +44 (0)1564 784312
Email  mowshill@farmline.com
Web    www.b-and-bmowshill.co.uk

Entry 536   Map 8

## Warwickshire

### Salford Farm House

Beautiful within, handsome without. Thanks to subtle colours, oak beams and lovely old pieces, Jane has achieved a seductive combination of comfort and style. A flagstoned hallway and an old rocking horse, ticking clocks, beeswax, fresh flowers: this house is well-loved. Jane was a ballet dancer, Richard has green fingers and runs a fruit farm nearby – you may expect meat and game from the Ragley Estate and delicious fruits in season. Bedrooms have a soft, warm elegance and flat-screen TVs, bathrooms are spotless and welcoming, views are to garden or fields. Wholly delightful.

| Price | £85. Singles £52.50. |
|---|---|
| Rooms | 2 twins/doubles. |
| Meals | Dinner £25. Restaurant 2.5 miles. |
| Closed | Rarely. |
| Directions | A46 from Evesham or Stratford; exit for Salford Priors. On entering village, right opp. church, for Dunnington. House on right, approx. 1 mile on, after 2nd sign on right for Dunnington. |

|  | Jane & Richard Beach |
|---|---|
|  | Salford Farm House, |
|  | Salford Priors, |
|  | Evesham, |
|  | Warwickshire WR11 8XN |
| Tel | +44 (0)1386 870000 |
| Email | salfordfarmhouse@aol.com |
| Web | www.salfordfarmhouse.co.uk |

✗ 🚂 🔊 🦊 🚜 ⚙️

Entry 537   Map 8

## Warwickshire

### Cross o' th' Hill Farm

Stratford in 12 minutes on foot, down a footpath across a field: from the veranda you can see the church where Shakespeare is buried. There's been a farm on this rural spot since before Shakespeare's time but part of the house is Victorian. Built around 1860, it's full of light, with wall-to-ceiling sash windows, glass panelling in the roof, large uncluttered bedrooms and smart, newly decorated bathrooms. The garden, full of trees and birds, dates from the same period – there's even a sunken croquet lawn. Decima grew up here; she and David are gentle hosts, and passionate about art and architecture.

Ethical Collection: Food. See page 412.

| Price | £90–£95. Singles £65–£70. |
|---|---|
| Rooms | 3: 2 doubles; 1 double with separate shower/bathroom. |
| Meals | Pubs/restaurants 20-minute walk. |
| Closed | 20 December–1 March. |
| Directions | From Stratford south on A3400 for 0.5 miles, 2nd right on B4632 for Broadway Rd for 500 yds. 2nd drive on right for farm. |

|  | Decima Noble |
|---|---|
|  | Cross o' th' Hill Farm, |
|  | Broadway Road, |
|  | Stratford-upon-Avon, |
|  | Warwickshire CV37 8HP |
| Tel | +44 (0)1789 204738 |
| Email | decimanoble@hotmail.com |
| Web | www.crossothhillfarm.com |

✗ 🔊 🚜

Entry 538   Map 8

# Warwickshire

## Drybank Farm

Behind the high, red-brick face of the farmhouse lies a cool, spacious hall, where Angela – warm and friendly – welcomes you in. Honey-coloured beams, a big sitting room overlooking the garden with cheerful fabrics and fresh flowers make for a perfectly serene feel, and the countrified bedrooms and bathrooms are reassuringly traditional: the separate bakery is quietly private and you can breakfast here à deux, or join the others in the main house. Shooting, riding and golf can all be arranged – and even RSC seats, tickets permitting. Return to a deep bath, a fluffy dressing gown and a feather duvet.

Travel Club offer. See page 414.

| | |
|---|---|
| Price | From £80. Singles £55. |
| Rooms | 3: 1 double, 1 twin/double, 1 suite. |
| Meals | Supper £18-£30. Packed lunch from £5. Pub 0.5 miles. |
| Closed | Christmas. |
| Directions | A422 from Stratford to Ettington; through village, past Chequers pub on left. Right at x-roads; house on left over brow of hill. |

Angela Winter
Drybank Farm,
Fosseway, Ettington,
Stratford-upon-Avon,
Warwickshire CV37 7PD
Tel   +44 (0)1789 740476
Email   drybank@btinternet.com
Web   www.drybank.co.uk

Entry 539   Map 8

# Warwickshire

## Sequoia House

A cat snoozes by the Aga in this smart Victorian townhouse – an easy stroll from Stratford and a civilised base for exploring Shakespeare country. Step into a pretty tiled hallway and discover high ceilings, deep bays, generous landings, handsome flagstones, a homely sitting room. The easygoing Evanses (Welsh-born) downsized from the hotel they used to run here, and are happy to treat just a few guests: trouser presses and piles of towels mingle with fine old furniture in immaculate rooms. A walkway runs past cricket grounds straight into town. Hotel touches but a warmly personal welcome, and so wonderfully convenient.

Travel Club offer. See page 414.

| | |
|---|---|
| Price | £125. Singles £85. |
| Rooms | 6 doubles. |
| Meals | Pub/restaurant 100 yds. |
| Closed | Christmas & New Year. |
| Directions | From north & M40 (junc. 15) to Stratford. Enter town, follow signs A3400 Shipston. Cross River Bridge, then 2nd exit off traffic island. House 100 yds on left. From south, join A3400 & enter Stratford. House on left 100 yds before traffic island. |

Jean Evans
Sequoia House,
51 Shipston Road,
Stratford-upon-Avon,
Warwickshire CV37 7LN
Tel   +44 (0)1789 268852
Email   reservations@sequoia-house.co.uk
Web   www.sequoia-house.co.uk

Entry 540   Map 8

# Warwickshire

## Blackwell Grange

Come for sheep-dotted views from mullioned windows and profound peace. The mellow stone farmhouse is homely in an old-fashioned way; there are flagstones, beams, floorboards that creak, and a guest sitting room stuffed with books, magazines, old sofas and an open fire. The best bedroom is in the house, cosy with afternoon sun, well-loved furniture and touches of chintz; the annexe room is on the ground floor and suitable for wheelchair users. Breakfast on eggs from the bantams (Lavender Perkin) who strut the summer lawns in the charming garden; take back some home-grown lamb for the freezer.

Travel Club offer. See page 414.

| | |
|---|---|
| Price | From £75. Singles from £45. |
| Rooms | 2 twins/doubles. |
| Meals | Pubs 1-1.5 miles. |
| Closed | Christmas Day & occasionally. |
| Directions | From Stratford, A3400 for Oxford. After 5 miles, right by church in Newbold-on-Stour & follow signs to Blackwell. Fork right on entering Blackwell. Entrance beyond thatched barn. |

|  | Didi Vernon Miller |
|---|---|
| | Blackwell Grange, |
| | Blackwell, Shipston-on-Stour, |
| | Warwickshire CV36 4PF |
| Tel | +44 (0)1608 682357 |
| Fax | +44 (0)1608 682856 |
| Email | didi@blackwellgrange.co.uk |
| Web | www.blackwellgrange.co.uk |

Entry 541   Map 8

# Warwickshire

## The Old Manor House

Jane runs her 16th- and 17th-century house with huge energy and efficiency. The A-shaped double in the main part of the house has ancient beams, oak furniture and a lovely bathroom; a newly decorated twin and a single in the other wing are private and self-contained with a large and elegant drawing and dining room for all visitors to share. Breakfasts are carefully prepared here and the river Stour flows through the beautiful landscaped garden. In warm weather enjoy a drink on the terrace surrounded by old, scented roses; dinner will be excellent and locally sourced. *Children over seven welcome.*

Travel Club offer. See page 414.

| | |
|---|---|
| Price | £85-£90. Singles from £50. |
| Rooms | 3: 1 double with separate bath; 1 twin, 1 single sharing bath (2nd room let to same party only). |
| Meals | Restaurants nearby. |
| Closed | Rarely. |
| Directions | From Stratford, A422 for 4 miles for Banbury. After 4 miles, right at r'bout onto A429 for Halford. There, 1st right. House straight ahead after 150 yds. |

|  | Jane Pusey |
|---|---|
| | The Old Manor House, |
| | Halford, Shipston-on-Stour, |
| | Warwickshire CV36 5BT |
| Tel | +44 (0)1789 740264 |
| Fax | +44 (0)1789 740609 |
| Email | info@oldmanor-halford.fsnet.co.uk |
| Web | www.oldmanor-halford.co.uk |

Entry 542   Map 8

# Warwickshire

## Oxbourne House

Hard to believe the house is new, with its beamed ceilings, fireplaces and antiques. Bedrooms are fresh, crisp, cosy and cared for, the family room with an 'in the attic' feel; lighting is soft, beds excellent, bath and shower rooms attractive and warm, and views far-reaching. In the garden are tennis, sculpture and Graeme's rambler-bedecked pergola. Wake to birdsong and fresh eggs from their own hens; on peaceful summer nights, watch the dipping sun. Posy and Graeme are hugely likeable and welcoming and the village pub is just down the road. A most comforting place to stay. *Dogs by arrangement.*

Ethical Collection: Community; Food. See page 412.

Travel Club offer. See page 414.

| Price | £65-£85. Singles from £45. |
|---|---|
| Rooms | 3: 1 double, 1 family room; 1 twin/double with separate bath. |
| Meals | Dinner from £20. Pub 2-minute walk. |
| Closed | Rarely. |
| Directions | A422 from Stratford for Banbury. After 8 miles, right to Oxhill. Last house on right on Whatcote Road. |

Graeme & Posy McDonald
Oxbourne House,
Oxhill,
Warwick,
Warwickshire CV35 0RA
Tel +44 (0)1295 688202
Email graememcdonald@msn.com
Web www.oxbournehouse.com

Entry 543   Map 8

# Warwickshire

## Shrewley Pools Farm

A charming, eccentric home and fabulous for families, with space to play and animals to see: sheep, bantams and pigs. A fragrant, romantic garden, too, and a fascinating house (1640), all low ceilings, aged floors and steep stairs. Timbered passages lead to large, pretty, sunny bedrooms (all with electric blankets) with leaded windows and polished wooden floors and a family room with everything needed for a baby. In a farmhouse dining room Cathy serves sausages, bacon, and eggs from the farm, can do gluten-free breakfasts and is happy with teas for children. Buy a day ticket and fish in the lake.

Travel Club offer. See page 414.

| Price | From £55. Singles from £40. |
|---|---|
| Rooms | 2: 1 family room (& cot), 1 twin. |
| Meals | Packed lunch £4. Child's high tea £4. Pub/restaurant 1.5 miles. |
| Closed | Christmas. |
| Directions | From M40 junc. 15, A46 for Coventry. Left onto A4177. 4.5 miles to Five Ways r'bout. 1st left, on for 0.75 miles; signed, opp. Farm Gate Poultry: track on left. |

Cathy Dodd
Shrewley Pools Farm,
Five Ways Road,
Haseley, Warwick,
Warwickshire CV35 7HB
Tel +44 (0)1926 484315
Email cathydodd@hotmail.co.uk
Web www.shrewleypoolsfarm.co.uk

Entry 544   Map 8

## Warwickshire

### Woolscott House

Scrunch across gravel to the tall, prosperous, well-kept Georgian house – a showcase for Juliet, interior designer. Warm and enthusiastic, she looks after dogs, guests, garden with equal talent. Bedrooms up steep stairs are not huge but madly comfortable, all rich textiles and subtle colours, family pieces and interesting pictures. Bed linen is divine, views are rural (the odd sheep), one bath is befriended by Venetian glass fish, another is reached down a flight of well-clad stairs. There are bags of sofas, books, magazines, a chatty parrot. In summer, dip in the pool or wave a tennis racquet. You'll love it.

| | |
|---|---|
| Price | From £80. Singles £60. |
| Rooms | 2: 1 double, 1 twin each with separate bath. |
| Meals | Pub/restaurant 0.5 miles. |
| Closed | Christmas. |
| Directions | A426 Rugby-Dunchurch; A45 towards Daventry. After 1 mile, right to Grandborough. 1.25 miles, then round sharp right-hand bend; house 3rd on left. |

Juliet Eckersley
Woolscott House,
Woolscott,
Rugby,
Warwickshire CV23 8DB
Tel +44 (0)1788 522154
Email julieteckersley@yahoo.co.uk

Entry 545  Map 8

## Warwickshire

### Marston House

A generous feel pervades this lovely family home; Kim's big friendly kitchen is the hub of the house. She and John are easy-going and kind and there's no standing on ceremony. Feel welcomed with tea on arrival, delicious homemade breakfasts, oodles of interesting facts about what to do in the area. The house is big and sunny; old rugs cover parquet floors, soft sofas tumble with cushions and sash windows look onto the smart garden packed with interesting plants and birds. Bedrooms are roomy, traditional and supremely comfortable. A special place with a big heart and great walks straight from the house.

Ethical Collection: Community; Food. See page 412.

 Travel Club offer. See page 414.

| | |
|---|---|
| Price | £85-£100. Singles from £60. |
| Rooms | 2: 1 twin/double with separate bath; 1 twin/double with separate shower. |
| Meals | Kitchen supper, 3 courses, £29.50. Dinner, in dining room, £35 (min. 4). Pub 5-minute walk. |
| Closed | Rarely. |
| Directions | M40 exit 11. From Banbury, A361 north for 7 miles; at Byfield village sign, left into Twistle Lane; on to Priors Marston; 5th house on left with cattle grid, after S-bend (3 miles from A361). |

Kim & John Mahon
Marston House,
Byfield Road, Priors Marston,
Southam, Warwickshire CV47 7RP
Tel +44 (0)1327 260297
Email kim@mahonand.co.uk
Web www.ivabestbandb.co.uk

Entry 546  Map 8

# Wiltshire

## Sarum College

This is very much a working, educational institution – not a luxurious B&B – but the setting in The Close is stunning: there are several museums with art and architecture from medieval to Georgian, you can listen to the choir sing at Evensong, stroll around the cloisters, or wander to good theatre and restaurants. Bedrooms are plain and comfortable, bathrooms functional and neat as a pin, there's a sitting room (no frills, but a magnificent view of the Cathedral) with TV if you want it, and a chapel you are welcome to attend. Food is hearty: they run courses here so at times it may be busy.

Travel Club offer. See page 414.

| | |
|---|---|
| Price | £105. Singles £80. |
| Rooms | 7: 3 doubles, 4 twins. |
| Meals | Lunch £10. Packed lunch £5. Dinner £10. (Rates for groups negotiable.) Pub/restaurant 100 yds. |
| Closed | Christmas. |
| Directions | A 10-minute walk from train & bus stations. From either New Street or Crane Street, enter the Close at the High Street gate and turn left. |

Linda Cooper
Sarum College,
19 The Close,
Salisbury, Wiltshire SP1 2EE
Tel +44 (0)1722 424800
Email hospitality@sarum.ac.uk
Web www.sarum.ac.uk

Entry 547   Map 3

---

# Wiltshire

## 85 Exeter Street

You are so central here that you can wander into town on foot (having parked by the house or walked from the station). Susan's Georgian house, facing the cathedral close, is on a main road but the bedrooms sit very quietly at the back and the upstairs drawing room has a lovely view of the spire. Enjoy a good breakfast of fresh fruit, local bacon and sausages, and homebaked bread downstairs at one big table. Bedrooms are simple and traditional: William Morris curtains, a five-foot bed and a shower cabinet in one, a single bed with a spare roll-out bed in the other. Good, solid city B&B. *French & German spoken.*

Travel Club offer. See page 414.

| | |
|---|---|
| Price | From £75. Singles from £60. |
| Rooms | 2: 1 double; 1 twin with separate bath/shower. |
| Meals | Pubs & restaurants nearby. |
| Closed | Rarely. |
| Directions | Ring road round Salisbury to south of city; past r'bout to Southampton; at next r'bout (Exeter St r'bout), 3rd exit on to Exeter St (signed Old George Mall). No 85 near city centre. Park opp. house; ask for permit on arrival. |

Susan Orr-Ewing
85 Exeter Street,
Salisbury,
Wiltshire SP1 2SE
Tel +44 (0)1722 417944
Email info@85exeterstreet.co.uk
Web www.85exeterstreet.co.uk

Entry 548   Map 3

## Wiltshire

### Little Langford Farmhouse

A rare treat to have your milk fresh from the cow – the Helyers have pedigree cattle. The bedrooms of this rather grand Victorian-gothic farmhouse are large and pretty with period furniture and crisp linen; there are impressive countryside views, a baby grand and a billiard room. Everything is elegant and polished yet cosy, and terrace doors are thrown open for delicious al fresco breakfasts in summer. The farm, part of which is an SSSI, is treasured for its glorious walks, wild flowers and butterflies, and the Helyers are immensely welcoming. *Minimum stay two nights at weekends. Children by arrangement.*

## Wiltshire

### The Mill House

In a tranquil village next to the river is a house surrounded by water meadows and wilderness garden. Roses ramble, marsh orchids bloom and butterflies shimmer. This 12-acre labour of love is the creation of ever-charming Diana and her son Michael. Their home, the time-worn 18th-century miller's house, is packed with country clutter – porcelain, foxes' brushes, ancestral photographs above the fire – while bedrooms are quaint and flowery, with firm comfy beds; organic breakfasts are served at small tables. Diana has lived here for many many years, and has been doing B&B for 27 of them! *Children over eight welcome.*

| | |
|---|---|
| Price | £75–£80. Singles £58–£70. |
| Rooms | 3: 1 double, 1 twin/double; 1 twin with separate shower. |
| Meals | Pub/restaurant 1.75 miles. |
| Closed | December & January. |
| Directions | Exit A303 at A36 junc; follow signs for Salisbury. 2 miles; right for The Langfords. In Steeple Langford, right for Hanging Langford. At T-junc. opp. village hall, left for Little Langford. House 0.75 miles on left. |

| | |
|---|---|
| Price | From £90. Singles from £60. |
| Rooms | 5: 3 doubles, 1 family room; 1 twin with separate bath. |
| Meals | Pub 5-minute walk. |
| Closed | Never. |
| Directions | From A303 take B3083 at Winterbourne Stoke to Berwick St James. Through village, past Boot Inn & church. Left into yard just before the sharp left bend. From A36 (B3083), house 1st on right. |

|  | |
|---|---|
| | **Patricia Helyer** |
| | Little Langford Farmhouse, |
| | Little Langford, |
| | Salisbury, Wiltshire SP3 4NP |
| Tel | +44 (0)1722 790205 |
| Fax | +44 (0)1722 790086 |
| Email | bandb@littlelangford.co.uk |
| Web | www.littlelangford.co.uk |

|  | |
|---|---|
| | **Diana Gifford Mead & Michael Mertens** |
| | The Mill House, |
| | Berwick St James, |
| | Salisbury, Wiltshire SP3 4TS |
| Tel | +44 (0)1722 790331 |
| Fax | +44 (0)1722 790753 |
| Web | www.millhouse.org.uk |

Entry 549   Map 3

Entry 550   Map 3

# Wiltshire

## The Duck Yard

Independence with your own terrace, your own entrance and your own sitting room. Peaceful too, at the end of the lane, with a colourful cottage garden, a summerhouse and roaming hens and ducks. Harriet makes wedding cakes, looks after guests and cheerfully rustles up fine meals at short notice; breakfasts promise delicious homemade bread. Your carpeted bedroom and aquamarine bathroom are tucked under the eaves; below is a sitting room cosy with wood-burner, books and old squashy sofas, leading to a terrace. Good for walkers – maps are supplied and you may even borrow a dog.

 Travel Club offer. See page 414.

| Price | £70. Singles £50. |
|---|---|
| Rooms | 1 twin/double & sitting room. |
| Meals | Dinner, 3 courses, £25. Packed lunch £7. Pub 2 miles. |
| Closed | Christmas & New Year. |
| Directions | A303 to Wylye, then for Dinton. After 4 miles left at x-roads, for Wilton & Salisbury. On for 1 mile, down hill, round sharp right bend, signed Sandhills Rd. 1st low red brick building on left. Park in space on left. |

Harriet & Peter Combes
The Duck Yard,
Sandhills Road,
Dinton,
Salisbury, Wiltshire SP3 5ER
Tel +44 (0)1722 716495
Fax +44 (0)1722 716163
Email harriet.combes@googlemail.com

Entry 551  Map 3

# Wiltshire

## Dowtys

A stunning setting and a recently converted farmhouse up a long drive, with fabulous views over the Nadder valley. Peaceful bedrooms are generously sized, very private – one ground-floor bedroom has its own garden room – and have rafters and beams, antiques, smart bathrooms, excellent beds. The guest sitting room has a contemporary feel with frameless windows, wood-burner, sliding oak patio windows and underfloor heating. Relax on the terrace, sit beneath the espaliered limes in the immaculate garden, dip into the National Trust woods. Footpaths start from the gate and the wildlife is abundant.

| Price | £68-£75. Singles from £48. |
|---|---|
| Rooms | 3: 1 double; 1 double, 1 twin both with separate bath/shower. |
| Meals | Packed lunch on request. Pub 0.25 miles. |
| Closed | Christmas & New Year. |
| Directions | B3089 approaching Dinton from east (Barford St Martin). Take 1st right after village sign & 30mph, signed Wylye. 100 yds; 1st right up Dowtys Lane to house. |

Mrs Di Verdon-Smith
Dowtys,
Dowtys Lane,
Dinton,
Salisbury, Wiltshire SP3 5ES
Tel +44 (0)1722 716886
Email dowtys.bb@gmail.com
Web www.dowtysbedandbreakfast.co.uk

Entry 552  Map 3

## Wiltshire

### Old Stoke

As pretty as thatched cottages come. This lovely old farmhouse is edged by an AONB filled with birdsong and wildlife, yet you are close to Salisbury. Guests have a book-filled sitting room with Dorset cream walls and pretty chairs and sofas to collapse onto: upstairs are fresh bedrooms with bright fabrics on headboards and window cushions, feathery beds and sparkling bathrooms. Tracie is charming and cooks well; good wholesome food using eggs from her own hens, vegetables from the garden and delicious flapjacks or cake for tea. Stroll down the fecund garden to a meadow and the river. *Children over eight welcome.*

## Wiltshire

### Oaklands

A comfortable townhouse, a south-facing garden, two dear dogs and a lovely old Silver Cross pram sitting under the stairs. It was the first house in Warminster to have a bathroom; the bathrooms have multiplied since and the interiors have had a delightful makeover – easy to see why this spacious 1880s house has been in the family forever. Andrew and Carolyn, relaxed and charming, serve delicious breakfasts in the beautiful new conservatory at the drawing room end. Bedrooms, desirable and welcoming, overlook churchyard and trees; fresh fabrics, soft colours, cosy bathroom, family antiques. And restaurants are a stroll.

Travel Club offer. See page 414.

| | |
|---|---|
| Price | £65–£70. Singles £45. |
| Rooms | 2: 1 twin/double; 1 double with separate bath. |
| Meals | Dinner £17.50–£22.50. Packed lunch £6. Pub 1 mile. |
| Closed | December-February. |
| Directions | SW from Salisbury on A354; right at Coombe Bissett dir. Bishopstone. 2nd left after White Hart, signed Stoke Farthing. In hamlet, sharp bend to right, 2nd house on left. Parking to left of house. |

| | |
|---|---|
| Price | £65–£85. Singles from £55. |
| Rooms | 2: 1 double, 1 twin/double (rooms can interconnect). |
| Meals | Occasional dinner (min. 4). Pub/restaurant 0.5 miles. |
| Closed | Christmas & rarely. |
| Directions | From Warminster centre direction Salisbury. On right, opp. end of St John's churchyard. |

| | |
|---|---|
| | Tracie Pickford |
| | Old Stoke, |
| | Stoke Farthing, Broadchalke, |
| | Salisbury, Wiltshire SP5 5ED |
| Tel | +44 (0)1722 780513 |
| Email | traciepickford@hotmail.co.uk |
| Web | www.oldstoke.co.uk |

| | |
|---|---|
| | Carolyn & Andrew Lewis |
| | Oaklands, |
| | 88 Boreham Road, |
| | Warminster, |
| | Wiltshire BA12 9JW |
| Tel | +44 (0)1985 215532 |
| Email | apl1944@yahoo.co.uk |

Entry 553   Map 3

Entry 554   Map 3

# Wiltshire

## The Old School House

Charmingly cluttered, sparklingly clean, this 1860 village house is filled with light, beautiful objects and lovely pieces of furniture. Find a comfy chair in the snug with its loaded book shelves on art, gardening and travel – Darea's passions. Your chintzy bedrooms (the double is larger) have wooden arched beams, excellent mattresses and a newly decorated bathroom with oatmeal tiles. Breakfast is in the smart kitchen with its humming black Aga: good sausages and bacon, local eggs. A little south-facing courtyard has colourful pots and a bench for idle gazing; Stonehenge, Longleat and Stourhead beckon.

| Price | £70–£80. Singles £40–£50. |
|---|---|
| Rooms | 2: 1 double, 1 twin sharing bath (let to same party only). |
| Meals | Pub 0.5 miles. |
| Closed | Rarely. |
| Directions | From London exit 303 at first Wylye turn off signed A36 Warminster, Salisbury. Take right fork, right at T-junction, then immediate left into Wylye village. Past pub, church and shop and house is immediately after. |

Mrs Darea Browne
The Old School House,
Wylye,
Warminster,
Wiltshire BA12 0QR
Tel +44 (0)1985 248228
Email dareabrowne@aol.com

Entry 555   Map 3

# Wiltshire

## The Manor

The house is as lovely inside as out and Isabel is a delight. She loves cooking, once ran a chalet in the Swiss Alps and is quite happy to chat by the Aga as she rustles up a delicious breakfast. She has also decorated her home in some style: beautiful bedrooms are papered in pale pink and blue, mattresses are of the highest quality. This is a treat of a 17th-century brick-and-flint manor in a beguiling spot by the river Avon, its walled garden and immaculate lawns fronted by the river. Breakfast is eaten at a polished oak table, glazed doors are thrown open in summer. There's good walking and loads of wildlife.

| Price | £90. Singles from £50. |
|---|---|
| Rooms | 2 twins/doubles. |
| Meals | Pub/restaurant 2-minute walk. |
| Closed | Rarely. |
| Directions | From Upavon towards Andover on A342. Manor 3rd house on right & last before bridge. |

Isabel Green
The Manor,
Upavon, Pewsey,
Wiltshire SN9 6EB
Tel +44 (0)1980 635115
Email themanorupavon@hotmail.co.uk
Web www.themanorupavon.co.uk

Entry 556   Map 3

## Wiltshire

### Puckshipton House

An intriguing name, Puckshipton: it means Goblin's Barn. The house is deep in the lush countryside of the Vale of Pewsey, reached by a long tree-lined drive. You stay in the Georgian end, with a private entrance that leads to a Regency-blue hall. Rooms are stylish and uncluttered, an attractive mix of old and new with good beds, crisp linen and bathrooms that are cossetting, one with a roll top bath. The dining and sitting rooms have wood-burners both. James, a forester, and Juliette have young children, a walled garden and a thatched hen house from which to fetch your breakfast egg.

| Price | £80. Singles £50. |
|---|---|
| Rooms | 2: 1 four-poster; 1 twin/double with separate bath/shower. |
| Meals | Pubs & restaurant 5-minute drive. |
| Closed | Christmas. |
| Directions | Devizes A342 towards Rushall; left to Chirton, right to Marden & through village. On for 0.25 miles; right into private drive. |

|  | Juliette & James Noble |
|---|---|
|  | Puckshipton House, |
|  | Beechingstoke, |
|  | Pewsey, Wiltshire SN9 6HG |
| Tel | +44 (0)1672 851336 |
| Email | noble.jj@gmail.com |
| Web | www.puckshipton.co.uk |

Entry 557   Map 3

## Wiltshire

### Upper Westcourt

Long views down Pewsey Vale, a stroll to the pub, bedrooms looking onto a beautiful garden. This is a relaxed, light-filled house surrounded by farmland that stretches away to Somerset, between Pewsey Downs and Martinsell Hill. Inside are rich curtains, polished old furniture, photographs and paintings; bedrooms and bathrooms are sunny with florals, pictures and books; drawing room sofas demand to be sunk into before a winter log fire; breakfasts may include fresh fruits and tomatoes from the garden. Come for traditional good taste and charming, welcoming, well-organised hosts.

 Travel Club offer. See page 414.

| Price | £75-£85. Singles £45-£55. |
|---|---|
| Rooms | 3: 1 twin/double; 1 twin, 1 single sharing separate bath (single let to same party). |
| Meals | Pubs within walking distance. |
| Closed | Christmas & Easter. |
| Directions | A346 or A338 to Burbage. In High St, turn west to Westcourt, over bypass and at sharp left hand bend, turn right (signed 'No Through Road'). 250 yds on left. |

|  | Peter & Carolyn Hill |
|---|---|
|  | Upper Westcourt, |
|  | Burbage, Marlborough, |
|  | Wiltshire SN8 3BW |
| Tel | +44 (0)1672 810307 |
| Email | prhill@onetel.com |
| Web | www.upperwestcourt.co.uk |

Entry 558   Map 3

# Wiltshire

## Westcourt Farm

Rozzie and Jonny left London to restore a medieval, Grade II* cruck truss hall house (beautifully) amid wildflower meadows, hedgerows, ponds, geese and hens. Delightful people, they love to cook and can spoil you rotten. Rooms are freshly decorated, crisp yet traditional, the country furniture is charming and the architecture fascinating. Bedrooms have comfortable beds and fine linen, bathrooms are spot-on, there's a lovely light drawing room and a barn for meetings and parties. Encircled by footpaths and fields, Westcourt is the oldest house in a perfect village, two minutes from a rather good pub.

| | |
|---|---|
| Price | £80. Singles £40. |
| Rooms | 2: 1 twin with separate bath; 1 double with separate shower. |
| Meals | Pub/restaurant in village. |
| Closed | Christmas & New Year. |
| Directions | A338 Hungerford-Salisbury; after 4 miles signed Shalbourne; through village & fork left at pub; 150 yds, 2nd drive on right. |

**Jonny & Rozzie Buxton**
Westcourt Farm,
Shalbourne,
Marlborough, Wiltshire SN8 3QE
Tel +44 (0)1672 871399
Email info@westcourtfarm.com
Web www.westcourtfarm.com

Entry 559  Map 3

# Wiltshire

## Fisherman's House

Watch ducks shoot the rapids of the Kennet River as it swooshes past the lawns of this exquisitely decorated home. It looks every inch a doll's house, but Jeremy and Heather add a deft human touch. The elegance of excellent breakfasts taken in the conservatory is balanced by the comforting hubbub emanating from the family kitchen. There's a guests' sitting room with an open fire and, upstairs, ornately and generously decorated bedrooms. Time slips by effortlessly here, many people come to visit the crop and stone circles and Marlborough is a hop away.

| | |
|---|---|
| Price | £80. Singles £50. |
| Rooms | 3: 1 double; 1 twin, 1 single sharing bath. |
| Meals | Lunch/packed lunch from £5. Pub 500 yds. |
| Closed | Christmas. |
| Directions | From Hungerford, A4 for Marlborough. After 7 miles, right for Stitchcombe, down hill (bear left at barn) & left at T-junc. On entering village, house 2nd on left. |

**Jeremy & Heather Coulter**
Fisherman's House,
Mildenhall, Marlborough,
Wiltshire SN8 2LZ
Tel +44 (0)1672 515390
Email heathercoulter610@btinternet.com
Web www.fishermanshouse.co.uk

Entry 560  Map 3

# Wiltshire

## Blue Barn

Jackie's gorgeous home is along a byway and surrounded by a lovely garden and paddocks with sweeping views. Through an avenue of trees you glimpse the stunning timber-framed green oak farmhouse. You have independence in your own annexe with a light and airy L-shaped sitting room, tartan sofa, lots of pictures, comfy chairs and a French daybed for an extra guest. Jackie brings your locally sourced breakfast here and you eat round a farmhouse table. The twin bedroom is fresh and pretty with rose-covered chintz headboards; the shower room spotless. You are right on the Ridgeway for fabulous walking.

| Price | £70. Singles £35–£45. |
| --- | --- |
| Rooms | 1 twin & sitting room. Extra beds available. |
| Meals | Pub 1 mile. |
| Closed | Never. |
| Directions | A346 Marlborough-Swindon. Turn for Ogbourne St George. Right after Crown Inn, continue to 'No Through' sign. At Ridgeway, left, then continue until Blue Barn. M4 motorway 5 miles. |

|  | Jacqueline Palmer |
| --- | --- |
|  | Blue Barn, |
|  | Ogbourne St George, |
|  | Marlborough, Wiltshire SN8 2NT |
| Tel | +44 (0)1672 841082 |
| Email | jax@capalmer.co.uk |
| Web | www.blue-barn.co.uk |

Entry 561   Map 3

# Wiltshire

## The Limes

Through the electric gates, past the gravelled car park and the pretty, box-edged front garden and you arrive at the middle part of a 1620 house divided into three. The beams, stone mullions and leaded windows are charming, and softly spoken Ellodie is an exceptional hostess. Light bedrooms have pretty curtains and fresh flowers, tiled bathrooms have good soaps and thick towels, logs glow in the grate, and breakfasts promise delicious Wiltshire bacon, prunes soaked in orange juice and organic bread. You are on the busy main road leading out of Melksham – catch the bus to Bath from right outside the door.

Travel Club offer. See page 414.

| Price | £75–£85. Singles £45–£50. |
| --- | --- |
| Rooms | 3: 2 twins/doubles, 1 single. |
| Meals | Dinner £20–£25. BYO. Packed lunch £6. Pub 1.5 miles. |
| Closed | Rarely. |
| Directions | Leave Melksham on A365 to Bath. After Victoria Motors, sharp right at school sign, brown gates will open slowly. Park on right, follow path to house. |

|  | Ellodie van der Wulp |
| --- | --- |
|  | The Limes, |
|  | Shurnhold House, |
|  | Shurnhold, |
|  | Melksham, |
|  | Wiltshire SN12 8DG |
| Tel | +44 (0)1225 790627 |

Entry 562   Map 3

# Wiltshire

## Lacock Pottery

In the heart of a National Trust village find this solid 1830s stone house – once a workhouse. Opposite the church, next to your hosts' working pottery, the front door opens to a sitting room with lots of oak, a log fire, pottery pieces, a simple, uncluttered feel. Ask for the Governor's House where the workhouse owners used to live, pretty with a brass bed, floral fabrics, marble-topped wash stand. It's set apart across a shrubby gravel garden scented by a climbing rose. There are cosy inns amid the village's half-timbered cottages and 13th-century abbey: art, architecture and history abound.

| Price | £76-£96. Singles £49-£59. |
|---|---|
| Rooms | 3: 2 doubles; |
| | 1 twin with separate shower. |
| Meals | Pub/restaurant 100 yds. |
| Closed | Christmas Day. |
| Directions | From Chippenham, A350 towards Melksham. Take signed left turning for Lacock. Once in village turn into Church Street. House opposite church, along the gravel drive. |

Simone & David McDowell
Lacock Pottery,
1 The Tanyard,
Church Street, Lacock,
Chippenham, Wiltshire SN15 2LB

| Tel | +44 (0)1249 730266 |
| Email | simone@lacockbedandbreakfast.com |
| Web | www.lacockbedandbreakfast.com |

Entry 563   Map 3

---

# Wiltshire

## Glebe House

The rogues' gallery of photographs up the stairs says it all: Glebe House is quirky and fun. Friendly Ginny spoils guests rotten with pressed linen and sociable dinners served on Wedgewood china. Charming, cosy and comfortable are the bedrooms, one with an Indian theme; delightful is the drawing room with its landscape oils, Bechstein piano and rugs from all over Asia; settle into a coral sofa and roast away by the fire. Breads, marmalades and jams are homemade, beautiful views shoot off down the valley, the garden trills with hundreds of birds and Mr Biggles (the grey parrot) chats by the Aga.

Travel Club offer. See page 414.

| Price | £70. Singles £40. |
|---|---|
| Rooms | 2: 1 double, 1 twin. |
| Meals | Dinner, 3 courses, from £23. |
| | Pub 4 miles. |
| Closed | Christmas. |
| Directions | From Devizes-Chippenham A342. Follow Chittoe & Spye Park. On over crossroads onto narrow lane. House 2nd on left. |

Bill & Ginny Scrope
Glebe House,
Chittoe, Chippenham, Wiltshire
SN15 2EL

| Tel | +44 (0)1380 850864 |
| Email | gscrope@aol.com |
| Web | www.glebehouse-chittoe.co.uk |

Entry 564   Map 3

# Wiltshire

## The Coach House

In an ancient hamlet a few miles north of Bath, an impeccable conversion of an early 19th-century barn. Bedrooms are fresh and cosy with sloping ceilings; the drawing room is elegant with porcelain and chintz, its pale walls the ideal background for striking displays of fresh flowers. Sliding glass doors lead to a south-facing patio... then to a well-groomed croquet lawn bordered by flowers, with vegetable garden, tennis court, woodland and paddock beyond. Helga and David are delightful and there's lots to do from here; the splendours of Bath, Castle Combe and plenty of good golf courses are all near.

# Wiltshire

## Manor Farm

Farmyard heaven in the Cotswolds. A 17th-century manor farmhouse in 550 arable acres; horses in the paddock, dozing dogs in the yard, tumbling blooms outside the door and a perfectly tended village, with duck pond, a short walk. Beautiful bedrooms are softly lit, with muted colours, plump goose down pillows and the crispest linen. Breakfast in front of the fire is a banquet of delights, tea among the roses is a treat, thanks to charming, welcoming Victoria. This is the postcard England of dreams, with Castle Combe, Lacock, grand walking and gardens to visit. *Children over 12 welcome.*

 Travel Club offer. See page 414.

| | |
|---|---|
| Price | £65–£80. Singles from £35. |
| Rooms | 2: 1 double with separate bath/shower; 1 twin/double let to same party only. |
| Meals | Dinner, 3 courses, from £20. Pubs/restaurants 1 mile. |
| Closed | Rarely. |
| Directions | From M4 junc. 17, A350 for Chippenham. A420 to Bristol (east) & Castle Combe. After 6.3 miles, right into Upper Wraxall. Sharp left opp. village green; at end of drive. |

**Helga & David Venables**
The Coach House,
Upper North Wraxall,
Chippenham, Wiltshire SN14 7AG
Tel     +44 (0)1225 891026
Email   david@dvenables.co.uk
Web     www.upperwraxallcoachhouse.co.uk

Entry 565   Map 3

| | |
|---|---|
| Price | From £80. Singles from £43. |
| Rooms | 3: 2 doubles; 1 twin with separate bath. |
| Meals | Pub 1 mile. Wild venison suppers by special arrangement. |
| Closed | Rarely. |
| Directions | From M4 A429 to Cirencester (junc. 17). After 200 yds, 1st left for Grittleton; there, follow signs to Alderton. Farmhouse near church. |

**Victoria Lippiatt-Onslow**
Manor Farm,
Alderton, Chippenham,
Wiltshire SN14 6NL
Tel     +44 (0)1666 840271
Email   victoria.lippiatt@btinternet.com
Web     www.themanorfarm.co.uk

Entry 566   Map 3

## Wiltshire

### Smokey Cottage

Super Susie looks after you with delightful ease in her 50s brick and flint house on a quiet country road. Flop in a lovely L-shaped sitting room with lots of pictures of dogs and horses and big windows overlooking the large garden; breakfast here on jolly days. Your bedroom is light, sunny and cosy with birds of paradise swooping over curtains and headboard; books, squishy cushions, bamboo tables and Chinese style lamps give character and your bathroom is functional but spotless. Eat in or walk to the pub; Susie, Dynamite the labrador and Bossy the Jack Russell will welcome you home afterwards.

| | |
|---|---|
| Price | £70. Singles £50. |
| Rooms | 1 twin/double with separate bath. |
| Meals | Dinner £25, and contribution for wine. Pub 0.25 miles. |
| Closed | Christmas & New Year. |
| Directions | M4 junction 16, then B4042. Through Brinkworth, then left to Somerfords, Clay Street. Left then immediate right, The Street. House 800 yds on right. |

Susie Brassey
Smokey Cottage,
Little Somerford,
Chippenham,
Wiltshire SN15 5JW
Tel +44 (0)1666 822255
Email susiebrassey@dsl.pipex.com

Entry 567   Map 3

## Wiltshire

### Manor Farm

The road through the sleepy Wiltshire village brings you to a Queen Anne house with a *petit château* feel, enfolded by a tranquil garden with tulip meadow, groomed lawns and... hens! Inside is as lovely; watercolourist Clare is a perfectionist behind the scenes and is charming. The bedroom is elegant and cosy, its soft-painted panelled walls hung with good pictures, its sash windows beautifully dressed. Scrumptious, all-organic breakfasts are served in a butter-yellow kitchen; the eclectically furnished drawing room, shared among guests, has a real fire and a delightful lived-in, family feel.

 Travel Club offer. See page 414.

| | |
|---|---|
| Price | £90. Singles by arrangement. |
| Rooms | 1 double. |
| Meals | Pub 200 yds. |
| Closed | Christmas & New Year. |
| Directions | M4 exit 17. North on A429 for Malmesbury, right on B4042. Right after 3 miles to Little Somerford. Past pub, right at crossroads, 50 yds on, house behind tall wall. |

Clare Inskip
Manor Farm,
Little Somerford,
Malmesbury,
Wiltshire SN15 5JW
Tel +44 (0)1666 822140
Email clareinskip@hotmail.com

Entry 568   Map 3

# Wiltshire

## Bullocks Horn Cottage

Up a country lane to this hidden-away house which the Legges have turned into a haven of peace and seclusion. Liz loves fabrics and mixes them with flair, Colin has painted a colourful mural – complete with macaws – in the conservatory. Bedrooms are quiet with lovely views, the sitting room with log fire has large comfy sofas, and the garden, which has been featured in various magazines, is exceptional. Home veg and herbs and local seasonal food are used at dinner which, in summer, you can eat in the cool shade of the arbour, covered in climbing roses and jasmine. *Children over 12 welcome.*

Ethical Collection: Food. See page 412.

| | |
|---|---|
| Price | From £75. Singles from £40. |
| Rooms | 2: 1 twin; 1 twin with separate bath. |
| Meals | Dinner £20–£25. BYO. Pub 1.5 miles. |
| Closed | Christmas. |
| Directions | From A429, B4040 through Charlton, past Horse & Groom. 0.5 miles, left signed 'Bullocks Horn No Through Road'. On to end of lane. Right; 1st on left. |

| | |
|---|---|
| | **Colin & Liz Legge** |
| | Bullocks Horn Cottage, |
| | Charlton, Malmesbury, |
| | Wiltshire SN16 9DZ |
| Tel | +44 (0)1666 577600 |
| Email | legge@bullockshorn.clara.co.uk |
| Web | www.bullockshorn.co.uk |

🐕 🐈

Entry 569   Map 3

# Wiltshire

## Manor Farm

Iron gates, a sweeping drive with fountain and lawn to an impressive Cotswold stone house, through an ancient oak door find a large hallway and Caroline who makes you feel truly welcome to roam the house. While away time in the enormous sitting room with its piles of good books, eat breakfast from the local shop in the kitchen – or by the wood-burner in the dining room, sleep in deep comfort and surrounded by beautiful things, wake to a cockerel crowing and church bells: wholly comfortable, deeply unpretentious. You are near to Tetbury for delightfully expensive antiques, and Westonbirt for wood walks. *French spoken.*

 Travel Club offer. See page 414.

| | |
|---|---|
| Price | £90. Singles £65. |
| Rooms | 2: 1 double, 1 twin with separate shared bath (let to same party only). |
| Meals | Pub/restaurant 100 yds. |
| Closed | Christmas & Boxing Day. |
| Directions | M4 junction 17, north on A429. Left to Hullavington/Sherston. Follow road through to Sherston. Straight over into Court Street. Drive on left after 100 yds. |

| | |
|---|---|
| | **Caroline Marcq** |
| | Manor Farm, |
| | Court Street, |
| | Sherston, |
| | Wiltshire SN16 0LL |
| Tel | +44 (0)1666 841102 |
| Email | phippsinteriors2@fsmail.net |

🐓 🍴 🚂 🐈

Entry 570   Map 3

# Wiltshire

## Alcombe Manor

Down a maze of magical lanes discover this hamlet and its 17th-century manor house: a deeply romantic hideaway with panelling, wooden floors, a couple of medieval windows, deep sofas, log fires, a galleried hall, shelves of books and plenty of places to sit. A fine oak staircase leads to large, light bedrooms, reassuringly old-fashioned; carpeted floors creak companionably and every ancient leaded window has a dreamy garden view... five acres of English perfection, no less, with topiary and a stream dashing through. Your hosts are kind and helpful, the peace is palpable, and you are just five miles from Bath.

| | |
|---|---|
| Price | From £80. Singles £50. |
| Rooms | 3: 2 twins, each with separate bath/shower; 1 single sharing bath. |
| Meals | Occasional dinner. Pubs nearby. |
| Closed | Rarely. |
| Directions | M4 junc. 17; A4 to Bath through Box; right for Middle Hill & Ditteridge; 200 yds, left signed Alcombe. Up hill for 0.5 miles, fork right; 200 yds on left. |

**Simon & Victoria Morley**
Alcombe Manor,
Box,
Corsham,
Wiltshire SN13 8QQ
Tel     +44 (0)1225 743850
Email   morley@alcombemanor.co.uk

Entry 571   Map 3

# Worcestershire

## Harrowfields

Tucked just off the high street this compact cottage is stylish, with contemporary colours and old beams, great books and a homely feel. The bedroom is large enough to lounge in with a comfy sofa, antique brass bed, crisp linen and your own cosy wood-burner; in the shower room the spoiling continues and there are lovely garden views. Susie and Adam (who cooks) are natural and charming, hens cluck around outside, breakfast is local and seasonal, you can walk for miles or just to the pub. Young, romantic couples will be in heaven here; uncork the wine, light the fire, turn up the music.

Travel Club offer. See page 414.

| | |
|---|---|
| Price | £70. Singles from £50. |
| Rooms | 1 double. |
| Meals | Pubs in village. |
| Closed | Rarely. |
| Directions | Enter Eckington from Bredon (M5 junc. 9). Turn 1st right by village shop. House on left before Anchor pub. |

**Susie Alington & Adam Stanford**
Harrowfields,
Cotheridge Lane, Eckington,
Worcestershire WR10 3BA
Tel     +44 (0)1386 751053
Email   susie@harrowfields.co.uk
Web     www.harrowfields.co.uk

Entry 572   Map 8

## Worcestershire

### Lower End House

They've piled on the chic here in this timber framed hall house in the middle of Eckington village, just outside Pershore: wide floorboards, huge fireplaces and leather sofas, cleverly mixed with bold fabrics, antler chandeliers and cow hide rugs. Bedrooms are all lavish and warm with the best mattresses and Siberian goose down; some have hand made wallpaper, one an explosion of beams, another a fabulous antique brocade sofa. Bathrooms will tempt you to flounce and preen; carved stone basins, the podgiest towels. Foodies will adore taking breakfast in the cookery school, walkers will find stunning countryside nearby.

| | |
|---|---|
| Price | £125. Singles £65. |
| Rooms | 5: 3 twins/doubles; 2 singles with shared bath (let to same party only). |
| Meals | Supper trays from £12.50. Packed lunch from £10. Pubs in village. |
| Closed | Christmas & New Year. |
| Directions | From Pershore, left onto A4104 for Upton. Left to Eckington on B4080, then 1st right in village into Drakesbridge Road; continue then right into Manor Road. |

Lucy Biltcliffe
Lower End House,
Manor Road, Eckington,
Worcestershire WR10 3BH
Tel     +44 (0)1386 751600
Fax    +44 (0)1386 751362
Email  info@lowerendhouse.co.uk
Web    www.lowerendhouse.co.uk

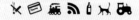

Entry 573   Map 8

## Worcestershire

### Bidders Croft

Completely rebuilt in 1995 from 200-year-old bricks, this solid house has a hand-carved mahogany hall pillar, oak-framed loggias and an enormous conservatory where you eat overlooking the garden, orchard, field and the Malvern Hills. Traditional bedrooms with padded headboards and dressing tables are warm and comfortable; bathrooms are spick and span. Bill and Charlotte give you a log fire, books and magazines in the drawing room, an Aga-cooked breakfast and candlelit dinner with home-grown vegetables and fruit. The hills beckon walkers, the views soar and you're near the Malvern theatres.

 Travel Club offer. See page 414.

| | |
|---|---|
| Price | £79–£89. Singles £49–£55. |
| Rooms | 2: 1 twin with separate bath; 1 double with separate shower. |
| Meals | Dinner, 4 courses, £29.50 (for min. 4). Pub/restaurant 250 yds. |
| Closed | Christmas & New Year. |
| Directions | From Upton-upon-Severn, A4104 for Little Malvern & Ledbury. After 3 miles, pass Anchor Inn on right; drive is 250 yds on left, signed. |

Bill & Charlotte Carver
Bidders Croft,
Welland,
Malvern,
Worcestershire WR13 6LN
Tel     +44 (0)1684 592179
Email  carvers@bidderscroft.com
Web    www.bidderscroft.com

Entry 574   Map 8

## Worcestershire

### Old Country Farm

Ella's passion for this remote, tranquil place – and the environment in general – is infectious. She believes the house was once home to a Saxon chief. Certainly, it has beams dating from 1400; now it's a rambling mix of russet stone and colour-washed brick, with a warm and delightfully cluttered kitchen, wooden floors, lovely rugs. Friendly, low-ceilinged bedrooms are simple and rustic. Ella's parents collected rare plants and the garden is full of hellebores and snowdrops; roe deer and barn owls flit about in the surrounding woods. A wonderful retreat for nature lovers, birdwatchers and walkers.

Ethical Collection: Community; Food. See page 412..

| Price | £60–£90. Singles £35–£55. |
|---|---|
| Rooms | 3: 1 double; 1 double with separate bath; 1 double with separate shower. |
| Meals | Pubs/restaurants 3 miles. |
| Closed | Rarely. |
| Directions | From Worcester A4103 for 11 miles; B4220 for Ledbury. After leaving Cradley, left at top of hill for Mathon, right for Coddington; house 0.25 miles on right. |

Ella Grace Quincy
Old Country Farm,
Mathon,
Malvern,
Worcestershire WR13 5PS
Tel +44 (0)1886 880867
Email ella@oldcountryhouse.co.uk
Web www.oldcountryhouse.co.uk

Entry 575  Map 8

## Worcestershire

### Home Farm

A half-moated farmhouse in a magical spot: the timbered part — 14th-century and listed — peeps through the trees as you approach. Gorgeous in summer (terrace, tennis, gardens, ducks) but light, relaxing and spacious all year round: antiques, soft colours and an open fire in the guest sitting room, fresh fabrics and carpeted comfort in the bedrooms, and peaceful views to the Abberley Hills and beyond. Roger and Anne are generous hosts and give you local bacon at breakfast and stewed fruits and jam from their plums. Make time for Great Witley, the most stunning baroque church in England. *Children over ten welcome.*

| Price | £80–£90. Singles £50–£55. |
|---|---|
| Rooms | 3: 1 twin; 1 single, 1 twin each with separate bath/shower. |
| Meals | Pubs within 5 miles. |
| Closed | Christmas & New Year. |
| Directions | On entering Great Witley from Worcester on A443, left onto B4197 to Martley; after 0.25 miles 1st right on sharp left-hand bend by grass triangle & chevrons; up hill 1st house on right. |

Roger & Anne Kendrick
Home Farm,
Great Witley,
Worcester,
Worcestershire WR6 6JJ
Tel +44 (0)1299 896825
Email info@homefarmbandb.com
Web www.homefarmbandb.com

Entry 576  Map 8

# Worcestershire

## The Hayloft

Beams galore – and photos too. Dennis is a photographer and your bedroom walls are lined with his colourful works; you get a jolly comfortable bed, posh robes, snazzy bathrooms with candles. plump towels and views across rolling fields. All is peaceful here: wake to a sizzling full English from cheery Maureen, with proper black pudding and homemade jams. You are near the Wychavon Way and the Droitwich Canal for walking, boating and birdwatching, but you could just pootle round the garden which slides down the hill into the countryside, or bubble gently in the hot tub. Excellent value, hearty suppers, lovely people.

🧳 Travel Club offer. See page 414.

| | |
|---|---|
| Price | £70–£80. Singles from £40. |
| Rooms | 2: 1 double; 1 double with separate bath. |
| Meals | Dinner, 2 courses, £15; 3 courses, £20. Packed lunch £5 (by arrangement). Pubs/restaurants 2-3 miles. |
| Closed | Rarely. |
| Directions | From Droitwich take the A442 Kidderminster road. After approximately 1 mile turn left into Doverdale Lane. Upper Hall is half a mile on right on the hill top. |

**Maureen & Dennis Alton**
The Hayloft,
Upper Hall, Hampton Lovett,
Droitwich, Worcestershire WR9 0PA
Tel +44 (0)1905 772819
Email maureen@hayloftbandb.com
Web www.hayloftbandb.com

✗ 🚂 🔊

# Worcestershire

## Brook Farm

A wonderful lost-in-the-country feel here with dogs bounding to greet you, a herd of cats lounging around and donkeys looking on. The farmhouse is surprisingly large: you get one end, Sarah and William have the other, so there's a private feel. Big armchairs and sofas are made for sprawling, a wood-burner keeps you shiver-free and there are masses of lovely books; you can have a ploughman's supper here if you want. Sleep soundly in a charming bedroom with fresh flowers, wake (with tea in bed if you like) to scrambled eggs and smoked trout. There are eight acres of woodland to explore and footpaths from the garden.

Ethical Collection: Environment.
See page 412.

🧳 Travel Club offer. See page 414.

| | |
|---|---|
| Price | From £65. Singles £50. |
| Rooms | 2: 1 double; 1 double with separate bath. |
| Meals | Supper, ploughman's, £7.50. Pub/restaurant 2 miles. |
| Closed | Rarely. |
| Directions | Leave Tenbury Wells direction Leominster. Right on bend after Pembroke House pub. At T-junc. left, 2 miles. At T-junc. right. Follow approx. 0.5 miles. House on left on right-hand bend opposite white railings, next to postbox. |

**Sarah & William Wint**
Brook Farm,
Berrington, Tenbury Wells,
Worcestershire WR15 8TJ
Tel +44 (0)1584 819868
Email sarah@brookfarmberrington.com
Web www.brookfarmberrington.com

✗ 🚂 🔊 🐾

## Yorkshire

### Dowthorpe Hall

Foodies will love it here: cooking is Caroline's passion and she trawls the county for the best ingredients; fresh fish and seafood from Hornsea, local game, Dexter or Lincoln Red beef, home-grown fruit and vegetables. All is served in the sumptuous Georgian dining room by flickering candlelight, and recovered from in a deeply comfortable drawing room – why not ask local friends to join you? Sleep peacefully on a luxuriously soft mattress, wake to warm bread, local bacon, sausages and eggs. There are acres of garden to roam, with mature trees, a pond with an ornamental bridge, potager and orchards.

Travel Club offer. See page 414.

| | |
|---|---|
| Price | £80-£90. Singles £50-£55. |
| Rooms | 2: 1 twin/double; 1 double with separate bath. |
| Meals | Dinner £25. Pubs 0.25-5 miles. |
| Closed | Never. |
| Directions | North on A165 for Bridlington, through Ganstead & Coniston. On right, white railings & drive to Dowthorpe Hall. |

**John & Caroline Holtby**
Dowthorpe Hall,
Skirlaugh,
Hull,
Yorkshire HU11 5AE
Tel       +44 (0)1964 562235
Email    john.holtby@farming.co.uk

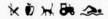

Entry 579   Map 13

## Yorkshire

### Village Farm

Tucked behind the houses and shops, this was once the village farm with land stretching to the coast; the one-storey buildings overlooking a courtyard are now large immaculate bedrooms in gorgeous colours with luxurious touches and music. Baths are deep, beds crisply comfortable, heating is underfoot. Delicious breakfasts are served at wooden tables in a cheerful, light room with a contemporary feel; wicker sofa and chairs, terracotta floors, white walls. Justin and Alison are friendly and helpful but give you complete privacy; stride the cliffs, watch birds at Flamborough Head or make for Spurn Point – remote and lovely.

| | |
|---|---|
| Price | £75. Singles from £39.95. |
| Rooms | 3: 2 doubles, 1 twin. |
| Meals | Pubs/restaurants within 15 miles. |
| Closed | Rarely. |
| Directions | A165 Beverley to Bridlington. At Beeford x-roads, right onto B1249 to Skipsea. There, pass church on left, at x-roads, straight across to Back Street. On right, opp. pub. |

**Justin & Alison Thorn**
Village Farm,
Skipsea,
Yorkshire YO25 8SW
Tel       +44 (0)1262 468479
Email    villagefarmskipsea@yahoo.com
Web      www.villagefarmskipsea.co.uk

Entry 580   Map 13

# Yorkshire

## The Wold Cottage

Drive down through mature trees, and a proper entrance with signs to an elegant Georgian Manor house in 300 glorious acres. Inside find a light and cheerful guest sitting room with thick carpets and plenty of sofas, a dining room with heartlifting views across the landscaped gardens, and gorgeous original features; fan-lights, high ceilings and broad staircases. Bedrooms in the house are sumptuous and comfortable, two in the barn are as neat as a pin. You are warmed by straw bale heating, food is local and delicious: a Yorkshire breakfast will set you up for discovering the unspoilt Wolds.

| | |
|---|---|
| Price | £90–£120. Singles £50–£60. |
| Rooms | 5: 1 double, 2 twins. |
| | Barn: 1 family room, 1 four-poster. |
| Meals | Supper £23. Wine from £12.95. |
| Closed | Rarely. |
| Directions | A64 onto B1249. Through Foxholes to Wold Newton. In village, take road between pond & pub; signed on right. |

|  | **Mrs Katrina Gray** |
|---|---|
| | The Wold Cottage, |
| | Wold Newton, |
| | Driffield, Yorkshire YO25 3HL |
| Tel | +44 (0)1262 470696 |
| Fax | +44 (0)1262 470696 |
| Email | katrina@woldcottage.com |
| Web | www.woldcottage.com |

Entry 581   Map 13

# Yorkshire

## Low Penhowe

With the Turners at the helm, you are on a safe ship. They see to everything so perfectly – the crispness of the breakfast bacon, the freshness of the eggs from their hens, the homemade bread, the bowls of flowers, the fire in the guest drawing room. Traditional, comfortable bedrooms face south and overlook the garden – lap up the views in summer while birds soar and twitter, Christopher's Highland cattle peer over the fence and the chickens strut and scratch. Castle Howard and the North Yorks Moors are in front of you and all around are abbeys, castles, rivers, ruins and woods. *Children over ten welcome.*

Ethical Collection: Community; Food. See page 412.

Travel Club offer. See page 414.

| | |
|---|---|
| Price | £72–£90. Singles £60. |
| Rooms | 2: 1 double; |
| | 1 twin/double with separate bath. |
| Meals | Packed lunch £6. Pubs 1.5 miles. |
| Closed | Christmas & New Year. |
| Directions | A64 at Whitwell on the Hill, right for Kirkham. Over crossing & Derwent, pass Kirkham Priory & Stone Trough Inn. Right at T-junc., left for Burythorpe, over x-roads, 700 yds; right up drive. |

| | **Christopher & Philippa Turner** |
|---|---|
| | Low Penhowe, |
| | Burythorpe, |
| | Malton, Yorkshire YO17 9LU |
| Tel | +44 (0)1653 658336 |
| Fax | +44 (0)1653 658619 |
| Email | lowpenhowe@btinternet.com |
| Web | www.bedandbreakfastyorkshire.co.uk |

Entry 582   Map 13

## Yorkshire

### Crown House

Scarborough… bracing walks, salty air, fresh fish and buckets and spades. But the Firths have one of those charming listed houses in respectable South Cliff, moments from the Esplanade. Inside find spacious light rooms with contemporary furniture, stunning art (Barbara's passion) and flowers everywhere. Barbara, thoughtful and fun, serves great breakfasts with juices just-squeezed at a large oval table. Bedrooms are cream and stylish with smart TVs and stereos, bathrooms luxurious and sparkling. Coastline and castles by day, home baking on your return, books and CDs to borrow, cats to admire, and a theatre just down the road.

 Travel Club offer. See page 414.

| Price | £80–£110. |
|---|---|
| Rooms | 3: 2 doubles, 1 twin/double. |
| Meals | Restaurants 10-minute walk. |
| Closed | Christmas to end of January. |
| Directions | From station, A165 signed Filey. Right over Valley Bridge, left at end; immed. right on Belmont Road. At green, right again; left into Crown Terrace. |

|  | Barbara Firth |
|---|---|
|  | Crown House, |
|  | 6 Crown Terrace, |
|  | Scarborough, |
|  | Yorkshire YO11 2BL |
| Tel | +44 (0)1723 375401 |
| Email | barbara@crownhousescarborough.co.uk |
| Web | www.crownhousescarborough.co.uk |

Entry 583   Map 13

## Yorkshire

### Holly Croft

Huge kindness and thoughtful touches (hot water bottles, lifts to the pub, cake and tea on arrival) make this home special. The décor is Edwardian plush – wallpapers striped and floral, curtains lavish – the comfort indisputable. The double has an elaborate floral-and-rose headboard with matching drapes, there are bathrobes in fitted wardrobes, big showers and generous breakfasts – own jams, Yorkshire teas, kippers if you choose – are served round the polished mahogany table. After a bracing clifftop walk return to a homely sitting room overlooking the garden. Whitby is 20 minutes away.

 Travel Club offer. See page 414.

| Price | From £75. Singles from £45. |
|---|---|
| Rooms | 2: 1 twin; 1 double with separate bath. |
| Meals | Evening meal by prior arrangement (minimum 4 people). Pub 600 yds. |
| Closed | Rarely. |
| Directions | A171 from Scarborough to Whitby; at Scalby x-roads, by tennis courts, take road on right. Signed 500 yds on right. |

|  | John & Christine Goodall |
|---|---|
|  | Holly Croft, |
|  | 28 Station Road, |
|  | Scalby, Scarborough, |
|  | Yorkshire YO13 0QA |
| Tel | +44 (0)1723 375376 |
| Email | christine.goodall@tesco.net |
| Web | www.holly-croft.co.uk |

Entry 584   Map 13

## Yorkshire

### Brickfields Farm

Down a long, quiet track but just a stone's throw from bustling Kirkbymoorside, this is a walker's paradise. Friendly Janet provides maps and information and sends you off to the North York Moors with a tasty breakfast, served at separate tables in the conservatory overlooking sheep and guinea fowl. Bedrooms are in the main house or in the long low barn and all are lovely; a French vintage bed, antiques, heavy curtains and sprung mattresses, fresh flowers and a hidden fridge. Bathrooms have big, open showers, thick towels and generous lotions and bubbles. *Not suitable for children.*

  Travel Club offer. See page 414.

| Price | £80–£110. |
|---|---|
| Rooms | 5: 1 twin, 4 suites. |
| Meals | Pub/restaurant 1 mile. |
| Closed | Rarely. |
| Directions | A170 east from Thirsk to Kirkbymoorside; continue past roundabout for 0.5 miles. Right into Kirkby Mills, signed. House 1st right along small lane. |

|  | Janet Trousdale |
|---|---|
|  | Brickfields Farm, |
|  | Kirkby Mills, Kirkbymoorside, |
|  | Yorkshire YO62 6NS |
| Tel | +44 (0)1751 433074 |
| Email | janet@brickfieldsfarm.co.uk |
| Web | www.brickfieldsfarm.co.uk |

Entry 585   Map 13

## Yorkshire

### Rectory Farmhouse

Walk from the door straight onto the North Yorkshire Moors and leave your car behind – it's only a 30-minute stride down the fields to the train station and Steam Railway. Michael, Heather and their son David have been here since 1997; along with dogs, cats, horses and bountiful hens. There's a relaxed, homely vibe with comfortable sofas and an open fire in the light lounge, comfy bedrooms and country florals. Enjoy proper Yorkshire dinner (organic and locally sourced); breakfasts in the guest dining room are just as good with Michael's homemade bread. Good value, superb walking and great riding, too. *Children over eight welcome.*

| Price | From £60. Singles £35. |
|---|---|
| Rooms | 4: 1 double, 1 twin. Apartment: 1 double, 1 twin sharing separate bath (let to same party only). |
| Meals | Dinner, 2 courses, £15. Packed lunch £5. Pub in village. |
| Closed | Christmas & New Year. |
| Directions | From A169 take Lockton/Levisham road. Once through Lockton, look for house sign after 0.75 miles on right, in Levisham. |

|  | Michael & Heather Holt |
|---|---|
|  | Rectory Farmhouse, |
|  | Levisham, Pickering, |
|  | Yorkshire YO18 7NL |
| Tel | +44 (0)1751 460491 |
| Email | stay@levisham.com |
| Web | www.levisham.com |

Entry 586   Map 13

## Yorkshire

### Flamborough Rigg Cottage

Even in the North York Moors it's rare to find a spot so remote – rarer still to find such luxury in an 1820s farmhouse set in fields of lambs. Philip and Caroline know how to delight guests with brilliant bathrooms, crisp linen, delicious meals from home-grown produce. They've melded modern touches with handsome antiques, like contemporary art around a grandfather clock in the vaulted dining room – it works. One bedroom has a sitting area; the others have French doors to an orchard garden; all gaze over hills that cry out for walking. Dogs are welcome, Whitby coast is ten miles, and there's fine food and company to round off the day.

| | |
|---|---|
| Price | £85. Singles £65. |
| Rooms | 3 doubles (1 with sitting room). |
| Meals | Packed lunch £5-£10. Dinner, 2 courses, from £15; 3 courses from £20. Pub 2 miles. |
| Closed | Rarely. |
| Directions | Leave Pickering passing the Steam Railway towards Newton-upon-Rawcliffe and Stape. Go through Newton in to Stape. 500 yards past phone box turn left, keep left. House 4th property along. |

**Philip & Caroline Jackson**
Flamborough Rigg Cottage,
Middlehead Road, Stape,
Pickering, Yorkshire YO18 8HR
Tel       +44 (0)1751 475263
Email    enquiries@flamboroughriggcottage.co.uk
Web     www.flamboroughriggcottage.co.uk

Entry 587   Map 13

## Yorkshire

### No. 54

The welcome tea and homemade cakes set the tone for your stay; this is a happy place. No 54 was once two cottages on the Duncombe estate; now it's a single house and Lizzie has made the most of the space. Buttermilk walls, be-rugged flagged floors, country furniture, open fires and a stylish lack of clutter. A single-storey extension has been fashioned into three extra bedrooms around a secluded courtyard. Thoughtful extras – a Roberts radio, fresh milk, hot water bottles – make you feel looked after, and the breakfasts will fuel the most serious of walks. Make a house party and bring your friends!

Travel Club offer. See page 414.

| | |
|---|---|
| Price | £88. Singles from £40. |
| Rooms | 4: 2 doubles, 1 twin; 1 single with separate shower. |
| Meals | Dinner, 2-3 courses, £28-£35. Restaurants 10-minute walk. |
| Closed | Christmas & New Year. |
| Directions | A170 to Helmsley; right at mini r'bout in centre, facing The Crown; house 500 yds along A170, on right. |

**Lizzie Would**
No. 54,
Bondgate, Helmsley,
Yorkshire YO62 5EZ
Tel       +44 (0)1439 771533
Email    lizzie@no54.co.uk
Web     www.no54.co.uk

Entry 588   Map 13

# Yorkshire

## Sproxton Hall

Drive through a stone archway into an old courtyard: the 17th-century beamed farmhouse, once attached to Rievaulx Abbey, is still part of a working farm – complete with rare-breed Belted Galloways. Inside, a handsome grandfather clock, log fire, fresh flowers and a genuine welcome from Margaret and Andrew. The guests' sitting and dining rooms have 18th-century country antiques and the bedrooms are traditional and comfortable, with lovely views; the double has a half-tester with floral canopy. Sensible, hearty breakfasts prepare you for a day on the peaceful North Yorkshire Moors. *Children over ten welcome.*

| | |
|---|---|
| Price | £74–£80. Singles £45. |
| Rooms | 3: 1 twin, 1 double; 1 twin with separate bath & shower. |
| Meals | Pubs/restaurants 1–3 miles. |
| Closed | Christmas & New Year. |
| Directions | From Thirsk A170 for 12 miles. Right onto B1257 (1 mile before Helmsley); 50 yds on, left by church. House at end of 'No Through Road'. |

Margaret & Andrew Wainwright
Sproxton Hall,
Sproxton,
Helmsley,
Yorkshire YO62 5EQ
Tel       +44 (0)1439 770225
Email     sproxtonhall@btinternet.com
Web       www.sproxtonhall.co.uk

Entry 589   Map 13

# Yorkshire

## Shallowdale House

Phillip and Anton have a true affection for their guests so you will be treated like angels. Sumptuous bedrooms dazzle in yellows, blues and limes, acres of curtains frame wide views over the Howardian Hills, bathrooms are gleaming and immaculate. Breakfast on the absolute best; fresh fruit compote, dry-cured bacon, homemade rolls – and walk it off in any direction straight from the house. Return to an elegant drawing room, with a fire in winter, and an enticing library. Dinner is out of this world and coffee and chocolates are all you need before you crawl up to bed. Bliss. *Children over 12 welcome.*

Ethical Collection: Food.
See page 412.

| | |
|---|---|
| Price | £95–£115. Singles £75–£85. |
| Rooms | 3: 2 twins/doubles; 1 double with separate bath/shower. |
| Meals | Dinner, 4 courses, £35. |
| Closed | Christmas & New Year. |
| Directions | From Thirsk, A19 south, then 'caravan route' via Coxwold & Byland Abbey. 1st house on left, just before Ampleforth. |

Anton van der Horst & Phillip Gill
Shallowdale House,
West End, Ampleforth,
Yorkshire YO62 4DY
Tel       +44 (0)1439 788325
Fax       +44 (0)1439 788885
Email     stay@shallowdalehouse.co.uk
Web       www.shallowdalehouse.co.uk

Entry 590   Map 12

# Yorkshire

## The Old Rectory

Once the residence of the Bishops of Whitby this elegant rectory has a comfortable lived-in air. Both Turner and Ruskin stayed here and probably enjoyed as much good conversation and comfort as you will. Bedrooms are pretty, traditional and with grand views; the drawing room is classic country house with a fine Venetian window and an enticing window-seat. The graceful, deep pink dining room looks south over a large garden of redwood and walnut trees – some are 300 years old. Caroline will give you a generous breakfast; wander at will to find an orchard, tennis court and croquet lawn. *Children over five welcome.*

# Yorkshire

## Hunters Hill

The moors lie behind this solid, stone farmhouse, five yards from the National Park, in farmland and woodland with fine views… marvellous walking country. The house is full of light and flowers; bedrooms are pretty but not overly grand. The attractive sitting room has deeply comfortable old sofas, armchairs and fine furniture, while rich colours, hunting prints and candles at dinner give a warm and cosy feel. The family has poured a good deal of affection into this tranquil house and the result is a home that's happy, charming and remarkably easy to relax in… Wonderful.

Travel Club offer. See page 414.

| | |
|---|---|
| Price | From £66. Singles from £40. |
| Rooms | 2: 1 double with separate bath & dressing room; 1 twin/double with separate bath & shower. |
| Meals | Pub opposite. |
| Closed | Rarely. |
| Directions | Take A168 (Northallerton road) off A19; over r'bout; left into village; house opp. pub, next to church. |

| | |
|---|---|
| Price | £80. Singles from £50. |
| Rooms | 2: 1 twin/double; 1 twin/double with separate bath. |
| Meals | Dinner, 3 courses, £30. Pub/restaurant 500 yds. |
| Closed | Rarely. |
| Directions | From A170 to Sinnington. On village green, keep river on left, fork right between cottages, sign to church. Up lane, bearing right up hill. House past church beyond farm buildings. |

Tim & Caroline O'Connor-Fenton
The Old Rectory,
South Kilvington,
Thirsk,
Yorkshire YO7 2NL
Tel    +44 (0)1845 526153
Email    ocfenton@talktalk.net

Jane Otter
Hunters Hill,
Sinnington,
York,
Yorkshire YO62 6SF
Tel    +44 (0)1751 431196
Email    ejorr@tiscali.co.uk

Entry 591    Map 12

Entry 592    Map 13

# Yorkshire

## Cundall Lodge Farm

Ancient chestnuts, crunchy drive, sheep grazing, hens free-ranging. This four-square Georgian farmhouse could be straight out of Central Casting. And there's tea and oven-fresh cake to welcome. Homely rooms of damask sofas and pretty wallpaper have views to Sutton Bank's White Horse or the river Swale. Bedrooms are comfy with family furnishings and inviting chairs. This is a working farm with typical farmers' breakfast: free-range eggs, homemade jams and local cured bacon. The garden and river walks guarantee peace. David and Caroline are sociable and generous. *Children over ten welcome.*

 Travel Club offer. See page 414.

| Price | £75–£90. |
|---|---|
| Rooms | 3: 2 doubles; 1 twin/double. |
| Meals | Packed lunch £5. Pubs/restaurants 2 miles. |
| Closed | Christmas & January. |
| Directions | Exit junc. 49 A1(M) onto A168 (Thirsk). Turn off 1st junc. for Cundall. Turn right at the Crab & Lobster. 2 miles on left. |

|  | Caroline Barker |
|---|---|
|  | Cundall Lodge Farm, |
|  | Cundall, York, |
|  | Yorkshire YO61 2RN |
| Tel | +44 (0)1423 360203 |
| Fax | +44 (0)1423 360805 |
| Email | info@lodgefarmbb.co.uk |
| Web | www.cundall-lodgefarm.co.uk |

Entry 593   Map 12

# Yorkshire

## North Dockenbush

An 1800s farmhouse transformed into a handsome B&B with a modern vibe. Animal skins and displays of flowers gleam in the mirrored light of chandeliers; dark red walls flicker in firelight. Sink into Siberian goose down, wake to waterfall showers and Molton Brown treats. Oliver loves country pursuits, housekeeper Jackie provides the feminine touch (and biscuits!) – both radiate energy. Breakfast bacon and eggs are farmyard fresh while port rounds off hearty British meals. Dogs and horses share the stables and the estate, close to Harrogate, is a walker's paradise: you're on the doorstep of the Yorkshire Dales.

Ethical Collection: Food. See page 412.

| Price | £90. Singles £65. |
|---|---|
| Rooms | 5: 3 doubles; 2 doubles sharing bath (let to same party only). |
| Meals | Dinner, 4 courses and half bottle of wine, £30 (min. 4 people). Pub/restaurant 2 miles. |
| Closed | Christmas. |
| Directions | Leave Harrogate on A61 (Ripon road). At 2nd r'bout, right onto B6156 to Knaresborough. Left to Brearton, past sign for village only, then next right on corner. |

|  | Oliver Whiteley |
|---|---|
|  | North Dockenbush, |
|  | Brearton, |
|  | Harrogate, |
|  | Yorkshire HG3 3DF |
| Tel | +44 (0)1423 797650 |
| Email | oliver@northdockenbush.co.uk |
| Web | www.northdockenbush.co.uk |

Entry 594   Map 12

# Yorkshire

### Braythorne Barn

Great independence here with your own entrance; inside are paintings, fine furniture, colourful fabrics and rugs. Floors are light oak, windows and doors hand-crafted and sunlight dances around the rooms. Both bedrooms are understatedly luxurious with beautiful rafters, glorious views and a fresh country feel. Bathrooms have Molton Brown toiletries and plump towels; the guest sitting room is gorgeous. Visit charming Harrogate or walk the Priests Way. Chickens in the field and great breakfasts – perhaps brandy-soaked fruit compote… this is a rural idyll with a contemporary twist. *Children over 12 welcome. Minimum stay two nights.*

| Price | £80–£90. Singles from £55. |
|---|---|
| Rooms | 2: 1 twin; <br> 1 double with separate shower. |
| Meals | Pubs/restaurants 2-4 miles. |
| Closed | Rarely. |
| Directions | From Pool-in-Wharfedale, A658 over bridge towards Harrogate. 1st left to Leathley; right opp. church to Stainburn (1.5 miles). Bear left at fork; house next on left. |

**Petrina Knockton**
Braythorne Barn,
Stainburn, Otley,
Yorkshire LS21 2LW
Tel     +44 (0)113 284 3160
Fax     +44 (0)113 2842297
Email   trina@home-relocation.co.uk
Web     www.braythornebarn.co.uk

Entry 595   Map 12

# Yorkshire

### Sunnybank

A Victorian gentleman's residence just a short walk up the hill from the centre of bustling *Last of the Summer Wine* Holmfirth, still with its working Picturedrome cinema (touring bands too), arts and folk festivals, restaurants and shops. Peter and Anne look after you beautifully. Big peaceful bedrooms are a fresh mix of contemporary, Art Nouveau and Art Deco pieces, caramel cream velvets and silks, spoiling bathrooms and lovely views. A huge Yorkshire breakfast will set you up for a lazy stroll round the charming gardens, or a brisk yomp through rural bliss. *Minimum stay two nights at weekends.*

| Price | £65–£90. Singles from £55. |
|---|---|
| Rooms | 3: 2 doubles, 1 twin/double (with extra single bed). |
| Meals | Supper snacks £12. Packed lunch £12. Pubs/restaurants 500 yds. |
| Closed | New Year & occasionally. |
| Directions | A6024 signed Glossop out of Holmfirth centre. Take right in between Ashley Jackson Studio & Worthingtons into Upperthong Lane. House is first drive on right after St John's Church. |

**Peter & Anne White**
Sunnybank,
78 Upperthong Lane,
Holmfirth,
Yorkshire HD9 3BQ
Tel     +44 (0)1484 684857
Email   info@sunnybankguesthouse.co.uk
Web     www.sunnybankguesthouse.co.uk

Entry 596   Map 12

## Yorkshire

### Field House

You drive over bridge and beck to this listed, 1713 farmhouse – expect comfort, homeliness and open fires. Pat and Geoff love showing guests their hens, horses, goats and lambs, and will tell you about the 14 circular walks or lend you a torch so you can find the pub across the fields! Ramblers will be in heaven – step out of the front door, past the lovely walled garden and you're in rolling, Bronte countryside. Good big bedrooms are in farmhouse style, one bathroom has a roll top bath, another a 70s blue suite, and Geoff's breakfasts are generous in the finest Yorkshire manner.

Ethical Collection: Community; Food. See page 412.

Travel Club offer. See page 414.

| | |
|---|---|
| Price | £60–£70. Singles £35–£44. |
| Rooms | 3: 1 double, 1 twin; 1 family room with separate bath/shower. |
| Meals | Dinner from £10. Packed lunch available. Pub/restaurant 200 yds. |
| Closed | Rarely. |
| Directions | 1 mile from Halifax on A58 Leeds road. Turn between Stump Cross Inn car park & white bungalow shop. 100 yds to gates. |

**Pat & Geoff Horrocks-Taylor**
Field House,
Staups Lane,
Stump Cross, Halifax,
Yorkshire HX3 6XW
Tel       +44 (0)1422 355457
Email    enquiries@fieldhouse-bb.co.uk
Web     www.fieldhouse-bb.co.uk

Entry 597   Map 12

## Yorkshire

### Thurst House Farm

This solid Pennine farmhouse, its stone mullion windows denoting 17th-century origins, is English to the core. Your warm, gracious hosts give guests a cosy and carpeted sitting room with an open fire in winter; bedrooms are equally generous, with inviting brass beds, antique linen and fresh flowers. Outside: clucking hens, two friendly sheep and a hammock in a garden with beautiful views. Tuck into homemade bread, marmalade and jams at breakfast, and good traditional English dinners, too – just the thing for walkers who've trekked the Calderdale or the Pennine Way. *Children over eight welcome.*

| | |
|---|---|
| Price | £80. Singles by arrangement. |
| Rooms | 2: 1 double, 1 family room. |
| Meals | Dinner, 4 courses, £25 (BYO). Packed lunch £5. Restaurants within 0.5 miles. |
| Closed | Christmas & New Year. |
| Directions | Ripponden on A58. Look for brown Beehive sign and then right up Royd Lane 100 yds before lights; right at T-junc. opp. Beehive Inn; on for 1 mile. House on right, gateway on blind bend, reverse in. |

**David & Judith Marriott**
Thurst House Farm,
Soyland, Ripponden,
Sowerby Bridge,
Yorkshire HX6 4NN
Tel       +44 (0)1422 822820
Email    judith@thursthousefarm.co.uk
Web     www.thursthousefarm.co.uk

Entry 598   Map 12

# Yorkshire

## Holme House

A delightful Georgian house in bustling Hebden Bridge: with its artists, musicians, book shops, real ale pubs and commitment to Fair Trade, it's the Totnes of the Pennines. Perfect if you enjoy the outdoor life – walks along the Calder Valley start from the door – but prefer to be based in town. Inside, you will be spoiled with classic proportions, a light-filled hallway, sometimes local art and a comfortable sitting room with leather sofas. Fresh flowers, chocolates, great beds and cool, creamy colours encourage you to linger in bed, but Sarah's locally sourced breakfasts will set you up for anything.

| | |
|---|---|
| Price | £70-£95. Singles £65. |
| Rooms | 3: 2 doubles, 1 twin. |
| Meals | Packed lunch from £7.50. Pubs/restaurants 100 yds. |
| Closed | Christmas Day & Boxing Day. |
| Directions | On corner of New Road (main road through town) & Holme Street. Car park on left as you turn into Holme Street, through black railings. |

Sarah Eggleston
Holme House,
New Road, Hebden Bridge,
Yorkshire HX7 8AD

| | |
|---|---|
| Tel | +44 (0)1422 847588 |
| Fax | +44 (0)1422 847354 |
| Email | mail@holmehousehebdenbridge.co.uk |
| Web | www.holmehousehebdenbridge.co.uk |

Entry 599   Map 12

# Yorkshire

## Ponden House

Bump your way up to Brenda's sturdy house, high on the wild Pennine Way. The spring water makes wonderful tea and the house hums with interest and artistic touches. Comfy sofas are jollied up with throws, there are homespun rugs and hangings, paintings, plants and a piano. Feed the hens, plonk your boots by the Aga, chat with your lovely leisurely hostess as she turns out fab home cooking; food is a passion. Bedrooms are exuberant but cosy, it's great for walkers and there's a hot tub under the stars (bookable by groups in advance). Good value with a lived-in, homely feel.

| | |
|---|---|
| Price | £60-£65. Singles £30-£45. |
| Rooms | 3: 2 doubles; 1 twin sharing bath. |
| Meals | Occasional dinner, 3 courses, £16. Packed lunch £5. Pub/restaurant 3 miles. |
| Closed | Rarely. |
| Directions | From B6142 for Colne. Pass through Stanbury village, cont. past Old Silent Inn. Access is either via Ponden Mill or Ponden reservoir. |

Brenda Taylor
Ponden House,
Stanbury,
Haworth,
Yorkshire BD22 0HR

| | |
|---|---|
| Tel | +44 (0)1535 644154 |
| Email | brenda.taylor@pondenhouse.co.uk |
| Web | www.pondenhouse.co.uk |

Entry 600   Map 12

# Yorkshire

## Knowles Lodge

Chris's father built this timber-framed house in 1938 on 18 acres of glorious hillside. It's a comfortable, comforting place to stay. Honey walls and polished floors give the sitting room a light, airy feel, cheerful throws on deep sofas make it cosy, a fine collection of modern art adds interest and there are views from large windows. Bedrooms are attractive with sprightly fabrics and fresh flowers; draw back the curtains and have your morning cuppa in peace. You're superbly well looked after, you can even get married here. Great walking and trout fishing, and the solitude a balm. *Children over seven welcome.*

| Price | £90. Singles £55-£60. |
|---|---|
| Rooms | 3: 2 doubles, 1 twin. |
| Meals | Packed lunch £5. |
| | Pubs/restaurants within 2 miles. |
| Closed | Never. |
| Directions | From Skipton A59 to Bolton Abbey. At r'bout, B6160 for Burnsall. 3 miles after Devonshire Arms, right immed. after Barden Tower for Appletreewick. Down hill, over bridge, up hill & on for 0.75 miles. Cross bridge; immed. on left. |

| | Pam & Chris Knowles-Fitton |
|---|---|
| | Knowles Lodge, |
| | Appletreewick, Skipton, |
| | Yorkshire BD23 6DQ |
| Tel | +44 (0)1756 720228 |
| Fax | +44 (0)1756 720381 |
| Email | pam@knowleslodge.com |
| Web | www.knowleslodge.com |

Entry 601   Map 12

# Yorkshire

## Brandymires

The Wensleydale hills lie framed through the windows of the time-warp bedrooms; no TV, no fuss, just calm. In the middle of the National Park, this is a glorious spot for walkers. Gail and Ann bake their own bread and make jams and marmalade, and their delicious, well-priced dinners are prepared with fresh local produce and served at your own table. Two bedrooms, not in their first flush of youth, have four-posters; all have the views. If you're arriving by car, take the 'over-the-top' road from Buckden to Hawes for the most stunning countryside. *Minimum stay two nights. Children over eight welcome.*

Ethical Collection: Food. See page 412.

 Travel Club offer. See page 414.

| Price | £52. Singles £31. |
|---|---|
| Rooms | 3: 1 twin, 2 four-posters, all sharing 2 bath/shower rooms (each floor can be let to same party only, by arrangement.) |
| Meals | Dinner, 4 courses, £18.50 (not Thurs). Pubs/restaurant 5-minute walk. |
| Closed | November-February. |
| Directions | 300 yds off A684, on road north out of Hawes, signed Muker & Hardraw. House on right. |

| | Gail Ainley & Ann Macdonald |
|---|---|
| | Brandymires, |
| | Muker Road, |
| | Hawes, |
| | Yorkshire DL8 3PR |
| Tel | +44 (0)1969 667482 |

Entry 602   Map 12

# Yorkshire

## Mallard Grange

Perfect farmhouse B&B. Hens, cats, sheepdogs wander the garden, an ancient apple tree leans against the wall, guests unwind and feel part of the family. Enter the rambling, deep-shuttered 16th-century farmhouse, cosy with well-loved family pieces, and feel at peace with the world. Breakfast is generous – homemade muffins, poached pears with cinnamon and a sizzling full Monty. A winding steep stair leads to big, friendly bedrooms, two cheerful others await in a converted 18th-century smithy and Maggie's enthusiasm for this glorious area is as genuine as her love of doing B&B. *Minimum stay two nights at weekends.*

# Yorkshire

## Lawrence House

A classically elegant, comfortable house run with faultless precision by John and Harriet – former wine importer and interior decorator respectively. The house is listed, and Georgian, the garden is formal, flagged and herbaceous, the position – by the back gate to Fountains Abbey and Studley Royal, overlooking long meadow and parkland – is supreme. There's a linen-sofa'd drawing room just for guests, and the promise of a very good dinner. Bedrooms and bathrooms are in a private wing: light, well-proportioned, full of special touches. Relaxed, peaceful and timeless. *Golf, riding & clay pigeon shooting can be arranged.*

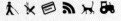 Travel Club offer. See page 414.

| | |
|---|---|
| Price | £75–£105. Singles from £70. |
| Rooms | 4: 1 double, 3 twins/doubles. |
| Meals | Pubs/restaurants 10-minute drive. |
| Closed | Christmas & New Year. |
| Directions | B6265 from Ripon for Pateley Bridge. Past entrance to Fountains Abbey. House on right, 2.5 miles from Ripon. |

| | |
|---|---|
| Price | £120. Singles £80. |
| Rooms | 2: 1 twin/double, 1 twin. |
| Meals | Dinner £30. Pub/restaurant 1 mile. |
| Closed | Christmas & New Year. |
| Directions | A1 to Ripon. B6265 & Pateley Bridge road for 2 miles. Left into Studley Roger. House last on right. |

**Maggie Johnson**
Mallard Grange,
Aldfield,
Ripon,
Yorkshire HG4 3BE
Tel       +44 (0)1765 620242
Email    maggie@mallardgrange.co.uk
Web      www.mallardgrange.co.uk

**John & Harriet Highley**
Lawrence House,
Studley Roger, Ripon,
Yorkshire HG4 3AY
Tel       +44 (0)1765 600947
Fax       +44 (0)1765 609297
Email    john@lawrence-house.co.uk
Web      www.lawrence-house.co.uk

Entry 603   Map 12

Entry 604   Map 12

# Yorkshire

## Park House

The soundtrack could be *Perfect Day*: a scenic drive, delicious cake on arrival, undisturbed peace in the converted estate cottages – partly built with stone from next door's stunning Cistercian Jervaulx Abbey, owned by your hosts. Antique gems stand out among leather bucket chairs, splashes of colour brighten a neutral palette, guest bedrooms are luxurious. Try Carol's bacon, egg and maple crumpets for breakfast – the menu lists local suppliers. Leave pets and children at home but take boots and binoculars for the glorious scenery of Nidderdale: an AONB and a fitting backdrop to a perfect country stay.

Travel Club offer. See page 414.

| Price | From £75. Singles from £55. |
| --- | --- |
| Rooms | 3: 2 doubles, 1 twin. |
| Meals | Packed lunch £3-£5. Pub 1.25 miles. |
| Closed | Never. |
| Directions | House is midway between Masham & Leyburn, about 25 minutes off A1. Full directions given on booking. |

Ian & Carol Burdon
Park House,
Jervaulx, Masham,
Ripon, Yorkshire HG4 4PH
Tel    +44 (0)1677 460184
Email  ba123@btopenworld.com
Web    www.jervaulxabbey.com

Entry 605  Map 12

# Yorkshire

## Mill Close

Country-house B&B in a tranquil spot among fields and woodland; spacious, luxurious and with your own entrance through a flower-filled conservatory. Beds are large and comfortable, there's a grand four-poster with a spa bath, and candle scones for flickering light. Be spoiled by handmade chocolates, fluffy robes, even your own 'quiet' fridge. A blue and cream sitting room has an open fire – but you are between the National Park and the Dales so walks are a must. Start with one of Patricia's famous breakfasts: bacon and sausages from the farm, smoked haddock or salmon, homemade jams. Bliss.

Travel Club offer. See page 414.

| Price | £80-£95. Singles £45-£65. |
| --- | --- |
| Rooms | 3: 2 doubles, 1 four-poster. |
| Meals | Pubs/restaurants 2 miles. |
| Closed | Christmas & New Year. |
| Directions | Follow the brown tourist signs from the village of Patrick Brompton on A684. Farm is 1 mile from village. |

Patricia Knox
Mill Close,
Patrick Brompton,
Bedale, Yorkshire DL8 1JY
Tel    +44 (0)1677 450257
Email  pat@millclose.co.uk
Web    www.millclose.co.uk

Entry 606  Map 12

# Yorkshire

## Lovesome Hill Farm

Who could resist home-reared lamb followed by sticky toffee pudding? This is a working farm and the Pearsons the warmest people imaginable; even in the mayhem of the lambing season they greet you with homemade biscuits and Yorkshire tea. Their farmhouse is as unpretentious as they are: chequered tablecloths, cosy and simple bedrooms (four in the old granary, one in the cottage) with garden and hill views, and a proper Victorian-style sitting room. The A167 traffic hum mingles with the odd sheepdog bark; you are brilliantly placed for the Moors and Dales. Good for walkers, families, business people.

Travel Club offer. See page 414.

| | |
|---|---|
| Price | £64–£76. Singles £35–£48. Gate Cottage: £70–£84. |
| Rooms | 5: 1 twin, 1 double, 1 family room, 1 single. Gate Cottage: 1 double. |
| Meals | Dinner, 2–3 courses, £15–£20. BYO. Packed lunch for walkers. Pub 4 miles. |
| Closed | Rarely. |
| Directions | From Northallerton, A167 north for Darlington for 4 miles. House on right, signed. |

**John & Mary Pearson**
Lovesome Hill Farm,
Lovesome Hill,
Northallerton, Yorkshire DL6 2PB
Tel +44 (0)1609 772311
Email lovesomehillfarm@btinternet.com
Web www.lovesomehillfarm.co.uk

Entry 607  Map 12

# Yorkshire

## The Old Rectory

The views are over glorious Teesdale, the village – solid in stone and 'twixt two borders – is perfect, and the cricket club bowls from one county to another! Across the pretty cobbled yard, up a steep stone stair, is an enchanting bedroom in the coach house: a lofty, cross-beamed ceiling, fresh fabrics at little windows, a country bathroom, coir and crisp linen, a big bed. Angela's watercolours add to the artistic mood and, outside, her green fingers have crafted a lovely walled garden. Inside the rectory, antiques and oils (mostly of horses). James and Angela are great hosts and you'll eat well.

Travel Club offer. See page 414.

| | |
|---|---|
| Price | £85–£90. |
| Rooms | Coach house: 1 double. |
| Meals | Supper £18.50. Pubs/restaurants 10-minute drive. |
| Closed | Christmas & New Year. |
| Directions | South off A66 for Barningham, 10 miles west of Scotch Corner. Immed. left for Barningham; 2 miles; left into courtyard 100 yds from T-junc. in village. |

**James & Angie Delahooke**
The Old Rectory,
Barningham,
Richmond,
Yorkshire DL11 7DW
Tel +44 (0)1833 621122
Email jdelahooke@aol.com

Entry 608  Map 12

## Hill Top

Books, magazines, bath essences, biscuits by the bed – and the charming, warm and welcoming Christina. Her pretty, listed, limestone farmhouse dates from 1820 and is deceptively big. Ivory walls are a perfect foil for some good furniture and paintings; the sitting room overlooks the charming garden and has a cosy fire. Bedrooms are comfy and conventional; food is fresh, interesting and as homemade as possible. Far-reaching views over rolling countryside in this AONB where waterfalls, moorland and castles beckon. Handy for Scotland or the south. *Babes in arms & children over ten welcome.*

| | |
|---|---|
| Price | £80. Singles £40. |
| Rooms | 2: 1 twin; 1 twin sharing bath (let to same party only). |
| Meals | Dinner, 2-3 courses, £15-£20. Pub/restaurant 1.5 miles. |
| Closed | Christmas & New Year. |
| Directions | From Scotch Corner west on A66. Approx. 7 miles on, down hill. Left to Newsham. Through village; 2nd left opp. sign on right for Helwith. House on right, name on gate. |

**Christina Farmer**
Hill Top,
Newsham,
Richmond,
Yorkshire DL11 7QX
Tel +44 (0)1833 621513
Email plow67@btinternet.com

Entry 609   Map 12

## Cliffe Hall

What remains is the Victorian section of an earlier mansion, added by Richard's family in 1858. Inside is a beautifully proportioned and charming family home: huge reception rooms, plasterwork ceilings, acres of sofas, family portraits, floor to ceiling shelves of books. Bedrooms are sunny, traditional and uncontrived, bathrooms carpeted and twin beds super-comfy; large windows look onto the glorious grounds (anyone for tennis?) and a croquet lawn that runs down to the Tees where you fish for trout. Soft, timeless grandeur, visiting thesps, a sweet dog and a hostess who is as special as her house.

Ethical Collection: Food. See page 412.

 Travel Club offer. See page 414.

| | |
|---|---|
| Price | £80. Singles £40. |
| Rooms | 2 twins/doubles, each with separate bath. |
| Meals | Pub 1 mile. |
| Closed | Rarely. |
| Directions | From A1, exit onto B6275. North for 4.2 miles. Into drive (on left before Piercebridge); 1st right fork. |

**Caroline & Richard Wilson**
Cliffe Hall,
Piercebridge,
Darlington, Yorkshire DL2 3SR
Tel +44 (0)1325 374322
Fax +44 (0)1325 374947
Email petal@cliffehall.co.uk

Entry 610   Map 12

Scotland

## Aberdeenshire

### Woodend House

Elegant riverside living at a fishing lodge by the river Dee – one of the most magnificent settings in Scotland. Outside, a wild, wonderful garden; inside, beautiful wallpapers, fabrics and rugs. The dining hall leads to the kitchen with an Aga, the drawing room has dreamy river views, the large bedrooms ooze comfort and more fabulous views, and the bathrooms have old cast-iron baths and fine toiletries. Breakfast and dinner are local, seasonal and first-class. All this, and a fishing hut and a secure rod room for salmon and sea trout fishing in season. *Minimum stay two nights.*

 Travel Club offer. See page 414.

| | |
|---|---|
| Price | £100. Singles £75. |
| Rooms | 3: 1 double, 1 twin; 1 twin with separate bath. |
| Meals | Dinner, 4 courses, £30. Packed lunch £5–£10. Pub 2 miles. |
| Closed | Christmas, New Year & occasionally. |
| Directions | 4 miles west of Banchory on A93. Entrance to drive on south side of road. |

**Miranda & Julian McHardy**
Woodend House,
Trustach, Banchory,
Aberdeenshire AB31 4AY
Tel       +44 (0)1330 822367
Email   miranda.mchardy@woodend.org
Web     www.woodend.org

Entry 611  Map 19

## Aberdeenshire

### Lys-na-Greyne House

Peace, tranquillity and a natural welcome – one of the loveliest places in this book. Expect a sweeping stair, sun-streamed rooms, log fires and the most comfortable beds in Scotland. Your room may be huge – two are; one with a dressing room and a balcony, all with family antiques, bathrobes, fine linen… and views of river, field, forest and hill where osprey and lapwing glide. Meg picks flowers and organic vegetables from the garden and her food is delicious; David is an enthusiastic naturalist and can advise on walking and wildlife. Nearby, golf, fishing and castles by the hatful.

Ethical Collection: Community. See page 412.

Travel Club offer. See page 414.

| | |
|---|---|
| Price | £90. Singles from £45. |
| Rooms | 3: 1 twin/double; 2 twins/doubles with separate bath/shower. Extra shower available. |
| Meals | Supper £25. Pub/bistro 15-minute walk. |
| Closed | Rarely. |
| Directions | From Aboyne, A93 west for Braemar. Just before 30mph sign, left down Rhu-na-Haven Rd. House 400 yds on, 4th gateway on right. |

**David & Meg White**
Lys-na-Greyne House,
Rhu-na-Haven Road, Aboyne,
Aberdeenshire AB34 5JD
Tel       +44 (0)1339 887397
Fax      +44 (0)1339 886441
Email   meg.white@virgin.net

Entry 612  Map 19

## Aberdeenshire

### Lynturk Home Farm

The stunning drawing room, with pier-glass mirror, ancestral portraits and enveloping sofas, is reason enough to come, while the food, served in a candlelit, deep-sage dining room, is delicious, with produce from the farm. You're treated very much as friends here and your hosts are delightful. It's peaceful, too, on the Aberdeenshire Castle Trail. The handsome farmhouse has been in the family since 1762 and you can roam the surrounding 300 acres of rolling hills. Inside, good fabrics and paints, hunting prints and some lovely family pieces. "A blissful haven," says a reader. *Fishing, shooting & golf breaks.*

 Travel Club offer. See page 414.

| | |
|---|---|
| Price | From £80. Singles £50. |
| Rooms | 3: 2 twins/doubles; 1 double with separate bath. |
| Meals | Dinner, 4 courses, £25. Pub 1 mile. |
| Closed | Rarely. |
| Directions | 20 miles from Aberdeen on A944 (towards Alford); through Tillyfourie, then left for Muir of Fowlis & Tough; after Tough, 2nd farm drive on left, signed. |

John & Veronica Evans-Freke
Lynturk Home Farm,
Alford,
Aberdeenshire AB33 8DU
Tel       +44 (0)1975 562504
Fax      +44 (0)1975 563517
Email   lynturk@hotmail.com

Entry 613    Map 19

## Aberdeenshire

### Ford of Clatt

A perfect, and peaceful, retreat for writers, artists and anybody wishing to hide away. Lucy and her family have a lovely, 19th-century former drovers' inn with an atmosphere of quiet serenity, tucked in below the Correen hills. Your bedroom is a warm, comfortable sanctuary with family photos, a spotted teapot, books and fresh flowers on antique tables; chill out on a striped sofa stool, watch the view from the cane chairs by the window or loll in a roll top with L'Occitane soaps. Breakfast is hearty, perfect for walkers, and there are interesting megalithic standing stones; Lucy, a qualified Swedish masseuse, offers massage to yomp-weary limbs.

| | |
|---|---|
| Price | £70. Singles £45. |
| Rooms | 1 twin/double. |
| Meals | Packed lunch on request. Pub/restaurants within 2 miles. |
| Closed | Rarely. |
| Directions | From Aberdeen A96. 7 miles after Invervrie left at Oyne fork. After Oyne, left to Clatt. After Leslie T-junc., house on corner on right; turn into courtyard. |

Lucy Aykroyd
Ford of Clatt,
Clatt,
Huntly, Aberdeenshire AB54 4PJ
Tel       +44 (0)1464 831115
Email   me@lucyaykroyd.co.uk
Web     www.fordofclatt.co.uk

Entry 614    Map 19

## Aberdeenshire

### Old Mayen

Follow narrow lanes crowded by beech trees and hedges, through high rolling hills and fast flowing rivers to this beautiful house perched next to a farm and overlooking the unspoilt valley below. You get classic country-house style in elegant bedrooms, spoiling bathrooms, a book-filled sitting room, cut flowers and a delicious candlelit dinner by a roaring fire. Fran and Jim are infectiously enthusiastic and kind; breakfasts are a moveable feast (outside in good weather) and the garden hums with birds. A fine retreat for tired and jaded souls – and there are castles, distilleries and gardens to visit.

Travel Club offer. See page 414.

| | |
|---|---|
| Price | £90. Singles £50. |
| Rooms | 2: 1 double; 1 double with separate shower. |
| Meals | Dinner £25. Supper £18. Packed lunch £8. |
| Closed | Rarely. |
| Directions | From A96, A97 to Banff. After crossing river Deveron (9 miles), left onto B9117; 3 miles, on left behind thick beech hedge. |

James & Fran Anderson
Old Mayen,
Rothiemay,
Huntly,
Aberdeenshire AB54 7NL
Tel    +44 (0)1466 711276
Fax    +44 (0)1466 711276
Email  oldmayen@tiscali.co.uk

Entry 615   Map 19

## Aberdeenshire

### Balwarren Croft

Thirty acres at the end of a farm track, a field of Highland cattle, mixed woodland, ancient dykes, a lochside full of birdlife, a herb garden with over 200 varieties and a burn you may follow down the hill. Hazel and James, warm, friendly, quietly passionate about green issues, came to croft 25 years ago and the whole place is a delight: cathedral roof, shiny wooden floors, cashmere blankets, sparkling bathrooms, log fires, delicious breakfasts (home eggs, jams and chutneys) and dinners are a treat. A beautiful, uplifting and peaceful place in glorious countryside. *Dry stone walling and herb courses.*

Travel Club offer. See page 414.

| | |
|---|---|
| Price | £70-£78. Singles £45-£50. |
| Rooms | 2: 1 twin, 1 double. |
| Meals | Dinner, 3 courses, £25. Pub/restaurant 10 miles. |
| Closed | Rarely. |
| Directions | North from Aberchirder on B9023. Right at Lootcherbrae (still B9023); 2nd left for Ordiquhill. After 1.7 miles, right at farm track opp. Aulton Farm; last croft up track. |

Hazel & James Watt
Balwarren Croft,
Ordiquhill, Banff,
Aberdeenshire AB45 2HR
Tel    +44 (0)1466 751688
Fax    +44 (0)1466 751688
Email  balwarren@tiscali.co.uk
Web    www.balwarren.com

Entry 616   Map 19

## Angus

### Newtonmill House

The house and grounds are in apple-pie order; the owners are charming and unobtrusive. This is a little-known part of Scotland, so explore the glens, discover deserted beaches and traditional fishing villages, and play a round or two of golf on one of the many good courses nearby. Return to a cup of tea in an elegant sitting room, then a proper supper of seasonal, local and home-grown produce. Upstairs are crisp sheets, soft blankets, feather pillows, fresh flowers, homemade fruit cake and sparkling, warm bathrooms with thick towels; you are beautifully looked after here.

 Travel Club offer. See page 414.

| | |
|---|---|
| Price | £96–£110. Singles from £60. |
| Rooms | 2: 1 twin; 1 double with separate bath. |
| Meals | Dinner, 4 courses, from £30. Supper, 2 courses, from £20. BYO. Packed lunch £10. Pub 3 miles. |
| Closed | Christmas. |
| Directions | Aberdeen–Dundee A90, turning marked Brechin/Edzell B966. Heading for Edzell, Newtonmill House is 1 mile on left, drive marked by pillars and sign. |

**Rose & Stephen Rickman**
Newtonmill House,
Brechin,
Angus DD9 7PZ

| | |
|---|---|
| Tel | +44 (0)1356 622533 |
| Email | rrickman@srickman.co.uk |
| Web | www.newtonmillhouse.co.uk |

✕ 🐾 📶 🐈

Entry 617   Map 19

---

## Angus

### Ethie Castle

Amazing. A listed Pele tower that dates to 1300 and which once was home to the Abbot of Arbroath, murdered in St Andrews on Henry VIII's orders. His private chapel remains, as does his secret stair. As for the rest of the house: turret staircases, beautiful bedrooms, a 1500s ceiling in the Great Hall, a Tudor kitchen with a walk-in fireplace that burns night and day. Kirstin has breathed new life into the house; the garden is now complete -- and something of a show-stopper. Lunan Bay, one of Scotland's most glorious beaches, is at the end of the road. There's a loch too.

| | |
|---|---|
| Price | From £95. Singles from £75. |
| Rooms | 3: 1 four-poster; 1 twin/double, 1 double, each with separate bath/shower. |
| Meals | Dinner, 4 courses with wine, £30. Packed lunch up to £10. Pub/restaurant 3 miles. |
| Closed | Rarely. |
| Directions | North from Arbroath on A92; right after Shell garage for Auchmithie; left at T-junc.; on for 2 miles; at phone box, private road to Ethie Barns in front. |

**Kirstin de Morgan**
Ethie Castle,
Inverkeilor, Arbroath,
Angus DD11 5SP

| | |
|---|---|
| Tel | +44 (0)1241 830434 |
| Fax | +44 (0)1241 830432 |
| Email | kmydemorgan@aol.com |
| Web | www.ethiecastle.com |

🍴 ✕ 🚂 🐾 🐈 ♨

Entry 618   Map 16+19

## Argyll & Bute

### Sithe Mor House

Terrific views from this lovely house on the shores of Loch Awe; its own bay and jetty below, acres of sky above and a winning pair at the helm. Patsy ensures all runs smoothly and John, a former oarsman of repute and the first man to row each way across Scotland, sweeps you along with joie de vivre. With ornate plasterwork, antlers and oils, lofty domed ceilings in the bedrooms and loch views, this 1880s house combines a baronial feel with massive luxury in bathrooms, beds and fabrics. Stay for home-grown and local dinners, borrow a kilt, marvel at the Oxford and Cambridge boat race memorabilia. *Minimum stay two nights.*

| | |
|---|---|
| Price | £110. Singles £60-£75. |
| Rooms | 2: 1 double, 1 twin/double. |
| Meals | Dinner, 4 courses, £35. Supper £25. Restaurants & pub 0.5-3 miles. |
| Closed | Rarely. |
| Directions | A82 from Glasgow; A85 from Tyndrum. At Taynuilt, left onto B845 to Kilchrenan village. After 1 mile, single track 'No Through Road' to Taychreggan. House is last on left. |

**Patsy & John Cugley**
Sithe Mor House,
Kilchrenan,
Loch Awe, Argyll & Bute PA35 1HF

| | |
|---|---|
| Tel | +44 (0)1866 833234 |
| Email | patsycugley@tiscali.co.uk |
| Web | www.sithemor.com |

Entry 619   Map 17

## Argyll & Bute

### Dun Na Mara

Twenty paces from the door, past the standing stone, a sweep of private beach and dazzling views to Mull. The Arts & Crafts house has been given a minimalist makeover by Mark and Suzanne — ex-architects and friendly, caring, interesting hosts. The result is a spotless, luminous interior of sumptuous beds, quilted throws, cream bucket chairs, sensual bathrooms, colourful cushions and sea views from three bedrooms. Breakfast on porridge with toasted almonds and honey, kedgeree, devilled kidneys, the full Scottish works; end the day with sherry in the little sitting room, DVDs, beautiful art and books. *Children over 12 welcome.*

| | |
|---|---|
| Price | £90-£115. Singles £50-£70. |
| Rooms | 7: 5 doubles, 2 singles. |
| Meals | Pubs 3 miles. |
| Closed | Christmas & New Year. |
| Directions | North from Oban on A828; over Connel Bridge; north for two miles; house signed left just after lay-by, before Benderloch village. |

**Mark McPhillips & Suzanne Pole**
Dun Na Mara,
Benderloch, Oban,
Argyll & Bute PA37 1RT

| | |
|---|---|
| Tel | +44 (0)1631 720233 |
| Email | stay@dunnamara.com |
| Web | www.dunnamara.com |

Entry 620   Map 17

## Argyll & Bute

### Barndromin Farm

Jamie and Morag run a cheerful, busy farmhouse that opens its arms to guests; hens cluck around the farmyard and Jamie will happily share his knowledge of butterflies, wild flowers and mushrooms. Bedrooms are carpeted and comfy with flowery duvets and Morag's art. There are places to flop in the elegant drawing room and a polished table for breakfast – tuck into croissants, bacon, sausages, black pudding, farm eggs. Set on the hillside with spectacular views over Loch Feochan, you can fish, walk, ride, spot grouse, otters, deer, red squirrels and rare butterflies. Gorgeous. *Children over ten welcome. Minimum stay two nights at weekends.*

| | |
|---|---|
| Price | £70-£80. Singles £40-£50. |
| Rooms | 2: 1 twin; 1 double with separate bath. |
| Meals | Pub/restaurant 4-6 miles. |
| Closed | December-February. |
| Directions | 6 miles south of Oban on A816 to Lochgilphead. Take 2nd entrance on left 200 yds after Knipoch Hotel. |

Jamie & Morag Mellor
Barndromin Farm,
Knipoch,
Oban, Argyll PA34 4QS

| | |
|---|---|
| Tel | +44 (0)1852 316297 |
| Email | mogsmellor@hotmail.co.uk |
| Web | www.knipochbedandbreakfast.com |

Entry 621   Map 17

## Argyll & Bute

### Glenmore

A pleasing buzz of family life and no need to stand on ceremony. The house was built in 1854 but it's the later 30s additions that set the style: carved doorways, red-pine panelling, Art Deco pieces, oak floors, elaborate cornicing and a curvy stone fireplace. Alasdair's family has been here for 140 years and much family furniture remains. One of the huge doubles is arranged as a suite with a single room and a sofabed; bath and basins are chunky 30s style with chrome plumbing. From the organic garden and the house there are magnificent views of Loch Melfort with its bobbing boats; you're free to come and go as you please.

| | |
|---|---|
| Price | £70-£90. Singles £40-£50. |
| Rooms | 2: 1 family suite; 1 double with separate bath/shower. |
| Meals | Pub 0.5 miles, restaurant 1.5 miles. |
| Closed | December & January. |
| Directions | From A816 0.5 miles south of Kilmelford; a private tree-lined avenue leads to Glenmore. House signed from both directions. Go past Lodge House at bottom of drive; follow drive for 0.25 miles to big house. |

Melissa & Alasdair Oatts
Glenmore,
Kilmelford, Oban,
Argyll & Bute PA34 4XA

| | |
|---|---|
| Tel | +44 (0)1852 200314 |
| Email | oatts@glenmore22.fsnet.co.uk |
| Web | www.glenmorecountryhouse.co.uk |

Entry 622   Map 17

## Argyll & Bute

## Melfort House

Enter a wild landscape of hidden glens, ancient oak woods and rivers that tumble to a blue sea. Find a Georgian-style, beautifully renovated house with views straight down the loch, exquisite furniture, designer fabrics, oak flooring and original paintings and prints. Bedrooms are sumptuous, with upholstered beds in soft plaids and superb views (especially the Loch suite with its toile de Jouy bathroom), warmth and comfort. Yvonne and Matthew (who cooks) are brilliant at looking after you; breakfast on fresh fruit, Stornoway black pudding, tattie scones fresh from the Aga – even chilli omelettes! Argyll at its finest.

| Price | £95-£115. Singles from £65. £15 for sofabed. |
|---|---|
| Rooms | 3: 1 double, 2 twins/doubles. |
| Meals | Dinner, 3 courses, from £28. Packed lunch £7. Pub/restaurant 400 yds. |
| Closed | Rarely. |
| Directions | From Oban A816 south, signed Campbeltown. After 14 miles, go through Kilmelford, then right to Melfort. Follow road & bear right after bridge. |

Yvonne & Matthew Anderson
Melfort House,
Kilmelford,
Oban, Argyll & Bute PA34 4XD

| Tel | +44 (0)1852 200326 |
|---|---|
| Email | relax@melforthouse.co.uk |
| Web | www.melforthouse.co.uk |

## Argyll & Bute

## Corranmor House

A radiant setting on the Ardfern peninsula. Barbara and Hew are as generous and committed to their guests as they are to the 400-acre farm, where they rear sheep and geese. The drawing room started life as a 16th-century bothy (you'd never guess!), the red dining room sparkles with silver, they enjoy dining with guests and the food is delicious: goose, mutton, lamb, or fish from local landings. Bedrooms are exceptionally private – the double across the courtyard, the suite with the log-fired sitting room. Wander and admire; the eye always comes to rest on the water and boats of Loch Craignish and the Sound of Jura.

| Price | £80. Suite £80-£135. Singles £45. |
|---|---|
| Rooms | 2: 1 double & sitting room; 1 family suite & sitting room. |
| Meals | Lunch £15. Dinner, 3 courses and cheese, £30; with lobster £45. Pubs/restaurants 0.75 miles. |
| Closed | 1 December-3 January; 4th week of August. |
| Directions | From A816, B8002 to Ardfern, & through village; 0.75 miles past church, long white house high on right. Right by Heron's Cottage, up drive. |

Hew & Barbara Service
Corranmor House,
Ardfern, Lochgilphead,
Argyll & Bute PA31 8QN

| Tel | +44 (0)1852 500609 |
|---|---|
| Fax | +44 (0)1852 500609 |
| Email | corranmorhouse@aol.com |

# Argyll & Bute

## Achamore House

No traffic jams here, tucked between the mainland and Islay. Despite its grandeur – turrets, Arts & Crafts doors, plasterwork ceilings – Achamore is not stuffy and neither is Don, your American host. A coastal skipper, he can take you to sea, or over to other islands in his diesel catamaran. Find warm wood panelling and light-washed rooms, huge bedrooms with shuttered windows, oversize beds, heavy antiques; all have iPods and music. You get the run of the house – billiard room, library, large lounge, TV room (great for kids). With 50 acres of gardens and a quiet beach it's ideal for big parties or gatherings.

| | |
|---|---|
| Price | £90–£130. Singles from £35. |
| Rooms | 9: 2 doubles, 1 family room; |
| | 2 doubles sharing bath; |
| | 2 twins/doubles sharing bath; |
| | 2 singles sharing bath. |
| Meals | Pub/restaurant 1 mile. |
| Closed | Rarely. |
| Directions | Uphill from ferry landing, turn left at T-junc.; 1 mile, stone gates on right, signed; house at top of drive. |

**Don Dennis & Emma Rennie**
Achamore House,
Isle of Gigha, Argyll & Bute PA41 7AD
Tel +44 (0)1583 505400
Fax +44 (0)1583 505 387
Email gigha@atlas.co.uk
Web www.achamorehouse.com

Entry 625   Map 14

# Ayrshire

## Langside Farm

Your hosts are intelligent, humorous and striving to be squeaky green in their family home: local (much organic) produce promises fine breakfasts and suppers; water comes from a private spring and you are kept cosy by a biomass woodchip boiler. Inside, a well-proportioned Georgian elegance – the main part dates back to 1745 – fresh contemporary artwork (some Elise's) and a snug kitchen. Deep red sofas, pale striped walls, books and lamps draw you in; pretty bedrooms have a period feel and long views. There's good walking and golf nearby. Chat in the kitchen, sit by the fire, make yourselves truly at home.

Ethical Collection: Environment; Community; Food. See page 412.

Travel Club offer. See page 414.

| | |
|---|---|
| Price | £79. Singles from £49.50. |
| Rooms | 2: 1 twin, 1 four-poster. |
| Meals | Packed lunch £5.50. Supper £15. Dinner £24.50. BYO. |
| Closed | January, February & November. |
| Directions | Langside Farm 0.7 miles from Dalry end of B784. B784 links B780 Dalry-Kilbirnie road to A760 Kilbirnie-Largs road. Train to Dalry or Glengarnock. |

**Nick & Elise Quick**
Langside Farm,
Dalry, Ayrshire KA24 5JZ
Tel +44 (0)1294 834402
Fax +44 (0)8700 569380
Email mail@langsidefarm.co.uk
Web www.langsidefarm.co.uk

Entry 626   Map 14

## Ayrshire

### The Carriage House

An avenue of limes, 250 acres of parkland, rhododendrons, wellingtonia – what a view to wake to! Luke's family have owned the estate and castle for 900 years. Their stylishly converted Carriage House, with its ochre walls, cobbled courtyard and delightful drawing room, is full of light and comfortable good taste; polished floors, handsome antiques, family photographs, contemporary fabrics. Aga-cooked breakfasts are taken in a huge kitchen with views of pottering hens. Tennis court, swimming pool, country walks: this is an elegant place to unwind. The Borwicks are confident and keen hosts.

| | |
|---|---|
| Price | £90. Singles £55. |
| Rooms | 3: 1 double, 1 twin/double, 1 twin. |
| Meals | Pubs/restaurants 3-7 miles. |
| Closed | Rarely. |
| Directions | From Beith enter Dalry on A737. First left (signed Bridgend Industrial Estate); uphill through houses, past farm on right at top of hill. First right into Blair Estate. |

| | |
|---|---|
| | Luke & Caroline Borwick |
| | The Carriage House, |
| | Blair, Dalry, Ayrshire KA24 4ER |
| Tel | +44 (0)1294 833100 |
| Fax | +44 (0)1294 834422 |
| Email | office@blairtrust.co.uk |
| Web | www.blairestate.com |

Entry 627   Map 14

## Ayrshire

### Heughmill

Five acres of fields and lawn with free-range hens that kindly donate for breakfast and views to the sea. The house is just as good, surrounded by old stone farm buildings, with climbing roses and a small burn tumbling through. Inside, a lovely country home with tapestries in an airy hall, an open fire in the sitting room and a terrace that sits under a vast sky. Country-house bedrooms are stylishly homely. Two have the view, one has an old armoire, another comes with a claw-foot bath; all have delightful art. Julia sculpts, Mungo cooks breakfast on the Aga. Rural Ayrshire waits, yet you are close to the airport.

| | |
|---|---|
| Price | £65-£80. Singles on request. |
| Rooms | 3: 2 twins/doubles, 1 twin. |
| Meals | Pubs/restaurants within 2 miles. |
| Closed | Christmas & New Year. |
| Directions | 3 miles south of Kilmarnock, turn east down B730 for Tarbolton. After 0.75 miles, right onto narrow road signed Ladykirk. House is 250 yds on right. |

| | |
|---|---|
| | Mungo & Julia Tulloch |
| | Heughmill, |
| | Craigie, |
| | Kilmarnock, |
| | Ayrshire KA1 5NQ |
| Tel | +44 (0)1563 860389 |
| Web | www.stayprestwick.com |

Entry 628   Map 14

# Clackmannanshire

## Kennels Cottage

Live the dream: tour Scotland by classic car. Sandy does Triumphs, Austin Healeys, convertible Beetles. Tanya spoils you, with big crisp beds, huge white towels, elegant blinds, orchids and oriental touches. The old gamekeeper's cottage is a stunningly fresh, stylish and immaculate place, all white walls, white sofas, books, paintings and the odd flash of gold. In the morning, feast on local bacon, Fair Trade coffees and eggs from their hens served at one convivial table. Take a picnic to the garden, wander through what was the Dollarbeg estate, replete with pheasant and deer... totally unwind.

# Dumfries & Galloway

## Knockhill

Fabulous Knockhill: stunning place, stunning position, a country house full of busts and screens, oils and mirrors, chests and clocks, rugs and fires. In the intimate drawing room, full of treasures, floor-to-ceiling windows look down the wooded hill. Fine stone stairs lead to country-house bedrooms that are smart yet homely: headboards of carved oak or padded chintz, books and views. Come for a grand farming feel and delicious Scottish meals; the Morgans are the most unpretentious and charming of hosts. Mellow, authentic, welcoming – an enduring favourite.

Travel Club offer. See page 414.

| | |
|---|---|
| Price | £70-£80. Singles £60. |
| Rooms | 3 doubles. |
| Meals | Packed lunch £10. Pub 2 miles. |
| Closed | December & January. |
| Directions | From Dollar take B913 towards Blairingone. House 2 miles from Dollar just before Blairingone. |

| | |
|---|---|
| Price | £80-£84. Singles £54. |
| Rooms | 2: 1 twin; 1 twin with separate bath. |
| Meals | Dinner £26. Pub 5 miles. |
| Closed | Rarely. |
| Directions | From M74 junc. 19, B725 for Dalton. Right by church in Ecclefechan, signed Hoddam Castle. After 1.2 miles right at x-roads towards Lockerbie. 1 mile on, right at stone [not whitewashed] lodge cottage. At top of long drive. |

**Tanya Worsfold & Sandy Stewart**
Kennels Cottage,
Dollarbeg, Dollar,
Clackmannanshire FK14 7PA
Tel   +44 (0)1259 742186
Fax   +44 (0)1259 743716
Email   tanya.worsfold@btinternet.com
Web   www.guesthousescotland.co.uk

**Yda & Rupert Morgan**
Knockhill,
Lockerbie,
Dumfries & Galloway DG11 1AW
Tel   +44 (0)1576 300232
Email   morganbellows@yahoo.co.uk

Entry 629   Map 15

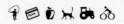

Entry 630   Map 15

## Dumfries & Galloway

### Applegarth House

Here is an old peaceful manse at the top of the hill, right next door to the church, with a 12th-century motte; the views from the pretty garden stretch for miles around. The house is a good size, with original pine floors and sweeping stairs. Off the large and light landing are three bedrooms with warm carpets, shuttered windows and glorious garden and country views. Let the tawny owls lull you to sleep then wake to freshly stewed fruits and excellent porridge. There are paths to wander through the flower beds, statues to admire and endless wildlife; a perfect stop off point for a trip north or south.

Travel Club offer. See page 414.

| | |
|---|---|
| Price | £84–£88. Singles from £54. |
| Rooms | 3: 2 twins; 1 double with separate bath. |
| Meals | Supper, 2 courses, £20. BYO. Hotel restaurant 1.5 miles. |
| Closed | Rarely. |
| Directions | M74 junc. 17 to Lockerbie, B7076 for Johnstonebridge. 1st right after 1.5 miles; after 100 yds left over m'way bridge. After 1 mile, right at T-junc., then 2nd left to church. Next to church. |

| | |
|---|---|
| | Frank & Jane Pearson |
| | Applegarth House, |
| | Lockerbie, |
| | Dumfries & Galloway DG11 1SX |
| Tel | +44 (0)1387 810270 |
| Fax | +44 (0)1387 811701 |
| Email | jane@applegarthtown.demon.co.uk |

Entry 631  Map 15

## Dumfries & Galloway

### Chipperkyle

Sink into the sofas without worrying about creasing them; this beautiful Scottish-Georgian family home has not a hint of formality, and the sociable Dicksons put you at your ease. Sitting and dining rooms connect through a large arch; there are family pictures, rugs on wooden floors and a log fire. Upstairs: a cast-iron bed dressed in good linen, striped walls, flowered curtains, lots of books and windows with views – this wonderful house just gets better and better. There are 200 acres, dogs, cats, donkeys and hens, and you can walk, play golf, visit gardens, sail or cycle – in magnificent countryside.

| | |
|---|---|
| Price | £94. |
| Rooms | 2: 1 double; 1 twin with separate bath/shower. Cot available. |
| Meals | Dinner available for groups. Pub 3 miles. |
| Closed | Christmas. |
| Directions | A75 Dumfries ring road for Stranraer. Approx. 12 miles to Springholm & right to Kirkpatrick Durham. Left at x-roads, after 0.8 miles, up drive on right by white lodge. |

| | |
|---|---|
| | Willie & Catriona Dickson |
| | Chipperkyle, |
| | Kirkpatrick Durham, Castle Douglas, |
| | Dumfries & Galloway DG7 3EY |
| Tel | +44 (0)1556 650223 |
| Email | special_place@chipperkyle.co.uk |
| Web | www.chipperkyle.co.uk |

Entry 632  Map 11

# Dumfries & Galloway

## Kirnaughtry House

With two dining rooms and a growing foodie reputation, it's no wonder the heart of this old church manse is the kitchen. Here Lynn serves a cheery breakfast and creates Slow food dinners with veg from the kitchen garden and fish from the Irish sea. Indulge around a French oak table in the plush main dining room, or in a smaller space with crystal chandelier and log fire (where canapés are served). Retire to the elegant sitting room and snooze to the sound of trees rustling in the wind. The house brims with wonderful details (handmade soap, a decanter of sherry, Persian rugs) but the abiding memory is your hosts' genuine warmth. Delightful.

| | |
|---|---|
| Price | £90–£100. Singles £65. |
| Rooms | 3: 2 doubles; |
| | 1 double with separate bath. |
| Meals | Dinner, 5 courses, £30. |
| | Pub/restaurant 3 miles. |
| Closed | Christmas & New Year. |
| Directions | 20 minutes south of Stranraer on the scenic route to the Mull of Galloway. Take A716 south of Stranraer. At Ardwell turn right. House is 1 mile on right. |

Lynn & Bob Malkin
Kirnaughtry House,
Ardwell, Stranraer,
Dumfries & Galloway DG9 9PA

| | |
|---|---|
| Tel | +44 (0)1776 860207 |
| Email | staywithbobandlynn@kirnaughtryhouse.co.uk |
| Web | www.kirnaughtryhouse.co.uk |

Entry 633   Map 14

# Dunbartonshire

## Blairbeich Plantation

Past swaying birches to a Swedish wonderland in the woods. It is a beautiful fusion of antique and modern and a mini-loch laps three feet from its walls. There are light stone floors and cathedral ceilings and delightful ground-floor bedrooms that look onto the loch – an enclave of wilderness that universities come to study. Despite all this it is the interior that knocks you flat: Malla – relaxed, friendly, a fine cook – has covered every inch with something spectacular and the sitting room is a private art gallery. Mosaic showers, orchids, woodpeckers… and curling on the loch in winter. Fabulous.

| | |
|---|---|
| Price | £80–£100. Singles from £70. |
| Rooms | 2 doubles. |
| Meals | Dinner, 4 courses, £40. |
| | Pub/restaurant 1.5 miles. |
| Closed | Rarely. |
| Directions | From west, A811 into Gartocharn; 1st right (School Road); 1.5 miles to T-junction, then left for 0.25 miles; house on right, signed. |

Malla Macdonald
Blairbeich Plantation,
Gartocharn, Loch Lomond,
Dunbartonshire G83 8RR

| | |
|---|---|
| Tel | +44 (0)1389 830257 |
| Email | macdonald@blairbeich.com |
| Web | www.blairbeich.com |

Entry 634   Map 14

## Dunbartonshire

### Finglen House

The Campsie Hills rise behind (climb them and you can see Loch Lomond), the Fin Burn takes a two-mile tumble down the hill into the garden, and herons and wagtails can be spotted from the breakfast table. All this 40 minutes from Glasgow. Sabrina's designer flair gives an easy, graceful comfort to the whole house: good beds in stylish rooms, proper linen, French touches, eclectic art, cast-iron baths and cream-painted wooden floors. A fresh, elegant drawing room with log fire is yours to share. Douglas, a documentary film maker, knows the Highlands and Islands well; he and Sabrina are fun and good company.

| | |
|---|---|
| Price | £80. Singles £50. |
| Rooms | 2: 1 double; |
| | 1 double with separate bath. |
| Meals | Pub 5-minute drive. |
| Closed | Christmas & New Year. |
| Directions | A81 from Glasgow right on A891 at Strathblane. 3 miles on, in Haughhead, look for a wall & trees on left, & turn in entrance signed Schoenstatt. Immed. left to house. |

Sabrina & Douglas Campbell
Finglen House,
Campsie Glen,
Dunbartonshire G66 7AZ
Tel +44 (0)1360 310279
Email sabrina.campbell@btinternet.com
Web www.finglenhouse.com

Entry 635 Map 15

## Edinburgh & the Lothians

### 24 Saxe Coburg Place

A ten-minute walk – or an even quicker bus ride – from the centre of Edinburgh, this 1827 house stands in a quiet, no-through road with a communal garden in the centre. There's a garden level entrance to three simple and luxurious bedrooms with extra long beds, good lighting, handsome antiques and spotless bathrooms – one with Paris metro tiling in white and green. Work up an appetite with a pretty walk along the Water of Leith, which is just behind the house; return to a delicious, generous continental breakfast which is served in the hall, or on the sunny terrace in summer. Marvellous!

| | |
|---|---|
| Price | £75–£120. Singles £40–£55. |
| Rooms | 3: 1 double, 1 twin/double, 1 single. |
| Meals | Continental breakfast. |
| | Restaurants/pubs 5-minute walk. |
| Closed | Rarely. |
| Directions | From George St, down Frederick St. Over 3 sets of lights, left at bottom of hill. Right up Clarence St; at junction, over to Saxe Coburg St. Saxe Coburg Place is at end. Ask about parking. |

Diana McMicking
24 Saxe Coburg Place,
Edinburgh EH3 5BP
Tel +44 (0)131 315 3263
Email diana@saxecoburgplace.co.uk
Web www.saxecoburgplace.co.uk

Entry 636 Map 15

## Edinburgh & the Lothians

## Edinburgh & the Lothians

### 7 Gloucester Place

A cantilevered staircase in walnut and mahogany, a soaring hand-painted cupola: the classic Georgian townhouse is five minutes from Princes Street. Rooms are cosy yet immaculate, sprinkled with paintings and decorative things from travels to far-flung places. Bedrooms are comfy, traditional and well-stocked with books and radio (and there are Z-beds for children). Bag the south-facing double with its stunning Art Deco bathroom and garden views. Naomi is pretty relaxed and happy to chat to you about the local music and art scene, or to leave you in peace. An interesting and hospitable place to unwind.

### 21 India Street

Portraits of the Macpherson clan beam down upon you at delicious breakfast served in a sunny and elegant dining room. In this house of great character you are cared for by Zandra, who offers guests the Laird's Room with its half-tester and the (smaller) Patio Room with its own front entrance. And it's just a hop and a skip up the majestic cobbled streets of New Town to Princes Street and the centre. Zandra plays the Scottish harp, loves to cook, has two beautiful black labs and has written about her life as wife of a clan chieftain – read up about it all in the spacious drawing room.

| | | | |
|---|---|---|---|
| Price | £90-£110. Singles from £50. | Price | £95-£130. Singles £60-£85. |
| Rooms | 3: 1 double; 1 double with separate bath; 1 double with separate shower. Extra child beds. | Rooms | 2: 1 double, 1 twin. |
| | | Meals | Restaurants close by. |
| | | Closed | Rarely. |
| Meals | Pubs/restaurants 300 yds. | Directions | Down South Queensferry Rd; left at Y-junc.; at 2nd Y-junc. left into Craig Leith Rd. through Stockbridge, over lights at bridge; 3rd right into Royal Circus; sharp right through Circus Gdns; left into India St. |
| Closed | Christmas & rarely. | | |
| Directions | From George St (city centre), down Hanover St, across Queen St at lights. Left into Heriot Row, right onto India St, then left. | | |

| | | | |
|---|---|---|---|
| | Naomi Jennings | | Mrs Zandra Macpherson of Glentruim |
| | 7 Gloucester Place, | | 21 India Street, |
| | Edinburgh EH3 6EE | | Edinburgh EH3 6HE |
| Tel | +44 (0)131 225 2974 | Tel | +44 (0)131 225 4353 |
| Email | naomijennings@hotmail.com | Email | zandra@twenty-one.co.uk |
| Web | www.stayinginscotland.com | Web | www.twenty-one.co.uk |

Entry 637   Map 15

Entry 638   Map 15

# Edinburgh & the Lothians

## 11 Belford Place

Guests love Susan's modern townhouse above the Water of Leith. A golden retriever wags his welcome in the wooden-floored entrance, a picture-lined staircase winds upward. Outside, New Zealand flax bursts into flower while herons and foxes share an exquisite sloping garden. Handsome rooms offer china cups and floral spreads; dazzling bathrooms have Molton Brown goodies. Taste Stornoway black pudding at the gleaming breakfast table – there are simple suppers and box lunches if you're on the trot. You hear owls at night yet you're a hop from the city, with free parking and a bus stop nearby. *Minimum stay two nights in August.*

Travel Club offer. See page 414.

| | |
|---|---|
| Price | £70–£120. |
| Rooms | 3: 1 double, 2 twins/doubles. |
| Meals | Supper £10. Packed lunch £10. Pub 200 yds. Restaurants 10-minute walk. |
| Closed | Christmas. |
| Directions | From city centre go to Belford Road; Belford Place is 1st left after Travelodge Hotel. House is down hill opposite Edinburgh Sports Club. Free parking. No 13 bus goes past top of lane. |

Lady Susan Kinross
11 Belford Place,
Edinburgh EH4 3DH
Tel +44 (0)131 332 9704
Email suekinross@blueyonder.co.uk
Web www.edinburghcitybandb.com

Entry 639   Map 15

# Edinburgh & the Lothians

## 12 Belford Terrace

Leafy trees, a secluded garden, a stone wall and, beyond, a quiet riverside stroll. Right on the doorstep of the Modern Art and Dean galleries with Edinburgh's theatres and restaurants just a 15-minute walk, this Victorian end terrace, beside Leith Water, oozes an easy-going elegance, helped by Carolyn's laid-back but competent manner. Garden level bedrooms have their own entrance and are big and creamy with stripy fabrics, antiques, sofas and huge windows. (The single has a *Boys Own* charm.) Carolyn spoils with crisp linen, books and biscuits and a delicious, full-works breakfast. After a day in town, relax on the sunny terrace.

Travel Club offer. See page 414.

| | |
|---|---|
| Price | £70–£100. Singles from £40. |
| Rooms | 3: 1 double, 1 twin/double; 1 single with separate shower. |
| Meals | Pub/restaurants 10-minute walk. |
| Closed | Christmas. |
| Directions | From Palmerston Place through 2 sets of lights, downhill on Belford Rd past Travelodge. Immediately left is Belford Terrace. Limited free parking, 2-minute drive. |

Carolyn Crabbie
12 Belford Terrace,
Edinburgh EH4 3DQ
Tel +44 (0)131 332 2413
Fax +44 (0)131 332 0224
Email carolyncrabbie@blueyonder.co.uk

Entry 640   Map 15

## Edinburgh & the Lothians

### Wallace's Arthouse Scotland

The apartment door swings open to a world of white walls, smooth floors, modern art, acoustic jazz, and smiling Wallace with a glass of wine – well worth the three-storey climb up this old Assembly Rooms building. Wallace – New York fashion designer and arts enthusiast, Glasgow-born, not shy – has created a bright, minimalist space sprinkled with humour and casual sophistication. Bedrooms capture light and exude his inimitable style; the kitchen's narrow bar is perfect for a light breakfast. Leith is Edinburgh's earthy side with its docks and noisy street life, but fine restaurants abound and the centre is close. Memorable.

## Edinburgh & the Lothians

### 2 Fingal Place

An elegant house on a Georgian terrace. The leafy park lies opposite (look upwards to Arthur's Seat). Bustling theatres, shops and the university are a stroll away, yet this is a very quiet house. Your hostess is sometimes away so you may be looked after by a housekeeper, but when at home Gillian can help plan your trips – or cater for celebrations and graduations with lunch and dinner; it's entirely flexible. Downstairs at garden level, the bedrooms have mahogany antique beds, floral curtains and bathrooms with good towels. Noodle the Llasa Apso and Gillian's cat will welcome you. *Parking metered until 5.30pm weekdays.*

Travel Club offer. See page 414.

| | | | |
|---|---|---|---|
| Price | £85-£95. Singles £65-£70. | Price | £80-£115 (£90-£130 during Festival). Singles from £55 (from £65 during Festival). |
| Rooms | 2 doubles. | | |
| Meals | Pubs/restaurants 10 yds. | Rooms | 2: 1 twin (with single room attached), 1 twin. |
| Closed | December. | | |
| Directions | From Princes Street, follow Leith Walk to the foot & left along Gt. Junction St. 1st right along Henderson St to Water of Leith traffic lights. Turn right along Bernard St; at next traffic lights right into Constitution St. | Meals | Pubs/restaurants 100 yds. |
| | | Closed | 22-27 December. |
| | | Directions | From centre, Lothian Rd to Tollcross (clock) & Melville Drive. At 2nd major lights, right into Argyle Place; immed. left into Fingal Place. Metered parking until 5.30pm weekdays, free at weekends. |

|  | | | |
|---|---|---|---|
| | Wallace Shaw | | Gillian Charlton-Meyrick |
| | Wallace's Arthouse Scotland, | | 2 Fingal Place, |
| | 41-4 Constitution Street, | | The Meadows, |
| | Edinburgh EH6 7BG | | Edinburgh EH9 1JX |
| Tel | +44 (0)131 538 3320 | Tel | +44 (0)131 667 4436 |
| Email | cawallaceshaw@mac.com | Email | gcmeyrick@fireflyuk.net |
| Web | www.wallacesarthousescotland.com | | |

Entry 641   Map 15

Entry 642   Map 15

### 20 Blackford Road

A 20-minute stroll from the Royal Mile is a substantial Victorian house with relaxed hosts and a touch of old-world luxury. From a cushioned window seat you gaze onto a lovely wildlife-filled walled garden where you can eat out on a warm day; breakfasts, though not cooked, are superb. Bedrooms, one up, one down, are tranquil and serene, with delicately papered walls and lush toile de Jouy; the drawing room, with cream sofas, soft lights, drinks tray and beautiful books, is elegant yet cosy. Lucas the rescue greyhound completes the picture – of a happy, charming place to stay. *Minimum stay two nights in August.*

### 1 Albert Terrace

A warm-hearted home with a lovely garden, an American hostess and two gorgeous Siamese cats. You are 20 minutes by bus from Princes Street yet the guests' sitting room overlooks pear trees and clematis and the rolling Pentland Hills. Cosy up in the winter next to a log fire; in summer, take your morning paper onto the terrace above the sunny garden. Books, fresh flowers, interesting art and ceramics and – you are on an old, quiet street – utter, surprising peace. Bedrooms are colourful, spacious and bright, one with an Art Deco bathroom and views over the garden. Clarissa is arty, easy, generous and loves having guests.

| | |
|---|---|
| Price | £70–£100. Singles from £60. |
| Rooms | 2: 1 twin/double, 1 twin, each with separate bath. |
| Meals | Restaurants 500 yds. |
| Closed | Christmas & New Year. |
| Directions | A720 city bypass, Lothianburn exit to city centre. On for 2.5 miles on Morningside Rd; right into Newbattle Terrace; 2nd left into Whitehouse Loan. Immed. right into Blackford Rd. House at end on left. |

| | |
|---|---|
| Price | £75–£90. Singles £50. |
| Rooms | 3: 1 double; 1 double, 1 single sharing bath. |
| Meals | Pubs/restaurants nearby. |
| Closed | Rarely. |
| Directions | From centre of Edinburgh, A702 south, for Peebles. Pass Churchill Theatre (on left), to lights. Albert Terrace 1st right after theatre. Metered parking on street, but non-metered area nearby. |

| | |
|---|---|
| | **John & Tricia Wood** |
| | 20 Blackford Road, Edinburgh EH9 2DS |
| Tel | +44 (0)131 447 4233 |
| Email | enquiries@grangebandb.co.uk |
| Web | www.grangebandb.co.uk |

| | |
|---|---|
| | **Clarissa Notley** |
| | 1 Albert Terrace, Edinburgh EH10 5EA |
| Tel | +44 (0)131 447 4491 |
| Email | canotley@aol.com |

Entry 643   Map 15

Entry 644   Map 15

## Edinburgh & the Lothians

### Craigbrae

Half a mile down a narrow winding lane and you wash up at the old stone farmhouse, with huge windows overlooking fields and a cooperage across the yard. The house has been recently renovated so there's a lovely new bathroom in New England style and bedrooms that ooze tranquillity and thoughtful touches. Your hosts are hospitable and great fun; the drawing room is warm, cosy and homely; there are books, china, family pieces and good oils. Edinburgh is 15 minutes by train from the village, the airport 12 minutes by taxi or car. And there's a pretty garden that catches the sun.

| Price | £70–£90. Singles from £35. |
|---|---|
| Rooms | 3: 1 double; 2 twins/doubles sharing 2 bath/shower rooms. |
| Meals | Pubs/restaurants 2 miles. |
| Closed | Christmas. |
| Directions | Please ask for directions when booking. |

Louise & Michael Westmacott
Craigbrae,
Kirkliston, Edinburgh EH29 9EL

| | |
|---|---|
| Tel | +44 (0)131 331 1205 |
| Fax | +44 (0)131 319 1476 |
| Email | louise@craigbrae.com |
| Web | www.craigbrae.com |

Entry 645   Map 15

## Edinburgh & the Lothians

### Highfield House

Although much of the house is grand, there's a relaxed feel to this 18th-century manse house; Jillian and Hugh enjoy their guests. Treat yourself to a quiet time in the large, light sitting room with family photos, lots of books and paintings, comfy sofas by the fire and a sunny window seat. Bedrooms are softly painted in yellows and blues, beds have good mattresses and bathrooms are spotless. Breakfast on old favourites, or haggis and black pudding, in a dining room with oodles of sunlight and Hugh's oil-clad ancestors watching; home cooking here in the evening is candlelit and cosy, or catch the train into town. *Dogs extra charge.*

Travel Club offer. See page 414.

| Price | £76–£80. Singles £50. |
|---|---|
| Rooms | 2 twins/doubles. |
| Meals | Packed lunch £6. Dinner £15–£25. Pub/restaurant 3 miles. |
| Closed | Christmas. |
| Directions | A71 from Edinburgh. 5 miles beyond city bypass left onto B7031 to Kirknewton. Next right then cross railway line. House is on left at top of hill. |

Jillian & Hugh Hunter Gordon
Highfield House,
Kirknewton, Midlothian EH27 8BJ

| | |
|---|---|
| Tel | +44 (0)1506 881489 |
| Fax | +44 (0)1506 885384 |
| Email | jill@hunter-gordon.co.uk |
| Web | www.highfield-h.co.uk |

Entry 646   Map 15

## Letham House

Sweep down the rhododendron-lined drive to enter a magical, secret world. This fine, early 17th-century mansion has elegant staircases, resplendent fabrics, gleaming antiques and roaring fires; generous, people-loving Barbara and Chris just want you to enjoy it all. They give you complete privacy and tranquillity in stunning south-facing bedrooms; the views over mature trees and impeccable parkland are the stuff of dreams. Eat robustly, sleep peacefully, indulge yourself in gorgeous bathrooms; this is a nurturing retreat. You won't want to leave, but there are beaches and golf nearby; Edinburgh is beyond.

## Eaglescairnie Mains

Wildlife thrives: eight acres of conservation headland have been created and wildflower meadows planted on this 350-acre working farm… you'd never guess Edinburgh is so close. The Georgian farmhouse sits in lovely gardens, its peace uninterrupted. There's a traditional conservatory for locally-sourced breakfasts, a perfectly gracious drawing room (coral walls, rich fabrics, log fire) for wintery nights, and beautiful big bedrooms full of books and kind extras. Barbara is warm and charming, Michael's commitment to the countryside is wide-ranging; you can now walk for miles from the front door.

Ethical Collection: Environment; Community. See page 412.

 Travel Club offer. See page 414.

| | | | |
|---|---|---|---|
| Price | £130–£180. Singles £55–£75. | Price | £60–£75. Singles from £45. |
| Rooms | 5: 2 doubles, 2 twins/doubles; 1 suite with separate bath. | Rooms | 3: 2 doubles, 1 twin. |
| Meals | Dinner, 3 courses, £35. Packed lunch £10. Guest kitchen. Pubs/restaurants 1 mile. | Meals | Pub 1 mile. |
| | | Closed | Christmas. |
| Closed | Rarely. | Directions | From A1 at Haddington, B6368 south for Bolton & Humbie. Right immed. after traffic lights on bridge. 2.5 miles on through Bolton, at top of hill, fork left for Gifford. Entrance 0.5 miles on left. |
| Directions | From A1 south, exit at Oak Tree junction. Follow signs for Haddington (B6471). Turn immediately right after 40mph signs, through large stone pillars. Straight down drive. | | |

| | | | |
|---|---|---|---|
| | Barbara Sharman | | Barbara & Michael Williams |
| | Letham House, | | Eaglescairnie Mains, |
| | Haddington, | | Gifford, Haddington, |
| | East Lothian EH41 3SS | | East Lothian EH41 4HN |
| Tel | +44 (0)1620 820055 | Tel | +44 (0)1620 810491 |
| Fax | +44 (0)1620 820056 | Fax | +44 (0)1620 810491 |
| Email | stay@lethamhouse.com | Email | williams.eagles@btinternet.com |
| Web | www.lethamhouse.com | Web | www.eaglescairnie.com |

Entry 647  Map 15

Entry 648  Map 16

## Edinburgh & the Lothians

### Glebe House

Gwen has lavished a huge amount of time and love on her 1780s manse. The perfect Georgian family house with all the well-proportioned elegance you'd expect, it is resplendent with original features – fireplaces, arched glass, long windows – that have appeared more than once in interiors magazines. Bedrooms are light and airy with pretty fabrics and lovely linen. The beach is a stone's throw away, views are leafy-green, and golfers have over 21 courses to choose from. There's also a fascinating sea bird centre close by – yet you are 30 minutes from Edinburgh! Regular trains take you to the foot of the castle.

| | |
|---|---|
| Price | £90–£100. Singles by arrangement. |
| Rooms | 3: 1 double, 1 twin, 1 four-poster. |
| Meals | Restaurants 2-minute walk. |
| Closed | Christmas. |
| Directions | From Edinburgh, A1 for Berwick. Left onto A198, follow signs into North Berwick. Right into Station Rd signed 'The Law', to 1st x-roads; left into town centre; house on left behind wall. |

**Gwen & Jake Scott**
Glebe House,
Law Road, North Berwick,
East Lothian EH39 4PL
Tel     +44 (0)1620 892608
Email     gwenscott@glebehouse-nb.co.uk
Web     www.glebehouse-nb.co.uk

Entry 649    Map 16

## Fife

### Blair Adam

If staying in a place with genuine Adam features is special, how much more so in the Adams' family home! They've been in this corner of Fife since 1733: John laid out the walled garden, son William was a prominent politician, Sir Walter Scott used to come and stay… you may be similarly inspired. The house stands in a swathe of parkland and forest overlooking the hills and Loch Leven, with big, friendly, light-flooded rooms filled with intriguing contents. The pretty bedroom is on the ground floor and you eat in the private dining room or with the family in the kitchen – you choose.

Travel Club offer. See page 414.

| | |
|---|---|
| Price | From £90. Singles from £50. |
| Rooms | 1 twin. |
| Meals | Dinner £25 including wine. Restaurants 5 miles. |
| Closed | December & January. |
| Directions | From M90 exit 5, B996 south for Cowdenbeath. Right for Maryburgh, through village, right through pillars onto drive, under bridge, then 0.5 miles up to house. |

**Keith & Elizabeth Adam**
Blair Adam,
Kelty,
Fife KY4 0JF
Tel     +44 (0)1383 831221
Fax     +44 (0)1383 839971
Email     adamofblairadam@hotmail.com

Entry 650    Map 15

# Fife

## Fincraigs

Immersed in delightful rolling hills, this characterful 18th-century farmhouse has an air of great comfort and warmth; Felicity and Tom make you feel instantly at home. There's a sunny drawing room with open fire and family antiques, and an upstairs sitting room for guests' own use. The pretty bedrooms have rural views and marvellous beds with lovely old linen. Wander through the orchard and walled garden, admire the free-range hens, visit the veggie patch: expect great home cooking and enthusiastic wine chat from Tom. You are near the sea, East Neuk fishing villages, the Tay estuary, Dundee and golf at St Andrews.

Travel Club offer. See page 414.

| Price | From £80. Singles from £40. |
|---|---|
| Rooms | 2: 1 double; 1 twin with separate bath. |
| Meals | Dinner, 3 courses, from £25. Pubs 3-5 miles. |
| Closed | Occasionally. |
| Directions | From A92 heading north, left after Rathillet, at Balmerino/Gauldry sign. Fincraigs 1 mile from main road on left. |

**Felicity & Tom Gilbey**
Fincraigs,
Kilmany, Cupar,
Fife KY15 4QQ
Tel    +44 (0)1382 330256
Email  anyone@fincraigs.freeserve.co.uk
Web    www.fincraigs.com

Entry 651   Map 15+19

# Fife

## 18 Queen's Terrace

So peaceful that it's hard to imagine that you're in the heart of St Andrews and a mere ten-minute walk from the Royal & Ancient golf club. Jill's stylish and traditional home shows off her artistic flair; the light, restful drawing room and elegant dining room are full of character, sunlight and flowers. Large bedrooms have especially comfortable beds, crisp linens, whisky and water, and poetry and prose on bedside tables. An enchanting place – and Jill, friendly and generous, is a mine of information on art, gardens and walks; sit on the terrace in summer and admire the water garden. *Children over 12 welcome.*

| Price | From £85. Singles £65-£70. |
|---|---|
| Rooms | 4: 3 doubles, 1 twin. |
| Meals | Dinner, 3 courses with wine, £20-£35. |
| Closed | Rarely. |
| Directions | Into St Andrews on A917; pass Old Course Hotel. Right at 2nd mini r'bout, left through arch at 2nd mini r'bout. 250 yds, right into Queens Gardens. Right at T-junc. On left opp. church. |

**Jill Hardie**
18 Queen's Terrace,
St Andrews, Fife KY16 9QF
Tel    +44 (0)1334 478849
Fax    +44 (0)1334 470283
Email  stay@18queensterrace.com
Web    www.18queensterrace.com

Entry 652   Map 15+19

# Fife

## Kinkell

An avenue of beech trees patrolled by guinea fowl leads to the house. If the sea views and the salty smack of St Andrews Bay air don't get you, step inside and have your senses tickled. The elegant drawing room has two open fires, rosy sofas, a grand piano – gorgeous. Bedrooms and bathrooms are immaculate, sunny and warm. There's great cooking too; Sandy and Frippy excel in the kitchen and make full use of local produce. From the front door head down to the beach, walk the wild coast, jump on a quad bike, try your hand at clay pigeon shooting. All this and wonderful hosts.

| | |
|---|---|
| Price | £90. Singles from £55. |
| Rooms | 3 twins/doubles. |
| Meals | Dinner £30. Restaurants in St Andrews, 2 miles. |
| Closed | Rarely. |
| Directions | From St Andrews, A917 for 2 miles for Crail. Driveway in 1st line of trees on left after St Andrews. |

**Sandy & Frippy Fyfe**
Kinkell,
St Andrews, Fife KY16 8PN
Tel       +44 (0)1334 472003
Fax      +44 (0)1334 475248
Email    fyfe@kinkell.com
Web      www.kinkell.com

Entry 653   Map 16+19

# Fife

## Falside Smiddy

The old smithy sits right on a bend (peaceful at night) but city dwellers won't mind. Saved from dereliction by Rosie and musical, chatty Keith, it is a home you are invited to share. Expect fresh flowers, maps on walls, books, boots and interesting ephemera – not for style seekers but this place is interesting and different. Small rooms have homemade biscuits and hat stands for clothes, bath and shower rooms are spotlessly clean. Rosie cooks a truly good breakfast and turns berries into jams, and the wood-burner makes winters cosy. Lovely walks from the door to the sea and you are close to golf courses.

| | |
|---|---|
| Price | £56–£65. Singles £40. |
| Rooms | 2 twins. |
| Meals | Pub 2 miles. St Andrews 4 miles. |
| Closed | Occasionally. |
| Directions | From St Andrews, A917 for Crail. After 4 miles, ignore turning for Boarhills, & continue to small river. Over bridge; house 2nd on left. |

**Rosie & Keith Birkinshaw**
Falside Smiddy,
Boarhills,
St Andrews,
Fife KY16 8PT
Tel       +44 (0)1334 880479
Email    rosiebirk@btinternet.com

Entry 654   Map 16+19

## Highland

### The Grange

A Victorian townhouse with its toes in the country: the mountain hovers above, the loch shimmers below and the garden slopes steeply to great banks of rhododendrons. Bedrooms, the one in the turret with a sumptuous new bathroom, are large, luscious, warm and inviting: crushed velvet, beautiful blankets, immaculate linen – all ooze panache. Expect decanters of sherry, ornate cornices, a Louis XV bed and a superb suite with contemporary touches. Elegant breakfasts are served at glass-topped tables; Joan's warm vivacity and love of B&B means guests keep coming back. And just a 10-minute walk into town.

| | |
|---|---|
| Price | £110–£118. |
| Rooms | 3: 2 doubles, 1 suite. |
| Meals | Restaurants 12-minute walk. |
| Closed | Mid-November to Easter. |
| Directions | A82 Glasgow–Fort William; 1 mile after 30mph sign into Fort William, turn right up Ashburn Lane, next to Ashburn guesthouse. On left at top. |

Joan & John Campbell
The Grange,
Grange Road, Fort William,
Inverness-shire PH33 6JF
Tel      +44 (0)1397 705516
Email   info@thegrange-scotland.co.uk
Web    www.thegrange-scotland.co.uk

Entry 655   Map 17

## Highland

### Tigh An Dochais

A contemporary, award-winning, 'see-through' house, quite unlike its neighbours, on a narrow strip of land between the busy town road and the rocky shoreline, with stunning views out the back across Broadford bay and the mountains beyond. Full-length windows and a cathedral ceiling allow light to flood in to an oak-floored sitting room with a wood-burner and super modern art. Downstairs are bedrooms with crisp white linen, tartan throws and modern bathrooms with underfloor heating. Try black pudding from Stornoway at breakfast, good fish and game for supper. Step straight onto the beach from here.

Travel Club offer. See page 414.

| | |
|---|---|
| Price | £70–£80. Singles £65–£70. |
| Rooms | 3: 2 doubles, 1 twin/double. |
| Meals | Dinner, 4 courses, £22–£25. BYO. Packed lunch £5. Pub/restaurant 200 yds. |
| Closed | Rarely. |
| Directions | Leave Skye Bridge & follow A87 to Broadford. After 6 miles pass Hebridean Hotel on left, house is 200 yds further up A87 on right. |

Neil Hope
Tigh An Dochais,
13 Harrapool, Harrapool,
Isle of Skye  IV49 9AQ
Tel      +44 (0)1471 820022
Email   hopeskye@btinternet.com
Web    www.skyebedbreakfast.co.uk

Entry 656   Map 17

## Highland

### The Berry

Drive through miles of spectacular landscape then bask in the final approach down a winding single-track road to the hamlet of Allt-Na-Subh – just five houses by the stunning loch. Joan, who paints, is friendly and kind, and her Rayburn-warmed kitchen the hub of this croft-style modern house. Inside is fresh and light with simple bedrooms – one up, one down; the sitting room has an open fire and south-facing views. Eat fish straight from the boats, stride the hills and spot golden eagles, red deer and otters. The perfect place for naturalists and artists, or those seeking solace. *Skye is a 20-minute drive.*

| | |
|---|---|
| Price | £65. Singles from £35. |
| Rooms | 2: 1 double with separate shower; 1 double sharing bath. |
| Meals | Dinner, 3 courses with wine, £30. Packed lunch £7. Pub 20-minute drive. |
| Closed | Rarely. |
| Directions | From A87 at Dornie follow signs for Killilin, Conchra & Salachy. House 2.7 miles on left. |

Joan Ashburner
The Berry,
Allt-Na-Subh,
Dornie,
Kyle of Lochalsh,
Highland IV40 8DZ
Tel      +44 (0)1599 588259

Entry 657   Map 17

## Highland

### Aurora

The perfect spot for walkers and climbers (single-track roads, lochs, rivers and mountains) and the perfect B&B for groups: three smart, uncluttered bedrooms have flexible sleeping arrangements and spick and span shower rooms. The guest sitting room is light and airy with binoculars, books to borrow, maps and a small fridge for your wine – stay put for glorious sunsets and views to Harris. Breakfast time is generously bendy and Thomas cooks delicious suppers; salads and herbs are home-grown. There's a drying room and bike storage, but those wanting to relax will love it here too. *Minimum stay two nights.*

Ethical Collection: Environment; Food.
See page 412.

| | |
|---|---|
| Price | £70-£80. Singles £65-£70. |
| Rooms | 3: 1 double, 2 twins/doubles (extra single bed). |
| Meals | Packed lunch £6. Dinner, 2 courses, £20. BYO. Pub/restaurant within 0.5 miles. |
| Closed | Occasionally between November-March. |
| Directions | From Inverness A9 north, follow signs 'Wester Ross Coastal Trail'. Left at Garve A832. Left at Kinlochewe A896. In Shieldaig at Heron sign 1st right; house 4th on left. |

Ann Barton
Aurora,
Shieldaig, Torridon,
Ross-shire IV54 8XN
Tel      +44 (0)1520 755246
Fax      +44 (0)1520 755285
Email    info@aurora-bedandbreakfast.co.uk
Web      www.aurora-bedandbreakfast.co.uk

Entry 658   Map 17

# Highland

## Tanglewood House

Down a steep drive through stunning landscape to this modern, curved house on the shore of Loch Broom – and distant views of the old fishing port of Ullapool. The drawing room is filled with antiques, fine fabrics, original paintings, flowers and a grand piano; bask in the views from the floor-to-ceiling window. Bedrooms are delightful: bold colours, crisp linen, proper bath tubs with fluffy towels. Anne gives you just-squeezed orange juice and eggs from her hens for breakfast, and delicious dinners; explore the wild garden then stroll to the rocky private beach for a swim in the loch. Superb. *Minimum stay two nights.*

| | |
|---|---|
| Price | £96–£110. Singles £73–£80. |
| Rooms | 3: 1 double, 2 twins. |
| Meals | Dinner, 4 courses, £36. BYO. Packed lunch £9. Pubs in village 0.5 miles. |
| Closed | Christmas, New Year & Easter. |
| Directions | On outskirts of Ullapool from Inverness on A835, left immed. after 4th 40mph sign. Take cattle grid on right & left fork down to house. |

|  | **Anne Holloway** |
|---|---|
| | Tanglewood House, |
| | Ullapool, |
| | Ross-shire IV26 2TB |
| Tel | +44 (0)1854 612059 |
| Email | anne@tanglewoodhouse.co.uk |
| Web | www.tanglewoodhouse.co.uk |

Entry 659  Map 17

# Highland

## Invergloy House

A peaceful, no-smoking home run by Margaret, a professional musician and James, a retired chemical engineer. It is a converted coach house with stables in the beautiful Great Glen and sits in 50 wild lochside acres of rhododendron, woodland and wonderful trees. Bedrooms are traditional, warm and welcoming; views of Loch Lochy and the mountains from the big picture window in the guest drawing room are spectacular. Walk to the private shingle beach on the loch, spot the wild roe deer in the grounds, savour the secluded peace and quiet. *Children over eight welcome.*

| | |
|---|---|
| Price | From £76. |
| Rooms | 2: 1 double, 1 twin. |
| Meals | Restaurants 2-5 miles. |
| Closed | Christmas & New Year. |
| Directions | From Spean Bridge north on A82. After 5 miles, house signed on left. |

|  | **Margaret & James Cairns** |
|---|---|
| | Invergloy House, |
| | Spean Bridge, |
| | Inverness-shire PH34 4DY |
| Tel | +44 (0)1397 712681 |
| Email | cairns@invergloy-house.co.uk |
| Web | www.invergloy-house.co.uk |

Entry 660  Map 18

## Highland

### The Old Ferryman's House

This former ferryman's house is small, homely and delightful, and just yards from the river Spey with its spectacular mountain views. Explore the countryside or relax in the garden with a tray of tea and homemade treats; there are plants tumbling from whisky barrels and baskets. The sitting room is cosy with a wood-burning stove and lots of books (no TV). Generous Elizabeth, a keen traveller who lived in the Sudan, cooks delicious and imaginative meals: herbs from the garden, eggs from her hens, heathery honeycomb, homemade bread and preserves. An unmatched spot for explorers, and very good value.

| | |
|---|---|
| Price | £55. Singles £27.50. |
| Rooms | 3: 1 double, 1 twin, 1 single, sharing 1 bath & 2 wcs. |
| Meals | Dinner, 3 courses, £20. BYO. Packed lunch £6. |
| Closed | Occasionally in winter. |
| Directions | From A9, follow main road markings through village, pass golf club & cross river. From B970 to Boat of Garten; house on left, just before river. |

Elizabeth Matthews
The Old Ferryman's House,
Boat of Garten,
Inverness-shire PH24 3BY
Tel +44 (0)1479 831370

Entry 661  Map 18

## Highland

### Craigiewood

The best of both worlds: the remoteness of the Highlands (red kites, wild goats) and Inverness just four miles. The landscape surrounding this elegant cottage exudes a sense of ancient mystery augmented by these six acres – home to woodpeckers, roe deer and glorious roses. Inside, maps, walking sticks, two cats and a lovely, family-home feel – what you'd expect from delightful owners. Bedrooms, old-fashioned and cosy, overlook a garden reclaimed from Black Isle gorse. Gavin is experimenting with solar panels, and runs garden tours: he can take you off to Inverewe, Attadale, Cawdor and Dunrobin Castle. Warm, peaceful, special.

Travel Club offer. See page 414.

| | |
|---|---|
| Price | £70–£80. Singles £40. |
| Rooms | 2 twins. |
| Meals | Pub 2 miles. |
| Closed | Christmas & New Year. |
| Directions | A9 north over Kessock Bridge. At N. Kessock junc. filter left to r'bout to Kilmuir. After 0.25 miles, right to Kilmuir; follow road uphill, left at top, then straight on. Ignore 'No Through Road' sign, pass Drynie Farm, follow road to right; house 1st left. |

Araminta & Gavin Dallmeyer
Craigiewood,
North Kessock, Inverness,
Inverness-shire IV1 3XG
Tel +44 (0)1463 731628
Email 2minty@craigiewood.co.uk
Web www.craigiewood.co.uk

Entry 662  Map 18

# Highland

## Milton Lodge

Arrive in the romantic night: plunge up a steep track in dense woodland, then swoop down a rhododendron-lined drive to spot the lights of this 1880 shooting lodge. Enter a large, candlelit, woodburner-warmed hall, with a convivial table for Barbara's good home cooking; sprawl in the sitting room afterwards with a book. Sleep well in light, comfortable bedrooms, with traditional fabrics and good beds; bathrooms are not state-of-the-art but spotless and with fluffy towels. Wake to breathtaking views south over the Highlands and a breakfast that will set you up for stalking, fishing or sublime walking.

Travel Club offer. See page 414.

| Price | From £80. Singles from £45. |
|---|---|
| Rooms | 3: 1 double; 1 double, 1 twin sharing bath. |
| Meals | Dinner, 3-4 courses (wine on request), £30-£35. Packed lunch £7.50. Pub/restaurant 3 miles. |
| Closed | Rarely. |
| Directions | From Inverness A9 north, 1st exit to Evanton from Cromarty Firth Bridge. Follow signpost to Swordale, 2.5 miles. Signed to Milton Lodge, rough track 0.5 miles. |

|  | Mrs Barbara Turner<br>Milton Lodge,<br>Swordale, Evanton,<br>Dingwall, Ross-shire IV16 9XA |
|---|---|
| Tel | +44 (0)1349 830216 |
| Email | barbara@mlbt.co.uk |
| Web | www.mlbt.co.uk |

Entry 663   Map 18

# Highland

## Wemyss House

The peace is palpable, the setting overlooking the Cromarty Firth is stunning. Take an early morning stroll and spot buzzards, pheasants, rabbits and roe deer. The deceptively spacious house with sweeping maple floors is flooded with light and fabulous views, big bedrooms are warmly decorated with Highland rugs and tweeds, there's Christine's grand piano in the living room, Stuart's handcrafted furniture at every turn, and a sweet dog called Bella. Aga breakfasts include homemade bread, preserves and eggs from happy hens. Dinners are delicious; Christine and Stuart are wonderful hosts.

Ethical Collection: Food. See page 412.

Travel Club offer. See page 414.

| Price | From £85. |
|---|---|
| Rooms | 3: 2 doubles, 1 twin. |
| Meals | Dinner, 4 courses, £30. Restaurants 15-minute drive. |
| Closed | Rarely. |
| Directions | From Inverness, A9 north. At Nigg r'bout, right onto B9175. Through Arabella; left at sign to Hilton & Shandwick; right towards Nigg; past church; 1 mile, right onto private road. House on right. |

|  | Christine Asher & Stuart Clifford<br>Wemyss House,<br>Bayfield, Tain,<br>Ross-shire IV19 1QW |
|---|---|
| Tel | +44 (0)1862 851212 |
| Email | stay@wemysshouse.com |
| Web | www.wemysshouse.com |

Entry 664   Map 18

## Highland

### Linsidecroy

Heaven in the Highlands with stunning valley and mountain views. The house, built in 1863 was part of the Duke of Sutherland's estate; Robert, a factor, first set eyes on it 20 years ago and now it is home. A sublime renovation gives you walls of books, valley views and an open fire in the airy drawing room. Super bedrooms come with rugs, crisp linen, books galore and fresh flowers. There are two terraces, one for breakfast, one for pre-dinner drinks; all around you Davina's remarkable garden is taking shape. You can fish and walk, play some golf, or head north to Tongue through Britain's wildest land. Magical.

## Highland

### St Callan's Manse

Fun, laughter and conversation flow in this warm, relaxed and happy home. You share it with prints, paintings, antiques, sofas and amazing memorabilia – and three dogs, nine ducks, 14 hens and 1,200 teddy bears of every shape, size and origin. Snug bedrooms have pretty fabrics, old armoires, sheepskin rugs, tartan blankets. Caroline cooks delicious breakfasts and dinners; Robert, a fund of knowledgeable anecdotes, can arrange just about anything. All this in incomparable surroundings: glens, forests, buzzards, deer and the odd golden eagle. A gem. *2.5% credit card charge. Dogs by arrangement.*

 Travel Club offer. See page 414.

| | |
|---|---|
| Price | £80. Singles £50. |
| Rooms | 2: 1 double, 1 twin. |
| Meals | Hotel 6 miles. |
| Closed | Christmas, Easter & occasionally. |
| Directions | A836 west out of Bonar Bridge. After 4 miles, left onto A837. Cross Shin river, then right towards Rosehall & Lochinver, 1.5 miles, double wooden gates on right. House is 150 yds up drive. |

| | |
|---|---|
| Price | £80. Singles £65. |
| Rooms | 2: 1 double with separate bath; 1 double with separate shower. |
| Meals | Dinner, 2-4 courses, £14.50-£25. BYO. Pub/restaurant in village, 1.5 miles. |
| Closed | Occasionally. |
| Directions | From Inverness, A9 north. Cross Dornoch bridge. 14 miles on, A839 to Lairg. Cross small bridge in Rogart; sharp right uphill, for St Callan's church. House 1.5 miles on, on right, next to church. |

|  |  |
|---|---|
| | Robert & Davina Howden |
| | Linsidecroy, |
| | Invershin, |
| | Lairg, |
| | Sutherland IV27 4EU |
| Tel | +44 (0)1549 421255 |
| Email | howden@linsidecroy.wanadoo.co.uk |

|  |  |
|---|---|
| | Robert & Caroline Mills |
| | St Callan's Manse, |
| | Rogart, |
| | Sutherland IV28 3XE |
| Tel | +44 (0)1408 641363 |
| Fax | +44 (0)1408 641313 |
| Email | caroline@rogartsnuff.me.uk |

Entry 665   Map 18

Entry 666   Map 21

## Moray

### Westfield House

Sweep up the drive to the grand home of an illustrious family: Macleans have lived here since 1862. Inside: polished furniture and burnished antiques, a tartan-carpeted hall, an oak stair hung with ancestral oils. John farms 500 acres while Veronica cooks sublimely; dinner is served at a long candelabra'd table, with vegetables from the vegetable garden. A winter fire crackles in the guest sitting room, old-fashioned bedrooms are warm and inviting (plump pillows, fine linen, books, lovely views), the peace is deep. A historic house in a perfect setting, run by the most charming people.

## Moray

### Blervie

The Meiklejohn coat of arms flies from the flagpole, an apple's throw from the orchard in which King Malcolm met his death. Blervie is a small 1776 mansion, "a restoration in progress", its finely proportioned rooms crammed with fresh flowers and splendid things to catch the eye. A large dresser swamped in china, a piano in the hall, books everywhere and the sweet smell of burnt beech from grand marble fireplaces. Big bedrooms have comfy old sofas at the feet of four-posters; bathrooms are eccentrically old-fashioned. Fiona and Paddy enjoy country pursuits and like to dine with their guests.

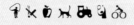

Travel Club offer. See page 414.

| | | | |
|---|---|---|---|
| Price | £80. Singles from £40. | Price | £80. |
| Rooms | 3: 1 twin; 1 twin with separate bath & shower; 1 single with separate bath. | Rooms | 2: 1 four-poster; 1 four-poster with separate bath. Extra single bed. |
| Meals | Dinner, 3 courses, £25. Pub 3 miles. | Meals | Dinner, 4 courses, £28. Pubs/restaurants 2-5 miles. |
| Closed | Rarely. | Closed | Christmas & New Year. |
| Directions | From Elgin, A96 west for Forres & Inverness; after 2.5 miles, right onto B9013 for Burghead; after 1 mile, signed right at x-roads. Cont. to 'Westfield House & Office'. | Directions | From A96 to Forres. South at clocktower, across r'bout onto B9010. Pass hospital; exactly 1 mile on, left at Mains of Blervie sign. Right at farm. (Do not use satnav.) |

| | | | |
|---|---|---|---|
| | **John & Veronica Maclean** | | **Paddy & Fiona Meiklejohn** |
| | Westfield House, | | Blervie, |
| | Elgin, Moray IV30 8XL | | Forres, |
| Tel | +44 (0)1343 547308 | | Moray IV36 2RH |
| Fax | +44 (0)1343 551340 | Tel | +44 (0)1309 672358 |
| Email | veronica.maclean@yahoo.co.uk | Email | meiklejohn@btinternet.com |

Entry 667   Map 18

Entry 668   Map 18

## Perth & Kinross

### Grenich Steading

Perched above silvery Loch Tummel is Lindsay's award-winning renovation of a once derelict barn. Inside, blue-and-white Portuguese tiles, seagrass matting and a wood-burning stove. You get a kitchen, dining and sitting room so you can self-cater too (minimum one week). Gaze upon mountain-to-loch views, walk in the unspoilt glen or visit the theatre at Pitlochry. Lindsay loves nurturing both garden and guests; her two Scottish deerhounds are welcoming too. The sunsets are fabulous, and there's so much to do you'll barely be inside. *Children over eight welcome. Minimum stay two nights at weekends May-October.*

| | |
|---|---|
| Price | From £80. Singles £60. |
| Rooms | 2: 1 double; 1 twin sharing bath & sitting room (2nd room let to same party only). |
| Meals | Dinner by arrangement, October to March only, £28 including wine. Pub 0.75 miles. |
| Closed | Christmas & New Year. |
| Directions | From A9 north of Pitlochry for Killiecrankie. Left, B8019 for Tummel Bridge to Loch Tummel Inn. After 0.75 miles right at sign, then up forestry road for 0.5 miles.. |

|  |  |
|---|---|
| | Lindsay Morison |
| | Grenich Steading, |
| | Strathtummel, |
| | Tummel Bridge, |
| | Pitlochry, |
| | Perth & Kinross PH16 5RT |
| Tel | +44 (0)1882 634332 |

Entry 669   Map 15 +18

## Perth & Kinross

### Beinn Bhracaigh

Here is a solid Victorian villa, with later wings, built for an Edinburgh family in the 1880s, when Pitlochry was hailed as the Switzerland of the North. Ann and Alf, generous hosts, have swept through with the cream paint and all is spanking new. Expect soft lighting, gleaming wooden floors, silk flowers, bowls of pot pourri and scented candles. The lounge is comfy and has an honesty bar with over 50 malt whiskies, good-sized bedrooms have excellent mattresses, padded head boards and views to the Tummel Hills, bathrooms are all new with thick towels and lovely lotions. Breakfast is a huge, imaginative feast.

| | |
|---|---|
| Price | £60-£90. Singles from £45. |
| Rooms | 10: 4 doubles, 6 twins/doubles. |
| Meals | Dinner £22.50-£30 (for groups only, by arrangement). Pubs/restaurants within 10-minute walk. |
| Closed | 23-28 December. |
| Directions | From A9, turn for Pitlochry. Under railway bridge, then right at scout hut & up East Moulin Road. 2nd left into Higher Oakfield; house almost immediately on left. |

|  |  |
|---|---|
| | Ann & Alf Berry |
| | Beinn Bhracaigh, |
| | 14 Higher Oakfield, Pitlochry, |
| | Perth, Perth & Kinross PH16 5HT |
| Tel | +44 (0)1796 470355 |
| Email | info@beinnbhracaigh.com |
| Web | www.beinnbhracaigh.com |

Entry 670   Map 15 +18

## Perth & Kinross

### Rock House

Prepare to fall hopelessly in love. Hard to know here, high above Loch Tay, whether the views are more beautiful outside or in. The cathedral ceiling in the sitting room allows light to soar upwards, there's a striking collection of modern art and an unfussy style: white sofas, painted furniture, and, here and there, a bit of quirky fun or a perfect antique. Sleep deeply in beds piled with linen cushions, soft woollen throws and cotton ticking, wake to grape and mint salad, Irish bread, kedgeree or anything else you want... Roland and Penny are passionate about their house, the land, and real food. *Minimum stay two nights.*

## Perth & Kinross

### Craighall Castle

The view from the balcony that circles the drawing room is simply stunning, and the deep gorge provides the fabulous walks where you might glimpse deer, red squirrels and otters. Nicky and Lachie, ever welcoming, battle to keep up with the demands of the impressive home that has been in the family for 500 years. Any mustiness or dustiness can be forgiven, as staying here is a memorable experience. Nothing is contrived, sterile or luxurious, and there's so much drama and intrigue it could be the setting for a film. Breakfast is served in the 18th-century library, and there's a Regency drawing room, too.

| | |
|---|---|
| Price | £115. Singles £85. |
| Rooms | 2 doubles. |
| Meals | Dinner, 2–3 courses, £25–£35. Packed lunch £12. Pub/restaurant 2.2 miles. |
| Closed | Rarely. |
| Directions | From Aberfeldy, A827 dir. Kenmore. At Loch Tay where main road turns sharp right, cont. along narrow road signed Acharn. Follow loch side for 2.2 miles. At top of hill, house on right. |

Roland & Penny Kennedy
Rock House,
Achianich, Kenmore, Aberfeldy,
Perthshire PH15 2HU

| | |
|---|---|
| Tel | +44 (0)1887 830336 |
| Fax | +44 (0)1887 830214 |
| Email | rockhouse@lochtay.co.uk |
| Web | www.lochtay.co.uk |

Entry 671   Map 15 +18

| | |
|---|---|
| Price | £80. Singles £45. |
| Rooms | 2: 1 four-poster; 1 twin (extra single bed) with separate bath. |
| Meals | Restaurant 3 miles. |
| Closed | Christmas & New Year. |
| Directions | From Blairgowrie, A93 for Braemar for 2 miles. Just before end of 30mph limit, sharp right-hand bend, with drive on right. Follow drive for 1 mile. |

Nicky & Lachie Rattray
Craighall Castle,
Blairgowrie,
Perth & Kinross PH10 7JB

| | |
|---|---|
| Tel | +44 (0)1250 874749 |
| Fax | +44 (0)1250 874749 |
| Email | lrattray@craighall.co.uk |

Entry 672   Map 15 +18

## Perth & Kinross

### Mackeanston House

They grow their own organic fruit and vegetables, make their own preserves, bake their own bread. Likeable and energetic – Fiona a wine buff and talented cook, Colin a tri-lingual guide – your hosts are hospitable people whose 1690 farmhouse combines informality and luxury in peaceful, central Scotland. Light-filled bedrooms have soft carpets, pretty fabrics, fine antiques; one has a canopied bed, a double shower (with a seat if you wish it) and a bath that overlooks fields. In the conservatory with views to Stirling Castle you may dine on salmon from the Teith and game from close by. *Local & battlefield tours.*

| | |
|---|---|
| Price | £92–£96. Singles £56–£58. |
| Rooms | 2: 1 double, 1 twin/double. |
| Meals | Dinner £28. Pub 1 mile. |
| Closed | Christmas. |
| Directions | From M9, north, junc. 10 onto A84 for Doune. After 5 miles, left on B826 for Thornhill. Drive on left after 2.2 miles, right off farm drive. |

Fiona & Colin Graham
Mackeanston House,
Doune, Stirling,
Perth & Kinross FK16 6AX
Tel      +44 (0)1786 850213
Email    info@mackeanstonhouse.co.uk
Web      www.mackeanstonhouse.co.uk

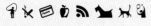

Entry 673   Map 15

## Perth & Kinross

### Old Kippenross

Pink since 1715 (a signal to Jacobites that the house was a safe haven), Old Kippenross rests in a wooded valley overlooking the river Allan – spot herons, dippers and otters. The Georgian part was built above the 500-year-old Tower House, and its rustic white-vaulted basement embraces dining room and sitting room, strewn with soft sofas and Persian rugs. Upstairs there are deeply comfortable sash-windowed bedrooms and warm, well-equipped bathrooms stuffed with towels. Sue and Patrick (who is an expert on birds of prey) are welcoming; breakfast and dinner are delicious. *Children over ten welcome. Dogs by arrangement.*

Travel Club offer. See page 414.

| | |
|---|---|
| Price | £95–£100. Singles from £62.50. |
| Rooms | 2: 1 double, 1 twin. |
| Meals | Dinner £28. BYO. Pub 1.5 miles. |
| Closed | Rarely. |
| Directions | M9 exit 11, B8033 for Dunblane. 500 yds, right over dual c'way, through entrance by stone gatehouse. Down drive, 1st fork right after bridge. House along gravelled drive. |

Sue & Patrick Stirling–Aird
Old Kippenross,
Dunblane,
Perth & Kinross FK15 0LQ
Tel      +44 (0)1786 824048
Fax      +44 (0)1786 824482
Email    kippenross@hotmail.com

Entry 674   Map 15

## Scottish Borders

### Over Langshaw Farm

A peaceful place in the rolling hills of the Scottish Borders, with an inspiring commitment to organic food and good husbandry. The energy here goes into Friesians and ewes, homemade farmhouse ice creams, bonny brown hens and guests. So, a cheery place for families and walkers, with unsophisticated bedrooms, old-fashioned bathrooms and a guest sitting room with a log fire and white shutters. Plus all the nooks and crannies you'd expect from a 1700s house, and a sweet smiling welcome from Sheila. She and Martyn have detailed walking maps and could not be more helpful. Authentic – and with views to die for.

## Scottish Borders

### Fauhope House

Near to Melrose Abbey and the glorious St Cuthberts' Walk, this solid 1890s house is immersed in bucolic bliss. Views soar to the Eildon Hills through wide windows with squashy seats; all is luxurious, elegant, fire-lit and serene with an eclectic mix of art. Bedrooms are warm with deeply coloured walls, thick chintz, pale tartan blankets and soft carpet; bathrooms are modern and pristine. Breakfast is served with smiles at a flower-laden table and overlooking those purple hills. A short walk through the garden and over a footbridge takes you to the interesting town of Melrose, with shops, restaurants and its own theatre.

🧳 Travel Club offer. See page 414.

| | |
|---|---|
| Price | £65. Family room £75. Singles £35. |
| Rooms | 2: 1 double; 1 family room with separate bath. |
| Meals | Dinner from £20. Packed lunch from £5. Pubs/restaurants 4-5 miles. |
| Closed | Never. |
| Directions | North from Galashiels, A7 past Torwoodlea golf course & right to Langshaw. After 2 miles, right at T-junc., then left at Earlston sign in Langshaw. White house, in trees, signed at farm road. |

| | |
|---|---|
| Price | From £80. Singles from £55. |
| Rooms | 3 twins/doubles. |
| Meals | Pub/restaurant 0.5 miles. |
| Closed | Rarely. |
| Directions | From A7, through Gattonside; at end of village, at sign on left 'Monkswood', immed. left; right up drive. |

| | |
|---|---|
| | **Sheila & Martyn Bergius** |
| | Over Langshaw Farm, |
| | Galashiels, |
| | Scottish Borders TD1 2PE |
| Tel | +44 (0)1896 860244 |
| Fax | +44 (0)1896 860668 |
| Email | overlangshaw@btconnect.com |

| | |
|---|---|
| | **Ian & Sheila Robson** |
| | Fauhope House, |
| | Gattonside, Melrose, |
| | Scottish Borders TD6 9LY |
| Tel | +44 (0)1896 823184 |
| Fax | +44 (0)1896 820188 |
| Email | fauhope@bordernet.co.uk |

Entry 675   Map 15

Entry 676   Map 15

## Scottish Borders

### Skirling House

An intriguing house with 1908 additions, impeccably maintained. The whole lovely place is imbued with the spirit of Scottish Arts & Crafts, augmented with Italianate flourishes. Colourful blankets embellish chairs; runners soften flagged floors; the carvings, wrought-ironwork and rare Florentine ceiling are sheer delight. Upstairs, a more English comfort holds sway: carpets and rugs, window seats and wicker, fruit and flowers. Bob cooks the finest local produce, Isobel shares a love of Scottish contemporary art and both look after you beautifully. Outside: 25,000 newly planted trees and grand walks from the door.

| Price | £110–£120. Singles £60. |
|---|---|
| Rooms | 5: 3 doubles, 1 twin, 1 twin/double. |
| Meals | Dinner £32. |
| | Pubs/restaurants 2 miles. |
| Closed | Christmas & January–February. |
| Directions | From Biggar, A702 for Edinburgh. Just outside Biggar, right on A72 for Skirling. Big wooden house on right opp. village green. |

**Bob & Isobel Hunter**
Skirling House,
Skirling, Biggar,
Scottish Borders ML12 6HD

| Tel | +44 (0)1899 860274 |
|---|---|
| Fax | +44 (0)1899 860255 |
| Email | enquiry@skirlinghouse.com |
| Web | www.skirlinghouse.com |

Entry 677   Map 15

## Scottish Borders

### Lessudden

A treat to stay in a great and historic tower house in the heart of the Scottish Borders. Your generous hosts give you big cosy bedrooms (one ground floor with an old-fashioned bathroom, one upstairs with a view), and a spacious sitting room with fine old rugs, heaps of books and a log fire. Memorable meals are served at a polished oak refectory table beneath the gaze of Sir Walter Scott's uncle and aunt, who used to live here. The 1680s white-stone stairwell is unique, the décor is traditional and homely, the living is relaxed and Alasdair and Angela care for their guests as open-heartedly as they do their cats, dogs, horses and hens.

Ethical Collection: Food. See page 412.

| Price | From £80. Singles from £55. |
|---|---|
| Rooms | 2: 1 double; |
| | 1 twin with separate bathroom. |
| Meals | Dinner, 3-4 courses, £25. |
| | Pub 0.5 miles. |
| Closed | Rarely. |
| Directions | North on A68 to St Boswells. Right opp. Buccleuch Arms Hotel, on through village; left up drive immediately beyond turning to golf course. |

**Alasdair & Angela Douglas-Hamilton**
Lessudden,
St Boswells,
Scottish Borders TD6 0BH

| Tel | +44 (0)1835 823244 |
|---|---|
| Email | alasdaird@lineone.net |
| Web | www.lessudden.com |

Entry 678   Map 16

# Scottish Borders

## New Belses Farm

Once lost by Lord Lothian in a game of backgammon, this Georgian farmhouse is safe in current hands. Delightful Helen divides her time between helping on the farm, gardening and caring for sundry pets, fan-tail doves, hens (fox permitting), family and guests. Bedrooms glow in a harmony of old paintings, lush chintzes and beautiful antiques; beds are extra long, towels snowy white. It's like home, only better. Discover great Border towns, stunning abbeys, fishing on the Tweed. Enjoy an excellent dinner locally then back to plump sofas by the log fire. Heaven.

Ethical Collection: Food. See page 412.

 Travel Club offer. See page 414.

| Price | From £80. |
|---|---|
| Rooms | 2: 1 double, 1 twin. |
| Meals | Pubs/restaurants 3.5-5 miles. |
| Closed | Christmas. |
| Directions | From Jedburgh, A68 for Edinburgh. Left after 3.5 miles to Ancrum; B6400 Ancrum to Lilliesleaf road; right after 4 miles, down drive (signed). |

Peter & Helen Wilson
New Belses Farm,
Ancrum, Jedburgh,
Scottish Borders TD8 6UR

| Tel | +44 (0)1835 870472 |
| Fax | +44 (0)1835 870482 |
| Email | wilson699@totalise.co.uk |

Entry 679   Map 16

# Stirling

## The Moss

Rozie loves fishing and Jamie keeps bees; they live in a charming listed house full of lovely things and are great hosts. Outside are 28 acres where deer prune the roses, pheasants roam and a garden seat sits with its toes in the water. Generous bedrooms are very private in their own wing and have big beds with feather pillows, books, flowers and long views to pastures and moorland. Expect walking sticks and the bell of HMS Tempest in the porch, rugs in the hall and smart sofas in the log-fired drawing room. Breakfast comes fresh from the Aga and is delivered to a big oak table, from which there are yet more views.

| Price | £90. Singles £45. |
|---|---|
| Rooms | 3: 1 twin; 2 doubles sharing bath (2nd room let to same party only). |
| Meals | Pubs/restaurants within 2 miles. |
| Closed | Rarely. |
| Directions | 4 miles west of Blanefield. Half a mile after Beech Tree Inn turn left off A81. After 300 yds, over bridge, 1st entrance on left. |

Jamie & Rozie Parker
The Moss,
Killearn,
Stirling G63 9LJ

| Tel | +44 (0)1360 550053 |
| Email | themoss@freeuk.com |

Entry 680   Map 15

# Stirling

## Quarter

This stately 1750s house commands views across Stirling's lush countryside and comes complete with crunching gravel drive and original ceiling dome. It was owned by the same family for generations until Pippa arrived, taking over its high ceilings, period features, sash windows. Pad your way upstairs to three comfortable bedrooms and bathrooms, brightened with a floral touch. Breakfast is a grand affair at a polished table; pecking hens provide the eggs and Pippa is determined to restore the kitchen garden to its former glory. The house is cocooned in extensive grounds and you've easy access to Stirling, Edinburgh and Perth. *Dogs by arrangement.*

Travel Club offer. See page 414.

| | |
|---|---|
| Price | £80. Singles £40. |
| Rooms | 3: 1 double, 1 twin/double, 1 twin. |
| Meals | Pub/restaurant 4 miles. |
| Closed | Christmas. |
| Directions | Stirling, exit 9 off M9. From roundabout take A872 towards Denny, after exactly 2 miles turn left (200 yds past Wellsfield Farm) through grey pillars up to house. |

Pippa Maclean
Quarter,
Denny,
Stirling FK6 6QZ
Tel      +44 (0)1324 825817
Email    pippa@edmonstone.com
Web      www.quarterstirling.com

Entry 681   Map 15

---

# Stirling

## Blairhullichan

So much to do here in the National Park: woodland walks, cycle tracks, your own fishing bay on the edge of Loch Ard, a private island to wade out to for picnics. The tranquil house sits high on a slope with fabulous loch views from the drawing room, comfortable with window bay, big fireplace and stacks of books. Reassuringly old-fashioned bedrooms have new mattresses and crisp linen; bathrooms have good towels and lotions. Be charmed by the 'Highlands in miniature' – plus resident labradors and welcoming Bridget, who gives you a grand breakfast and the best of her local knowledge. *Minimum stay two nights.*

Travel Club offer. See page 414.

| | |
|---|---|
| Price | £75-£80. Singles £40. |
| Rooms | 3: 1 double with sitting room, 1 twin; 1 double with separate bath/shower. |
| Meals | Dinner, with wine, £25-£35. Restaurant 10 miles. |
| Closed | Rarely. |
| Directions | A81 to Aberfoyle; at Bank of Scotland, onto B829 to Kinlochard; on for 4.5 miles, pass Macdonald Hotel; left at shop, road becomes unpaved, pass wooden house on right. On left, signed. |

John & Bridget Lewis
Blairhullichan,
Kinlochard,
Aberfoyle, Stirling FK8 3TN
Tel      +44 (0)1877 387341
Email    jablewis@aol.com
Web      www.blairhullichan.net

Entry 682   Map 15

# Stirling

## Cardross

Dodge the lazy sheep on the long drive to arrive (eventually!) at a sweep of gravel and lovely old Cardross, in a gorgeous setting with its 15th-century tower. Bang on the enormous old door and either Archie or Nicola (plus labradors and Jack Russells) will usher you in. And what a delight it is; light and space, long views, exquisite furniture, wooden shutters, towelling robes, fresh flowers, crisp linen, a cast-iron period bath – and that's just the bedrooms. It all feels warm, kind and generous, the drawing room is vast, the house is filled with character and the Orr Ewings can tell you all the history. *Young people over 14 welcome.*

| | |
|---|---|
| Price | £100–£110. Singles £50–£55. |
| Rooms | 2: 1 twin; 1 twin with separate bath. |
| Meals | Occasional dinner £28. Pubs/restaurants 2.5-6 miles. |
| Closed | Christmas & New Year. |
| Directions | A811 Stirling-Dumbarton to Arnprior; B8034 towards Port of Menteith; 2 miles, then cross Forth over humpback bridge. Drive with yellow lodge 150 yds from bridge on right. 1st exit on right from drive. |

**Sir Archie & Lady Orr Ewing**
Cardross,
Port of Menteith,
Kippen, Stirling FK8 3JY

| | |
|---|---|
| Tel | +44 (0)1877 385223 |
| Fax | +44 (0)1877 385223 |
| Email | cardrossestate@googlemail.com |
| Web | www.cardrossholidayhomes.com |

Entry 683  Map 15

# Western Isles

## Kinloch

Meander across the flower-filled machair to the wide open spaces of South Uist – home to waders, hen harriers, corncrakes and talkative Wegg. The house, built 20 years ago, is comfy with books, photos, easy chairs, pictures and angling paraphernalia. Bedrooms – the upstairs double the best – have patchwork and pine and a general junk-shop chic; views across the loch are enormous, sunrises are spectacular. Wegg loves cooking, especially barbecued fish and game; his breakfasts and dinners are sociable occasions and you are surrounded by a clever acre of garden. Nature lovers will adore it. *Shoes off at the front door!*

| | |
|---|---|
| Price | £76. Singles £38. |
| Rooms | 3: 1 twin/double; 1 twin/double, 1 single each with separate bath. |
| Meals | Dinner £22. Packed lunch £8. Restaurant 5 miles. |
| Closed | Rarely. |
| Directions | 30 mins from Benbecula airport; 30 mins from Lochboisdale ferry; 45 mins from Lochmaddy. |

**Wegg Kimbell**
Kinloch,
Grogarry,
Isle of South Uist,
Western Isles HS8 5RR

| | |
|---|---|
| Tel | +44 (0)1870 620316 |
| Email | wegg@kinlochuist.com |
| Web | www.kinlochuist.com |

Entry 684  Map 20

## Western Isles

### Airdabhaigh

A rare 'undiscovered' corner of Britain… moody hills, lochs and acres of treeless blowy shores are wildly atmospheric. Miles of white sandy beaches too, and vast skies. Flora is inspirational; she's involved in Community Arts and runs dyeing and weaving workshops – a unique island experience. Wood panelling, thick walls, a peat fire, a warm kitchen, the wind whistling outside – and now, just below the house, a restored thatched shieling for writing, reading, painting. Sweet bedrooms are a haven of warmth and simplicity. It's utterly peaceful, 100% authentic, a step back in time. *Ask about creative workshops.*

| Price | £50. Singles £26. |
|---|---|
| Rooms | 2: 1 double, 1 twin sharing shower. |
| Meals | Hotel within walking distance. |
| Closed | Rarely. |
| Directions | From Lochmaddy ferry, left on A867 for 8.6 miles to T-junc. Left on A865 for 2.4 miles (ignore signs to Carinish), then right at church. Up track. House 1st on left. |

Flora Macdonald
Airdabhaigh,
Uppertown, Carinish,
Isle of North Uist,
Western Isles HS6 5HL
Tel +44 (0)1876 580611
Email floraidh@hebrides.net
Web www.calanas.co.uk

Entry 685   Map 20

## Western Isles

### Pairc an t-Srath

Richard and Lena's lovely home overlooks the beach at Borve, another absurdly beautiful Harris view. Inside, smart simplicity abounds: wooden floors, white walls, a peat fire, colourful art. Airy bedrooms fit the mood perfectly: trim carpets, chunky wood beds, Harris tweed throws, excellent shower rooms (there's a bathroom, too, if you want a soak). Richard crofts, Lena cooks, perhaps homemade soup, venison casserole, wet chocolate cake with raspberries. Views from the dining room tumble down hill, so expect to linger over breakfast. You'll spot otters in the loch, while the standing stones at Callanish are unmissable.

| Price | £100. Singles from £50. |
|---|---|
| Rooms | 4: 2 doubles, 1 twin, 1 single. |
| Meals | Dinner, 3 courses, £35. Restaurant 3 miles; pub 7 miles. |
| Closed | Rarely. |
| Directions | South from Tarbet ferry and first house on left in village; or north from Leverburgh ferry and last house on right. |

Lena & Richard MacLennan
Pairc an t-Srath,
Borve,
Isle of Harris HS3 3HT
Tel +44 (0)1859 550386
Email info@paircant-srath.co.uk
Web www.paircant-srath.co.uk

Entry 686   Map 20

# Western Isles

## Broad Bay House

In a wild landscape, 21st-century style and sophistication. Built in 2007, the house rises on graceful flights of decking above the beach. On an otherwise deserted shore, there is a villa right next door – but it disappears the moment you're inside. A stunning hall leads to a vaulted living room, whose windows face the waves on three sides... wow! More intimate boutique hotel than B&B – subtle lighting, oak doors, original art – Broad Bay has been designed with sheer, unadulterated comfort in mind. Ian and Marion are considerate, generous, flexible hosts and the food, served at candlelit tables, is heavenly.

| | |
|---|---|
| Price | £129-£170. |
| Rooms | 4: 2 doubles, 2 twins/doubles. |
| Meals | Dinner, 3 courses, £32.<br>Packed lunch £7-£10.<br>Pub/restaurant 7 miles. |
| Closed | Rarely. |
| Directions | A867 from Stornoway towards Barvas & Ness. On edge of Stornoway, right onto B895. After 6 miles, house on right, between Back & Gress. |

|  |  |
|---|---|
| | Ian Fordham |
| | Broad Bay House, |
| | Back, |
| | Stornoway, |
| | Isle of Lewis HS2 0LQ |
| Tel | +44 (0)1851 820990 |
| Email | stay@broadbayhouse.co.uk |
| Web | www.broadbayhouse.co.uk |

Wales

## Anglesey

### Cleifiog

Liz moved here for the view: you can see why. The creamy Georgian monks' hospice, later an 18th-century customs house, looks across to the whole Snowdon massif – spectacular with the Menai Strait between; the masts of Beaumaris Bay chink in the wind. As well as being a keen gardener, Liz paints and exhibits; her bold, striking pictures are dotted through the house. Big, bright, elegant rooms, are sprinkled with tapestries, antique samplers and fresh flowers. Be charmed by the welcome, the soft linens, the ample breakfasts and the wonderful soft sea air. *Children over three welcome. Minimum stay two nights at weekends.*

Travel Club offer. See page 414.

| | |
|---|---|
| Price | £75–£95. Singles £45–£65. |
| Rooms | 3: 2 twins/doubles, 1 suite. |
| Meals | Pub/restaurant 200 yards. |
| Closed | Christmas & New Year. |
| Directions | A55 over Britannia Bridge to Anglesey. A545 to Beaumaris. Past 2 left turns, house is 5th on left facing the sea. Bus stop outside. |

| | |
|---|---|
| | Liz Bradley |
| | Cleifiog, |
| | Townsend, Beaumaris, |
| | Anglesey LL58 8BH |
| Tel | +44 (0)1248 811507 |
| Email | liz@cleifiogbandb.co.uk |
| Web | www.cleifiogbandb.co.uk |

Entry 688  Map 6

## Carmarthenshire

### The Drovers

The ice-cream pink Georgian townhouse looks good enough to eat – as do the leek and cheese cakes; Jill is a superb cook. A fabulous Welsh hospitality pervades this B&B, along with antiques, gas log fires and peaceful, cosy rooms. Downstairs areas are spacious, with a rambling hotel feel; sunny bedrooms are laced with books and floral wallpapers; bathrooms come in contemporary white and cream, stocked with spoiling towels. Over breakfast (relaxed, delicious, locally sourced) you gaze through deep sash windows onto the town square; order a packed lunch and head for the hills. *Minimum stay two nights at weekends in high season.*

Travel Club offer. See page 414.

| | |
|---|---|
| Price | £65–£70. Singles from £45. |
| Rooms | 3: 2 doubles, 1 twin/double. |
| Meals | Dinner, 3 courses, £20. |
| | Packed lunch £5. Inns 50 yds. |
| Closed | Christmas & New Year. |
| Directions | In town centre, opposite fountain. |

| | |
|---|---|
| | Mrs Jill Blud |
| | The Drovers, |
| | 9 Market Square, Llandovery, |
| | Carmarthenshire SA20 0AB |
| Tel | +44 (0)1550 721115 |
| Email | jillblud@aol.com |
| Web | www.droversllandovery.co.uk |

Entry 689  Map 7

## Carmarthenshire

### Mount Pleasant Farm

Wake up to circling Red Kites with a breathtaking backdrop of the Black Mountain: your bedroom view is one of the best in this book. Sue and Nick are warm and delightful hosts and Sue is a brilliant cook – only the best local lamb and beef will do. The veg is organic and the eggs (deep yellow!) are from up the hill; vegetarians are spoiled too. After dinner there's snooker, a log fire, a cosy sofa; then a seriously comfortable bed in a room with a lovely country-house feel. Aberglasney and the National Botanic Gardens are nearby, coastal walks less than an hour away. *Children over 12 welcome. 1.5 hours from Pembroke Dock.*

| | |
|---|---|
| Price | £70. Singles £35–£38. |
| Rooms | 3: 1 twin/double; 1 twin/double, 1 single, sharing bath (2nd room let to same party only). |
| Meals | Dinner, 3 courses with wine, £18.50. Packed lunch £7.50. |
| Closed | Christmas. |
| Directions | A40 Llandovery-Llandeilo. At Llanwrda, right for Lampeter (A482). Out of village, 1st right after mounted pillar box in lay-by on left. Over bridge & up hill; 1st left. House 1st on right. |

Sue, Nick & Alice Thompson
Mount Pleasant Farm,
Llanwrda,
Carmarthenshire SA19 8AN
Tel    +44 (0)1550 777537
Fax    +44 (0)1550 777537
Email  rivarevivaluk@aol.com

Entry 690   Map 7

## Carmarthenshire

### Mandinam

On a heavenly bluff on the edge of the Beacons, beneath wheeling red kites and moody Welsh skies, lies Mandinam, the 'untouched holy place'. Delightful artistic Marcus and Daniella are its guardians, the farm is now mostly conservation land and they look after you as friends. Be charmed by bold rugs on wooden floors, weathered antiques, lofty ceilings, shutters, fires… and scrumptious meals in a red dining room. The rustic coach house studio, with hillside terrace and wood-burner, is for dreamers; the serene four-poster room has underfloor heating. Watch the sun go down before dinner, revel in the peace.

Ethical Collection: Environment; Community; Food. See page 412.

Travel Club offer. See page 414.

| | |
|---|---|
| Price | £70–£80. Singles by arrangement. |
| Rooms | 2: 1 studio twin/double, 1 four-poster. |
| Meals | Lunch or picnic from £7.50. Dinner with wine, £25. Restaurants & pubs 2 miles. |
| Closed | Christmas. |
| Directions | Left at Llangadog village shop; 50 yds, right for Myddfai. Past cemetery, 1st right for Llanddeusant; 1.5 miles, through woods on left. Or, by train to Llangadog. |

Daniella & Marcus Lampard
Mandinam,
Llangadog,
Carmarthenshire SA19 9LA
Tel    +44 (0)1550 777368
Email  info@mandinam.co.uk
Web    www.mandinam.co.uk

Entry 691   Map 7

## Carmarthenshire

### Plas Alltyferin

Wisteria-wrapped and delightfully creaky in parts, this Georgian family house comes with 270 secluded acres in the handsome Towy Valley, close to the superb gardens of Aberglasney and The National Botanical Gardens. The dining room, where you breakfast, has the original panelling; the bedrooms have an old-fashioned charm. Not the place for you if you like spotlessness and state-of-the-art plumbing, but the views across the ha-ha to the Norman hill fort are timelessly lovely and the welcome is heartfelt. Gerard and Charlotte are the easiest, kindest and dog-friendliest of hosts. *Children over ten welcome.*

 Travel Club offer. See page 414.

| | |
|---|---|
| Price | £60–£70. Singles £35–£40. |
| Rooms | 2: 1 twin; 1 twin with separate bathroom. |
| Meals | Pubs/restaurants within 2 miles. |
| Closed | Rarely. |
| Directions | From Carmarthen A40 east to Pont-ar-gothi. Left before bridge & follow narrow lane for approx. 2 miles keeping to right-hand hedge. House on right, signed. Call for precise details. |

Charlotte & Gerard Dent
Plas Alltyferin,
Pont-ar-gothi, Nantgaredig,
Carmarthen,
Carmarthenshire SA32 7PF
Tel/Fax    +44 (0)1267 290662
Email      dent@alltyferin.co.uk
Web        www.alltyferin.co.uk

Entry 692   Map 6

## Carmarthenshire

### Sarnau Mansion

Listed and Georgian, the house has its own water supply. Play tennis and revel in 16 acres of beautiful grounds complete with pond, walled garden and woodland with nesting red kites. Bedrooms are simply furnished in heritage colours; bathrooms are big. The oak-floored sitting room with chesterfields has French windows onto the garden, the dining room is simpler with separate tables and there's good, fresh home cooking from Cynthia. One mile from the A40, you can hear a slight hum of traffic if the wind is from that direction. You are 15 minutes from the National Botanic Garden of Wales. *Children over five welcome.*

 Travel Club offer. See page 414.

| | |
|---|---|
| Price | £70–£80. Singles £50. |
| Rooms | 3: 2 doubles, 1 twin. |
| Meals | Dinner, 3 courses, around £20. BYO. Pub 1 mile. |
| Closed | Rarely. |
| Directions | From Carmarthen A40 west for 4 miles. Right for Bancyfelin. After 0.5 miles, right into drive on brow of hill. |

Cynthia & David Fernihough
Sarnau Mansion,
Llysonnen Road, Bancyfelin,
Carmarthen,
Carmarthenshire SA33 5DZ
Tel/Fax    +44 (0)1267 211404
Email      fernihough@so1405.force9.co.uk
Web        www.sarnaumansion.co.uk

Entry 693   Map 6

# Ceredigion

## Broniwan

Carole and Allen have created a model organic farm, and it shows. They are happy, the cows are happy and the kitchen garden is the neatest in Wales. With huge warmth and a tray of Welsh cakes they invite you into their cosy, ivy-clad house of natural browns, reds and the odd vibrant flourish of local art. Another passion is literature; call to arrange a literary weekend. Plentiful birdlife in the wonderful garden with views to the Preseli hills adds an audible welcome from tree-creepers, redstarts and wrens. The National Botanic Garden of Wales and Aberglasney are nearby, the coastal paths a quick drive.

| Price | £66–£70. Singles £35. |
|---|---|
| Rooms | 2: 1 double; 1 double with separate bath. |
| Meals | Dinner £25–£30. BYO. Restaurant 7-8 miles. |
| Closed | Rarely. |
| Directions | From Aberaeron, A487 for 6 miles for Brynhoffnant. Left at B4334 to Rhydlewis; left at Post Office & shop, 1st lane on right, then 1st track on right. |

**Carole & Allen Jacobs**
Broniwan,
Rhydlewis, Llandysul,
Ceredigion SA44 5PF
Tel    +44 (0)1239 851261
Fax    +44 (0)1239 851261
Email  broniwan@btinternet.com
Web    www.broniwan.com

Entry 694  Map 6

# Ceredigion

## Ffynnon Fendigaid

Arrive through rolling countryside – birdsong and breeze the only sound; within moments you will be sprawled on a leather sofa admiring modern art and wondering how a little bit of Milan arrived here along with Huw and homemade cake. A place to come and pootle, with no rush; you can stay all day to stroll the fern fringed paths through the acres of wild garden to a lake and a grand bench, or opt for hearty walking. Your bed is big, the colours are soft, the bathrooms are spotless and the food is local – try all the Welsh cheeses. Wide beaches are minutes away, red kites and buzzards soar above you. Pulchritudinous.

 Travel Club offer. See page 414.

| Price | From £70. Singles from £40. |
|---|---|
| Rooms | 2 doubles. |
| Meals | Dinner, 2-3 courses, £15–£18. Packed lunch £6. Pub 1 mile. |
| Closed | Rarely. |
| Directions | From A487 Cardigan & Aberystwth coast road, take B4334 at Brynhoffnant towards Rhydlewis. 1 mile to junction where road joins from right & lane to house on left. |

**Huw Davies**
Ffynnon Fendigaid,
Rhydlewis,
Llandysul,
Ceredigion SA44 5SR
Tel    +44 (0)1239 851361
Email  ffynnonf@btinternet.com
Web    www.ffynnonf.co.uk

Entry 695  Map 6

## Conwy

### Pengwern Country House

The steeply wooded Conwy valley snakes down to this stone and slate gabled property set back from the road in Snowdonia National Park. Inside has an upbeat traditional feel: a large sitting room with floor-to-ceiling bay windows and pictures by the Betws-y-Coed artists who once lived here. Settle with a book by the wood-burner; Gwawr and Ian know just when to chat and when not. Bedrooms have rough plastered walls, colourful fabrics and super bathrooms, one with a double-ended roll top and views of Lledr Valley. Breakfast on fruits, yogurts, herb rösti, soda bread – gorgeous. *Minimum stay two nights at weekends in summer.*

| | |
|---|---|
| Price | £72–£84. Singles from £62. |
| Rooms | 3: 1 double, 1 four-poster, 1 twin/double. |
| Meals | Pubs/restaurants within 1.5 miles. Packed lunch £5.50. |
| Closed | Christmas & New Year. |
| Directions | From Betws-y-Coed, A5 towards Llangollen for 1 mile. Driveway on left, opposite small stone building. |

| | |
|---|---|
| | Gwawr & Ian Mowatt |
| | Pengwern Country House, |
| | Allt Dinas, Betws-y-Coed, |
| | Conwy LL24 0HF |
| Tel | +44 (0)1690 710480 |
| Email | gwawr.pengwern@btopenworld.com |
| Web | www.snowdoniaaccommodation.co.uk |

## Denbighshire

### Plas Efenechtyd Cottage

Efenechtyd means 'place of the monks' but there's nothing spartan about Dave and Marilyn's handsome brick farmhouse: breakfasts of local sausages, eggs from their hens, salmon fish cakes with mushrooms and homemade bread, are served at a polished table in the dining room with exotic wall hangings from Vietnam and Laos. Light bedrooms have a clear, uncluttered feel, excellent mattresses and good linen; bathrooms are surprisingly bling and warm as toast with plump towels. Motor or walk to Ruthin with its windy streets and interesting shops, or strike out for Offa's Dyke with a packed lunch; this is stunning countryside.

Travel Club offer. See page 414.

| | |
|---|---|
| Price | £60. Singles £40. |
| Rooms | 3: 2 doubles, 1 twin. |
| Meals | Packed lunch £6. Pub 1.6 miles. |
| Closed | Rarely. |
| Directions | From Ruthin follow signs for Bala. Straight over mini roundabout onto B5105. Take first left after 1 mile. Right at T-junction; house is 50 yds on right. |

| | |
|---|---|
| | Dave Jones & Marilyn Jeffery |
| | Plas Efenechtyd Cottage, |
| | Efenechtyd, Ruthin, |
| | Denbighshire LL15 2LP |
| Tel | +44 (0)1824 704008 |
| Email | info@plas-efenechtyd-cottage.co.uk |
| Web | www.plas-efenechtyd-cottage.co.uk |

## Flintshire

### Golden Grove

Huge, Elizabethan and intriguing – Golden Grove was built by Sir Edward Morgan in 1580. The Queen Anne staircase, oak panelling, faded fabrics and fine family pieces are enhanced by jewel-like colour schemes: rose-pink, indigo, aqua. In summer the magnificent dining room is in use; in the winter the sitting room fire counters the draughts. The two Anns are charming and amusing, dinners are delicious and the family foursome tend the garden – beautiful, productive and well-kept. They also find time for a nuttery and a sheep farm as well as their relaxed B&B. Many return to this exceptional place.

Travel Club offer. See page 414.

| | |
|---|---|
| Price | £100. Singles £60. |
| Rooms | 3: 1 double; 1 double, 1 twin, each with separate bath. |
| Meals | Dinner £28. Pubs within 2 miles. |
| Closed | November-February. |
| Directions | Turn off A55 onto A5151 for Prestatyn. At Texaco before Trelawnyd, right. Branch left immed. over 1st x-roads; right at T-junc. Gates 170 yds on left. |

**Ann & Mervyn and Ann & Nigel Steele-Mortimer**
Golden Grove,
Llanasa, Holywell,
Flintshire CH8 9NA
Tel     +44 (0)1745 854452
Email   golden.grove@lineone.net

Entry 698   Map 7

## Flintshire

### Plas Penucha

Swing back in time with polished parquet, tidy beams, a huge Elizabethan panelled lounge with books, leather sofas and open fire – a cosy spot for tea in winter. Plas Penucha – 'the big house on the highest point in the parish' – has been in the family for 500 years. Airy, old-fashioned bedrooms have long views across the garden to Offa's Dyke and one has a shower in the corner. The L-shaped dining room has a genuine Arts & Crafts interior; outside, rhododendrons and a rock garden flourish. Beyond is open countryside and St Asaph, with the smallest medieval cathedral in the country.

Travel Club offer. See page 414.

| | |
|---|---|
| Price | From £60. Singles from £32. |
| Rooms | 2: 1 double, 1 twin. |
| Meals | Dinner £18.50. Packed lunch £4.50. Pub 2 miles. |
| Closed | Rarely. |
| Directions | From Chester, A55, B5122 left for Caerwys. 1st right into High St. Right at end. 0.75 miles to x-roads & left, then straight for 1 mile. House on left, signed. |

**Mrs Nest Price**
Plas Penucha,
Peny Cefn Road, Caerwys, Mold,
Flintshire CH7 5BH
Tel     +44 (0)1352 720210
Email   info@plaspenucha.co.uk
Web     www.plaspenucha.co.uk

Entry 699   Map 7

# Gwynedd

## Lympley Lodge

The solid Victorian exterior belies a surprising interior. Welcoming Patricia, a former restorer, has brought together a gorgeous collection of furniture, while her meticulous paintwork adds light and life to her seaside home. Above is the Little Orme; below, across the main coast road, the sweep of Llandudno Bay. Bedrooms strike the perfect balance between the practical and the exotic; all have crisp linen, rich fabrics, fresh flowers, lovely views. There's an elegant sitting room for guests, a stunning dining room with a Renaissance feel and breakfasts full of local and homemade produce. Wonderful.

| Price | £80. Singles £50–£55. |
|---|---|
| Rooms | 3: 2 doubles, 1 twin. |
| Meals | Restaurants/pubs 5-minute drive. |
| Closed | Mid-December to end of January. |
| Directions | From Llandudno Promenade, turn right and follow B5115 (Colwyn Bay) up the hill. Pass right turn for Bryn Y Bia. House entrance (board on side of building) on right. |

|  | Patricia Richards |
|---|---|
|  | Lympley Lodge, |
|  | Colwyn Road, Craigside, |
|  | Llandudno, Gwynedd LL30 3AL |
| Tel | +44 (0)1492 549304 |
| Email | patricia@lympleylodge.co.uk |
| Web | www.lympleylodge.co.uk |

✗ 🚂 🚲

Entry 700   Map 7

# Gwynedd

## Abercelyn Country House

The 1729 rectory comes with rhododendron-rich grounds, an immaculate kitchen garden and a mountain stream. In spite of the rugged setting Abercelyn is a genteel retreat. Shutters gleam, logs glow and bedrooms are spacious and light with smart bathrooms and luscious views. You are well looked after: the drawing room overflows with outdoor guides, Ray orchestrates adventure trips to Snowdonia National Park and Lindsay cooks a great breakfast with eggs from their own hens. Bala Lake is a ten-minute stroll – or you can strike off round it for the whole 14 miles – bracing indeed! *Guided walks & canoeing.*

Ethical Collection: Environment; Community; Food. See page 412.

🧳 Travel Club offer. See page 414.

| Price | £70–£80. Singles £50. |
|---|---|
| Rooms | 3: 2 doubles, 1 twin/double. |
| Meals | Pub 10-minute drive. Restaurant 15-minute walk; free return taxi service. |
| Closed | Rarely. |
| Directions | On A494 Bala-Dolgellau road, 1 mile from centre of Bala, opp. Llanycil Church. Bus service: Wrexham - Bala - Llanycil - Dolgellau - Bamouth. |

|  | Ray & Lindsay Hind |
|---|---|
|  | Abercelyn Country House, |
|  | Llanycil, Bala, |
|  | Gwynedd LL23 7YF |
| Tel | +44 (0)1678 521109 |
| Email | info@abercelyn.co.uk |
| Web | www.abercelyn.co.uk |

🎁 ✗ 📖

Entry 701   Map 7

# Gwynedd

## Dolgadfa

Gasp at the beauty of the road to Dolgadfa, every bend revealing yet another perfect frame of southern Snowdonia – the gentle prelude to the ragged peaks. The youthful Robertsons' slice of this bliss is unexpectedly luxurious. The deep limpid river winds past the listed guest barn where bedrooms – one with stone steps straight onto the riverside garden – are fresh and country-cosy, with gingham curtains and all the trimmings. A bright living room with roaring fire, sofas and Welsh oak floor is yours, and Louise does a fine breakfast. For a couple or a party, a superb place. *Fishing & shooting available.*

 Travel Club offer. See page 414.

| | |
|---|---|
| Price | £70. |
| Rooms | 3: 1 double, 1 twin; 1 double with separate bath. |
| Meals | Pub/restaurant in village, 1 mile. |
| Closed | Christmas. |
| Directions | B4401; after Llandrillo, 2nd right. Single track road; over bridge; at T-junc. left, on for 1.5 miles; 2nd farmhouse on left. White gate. |

|  |  |
|---|---|
| | **Louise Robertson** Dolgadfa, Llandderfel, Bala, Gwynedd LL23 7RE |
| Tel | +44 (0)7708 249537 |
| Email | dolgadfa@btinternet.com |
| Web | www.dolgadfa.co.uk |

Entry 702   Map 7

# Gwynedd

## Bryniau Golau

Under clear skies, there are few more soul-lifting views: the long lake and miles of Snowdonia National Park. Each generous room is beautifully furnished – traditional with a contemporary twist, and more glorious views to the garden and lake. Katrina, friendly and adaptable, spoils you with open fires in the sitting room, goose down duvets on the beds, spa baths, underfloor heating and scrumptious breakfasts that set you up for the day. Linger on the lawn, perhaps with a drink as the sun sets, and try your hand at fly fishing or white water rafting. A wonderful place for a house party – and the walking is superb.

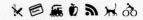 Travel Club offer. See page 414.

| | |
|---|---|
| Price | £80-£90. Singles £55-£65. |
| Rooms | 3: 2 four-posters, 1 twin/double. |
| Meals | Supper available. Pubs/restaurants within 2 miles. |
| Closed | Rarely. |
| Directions | From Bala B4391; 1 mile, B4403 Llangower. Pass Bala Lake Hotel; look for sign showing left turn; 20 yds after tree, sign on right; left up hill, over cattle grid; 1st on right. |

|  |  |
|---|---|
| | **Katrina le Saux** Bryniau Golau, Llangower, Bala, Gwynedd LL23 7BT |
| Tel | +44 (0)1678 521782 |
| Email | katrinalesaux@hotmail.co.uk |
| Web | www.bryniau-golau.co.uk |

Entry 703   Map 7

# Gwynedd

## The Old Rectory - on the lake

The drive to get here is fantastic and the approach truly beautiful – The Old Rectory waits for you on the other side of the lake. The owners are full of enthusiasm for their fabulous B&B and spoil guests rotten – comfy beds with smooth Egyptian cotton sheets, binoculars for bird spotting and luxurious baths. Fabulous photos of mountains and lake decorate the dining room, there are views from every window to the luminous lake, and you can climb Cadair Idris from the front door. Return, weak-limbed, to a delicious, home-cooked meal and a bit of cossetting… maybe a wallow in the hot tub under the stars. *Minimum stay two nights at weekends.*

| | |
|---|---|
| Price | £90. Singles £60. |
| Rooms | 3 doubles. |
| Meals | Dinner £25. Pub 4 miles. |
| Closed | Rarely. |
| Directions | A470 from Dolgellau. A487 from Cross Foxes Inn, then B4405 (signposted Tywyn). Follow along lakeside; turn right at head of lake and cont. 0.25 miles. House illuminated by blue lights at night. |

Ricky Francis
The Old Rectory - on the lake,
Talyllyn,
Gwynedd LL36 9AJ

| | |
|---|---|
| Tel | +44 (0)1654 782225 |
| Email | enquiries@rectoryonthelake.co.uk |
| Web | www.rectoryonthelake.co.uk |

🐾 🍴 🏠 🐕 📶 🍷 🚴

Entry 704   Map 7

# Gwynedd

## Y Goeden Eirin

A little gem tucked between the sea and the mountains, an education in Welsh culture, and a great place to explore wild Snowdonia, the Llyn Pensinsula and the dramatic Eifl mountains. Inside presents a cosy picture: Welsh-language and English books share the shelves, paintings by contemporary Welsh artists enliven the walls, an arty 70s décor mingles with sturdy Welsh oak in the bedrooms – the one in the house the best – and all bathrooms are super. Wonderful food is served alongside the Bechstein in the beamed dining room – the welcoming, thoughtful Eluned and John have created an unusually delightful space.

Ethical Collection: Environment; Food. See page 412.

🧳 Travel Club offer. See page 414.

| | |
|---|---|
| Price | £80–£100. Singles from £60. |
| Rooms | 3: 2 doubles, 1 twin. |
| Meals | Dinner, 3 courses, £28. Wine from £14. Packed lunch £12. Pub/restaurant 0.75 miles. |
| Closed | Christmas to New Year & occasionally. |
| Directions | From Caernarfon onto Porthmadog & Pwllheli road. A487 through Bontnewydd, left at r'bout, signed Dolydd. House 0.5 miles on right, last entrance before garage on left. |

Dr John & Mrs Eluned Rowlands
Y Goeden Eirin,
Dolydd,
Caernarfon, Gwynedd LL54 7EF

| | |
|---|---|
| Tel | +44 (0)1286 830942 |
| Email | john_rowlands@tiscali.co.uk |
| Web | www.ygoedeneirin.co.uk |

🍴 🚂 🐕 📶 🍷 🐈

Entry 705   Map 6

# Gwynedd

## Plas Tan-yr-allt

Who shot Shelley in the drawing room? The poet fled in 1813, the mystery unsolved. The listed house has a colourful history, irresistible to the owners who have just finished a glorious restoration: roll top baths, deep luscious colours, underfloor heating, handsome furniture. *The Daily Telegraph* said Tanny exemplifies "contemporary country-house style"... and there's country-house cooking too. Nick uses local ingredients, and guests eat together at an impressive oak and slate table for dinner – a convivial treat. Wonderful views stretch from the terrace and gardens over the estuary and bay.

Travel Club offer. See page 414.

| | |
|---|---|
| Price | £120-£175. Singles £100-£140. |
| Rooms | 6: 3 doubles, 1 twin, 2 four-posters. |
| Meals | Dinner, 3 courses, £38.50 (Wednesday-Sunday). Pubs/restaurants 10-minute walk. |
| Closed | 4 weeks in January/February. |
| Directions | Leave Tremadog on A498 for Beddgelert. Signed on left after 0.5 miles. House at top of hill. |

Michael Bewick & Nick Golding
Plas Tan-yr-allt,
Tremadog, Porthmadog,
Gwynedd LL49 9RG
Tel        +44 (0)1766 514545
Email    info@tanyrallt.co.uk
Web      www.tanyrallt.co.uk

Entry 706   Map 6

# Gwynedd

## The Old Rectory

In the heart of the Llyn Peninsula, an immaculate Georgian rectory in its own grounds. There are gardens to relax in, a horse in the paddock and wonderful art on the walls – Gabrielle has created delightful interiors. Seagrass floors and toile de Jouy, big mirrors and family antiques, a log fire for cool evenings, a guest drawing room with sofas and books... the mood is one of easy elegance and you can come and go as you please. Gabrielle rides, Roger sails and both are relaxed and charming hosts. The area is stunning, walks start from the door; no wonder guests return. *Pets by arrangement. Minimum stay two nights bank holidays.*

Travel Club offer. See page 414.

| | |
|---|---|
| Price | From £90. Singles from £65. |
| Rooms | 3: 2 twins/doubles, 1 double. |
| Meals | Packed lunch £6.50. Pub/restaurant 2 miles. |
| Closed | Christmas. |
| Directions | From Pwllheli, A499 to r'bout. Right onto A497 Nefyn & Boduan road for 3 miles; left opp. church; house set back, on right. |

Gabrielle & Roger Pollard
The Old Rectory,
Boduan, Pwllheli, Gwynedd LL53 6DT
Tel        +44 (0)1758 721519
Fax       +44 (0)1758 721519
Email    thepollards@theoldrectory.net
Web      www.theoldrectory.net

Entry 707   Map 6

# Monmouthshire

## Penpergwm Lodge

On the edge of the Brecon Beacons, a large and lovely Edwardian house. Breakfast round the mahogany table, relax by the fire in the sitting room with books to read and piano to play. The Boyles have been here for years and pour much of their energy into three beautiful acres of parterre and potager, orchard and flowers. Bedrooms are gloriously traditional – ancestral portraits, embroidered bed covers, big windows, good chintz – with garden views; bathrooms are a skip across the landing. A pool and tennis for the sporty, two summer houses for the dreamy, a good pub you can walk to. Splendid, old-fashioned B&B.

| | |
|---|---|
| Price | £70-£75. Singles £40. |
| Rooms | 2 twins, each with separate bath. |
| Meals | Pub within walking distance. |
| Closed | Rarely. |
| Directions | A40 to Abergavenny; at big r'bout on SE edge of town, B4598 to Usk for 2.5 miles. Left at King of Prussia pub, up small lane; house 200 yds on left. |

|  | Catriona Boyle |
|---|---|
| | Penpergwm Lodge, |
| | Abergavenny, Monmouthshire NP7 9AS |
| Tel | +44 (0)1873 840208 |
| Fax | +44 (0)1873 840208 |
| Email | boyle@penpergwm.co.uk |
| Web | www.penplants.com |

Entry 708   Map 7

# Pembrokeshire

## Penfro

This is fun – idiosyncratic and a tad theatrical, rather than conventional and uniformly stylish. The Lappins' home is a tall, impressive Grade II*-listed Georgian affair, formerly a ballet school. Judith's taste – she's also a WW1 expert – is eclectic verging on the wacky and she minds that guests are comfortable and well-fed. You eat communally, and very well, at the big scrubbed table in the flagged, Aga-fired kitchen at garden level... the garden's big and beautiful so enjoy its conversational terrace and hammocks. And discuss which of the three very characterful bedrooms will suit you best, plumbing and all!

Ethical Collection: Food. See page 412.

Travel Club offer. See page 414.

| | |
|---|---|
| Price | £65-£90. Singles from £45. |
| Rooms | 3: 1 double; 1 double, 1 twin both with separate bathroom. |
| Meals | Packed lunch from £8. Pub 250 yds. |
| Closed | Rarely. |
| Directions | A4075 Pembroke; 2 miles to mini r'bout. Straight ahead, down hill, bear right. Right lane past castle; T-junc. bear right. Road widens by Chapel Pembroke Antique Centre. House on right. |

|  | Judith Lappin |
|---|---|
| | Penfro, |
| | 111 Main Street, Pembroke, |
| | Pembrokeshire SA71 4DB |
| Tel | +44 (0)1646 682753 |
| Email | info@penfro.co.uk |
| Web | www.penfro.co.uk |

Entry 709   Map 6

## Pembrokeshire

### Furzehill Farm

Val and Paul's recently built farmhouse is a friendly and characterful place for families and walkers. The Aga-driven kitchen is the hub and Paul will do you a grand breakfast, and something tasty and local for supper too. There are hunting prints, a modern leather sofa and a brick-surround open fire in the sitting room, and cosy carpeted bedrooms upstairs – one with a shower, two sharing a jazzy jacuzzi. Eco credentials include ground-sourced heating and the young garden promises an above-ground pool. This is a deeply rural spot with a good pub to walk to and the birds of the lovely Cleddau Estuary to admire.

Ethical Collection: Environment; Food. See page 412.

Travel Club offer. See page 414.

| | |
|---|---|
| Price | £60–£90. Singles from £30. |
| Rooms | 3: 1 family for 4 or 5; 1 double, 1 room with bunk beds, sharing separate bath. |
| Meals | Dinner, 3 courses, £18. Supper from £12. Packed lunch £5. Pub/restaurant 3 miles. |
| Closed | Christmas Day. |
| Directions | A40 to Canaston Bridge; A4075 for Pembroke. Right at Crosshands; after sharp bend, left for Cresswell Quay; left again at T-junc. for C. Quay; 2nd entrance on left. |

| | |
|---|---|
| | E V Rees |
| | Furzehill Farm, |
| | Martletwy, Narberth, |
| | Pembrokeshire SA67 8AN |
| Tel | +44 (0)1834 891480 |
| Email | val@furzehillfarm.com |
| Web | www.furzehillfarm.com |

Entry 710    Map 6

## Pembrokeshire

### Knowles Farm

The Cleddau estuary winds its way around this 1,000-acre organic farm – its lush grasses feed the cows that produce milk for the renowned Rachel's yoghurt. Your hosts love the area, are passionate about its conservation and let you come and go as you please; picnic in the garden, wander through bluebell woods, discover a pond – dogs love it too! Gini rustles up scrumptious, candlelit dinners; food is fully organic or very local (five miles!). You have your own entrance to bedrooms which are old-fashioned but well-maintained, with comfy beds, fresh flowers and glorious views. Traditional, real-farmhouse B&B.

Travel Club offer. See page 414.

| | |
|---|---|
| Price | From £65. |
| Rooms | 3: 2 doubles; 1 twin with separate bath. |
| Meals | Supper from £12. Dinner, 4 courses, £22. Packed lunch £6. Pub 1.5 miles, restaurant 3 miles. |
| Closed | Rarely. |
| Directions | A4075 to Cresselly; turn right. Follow signs for Lawrenny to first x-roads; straight over; next x-roads right; 100 yds on left. |

| | |
|---|---|
| | Ms Virginia Lort Phillips |
| | Knowles Farm, |
| | Lawrenny, Pembrokeshire SA68 0PX |
| Tel | +44 (0)1834 891221 |
| Fax | +44 (0)1834 891221 |
| Email | ginilp@lawrenny.org.uk |
| Web | www.lawrenny.org.uk |

Entry 711    Map 6

# Pembrokeshire

## Boulston Manor

A lush descent through ancient woodland, with tantalising glimpses of open water,takes you to the ivy-clad 1790s house and a great place to stay. A country-house drawing room with veranda and Cleddau views is yours to use; soft sofas, horsey pictures, fresh flowers and a grand piano set the tone. Perfectly refurbished bedrooms and bathrooms are roomy and glamorous: yards of thick fabrics, dazzling white linen, stone fireplaces, marble tiling, and, in one, a jucuzzi with the grandest parkland views. Generous Jules and Rod are lively and fun, you will eat good, local food and there's miles of walking in the National Park.

| | |
|---|---|
| Price | £60-£100. |
| Rooms | 3 doubles. |
| Meals | Supper £15. Dinner from £25. |
| Closed | Never. |
| Directions | From Salutation Square (County Hotel) Haverfordwest, take Uzmaston Road past Popes Garage. Through Uzmaston, past Goodwood (signed Boulston). Continue for 1.5 miles and follow Boulston signs. |

**Mr & Mrs Roderick Thomas**
Boulston Manor,
Haverfordwest,
Pembrokeshire SA62 4AQ
Tel +44 (0)1437 764600
Email info@boulstonmanor.co.uk
Web www.boulstonmanor.co.uk

Entry 712   Map 6

# Pembrokeshire

## Pentower

Curl up with a cat and watch the ferries – or sometimes a porpoise – coasting to Ireland; French windows open onto the terrace and a glorious vista. Mary and Tony are welcoming; they've done an excellent restoration on the turreted 1898 house, keeping its quarry tiled floors, decorative fireplaces and impressive staircase. Spotless bedrooms are light and airy, with large showers; the Tower Room has the views. There's a tiled dining/sitting room for full English (or Welsh) breakfasts – also with views, a 'temple' in the garden for summer, Fishguard is a short stroll, and the stunning coastal path nearby.

 Travel Club offer. See page 414.

| | |
|---|---|
| Price | £70-£75. Singles £45. |
| Rooms | 3: 2 doubles, 1 twin. |
| Meals | Packed lunch £5. Pubs/restaurants 500 yds. |
| Closed | Occasionally. |
| Directions | A40 to Fishguard town; at r'bout, 2nd exit onto Main Street. Before sharp left bend, right fork onto Tower Hill; 200 yds on, through house gates. |

**Tony Jacobs & Mary Geraldine Casey**
Pentower,
Tower Hill, Fishguard,
Pembrokeshire SA65 9LA
Tel +44 (0)1348 874462
Email sales@pentower.co.uk
Web www.pentower.co.uk

Entry 713   Map 6

## Pembrokeshire

### Merton Hall

In front of this intriguing triple-peaked Victorian house lies manicured parkland; behind, a wild, wonderful hill offering stunning sea views. Nigel and Rowena are busy refurbishing Dinas's 'Ty Hen' (Old House), which was pieced together over centuries. Family heirlooms (with matching anecdotes) and naval prints and paintings give the sitting room a certain charm; the dining area's bay windows overlook distant gorse-covered hills. On sunny mornings, join the birds for breakfast in a pretty wisteria-strewn courtyard. You can walk to Aberbach cove, explore Preseli hills, return to comfortable beds and capable, caring hosts.

Travel Club offer. See page 414.

| | |
|---|---|
| Price | £70–£90. Singles £45–£55. |
| Rooms | 2: 1 double, 1 twin. |
| Meals | Packed lunch for walkers £5. Pub 0.75 miles; restaurants 3.5 miles. |
| Closed | Christmas, New Year & occasionally. |
| Directions | From Fishguard, A487 for Cardigan. After 3 miles enter Dinas Cross. Left down track just after 30mph limit sign. House is on left after 50 yds. |

**Rowena Corlett**
Merton Hall,
Dinas Cross, Newport,
Pembrokeshire SA42 0XN
Tel    +44 (0)1348 811223
Email  info@mertonhall.co.uk
Web   www.mertonhall.co.uk

Entry 714   Map 6

## Powys

### Llangattock Court

Built in 1690 and mentioned in Pevsner as an 'outstanding example of a country house in this style', this is indeed grand and sits in the middle of the sleepy village, surrounded by a large garden. Both bedrooms are a good size (one has a big French bed and a small shower room) with lovely antiques and a fresh feel; views from one soar across to the Black Mountains. Breakfast in style in the enormous dining room overlooked by framed relatives, stroll through the rose garden, visit a castle or historic house, walk to the local pub for dinner. Morgan is a painter; some of his paintings are on display.

Travel Club offer. See page 414.

| | |
|---|---|
| Price | £50–£80. Singles £45. |
| Rooms | 2: 1 double, 1 suite with four-poster and twin. |
| Meals | Restaurants/pubs within 1 mile. |
| Closed | Christmas & New Year; 1-2 weeks October. |
| Directions | From A465, B4777 into Gilwern, follow signs to Crickhowell. In Legar, left at Vine Tree Inn. Pass Horse Shoe Inn on right; after 60 yds right, then right again 50 yds beyond church signed to Dardy. 1st on left. |

**Polly Llewellyn**
Llangattock Court,
Llangattock, Crickhowell,
Powys NP8 1PH
Tel    +44 (0)1873 810116
Email  morganllewellyn@btinternet.com
Web   www.llangattockcourt.co.uk

Entry 715   Map 7

# Powys

## Tyr Chanter

Warmth, colour, children and activity: this house is fun. Tiggy welcomes you like family; help collect eggs, feed the lambs or the pony, drop your shoes by the fire. The farmhouse and barn are stylishly relaxed; deep sofas, tartan throws, heaps of books, views to the Brecon Beacons and Black Mountains. Bedrooms are soft, simple sanctuaries with Jo Malone bathroom treats. Children's rooms zing with murals; toys, kids' sitting room, sandpit – child heaven. Walk, fish, canoe, book-browse in Hay or stroll the estate. Homemade cakes, whisky to help yourself to: fine hospitality.

| | |
|---|---|
| Price | £90. Singles £55. |
| Rooms | 4: 1 double; 1 double with separate bath/shower; 2 children's rooms. |
| Meals | Packed lunch £8. Pub 1 mile. |
| Closed | Christmas. |
| Directions | From Crickhowell, A40 towards Brecon. 2 miles left at Gliffaes Hotel sign. 2 miles, past hotel, house is 600 yds on right. |

| | |
|---|---|
| | Tiggy Pettifer |
| | Tyr Chanter, |
| | Gliffaes, |
| | Crickhowell, Powys NP8 1RL |
| Tel | +44 (0)1874 731144 |
| Email | tiggy@tyrchanter.com |
| Web | www.tyrchanter.com |

Entry 716   Map 7

# Powys

## The Old Store House

Unbend here with agreeable books, chattering birds, and twinkling Peter, who asks only that you feel at home. Downstairs are a range-warmed kitchen, a sunny conservatory overlooking garden, ducks and canal, and a charmingly ramshackle sitting room with a wood-burner, sofas and a piano – no babbling TV. Bedrooms are large, light and spotless, with more books, soft goose down, new bathrooms, and armchairs facing views. Breakfast, without haste, on toothsome scrambled eggs, local bacon and sausages, blistering coffee. Bliss – but not for those who prefer the comfort of rules. *Minimum stay two nights at weekends.*

Travel Club offer. See page 414.

| | |
|---|---|
| Price | £75. Singles £40. |
| Rooms | 4: 3 doubles, 1 twin. |
| Meals | Packed lunch £4. Pub/restaurant 0.75 miles. |
| Closed | Rarely. |
| Directions | From Brecon, Abergavenny A40. After 1 mile, left for Llanfrynach B4558. Cross narrow stone bridge. House is 1.3 miles on right. |

| | |
|---|---|
| | Peter Evans |
| | The Old Store House, |
| | Llanfrynach, |
| | Powys LD3 7LJ |
| Tel | +44 (0)1874 665499 |
| Email | p.e@tesco.net |
| Web | www.theoldstorehouse.co.uk |

Entry 717   Map 7

# Powys

## The Old Post Office

Unpretentious, simple B&B in the most glorious surroundings. Bedrooms are large, colourful and delightfully quiet; beds are comfortable. Fresh flowers and good books abound, there's a guests' sitting room in which exhausted hikers – and their dogs – can collapse after a recce in the Black Mountains, and it's a two mile walk across fields for all the delights of Hay-on-Wye. Whatever you do, you'll be captivated by the region. Linda serves delicious, cooked vegetarian breakfasts at a long communal table; she and Ed tend to keep to their own part of the house and you come and go as you please.

# Powys

## Hafod Y Garreg

A unique opportunity to stay in the oldest house in Wales – a 1402 cruck-framed hall house, built for Henry IV as a hunting lodge. Annie and John have filled it with a fascinating mix of Venetian mirrors, Indian rugs, pewter plates, gorgeous fabrics and oak furniture. Dine by candlelight – maybe pheasant pie with chilli jam and hazelnut mash: delicious. Bedrooms are stylish and comfortable with Egyptian cotton bed linen. You reach the Grade II*-listed house by a bumpy track across gated fields crowded with chickens, cats, goats, birds... a very special, peaceful and secluded place.

 Travel Club offer. See page 414.

| | | | | |
|---|---|---|---|---|
| Price | £70. Singles from £35. | | Price | £72. Singles from £68. |
| Rooms | 3: 1 double, 1 twin/double, 1 double (extra bed). | | Rooms | 2 doubles. |
| Meals | Pub 2 miles. Pubs/restaurants in Hay-on-Wye. | | Meals | Dinner, 3 courses, £21.50. BYO. Pubs/restaurants 2.5 miles. |
| Closed | Rarely. | | Closed | Christmas. |
| Directions | Hay-on-Wye to Brecon; 0.5 miles, left, for Llanigon; on for 1 mile, left before school. On right opp. church. | | Directions | From Hay-on-Wye, A479 then A470 to B. Wells. Through Llyswen, past forest on left, down hill. Next left for Trericket Mill, then immed. right & up hill. Straight through gate across track to house. |

|  | | |  | |
|---|---|---|---|---|
| | Linda Webb & Ed Moore | | | Annie & John McKay |
| | The Old Post Office, | | | Hafod Y Garreg, |
| | Llanigon, | | | Erwood, |
| | Hay-on-Wye, | | | Builth Wells, Powys LD2 3TQ |
| | Powys HR3 5QA | | Tel | +44 (0)1982 560400 |
| Tel | +44 (0)1497 820008 | | Email | john-annie@hafod-y.wanadoo.co.uk |
| Web | www.oldpost-office.co.uk | | Web | www.hafodygarreg.co.uk |

Entry 718  Map 7

Entry 719  Map 7

## Powys

### Trericket Mill Vegetarian Guesthouse

Part guest house, part bunk house, all very informal – all Grade II*-listed. The dining room has been created amid a jumble of corn-milling machinery: B&B guests, campers and bunkers pile in together to fill hungry bellies with Nicky and Alistair's delicious and plentiful veggie food from a chalkboard menu. Stoves throw out the heat in the flagstoned living rooms with their comfy chairs; the bedrooms are simple pine affairs. Set out to explore from here on foot, horseback, bicycle or canoe; lovers of the outdoors looking for good value and a planet-friendly bias will be in heaven.

Ethical Collection: Environment; Food.
See page 412.

Travel Club offer. See page 414.

| Price | £60–£75. Singles £40–£52.50. |
|---|---|
| Rooms | 3: 2 doubles, 1 twin. |
| Meals | Dinner, 3 courses, £18.50. BYO. Simple supper £8. Pub/restaurant 2 miles. |
| Closed | Christmas & occasionally in winter. |
| Directions | 12 miles north of Brecon on A470. Mill set slightly back from road, on left, between Llyswen & Erwood. Train to Llandrindod Wells; bus to Brecon every 2 hrs will drop at mill on request. |

**Alistair & Nicky Legge**
Trericket Mill Vegetarian Guesthouse,
Erwood, Builth Wells,
Powys LD2 3TQ
Tel   +44 (0)1982 560312
Email   mail@trericket.co.uk
Web   www.trericket.co.uk

Entry 720   Map 7

## Powys

### Rhedyn

Come here if you need to remember how to relax. Such an unassuming little place, but with real character and soul: great comfort too with exposed walls in the bedrooms, funky lighting, pocket sprung mattresses, lovely books to read, and calm colours; bathrooms are modern and delightfully quirky. But the real stars of this show are Muiread and Ciaran: wonderfully warm, enthusiastic and engaging, with a passion for good, local food and a desire for more self-sufficiency – pigs and bees are planned next. This is a totally tranquil place, with agreeable walks through the Irfon valley and bog snorkelling too!

| Price | £65. Singles £60. |
|---|---|
| Rooms | 3 doubles. |
| Meals | Dinner, 3 courses, £25. Packed lunch £7.50. Pub/restaurant 1 mile. |
| Closed | Rarely. |
| Directions | From Builth Wells A483 towards 'Garth'. Pass Cilmery village, Rhedyn signpost is one mile on right. House is in middle of field. |

**Muiread & Ciaran O'Connell**
Rhedyn,
Cilmery, Builth Wells,
Powys LD2 3LH
Tel   +44 (0)1982 551944
Email   info@rhedynguesthouse.co.uk
Web   www.rhedynguesthouse.co.uk

Entry 721   Map 7

# Powys

## The Old Vicarage

Blessed are those who enter... especially devotees of Victoriana. The house, designed by Sir George Gilbert Scott, is a delight. Your host, charming and fun, ushers you in to a rich confection of colours, dark wood and a lifetime's collecting: splendid brass beds, cast-iron radiators, porcelain loos, sumptuous bedspreads and a garden with grotto, waterfall and rill. Dine by candle or gas light (the food is superb), ring the servants' bell for early morning tea. You are on the English side of Offa's Dyke: look north to the heavenly Radnorshire hills, south to all of Herefordshire. *Minimum stay two nights weekends & bank holidays.*

Travel Club offer. See page 414.

| | |
|---|---|
| Price | From £98. |
| Rooms | 3: 2 doubles, 1 twin. |
| Meals | Dinner, 4 courses, £34. Restaurant 10-minute drive. |
| Closed | Rarely. |
| Directions | B4355, between Presteigne & Knighton; in village of Norton, immed. north of church. |

Paul Gerrard
The Old Vicarage,
Norton, Presteigne,
Powys LD8 2EN
Tel +44 (0)1544 260038
Email paul@nortonoldvic.co.uk
Web www.oldvicarage-nortonrads.co.uk

Entry 722  Map 7

# Powys

## The Old Vicarage

Come for vast skies, forested hills and quilted fields that stretch for miles. This Victorian vicarage is a super base: smart, welcoming, full of comforts. You get a log fire in a cosy sitting room, a super-smart dining room with long country views and fancy bedrooms that spoil you all the way. Tim's food is just as good. Local suppliers are noted on menus, but much is grown in the garden, where chickens run free. Resist laziness and take to the hills – the Kerry Ridgeway is on your doorstep as is Powis Castle – for glorious walking, then home and afternoon tea. *Children over 12 welcome.*

Ethical Collection: Environment; Food. See page 412.

Travel Club offer. See page 414.

| | |
|---|---|
| Price | £95. Singles £65. |
| Rooms | 3: 1 twin/double, 2 doubles. |
| Meals | Dinner, 3 courses, £28. Packed lunch available. Pub 4 miles. |
| Closed | Rarely. |
| Directions | A483, 3.5 miles from Newtown for Llandrindod Wells, left on sharp right bend, house first on left. |

Tim & Helen Withers
The Old Vicarage,
Dolfor, Newtown,
Powys SY16 4BN
Tel +44 (0)1686 629051
Email tim@theoldvicaragedolfor.co.uk
Web www.theoldvicaragedolfor.co.uk

Entry 723  Map 7

## Powys

### Talbontdrain

Way off the beaten track, remote and wild, sits a white-painted stone farmhouse. The Cambrian mountains stretch to the south, the river Dovey lies in the vale below and kind Hilary knows all the walks and can sort special routes for you. She cooks a hearty breakfast too, or a farmhouse supper, and gives you colourful bedrooms – not swish, but with everything you need. There are photographs of garden plants, a pianola, and furniture in such a mix of styles that it all gives a feeling of great informality. The peace is deep – even the cockerel stays quiet until a respectable time – and walkers will adore it.

Travel Club offer. See page 414.

| | |
|---|---|
| Price | £56–£66. Singles £28. |
| Rooms | 4: 1 double, 1 family room for 3; 1 twin/double, 1 single sharing shower. |
| Meals | Dinner, 2 courses & coffee, £18. Packed lunch £6. |
| Closed | Christmas & Boxing Day. |
| Directions | Leaving Machynlleth on A489, 1st right signed Forge. In Forge bear right to Uwchygarreg up 'dead end'. 3 miles, pass phone box on left, up steep hill. House on left at top. |

|  |  |
|---|---|
| | **Hilary Matthews** |
| | Talbontdrain, |
| | Uwchygarreg, Machynlleth, Powys |
| | SY20 8RR |
| Tel | +44 (0)1654 702192 |
| Email | hilary@talbontdrain.co.uk |
| Web | www.talbontdrain.co.uk |

Entry 724   Map 7

## Swansea

### Blas Gŵyr

Sleepy Llangennith was once a well-kept secret – now walkers, riders, surfers and beach lovers of all ages flock here. Tucked back from the bustling bay is an extended 1700s cottage with a boutique hotel facelift. All is simple but stylish: bedrooms are modern and matching with tiled floors and contemporary paintings, while bathrooms come with warm floors and fluffy towels. Everything from the bedspread to the breakfast is local: make sure you try the lava bread. After a day at sea fling wet gear in the drying room and linger over a coffee on the front deck, or walk to the pub for a sun-kissed pint. Bliss. *Welsh spoken.*

Travel Club offer. See page 414.

| | |
|---|---|
| Price | £100–£110. Singles £85. |
| Rooms | 4: 1 double, 1 double (with sofa bed), 1 twin/double, 1 suite for 2-4. |
| Meals | Packed lunch £5. Dinner, 3 courses, £20 (Fri/Sat, for groups of 6+, by arrangement). Pub 150 yds. |
| Closed | Never. |
| Directions | M4 junc. 47, 2nd exit, A483. At next 2 r'bouts 3rd exit, A484. Dual c'way then at r'bout, 1st left, B4296. Right at lights. On to Llangennith, pass pub, at mini r'bout, right, then immed. right into car park. |

|  |  |
|---|---|
| | **Dafydd & Kerry James** |
| | Blas Gŵyr, |
| | Plenty Farm, Llangennith, |
| | Swansea SA3 1HU |
| Tel | +44 (0)1792 386472 |
| Email | info@blasgwyr.co.uk |
| Web | www.blasgwyr.co.uk |

Entry 725   Map 2

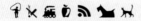

# Wrexham

## The Garden House

Unbelievable that a few years ago this was bare farmland. Simon and Susie have worked magic: Simon building the handsome brick house, his mother transforming the land into a symphony of lawns, boxed hedges, hideaways, a bridged pond with views to the river, sculptures here and there, hordes of hydrangeas, a greenhouse for afternoon tea. One of Simon's passions is art and antiques so inside is equally creative: the smart double room in the main house and separate Orangery suite are bursting with artworks and original pieces. Eat in the wonderfully chaotic family kitchen or walk to the pub, wake to a dawn chorus, revel in the enthusiasm of it all.

Travel Club offer. See page 414.

| | |
|---|---|
| Price | £100. Singles £60. |
| Rooms | 2: 1 double with sitting room. Orangery: 1 double with sitting room. |
| Meals | Supper £20-£30. Pub/restaurant 0.75 miles. |
| Closed | Occasionally. |
| Directions | A483 to Chester, turn on to A539 (Whitchurch). Turn right on A528; right by Cross Foxes pub. Follow Gardens sign. House 0.75 miles on right. |

Simon Wingett
The Garden House,
Erbistock,
Wrexham LL13 0DL
Tel       +44(0)1978 781149
Email    art@simonwingett.com
Web      www.simonwingett.com

Entry 726   Map 7

# Wrexham

## Worthenbury Manor

Homemade bread and Hepplewhite! This is a good, solid house of generous proportions and your hosts live in part of it. Wallow in antique oak four-posters in rose-carpeted chandeliered bedrooms, full of comfort (books, games and flowers adding a cosy touch) and breakfast on fresh fruit (some from the garden) local bacon and sausages. Ian, history buff and former chef, is gentle, thoughtful and looks after you properly; dinner is quite an occasion. The listed house is close to Chester yet in a quiet, birdsung setting; the original building was enlarged in the 1890s in the William and Mary revival style.

Travel Club offer. See page 414.

| | |
|---|---|
| Price | £60-£85. Singles £38-£49. |
| Rooms | 2: 1 four-poster; 1 four-poster with separate bath. |
| Meals | Dinner, 3 courses, £25. Lunch £15. |
| Closed | December-February. |
| Directions | Between A525 Whitchurch-Wrexham & A41 Whitchurch-Chester, on B5069 between Bangor-on-Dee (also called Bangor-is-y-coed) and Malpas. On right before bridge. |

Elizabeth & Ian Taylor
Worthenbury Manor,
Worthenbury,
Wrexham LL13 0AW
Tel       +44 (0)1948 770342
Email    enquiries@worthenburymanor.co.uk
Web      www.worthenburymanor.co.uk

Entry 727   Map 7

Many of you may want to stay in environmentally friendly places. You may be passionate about local, organic or home-grown food. Or perhaps you want to know that the place you are staying in contributes to the community? To help you we have launched our Ethical Collection, so you can find the right place to stay and also discover how each owner is addressing these issues.

The Collection is made up of places going the extra mile, and taking the steps that most people have not yet taken, in one or more of the following areas:

• Environment Those making great efforts to reduce the environmental impact of their Special Place. We expect more than energy-saving light bulbs and recycling – in this part of the Collection you will find owners who make their own natural cleaning products, properties with solar hot water and biomass boilers, the odd green roof and a good measure of green elbow grease.

• Community Given to owners who use their property to play a positive role in their local and wider community. For example, by making a contribution from every guest's bill to a local fund, or running pond-dipping courses for local school children on their farm.

• Food Awarded to owners who make a real effort to source local or organic food, or to grow their own. We look for those who have gone out of their way to strike up relationships with local producers or to seek out organic suppliers. It is easier for an owner on a farm to produce their own eggs than for someone in the middle of a city, so we take this into account.

## How it works

To become part of our Ethical Collection owners choose whether to apply in one, two or all three categories, and fill in a detailed questionnaire asking demanding questions about their activities in the chosen areas. You can download a full list of the questions at www.sawdays.co.uk/about_us/ethical_collection/faq/

We then review each questionnaire carefully before deciding whether or not to give the award(s). The final decision is subjective; it is based not only on whether an owner ticks 'yes' to a question but also on the detailed explanation that accompanies each 'yes' or 'no' answer. For example, an owner who has tried as hard as possible to install solar water-heating panels, but has failed because of strict conservation planning laws, will be given some credit for their effort (as long as they are doing other things in this area).

We have tried to be as rigorous as possible and have made sure the questions are demanding. We have not checked out the claims of owners before making our decisions, but we do trust them to be honest. We are only human, as are they, so please let us know if you think we have made any mistakes.

The Ethical Collection is still a new initiative for us, and we'd love to know what you think about it – email us at ethicalcollection@sawdays.co.uk or write to us. And remember that because this is a new scheme some owners have not yet completed their questionnaires – we're sure other places in the guide are working just as hard in these areas, but we don't yet know the full details.

## Ethical Collection in this book

On the entry page of all places in the Collection we show which awards have been given.

A list of the places in our Ethical Collection is shown below, by entry number.

### Environment

23 • 30 • 44 • 49 • 61 • 74 • 77 • 83 • 84 • 97 • 105 • 127 • 139 • 161 • 215 • 248 • 249 • 250 • 254 • 340 • 398 • 416 • 420 • 424 • 429 • 463 • 480 • 575 • 578 • 626 • 648 • 658 • 691 • 701 • 705 • 710 • 720 • 723

### Community

28 • 77 • 84 • 105 • 111 • 156 • 340 • 412 • 421 • 445 • 480 • 493 • 543 • 546 • 582 • 597 • 612 • 626 • 648 • 691 • 701

### Food

4 • 23 • 28 • 30 • 36 • 38 • 44 • 49 • 58 •

61 • 74 • 75 • 77 • 81 • 84 • 94 • 103 • 105 • 107 • 111 • 112 • 127 • 128 • 143 • 148 • 156 • 158 • 159 • 160 • 192 • 207 • 215 • 227 • 239 • 248 • 249 • 250 • 254 • 259 • 268 • 328 • 340 • 360 • 376 • 382 • 412 • 416 • 420 • 421 • 424 • 429 • 430 • 432 • 441 • 463 • 474 • 480 • 491 • 493 • 511 • 538 • 543 • 546 • 569 • 575 • 582 • 590 • 594 • 597 • 602 • 610 • 626 • 658 • 664 • 678 • 679 • 691 • 701 • 705 • 709 • 710 • 720 • 723

## Ethical Collection online

There is stacks more information on our website, www.sawdays.co.uk. You can read the answers each owner has given to our Ethical Collection questionnaire and get a more detailed idea of what they are doing in each area. You can also search for properties that have awards.

Photo: Lys-na-Greyne House, entry 612

Becoming a member of Sawday's Travel Club opens up hundreds of discounts, treats and other offers at many of our Special Places to Stay in Britain and Ireland, as well as promotions on Sawday's books and other goodies.

Where you see the 💼 symbol in this book it means the place has a special offer for Club members. It may be money off your room price, a bottle of champagne or a day's trout fishing. The offers for each place are listed on the following pages. These were correct at the time of going to print, but owners reserve the right to change the listed offer. Latest offers for all places can be found on our website, www.sawdays.co.uk.

Membership is only £25 per year. To see membership extras and to register visit www.sawdays.co.uk/members. You can also call +44 (0)1275 395433 to set up a direct debit.

### The small print

You must mention that you are a Travel Club member when booking, and confirm that the offer is available. Your Travel Club card must be shown on arrival to claim the offer. Sawday's Travel Club cards are not transferable. If two cardholders share a room they can only claim the offer once. Offers for Sawday's Travel Club members are subject to availability. Alastair Sawday Publishing cannot accept any responsibility if places fail to honour offers; neither can we accept responsibility if a place changes hands and drops out of the Travel Club.

### England

#### Bath & N.E. Somerset

4     Half decanter of sherry in your room. 10% off room rate Monday-Thursday.
6     3 nights for the price of 2 Monday-Thursday. Home-made Austrian cakes in room.
7     Guidebook of Bath.
8     Free pick-up from local bus/train station. Taxi fare reimbursed up to £8.
9     10% off room rate Monday-Thursday.

#### Brighton & Hove

15a   10% off stays of 3 or more nights Monday-Thursday.
16    10% off room rate Monday-Thursday. Bottle of wine in your room for returning guests.

## Buckinghamshire

19   Bottle of wine with dinner on first night.

## Cambridgeshire

22   10% off stays of 2 or more nights Monday-Thursday.
23   Chapel cocktail on arrival or Bucks Fizz with breakfast.

## Cheshire

27   Bottle of wine in your room.
28   Local 'goodies' in the room.

## Cornwall

30   Cream tea on arrival 4-6pm; glass of wine or gin and tonic after 6pm
     (for stays of 2 or more nights).
31   Cornish cream tea on arrival.
32   Cornish cream tea on arrival.
36   Stay for 4 nights and get the 5th night free.
38   Arrangement for St Enodoc golf (green fee not included). Talk about Cornish
     gardens or coastal and moor walks over a glass of wine.
41   Tea/coffee on arrival. Bottle of wine with dinner. 12pm checkout.
43   10% off stays of 2 or more nights.
44   Drink on arrival.
45   Bottle of wine in your room. Free pick-up from local bus/train station.
46   Talk about St Ives artists with a glass of wine.
47   Cornish cream tea in the afternoon. Free pick-up from local bus/train station.
     Local food/produce in your room.
49   Truffles & glass of champagne on arrival.
51   Use of owner's studio.
52   Tea and cakes/biscuits and sherry on arrival.
54   Local food/produce in your room.
55   Homemade cake on arrival. Bottle of wine with dinner. Discounts on Jane and
     John's books.
58   10% off room rate Monday-Thursday in low season. Drinks or tea, coffee and
     biscuits on arrival.
59   Key to 'secret' clifftop garden.
61   Reiki or reflexology therapy session per room on minimum 7 nights stay.
64   10% off minimum 5 nights. Free pick-up from Penryn station. Decanter of
     sherry in your room.
68   Fruit bowl in your room.

73   Cornish fare. Luxury toiletries.
74   10% off stays of 3 or more nights (except July & August). Free pick-up from local train station. Maps of local walks. Advance purchase of Eden Project tickets which saves you queuing (the ticket cost will be added to your bill).
75   10% off room rate. Late checkout (12pm). Free pick-up from Torpoint ferry.
77   Drinks on arrival.
78   Free pick-up from local bus/train station. 10% off room rate Monday-Thursday. No charge for dogs.

## Cumbria

83   A bottle of wine in your room for stays of 3 or more nights Sunday-Thursday.
85   10% off room rate.
86   Bottle of Moët champagne for stays of 2 or more nights.
87   Drinks on arrival. Late checkout (12pm).
89   20% off dinner at Lindeth Howe Hotel and use of leisure facilities when booking dinner. 20% off Mountain Goat Tours.
90   Free pick-up from local bus/train station. Late checkout (12pm).
91   Guided woodland/nature walks in owners' woodland, including badger watching. Local maps available on loan and help planning days in the Lake District.
94   Late checkout (12pm). 20% off purchases of our sausage, bacon and eggs to take home.
95   Bottle of organic wine with 2-night stay. 10% off stays of 2 or more nights. Free pick-up from local bus/train station.
97   Bottle of wine with 2-night stay.
98   10% off room rate Monday-Thursday.

## Derbyshire

100  Bottle of wine in your room.
101  10% off room rate Monday-Thursday. Bottle of wine in your room.
103  10% off stays of 2 or more nights in a double en suite room, Monday-Thursday.
104  10% off room rate Monday-Thursday. 15% off stays of 3 or more nights. Afternoon organic tea. Bottle of wine with dinner on first night. Free pick-up from local bus/train station. Late checkout (12pm).

## Devon

107  10% off room rate Monday-Thursday. Drinks on arrival. Relax with a 'spoil yourself' day: massage; seaweed bath with scented candles (£25 for a single treatment).
108  Cream tea on arrival or following afternoon.

109  10% off room rate Monday-Thursday.

111  Tea/coffee and homemade cake served on arrival.

112  Bottle of wine with dinner on first night (if it's a night when not cooking, then bottle of wine with meal on second night).

115  Bottle of wine with dinner on first night.

116  Bottle of wine with first dinner. 15% off stays of 3 or more nights.

118  Afternoon tea. Fruit and chocolates in your room.

120  Bottle of champagne for bookings of 2 or more nights.

121  Drink on arrival. 10% off stays Monday-Thursday. Transport to foot ferry.

122  10% off room rate Monday-Thursday. 10% off stays of 2 or more nights.

123  10% off stays of 2 or more nights Monday-Thursday.

124  10% off stays of 2 or more nights Monday-Thursday. Late checkout (12pm). Lift to local pubs.

126  Delicious afternoon tea on arrival, by the log fire in the drawing room.

128  10% off room rate Monday-Thursday. 10% off stays of 2 or more nights. Drinks on arrival. Late checkout (12pm). Drive in carriage with pair of Dartmoor Hill ponies.

130  10% off room rate Monday-Thursday.

134  Free pick-up from local bus/train station. Late checkout (12pm). Local food/produce in your room.

136  Slice of homemade cake or fruit bun on arrival. 5% off stays of 2 or more nights.

139  Sunday-Thursday nights – either upgrade when available or 10% discount.

143  Late checkout (12pm).

144  10% off stays of 2 or more nights. Welcome drinks tray.

146  10% off stays of 2 or more nights. Afternoon tea on arrival. Bottle of house wine with first dinner. Free pick-up from Exeter St Davids mainline train station.

149  Bottle of house wine with dinner.

150  A Devon cream tea on arrival, 4-6pm. After 6pm a glass of wine.

151  10% off room rate Monday-Thursday. Drinks on arrival. Free pick-up from local bus/train station. Late checkout (12pm).

153  10% off stays of 2 or more nights. Glass of wine on arrival and/or homemade tea.

154  Drinks on arrival. Glass of wine, gin and tonic or equivalent for each night of your stay.

156  Waived charge for dogs or decanter of port.

158  Bottle of wine with dinner on first night.

159  Late checkout (12pm).

160  Drinks on arrival.

## Dorset

161  Homemade organic Dorset cream tea or aperitif with nibbles on one night of your stay, served on sunny terrace or by log fire.

162  3 nights for the price of 2 Monday-Thursday. Wine on arrival.

164  Half a bottle of bubbly on arrival. 10% off stays of 3 or more nights Sunday-Thursday.

165  A jar of Susie's homemade marmalade or jam to take home. Or free pick-up from Yeovil train station.

166  Locally made chocolate truffles and a bottle of truffle oil in your room.

168  Bottle of wine in your room.

170  Bottle of wine in your room.

171  Glass of wine on arrival.

176  10% off stays Monday-Thursday. Free pick-up from local train station. Welcome drink and guided tour of local area.

183  10% off stays Monday-Thursday.

185  Bottle of wine in your room.

186  10% off stays of 2 or more nights. Drinks on arrival.

187  10% off double room rate Monday-Thursday.

188  Free pick-up from local bus/train station.

189  Local food/produce in your room.

190  10% off stays of 2 or more nights Monday-Thursday.

191  Afternoon tea on arrival. Free pick-up from Gillingham train/bus station (20-minute drive).

192  10% off stays of 2 or more nights Monday-Thursday. Free pick-up from local bus/train station. Local food/produce in your room.

## Essex

197  Welcome drink on arrival – tipple depending on season, weather and hour! 10% off stays of 2 or more nights.

198  Tea and homemade cake on arrival.

200  10% off room rate Monday-Thursday. 15% off room rate for stays of 2 or more nights Monday-Thursday. House cocktail before 3-course dinner. Drinks on arrival. Late checkout (12pm).

## Gloucestershire

201  Tea and hot all-butter scones on arrival.

205  10% off stays of 2 or more nights. Free pick-up from local bus/train station. Afternoon tea and cake.

207  10% off stays of 3 or more nights.

208  10% off stays of 3 or more nights November-April.

214  10% off stays of 2 or more nights. Bottle of wine in your room. Free pick-up from local bus/train station. Local food/produce in your room.

216  10% off room rate Monday-Thursday. Bottle of champagne for bookings of 2 nights or more.

218  Bottle of wine in your room.

221  Coffee & tea on arrival. Glass of wine with dinner. 10% off room rate Mon-Thurs.

225  10% off stays of 3 or more nights. Stay 3 nights, 4th free. Drinks on arrival.

## Hampshire

227  10% off room rate.

230  10% off room rate Monday-Thursday. Free pick-up from local bus/train station.

231  10% off stays of 3 or more nights Monday-Thursday

232  Bottle of wine in your room.

237  Drinks on arrival. Local food/produce in your room. Free pick-up from local bus/train station. Late checkout (12pm).

238  Glass of champagne on arrival. 10% off stays of 2 or more nights Monday-Thursday. Farm tour by John.

239  Tea and homemade cake on arrival.

## Herefordshire

246  Pot of tea or coffee with cake and biscuits on arrival. Bottle of wine with dinner on first night.

247  Bottle of local cider or chocolates if celebrating a birthday, honeymoon or anniversary.

251  Evening drink or afternoon tea and cakes on arrival.

253  10% off room rate Monday-Thursday. Cream tea on arrival.

## Kent

257  3 nights for 2 Monday-Thursday.

258  Drinks on arrival. Free pick-up from local bus/train station.

259  10% off second night (double occupancy) at weekends.

263  Bottle of wine with dinner on first night. Drinks on arrival.

265  Bottle of wine for minimum 2-night stays. Free pick-up from local bus/train station. Late checkout (12pm).

266  Bottle of wine. Morning newspaper. Checkout at 11am with snack for journey.

267  10% off stays of 2 or more nights. Free pick-up from local bus/train station. Late checkout (12pm). Local food/produce in your room.

269  10% off stays of 3 or more nights.

271   10% off stays of 2 or more nights. Drinks on arrival. Bottle of wine with dinner on first night.

272   Late checkout (12pm). Bottle of house wine with dinner if requested.

276   Lift to and from local pub or restaurant. A bottle of Sally's famous Benenden Sauce.

278   Locally made chocolate truffles, Kentish Hills water, towelling slippers and range of Neutrogena toiletries in your room. Lift to local restaurants (by arrangement).

279   Bottle of wine with dinner on first night.

280   6 greeting cards of your choice drawn by your host David Gurdon.

281   Bottle of wine with dinner on first night.

282   Sherry and homemade biscuits in your room. Pot of homemade jam or marmalade to take home.

283   Free pick-up from local train station.

285   10% off stays of 2 or more nights. Free pick-up from local bus/train station.

## Lancashire

287   Free pick-up from local train station. Fridge full of beverages. Late checkout.

288   Local food/produce in your room.

## Leicestershire

291   Bottle of wine with dinner on first night. Late checkout (12pm). Drinks on arrival.

292   Glass of wine each night of your stay.

## Lincolnshire

296   Tea on arrival. House drink per person for each night of stay. Free pick-up from local train station.

298   10% off room rate Monday-Thursday.

299   Home-grown produce, as in season and available.

301   10% off room rate Monday-Thursday, not July and August.

303   Locally produced Belvoir cordials in your room. Free pick-up from local bus/train station. 10% off room rate Monday-Thursday. Late checkout (12pm).

304   10% off room rate Monday-Thursday. 10% off stays of 2 or more nights.

305   10% discount on third night Monday-Thursday.

306   Drinks on arrival.

## London

309   Evening drink or afternoon tea on arrival.

313   Half bottle of champagne for stays of 2 or more nights.

316   Gin and tonic, glass of wine or other refreshment on arrival.

317  10% off stays of 2 or more nights.

318  Late checkout (12pm).

322  10% off room rate Monday-Thursday. 10% off stays of 2 or more nights.

323  Jar of house preserve in room. Free pick-up from local station. Bottle of house wine with dinner.

324  10% off stays of 2 or more nights.

331  Late checkout (12pm). Discounts for longer stays.

## Middlesex

334  10% off stays of 2 or more nights.

## Norfolk

341  Chilled bottle of wine. Late checkout (12pm).

342  10% off room rate Sunday-Thursday. Bottle of wine on arrival.

343  Bottle of house wine per room.

347  10% off room rate Monday-Thursday. Bottle of wine in your room. Drinks on arrival. Free pick-up from local bus/train station.

348  10% off room rate Monday-Thursday.

349  10% off stays of 4 nights Monday-Thursday inclusive. Norfolk handmade soap.

350  10% off room rate Monday-Thursday. Free pick-up from local bus/train station.

351  10% off stays of 2 or more nights. Tea on arrival.

353  Bottle of wine in your room. Late checkout (12pm). 20% off stays of 3 or more nights Monday-Thursday.

354  Bottle of wine.

355  Coffee/tea and biscuits on arrival. Late checkout (12pm) Monday-Friday.

356  10% off stays of 2 or more nights.

## Northamptonshire

361  Bottle of wine, selected by the Wine Society, in your room.

362  10% off stays of 2 or more nights.

364  Late checkout (12pm).

365  Good bottle of wine for stays of 2 nights.

## Northumberland

367  10% off room rate Monday-Thursday,

368  Bottle of wine with dinner on first night. Late breakfast (11 am) on Saturday & Sunday. Free packed lunch.

369  Tea and homemade cake on arrival.

370  Drinks on arrival. 10% off room rate.

371 Guided tour of antique furniture restoration workshops and advice on any furniture-related subject.

372 Free pick-up from local station. Late checkout (12pm).

374 Bottle of wine in your room.

376 10% off room rate Monday-Thursday. Bottle of champagne for bookings of 2 or more nights. A drive into the College Valley with Martin.

### Nottinghamshire

379 Occasionally fruit and vegetables from the garden for guests to take home. Drink on arrival. 10% off stays of 3 or more nights.

380 Bottle of wine in your room.

381 A chunk of your favourite cheese to take home!

### Oxfordshire

384 Tea and cake on arrival. Drink before dinner.

385 10% off room rate Monday-Thursday. 10% off stays of 3 or more nights. Late checkout (12pm).

389 Tea and cake on arrival (4pm-6pm). Bowl of fruit, chocolates and flapjacks in your room.

392 10% off room rate Monday-Thursday.

393 10% off stays of 3 or more nights Monday-Thursday.

397 Bottle of wine in your room.

398 25% discount on pilates or Alexander Technique lesson.

399 10% off room rate Monday-Thursday.

400 5% off room rate Monday-Thursday.

### Rutland

401 10% off room rate Monday-Thursday.

### Shropshire

405 Bottle of sparkling wine, minimum 2-night stay.

406 10% off room rate Monday-Thursday. 10% off stays of 2 or more nights.

408 10% off room rate Monday-Thursday. 10% off stays of 2 or more nights.

410 Bowl of fruit in your room.

412 10% off stays of 2 or more nights. Pot of tea/coffee and homemade cake on arrival.

413 Flexible breakfast until midday. Free drop off within 10 mile radius to enable walk home. Fair trade chocolate in your room. Bottle of wine with dinner on first night. Drinks on arrival. Free pick-up from local bus/train station. Late checkout (12pm).

415  5% off room rate Monday-Thursday.

416  10% off room rate Monday-Thursday.

418  Afternoon tea on arrival. Guided tour of the heronry when appropriate. 10% off stays of 2 or more nights.

419  Home-grown vegetable goodie bag. Free pick-up from local bus/train station.

420  Bottle of wine with dinner on first night. Drinks on arrival. Local food/produce in your room. Homemade muffins to take away.

421  Free pick-up from local train station. Glass of wine on arrival. Fruit in your bedroom.

422  Free pick-up from local bus/train station.

423  Tea and homemade cake on arrival.

424  Free pick-up from local bus/train station.

425  10% off stays of 3 or more nights.

## Somerset

428  20% off room rate Monday-Thursday. Afternoon tea on arrival. Free pick-up from local bus/train station.

429  10% off stays Monday-Friday. Selection of local food on arrival. Late checkout (12pm). Free pick-up from local station. Lifts to walking start points with advice, map and guide. Laundry service.

430  Free pick-up from Dunster station. Drink per person per night. Jar of Exmoor honey and 1/2 dozen free-range eggs (when available).

432  10% off room rate. Welcome tea tray with homemade cake. Tin of homemade biscuits in your room. Fresh flowers in your room.

433  Tea and homemade biscuits or cake on arrival.

434  3 nights for the price of 2. 10% off room rate.

438  10% off room rate Monday-Thursday. Free pick-up from local bus/train station.

440  Bottle of wine per couple on arrival. Pick-up from airport and Yatton station. 10% off stays of 2 or more nights.

441  10% off room rate Monday-Thursday. Aperitif before dinner. 3-course dinner for the price of 2 courses per person.

442  10% off room rate Monday-Thursday.

443  Pick-up from Keynsham station and Bristol Airport. 10% off room rate Monday-Thursday. Late checkout (12pm).

445  Luxury 3-course breakfast for stays of 2 nights (see website).

446  Escorted local walks. Tour of Wells Cathedral or Wells Bishop's Palace. Drinks on arrival. Free pick-up from local bus/train station. Late checkout (12pm).

447  10% off stays of 4 or more nights. Free pick-up from local bus/train station.

449  10% off room rate Monday-Thursday.

450  10% off room rate Monday-Thursday.

452  10% off room rate Monday-Thursday. Drinks on arrival.

453  10% off room rate.

456  10% off room rate Monday-Thursday. Bottle of wine in your room. Late checkout (12pm).

457  10% off stays of 3 or more nights Monday-Thursday. Drinks on arrival. Free pick-up from local bus/train station. Late checkout (12pm).

459  10% off room rate Monday-Thursday.

460  10% off room rate Monday-Thursday.

464  10% off room rate Monday-Thursday. Local food in your room on arrival. Late checkout (12pm). Bottle of wine with dinner.

465  10% off room rate. Drinks on arrival. Use of studio area. Tour of house — a very interesting collection of pictures and furniture. Tour of garden with owner. Late checkout (12pm).

467  Home-grown produce. Bottle of champagne for bookings of 2 or more nights. Free pick-up from local bus/train station. Late checkout (12pm).

468  Free pick-up from local bus/train station. Late checkout (12pm). Tea and cake on arrival. 10% off stays of 3 or more nights.

469  10% off room rate Monday-Thursday.

470  Bottle of house wine with dinner.

471  10% off stays of 3 or more nights. Refreshments on arrival. Drop-off service for coastal walks.

## Staffordshire

472  Late checkout (12pm). Tea and coffee and homemade shortbread.

473  10% off stays of 2 or more nights. Bottle of wine in your room.

474  10% off room rate Monday-Thursday.

## Suffolk

478  10% off room rate Monday-Thursday. Free pick-up from local bus/train station. Late checkout (12pm). Local produce in your room.

481  10% off first night, minimum 2-night stay.

482  Pick-up from local station.

486  Tea and homemade cakes on arrival. 10% off stays of 2 or more nights. Free pick-up from local bus/train station. Local food/produce in your room.

487  Bottle of wine with dinner on first night. 10% off stays of 2 or more nights Monday-Thursday.

489  Free pick-up from local bus/train station. Bottle of wine for 3+ nights.

490  Selection of home-grown produce in season to take home. 10% off stays of 3 or more nights. Tea and homemade cake during your stay.

491 Will babysit. In season Hugh will give lessons on preparation of game or fish. Free pick-up from local bus/train station. Late checkout (12pm).

493 10% off room rate Monday-Thursday, except during August and Aldeburgh Festival.

496 For two night stays including Saturday, third night charged at single rate. 25% off room rate Monday-Thursday.

497 Half a bottle of wine or Aspall apple juice in room on arrival.

## Surrey

500 Drink of spirits, beer or wine each evening. Drinks on arrival. Free pick-up from local bus/train station.

502 10% off room rate Monday-Thursday.

## Sussex

510 Tea and cake on arrival. Free pick-up from local pubs or stations.

511 Drinks on arrival. Bottle of wine in your room. Local food/produce in your room.

513 10% off room rate Monday-Thursday.

515 Local food/produce in your room.

523 10% off room rate Monday-Thursday. Bottle of wine in your room.

525 Biscuits and fresh fruit in your room. Bottle of wine for stays of 2 or more nights.

529 Drinks on arrival. Free pick-up from local bus/train station. Late checkout (12pm).

530 Bottle of wine from a local vineyard.

531 Glass of wine at dinner. Late checkout.

533 20% off room rate Monday-Thursday for 3-night stays (some date restrictions).

## Warwickshire

539 Bottle of wine in your room.

540 10% off room rate Monday-Thursday.

541 10% off room rate Monday-Thursday.

542 10% off room rate Monday-Thursday.

543 10% off stays of 3 or more nights.

544 10% discount for members of the armed forces. Free pick-up from local bus/train station.

546 10% off room rate Monday-Thursday. Bottle of house wine with dinner.

## Wiltshire

547 10% off stays of 2 or more nights.

548 10% off stays of 2 or more nights.

551  10% off room rate Monday-Thursday.

553  Bottle of wine with dinner on first night.

558  10% off stays of 2 or more nights Monday-Thursday.

562  10% off room rate Monday-Thursday and for 3-night stays over a weekend.
A selection of fresh fruit in your room.

564  On arrival a cup of tea and Glebe Home Fruit Cake. On departure homemade
jam or marmalade.

565  Postcards. Bottle of house wine with dinner. Late checkout (12pm).
Free pick-up from local train station.

568  10% off room rate Monday-Thursday. Drinks on arrival.

570  10% off stays of 2 or more nights.

### Worcestershire

572  Free pick-up from local bus/train station.

574  Bottle of vintage Cava for bookings of 2 or more nights.

577  10% off stays of 2 or more nights. Free pick-up from local bus/train station.

578  10% off stays of 2 or more nights.

### Yorkshire

579  Drinks on arrival.

582  Bottle of house wine for a minimum 2-night stay.

583  10% off stays of 2 or more nights Monday-Wednesday.

584  10% off room rate Monday-Thursday. Drinks on arrival.

585  6 breakfast eggs: extra fresh, free-range.

587  10% off stays of 2 or more nights.

591  Drinks on arrival.

593  10% off room rate Monday-Thursday.

597  Jar of local honey or 6 eggs from the farm.

602  Choice of any bottle of wine from list with first dinner.

603  10% off room rate Monday-Thursday (does not apply to online bookings).

605  Tea and homemade cake on arrival. Entrance to Jervaulx Abbey.

606  Bottle of wine for stays of 3 or more nights.

607  Tour of the working farm.

608  10% off stays of 2 or more nights.

610  Drink on arrival and late checkout.

## Scotland

### Aberdeenshire

611  Freshly made scones and afternoon tea on arrival 4pm-6pm.

612  Fresh flowers in your room. Afternoon tea or a glass of wine or whisky on arrival.

613  Tea and cakes or drinks on arrival. A drink before dinner. Bottle of wine with dinner.

615  Afternoon tea for early arrivals. Pre-dinner drink and house wine with dinner.

616  10% off stays of 2 or more nights.

## Angus

617  One free supper for stays of 3 or more nights (November-May).

## Ayrshire

626  Afternoon tea on arrival. Free transport to Braidwoods, our local 'Michelin Star' restaurant. Free pick-up from local bus/train station.

## Clackmannanshire

629  10% off room rate Monday-Thursday. 10% off mini tour package (classic car hire plus bed & breakfast).

## Dumfries & Galloway

631  10% off stays of 2 or more nights. Free pick-up from local bus/train station.

## Edinburgh & the Lothians

639  Bottle of wine and chocolates in your room on arrival.

640  Fresh flowers and bottle of wine in your room.

641  10% off room rate Monday-Thursday. Drinks on arrival.

646  10% off room rate. 10% off stays of 2 or more nights. Bottle of wine in your room.

647  10% off room rate Monday-Thursday. 10% off stays of 2 or more nights. Bottle of wine with dinner on first night. Drinks on arrival. Free pick-up from local bus/train station. Late checkout (12pm). Special rates for exclusive use of house.

## Fife

650  Tea and cake on arrival. Drinks before and wine with dinner. 10% off stays of 2 or more nights.

651  Decanter of whisky, supplies of tea and coffee, homebaking available in guests' sitting room. Bottle of house wine with dinner. No set checkout time. 10% off stays of 2 or more nights (doubles only). Drinks on arrival.

## Highland

655  50% off 4th night.

662  Glass of wine or whisky on arrival.

663   10% off stays of 2 or more nights. Bottle of wine with dinner on first night.

664   Bottle of wine with dinner on first night.

666   Drinks on arrival. Free pick-up from local bus/train station. Late checkout (12pm). Local food/produce.

667   10% off room rate Monday-Thursday.

674   Bottle of wine with dinner on first night. Free salmon fishing on the river Allan, by arrangement.

675   Toasted teacakes with homemade jams and tea or coffee on arrival.

679   10% off stays of 2 or more nights.

681   Tea and drink on arrival. Fruit and fresh flowers in your room. Free pick-up from local bus/train station.

682   Bottle of wine with dinner on first night. Drinks on arrival. Late checkout (12pm).

## Wales

### Anglesey

688   Bottle of wine in your room.

### Carmarthenshire

689   10% off room rate Monday-Thursday.

691   Bottle of wine with dinner. Free pick-up from local train station. Maps drawn to order for walkers. Late checkout (12pm).

692   10% off stays of 3 or more nights. Drinks on arrival. Free pick-up from local bus/train station. Late checkout (12pm).

693   10% off stays of 4 or more nights.

### Ceredigion

695   Bottle of wine on first night (either at dinner or in your room).

### Denbighshire

697   10% off stays of 2 or more nights Monday-Thursday.

### Flintshire

698   Afternoon tea on arrival.

699   10% off stays of 2 or more nights.

### Gwynedd

701   Stay 4 or more nights for a guided walk (half day) with a mountain guide.

702   Free fishing for stays of 2 or more nights. Packed lunch for stays of 2 or more nights.

Photo: Gower's Close, entry 386

703  10% off room rate Monday-Thursday. Bottle of wine in your room.

705  Bottle of house wine with dinner.

706  Bottle of champagne for bookings of 2 or more nights.

707  Free pick-up from local bus/train station.

## Pembrokeshire

709  Penfro jam or similar. Subsequent visits of 2 or more nights £5 per night discount.

710  10% off stays of 2 or more nights.

711  Glass of wine with dinner, or evening of first night if dining out.

713  Homemade Welsh recipe cakes in room. Bottle of wine in room for stays of 2 or more nights.

714  Bottle of wine for stays of 2 or more nights.

## Powys

715  10% off room rate Monday-Thursday. Free pick-up from local bus/train station.

717  Free pick-up from local bus/train station.

719  Drinks on arrival.

720  Bottle of fairtrade wine.

722  Bottle of house champagne for stays of 2 nights with dinner on one night.

723  25% off stays of 2 or more nights.

724  Free entry to the Centre for Alternative Technology if staying two or more nights.

## Wrexham

726  Drinks on arrival.

727  3 nights for the price of 2. For stays of 2 or more nights half a bottle of house wine per person with dinner.

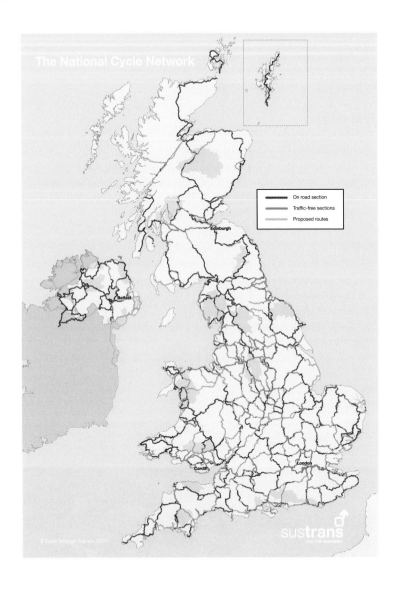

The National Cycle Network

| | On road section |
| | Traffic-free sections |
| | Proposed routes |

Edinburgh

Belfast

Cardiff

London

sustrans

For route information see www.sustrans.org

Quick reference indices

Quick reference indices

## Wheelchair-accessible
At least one bedroom and
bathroom accessible for
wheelchair users. Phone for
details.

## Stay all day
You can stay all day at these
places if you wish.

## Scotland

## Wales

Quick reference indices

Quick reference indices

## On a budget?
These places have a double room for £70 or under.

# Special Places series

Have you enjoyed this book? Why not try one of the others in the Special Places series and get 35% discount on the RRP *

| | | |
|---|---|---|
| British Bed & Breakfast (Ed 14) | RRP £14.99 | Offer price £9.75 |
| British Bed & Breakfast for Garden Lovers (Ed 5) | RRP £14.99 | Offer price £9.75 |
| British Hotels & Inns (Ed 11) | RRP £14.99 | Offer price £9.75 |
| Devon & Cornwall (Ed 1) | RRP £9.99 | Offer price £6.50 |
| Scotland (Ed 1) | RRP £9.99 | Offer price £6.50 |
| Pubs & Inns of England & Wales (Ed 6) | RRP £14.99 | Offer price £9.75 |
| Ireland (Ed 7) | RRP £12.99 | Offer price £8.45 |
| French Bed & Breakfast (Ed 11) | RRP £15.99 | Offer price £10.40 |
| French Holiday Homes (Ed 4) | RRP £14.99 | Offer price £9.75 |
| French Hotels & Châteaux (Ed 5) | RRP £14.99 | Offer price £9.75 |
| Paris (Ed 1) | RRP £9.99 | Offer price £6.50 |
| Italy (Ed 5) | RRP £14.99 | Offer price £9.75 |
| Spain (Ed 8) | RRP £14.99 | Offer price £9.75 |
| Portugal (Ed 4) | RRP £11.99 | Offer price £7.80 |
| Croatia (Ed 1) | RRP £11.99 | Offer price £7.80 |
| India (Ed 2) | RRP £11.99 | Offer price £7.80 |
| Green Europe (Ed 1) | RRP £11.99 | Offer price £7.80 |
| Green Places to Stay (Ed 1) | RRP £13.99 | Offer price £9.10 |
| Go Slow England | RRP £19.99 | Offer price £13.00 |
| Go Slow Italy | RRP £19.99 | Offer price £13.00 |

*postage and packing is added to each order

To order at the Reader's Discount price simply phone +44 (0)1275 395431 and quote 'Reader Discount BBB'.

## Special places to stay, slow travel and slow food

The Slow Food revolution is upon us and these guides celebrate the Slow philosophy of life with a terrific selection of the places, recipes and people who take their time to enjoy life at its most enriching. In these beautiful books that go beyond the mere 'glossy', you will discover an unusual emphasis on the people who live in Special Slow Places and what they do. You will meet farmers, literary people, wine-makers and craftsmen – all with rich stories to tell. *Go Slow England* and our new title *Go Slow Italy* celebrate fascinating people, fine architecture, history, landscape and real food.

RRP £19.99. To order either of these titles at the Reader's Discount price of £13.00 (plus p&tp) call +44 (0)1275 395431 and quote 'Reader Discount BBB14'.

*"Go Slow England* is a magnificent guidebook" *BBC Good Food Magazine*

If you have any comments on entries in this guide, please tell us. If you have a favourite place or a new discovery, please let us know about it. You can return this form or visit www.sawdays.co.uk.

## Existing entry

Property name: _____

Entry number: _____ Date of visit: _____

## New recommendation

Property name: _____

Address: _____

_____

Tel/Email/Web: _____

## Your comments

What did you like (or dislike) about this place? Were the people friendly? What was the location like? What sort of food did they serve?

_____

_____

_____

_____

## Your details

Name: _____

Address: _____

_____

_____ Postcode: _____

Tel: _____ Email: _____

Please send completed form to:
BBB, Sawday's, The Old Farmyard, Yanley Lane, Long Ashton, Bristol BS41 9LR, UK

# Fragile Earth series

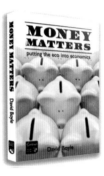

## Money Matters
Putting the eco into economics
David Boyle
£6.99

## Do Humans Dream of Electric Cars?
Your journey to sustainable travel
£4.99

This well-timed book will make you look at everything from your bank statements to the coins in your pocket in a whole new way. It holds the potential to change your life. In a world where the richest man is able to amass a fortune of over $50 billion, but over half the population of the planet live on less than $2 a day, this book discloses alternative and fairer ways. In his pithy and well argued style, author David Boyle sheds new light on our money system and exposes the inequality, greed and instability of the economies that dominate the world's wealth.

*Money Matters* is an easy-to-understand guide that demystifies the economic system that has us all caught in its tentacles, from hedge funds to hyperinflation, credit cards to the credit crunch.

It is estimated that there are over 600 million motor vehicles being driven on the streets of the earth. This figure is expected to double in the next 30 years. But oil is running out and bio-fuels are no longer seen as a viable alternative to fossil fuels.

This guide provides a no-nonsense approach to sustainable travel and outlines the simple steps needed to achieve a low carbon future. It highlights innovative and imaginative schemes that are already working, such as car clubs and bike sharing and is published to coincide with Sustrans's Change Your World Campaign 2009.

Sustrans is the UK's leading sustainable tranport charity. Their vision is a world in which people choose to travel in ways that benefit their health and the environment.

## The Big Earth Book £12.99
### Updated paperback edition

This book explores environmental, economic and social ideas to save our planet. It helps us understand what is happening to the planet today, exposes the actions of corporations and the lack of action of governments, weighs up new technologies, and champions innovative and viable solutions.

## What About China? £6.99
### Answers to this and other awkward questions about climate change

A panel of experts gives clear, entertaining and informative answers arguing that the excuses we give to avoid reducing our carbon footprint and our personal impact on the earth are exactly that, excuses.

## The Book of Rubbish Ideas   £6.99

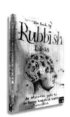

Every householder should have a copy of this guide to reducing household waste and stopping wasteful behaviour. Containing step-by-step projects, the book takes a top-down guided tour through the average family home.

## Ban the Bag £4.99
In May 2007 Modbury in Devon became Britain's first plastic bag-free town. This book tells their story and highlights the struggles.

## One Planet Living £4.99
Based on 10 guiding principles, which address key human needs, this little book suggests easy, ingenious and affordable ways in which we can lessen our impact on the planet and other people.

## Little Food Book £6.99
Original, stimulating mini essays about what is wrong with our food today, and about one of the greatest challenges of the new century: how to produce enough food without further damaging our health and our environment.

To order any of the books in the Fragile Earth series call +44 (0)1275 395431 or visit www.fragile-earth.com

**Alastair**

# Sawday's

## British self-catering

A whole week self-catering in Britain with your friends or family is precious, and you dare not get it wrong. To whom do you turn for advice and who on earth do you trust when the web is awash with advice from strangers? We launched Special Escapes to satisfy an obvious need for impartial and trustworthy help – and that is what it provides. The criteria for inclusion are the same as for our books: we have to like the place and the owners. It has, quite simply, to be 'special'. The site, our first online-only publication, is featured on www.thegoodwebguide.com and is growing fast.

Cosy cottages • Manor houses
Tipis • Hilltop bothies
City apartments and more

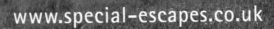

Photo: www.istockphoto.com

## Warwickshire

### Oxbourne House

Hard to believe the house is new, with its beamed ceilings, fireplaces and antiques. Bedrooms are fresh, crisp, cosy and cared for, the family room with an 'in the attic' feel; lighting is soft, beds excellent, bath and shower rooms attractive and warm, and views far-reaching. In the garden are tennis, sculpture and Graeme's rambler-bedecked pergola. Wake to birdsong and fresh eggs from their own hens; on peaceful summer nights, watch the dipping sun. Posy and Graeme are hugely likeable and welcoming and the village pub is just down the road. A most comforting place to stay. *Dogs by arrangement.*

Ethical Collection: Community; Food. See page 412.

Travel Club offer. See page 414.

| | |
|---|---|
| Price | £65-£85. Singles from £45. |
| Rooms | 3: 1 double, 1 family room; 1 twin/double with separate bath. |
| Meals | Dinner from £20. Pub 2-minute walk. |
| Closed | Rarely. |
| Directions | A422 from Stratford for Banbury. After 8 miles, right to Oxhill. Last house on right on Whatcote Road. |

Graeme & Posy McDonald
Oxbourne House,
Oxhill,
Warwick,
Warwickshire CV35 0RA
Tel     +44 (0)1295 688202
Email   graememcdonald@msn.com
Web     www.oxbournehouse.com

Entry 543   Map 8

## Warwickshire

### Shrewley Pools Farm

A charming, eccentric home and fabulous for families, with space to play and animals to see: sheep, bantams and pigs. A fragrant, romantic garden, too, and a fascinating house (1640), all low ceilings, aged floors and steep stairs. Timbered passages lead to large, pretty, sunny bedrooms (all with electric blankets) with leaded windows and polished wooden floors and a family room with everything needed for a baby. In a farmhouse dining room Cathy serves sausages, bacon, and eggs from the farm, can do gluten-free breakfasts and is happy with teas for children. Buy a day ticket and fish in the lake.

Travel Club offer. See page 414.

| | |
|---|---|
| Price | From £55. Singles from £40. |
| Rooms | 2: 1 family room (& cot), 1 twin. |
| Meals | Packed lunch £4. Child's high tea £4. Pub/restaurant 1.5 miles. |
| Closed | Christmas. |
| Directions | From M40 junc. 15, A46 for Coventry. Left onto A4177. 4.5 miles to Five Ways r'bout. 1st left, on for 0.75 miles; signed, opp. Farm Gate Poultry: track on left. |

Cathy Dodd
Shrewley Pools Farm,
Five Ways Road,
Haseley, Warwick,
Warwickshire CV35 7HB
Tel     +44 (0)1926 484315
Email   cathydodd@hotmail.co.uk
Web     www.shrewleypoolsfarm.co.uk

Entry 544   Map 8